# Reading Contemporary Performance

As the nature of contemporary performance continues to expand into new forms, genres and media, it requires an increasingly diverse vocabulary. *Reading Contemporary Performance* provides students, critics and creators with a rich understanding of the key terms and ideas that are central to any discussion of this evolving theatricality.

Specially commissioned entries from a wealth of contributors map out the many and varied ways of discussing performance in all of its forms – from theatrical and site-specific performances to live and New Media art. The book is divided into two sections:

- Concepts – key terms and ideas arranged according to the five characteristic elements of performance art: time, space, action, performer, and audience.
- Methodologies and turning points – the seminal theories and ways of reading performance, such as postmodernism, epic theatre, feminisms, happenings, and animal studies.

Entries in both sections are accompanied by short case studies of specific performances and events, demonstrating creative examples of the ideas and issues in question.

Three different introductory essays provide multiple entry points into the discussion of contemporary performance, and cross-references for each entry encourage the plotting of one's own pathway. *Reading Contemporary Performance* is an invaluable guide, providing not just a strong grounding, but an exploration and contextualization of this broad and vital field.

**Meiling Cheng** is Associate Professor of Dramatic Arts/Critical Studies and English at the University of Southern California and Director of Critical Studies at USC School of Dramatic Arts, USA.

**Gabrielle H. Cody** is Professor of Drama on the Mary Riepma Ross Chair at Vassar College., USA. She concentrates her areas of teaching in performance studies, environmental studies, and performance.

# Reading Contemporary Performance

## Theatricality Across Genres

Edited by

Meiling Cheng and Gabrielle H. Cody

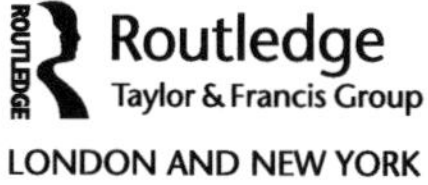

LONDON AND NEW YORK

First published 2016
by Routledge
2 Park Square, Milton Park, Abingdon, Oxon OX14 4RN

and by Routledge
711 Third Avenue, New York, NY 10017

*Routledge is an imprint of the Taylor & Francis Group, an informa business*



*British Library Cataloguing-in-Publication Data*
A catalogue record for this book is available from the British Library

*Library of Congress Cataloguing-in-Publication Data*
Reading contemporary performance : theatricality across genres / edited by Meiling Cheng and Gabrielle Cody.
pages cm
Includes bibliographical references.
1. Performing arts –Philosophy. 2. Performance art – Philosophy.
3. Theater – Philosophy. I. Cheng, Meiling, 1960– editor.
II. Cody, Gabrielle, 1956– editor.
PN1584.R43 2015
791.01-dc23 2015012992

ISBN: 978-0-415-62497-8 (hbk)
ISBN: 978-0-415-62498-5 (pbk)
ISBN: 978-0-203-10383-8 (ebk)

Typeset in Arno and Interstate
by HWA Text and Data Management, London

**To Willa Jane Velasquez Sio-Cody, a.k.a. Mootchie**
**Right up to the moon and back**

**To Master Riro, the multicentric ear for my writing**

# Contents

# Figures

# Contributors

**Chelsea Adewunmi** joined the Department of English Literature at Princeton University in 2008. She earned her BA (cum laude) from Vassar College, where she focused on English Literature, and her MA in Performance Studies from NYU's Tisch School of the Arts. Chelsea's areas of intellectual commitment include Performance Studies, African-American Literature and Culture, 19th Century Literature, Sound Studies, Visual Culture, Avant Garde and Experimental Aesthetics, Feminist, Gender and Sexuality Studies, and Studies of Corporeality and the Body.

**Daniel Albright** is Ernest Bernbaum Professor of Literature at Harvard where he teaches in the Music Department as well as the English Department. He is particularly interested in the ways in which artistic media—poetry, music, painting—interact with one another; in 2000 his book *Untwisting the Serpent: Music, Literature, and the Visual Arts* won the Susanne M. Glasscock Humanities Book Prize for Interdisciplinary Scholarship. At Harvard he teaches courses on Modernism, and the history of the English Language. He also teaches courses on opera, drama, Victorian and Modernist poetry and fiction, and the relation of physics to literature.

**Gwendolyn Alker** is on the faculty in the Department of Drama at New York University where she teaches courses on gender and performance, Latina/o theatre and embodiment. She has published articles and book chapters in *TDR, Dance Research Journal, Theatre Journal, Women & Performance* and *Theatre Topics* where she is currently the co-editor. She also acts as dramaturg and curator of public events such as the 2010 Fornes Festival, and the 25th Anniversary Conference of ATHE (Association of Theatre in Higher Education).

**Jessica Applebaum** is Literary Manager for One Year Lease Theater Company and specializes in devised performance practices. In the spring of 2014 she presented "Dramaturg for Hire: Contextual Dramaturgy for a Global (St)age" at the conference Alternative Dramaturgies of the New Millennium in Tangiers, Morocco, and curated and led a discussion on Devised Performance Dramaturgy at LMDA's annual conference. Her article "Finding the Hyphenate—Embodying Dramaturgy" appears in the *The Routledge Companion to Dramaturgy* (2014), edited by Magda Romanska. Jess holds an MFA in Dramaturgy from Columbia University and an MA in Performance Studies from NYU.

**Philip Auslander** is a Professor in the School of Literature, Media, and Communication of the Georgia Institute of Technology. He writes on performance, popular music, media, and visual art. His books include: *Presence and Resistance: Postmodernism and Cultural Politics in Contemporary American Performance* (1992), *From Acting to Performance: Essays in Modernism and Postmodernism* (1997), *Liveness: Performance in a Mediatized Culture* (1999, 2008), for which he received the prestigious Callaway Prize, and *Performing Glam Rock: Gender and Theatricality in Popular Music* (2006). Auslander is also a working film actor.

**Emily Ball Cicchini** practices and studies across the boundaries of art, education, and technology. She holds a BFA from the Theatre School/DePaul University, an MFA from the University of Texas at Austin, and is pursuing a PhD in communication. Her web-based projects include Massive Open Online Courses (MOOCs) and online resources through the Center for Open Educational Resources in Language Learning (COERLL). She writes for a variety of publications and is resident playwright of The Pollyanna Theatre Company. Her plays include *Becoming Brontë, Mays & Terese*, and *Like a Metaphor*.

**Demir Barlas** has nearly a decade of experience in business writing and editing, marketing communications, and online community building. He holds a BA from Cornell University and an MFA from UCLA Film School. Barlas is a freelance writer for LifeWire, a part of The New York Times Company that provides original and syndicated online lifestyle content.

**Sarah Bay-Cheng** is Professor of Theatre and Director of Graduate Studies in Theatre and Performance at the University at Buffalo, where she also serves as the Founding Director for the Technē Institute for Art and Emerging Technologies. Her research includes avant-garde theatre and film, digital historiography, and intersections among technology and performance. She is currently completing a new book *Performance and Media: Technologies for a Changing Field* with Jennifer Parker-Starbuck and David Saltz, and a new project on digital historiography and performance.

**John Bell** is the Director of the Ballard Institute and Museum of Puppetry and an Associate Professor of Dramatic Arts at the University of Connecticut. He is a founding member of the Great Small Works theater company; he was a member of the Bread and Puppet Theater company from 1976 to 1986. He is the author of *American Puppet Modernism* (2008), the editor of *Puppets, Masks, and Performing Objects* (2001); and, with Dassia Posner and Claudia Orenstein, the editor of *The Routledge Companion to Puppetry and Material Performance* (2014).

**Henry Bial** is Professor of Theatre and Director of the School of the Arts at the University of Kansas. His work has appeared in *TDR, Theatre Topics, The Journal of American Drama and Theatre*, and *The Journal of Dramatic Theory and Criticism*. He is the author, editor, or co-editor of several books, including *Acting Jewish: Negotiating Ethnicity on the American Stage and Screen* (2005), *The Performance Studies Reader* (2004, 2007), *Theater Historiography: Critical Interventions* (2010), and *Brecht Sourcebook* (2000).

**Johannes Birringer** is a choreographer/media artist and co-director of DAP-Lab at Brunel University where he is a Professor of Performance Technologies. He has created numerous dance-theatre works, films and video installations that have been shown in Europe, the Americas, China, and Japan. DAP-Lab's *Suna no Onna* was featured at festivals in London; the mixed-reality installation *UKIYO* went on European tour in 2010. The dance opera *for the time being [Victory over the Sun]* premiered at Sadler's Wells (2014). His books include *Media and Performance* (1998), *Performance on the Edge* (2000), *Performance, Technology and Science* (2008), *Dance and Cognition* (2005), and *Dance and Choreomania* (2011).

**Claudia Bucher** is a Los Angeles-based artist who works with performance, digital media, sculpture, and installations to explore ideas about extended sentience. She is interested in the crossover between art, science and technology, architecture, mysticism and science fiction. Her recent work is inspired by space exploration, the Mojave Desert, biomorphic design and DIY culture. She has an MFA from Art Center College of Design and has taught sculpture and 3D printing at UCLA, Otis College of Art and Brandeis University. She is a cofounder of the Museum of OMMMMM (MoOM), along with Meiling Cheng and Rolf Hoefer.

**Sharon Carnicke** is Professor of Theatre and Slavic Languages and Literatures at the University of Southern California. She is internationally known for her groundbreaking book *Stanislavsky in Focus* (2009), now in its second edition. Her other books include *Anton Chekhov: 4 Plays and 3 Jokes* (2009), *Checking out Chekhov* (2013), *The Theatrical Instinct: The Work of Nikolai Evreinov* (1989), and with Cynthia Baron, *Reframing Screen Performance* (2008). She is a widely published author on acting methods and theories, film performance, and Russian theatre. Her honors include grants and awards from the Rockefeller Foundation, the NEH, the National Science Foundation, and the Kennedy Center.

**Cynthia Carr** is the author of three books, most recently *Fire in the Belly: The Life and Times of David Wojnarowicz* (2012). Her previous books are *Our Town: A Heartland Lynching, a Haunted Town, and the Hidden History of White America* (2006) and *On Edge: Performance at the End of the Twentieth Century* (1993). Carr chronicled the work of contemporary artists as a *Village Voice* writer (with the byline C. Carr) in the 1980s and 1990s. Her work has also appeared in *Artforum, The New York Times, TDR: The Drama Review,* and other publications. She was awarded a Guggenheim in 2007.

**Mariel Carranza** was born in Peru and has lived and worked in Los Angeles since she received her MFA in sculpture in 1989 from UCLA. She has exhibited her work at Highways Performance Space in Santa Monica, L.A.C.E. (Los Angeles Contemporary Exhibitions), The Hammer Museum, and Track 16 Gallery. Carranza has also performed internationally, including L7 Studio, Santo Domingo, Dominican Republic (2014), Sierra Tarahuamara, Norogachi, Mexico, First International Festival, Chihuahua, Mexico (2013), the Belfast International Performance Art Festival, Northern Ireland (2013), The Festival Hall, London (2012), The Erarta Museum, St. Petersburg, Russia (2011), and Crossing Zones = Language = Land, Stanglinec, Croatia (2011).

**T. Nikki Cesare Schotzko** is Assistant Professor at the University of Toronto's Centre for Drama, Theatre, and Performance Studies. In 2010 she co-guest edited a special issue of *TDR*, "Caught Off-Garde: New Theatre Ensembles from NYC (mostly)," with Mariellen R. Sandford, and, in 2015, the special issue of *CTR* titled "Performing Products: When Acting Up Is Selling Out," with Isabel Stowell-Kaplan and Didier Morelli. Her first book, *Learning How to Fall: Art and Culture after September 11* (2014), considers the skewed relationship between 21st-century digital technologies, perception, and pop culture. She is currently exploring digital utopias.

**Sudipto Chatterjee** is a scholar/playwright/performer/singer/director born in Calcutta, who received his PhD in Performance Studies from NYU. *The Colonial Staged*, his book on 19th-century Bengali theatre history, was published in 2007. Author of sixteen plays in Bengali and English, he has also directed internationally in several languages. He wrote and solo-performed *Man of the Heart*, a performance-research-archiving project, which was seen at various international venues including London's Barbican Centre. He completed the first full English translation of Rabindranath Tagore's play *Bisarjan*. Chatterjee is currently Senior Lecturer of Drama at Loughborough University, U.K. and a research partner in the Global Theatre Histories project at Ludwig Maximilians-Universität München.

**Una Chaudhuri** is Professor of English, Drama, and Environmental Studies at New York University. Author of *No Man's Stage: A Study of Genet's Drama* and *Staging Place*, and co-editor, with Elinor Fuchs, of *Land/Scape/Theater*, she helped launch the field of "eco-theatre" when she guest-edited a special issue of Yale's *Theater* journal in 1994. She was among the first theatre scholars to engage with Animal Studies, guest editing a special issue of *TDR* on "Animals and Performance." In 2014, she published books in both these fields: *Animal Acts: Performing Species Today* (co-edited with Holly Hughes) and *The Ecocide Project: Research Theatre and Climate Change* (with Shonni Ennelow).

**Meiling Cheng** is the author of *In Other Los Angeleses: Multicentric Performance Art* (2002) and *Beijing Xingwei: Contemporary Chinese Time-Based Art* (2013). With Gabrielle H. Cody, she co-edited *Reading Contemporary Performance: Theatricality Across Genres* (2016). Dr. Cheng is currently teaching at USC School of Dramatic Arts, in Los Angeles, California, U.S.A. With Claudia Bucher and Rolf Hoefer, she cofounded the Museum of OMMMMM (MoOM, 2010–). She serves as an occasional artistic consultant for amphibianArc Design Studio, founded by architect Nonchi Wang.

**Jane Chin Davidson** is a researcher of the signification of race, gender and sexuality in performance works and in global expression. Her essays have been published in numerous edited collections and journals including *Journal of Visual Culture, Third Text*, and *Interventions*. She is also a curator of art exhibitions, including *Inner Space, Global Matter* (2012–2013) and for the following three sites: Johnson Space Center, University of Houston, and Miami International University. Chin Davidson was a British ESRC fellow with the Cultural Theory Institute at the University of Manchester, and is currently Assistant Professor of Art History and Contemporary Art at California State University, San Bernardino.

**Gabrielle H. Cody** is Mary Riepma Ross Professor and Chair in the Department of Drama at Vassar College. Her articles on contemporary performance have appeared in *Theatre Journal, TDR, The Journal of Women and Performance, PAJ*, Yale's *Theater*, and *Diacritics*. Her books include *Impossible Performances: Duras as Dramatist* (2000) and *Hard Core From the Heart: Annie Sprinkle Solo* (2001); with Rebecca Schneider she co-edited *RE:DIRECTION, a Theorectical and Practical Guide* (2001); with Evert Sprinchorn she co-edited *The Columbia Encyclopedia of Modern Drama* (2007); and with Meiling Cheng she co-edited *Reading Contemporary Performance: Theatricality Across Genres* (2015).

**Jeanne Colleran** is Provost and Academic Vice President at John Carroll University in Cleveland, Ohio. She is the author of *Theater and War* (2012) and co-editor, with Jenny Spencer, of *Staging Resistance: Essays in Political Theatre* (1998) as well as numerous essays on South African literature and contemporary theatre.

**Svetlana Darsalia (Tshvaradze)** is an art curator who has lived in the USSR, Los Angeles, and Mexico City. She took an active part in the movement of Noncomformist artists in the former USSR for the freedom of self-expression in the 1970s in Moscow. In LA Darsalia curated and directed art exhibitions around the country, and also wrote or contributed to several photography and poetry publications, including *Eugene Rukhin* (2009), *All is One* (2007), *Every Day the Day, ETC.* (2006), and *Meditation on America* (1987). Her filmography includes *Cage Free Born Free* (2008), *365 Days and 365 Plays*, and *2010 Mother Sela* (2012).

**Elin Diamond** is the author of *Unmaking Mimesis: Essays on Feminism and Theater* (1997) and *Pinter's Comic Play* (1985); she is also the editor of *Performance and Cultural Politics* (1996). Her many journal publications include essays on 17th- and 20th-century drama, and Freudian, Brechtian, and feminist theory. Her work continually explores the connection between performance and feminist or critical theory, using texts from early modernism through postmodern art. She is currently at work on a book on modernism and transatlantic performance.

**Jill Dolan** is the Annan Professor of English and Professor of Theatre at Princeton University. Among other books, she is the author of *The Feminist Spectator as Critic* (1988, rereleased in a 2012 anniversary edition); *Utopia in Performance: Finding Hope at the Theatre* (2005); and *The Feminist Spectator in Action: Feminist Criticism for the Stage and Screen* (2013). Her blog, *The Feminist Spectator*, won the 2010–2011 George Jean Nathan Award for Dramatic Criticism. She received the 2013 American Society for Theatre Research career achievement award and the 2011 Association for Theatre in Higher Education Outstanding Teacher award.

**Sean Edgecomb** is Assistant Professor of Theatre at the City University of New York, College of Staten Island. He also serves as a member of CLAGS: Center for LGBTQ Studies and teaches at the CUNY Graduate Center. His work primarily investigates the intersection of performance and queerness as an act of ambivalent agency. He has published articles in *Theatre Journal, Popular Entertainment Studies* and *Modern Drama* and book chapters in collections from Palgrave, McFarland and Routledge. His book on the queer legacy of Charles Ludlams Ridiculous Theatre is forthcoming from the Triangulations Series at the University of Michigan Press.

**Eleonora Fabião** is a performer and performance theorist, and Associate Professor at the Federal University of Rio de Janeiro, School of Communication. In 2011 she received the "Art in the Streets Award" from the Brazilian National Foundation of the Arts, and in 2014 the "Rumos Itaú Cultural Grant." Fabião is a member of the Hemispheric Institute of Performance and Politics Council, and was the researcher on Latin American performance art for the Berlin-based *Re.act.feminism Performing Archive*. She has been publishing, teaching, and performing in the Americas and Europe.

**Elinor Fuchs** is the author or editor of five books, including *The Death of Character: Reflection on Theater After Modernism* (1996), winner of the George Jean Nathan Award in Dramatic Criticism; *Making an Exit* (2005), a family memoir; and *Land/Scape/Theater* (2002), coedited with Una Chaudhuri. She has published numerous scholarly articles in anthologies and journals as well as theater criticism in American Theatre and The Village Voice. She is a Professor of Dramaturgy and Dramatic Criticism at the Yale School of Drama. She has also taught at Harvard, Columbia, NYU, Emory, and at the Institut für Theatrewissenschaft of the Free University in Berlin and has been awarded two Rockefeller Foundation fellowships.

**Marcela A. Fuentes** is Assistant Professor in the Department of Performance Studies at Northwestern University. Her research focuses on late 20th- and early 21st-century activism and interventionist art. Her book manuscript "In the Event of Performance: Bodies, Tactical Media, and Politics in the Americas," under contract with the University of Michigan Press, investigates the changing relationship between embodied performance and mediation as techniques of control and resistance within neoliberal states. Fuentes analyzes how the relationship between bodily performance and digital mediation has evolved from complementarity to synergy constituting "constellations of performance." Fuentes also works as a performer and dramaturg.

**Charles R. Garoian** is Professor of Art Education at Penn State University. He has performed, lectured, and conducted workshops in festivals, galleries, museums, and university campuses in the United States and internationally. In addition to his scholarly publications in leading journals on art and education, Garoian is the author of *Performing Pedagogy: Toward an Art of Politics* (1999); and co-author of *Spectacle Pedagogy: Art, Politics, and*

*Visual Culture* (2008) and *The Prosthetic Pedagogy of Art: Embodied Research and Practice* (2013).

**Shawn-Marie Garrett** has developed and taught a variety of classes in writing, editing, cultural history, critical theory, and allied subjects in the course of her career. She has also worked in directorial and dramaturgical capacities on dozens of professional and university theater productions as well as on films in development in the U.S., Canada, and Europe. Since 1999, she has served as a Contributing Editor for *THEATER* magazine (Duke University Press). She taught for over a decade at Yale and Barnard College, Columbia University.

**Arianna Gass** is a Philadelphia-based interdisciplinary artist. A graduate of Vassar College with degrees in both English and Drama and member of Phi Beta Kappa, her scholarship focuses on the intersection of live performance and new media. She is the Program Manager at Drexel University's Entrepreneurial Game Studio where she works with graduate and undergraduate students to design and ship video games. More of her writing and work can be found at www.ariannagass.com.

**Yvonne M. Gaudelius** is an Associate Vice President and Senior Associate Dean of Undergraduate Education and a Professor of Art Education and Women's Studies at Penn State. She has received numerous grants and awards including the invited *Studies in Art Education* lecture and the June King McFee Award from the Women's Caucus of the National Art Education Association. Dr. Gaudelius has presented at numerous national and international conferences, and her writings include the co-authored book *Spectacle Pedagogy: Art, Culture and Visual Politics* (2008), the co-edited book *Contemporary Issues in Art Education* (2001), articles in leading research journals, and chapters in several books.

**Cheri Gaulke**'s art and life were profoundly changed in 1975, when she moved from the Midwest to Los Angeles to join the Feminist Studio Workshop at the Woman's Building. She works in performance, video, installation and artists' books and co-founded collaborative performance groups Feminist Art Workers and Sisters Of Survival. In recent years, she created a number of public art works. Gaulke has been honored by grants from the National Endowment for the Arts, California Arts Council, California Community Foundation and LA's Cultural Affairs Department. In 2011–2012, her solo and collaborative work was featured in Getty-sponsored Pacific Standard Time exhibitions at LACE and Otis. As an educator, Gaulke has mentored hundreds of award-winning youth videos.

**Guillermo Gómez-Peña** is a performance artist, writer, activist, pedagogue, and Director of the performance troupe La Pocha Nostra. His performance work and ten books have contributed to debates on cultural diversity, border culture, and U.S.–Mexico relations and have been presented internationally. A MacArthur fellow, Bessie, and American Book Award winner, he is a contributor to publications in the U.S., Mexico, and Europe, and an editor for *The Drama Review*. Gómez-Peña is a senior fellow in the Hemispheric Institute of Performance and Politics, a Patron for the Live Art Development Agency, and was named Samuel Hoi fellow by USA Artists.

**Rachel Haidu** is Associate Professor of Art History Arts at the University of Rochester. Her areas of expertise are modern European and American art, contemporary art, critical theory, postwar Europe, postcommunist and Eastern European art. She has published a book, *The Absence of Work: Marcel Broodthaers*, 1964–1976 (2010), and numerous articles on artists such as Daniel Buren, Gerhard Richter, Edward Krasinski, and Thomas Hirschhorn. She is currently completing a second book.

**Jack Halberstam** is Professor of American Studies and Ethnicity at the University of Souther California, and is the author of numerous articles and five books including: *Skin Shows: Gothic Horror and the Technology of Monsters* (1995), *Female Masculinity* (1998), *In A Queer Time and Place* (2005), *The Queer Art of Failure* (2011), and *Gaga Feminism: Sex, Gender, and the End of Normal* (2012). Halberstam is currently working on a book on "wildness."

**Andrew J. Henkes** is currently a research fellow at the Interdisciplinary Humanities Center at the University of California, Santa Barbara as well as a part-time Assistant Professor at the University of Southern California and the University of California, Riverside. He writes on the history of theatre, popular entertainment, and LGBTQ performance. His first book will examine the delineation of gay and lesbian identities in Los Angeles nightlife through theatre, dance, drag, and fetish performances.

**Brian Herrera** is Assistant Professor of Theater at Princeton University. Herrera's academic and creative work examines the history of gender, sexuality, and race within and through popular performance. He is the author of *The Latina/o Theatre Commons 2013 National Convening: A Narrative Report* (2014) and *Latin Numbers: Playing Latino in 20th Century US Popular Performance* (2015). Herrera has authored articles in *Theatre Journal*, *Modern Drama* and *TDR: The Drama Review*. He is presently developing a scholarly history of casting in American entertainment.

**Rolf Hoefer** is a PhD student at INSEAD. He holds a BA in Theatre (focus: Performance Studies) and a BS in Business Administration (focus: Entrepreneurship) from the University of Southern California. With Claudia Bucher and Meiling Cheng, he cofounded the Museum of OMMMMM (MoOM 2010).

**Nicole Hodges Persley** is an Assistant Professor of Theatre at the University of Kansas. She received her PhD from the University of Southern California's Department of American Studies and Ethnicity. Dr. Hodges Persley's research explores the impact of racial, ethnic and national identity on performance practices in theatre, television and film. Her forthcoming book, *Sampling and Remixing Blackness* (under contract with The University of Michigan Press), covers the artistic practices of non-African-American artists who create works in theatre, conceptual art, and dance that are inspired by hip-hop culture. Dr. Hodges Persley teaches courses on race and performance, acting, improvisation theory, hip-hop, and transnationalism. She is a proud member of SAG-AFTRA.

**Sharon Irish** is an art and architectural historian at the University of Illinois, Urbana-Champaign (UIUC). *Suzanne Lacy: Spaces Between* (2010) is her most recent book. Her research focuses on intersections of urban and architectural spaces with contemporary art, conceptual art's links to social practice, and second-order cybernetics. Her previous publications include a book-length bibliography on medievalism in North American art and architecture, and a monograph on the architect Cass Gilbert, as well as a number of articles and book chapters on Gilbert, and essays on artists Anish Kapoor, Suzanne Lacy, Nek Chand Saini, Le Corbusier, and Stephen Willats.

**Kimberly Jannarone** is Professor of Theater Arts, Digital Arts and New Media, and History of Consciousness at the University of California, Santa Cruz, where she holds the Gary D. Licker Memorial Chair. She is the author of *Artaud and His Doubles* (2010), winner of the Honorable Mention for the Joe Callaway Prize for best book in drama. Forthcoming books include *Mass Performance, History, and the Invention of Tradition* and the edited volume *Vanguard Performance Beyond Left and Right* (forthcoming University of Michigan Press). Jannarone also directs, dramaturgs, and translates experimental drama, including the recent Gynt Project in Santa Cruz, California.

**Susan Jarosi** is Associate Professor of Contemporary Art History and Theory in the Women's and Gender Studies and Fine Arts

Departments at the University of Louisville. Her critical writing on performance art and expanded cinema has been published in the journals *Art History*, *Screen*, and *Art and Documentation*; and in anthologies such as *The Fluxus Reader* (1998), *Not a Day Without a Line—Understanding Artists' Writings* (2013), and *Interactive Contemporary Art: Participation in Practice* (2014). She is currently completing projects on vitrines and holography.

**Amelia Jones** is the Robert A. Day Professor in Art and Design, and Vice-Dean of Critical Studies at the Roski School of Art and Design at University of Southern California. A curator, and a theorist and historian of art and performance, her recent publications include *Perform Repeat Record: Live Art in History* (2012), co-edited with Adrian Heathfield, and a single-authored book *Seeing Differently: A History and Theory of Identification and the Visual Arts* (2012). Her exhibition *Material Traces: Time and the Gesture in Contemporary Art* took place in 2013 in Montreal, and her edited volume *Sexuality* was released in 2014 in the Whitechapel "Documents" series.

**Jenn Joy** is a co-founder with Kelly Kivland of collective address, a choreographic research space in Brooklyn, and teaches in Sculpture at Rhode Island School of Design. She curated *Conversations without Walls*, and co-edited *Diary of an Image* (2014) and *JUDSONOW* (2012) with Judy Hussie-Taylor for Danspace Project. She is a Contributing Editor for *BOMB* magazine and edited *Planes of Composition: Dance, Theory and the Global* with André Lepecki (Seagull Press, 2009). Her recent writing has been published in *DANSE: An Anthology* (Les Presses du Réel, 2014), *DANCE* (Whitechapel/MIT Press, 2012) and her book, *The Choreographic*, was published by MIT Press in October 2014.

**Jennie Klein** is Associate Professor of Art History at Ohio University. She specializes in contemporary art, theory, performance studies, and new genre art. Her current research interests include feminist performance and video in the 1970s, inSITE and the politics of international exhibitions on the U.S./Mexico border, and the representation and politics of motherhood in video, performance, and photography. She has published in *New Art Examiner*, *Afterimage*, *Art Papers*, *Art History*, *N.Paradoxa*, *Artweek*, *Sculpture*, and *Performing Art Journal* (*PAJ*), for whom she is a contributing editor. She is the editor of *Letters from Linda M. Montano*, the most recent book of writings by Linda Montano. She is also the co-curator and catalogue essayist for the Barbara T. Smith retrospective at the Pomona College Museum of Art.

**Michaël La Chance** PhD (Paris-VIII), DEA (EPHSS), is a philosopher of aesthetics, a writer and Art Theory and History Professor at UQAC, University du Québec à Chicoutimi, Canada, with a special interest in Performance Art and Digital Arts. He is head of the Departement des arts et lettres. He also taught in UQAM's Philosophy Departement and Doctoral Program in Art Study and Pratice. Member of CELAT, Centre Interuniversitaire d'Étude sur les Lettres, les Arts et les Traditions, La Chance is the author of numerous books and artist's catalogs, and has published an extensive body of poetical works. He is Senior Editor of *Inter Art Actuel*.

**Suzanne Lacy**'s work includes large-scale performances, photography, installations, videos, and critical writing on art and the public realm. She is founding chair of the MFA program in Public Practice at Otis College of Art and Design, Los Angeles. Her works range from intimate explorations of the body to performances with hundreds of participants staged before live audiences numbering in the thousands like the recent project, *Between the Door and the Street* (2013) with Creative Time and the Brooklyn Museum. Her publications include *Mapping the Terrain: New Genre Public Art* (1995) and *Leaving Art: Writings on Performance, Politics, and Publics, 1974–2007* (2010).

**André Lepecki** is Associate Professor at the Department of Performance Studies at New York University. He is also a curator, writer and dramaturg. He is the author of *Exhausting Dance: Performance and Politics of Movement* (2006), currently translated into six languages. He edited the anthologies *Of the Presence of the Body* (2004), *The Senses in Performance* (with Sally Banes, 2007), and *Planes of Composition: Dance Theory and the Global* (with Jenn Joy, 2010), and *Dance* (2012). His writing has also appeared in *Performance Research, The Drama Review, Art Forum, Nouvelles de Danse, Dance Research Journal,* among other publications in Europe, Brazil, and the Middle East.

**Debra Levine** is an Assistant Professor of Theatre at NYU Abu Dhabi and affiliated with The Hemispheric Institute for Politics and Performance. Her work explores the intersection between performance, politics, and new media/digital humanities through feminist and queer theory, disability studies, and visual studies. With Pamela Cobrin, she co-edited the 2012 issue on "Aging and Performance," for *Women and Performance* and edited the 2008 issue on "Wasting." Debra has contributed articles to *GLQ, Women & Performance, e-misférica, Theatre Research International,* and *The Disability Studies Quarterly.* Currently she is finishing *Demonstrating ACT UP*—a web-based book with multimedia essays and an archive of documentation that acts as a finding aid to understand historical demonstrations of AIDS activism.

**Steve Luber** is Adjunct Assistant Professor of Theater, Associate Director of Curriculum and Student Research, Ammerman Center for Arts and Technology. He specializes in multimedia performance, avant-garde and experimental performance, performance art, and the history of scenography. His most recent article, "The Theatre of a Two-Headed Calf: Simulacral Performance and the Deconstruction of Orientalism," appeared in *Theatre Survey*. Luber has also worked with The Builders Association, David Byrne, and the Mabou Mines Suite, in addition to creating solo works, "Steve Sells Out" (2005) and "Rock Star" (2001). He is co-founder and author of "Obscene Jester: the performance art blog."

**Llewyn Máire and Lisa Newman** The gyrl grip was founded in 2001 by collaborators and co-directors of 2 Gyrlz Performative Arts, Llewyn Máire and Lisa Newman. Using video, movement, sound sculpture, endurance, conceptual and text-based performance, the gyrl grip explores new modes of body-based communication. *We discover new languages through any means necessary and encourage our audiences to try on different tongues.* The most recent series, *Surgemony*, manifested at the PSi #13 Conference (Copenhagen, DK), 5th International Art Action Festival (Monza, Italy), Rdece Zore festival (Ljubljana, Slovenia), PSI #11 (Providence, Rhode Island), and Lewis & Clark College's annual Gender Symposium (Portland, Oregon).

**Lynn Manning** is an award winning poet, playwright, actor, and former World Champion of blind judo. He accomplished all of this after being shot and blinded aged 23. A graduate of LACC, Lynn honed his playwriting skills in Center Theatre Group's Blacksmiths and Mentor Playwrights workshops, and The Actors' Studio Writers/Directors Unit/West. Lynn's autobiographical, solo play, *WEIGHTS*, received three NAACP Theater awards (including "Best Actor" for Lynn) and an Edinburgh Fringe Review "Teapot Award" for "Excellence In Theatre." In 1996, Lynn co-founded Watts Village Theater Company, dedicated to providing professional live theatre and theatre arts education to the communities of South Los Angeles and Watts.

**Bonnie Marranca** is founding publisher and editor of the Obie-Award winning *PAJ* Publications/*PAJ: A Journal of Performance and Art*, and a recent recipient of the Association for Theatre in Higher Education Excellence in Editing Award for Sustained Achievement. She is the author of three volumes of criticism—*Performance Histories* (2008), *Ecologies of Theatre* (1996), and *Theatrewritings* (1984)—and editor of several play anthologies and essay collections, including *New Europe: Plays from the Continent* (2009), *Interculturalism and Performance* (1991), and *Plays* *for the End of the Century* (1996). Her most recent book is *Conversations with Meredith Monk* (2014). Bonnie Marranca is Professor of Theatre at The New School for Liberal Arts/Eugene Lang College.

**Paige McGinley** is Assistant Professor of Performing Arts at Washington University in St. Louis. Her research and teaching examine histories of theater and performance in the 20th century United States, with a particular focus on African American theater and popular entertainment. Her published articles have appeared in *TDR, Performance Research,* and *Theatre Survey.* She is the author of *Staging the Blues: From Tent Shows to Tourism* (Duke, 2014).

**Erin Mee**'s book *The Theatre of Roots: Redirecting the Modern Indian Stage* was published in 2008 by Seagull Books and Palgrave-McMillan. She is co-editor (with Helene Foley of Barnard College) of Antigone on the Contemporary World Stage, which examines the reasons and ways Antigone has been mobilized in a wide variety of historical, political, and cultural contexts around the world; and editor of *DramaContemporary: India,* a collection of modern Indian plays published in the United States by Johns Hopkins University Press and in India by Oxford University Press. Her articles have appeared in *TDR, Theater Journal, Performing Arts Journal, Seagull Theatre Quarterly, American Theatre Magazine,* and in numerous edited books.

**Linda Mary Montano** is a performance artist whose raffish practices include endurance; blurring the edge between art and life; witnessing the inherent humor of the human situation; death; recognizing the autobiographical need to fix life through art; the aging body; changing the mind; and using Catholic imagery to speak to the mystery of the everyday. In 1976, Montano began videotaping herself as seven different mythical personas, and in the last seven years, Montano has acted as doppelgänger to real, living beings, including Mother Teresa, Bob Dylan, and Woodstock rock 'n' roll artist, Paul McMahon. These transformations have allowed her to question the uncertainty of the human ego and the flexibility of shape shifting. Montano has taught performance art internationally and has written four books on the subject.

**Elise Morrison** is currently a Mellon postdoctoral fellow in Interdisciplinary Performance Studies at Yale University. She writes and teaches about surveillance technologies and their theatrical uses in art-making and everyday life. She has created and performed a number of surveillance art pieces in Providence, Boston, and New York, using surveillance technologies from publicly installed CCTV cameras to re-engineered drones. Her book, *Discipline and Desire: Surveillance Technologies in Performance* is under contract with University of Michigan Press.

**José Esteban Muñoz** was an American academic in the fields of performance studies, visual culture, queer theory, cultural studies, and critical theory. His book *Disidentifications: Queers of Color and the Performance of Politics* (1999) examines queer and racial minority issues from a performance studies perspective. His second book, *Cruising Utopia: the Then and There of Queer Futurity,* was published by NYU Press in 2009. He also co-edited *Pop Out: Queer Warhol* (1996) with Jennifer Doyle and Jonathan Flatley, and *Everynight Life: Culture and Dance in Latin/o America* (1997) with Celeste Fraser Delgado. Muñoz was Professor in, and former Chair of, the Department of Performance Studies at New York University's Tisch School of the Arts. With great respect and affection, the *RCP* editorial team remembers José Muñoz, who passed away in New York City in December 2013.

**Pramod K. Nayar** teaches at the Dept. of English, University of Hyderabad, India. His newest books include *Frantz Fanon* (2013), *Posthumanism* (2014), and *Citizenship and Identity in the Age of Surveillance* (2015). His forthcoming works include *The Postcolonial Studies Dictionary* for Wiley-Blackwell and *The Transnational in English Literature: Shakespeare to the Modern* for Routledge, along with a book on the Indian graphic novel. He is currently at work on a book on Human Rights and Literature. His essays have appeared in *Modern Fiction Studies, Celebrity Studies, Prose Studies, Journal of Postcolonial Writing, Postcolonial Text, Ariel, Kunapipi*, and other journals.

**Tavia Nyong'o** is Associate Professor of Performance Studies at New York University. His areas of interest include black studies, queer studies, critical theory, popular music studies and cultural critique. His first book, *The Amalgamation Waltz: Race, Performance, and the Ruses of Memory* (Minnesota, 2009), won the Errol Hill Award for best book in African American theatre and performance studies. He is co-editor of the journal *Social Text.*

**Kathy O'Dell** is Associate Professor of Visual Arts at the University of Maryland, Baltimore County (UMBC), where she served as Associate Dean of Arts, Humanities, and Social Sciences from 2001 to 2014. She writes on modern and contemporary art, with a focus on performance and global art. She is the author of *Contract with the Skin: Masochism, Performance Art, and the 1970s* (1998), and an in-progress book titled *The Dot: A Small History of a Big Point.* She and Kristine Stiles are completing their manuscript *World Art Since 1945.*

**Lissette Olivares** is a liminal entity fascinated by and invested in performance. As a feminist, artist, theorist, curator, and multispecies storyteller she pursues interdisciplinary approaches to knowledge production. She is an Assistant Professor and faculty fellow at NYU, and a doctoral candidate in the History of Consciousness Department. She is the co-founder and Director of MACS, Laboratorio de Piel/Skin Laboratory, and the Transmedia Network. She has curated many international performance events and is interested in exploring experimental curatorial formats that consider performance and its traces. Her own interventions have been presented in: Christie's Auction House, the Museum of Contemporary Art, Santiago, the Western Front Society, and most recently, Kara Walker's 6–8 month project.

**Allison Pearl** is a current student at Vassar College, where she has worked for Gabrielle H. Cody as a research and editorial assistant. Working on this book with Gabrielle, Meiling, Arianna, Kelly, and Arden was an inspiring and rewarding experience for Allison, and she hopes to continue being involved in writing and editing processes throughout her time at Vassar and beyond. Assisting and collaborating with the many brilliant contributors to this book, especially Professor Daniel Albright, was an honor and Allison is very proud to have been a part of the process of this book's publication.

**Ann Pellegrini** is Professor of Performance Studies and Social and Cultural Analysis at New York University, where she also directs the Center for the Study of Gender and Sexuality. Her books include *Performance Anxieties: Staging Psychoanalysis, Staging Race* (1997); *Love the Sin: Sexual Regulation and the Limits of Religious Tolerance*, co-authored with Janet R. Jakobsen (2003); and *"You Can Tell Just By Looking" and 20 Other Myths About LGBT Life and People*, co-authored with Michael Bronski and Michael Amico (2013). She co-edits the "Sexual Cultures" series at New York University Press.

**Tylar Pendgraft** is a Los Angeles-based African American female playwright whose work is concerned with creating roles for female minorities as a means of decolonizing the Black female body. Tylar will receive her MFA in Dramatic Writing at USC's School of Dramatic Arts in 2015. Her other fields of work include interactive and multimedia theatre experiences as well as critical studies in regards to disability and performance.

**Cynthia Port** is Associate Professor of English at Coastal Carolina University. Her research centers on age, value, and temporality in modernist and contemporary fiction and film. Recent work has appeared in *Occasion* and *International Journal of*

*Ageing and Later Life* (IJAL). Dr. Port is co-editor of *Age, Culture, Humanities: An Interdisciplinary Journal* as well as an executive council co-chair of the North American Network in Aging Studies (NANAS).

**Moira Roth** was born in London in 1933 and is an art historian, writer, and playwright. She holds the Trefethen Chair of Art History at Mills College in Oakland (previously she taught at various University of California campuses). Since the early 1970s she has written on U.S. performance history and feminism, and from the 1980s onward, has worked increasingly cross-culturally, and internationally (in 2012 she was the blogger for the 18th Biennale of Sydney, Australia). In 2001, she began to write *Through the Eyes of Rachel Marker*, a sprawling narrative about European history seen through the eyes of a fictional character.

**Erika Rundle** is a dramaturg, translator, and Associate Professor of Theatre Arts and Gender Studies at Mount Holyoke College, where she is also a member of the program in Critical Social Thought. Her articles and reviews have been published in *TDR, PAJ, Theater, Theatre Journal*, and the *Eugene O'Neill Review*, as well as numerous anthologies—most recently *Animal Acts: Performing Species Today* (2014). Her translation of Marie Ndiaye's *Hilda* was performed off-Broadway as part of the Act French festival, and at regional theatres. *Drama after Darwin*, her study of 20th-century "primate drag," is forthcoming in 2016.

**Kathleen Ryan** is Assistant Professor of Rhetoric and Composition in the English Department at Montana State University where she has directed the Composition Program for almost a decade. Her areas of specialization are feminist rhetorical studies and writing program administration. Her publications include "Taking Ecological Location into Account: Theorizing a Rhetorical Ecological Feminist Agency for WPAs" (2012); *GenAdmin: Theorizing WPA Identities in the Twenty-first Century* co-authored with Colin Charlton, Jonikka Charlton, Tarez Samra Graban, and Amy Ferdinandt Stolley (2011); and *Walking and Talking Feminist Rhetorics: Landmark Essays and Controversies*, co-edited with Lindal Buchanan (2009).

**Daniel Sack** is Assistant Professor of English at the University of Massachusetts in Amherst. He is the author of *After Live: Possibility, Potentiality, and the Futures of Performance* (2015). His reviews and essays on Romeo Castellucci and other contemporary artists have been published in journals such as *PAJ: a Journal of Art and Performance, Studies in Theatre and Performance, Theater, Theatre Journal,* and *TDR: the Drama Review*, and have been included in various edited collections.

**Mariellen Sandford** is Associate Editor of *TDR: The Drama Review*. She is editor of a special issue of *TDR* on new theatre ensembles in New York (54:4), *Happenings and Other Acts* (Routledge), and, as a freelance editor, numerous academic books on performance.

**Richard Schechner** is University Professor and Professor of Performance Studies, Tisch School of the Arts, New York University. He is editor of *TDR: The Journal of Performance Studies*. Among his books are *Environmental Theater* (1973), *The End of Humanism* (1982), *Between Theater and Anthropology* (1985), *Performance Theory* (latest edition, 2003), *Performance Studies An Introduction* (latest edition, 2013), and *Performed Imaginaries* (2014). Schechner founded The New Orleans Group, The Performance Group, and East Coast Artists. His theatre productions have been seen in the U.S., Romania, Poland, France, India, China, Taiwan, the U.K., and the Republic of South Africa.

**Timothy Scheie** has been a faculty member in the Humanities Department at the Eastman School of Music since 1994, serving as department chair from 2005–2011. He has published articles on performance and identity in French and American production, and a book-length study on the place of theatre and performance in the writings of Roland

Barthes. More recently his research bears on national narratives in film genre. Prior to his appointment at the Eastman School he taught at the University of Oregon and in France. At the Eastman School, in addition to his role as a French Professor he also serves as Director of Foreign Language Instruction and Fulbright Program Advisor.

**Rebecca Schneider** is Professor of Theatre Arts and Performance Studies at Brown University and author of *Theatre and History* (2014); *Performing Remains: Art and War in Times of Theatrical Reenactment* (2011); and *The Explicit Body in Performance* (1997). She is the author of numerous essays including "Hello Dolly Well Hello Dolly: The Double and Its Theatre," "Solo Solo Solo," and "It Seems As If I am Dead: Zombie Capitalism and Theatrical Labor." She is co-editor, with Gabrielle H. Cody, of *Re:Direction,* and of the book series "Theatre: Theory/Text/Performance" with University of Michigan Press. She is also a consortium editor of *TDR*.

**Mike Sell** is Professor of English at Indiana University of Pennsylvania. His publications include *The Avant-Garde: Race Religion War* (2011) and *Avant-Garde Performance and the Limits of Criticism* (2005), along with essays in *New Literary History, African American Review, Modernism/Modernity, Theatre Journal*, and *TDR*.

**Megan Shea** received her PhD in Theatre Arts from Cornell University and is a Language Lecturer in the Expository Writing Program at New York University. She is currently developing a production of her translation of Euripides' *Cyclops*, which premiered in a workshop at Dixon Place. Shea has published in *Theatre Topics, The Journal of Dramatic Theory and Criticism*, and *TheatreForum* and has served as Focus Group President for ATHE's Performance Studies Focus Group.

**Arden Shwayder** is a student at Vassar College studying Drama, Film and Art History where she is also Gabrielle H. Cody's research and editorial assistant. It has been an exciting, challenging and rewarding process to work on this book with Gabrielle, Meiling, Kelly, and Allison. The experience has been invaluable, both supporting and reinforcing her plans to pursue writing and editing after Vassar. She cannot thank them enough for the opportunity and their guidance throughout the journey.

**Matthew Smith** is Associate Professor of Theatre at Boston University where he teaches courses on Modern theater history and theory, relations between theatre and film, and digital performance. His published writing includes "Virtual Journeys and Virtual Walls: The Digital Art of Tamiko Thiel" (2010), "American Valkyries: Richard Wagner, D.W. Griffith, and the Birth of Classical Cinema" (2008), and "Orson Welles' Shakespeare" (2008). He was the co-editor, of *Modern Drama* Fiftieth Anniversary Issue (2007), "Laughing at the Redeemer: Kundry and the Paradox of *Parsifal*" (2007), and *The Total Work of Art: From Bayreuth to Cyberspace* (2007).

**Kelly Speca** is a recent graduate of the University of Southern California in Narrative Studies and Classics. Her senior thesis focused on the Beijing East Village Artists with support from her mentor and adviser, Meiling Cheng of the USC School of Dramatic Arts. She has served as Professor Cheng's research assistant on her anthology with Professor Gabrielle H. Cody, *Reading Contemporary Performance: Theatricality Across Genres*. She volunteers at the Museum of Tolerance and the Daniel Pearl Foundation.

**Kristine Stiles** is France Family Professor of Art, Art History and Visual Studies at Duke University. She specializes in contemporary global art, focusing on performance art, artists' writings, trauma and destruction in art. Among her books are *Theories and Documents of Contemporary Art* (1996, 2012), *Correspondence Course: An Epistolary History of Carolee Schneemann and Her Circle* (2010), and *Concerning Consequences: Studies in Art, Destruction, and Trauma* (2015). Stiles and Kathy O'Dell, are completing their manuscript *World Art Since 1945*. As a curator, Stiles' recent exhibition is *Rauschenberg: Collecting and Connecting*: http://shuffle.rauschenbergfoundation.org/exhibitions/nasher/ Stiles is also an artist and equestrian.

**Amy Strahler Holzapfel** is Associate Professor of Theatre at Williams College, where she teaches courses in theatre history and literature, performance studies, and dramaturgy. Her recent book *Art, Vision and Nineteenth-Century Realist Drama: Acts of Seeing* (2014) explores how modern theories of vision in art and science impacted the rise of the realist movement in theatre. She has published articles *Contemporary Theatre Review*, *PAJ: A Journal of Performance and Art*, *The Journal of Dramatic Theory & Criticism*, *Modern Drama*, and *Theater*, as well as the anthologies *Spatial Turns: Space, Place and Mobility in German Literary and Visual Culture* (2010) and *The Oxford Handbook on Dance and Theatre* (Oxford, forthcoming).

**Peta Tait** is Professor at La Trobe University, Australia, and Visiting Professor at the University of Wollongong. She was elected a fellow of the Australian Academy of the Humanities, and served as a member of the ARC ERA HCA panel in 2010 and 2012 and PSi executive 2005–2009. She has published over 50 articles on body-based performance and phenomenology, and cultural languages of emotion, affect, and on species. She is also a playwright and her recent books are *Wild and Dangerous Performances: Animals, Emotions, Circus* (2012) and *Circus Bodies* (2005); her forthcoming book is *Fighting Nature*.

**Tina Takemoto** is an artist and Associate Professor of Visual Studies at California College of the Arts. She presents artwork and performances internationally and has received grants funded by Art Matters, James Irvine Foundation, and San Francisco Arts Commission. Her film *Looking for Jiro* (2011) received Best Experimental Film Jury Award at Austin Gay and Lesbian Film Festival. Takemoto's writing appears in *Afterimage*, *Art Journal*, *GLQ*, *Performance Research*, *Radical Teacher*, *Theatre Survey*, *Women and Performance*, and the anthology *Thinking Through the Skin*. Takemoto is Board President of the Queer Cultural Center and co-founder of Queer Conversations on Culture and the Arts.

**Diana Taylor** is University Professor and Professor of Performance Studies and Spanish at NYU. She wrote *Theatre of Crisis: Drama and Politics in Latin America* (1991), which won the Best Book Award given by New England Council on Latin American Studies and Honorable Mention in the Joe E. Callaway Prize for the Best Book on Drama; *Disappearing Acts: Spectacles of Gender and Nationalism in Argentina's "Dirty War"* (1997); and *The Archive and the Repertoire: Performing Cultural Memory in the Americas*, which won the ATHE Research Award in Theatre Practice and Pedagogy and the Modern Language Association Katherine Singer Kovacs Prize for the best book in Latin American and Spanish Literatures and Culture (2004). *The Archive and the Repertoire* has been translated into Portuguese by Eliana Lourenço de Lima Reis and Spanish by Anabelle Contreras (2015).

**Arden Thomas** is the Executive Director of MACH 33: The Festival of New Science-Driven Plays at Caltech, and a Teaching Artist at The Huntington Library and Art Galleries. Her writings on contemporary theater and dance have been published in *Readings in Performance and Ecology*, *Theatre Journal*, and *InDance*, and an essay is forthcoming in *Staging Motherhood in North American Drama*. She is active as a dramaturg and director, with particular interests in theater and performance-making that catalyze the national conversation about climate change and other environmental issues.

**Philip Tinari** is Director of the Ullens Center for Contemporary Art in Beijing. There he oversees an exhibition program devoted to established figures and rising talents both Chinese and international, aimed at an annual public of nearly a million visitors. He has written extensively on contemporary art in China. Prior to joining UCCA in 2011 he was founding editorial director of the bilingual art magazine *LEAP*. He previously served as China advisor to Art Basel, founding editor of *Artforum*'s Chinese-language edition, and lecturer at the Central Academy of Fine Arts.

**Jeff Watson** is an award winning artist, designer, and Assistant Professor of Interactive Media and Games at the University of Southern California School of Cinematic Arts. His work investigates how game design, pervasive computing, and social media can enable new forms of storytelling, participation, and learning.

**Winnie Wong** is a historian of modern and contemporary art and visual culture, with a special interest in fakes, forgeries, frauds, copies, counterfeits, and other non-art challenges to authorship and originality. She is currently Assistant Professor teaching visual culture in the Rhetoric department at the University of California, Berkeley. Her research is based in the southern Chinese cities of Hong Kong, Guangzhou, and Shenzhen, and her writing engages with Chinese and Western aesthetics, intellectual property law, and popular culture. She is the author of *Van Gogh on Demand: China and the Readymade*, published by the University of Chicago Press (2014). Winnie is currently writing a second book, a new art history of export painting and the Canton Trade, 1760–1842.

**Haiping Yan** was formerly Professor of UCLA and Cornell University in Theatre/Performance Studies, Comparative Literature and East Asian Literature, and is presently University Professor of Cross-cultural Studies and the Director of the Institute for World Literatures and Cultures at Tsinghua University, and EAP fellow at Cornell University. Her specialties include modern and contemporary theatre and cinema, literary and cultural history, critical theory, and transnational performance studies. Her book publications include *Theatre and Society* (Routledge, 1998), *Chinese Women Writers and the Feminist Imagination* (Routledge, 2006), "Other Transnationals" (*Modern Drama*, 2005), and *A Journey of Homecoming*. She recently completed her manuscript on Chinese artistic culture and cosmopolitanism and is working on a memoir titled *Class of 77: The Making of Global China*.

**Midori Yoshimoto** is Associate Professor of Art History at New Jersey City University, who specializes in post-1945 Japanese art and its global intersections. Her publications include *Into Performance: Japanese Women Artists in New York* (2005); an essay in *Yayoi Kusama* (Centre Pompidou, 2011); an essay in *Yoko Ono One Woman Show* (MoMA, 2015); "*From Space to Environment*: The Origins of Kankyō and the Emergence of Intermedia Art in Japan" in *Art Journal* (2008); and an essay in *Gutai* (Guggenheim, 2013). She guest-edited an issue on "Women and Fluxus" for the *Women and Performance* journal (2009).

**Yvonne Zeeb** is a cognitive neuroscientist and the Director of The Center for Trans-Cognitive Imaging in Los Angeles, California. Founded in 2001, CTCI studies cognition and neurophysiology in posthuman organisms. Zeeb has a background in linguistics, philosophy and neuroscience and is the author of numerous research papers including the landmark "Systems Poetics of a Physiological Imaginary as applied to *Kinocognophore*." She is currently a consultant to Spacetime Applied Research Systems on the metacognitive effects of space travel on bionic organisms. She is a staunch advocate for the transition from a consciousness of "humanity" to one of "organity."

**Bo Zheng** is Assistant Professor at the School of Creative Media, City University of Hong Kong. He has been making and writing about socially engaged art since 2003. He is an editorial board member of *Journal of Chinese Contemporary Art*. He received his PhD from the Visual and Cultural Studies program at the University of Rochester, and taught at China Academy of Art in Hangzhou from 2010–2013. His artworks and writings can be accessed at www.tigerchicken.com

# How to use this book

*Meiling Cheng and Gabrielle H. Cody*

*Reading Contemporary Performance: Theatricality Across Genres* provides students, academics, practitioners, and general readers with an enriched understanding of how theatricality across genres, media, and experiential platforms can be considered part of a performance continuum. As coeditors, we enact our belief that there are multiple entry points into today's expanded field of performance by offering our readers three introductory essays. These three essays reflect the thematic order of our book's main title, subtitle, and the body of its text; each guides the reader to approach contemporary performance from a particular direction. The reader may also choose to bypass these essays and go straight into their following sections.

- For those who prefer to learn about contemporary performance by experiencing it: go to the first introductory essay "Reading performance: A physiognomy" and follow our lead to access, view, and read a case study of a selected performance, Ann Hamilton's *(aleph • video)* (1992/93), whose image adorns our book cover.
- For those who enjoy contemplating a major performance concept in depth: go first to the second introductory essay "Theatricality across genres" to explore the concept's relevance to the multicentric, genre-elusive contemporary performance scene.
- For those who wish to discover how we organize this book's more than 130 entries: go first to the third introductory essay "Performing the theatrical matrix" to sample the multiple pathways that this vibrant conceptual lens has helped us envision so as to present them in this volume.
- For those who favor partially charted ways of navigating this book: go first to any title included in the volume and then follow its trail of *Cross references* to other related entries.

# Acknowledgments

First and foremost, we wish to thank Talia Rogers for her steadfast support and patience over a number of years—as this manuscript emerged out of another project, and took its own amazing shape. We are especially indebted to Talia for suggesting "Reading Contemporary Performance" as our book's main title, which set our theorizing engine going a couple of years ago. Thanks also to Ben Piggott and Harriet Affleck for helping us navigate this massive, and at times, unwieldy ship.

Gabrielle would like to thank the brilliant Meiling Cheng beyond words for joining her on this massive journey, helping her to map a solid course, and being such a generous collaborator. She is also grateful to Vassar College for two Research grants, a Ford Foundation grant, and to Jon Chenette, Dean of the Faculty, for his additional funding to help defray the cost of images and image rights.

Over the years, several smart, resourceful, and incredibly dedicated Vassar students have helped me through the different stages of this book: Marc Etlin, Charlie O'Malley, Arianna Gass, Allison Pearl, and Arden Shwayder. You made it happen. Allison, you have been an angel of mercy. My deep thanks also to Kelly Speca from USC for her incredible work and commitment to our project.

I am always indebted to my beyond generous friend and partner Hilary Sio, my ever inquisitive daughter Willa Sio-Cody, and two canine friends, whose collective sweetness and wisdom have kept me going through the good and bad days.

For Meiling: I would like to thank the fabulous Gabrielle H. Cody for inviting me to join her as coeditor to reshape a project that she had initiated and for the tremendous trust, respect, enthusiasm, and generosity that she has given me during our joyous four-year partnership in making this book. Working on *RCP* offered me the intellectual stimuli needed to recover from the mental and physical depletion that I experienced right after I finished my book *Beijing Xingwei* (2013). I am also grateful for the privilege of returning to the theatrical matrix—a theoretical proposition noted in my first book *In Other Los Angeleses* (2002)—and of developing the theory much further in this book with the contributions of Gabrielle and our *RCP* editorial team. We retrieved three grains of sand there and built a dome with lots of stones here.

Many thanks are due to University of Southern California's Undergraduate Research Associate Program, which offered me two grants (2013–14; 2014–15) and the opportunity of working with Kelly Speca, my Undergraduate Research Associate who provided competent editorial assistance during her intensive one-year (2014) involvement with *RCP*. Responsive and efficient,

Kelly, with the help of Arden Shwayder, obtained most photo permissions for our image illustrations and, together with Allison Pearl, worked on an important feature—cross-references among entries—for *RCP*. I give heartfelt thanks also to Allison Pearl from Vassar College for returning to *RCP* during the final critical month to help the editorial team—in Allison's words—"power through" our hefty manuscript. As always and once again, I bow to amphibianArc Design Studio for the problem-solving grant to make this and many other events pleasantly accomplishable.

My life would have been a nonsensical automatic performance without the interventions of many loving significant others. I owe happiness, sustenance, and solace to my closest family: my beloved mother Yu-Jen Su, sister Judy Cheng, brother Kai Cheng, my life partner and mind mentor Nonchi Wang, our son the indomitable Ashtin Wang, and our "dry daughter" Xin Yi. I hold many fond memories of my father Shu-King Cheng and wish he could have seen this book. I am indebted to the curiosity and inspirations of my USC students, who have served to model a particular group of *RCP* readers for me. Among all my former students and current friends, my deepest gratitude goes to Rolf Hoefer, whose brilliance, acute judgment, and unfailing wordsmithery have helped push my writing to its most lucid persuasion.

As coeditors, we owe our greatest debt to the many contributors to *RCP*. Corresponding with them and learning about contemporary performance from working on their entries have made our process of generating *RCP* an invigorating matrix: we feel alive and thriving within an ongoing performance genealogy.

* * *

The *RCP* editorial team and our publisher gratefully acknowledge the permission granted to reproduce published copyrighted material in adapted forms in our book:

"Boychild": Halberstam, Jack. 2015. "Boychild." In *Stand Close, It's Shorter Than You Think: A Show on Feminist Rage*, edited by Katherine Brewer Ball and David Frantz. Exhibition catalogue, printed by ONE Archives at the USC Libraries.

"Fifteen Principles of Black Market International": La Chance, Michäel. 2005. "Les 15 principes du Black Market International." In *The Principles of Black Market International 1985–2005*, edited by Boris Nieslony and Marco Teubner, 22. Köln: E.P.I. Zentrum, unpaginated.

"Gaga Feminism": Halberstam, Jack. 2013. "Charming for the Revolution: A Gaga Manifesto." In *E-flux* 44. http://www.e-flux.com/journal/charming-for-the-revolution-a-gaga-manifesto/.

"He Yunchang's Limit Acts": Cheng, Meiling. 2006. "Extreme Performance and Installation from China." *TheatreForum* (Summer): 88–96.

"Memoirs of Bjork-Geisha": Takemoto, Tina. 2015. "Drawing Complaint: Orientalism, Disidentification, and Performance." *Asian Diasporic Visual Cultures and the Americas* 1: 84–107.

"The Wooster Group's *TO YOU THE BIRDIE!*": Cody, Gabrielle H.. 2003. *Theatre Journal: A Special Issue on Ancient Theatre* 55.1: 173–175.

# Part I

# Introductions

# Reading performance

## A physiognomy

*Meiling Cheng and Gabrielle H. Cody*

> And every "form" is a face looking at us.
>
> Serge Daney, "The Tracking Shot in Kapo" (1992)

Serge Daney, a self-proclaimed "cinephile," had a specific referent in mind when he made the general analogy between a form and a face. He later named this referent, "And then I see clearly why I have adopted cinema: so it could adopt me in return" (1992, online). Daney's statement, however, carries greater resonance than the particular genre of his address, for his analogy redirects our modernist interest in knowing a given artwork's intrinsic qualities to performative dynamics: the reciprocal impacts borne by the artwork and its beholder through their encounter. This transition from the ontological (the nature of an artwork) to the interactive (an artwork's relationship with its beholder) implied by Daney's remark opens up the cultural space for our book, *Reading Contemporary Performance: Theatricality Across Genres*, to claim that performance has emerged as one of the most mobile, adaptable, and sharable ways for us to experience the world, look into ourselves, and communicate with others. We have entered an era in which we care less about what a performance is than about what it does for us and how we can return the favor.

But does performance have a form that can serve as its face? Daney's daring metaphorical schema (every form = its face) asserts that it does: even formlessness is a form. By giving a face to an art form, Daney evokes certain attributes—such as agency, affect, and expression—that we usually associate with a face in the act of looking and effectively makes the artwork, in whatever form it takes, an entity equivalent in status to the human agent who engages with it. Daney's conceptual paradigm relocates an artwork's purpose from exercising its unique being to its dialogic function, as it develops a relationship with us, the people who choose to experience it. Simultaneously, the same paradigm exposes our role in this relationship as not always the subjects actively doing the "looking," but also the objects being "looked at" by the artwork. At the heart of Daney's premise lies the mystery of the encounter between two parties, who share equal status as reciprocal partners and interacting performers, even though they may reside within different levels of reality.

Since Daney's paradigm defines this meeting from the perspective of the artwork itself as a looking subject, we might approach the same process from our position as the one in thrall to the look. Thus, let's consider our options: If indeed every form—including this book, *Reading Contemporary Performance* (alias, *RCP*)—is a face looking at us, then why and how do we look back?

The answers to the "Why ... ?" question are likely to be existential and relatively unique to each individual. Why do we want to know about performance? Why do we read this book? Why do we dance to a sad song and weep from happiness? Why do we brave through our constant aging and incremental dying to still try to "perform our best" every day, documenting our transitory faces with countless selfies and sending them tumbling through electronic ether? Why not—if that's the way we greet the world and amuse our friends, while investing in our digital immortality. What does Serge Daney say?

Our average guru's answer to the "Why ... ?" question pivots on the consensual pleasure of mutual adoption: "I've adopted cinema, so cinema could adopt me!" Provocatively, Daney's answer echoes a simple calculation in physics: I cannot see my own face without being seen by another face—the face of a mirror, the face of water, or the face of my reflection inside another person's pupils. Even when I don't see my face literally reflected on the face of, say, a rock, I might trace the rock's sedimented patterns and recognize how time has produced similar wrinkles on my face to make me as stoic, solid, still, and enduring as a rock. Consciously or not, we look into and look back at the face looking at us in search of our own possible faces. In other words, we would read this particular face, *RCP*, to see how the reading may change us and how we may in turn change *RCP*. What happens between *RCP* and us during the protracted reading process is a contingent concatenation of performances, which promise, if nothing else, to change our perceptions about the world around us.

Compared with the idiosyncratic "Why ... ?" question, the "How ... ?" question is collaborative. Answers to the "How ... ?" will multiply, evolve, migrate, mutate, proliferate, and accumulate upon one another through their respondents' aggregated labors and for the sake of their common benefits. It surely takes more than one book and a few centuries to respond to the "How ... ?" question. So we might as well begin again, here and now, by raising the question that we earlier put off: "What is the face of the form that *RCP* desires to look back at, to reflect, to touch, and to talk to, to draw on, to play with, to tear apart, to ponder, to imitate, and to read?" Suppose that the face has no eyes, no nose, no ears, nor jaw, how do we start?

> From a video still image, you see the close-up shot of a mouth, with lips ajar and a number of stone marbles weighing on its tongue. You click your computer cursor on the triangular sign activating "Play" and the mouth begins moving, bringing the stones inside its orifice into rolling motions. These stones orbit around one another like an acrobatic ensemble and constantly shift their positions on the mobile bridge of a tongue, making dull grating sounds as their moist surfaces touch. Revolving rhythmically in their discrete but intimate proximity, these spherical players can barely remain on their stage—two just slip past the guardian teeth and almost fall from the lips' edge, while others sway precariously against the backdrop of a larynx.

Spotlighted with a framing border and a sans-serif font, our narrative offers a brief case study of a viewer's encounter with one of many faces of contemporary performance. In this context, the "viewer" is anyone who has the means of interfacing with a digitized video sequence accessible on the Internet and who has an interest in initiating a fleeting sensory contact with what the online portal might proffer. To launch this "sensory contact" entails a viewer's own performance through several actions: (1) make a choice to access a virtual object (a face/form) that promises something more than its initial still image; (2) engage with the haptic experience of holding the computer devices required for the access; (3) watch a recording of an action executed by a troupe of performers, including an acrobatic mouth, two rows of teeth, a skillful tongue, a bunch of stones set to occupy the mouth, and a tantalizing larynx. After most likely a private screening from a computer monitor, the viewer, if seduced by these apparently constricted yet all-the-more-so virtuosic performers, might choose to generate more follow-up actions. *RCP* suggests that the act of *reading a performance* usually happens not with the first but rather with the follow-up set of a viewer's performance. Reading a performance is *a repeat performance.*

In a world suffused with traces of performance—such as pop-up ads, Facebook postings, Twitter tweets, movie previews, YouTube videos, even a sad lost dog poster with a guaranteed reward and a detachable list of phone numbers—a person's choice to experience more than haphazard fragments of a particular performance will often produce an instant series of shifting roles. By giving permission to linger with the face of another form, the person changes from a random passer-by to a volitional actor, from an embodied sentient being who performs the tasks of daily living to one who interrupts the flow of quotidian routines so as to pay attention to another being, from a perceiver of information and a consumer of data streams to a reader, one potentially able to process, interpret, question, critique, and make something out of that same information, henceforth altering the information.

If our exemplary viewer serves as a prototypical reader addressed by *RCP*, then how can we characterize the video piece we described earlier as a face of contemporary performance? At our spectacle-saturated contemporary moment, we often encounter the face of a performance first as an anonymous image: a mouth strangely stuffed with stones, for example. Something about this image—perhaps the slight dread of suffocation it evokes, or the cunning configuration of those stones—compels our attention, urging us to find out more, if only to make sense of this peculiar sight. As *RCP* proposes, the instant we transition from indifference, to interest, to initiating a relationship with what that image might bring establishes the condition for us to begin conceptualizing what we experience subsequently as a performance. Specifically, we understand a performance as an intentional construct emerging out of the creative ecology of five irreducible, interwoven, and mutually affecting elements: the "*time-space-action-performer-audience* matrix" of theatricality (Cheng 2002: 278). Any element in this dynamic theatrical matrix may function as an entry point to stimulate the concomitant formation and motion of the other four elements, thereby constituting an experiential event that we appreciate as a performance.

In our opening case study, for instance, the entry point is the viewer, or an audience of one. This audience's choice to instigate an exchange with an intriguing image triggers at least two simultaneous performances. As we explored earlier, one of these performances is self-generating, when the audience doubles as the performer to execute a durational action of observing a video recording. The time for this performance coincides with the audience-performer's chosen duration, which might last from a few seconds to the roughly one-minute length of the video sequence, or longer, with repeated viewings. The space is the virtual interface as well as the actual place where the mechanism enabling this interface resides. The *site* of this performance emerges as the conjunction of space and time designated by the performed action: while the virtual site engaged by the audience-performer's observation is both somewhere out there (on the Web) and in here (inside the viewer's mind), the actual site might be as small, near, and dear as a smart phone screen, along with the tinier cognitive nerves fired up by synapses within the observer's brain.

Meanwhile, concurrent with this audience-performer's enactment is a parallel performance by our case study's other subject, faces of which adorn the cover of *RCP*. The mouth starts moving, the stones on its tongue spinning, making grating sounds. After approximately one minute, the performance stops, while the mouth remains agape, restored to its former anonymity, which suddenly feels unbearable to us. We succumb to this scene of seduction by searching further; now we want to be able to *read the performance.*

*Reading as a query for facts*: what we watched and described in our case study is an excerpt from *(aleph • video)* (1992/93), made by artist Ann Hamilton (annhamiltonstudio.com 2014). Hamilton first shot on a beta tape her own mouth, teeth, and tongue manipulating a number of stone marbles to produce a thirty-minute video piece, shown in a continuous loop from a small television monitor (with a 3.5 × 4.5 inches screen) inset onto a wall, to form part of her site-specific installation *aleph* (1992) at the List Visual Arts Center, Massachusetts Institute of Technology.

*Reading as historiographic investigation*: Although Hamilton's 1992 installation is no longer extant, *(aleph • video)* has been converted into a digital format and, in its limited version, is available for online public access in a virtual gallery via the artist's website. The video excerpt serves as both a mnemonic reference to the ephemeral scenographic environment in which it once participated and an archival sampling of a collectible video piece, editioned by the artist and acquired by a museum (Guggenheim, see Ragheb 2015). The migratory path that the video has taken (studio -> installation -> internet -> any conceivable elsewhere) typifies how performative artworks might travel and circulate in our globalized technological economy. A transient performance piece may now lead an afterlife as variously reconfigured commodities branded with an artist's signature.

*Reading as comparing clues*: According to Hamilton, her piece's title was inspired by Ivan Illich and Barry Sanders's explication that "the sound and the name of the [Semitic] letter 'aleph' derive from the shape the larynx takes as it moves from silence to speech" (Simon 2006; see also Illich and Sanders 1989). Our previous reading approaches the action of *(aleph • video)* as a performance of competence, in which an ensemble of stones behave like autonomous performers to accomplish clever relational routines in a theatre made of human organs. The stones play for our diversion. The new clue from the artist's statement, however, recasts the piece's action in a linguistic framework, calling attention, instead, to its drama of necessity, a suspenseful labor through which a speaker strives to move "from silence to speech." In this light, the stones, with the lips and tongue, teeth and gums, and even the larynx, all become supporting players for the featured performance of the speaking subject.

*Reading as decipherment*: Our newly clued reading of *(aleph • video)* as a performer's gestural production of sounds guides us to see her mouth less as a site where performance happens than as an instrument with which the speaker plays, vacillating between silences and speeches. We already knew that the mouth in *(aleph • video)* belongs to Hamilton—who wears a dark lipstick—but why didn't she show her entire face? This exclusive focus on a mouth-in-action, as we may reasonably decipher, serves to obscure the performer's individual identity and heighten the mouth's status as a common facial organ through which we, the human species, produce speech and develop language. Thus, Hamilton chose a small and relatively anonymous (being eyeless/soulless, etc.) part of her face to substitute for the highly evolved mouth of Homo sapiens, capable of producing silence and speech, plus many other oral variations in between. If so, then what do those stones stand for?

*Reading as all you can take*: There are no stones in *(aleph • video)*, for all is digital! As homage to one of the best contemporary film epics of our time, *The Matrix* (1999), we sample and remix a line from it—"There is no spoon"—to characterize the mutability of those stones rolling in the mouth on the cover/face of *RCP*. Once upon a time, those stones were real! They were the building blocks, if not the alphabet, for Hamilton's self-invented hybrid speech in her initial recorded live performance. This hybrid speech comprises disparate elements rarely used in the so-called conventional human tongues: the speaker's conjoint senses of touch and taste; the athleticism of nerves-laden labial muscles around the lips; and the insertion of material sonic components (the actual stones) into the speech system. Yet, insofar as Hamilton's hybrid speech is not widely recognized, practiced, and exchanged as such, the stones interspersed in her system of orature exist merely as linguistic embryos, or premature signifiers, those sign-objects that may potentially become codified as the signified, as the meaning-carrying entities capable of facilitating linguistic communication. At present, these stones are more like slippery notes in a song than legible letters in a speech.

*RCP* delights in collecting and cultivating these not-quite-stones. Precisely because of their embryonic state, the stones inhabit the realm of the *edgy imaginable*, a delirious liminal zone where symbols sit next to tools neighboring similes side by side icons flanking metaphors across hypotheses and adjacent to functions. Infinitely malleable, these stones are ready to be adopted by those who are ready to adopt and be adopted by contemporary performance.

# Theatricality across genres

Gabrielle H. Cody and Meiling Cheng

"Theatricality" was the title of the 20th episode of the television series *Glee,* which premiered in 2010, and featured its female club members paying homage to Lady Gaga. The *Glee* cast performed in a selection of Mother Monster's costumes, including her *Haus of Gaga* bubble dress, the *Armani prive orbit* dress she wore to the 52nd Grammy Awards, and a knock–off of the dress she wore to meet Elizabeth II. That Lady Gaga and her wardrobe should be the inspiration for an episode about the pleasures of over-the-top, fake ontologies—an episode watched by 11.5 million 18 to 49 year-old Americans, securing a 4.8 Nielson rating—(Russell and Cohn 2012, 5–7) affirms pop culture's valorization of the illusory, embracing a concept of theatricality as irrepressible, subversive. Lady Gaga's "Meat Dress," made of flank steak, and worn at the MTV Video Awards that same year—an idea whose initial provenance was most likely Canadian sculptor Jana Sterback's *Vanitas: Fresh Dress for an Albino Anorexic* (1987) and more recently seen in Chinese artist Zhang Huan's *My New York* (2002)—also spoofs the myth of authenticity and originality.

In contrast to popular culture's campy, even salacious, flirtation with theatricality in its most histrionic extreme, Euro-American philosophical discourses on this elusive concept have been fraught from Plato's antitheatricality to the present. Jonas Barish picked up this thread almost three decades ago in his voluminous classic, *The Antitheatrical Prejudice* (1981), which comprehensively documents the bias and suspicion against theatricality throughout Western history. The "theatrical" assumes a heightening, even an unmasking and denuding, of the so-called "natural" and "decent" through exaggeration, explicit eroticism, sentimentality, and blatant or subtle disguise, all of which dramatize age-old fears of excess, artificiality, and inauthenticity—traits that have also animated a range of deadly binaries. "All things theatrical," as Tracy Davis and Thomas Postlewait observe, "are on the negative end of the polarity [ ... ] this opposition has also been used to distinguish between masculine and feminine traits, with women portrayed (from the perspective of patriarchy) as duplicitous, deceptive, costumed, showy, and thus as a sex inherently theatrical" (2003, 17).

When "theatricality" fares well discursively, it is considered "pre-aesthetic," "a metaphor for life itself" (Evreinov 1927, 24), "universal" (Phelan and Lane 1998, 3). When it does not, its worth is that of emptiness, deceit, campy surplus. The concept's contradictory value-designation prompts Davis and Postlewait to remark that theatricality "is a sign empty of meaning; it is the meaning of all signs" (2003, 1). This provocative statement from the coeditors of a volume devoted to reassessing "theatricality" as a critical term reflects the resurgence of interest in this historically contested concept among U.S. scholars. For the most part, however, their scholarly interest in theatricality appears in reaction to their more vigorous engagement with the concepts of performance and performativity. As Shannon Jackson puts it, for Anglo-American "theater scholars, the relation between theatricality and performativity is more pressing, and cause for defensiveness, in a theoretical context where the latter term has intellectual currency" (2003, 209; see also McGillivray 2009, 112). Janelle Reinelt has attributed this implicit intellectual hierarchy to the relatively convoluted history of theatricality, for there have been "widely distributed metaphorical usages of the theatrical and of theatricality," which "threaten to dilute any prospective genealogy of this discourse" (2002, 205). What's clear is that there can be no one definition for theatricality, since the term is steeped in specific periods, cultures, and practices. Thus, as Davis and Postlewait recommend, the idea of theatricality in its multiple incarnations and "the wide range of possible applications" is "more efficacious" as a "starting point" (2003, 3). In other words, "theatricality," as a starting point of reference, carries implications that are relative and would change according to whether it is used in European, Anglo-American, Latin American, or non-Western contexts (Reinelt 2002, 205, 211).

While contemporary Anglo-American theorists have located "performance and performativity as central organizing concepts" (Reinelt 2002, 207) in the field of performing arts, Europeans have been inclined to embrace the "specificity of theatrical language," revealing an affinity with the early 20th-century avant-garde's re-ordering of semiotic principles in cultural and discursive spheres (Féral 2002, 94; Fischer-Lichte 1995, 98). German scholar Erika Fischer-Lichte, for instance, locates a specific language of theatricality in the trend for "re-theatricalization" of the stage, which began happening in various productions that preceded more radical avant-garde experiments at the turn of the twentieth century (Fischer-Lichte 1995, 98). Reflecting on Max Reinhardt's *Sumurin* (1910)—a drama based on an imaginary Orient and staged simultaneously in multiple areas, including a *hanamichi*—Fischer-Lichte notes that the "role of the [spectators] was no longer to [...] understand one representation of reality, but, instead, to create their own reality":

> As a consequence, theater was no longer to be defined through its representations but through the processes of construction which it triggers. Since this capacity is not restricted to theater (or art in general), yet is explicitly focused and marked by it, I call it theatricality. (1995, 103)

Similar to Fischer-Lichte, French Canadian Josette Féral also relates theatricality to a beholder's perceptual construction rather than to the medium of theatre per se. As Féral states, "theatricality is not strictly a theatrical or stage related phenomenon" but rather "emerges through a cleft in quotidian space" (2002, 97). According to Féral, an empty stage in a theatre before the arrival of actors has already been read as a semiotic object—"certain signs are already in place" (2002, 95)—because it addresses and regards the spectator *as* spectator, as a particular role/sign in a semiotic process. The spectator's "exercise of watching" a dramatic artwork unfolding on a stage "reassigns gestures to theatrical space" through the "process" of "a 'gaze' that postulates and creates a distinct, virtual space belonging to the other, from which *fiction can emerge*" (2002, 97, *emphasis ours*). Likewise, using the example of a person watching passers-by from a sidewalk café, Féral points out that our "gaze" in quotidian space also functions to frame events. Both settings—quotidian or artistic—reinforce Féral's analysis that theatricality is "the result of a perceptual dynamics linking the onlooker with someone or something that is looked at" (2002, 105). The experience of theatricality here hinges on the conceptual and situational affiliation between the performer and the spectator, who essentially co-create the meaning of the scene watched, whether it's an accidental event observed from a café, or an intentional spectacle produced on a stage.

In the expansive view shared by Fischer-Lichte and Féral, "theatricality [is] not strictly a theatrical phenomenon" (Féral 2002, 98); rather, theatricality emerges from the fissure between the onlooker's eyes and the object being watched. Whereas Fischer-Lichte's theory of theatricality focuses on an onlooker's hermeneutic construction of the scene observed, Féral regards theatricality as a process of recognition: "a process that recognizes subjects in process; it is a process of looking at or being looked at." In other words, the agents linked through this process of reciprocal recognition become mutually implicated theatrical subjects. Further, Féral conceptualizes this "subject" as not necessarily human: "the presence of the actor is not a prerequisite to theatricality"; instead, "space is the vehicle of theatricality" (2002, 96). To extend Féral's thesis, this space is the cleft— the interpretive distance—that enables the onlooker to experience the performative dynamic we call "theatricality."

Such radical claims that detach theatricality from theatre offer myriad possibilities for how this perceptual dynamic can be deployed *across* various performance genres, including theatrical performance, visual art-centered conceptual performance, sound-and-movement-based kinetic performance, site-specific environmental or architectural performance, digital media-oriented interactive performance, and technological prostheses-enabled immersive performance, in addition to performances in everyday life. Féral's proposition anticipates Meiling Cheng's appropriation of theatricality to theorize multicentric performance art. To Cheng, however, theatricality signifies more than the process of intersubjective recognition and extends beyond the instrumentality of space to involve the creative ecology of five irreducible, interwoven, and mutually affecting elements: "the *time-space-action-performer-audience* matrix" (2002, 278). With such specifications, Cheng delineates performance as an intentional construct arising from the interactive kinetics of the five structural units that constitute the theatrical matrix—"theatricality is both the *quintessence* and the *culmination*" of this matrix (2002, 278). In *RCP*, we extend and substantiate Cheng's hypothesis to prioritize the multiple points of access for a self-reflexive onlooker/reader to activate the theatrical matrix from any of its pentagonal nodes. To reiterate our succinct premise here: "Any element in this dynamic theatrical matrix may function as an entry point to stimulate the concomitant formation and motion of the other four elements, thereby constituting an experiential event that we appreciate as a performance" (Cheng and Cody in *RCP*, 5).

Shannon Jackson is mindful of precisely this kind of interdisciplinary hybridization when she suggests that a number of "performative turns" (2011, 28) have taken place through a renewed interest in sociality and participation. While in the previous century, modernist art critic Michael Fried could still un-self-consciously express his virulent antitheatrical prejudice by announcing that, "*Art degenerates as it approaches the condition of theatre*" (1967, 8; original emphasis), the past two decades have seen art galleries become theatricalized through relational procedures and organized types of sociability, as predicted and popularized by the French curator Nicolas Bourriaud's practice of *Relational Aesthetics* (1998). Visual artists are "re-imagining the theatrical event" through "exploring the durational, embodied, social and extended spatiality of theatrical forms in work such as Rirkrit Tiravanija's cooking installations, [or] Santiago Sierra's use of local laborers to pose as statues" (Jackson 2011, 1). Concurrently, there has been "a movement towards painting and sculpture" in most postdramatic theatre works (Jackson 2011, 2). Creative cross-pollination is the imaginary ethos of contemporary performance. In these genre-busting formulations, the theatrical matrix offers a generative framework for the reader to experience the event of performance as theatricality.

# Performing the theatrical matrix

*Meiling Cheng and Gabrielle H. Cody*

*Reading Contemporary Performance: Theatricality Across Genres* explores intermedial, multidisciplinary, and cross-platform performance in the 21st century, encompassing theatrical performance, live art, time-based art, postmodern dance, and experimental music, animal acts, expanded cinema, mediated ceremonies, and alternative reality games, transgender rituals, queer brigades, inter-ethnic identity events, installation and interactive sculpture, site-specific, ecology-centered relational actions, pop-cultural activism, and posthuman technological art. We subsume these simultaneously multiplying, crisscrossing, and hybridizing genres of performance artworks under the common term of theatricality, so as to track these diverse expressions in a spectrum of imaginative possibilities. For us, *theatricality* is not a quality specifically produced by a proscenium-framed theatre work; instead, it is a floating *affect* occasioned by the interplay among the five constitutive elements in any performance artwork: the *time-space-action-performer-audience matrix of theatricality* (see Cheng 2002). As a perceptual and interactive sensory output, theatricality may emanate from a performance produced on the literal stage, but it may also erupt from various performative acts happening on the stage of the body, the street, the open field, the gallery, the petri dish, the canvas, the screen, and the sound—even from the shimmering surface of a meteorite, or the interior of a mouth.

If for nothing else but the concept's alleged flamboyant and campy perversity, we have selected theatricality—in its guise as a palpable, if also random, fluid, and volatile, outcome from *the theatrical matrix*—to be our organizing principle for the more than 130 entries that we collected in *RCP*, our treasure chest of performing, performable, and reperformable "stones" made of paper, thought, text, and digitalia. We set out to investigate how performance practitioners across genres relate to the contradictory nature and multiple lineages of theatricality, which, as our second introductory essay traces, have offered a rich practical and theoretical resource for the evolving language of performance. How are contemporary practitioners exploring and exploiting, devising and deploying, manipulating and negating their particular use of theatricality, and to what ends? How has theatricality, as both a human and supra-human effect from a structural constancy (its five-elemental matrix), inspired theatre and art creators, critics, poets, curators, scholars, and other genre-benders to enhance the relevance of performance to contemporary cultural productions as well as to everyday life? And how would theatricality jumpstart an inert strip of quotidian behavior to make the act of reading as agonizingly delicious as that of creating a performance?

In our opening essay, we guided our readers to become aware of the pervasive interventions of performance into contemporary life and their own active participations in this trending style of living. We offered *the theatrical matrix* as a conceptual compass for our readers to identify and generate performances whenever they so desire. Furthermore, we took our readers through the time-based and space-flexible action of deeply reading Ann Hamilton's *(aleph • video)*, our incipient case study. We conduct this joint pondering process—with a whiff of self-reflexive irony—to put the equation of *performance* and *the theatrical matrix* (*p* = *ttm*™) into the minds of those already inclined to receiving the idea (see *Inception* 2010). In sum, *RCP* aims to empower our readers with a technology of recognizing, unraveling, knowing, exploiting, initiating, and recreating contemporary performance pieces whenever they chance upon those *p* = *ttms* on their daily paths; the baseline of this reading technology is the ever-adaptable—and potentially App-convertible—*theatrical matrix*: our *RCP*™.

Sustaining *the theatrical matrix*, however, is a massive and protean heritage of performance practices and scholarships, a glocalizing heritage molded by—to name but a few more visible disciplines—theatre studies; art history; cultural studies; performance studies; visual anthropology; ecology and sociobiology; economics, genetics, and politics; communication studies; information technology; and interactive media studies. This heritage for contemporary performance education is variously pluralistic, divergent, syncretic, contradictory, and complex—a multicentric living legacy. Without prior immersion in this heritage, we, as editorial emissaries from *Planet RCP*, cannot even move our tongues, let alone push conceptual stones, to chew over *(aleph • video)*. We reveal our affiliation with that multicentric heritage by embedding many of our inherited terms as essential critical vocabulary with which we enact our performative reading.

This bountiful living legacy for contemporary performance production, curation, and critique contains roughly three major heuristic trends. We mimic these trends in *RCP* by organizing our entries in a tripartite structure.

1 **Concepts:** This section includes brief explications of those innovative, multivalent, and easily portable cognitive-entities that we call "concepts." Most of them may be modified from their initial contexts to become recombined with other concepts in addressing emergent contemporary issues.
2 **Methodologies/turning points:** Most entries in this section discuss concepts that have developed through longer historical periods to become applicable "methodologies" in reading and making performances. Also included are entries on theoretical principles that may be considered aesthetic and cultural "turning points," which have radically affected the evolving course of performance.
3 **Case studies:** Dispersed throughout the book is a collection of case studies, which include both textual embodiments of certain performance practices and focused analyses. Topics range from an artist's reflection of her/his/zir creative process, a critic's account of a theatre company's oeuvres, to a choreographer's reminiscence of an awe-inspiring predecessor, from the editors' excerpt of an existing performance piece, a team of theorists' contemplation of a single performance genre, to a quasi-manifesto from an ad-hoc global performance collective.

We have half-jokingly referred to *the theatrical matrix* (*ttm*) as *RCP*'s trademark technology for reading contemporary performance across genres. In earnest, we propose *the theatrical matrix* as an accessible and malleable way to engage with myriad daily performative incidents. Indeed with a *ttm* lens, reading *RCP* may itself become a performance. We also submit that *the theatrical matrix*, like an alphabet, facilitates the formation of a vernacular with which we may approach and talk back to performance artworks made in explicit creative contexts.

The *ttm* alphabet has a total of five "letters," which always operate together, supporting and subverting one another in generating a multitude of performance texts. In any given performance circumstance, "one [letter] may be prioritized over another, or one maybe diminished, but none can be entirely eliminated" (Pearl 2014, 1). In the theatrical matrix, *time* is not only the designated hour and the length/duration of a performance, but also the sense of time constructed by the action. The *space* indicates the determined performance locale and the particular use of its expanse, depth, areas, and dimensions as well as the molding of space as a negative presence or a virtual emergence in the action. Accordingly, what is usually called the "site" of a performance involves at least two elements: the space enlivened and animated by time during the performing process. The *action* refers to the nature and types of activities involved in a performance, including the ways in which the performer manipulates the site, relates to the audience, and multiplies the interactive opportunities between them. The *performer* is the entity executing the action; the entity may comprise a solo artist, an ensemble of collaborating artists, or a group of involuntary nonhuman actors—corralled, coerced, or coded into the action. The *audience* for a performance ranges from one resembling a theatre audience, which sees, hears, experiences, evaluates, and sometimes participates in the action, to one who only engages with the action after the fact and via documentation, in the conceptual realm of virtual witnessing and reenactment.

To turn *RCP* into both a showcase and a test case for *the theatrical matrix*, we have assigned ourselves a series of invigorating, if somewhat perilous, tasks: categorization; puzzle challenges; and theatrical pairing. We overtly enlist *the theatrical matrix* to organize our **Concepts** section by subsuming under each *ttm* category a set of concept-entries. Our selections help us define, substantiate, and expand the significance and applicability of the given *ttm* category. "The Internet" (Auslander in *RCP*, 41), for instance, has emerged as a contemporary engineered version of *Space*, offering new performance possibilities to be accessed by a random grouping of virtual *Audience* (Cody in *RCP*, 136). Occasionally we classify a certain concept as a counter-intuitive supplement to a chosen *ttm* category, thereby confronting our assumptions about that category. Associating "Cultural Production" (Colleran in *RCP*, 111) with *Performer*, for instance, transfers our attention from the conglomerate results of many concurrent and seemingly anonymous *Actions* to the individual and collective agents who have manufactured those cultural products with vested commercial, political, and ideological interests. The majority of concepts are elastic and applicable to more than one category. Is "Celebrity" (Nayar in *RCP*, 110) an eroticized stylistic signature from an alluring *Performer*, the effect of orchestrated media *Action*, or the longing projection by an adoring *Audience*? As a provisional solution to this dilemma, we offer a copious and suggestive list of *Cross references*, in order to point our readers to other related *RCP* entries similarly or otherwise categorized.

In **Methodologies/turning points**, we deliberately withhold *ttm* as an ordering principle for several reasons. First, we want this section to stand as a contrast to **Concepts** in order to test—*via negativa*—the efficacy of *ttm* as an epistemological scheme. Is "Aging" (Port in *RCP*, 177), for instance, a natural result of *Time*, its durational corporeal script, or its cumulative behavioral expectations? Does *Space* become increasingly constricted or expansive with "Aging"? Does "Aging" command a specialized series of *Action*? Is "Aging" an attribute, a decoration, a mask, a costume, an attitude, a physiology, or a pervasive but unreliable cultural lore for a *Performer*? Does "Aging" as a spectacle exist mostly in the eyes of the beholding *Audience*? Can we exercise similar *ttm* scanning with other entries? Second, we align our selections by their titles alphabetically to suggest that these entries constitute a miniature lexicon of viable methodologies and conceptual turning points for contemporary performance. While the entries do not follow a chronological order, they do reflect topics of interest that have rejuvenated performance history since at least the early twentieth century. Third, we present this assemblage of terms as our "puzzles" for our readers to play with their own *ttm* categorization.

Our **Case studies** selections exemplify the stunning diversity of *ttm*. Different from the other two sections, entries from **Case studies** appear intermittently throughout *RCP.* We also mark their distinct identities by adopting a consistent typographic style, as presaged by our incipient treatment of *(aleph • video)*. By dispersing the illustrative case studies among our more abstract entries, we manifest our theory that contemporary performance is no longer bound by specificity of genres, even when there is paradoxically an upsurge in the heterogeneous voices speaking in performance tongues.

Thus, in *RCP*, our readers may encounter performance in the form of a theoretical précis about "Precariousness" (Fabião in *RCP*, 30), for example, and then see how, in the next entry, precariousness and ephemerality become indistinguishable in curator Philip Tinari's analysis of Wang Wei's *Temporary Space* (*RCP*, 31), which pushes the capitalist conspiracy of planned obsolescence to the extreme. The readers may observe how performance artists proactively exercise civic responsibilities through "Intervention" (Olivares in *RCP*, 69) and then witness one such intervention in the following entry, "Sisters of Survival Signal S.O.S." (Gaulke in *RCP*, 71), which recounts the globetrotting performance protests against the proliferation of nuclear weapons initiated by a group of U.S. feminist artists and joined by fellow European artists. The readers may be enraged—yet again—by "Global censorship" (Shea in *RCP*, 138) in the form of a Taliban assassination that Malala Yousafzai suffered and then recall how Ai Weiwei, after his censorious imprisonment by the Chinese government, has risen to be a mega art star in "Transnational public spheres" (Zheng in *RCP*, 140). Or, the readers may feel intrigued by the recent scholarly exposure of "Whiteness" (Jones in *RCP*, 278) as a performative ethnic marker and then realize next that the religious practice of veiling, just like whiteness, may also become denaturalized, even repurposed, to work as a feminist stylistic rhetoric in the putatively all-pious idiom of "The Muslim performative" (Barlas in *RCP*, 280).

Similar to our categorization, our primary logic in pairing disparate entries is to underscore their thematic affinities. Therefore, for instance, we match "New genre public art" (Irish in *RCP*, 79) with Excerpts from Suzanne Lacy's *Prostitution Notes* (1974), because Lacy first introduced the term "New genre public art" in 1995, roughly two decades after she enacted *Prostitution Notes*, which manages, in retrospect, to prefigure the type of art practice that she subsequently named and popularized. In a few cases, we pair entries that might not appear to be immediate matches, but their linkages evoke latent thematic patterns. Pairing "Prosthetic performance" (Gass in *RCP*, 154) with "Gyrl grip" (Máire and Newman in *RCP*, 156), for instance, reveals how Llewyn Máire's body in ongoing transsexual transformation consists of no original versions, but a series of prosthetic alterations. Pairing "Reenactment" (Bay-Cheng in *RCP*, 89) with "Heather Cassils' indeterminate body" (Jones in *RCP*, 90) doubly annotates Cassils' durational appropriation of corporeal prosthetic performances as a means of citing, reenacting, and altering the iconic performances by selected predecessors. Heightening such exchange of discursive currency, we pair "Semiotics/semiology" (Scheie in *RCP*, 264) with "Bodies in action" (Stiles and O'Dell in *RCP*, 265) to display the field of semiotic performances as the ground in which performance theorists plow to plant their seeds of elegant arguments.

By mobilizing *the theatrical matrix* as an operating system for our tripartite platform, we expose the limits of our judgments, risk controversy and arbitrariness in our categorization, and appear to treat *ttm*, an intrinsically porous, pliable, and dynamic conceptual system, as a stable taxonomy. We commit ourselves to these potential intellectual liabilities, along with their attendant cognitive excitements, to both acknowledge and demonstrate that making knowledge about performances is as chancy, transitory, and prone to accidental misalignment as making performances. Our failings supply the soil and compost for our readers to grow their own "stones."

# Introductory essays bibliography


Barish, Jonas A. 1981. *The Antitheatrical Prejudice.* Berkeley, CA: University of California Press.

Bourriaud, Nicolas. 1998. *Relational Aesthetics.* France: Les Presses Du Reel.

Cheng, Meiling. 2002. *In Other Los Angeleses: Multicentric Performance Art.* Berkeley, CA: University of California Press.

Daney, Serge. 1992. "The Tracking Shot in Kapo." *P.O.L./Trafic* No. 4, translated by Laurent Kretzschmar. Accessed January 18, 2015. http://kit.kein.org/files/kit/daney.pdf

Davis, Tracy and Thomas Postlewait. 2003. *Theatricality.* Cambridge: Cambridge University Press.

Evreinov, Nikolai. 1927. *The Theatre in Life.* Translated by Alexander I. Nazaroff. New York: Brentano.

Féral, Josette and Ronald P. Bermingham. 2002. "Theatricality: The Specificity of Theatrical Language." In *SubStance,* Vol. 31, Special Issue Theatricality: 94–108.

Fischer-Lichte, Erika. 1995. "From Theatre to Theatricality – How to Construct Reality." In *Theatre Research International,* 20.2: 97–105.

Fried, Michael. 1967. "Art and Objecthood." In *Art and Objecthood: Essays and Reviews.* Chicago, IL: University of Chicago Press, 1998.

Fried, Michael. 1998. *Art and Objecthood: Essays and* Reviews. Chicago, IL and London: University of Chicago Press, 148–172.

Hamilton, Ann 1993. *aleph • video.* Accessed January 18, 2015. http://www.annhamiltonstudio.com/videosound/aleph_video.html

Illich, Ivan and Barry Sanders. 1989. *ABC: Alphabetization of the Popular Mind.* New York: Vintage.

*Inception,* film. 2010. Directed by Christopher Nolan. Performed by Leonardo DiCaprio, Joseph Gordon-Levitt, Ellen Page. Screenplay by Christopher Nolan. Warner Brothers.

Jackson, Shannon (2003). "Theatricality's proper objects: genealogies of performance and gender theory." In Tracy C. Davis and Thomas Postlewait, eds. *Theatricality.* Cambridge: Cambridge University Press, 186–213.

Jackson, Shannon. 2011. *Social Works, Performing Art, Supporting Publics.* New York and London: Routledge.

*The Matrix,* film. 1999. Directed by Andy Wachowski and Lana Wachowski. Performed by Keanu Reeves, Laurence Fishburne, Carrie-Anne Moss. Warner Brothers, Village Roadshow Pictures, Groucho II Film Partnership.

McGillivray, Glen. 2009, "The Discursive Formation of Theatricality as a Critical Concept." *Metaphorik.de* 17: 101–11. Accessed June 13, 2015. http://www.metaphorik.de/17/mcgillivray.pdf (last).

Pearl, Allison. 2014. "The Five Categories of Theatricality." Paper written, August 1, for *Reading Contemporary Performance*.

Phelan, Peggy and Jill Lane. 1998. "Introduction: The Ends of Performance." In Peggy Phelan and Jill Lane. *The Ends of Performance* 1–19. New York and London: New York University Press.

Ragheb, J. Fiona. 2015. "Ann Hamilton (*aleph • video*)." Guggenheim Collection Online. Accessed January 18, 2015. http://www.guggenheim.org/new-york/collections/collection-online/artwork/1608

Reinelt, Janelle. 2002. "The Politics of Discourse: Performativity Meets Theatricality." In *SubStance* Vol. 31, Special Issue Theatricality: 201–215.

Russell, Jesse and Ronald Cohn. 2012. *Theatricality*, 5–7. Edinburgh: LENNEX Corp.

Simon, Joan, ed. 2006. *Ann Hamilton: An Inventory of Objects*. New York: Gregory R. Miller & Co. Accessed January 18, 2015. http://www.annhamiltonstudio.com/videosound/aleph_video.html

# Part II

# Concepts and paired case studies

# Time

## Communitas

Debra Levine

Anthropologist Victor Turner uses the term "communitas" to describe a sensation of shared humanity that occurs during the liminal phase of a rite of passage. Communitas is a "structure of feeling," a term Raymond Williams employs to describe an affect that reflects a community's lived experience "in solution" (1977, 133). In Turner's example of Ndembu ritual, communitas arises between participants in the throes of an upheaval or transition as they simultaneously labor to discard the roles that have previously supported their phenomenological understanding of how they are embedded in a social matrix and begin to formulate a different mode of subjectivity.

Rites of passage are scenarios created to negotiate interpersonal conflicts or breakdowns in social relations. The ritual expression of those rites is a mode of performance, an expressive act and set of actions devised to shatter the participant's relationship to her or his prior subjectivity and strip away all previous privilege and status. When that occurs, the subject literally and symbolically acts out the transition from one state of being to another together with other ritual subjects. As this smaller community understands itself to be temporarily equal in status, it engages in imaginative play that sometimes is coupled with great hardship and can last for an extended time. This period, bracketed out from quotidian life, is an encounter that participants experience as of being "in and out of time," and in an "eternal now" (Turner 1987, 238). Sharing the experience strengthens comradeship and intensifies interdependence.

Communitas is the feeling that arises between liminal subjects. It is sometimes understood as communion, ecstasy, or what John Dewey termed a "heightened vitality" (Schechner and Appel 1990, 13). The feeling has also been described as a fleeting sense of harmony achieved by subjects acting in concert as they work through a social drama that plays out the conflicts and fissures inherent in any formation of communal existence (Schechner and Appel 1990, 13).

Because communitas can only be generated when existing social mores and hierarchical relationships have been suppressed, a framework Turner terms "anti-structure," it arises only if participants perceive the field of play as democratic. The collapse of hierarchical standing, where actors are neither higher nor lower in status than any other and there is no other designated authority over them, creates what philosopher

Jean Luc Nancy calls the state of "being-in-common" (Nancy 1991, 58). Turner describes this comradeship as "a relationship which nevertheless does not submerge one in the other but safeguards their uniqueness in the very act of realizing their commonness" (1987, 274). The structure of feeling prompts a recognition and appreciation of a common purpose between social actors but notes their individuality.

Communitas as a somatic knowledge of ephemeral commonality is performative; it depends on the reiteration of individuals acting together in order to sustain itself. Its presence is wholly tied to the dissolution of social frameworks. Therefore, communitas can never be permanent or stable because as Turner notes, structure always returns. Communitas differs from the materiality of community in that it cannot be separated from the transient set of acts and perception of egalitarianism that engenders its intensified sensation of vivacity and commonality.

Turner distinguishes three manifestations of communitas: spontaneous (happening inadvertently during the course of an event like a sacred ritual or a secular rehearsal or workshop); ideological (revealed retrospectively after reflection on an historical experience that comes to embody a standard or ideal of communal behavior); and normative (that "attempts to build the spontaneous model of communitas into everyday life"—Holm and Bowker 1994, 7).

Anti-capitalist political networks like the Zapatista Army of National Liberation, events structured as festivals or celebrations like Critical Mass Bike Rides, and cultural movements such as the Situationists have deliberately designed anti-structural performance-based scenarios in order for participants to feel the possibilities of egalitarianism, creativity, and joy through acting in concert with everyday life. These movements of resistance, not merely oppositional, deconstruct how the quotidian sensation of disempowerment and enervation is naturalized through an enforcement of atomism under dominant state and kinship systems. This performative use of communitas politically interrogates how affective states reinforce modes of social relations. As "feeling bad" can be linked to hegemony's dependence on feeling divided to instantiate power relations, communitas becomes an intervention that manifests modes of commonality, which by feeling more than oneself, can interrupt that reality.

*Further reading*

Debord (1967); Turner (1987); Williams (1977).

*References*


Debord, Guy. 1967. *The Society of Spectacle.* New York: Zone.

Holm, Jean and John Bowker, eds. 1994. *Rites of Passage.* London: Continuum International Publishing Group.

Nancy, Jean Luc. 1991. *The Inoperative Community.* Minneapolis, MN: University of Minnesota Press.

Turner, Victor. 1987. *The Anthropology of Performance.* New York: PAJ.

Williams, Raymond. 1977. *Marxism and Literature.* Oxford: Oxford University Press.


*Cross references*

"**Event**" by Fuentes; "**Fifteen principles of Black Market International**" by La Chance; "**Intervention**" by Olivares; "**Liminality**" by Levine; "**Multicentricity**" by Cheng; "**Play**" by Schechner.

## Endurance performance

Jennie Klein

"Endurance Performance," also known as "masochistic art" (O'Dell 1998), or "hardship/ordeal art" (Phelan 1993), involves the artist using her or his body to the point of privation, discomfort, corporeal danger, or even pain for long periods of time, ranging from several hours/days to a year or longer. Informed by action art, destruction art, conceptual art, process art, and site-specific art, endurance performance is generally considered within the larger context of body art. Lea Vergine's seminal text *The Body as Language: "Body Art" and Performance* (1974/2001), for example, profiled a number of artists associated with endurance work, such as Günter Brus, Otto Muehl, and Hermann Nitsch.

Vergine's inclusion of the Vienna Actionists, whose work was based on Catholic ritual and mysticism, points to the spiritual and ritualistic dimensions of endurance performance. Artists such as Barbara T. Smith, Linda M. Montano, Tehching Hsieh, Alastair MacLennan, and Joseph Beuys viewed their work as a spiritual response to a secular culture that had become increasingly out of balance. Vergine compared endurance artists to mystics, noting that they created a religious experience for themselves and for the viewer. Although endurance performance was a product of the anti-establishment, counter-culture, postmodern zeitgeist of the 1960s,it was also beholden to modernist constructions of the artist as seer/visionary, a stereotype that Vergine did not refute and which is still very much a part of the construction of endurance art. *The Artist's Body*, edited by Tracey Warr (2000/2012), includes many artists known for endurance performance under the heading "Ritualistic and Transgressive Bodies": Gina Pane, Ana Mendietta, Paul McCarthy, Chris Burden, Ron Athey, Franko B, Marina Abramović, and the Vienna Actionists. Karen Gonzalez Rice (2010) has theorized a connection between endurance performance, trauma, and religious beliefs in the work of Montano. In endurance art, piety and pain go hand in hand. It is not by chance that Vergine make reference to St. Simeon, an early Christian saint who spent the latter part of his life living on a column in the desert while subsisting on a handful of seeds a day.

In popular parlance, endurance performance refers to the ability of an organism to exert itself and remain active for a long period of time while resisting the ill effects of trauma, fatigue, and injury. Like extreme performance, a genre well elucidated by Meiling Cheng (2006), endurance performance is associated with athletic fitness and ability. But it is duration—rather than corporeal suffering or competence—that separates endurance performances from other manifestations of body art. Durational aesthetics employ a temporal measure that undermines the notion of linear clock time promulgated by global capitalism. Adrian Heathfield writes, "aesthetic duration is a wasteful form of labor; it saves nothing, and as such it is often deployed as a means to disturb or suspend narrative resolutions or consolidated identities" (Heathfield and Hsieh 2009, 22). Tehching Hsieh's *One Year Performance 1980–1981*, in which he punched a time clock every hour on the hour for one year, can be read as a wasteful form of labor, one that mimics the time of labor, measured by clocking in and clocking out. Lara Shalson (2012) argues that endurance performance, which takes place in real time and space, stands in contradistinction to the make-believe artificiality of conventional theatrical performance. Alastair MacLennan's *actuations*, for example, last eight hours to six days. A practicing Buddhist, MacLennan sharpens his awareness of "presentness" during his *actuations* by refraining from eating and sleeping for the duration of the performance. "For MacLennan," as Gray Watson observes, "an engagement with the physicality of time is in a sense an engagement with the reality of being alive, something which normal, habitual behavior can easily mask" (2003, 16).

Endurance performance's combination of corporeal excess/pain, extended duration, and quasi-mystical origins reinstate the artist, regardless of her or his gender and ethnic/racial origin, at the pinnacle of the creative hierarchy. Endurance art, as Warr (2012) notes, makes apparent the fragility and temporality of our bodies. Stelarc, Traci Kelly, Richard Hancock, Kira O'Reilly, Yann Marussich, and Franko B have injured and/or penetrated their bodies repeatedly during performance so that the transgression of the body's boundaries become part of the piece. Significantly, many artists whose bodies are in fact more "fragile" than most due to physical limitations choose to practice endurance performance. The late Bob Flanagan, who suffered from Cystic Fibrosis, partnered with Sheree Rose in pieces that were physically taxing. Rose has partnered recently with Martin O'Brien, an artist with CF whose performance work is premised upon expelling and using the viscous mucus that is the result of his disease.

*Further reading*

Cheng (2006); Heathfield and Hsieh (2009); Jones (1998).

*References*

Cheng, Meiling. 2006. "Extreme Performance and Installation from China." *TheatreForum*, 29: 88–96.

Heathfield, Adrian and Tehching Hsieh. 2009. *Out of Now: The Lifeworks of Tehching Hsieh.* London: Live Art Development Agency.

Jones, Amelia. 1998. *Body Art/Performing the Subject.* Minneapolis, MN: University of Minnesota Press.

Shalson, Lara. 2012. "On the Endurance of Theatre in Live Art." *Contemporary Theatre* Review, 22.1: 106–119.

Vergine, Lea. 1974. *The Body as Language: "Body Art" and Performance.* Reprint, 2001. Milan: Skira.

Warr, Tracy and Amelia Jones. 2000. *The Artist's Body (Themes and Movements).* Reprint, 2102. London: Phaidon Press.

Watson, Gray. 2003. "Alastair MacLennan: A Poetic Invitation." In *Alastair MacLennan Knot Naught.* Belfast: Ormeau Baths Gallery.

*Cross references*

"**35 Years of Living Art (Excerpts from Linda Mary Montano's blog, Thursday, December 6, 2012)**" by Montano; "**Becoming *Kinocognophore***" by Bucher and Zeeb, with Cheng; "**Body Art Still Image Event: *OFFERING***" by Carranza, Darsalia and Cheng; "**Extreme performance**" by Cheng; "**Marina Abramovic's durational opus**" by Carr; "**Masochism**" by O'Dell; "**The Muslim performative**" by Barlas; "**Performing body modifications**" by Henkes.

## Marina Abramovic's durational opus

Cynthia Carr

Halfway up the wall at New York's Sean Kelly Gallery were three open platforms where Marina Abramovic intended to live for twelve days without eating or speaking. Designated as a sleeping space, a sitting room, and a bathroom, they looked like balconies. Ladders leaning against each platform had rungs made of butcher knives, sharp edge up. Gaps of 18 inches separated the platforms so falling would be possible, especially after she'd grown weak and dizzy from lack of food. She intended this; danger would help her to focus. A few days before Abramovic began this twelve-day piece, *The House with the Ocean View* late in 2002, she woke in a panic. That was a good sign, she thought.

In her forty years of work, Abramovic has been remarkably consistent in her attitudes and self-imposed rules. In 1988, when I joined her and her then-partner Ulay for part of their walk across the Great Wall of China, Abramovic told me that if she did not feel panic and fear about doing a piece, she would not do it, and that this had been true since she began her performance work in Belgrade in the 1970s.

Danger, deprivation (fasting, for example), and duration (pieces that last for hours, days, even months) have been hallmarks of her work, but also her tools. She believes that art has to be made from that extraordinary state of mind one can only get to through exhaustion or pain or repetition. Abramovic has described the body in extremis as a gate into altered consciousness, "a higher self." What has changed over the years is how she relates this to an audience.

Her early work was about confronting her own fears and limitations. For example, because she was afraid of bleeding, she cut herself in performance with a razor blade (*Lips of Thomas*, 1975) and a knife (*Rhythm 10*,

1973). This was the decade when performance art was almost synonymous with ordeal art, frequently including self-injury and genuine risk. Abramovic often created situations in which spectators might fear for her safety. In *Rhythm 0* (1974), she announced that she would be a passive object for six hours—and laid out 72 objects the audience could use on her, including a loaded gun. A fight broke out among spectators when someone tried to use it.

In 1975, Abramovic met Ulay (Uwe Laysiepen). They shared the same birthday, the same profile, the same values and resolve, and soon designated their shared persona as "UMA" or "that self." For four years they lived in their car, traveling to performance sites and adhering to a strict set of guidelines: no rehearsal, no repetition, no predicted end, no fixed living place, permanent movement. During their legendary twelve-year partnership, they created many tough, and now classic, body art pieces illustrating and dependent upon their relationship: sitting back to back with their hair tied together for 17 hours, running at each other naked and colliding at top speed, breathing each other's breath until they felt queasy, and so on. Abramovic and Ulay called this "Relation Work."

In 1980, feeling they'd exhausted the possibilities of this work, they spent six months in the Australian desert. Forced into stillness by the intense heat, they discovered the energy and the sensitivity they could generate while motionless. They turned away from aggressive physicality to work with the "nightsea" of the subconscious. Abramovic and Ulay performed *Nightsea Crossing* ninety times in museums all over the world—sitting for seven hours at either end of a long table, trying not even to blink. It proved to be the most painful and difficult work they ever did, always leading to intense muscle cramps. Observing *Nightsea Crossing* on each of the three days the artists performed it in New York at the New Museum in 1986, I could almost see their connection, like a filament between them that grew stronger each day.

They had also decided, in Australia, that they would walk the length of the Great Wall of China, starting from opposite ends to meet in the middle—an epic unobserved by an art audience, in addition to being

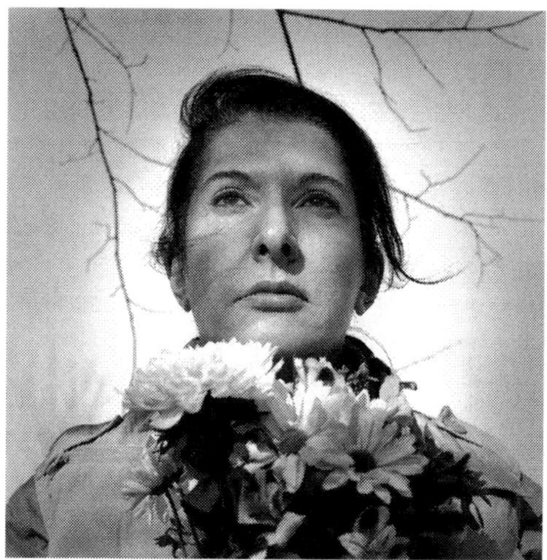

**Figure 1** Marina Abramovic. *Portrait With Flowers.* Black and white pigment print 135.6 x 137.6cm. 2009. © 2014 Marina Abramovic. Courtesy of Sean Kelly Gallery / (ARS), New York.

the last piece that they would do together. During the nomadic years with Ulay, Abramovic decided that constant travel or what she calls "the space inbetween" was a necessary condition for her. That was where she got ideas and she could avoid creating patterns. Long interested in the way spiritual practitioners develop themselves through silence, fasting and ritual, she began as a solo artist to spend extended time isolated in remote locations—a monastery near Dharamsala, for example—to prepare for her performances.

In her new solo work, Abramovic began trying to establish an "energy dialogue" with spectators. *Luminosity* (1997), for example, was clearly an effort to radiate. She stood naked and motionless on two support beams about five feet up the wall at Sean Kelly Gallery, occasionally sitting down to rest on a bicycle seat. "Nothing" happened, yet something seemed to manifest. Though it lasted just two hours, an eyeblink by Abramovic standards, she told me later that she felt "this kind of magnetic field with the public" but couldn't sustain it, couldn't take the tension.

*The House with the Ocean View* extended this effort. "The ocean is in my head," she told me. "This is about consciousness. An experiment. If I purify myself, can

I change the energy in the space and the energy in the audience?" On each of the twelve days, I spent at least one hour observing. For the first couple of days, she was restless. By day three she looked shaky and vulnerable. By day five, her energy had changed, as if she'd sunk into her deep reserves of willpower. She spent time focusing on certain spectators, some of whom were coming every day. On day seven, a woman came forward to engage Abramovic in staring. The artist put her palms out away from her body. The woman stepped out of her shoes. That moment of silent connection seemed very dramatic to me. By day eleven, Abramovic was clearly suffering, expending great energy even to stand. Later she explained she'd just been extremely dizzy. On day twelve, the gallery filled with spectators to watch her finish, and this seemed to energize her. After climbing down from the platforms, she addressed the audience–the first time she'd ever done so after a performance–but, she explained, she owed it to them. Without the audience, the performance wouldn't have worked.

In the back room at Sean Kelly Gallery, imbibing her first food in twelve days (a glass of carrot juice), Abramovic told me that she had developed a new idea during the course of the performance. She didn't like the three platforms up on the wall; they were too much like altars. Next time, she wanted to be on the same level, "to establish a situation of equality between me and the public."

Abramovic went on to do *The Artist is Present* (2010) at MOMA, creating that energy dialogue one-on-one with some 1400 spectators. There she manifested what she had described to me about *Nightsea Crossing* during our first interview, in 1986: "We believe in the art of the 21st century. No object between the artist and observer. Just direct transmission of the energy. When you develop yourself strongly inside, you can communicate your idea directly."

## Event

Marcela A. Fuentes

The concept of event is closely related to performance, specifically as a happening that is framed in space and time. The ontological similarity between performance and event has caused a conflation between these terms, with "event" being used to refer to a specific sub-set of performance. Performance as event implies an approach that could be associated with what anthropologist Victor Turner calls the liminoid aspect of performance, or the way in which aesthetic performance mirrors the liminality or separateness that characterizes rituals (1974). In this sense, the term "performance event" is employed to differentiate framed, live cultural productions, from quotidian notions of performance, such as gender identity and national belonging, which are not enclosed within a specific space-time continuum.

Taking the event's bracketing of space-time a step further to include the affective and disruptive elements of performance, Adrian Heathfield uses the term "eventhood" to refer to the "charging of attention" through which artists engage spectators in "varied deployments of altered time" (2004, 9). Importantly, Heathfield's concept of eventhood troubles a stable understanding of co-presence between artists and spectators as the defining element of performance. Heathfield's approach to eventhood accounts for the audience's desire to live in the present moment of the making and unmaking of meaning while preserving it from its elusive and transient nature. Thus, eventhood is entangled with liveness and ephemerality—characteristics that distinguish performances and events from works that organize around the production and display of aesthetic objects. Focusing on this aspect, Branislav Jakovljevic states that while material objects exist, performance and events happen. In an attempt to distinguish performance from event, Jakovljevic addresses performance's focus on embodied action and doing, with the body as agent or patient. In contrast, events are concerned with becomings, potentiality, and contingency. This definition of the event draws from the philosophy of Gilles Deleuze, who, together with Alain Badiou, has influenced contemporary thinking on the event in its relation to change, whether contained within the situation as inherent virtuality (Deleuze 1990) or conceived as a radical break from our understanding of reality (Badiou 2005).

Drawing from this body of work, performance scholar Marcela A. Fuentes explores the relationship between performance and event as they are reshaped in digital culture. Fuentes uses the term "performance constellations" (2015) to theorize the changing modalities of eventhood assembled by activists and artists who utilize digital networks as tools of intervention. The concept of performance constellations maps out ways in which, through relations of convergence and divergence, digital networks redefine traditional understandings of live art as an event of co-presence between performers and spectators. Through dynamics of complementarity and synergy, embodied behavior and digital mediation combine in performance constellations to produce synchronous and a-synchronous action from remote participants.

By involving digital networks in the constitution of a collective, distributed act, performance constellations include a central aspect of the event: non-human agency. Theorizing this phenomenon as digital liveness (2012), Philip Auslander argues that liveness or the time-based execution of a performance in the time of its consumption, can no longer be defined by the co-presence of humans before each other, but rather as people's affective response to the claims technological entities make on us, demanding that we interact with them in real time. Digital liveness is thus defined as a phenomenological accomplishment between humans and machines rather than as a fixed ontology of mediated performance. As Fuentes demonstrates through the concept of performance constellations, digital media, specifically digital networks, redefines the event as de-centered or distributed liveness in which embodied, programmed action combines with forms of eventhood as happenstance, chance, and possibility.

*Further reading*

Heathfield (2004); Jakovljevic (2009).

*References*

Auslander, Philip. 2012. "Digital Liveness: A Historico-Philosophical Perspective." *PAJ: A Journal of Performance and Art*, 34.3: 3–11.

Badiou, Alain. 2005. *Being and Event.* Translated by Oliver Feltham. London and New York: Continuum.

Deleuze, Gilles. 1990. "Societies of Control." *L'autre journal* 1 (May 1990): 3–7.

Fuentes, Marcela. 2015. "Performance Constellations: Memory and Event in Digitally Mediated Protest in the Americas." *Text and Performance Quarterly*, 35.1: 24–42.

Heathfield, Adrian, ed. 2004. *Live: Art and Performance.* New York: Routledge.

Jakovljevic, Branislav. 2009. *Daniil Kharms: Writing and the Event.* Evanston, IL: Northwestern University Press.

Turner, Victor. 1974. "Liminal to Liminoid, in Play, Flow, and Ritual: An Essay in Comparative Symbology." *The Rice University Studies*, 60.3: 53–92.

*Cross references*

"**Fluxus**" by Stiles; "**Happenings**" by Sandford; "**Invisible theatre**" by Cody; "**Liveness**" by Auslander; "**New genre public art**" by Irish; ***"Reality Ends Here"*** by Watson.

## Liminality

Debra Levine

The term "liminal" is derived from the Latin root "limen," signifying a material threshold or a passage from one stage to another. Performance research employs the expansive version of the term liminal—liminoid—to acknowledge a transitional state of being, a symbolic as well as spatial site (lintel, door, rehearsal space), a period of duration that is often described as "suspended," and a sensory excitation or stimulus that results in a bodily/psychic transformation. Both the liminal and liminoid as periods of durational change are frequently likened to death or gestation. At the end of the liminal phase, the subject is reconstituted into a different formation of social being.

The concept of a liminal state was derived from the observations of anthropologist and folklorist Arnold van Gennep, whose seminal 1909 work on rites of passage declared that ritual ceremonies are "characterized by three phases: separation, transition and aggregation" (1909, 93–111). Performance studies scholar Richard Schechner takes up this notion by citing from anthropologist Victor Turner's *The Ritual Process* (1969), which elaborates and extends van Gennep's work. Writing about the performance of rituals in pre-modern and traditional societies, Turner describes liminal subjects as "neither here nor there; they are betwixt and between the positions assigned and arrayed by law, custom, convention and ceremonial" (Schechner 2006, 66). Schechner analogizes this suspended state from which the ritual subject emerges, having undergone a reversal or transformation, to the "workshop rehearsal phase of performance composition" (2006, 66). Schechner argues that bracketing off a liminoid period in secular theatre is essential to generate creative praxis, for that time is crucial to develop a liberatory state in which participants are unmoored from the cares of quotidian life. It is an "anti-structure" in which they share an intense self-shattering experience with the other participants, engendering "communitas," Turner's term for "the charged field [...] a relationship which nevertheless does not submerge one in the other but safeguards their uniqueness in the very act of realizing their commonness" (Schechner 2006, 66).

Diverging from Schechner, who primarily employs the liminal as a rehearsal stage in performance, Susan Broadhurst has theorized performance itself as inherently liminoid. Liminoid performances are distinguished by hybridization, indeterminacy, a lack of aura [specifically referring to Benjamin's definition of the term] and the collapse of distinction between high and popular culture (1999, 1). In this respect, performance as it embodies this liminoid state can challenge hetero-normative social order by dissolving discrete formal elements and polluting disciplinary boundaries. As Mary Douglas theorizes in *Purity and Danger* (2004), liminal objects are most dangerous because they not only are outside of an organized structure but also decompose into formlessness.

Franz Kafka, in "The Cares of A Family Man," (1971) writes of Odradek, a semi-animate piece of detritus who inhabits passageways (stairways, lobbies, entrance halls). Odradek is an unraveled spool who changes from a creature, to an "it," and then a "he": his morphology embodies the ambiguity of the "liminal" with respect to gender and species. The story's narrator expresses anxiety that Odradek, unlike him as a family man, can exist indefinitely without any loss of potency. Through Odradek, Kafka interrogates Turner and van Gennep's understanding of the liminal as a transitory but finite suspended state between past and future to instead posit modernity itself as a mode of liminal temporality that is self-sustaining and denies its living human subjects any guarantee of change.

Odradek's liminoid ontology challenges the Enlightenment's progress narrative and bourgeois time's aim-directed existence. His paradoxical state of flux and stability, animation and objecthood threaten to collapse the disciplinary boundaries of social order, much like liminoid performances that allow human subjects to "play to the edge of the possible" (Broadhurst 1999, 1). Maddeningly, Odradek, as an intransient state of liminality, will far survive our lifetime and foreshadows, as Winnie says, in *Happy Days*, a "world without end, Amen" (Beckett 1961, 8).

### *Further reading*

Douglas (2004); Schechner (2006).

*References*


Beckett, Samuel. 1961. *Happy Days: A Play in Two Acts*. New York: Grove Press.

Broadhurst, Susan. 1999. *Liminal Acts: A Critical Overview of Contemporary Performance and Theory*. London and New York: Cassell.

Douglas, Mary. 2004. *Purity and Danger: An Analysis of Concept of Pollution and Taboo*. London and New York: Routledge.

Kafka, Franz. 1971. *The Complete Stories*. Translated by Willa and Edwin Muir. New York: Schocken Books.

Schechner, Richard. 2006. *Performance Studies: An Introduction*. New York: Routledge.

Turner, Victor W. (1969). *The Ritual Process: Structure and Anti-Structure*. Chicago, IL: Aldine

Van Gennep, Arnold. 1909. *The Rites of Passage*. Chicago, IL: University of Chicago Press.


*Cross references*

"**Communitas**" by Levine; "**Emotions**" by Tait; "**Hierarchy**" by Luber; "**Identification/dis-identification**" by Muñoz; "**Play**" by Schechner; "**Proxemics**" by Cody; "**Scenario**" by Taylor.

## Post-linearity

Sarah Bay-Cheng

Post-linearity follows the tendencies of postmodern and post-structural theory as an epistemological break with linear narrative structure. Rooted in modernist revisions of narrative (James Joyce's *Ulysses*, for instance), contemporary post-linearity articulates a radical reworking of previously accepted patterns of time and space, reflecting the influence of chaos theory (a theory of physics in which apparently random and unstructured systems nevertheless obey particular rules) and trends in electronic literature, in which information (expressed either as data or language) eschews a single, linear progression, but is shaped uniquely in time by the reader.

In performance, we may broadly define nonlinearity within a long theatrical history, including Shakespeare's multi-plot episodic plays, dramatic flashbacks (analepsis), as well as more radical experimentation as in Georg Büchner's deliberately fragmented play, *Woyzeck* (1836). European artists of the avant-garde, particularly Dada, Surrealism, and Futurism explicitly rejected the compressed, linear time of the late nineteenth-century well-made play. In an attempt to undermine the causal expectations of the audience, avant-garde dramatists often ordered dramatic events randomly, introduced linguistic non-sequiturs, and used simultaneity and repetition throughout their dramas. Gertrude Stein used all of these devices in her plays. Perhaps the most effective use of nonlinearity appeared in their films, which not only overturned linear time, but also undermined the basic assumptions of cause and effect. In their now-iconic film *Un Chien Andalou* (1928), Salvador Dali and Luis Buñuel famously juxtaposed contradictory images to eliminate any suggestion of causal, linear, or thematic connection.

Although similar to nonlinearity in drama, physics, and electronic literature, post-linearity in contemporary performance goes beyond a simple rejection of linear plot structure. Post-linear performance is less a rejection of linearity than it is the explicit acknowledgment of multiple, simultaneous, and competing linearities within *and exceeding* the domain of a particular performance. As Lizbeth Goodman argues in the *Routledge Reader in Politics and Performance* (1998), post-linear performance includes and "engulfs the many positions of the viewer, the actors, the critics. [It] acknowledges that the play plays on after the curtain goes down and began long before the audience took their seats" (1998, 259). Such a perspective suggests that while all performance unfolds in time and therefore adheres to some sort of linear progression (even if the representation of events does not), this sense of linearity is highly contingent and constructed within a particular viewing position and moment.

*Further reading*

Büchner (1836); Goodman and deGay (1998).

*References*

Büchner, Georg. 1836. *Woyzeck*. London: Eyre Methuen.

Goodman, Lizbeth and Jane deGay, eds. 1998. *The Routledge Reader in Gender and Performance*. New York: Routledge.

*Cross references*

"**Fluxus**" by Stiles; "**Happenings**" by Sandford; "**Landscape theatre**" by Holzapfel; "**Postdramatic theatre**" by Fuchs; "**Postmodernism**" by Chin Davidson.

## Precariousness

Eleonora Fabião

In a performative sense, the philosophical, aesthetical, and political force of precariousness derives from the ways it differs from, as well as adds to, the notion of "ephemerality"—a term frequently applied to conceptualize the temporal aspect of performance. If the ephemeral is transient, momentary, brief (the opposite of what is permanent), the precarious is unstable, risky, dangerous (the opposite of what is secure, stable, and safe). If the ephemeral is diaphanous, the precarious is shaky. If "ephemerality" denotes disappearance and absence (thus, predicating that at a certain moment, something was fully given to view), "precariouness" denotes the incompleteness of every apparition as its corporeal, moving, constitutive condition. If the ephemeral can open spaces of melancholy, the material urgency of precariousness innerves both bodies and spaces. If the ephemeral rehearses death, precariouness lives life. If the ephemeral refers to the non-lasting, the precarious discovers that "what is under construction is already a ruin" (Veloso 1991), thus revealing the generalized shakiness of capital. If the ephemeral leaves traces, the precarious is by itself a remainder and leaves what it is. The precarious does not exactly announce or resemble its disappearance; rather, it performs the intertwinement of past, present, and future as the only mode for presencing presence. A poetics and politics of precariousness approximate time and matter in such a way that it dilutes their claims for autonomy; indeed, precariousness is the performance of time and matter's distinct sameness: time becomes a force of matter and matter becomes a force of time.

It is no wonder then that the word-concept "precariouness"—both as a critical tool to analyze performance and a conceptual strategy to create performance as proposed here—springs from a post-colonial, South-American context. More specifically, from a so-called "third-world/under developed/developing/emergent-country": Brazil. In a 1983 manifesto written by Brazilian artist Lygia Clark—one year before the end of a brutal, 20 year long military dictatorship, and barely one hundred years after the abolition of slavery in Brazil—Clark proposed "the precarious as a new concept of existence against any form of static crystallization in duration" (1998, 211). In Clark's case this meant the abandonment of her career as a visual artist, of the art world's modes of production and reception, and the full and explicit embracing of a poetics of radical precariousness. Her final project "The Structuring of the Self" leads not only to the deconstruction of art's conventional definitions and delimitations but also to the emancipation of aesthetics from art making. It is precarious, precarious, precarious.

*Further reading:*

Clark (1997); Fabião (2006 and 2014).

*References*

Clark, Lygia. 1997. *Lygia Clark*. Reprint, Barcelona: Fundació Antoni Tàpies, 1998.

Fabião, Eleonora. 2006. *Precarious, Precarious, Precarious: Performative Historiography and the Energetics of the Paradox*. New York: New York University Press.

Fabião, Eleonora. 2014. "The Making of a Body: Lygia Clark's Anthropofagic Slobber." In *Lygia Clark: The Abandonment of Art,* edited by Cornelia Butler and Luis Pérez-Oramas. New York: The Museum of Modern Art.

Veloso, Caetano. 1991. *Fora da Ordem.* Circuladô: Nonesuch.

*Cross references*

"**Appropriation**" by Wong; "**Framing**" by Smith; "**Liveness**" and "**Virtual reality**" by Auslander; "**Mimicry**" by Applebaum; "**Performativity**" by Pendgraft; "**Readymade**" by Hoefer; "**Remains**" by Morrison.

## Wang Wei's *Temporary Space*

Philip Tinari

Over the course of three July weeks in 2003, Wang Wei (王卫) found the itinerant brick collectors he had photographed as a photojournalist for the *Beijing Youth Daily* a year earlier. They were amidst the remains of a village called Dongba, east of the East Fourth Ring and west of the East Fifth Ring in Beijing, in one of countless stands of one-story *pingfang* dwellings, inevitably made of brick and mortar. Wang Wei's idea for this, his first solo show, was simple: he would hire these brickmongers to haul donkey-cartloads of collected bricks to the newly christened Factory 798 art district, where inside the white cube of a gallery they would construct a brick box ten meters by ten meters, leaving only one meter of clearance between this bizarre structure and the gallery walls. The box would be photographed as it grew. An opening would be held when it was complete (although no one would really be able to enter the gallery). And the next day, the whole thing would be destroyed, its component bricks sold back to the brickmongers, loaded back onto their donkey carts, and moved further out into the urban frontier, where they would no doubt be sold once again and incorporated into the makeshift built environment of the constantly shifting area where urban core meets rural periphery.

As a project, *Temporary Space* was at once transactional, narrative, and architectural. It was also deeply contextual, voicing an implied fear—prevalent at that time if seemingly ridiculous now—that the 798 gallery district would prove similarly fleeting. Beijing itself was then likewise in the midst of its most intense moment of urban transformation. The name Wang Wei chose for the series of twelve photographs that would accompany the project, "What does not stand cannot fall," was a pun on Mao's maxim that "if [the old] is not broken down, [the new] cannot be erected." (In Chinese, both of these expressions are rendered by coyly reversing the order of the same four characters.) In recent years, the work has been discussed mostly as a serious work of social critique, but it was also something of a joke: when everything around seems at risk of being torn down, what better to do than build something for that express purpose?

Wang Wei is a native Beijinger, a Central Academy graduate, and a veteran of the *Post-Sense Sensibility* series of basement shows of 1999-2001, which brought together a generation of artists then in their mid- and late twenties. His installation for the first *Post-Sense* show, *1/30th of a Second Under Water*—later widely reproduced and included in the 2004 photographic survey *Between Past and Future*—involved large-scale facial portraits of friends and associates with their heads submerged in water, shot from below a glass basin to produce an effect whereby the subjects appeared to be peering out from the floor, blowing bubbles. Later projects turned more architectural, notably *Empty Space*, realized for the warehouse exhibition *Twins*, which took place during the opening of the Shanghai Biennale in 2002. This work entailed a hollow box made of metal framing and a 360-degree jet-printed panorama of the warehouse pre-exhibition, empty save for white square structural columns. The size of the box, three by five by three meters, aped the dimensions of his Beijing living room. This box was set on wheels and pushed back and forth by a team of students, never staying still. It was paired with a set of ten white columns, also on wheels and in metal and vinyl, replicas of those that held up the warehouse roof. At the end of that exhibition, performers sawed the columns into segments.

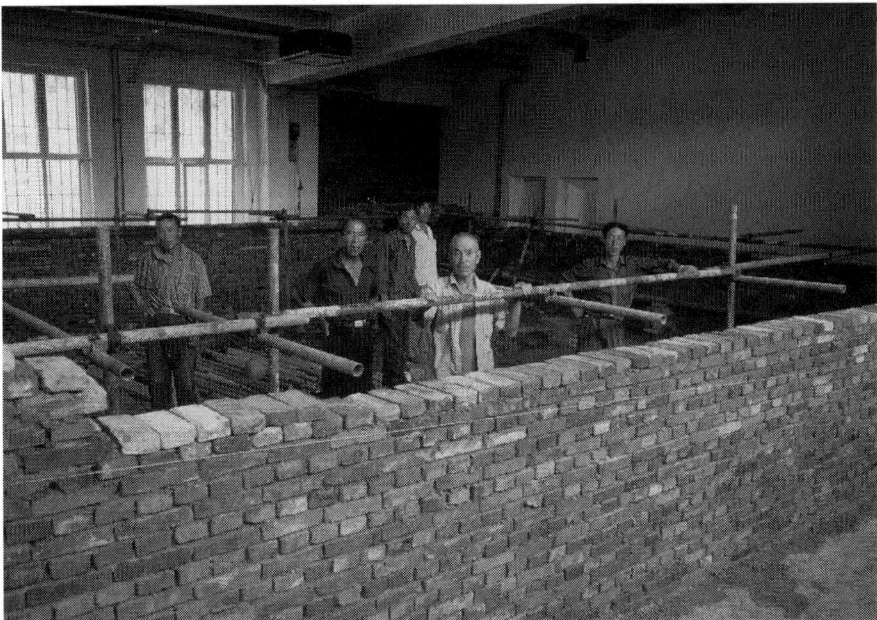

**Figure 2** Wang Wei's *Temporary Space* (30 June–19 July 2003), an exhibition curated by Philip Tinari in 25,000 Cultural Transmission Center/Long March Space, in Beijing. Image courtesy of the artist.

The original installation of *Temporary Space* included three works. The first was the building itself, which was categorized as an installation and named *25000 Bricks*. The second was a video projection in one dark corner of the space, an eight-minute piece entitled *Dong Ba*, after the former village whence the workers collected the bricks. The sounds of cleavers hacking mortar from old bricks waft from a pair of speakers, in subtle contrast to the sounds of the same brickmongers, physically present in the space, putting what may be the same bricks together again. The video's tone is lyrical and documentary. The only text comes in the opening shot of a sign proclaiming the area "the backyard of the Central Business District," and in a closing panel that explains that "around Beijing, three thousand people survive on the city's destruction." The final shot is a 360-degree panorama, a classic vista of workers whipping horses, piled debris, and new apartment buildings–still swathed in green mesh–rising in the distance.

The third and only enduring work was a black and white twelve-part photographic cycle, *What Does Not Stand Cannot Fall*. Like Wang Wei's earlier works, the photos, displayed originally on the gallery's back wall, behind the building they depict, are studies of people (in this case the peasant workers he has hired for a construction project) in an environment (in this case the 25000 Cultural Transmission Center, and the *25000 Bricks*). The photos chart the rise and fall of the brick box. Beginning with and returning to the empty white cube of the gallery, they hint at the instability that has become one of the few constants of the visual landscape of Beijing. But they also humanize and obscure its creators: the workers, present in the first few images, disappear behind what they build.

*Temporary Space* marked a milestone in Wang Wei's budding career, mainly by drawing out a temporal element that had already been central to works like *1/30th of a Second* (named for the shutter speed of his camera). Given a full three-week interval and the luxury of the 300 square-meter Long March Foundation gallery space (still a rarity in 2003), he was able to create a work that smartly mixed performance and documentation, sculpture and photography, social commentary and formal experimentation.

## Remains

Elise Morrison

The field of performance studies has hosted several noteworthy debates over the ways in which performance does or does not remain, the extent to which the embodied, contingent nature of performance can or should be defined in opposition to material, archival remains, and the status of ephemera and ephemerality in relation to both performance and the archive. Performance has often been placed in binary distinction to the material record, delineating the archive (remains) from the repertoire (performance), and positing live performance as ephemeral, as that which does not, cannot, and should not remain beyond its singular enactment (see Schechner 2001; Blau 1982; Kirschenblatt-Gimblett 1998; Taylor, 2003). At the heart of these arguments stands the vexed relationship between the live, contingent body in performance and the archival documents that traditionally compose historical record, problematizing the status of performance in relation to archive-based history-making and traditional genealogies of knowledge in the West (Derrida 1994; Foucault 1971).

Peggy Phelan argues that live performance is uniquely characterized by acts of embodied representation that disappear after the moment of enactment and are thus inherently non-reproducible. This central feature of ephemerality distinguishes live performance from other modes of representation in visual culture that produce material records (such as film and photography). Phelan claims that through its ephemeral nature, the live performing body possesses an inherent resistance to the reproductive ideology embedded in archival forms of visual representation, and that this understanding of performance has great political potential for feminist theorists and performance artists working to critique and counterbalance male-dominated forms of representation and reproduction in visual culture. She identifies "an *active* vanishing, a deliberate and conscious refusal to take the payoff of visibility" that characterizes the various feminist performance art pieces she examines (1993, 19). In this way, live performance that does not produce a stable, reproducible material object allows the performer to author her own immediate representation while resisting commodification and objectification, thereby radically deploying an "unmarked" body within the politicized field of vision.

Rebecca Schneider's essay "Performance Remains" (2001) takes on the claims of Phelan and others who argue that performance is ephemeral and located at the vanishing point of cultural record. Schneider asks, "if we consider performance as a process of disappearance, of an ephemerality read as vanishment (versus material remains), are we limiting ourselves to an understanding of performance predetermined by our cultural habituation to the logic of the archive?" (2001, 100). Schneider suggests instead that through other modes of knowing and remembering, such as reenactment, repetition, gestural memory, and embodied ritual, performance does remain as part of an ongoing historical record that is passed on through non-archival materials and processes. In proposing a different understanding of remaining and the ability of performance to do so, she argues that performance can interrogate and disrupt archival thinking and its attendant patriarchal logic.

Schneider's feminist arguments simultaneously engage questions of colonialism and imperialism embedded in the logic of the archive. Her suggestions that performance can function as a legitimate means of tracing historical record aligns her project with Joseph Roach's *Cities of the Dead* (1996). In this marriage of theatre historiography and performance studies, Roach argues that "performances so often carry within them the memory of otherwise forgotten substitutions," substitutions that may have escaped or been erased from the official archive of material remains (1996, 5). Thus, Roach moves fluidly between archival records and live performance traditions, tracing the interplay of orature, embodied performance, law, and literature in formations and enactments of collective memory and processes of cultural transmission.

*Further reading*

Roach (1996); Schneider (2001/2011).

*References*

Blau, Herbert. 1982. *Take Up the Bodies: Theater at the Vanishing Point*, Urbana, IL: University of Illinois Press.

Derrida, Jacques. 1994. *Specters of Marx: The State of the Debt, the Work of Mourning, and the New International*. New York: Routledge.

Foucault, Michel. 1971. "The Discourse of Knowledge" In *The Archaeology of Knowledge*, translated A.M. Sheridan Smith, 215–237. New York: Pantheon.

Kirshenblatt-Gimblett, Barbara. 1998. *Destination Culture: Tourism, Museums, and Heritage*. Berkeley, CA: University of California Press.

Phelan, Peggy. 1993. *Unmarked: The Politics of Performance*. New York: Routledge.

Roach, Joseph. 1996. *Cities of the Dead: Circum-Atlantic Performance*. New York: Columbia University Press.

Schechner, Richard. 2001. "What is Performance Studies?" Interview with Diana Taylor. November 27. http://hidvl.nyu.edu/video/003305515.html

Schneider, Rebecca. 2001. "Performance Remains." In *Performing Remains: Art and War in times of Theatrical Reenactment*, 100–108. Reprint, Abingdon, Oxon: Routledge, 2011.

Taylor, Diana. 2003. "Bush's Happy Performative." *TDR: The Drama Review*, 47.3: 5–8.

*Cross references*

"**Archive and repertoire**" by Taylor; "**Cindy Sherman's real fakery**" by Schneider; "**Emotions**" by Tait; "**Historicity**" by Colleran; "**Performing the archive**" by Nyong'o; "**Postdramatic theatre**" by Fuchs; "**Prosthetic performance**" by Gass; "**Through the Eyes of Rachel Marker**" by Roth.

## Reproduction

Sarah Bay-Cheng

Most simply, reproduction is the biological process by which a living organism creates its progeny. Since the advance of studies in genetic mapping, reproduction has been widely understood as an increasingly malleable process in which the characteristics passed down from generation to generation can be subject to a variety of manipulations designed to create a more deliberate and desirable offspring, as well as exact genetic copies of original organisms. Such manipulations have provoked no small amount of anxiety and political opposition, particularly in the area of human cloning.

Within performance contexts, reproduction is closely related to reenactment and documentation of time-based art. Walter Benjamin's "The Work of Art in the Age of Mechanical Reproduction" praises mechanical reproduction (i.e., photography and cinema) as "the technique of reproduction" that will detach "the reproduced object from the domain of tradition" (1936, 221), thereby democratizing the art object. Though enthusiastic, his embrace of mechanical reproduction is not unqualified. In a key footnote, Benjamin notes that the new recording technologies equally may favor the star and the dictator, suggesting the potential of mechanical reproduction to both animate (in the case of mass political movements) and subvert (in the case of the media-savvy dictator) radical politics.

Writing nearly 60 years after Benjamin, Peggy Phelan returns to the question of reproduction in her influential book, *Unmarked: The Politics of Performance* (1993). Phelan argues that the key characteristic of performance is its very irreproducibility, stating that "Performance cannot be saved, recorded, documented, or otherwise participate in the circulation of representations: once it does so, it becomes something other than performance" (1993, 122). This passage has been widely cited and challenged in the ongoing debate regarding digital recording technology and live performance (Auslander 1999). Phelan's book also addresses the role of performance in light of the debate over reproductive rights, in particular the anti-abortion group Operation Rescue's efforts to perform in the role of fetuses as a means to dissuade women seeking abortions.

In both instances, biological forces are affected by and in turn affect technology. Reproduction therefore occupies a prominent place in contemporary performance debates, one that seems likely to increase as more sophisticated reproductive technologies emerge.

### Further reading

Benjamin (1936); Phelan (1993).

### References

Auslander, Philip. 1999. *Liveness: Performance in a Mediatized Culture*. London and New York: Routledge.

Benjamin, Walter. 1936 [1969]. "The Work of Art in the Age of Mechanical Reproduction." In *Illuminations: Essays and Reflections*, edited by Hannah Arendt and translated by Harry Zohn. New York: Schocken.

Phelan, Peggy. 1993. *Unmarked: The Politics of Performance*. New York: Routledge.

### Cross references

"**Appropriation**" by Wong; "**Modernism**" by Albright, Pearl, and Speca; "**Precariousness**" by Fabião; "**Readymade**" by Hoefer; "**Reenactment**" by Bay-Cheng; "**Remains**" and "**Rhetoric**" by Morrison; "**Sampling**" by Hodges Persley; "**Simulacrum**" by Cesare Schotzko.

# Space

## Environmental Theatre

Gwendolyn Alker

Environmental Theatre refers to performances that call into question the fixed conventions of viewing the stage through a so-called "fourth wall," and those that challenge the standard relationships between actor and audience. Often interchangeable with "site-specific theatre," Environmental Theatre frequently turns found spaces into theatres and shifts the regular architecture of theatres into more malleable spaces. While Environmental Theatre can refer to popular entertainments, performance art, or more contemporary theatrical productions that utilize such staging techniques or training processes, the term arose and is generally associated with the American avant-garde theatre of the late 1960s and 1970s. Even this more narrow idea of Environmental Theatre can be extended to Allan Kaprow's happenings in the 1950s, through Maria Irene Fornes' *Fefu and Her Friends,* staged in 1977 at the Relativity Media Lab, to Reza Abdoh's *Father Was a Peculiar Man,* staged in NYC's meatpacking district in 1990. With *Fefu,* Fornes utilized all the spaces of a SoHo loft, staging differing scenes in various rooms and dividing the audience into smaller groups that moved separately to view each scene.

The term was codified by Richard Schechner in "Six Axioms for Environmental Theatre," published in *The Drama Review* (1968), followed by his book *Environmental Theatre* (1973). "Six Axioms" is still an immensely useful summary of central aspects of Environmental Theatre. Schechner delineates six elements that comprise the core of environmental work: "the theatrical event is a set of related transactions; all the space is used for the performance; the theatrical event can take place either in a totally transformed space or in 'found space'; focus is flexible and variable; all production elements speak their own language; the text need be neither the starting point nor the goal of a production. There may be no verbal text at all" (Schechner 1973, xix–xli). Schechner's larger work draws primarily on the experimentation he was engaged in as director of The Performance Group for *Dionysus in 69, Makbeth,* and Sam Shepard's *The Tooth of Crime.* This later production brought to the fore the issue of anti-textuality that is often associated with Environmental Theatre. While many proponents of Environmental Theatre sought to challenge the centrality of the playwright, Schechner insists that the genre does not seek to disregard the playwright's voice, but rather to heighten the other aspects of the theatrical production to achieve similar authorial status. Thus, the ensuing work of The Wooster Group and its legal battles with Arthur Miller over *L.S.D. (... Just the High Points ...)*, which incorporated portions of *The Crucible*, can be seen as an example of the legal battles that true environmental staging can create for mainstream theatrical production.

Another debatable aspect of Environmental Theatre is the degree to which a political agenda is wrapped up in the spatial and social elements of this genre. In the 1960s and 1970s, experiments by The Performance Group, The Living Theatre, and other group theatres undoubtedly tied Environmental Theatre to a political agenda that included a leveling of the actor/spectator relationship, a heightening of group consciousness, and a questioning of all forms of authority. Such elements could be traced through the rise of performance art as a dominant form of experimental performance in the 1980s and 1990s. However, many contemporary pieces that are staged environmentally, such as *Tony n' Tina's Wedding*, make little effort to capture or promote any political agenda. One political aspect of Schechner's revised treatise in 1994 was his brief foray into the ecological undertones of Environmental Theatre. Noting that humankind may influence the environment in ways that we can't yet begin to understand, Schechner presciently argued for "discover[ing] more and finer links between human agency, the agency of other living beings, and what was not so long ago believed to be a separate, dumbly operating nature" (1994, x). Perhaps this is another, if less spoken of, way in which Environmental Theatre has and will challenge Theatre as a political art.

### *Further reading*

Kaprow (1966a); Schechner (1973).

### *References*

Kaprow, Allan. 1966a. *Some Recent Happenings.* New York: Something Else Press.

Schechner, Richard. 1968. "6 Axioms for Environmental Theatre," *The Drama Review: TDR*, 12.3: pp. 41–64.

Schechner, Richard. 1973. *Environmental Theater: An Expanded New Edition including "Six Axioms for Environmental Theater."* Reprint, New York: Applause, 1994.

### *Cross references*

"**Ecodramaturgy**" by Thomas; "**Framing**" by Smith; "**Grace notes: Meredith Monk's *Songs of Ascension***" by Marranca; "**New genre public art**" by Irish; "**Performance in the digital age**" and "**Virtual reality**" by Auslander; ***"Reality Ends Here"*** by Watson; "**Scenario**" by Taylor; "**Surveillance**" by Morrison.

## Marc Bamuthi Joseph's *red, black, & GREEN: a blues*

Arden Thomas

I had read much about Marc Bamuthi Joseph's *red, black, and GREEN: a blues*, before seeing it, but nothing could have prepared me for the experience of the performance. In short, I was floored. Through a mesmerizing, heart-quickening hybridization of hip-hop aesthetics, dance, spoken word, visual art, rhythm, song, theater, and film, *red, black, and GREEN: a blues* (*rbGb*) offers a provocative and poetic, socially-engaged performance piece unlike anything I'd seen before. This dynamic performance raises issues of survival, urban wastelands, violence, food scarcity, poverty, homelessness, toxic dumping, and intergenerational health in critical and stunningly artful ways that challenge the audience to root more deeply in their community, to fight for environmental justice, and to change their relationships with each other, with their urban environment, with animals, and the land.

Bamuthi created and performed *rbGb* in collaboration with visual artist/set designer Theaster Gates as well as actor/dancer Traci Tolmaire; drummer/beat boxer/turntablist Tommy Sheppard, aka Emcee Soulati; and vocalist Yaw.

Instead of starting with an identifiably "green" question (like, how can we stage the relationships between humans and the environment), Bamuthi broadens the ecological question by asking, "What sustains life in your community?" He came to that question indirectly, and *rbGb* stages the paths he traveled, and the partners he traveled with, to get to that question and its many answers.

Before creating the piece, Bamuthi worked with the organization Youth Speaks to mount festivals called *Life is Living* in public parks to promote environmental awareness in under-resourced urban neighborhoods. *Life is Living* festivals started in Oakland and New York, featuring hip-hop artists such as Mos Def who performed on solar-powered stages and used equipment fueled by bicycle power; the festival staged graffiti battles, painted murals, and sponsored tree-planting. Bamuthi learned through these festivals, however, that "going green" was only one concern among the audience's more immediate issues of survival, literacy, violence, and getting enough food on the table. So Bamuthi shifted the tone of the festivals and began asking larger questions about sustainability. The performance *rbGb* documents this shift from "green" to "life," bringing together stories and impressions from the *Life is Living* festivals.

As audience members of *rbGb*, we experience the festivals in the murals, videos, and photographs embedded, projected, and pinned onto the set of *rbGb*. In the first of the three sections of the performance, titled *the colored museum* (a tribute to George C. Wolfe's iconic play), we enter the theater and walk directly onto the stage where we peer into the windows of a small cube-like, weather-beaten house while the performers sing and talk within. Slowly, the actors pull

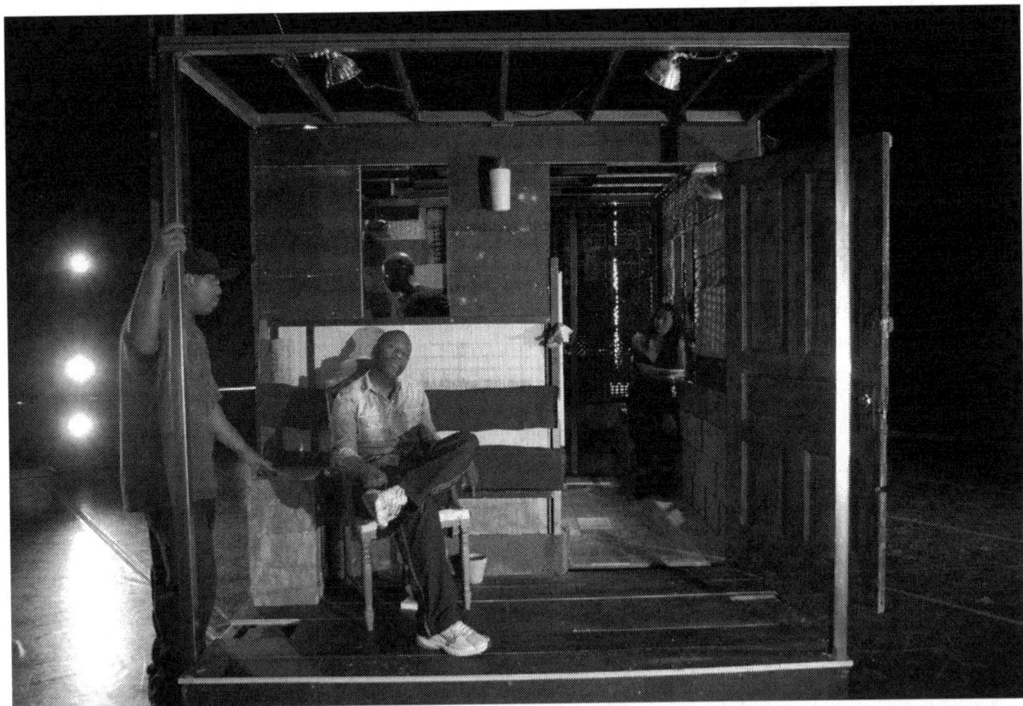

**Figure 3** *red, black & GREEN: a blues*, dir. Marc Bamuthi Joseph, set by Theaster Gates, 2011. MAPP International Productions. Photograph by Bethanie Hines.

and push apart the cube, splitting it into four separate modules. We find ourselves both inside and outside four separate houses surrounded by the performers, stories, and music.

Set designer Theaster Gates explains that he constructed the set entirely of found materials, "garbage," he says: old mattresses, denim, hoses, astroturf, sneakers, raw timber, packing crates, canvas, fire hoses. The entire set becomes a musical instrument itself, Soulati's kinetic compositions drummed and stomped and danced on boards, beams, walls, and steel poles. Yaw raps from the roof of a shack while Tolmaire sings, dances, and engages with an audience member. As the audience moves around and through the set pieces, the performers also move, singing, guiding, inviting, dancing, telling a story. The performers rotate the set pieces, turning an interior parlor into an exterior porch, turning the outside inside, the architectural movements of the piece signifying the festival's transformational movements from space to place, from "green" to "life," from "environment" to "environmental justice." The piece moves multi-directionally, dance to voice to drum, news report to rap to call-and-response, a story told from the roof of a shack to a group dance on a front porch, song to tap to the shaking of a paint can, a man chanting "I feel like tagging" to the beat of the rattle of a ball in can.

As the performers guide us into our seats, the second section, *colors and muses*, begins. The performers continue to inhabit the four set pieces as they more fully inhabit the stories, gestures, and vocal inflections we just witnessed while we were on the stage. Repeating a snippet of conversation we just heard in the first section, Tolmaire develops it into a monologue telling the story of an urban farm organizer in Houston who provides meals in return for farm labor. As she riffs on "food insecurities," she says, "you have the right to education, clean water, you should have the right to fresh food." Later Tolmaire becomes the old man we already know as "the flower man," morphing her body to evoke addiction and old age. Yaw croons the blues in counterpoint to Bamuthi's raps; Bamuthi spins a tale of talking to his nine-year old son about the complicated legacies of Tupac and the Black Panthers; narratives build on each other as the performers dance powerful duets together. We bear witness to mothers, fathers, addicts, grievers, farmers, teens, and activists, all telling their stories, their stories moving as the set moves, resonating through the audience.

In the third section, *back talk*, the performers invite the audience members back up onto the stage, this time for an informal discussion with the performers. As we talk, we move together in a shared space, a newly formed community reflecting on what sustains life–in our own lives, the environment, and the lives of others. We begin to ask how city-building practices and human attitudes and behaviors together define the capacity of urban ecologies to support life. Spinning a story of the intersections between health, education, literacy, clean water, and access to fresh food, *red, black, and GREEN: a blues* redefines what it means to really be "green," to be sustainable, to affirm life.

## Hierarchy

Steve Luber

Hierarchy, derived from the Greek word for "high priest," with its root meaning "sacred," is an ordered set of elements, usually ranked in order of ideological system of values. Hierarchies therefore pervade social ordering, in politics, gender, race, class, species, etc.

Although this system theoretically allows room for mobility and status changes, cultural theory has sought to undermine what it considers to be arbitrary sets of relationships that impose oppressive power structures upon social relations and ordering. This structure is vividly and thoroughly exposed in Foucault's *The Order of Things: An Archaeology of the Human Sciences* (1966), which examines underlying ideologies of societal truths that create, promote, and enforce normative discourses.

Hierarchies in performance do contribute to hegemonic discourse (aesthetics itself a strict set of rules on beauty and quality), but often have a more fluid nature, as exemplified by the avant-garde movements of the twentieth century, which constantly rejected the aesthetic of the period, from Craig's rejection of naturalism in stage design, to the futurists' and dadaists' rejection of the literary sublime and antagonism of audiences, to the constructivists' rejection of romanticism for industrial material and the staging of workers' struggles. It is important to note, though, that even these lead to a restructuring, not the destruction, of hierarchies, creating an ouroboros of power dynamics.

### *Further reading*

Conquergood (2002); Foucault (1977); Hall (1993).

### *References*


Conquergood, Dwight. 2002. "Lethal Theatre: Performance, Punishment, and the Death Penalty." *Theatre Journal*, 54.3: 339–367.

Foucault, Michel. 1966. *The Order of Things: An Archaeology of the Human Sciences*. Reprint, London: Tavistock Publication, 1970.

Foucault, Michel. 1977. *Discipline and Punish: The Birth of the Prison*. Translated by Alan Sheridan. New York: Vintage.

Hall, Stuart. 1993. "Cultural Identity and Diaspora." In *Colonial Discourse and Post-Colonial Theory. A Reader*, edited by Patrick Williams and Laura Chrisman, 392–403. New York: Harvester Wheatsheaf.


### *Cross references*

"**Framing**" by Smith; "**Historicity**" by Colleran; "**Historiography**" by Fabião; "**Postcolonial performance inquiry**" by Chatterjee; "**Quotation**" by Garrett.

## Installation art

Rachel Haidu

Installation art can look lazy, chaotic, and meaningless (what's the point of a jumble of objects, particularly if few or none of them are handmade?). And sometimes it's not only supposed to look but *be* those things, forcing us to find meaning in a jumble, in discordance, or literally in nothing: the gap in between.

One important antecedent to installation art is early twentieth century radical exhibition practices, epitomized by the dozens of artists who participated in the 1938 *Exposition Internationale du Surréalisme*. These artists blurred the lines between their individual contributions and decorating, for example, by exhibiting a series of dress mannequins standing in front of street signs. Another antecedent is Minimalism, which orients viewers towards the ways they share a sculpture's space.

Installation art questions the nature of "negative space" by incorporating it into the artwork itself. One way to understand installations is to accept them as negative or hostile occupations—perhaps even takeovers—of a traditional museum or gallery space. Mike Kelley, for instance, diminishes or even destroys the worth and value of "the art object" through his use in various installations of stuffed animals, cheap carpet, and, famously, air deodorizers. Is Kelley out to "shock" the bourgeois museum or infiltrate its very atmosphere? Or is Kelley using those objects to point us towards the space *between* paintings and sculptures in a gallery or museum? Either way, he shows us how their value and differences from one another cocoon them, sheltering art objects from receiving other kinds of meaning.

But to the degree that Minimalism is also a key precedent to installation art, it allows us to perceive that negative space in another important manner. The work of an artist like Fred Sandback, which bridges Minimalism and installation art, is instructive. Sandback's medium is colored acrylic yarn, stretching from floor to ceiling or wall to wall, creating lines, columns, rhomboids, and triangles that the viewer walks through and perceives as both missing shapes, or an extension of her own body. The tension of the yarn against the body makes it a three-dimensional equivalent to lines drawn on a piece of paper or in a painting, but its presence in our space also shifts it away from such a purely symbolic role. We are allowed, in the presence of Sandback's work, to experience both the missing mass *as missing* and also as *with us*, or a part of ourselves: hence, as the artist Andrea Fraser has pointed out, Sandback's work can make us cry. Negative space can offer installation art its mode of critique, but it can also offer access to a viewer's emotional reserves, which are usually defended by the conventional pattern of me/not-me, and repeated in the patterns of painting-wall-painting; thing-not thing-thing. By conferring value on the space as well as the combination of objects, lines, or other elements of the installation, artists can dis-align us with our coherent and habitual system of differentiating between objects, or selves, and bring us into another "space" altogether.

### *Further reading*

Haidu (2010); Welchman (2003).

### *References*

Haidu, Rachel. 2010. *The Absence of Work: Marcel Broodthaers, 1964–1976*. Cambridge, MA: MIT Press.

Welchman, John. 2003. *Art After Appropriation: Essays on Art in the 1990s*. London: Gordon and Breach Publishing Group.

### *Cross references*

"**Becoming *Kinocognophore***" by Bucher and Zeeb, with Cheng; "**Body Art Still Image Action: *OFFERING***" by Carranza, with Darsalia and Cheng; "**Elevator Girls Return: Miwa Yanagi's border crossing between photography and theatre**" by Yoshimoto; "**Heather Cassils' indeterminate body**" by Jones; "**Memoirs of Björk-Geisha**" by Takemoto; "**Minimalism**" by Lepecki; "**Readymade**" by Hoefer; "**Theatre of images**" by Marranca; "**Through the Eyes of Rachel Marker**" by Roth; "**Wang Wei's *Temporary Space***" by Tinari.

## The Internet

Philip Auslander

Although the Internet is actually an informal series of electronic connections among globally distributed computer networks, it is often described using implicitly spatial metaphors like cyberspace, surfing, and searching. Following this construction, the Internet can be understood as a performance space for both aesthetic and social performances.

Websites are now often used for displaying recordings of performances (such as streaming videos) and archival information about performances and performance venues. Arguably, such uses, while valuable, simply replicate earlier technologies, albeit with the potential to reach a global audience. There have also been attempts to use the Internet as a performance space rather than an archive by staging performances *on* the Internet. The BMW Tate Live Performance Room at the Tate Modern in London, active since 2012, combines both. The room itself is a performance space devoted solely to art performances to be streamed live on the Internet. The performances are then archived on the website and remain available for subsequent viewing.

Whereas the performances at the Tate Modern's Performance Room are streamed to an audience that resides outside of virtual space, other performances have engaged with audiences that are contained within the digital environment itself. When Suzanne Vega performed live in 2006 in Second Life, an "online virtual world" that "opened to the public" in 2003, her avatar, a digital representation of herself, sang in a virtual theatre for an audience of fellow avatars representing those who participate in Second Life. Viewers watching from outside of Second Life constituted a second layer of spectatorship.

The ubiquity of the Internet in contemporary life has led artists other than performers to treat it as a platform for their work. Although Internet Art (or Net Art) has existed as a practice only since the mid-1990s, it can be said to have gone through three phases. In the first, artists built websites, often with the intent either of exposing or disrupting the Internet's underlying electronic infrastructure or to reveal social inequities surrounding access to the Internet and its growing corporatization. Around the turn of the Millennium, the website started to seem too conventional a form, and artists turned their attention to developing software that reconfigures existing sites and other gestures designed to make Internet consumption more self-reflexive and creative. In its most recent phase, Net Art has largely moved off the net as artists seek ways of creating sculptural objects, installations, and environments in gallery settings that respond to the culture of the Internet.

Arguably, the Internet has proved to be even more successful as a platform for social performance than artistic performance. The construction and deployment of an avatar is a kind of social performance, a "presentation of self," to use Erving Goffman's phrase. An oft-cited *New Yorker* cartoon by Peter Steiner from 1993 that has achieved the status of a "meme," emphasizes both the anonymity of the Internet and the possibilities it offers for self-construction. It shows a dog sitting at a computer and saying to another dog, "On the Internet, nobody knows you're a dog." With the development of personal blogs, vlogs, and popular social media sites such as Facebook, the Internet has become ever more centrally a space for the performance of identity, even multiple identities geared to specific online contexts. Corinne Weisgerber describes this effect: "Facebook Corinne and Twitter Corinne are not the same persona. And they're also slightly different from Corinne, the blogger. I'm a lot pickier about who I let join my Facebook network and I rarely let mere acquaintances in. If you want to connect with me on Facebook, I have to know you fairly well. As a result, you'd probably get to see a much more unfiltered version of Corinne than you would on Twitter" (2011).

Since Goffman himself suggests that we have no single identity but present ourselves differently for different social audiences, his work provides a promising framework for analyzing social performance online. Inasmuch as Goffman takes face-to-face interaction as his default scenario, however, a number of researchers have found it necessary to adapt his framework somewhat to accommodate social interaction on the Internet, which lacks physical co-presence and is often asynchronous.

### *Further reading*

Aspling (2011); Auslander (2001); Goffman (1959).

### *References*

Aspling, Fredrik. 2011. "The Private and the Public in Online Presentations of the Self: A Critical Development of Goffman's Dramaturgical Perspective." Thesis, Stockholms Universitet. http://www.diva-portal.org/smash/get/diva2:431462/FULLTEXT01.pdf

Auslander, Philip. 2001. "Cyberspace as a Performance Art Venue." *Performance Research*, 38.2: 123–126.

Goffman, Erving. 1959. *The Presentation of Self in Everyday Life*. New York: Anchor.

Weisgerber, Corinne. 2011. "Negotiating Multiple Identities on the Social Web: Goffman, Fragmentation, and the Multiverse." Keynote Address, WebCom Montréal from Montréal, 2011. http://academic.stedwards.edu/socialmedia/blog/2011/11/16/negotiating-multiple-identities-on-the-social-web-goffman-fragmentation-and-the-multiverse/

### *Cross references*

"**Feminist blogging as activism and pedagogy**" by Dolan; "**Media**" by Colleran; "**Mediaturgy**" by Marranca; "**Performance in the digital age**" and "**Virtual reality**" by Auslander.

## Landscape theatre

Amy Strahler Holzapfel

The term "landscape" evades a single definition or theorization. Studies in the formalist vein seek to define landscape as an artistic genre, appearing in the western lexicon as early as the fifteenth century via Dutch and German words for "setting" or "picture of land," and loosely defined thereafter as any representation of land, place, or the "natural" world. In the mid-twentieth century, art historians focused on landscape as a genre of painting interpretable via stylistic modes—ideal, heroic, picturesque, romantic, etc. (Clark 1949)—or through psychological and symbolic terms (Gombrich 1961). In contrast, visual theorist W.J.T. Mitchell defines landscape not as a genre but as "a medium of cultural expression," that is, as discourse. In *Landscape and Power*, Mitchell considers how landscape can refer simultaneously to "a represented and presented space, both a signifier and a signified, both a frame and what a frame contains, both a real place and its simulacrum, both a package and the commodity inside the package" (1994, 5). For cultural theorists, what matters most is not what a landscape *is* but what it *does*—in Mitchell's words, "how it works as a cultural *practice*" (1994, 1).

Whether viewed as genre of art or medium of cultural exchange, landscape has increasingly entered into theorizations about theatre and performance. In their critical anthology *Land/Scape/Theatre* (2002), Una Chadhuri and Elinor Fuchs go so far as to suggest that landscape "names the modern theatre's new spatial paradigm" (2002, 2). In her chapter on American drama, Fuchs views the rise of landscape's role in theater as a fundamentally modernist development. She suggests that "the signs of a shift from preconscious to conscious *landscape poetics* are everywhere to be found in the European dramatic texts of the end of the nineteenth century" (Chadhuri and Fuchs 2002, 30), such as those of Ibsen, whose *plein air* dramas stage the fjords, seascapes and peaks of his native Norway, or Chekhov, whose prescient ecological sensibility is reflected by the fragile ecosystems of his four major plays (Chaudhuri 1996).

After the turn of the nineteenth century, American artists like Gertrude Stein, Thornton Wilder and Eugene O'Neill employed landscape as an organizing principle for their theatrical structures and designs. Influenced by the Cubism of Picasso, for example, Stein famously coined the expression "*landscape play*" to define the non-linear compositions of her own short plays and operas (Bowers 1991). Stein, who claimed she felt "nervous" as an audience member trying to keep up with the climactic action of a traditional dramatic plot, theorized that "sight and sound and its relation to emotion and time" could become the meaning of a play (1935b, 35). She suggested that in the same way that a landscape "is the thing," so, too, could a play be its own "thing," freeing the audience from struggling to "make acquaintance" with the persons, places, and events occurring on stage (1935b, 37). Instead of a work of representation striving to achieve a linear narrative, a play could be simply a series of "relations between things"—imparted visually, sonically, and in other sensory ways. Stein's idea of a "play as landscape" provided a new and radical paradigm shift in the conception of stage itself, laying a foundation for theatre of the experimental avant-garde. In the last decades of the twentieth century, major studies of postmodern performance—such as Bonnie Marranca's *Theatre of Images* (1977) and Elinor Fuchs' *The Death of Character* (1996)—sought to frame the Steinian emphasis on visual elements (tableaux, frames, images, video, etc.) in the dramaturgy of artists like Richard Foreman, Robert Wilson, Elizabeth LeCompte, and Meredith Monk, in relation to landscape compositionality. Hans-Thies Lehmann's intervention of the "post-dramatic" theatre is also indebted to Stein's concept of the "landscape play."

The paradigm of landscape has terminologically morphed into many other directions, as well—beyond space, setting, environment, and site, into linguistic and sonic areas "langscapes" (Bowers 1991) and "soundscapes" (R. Murray Schafer 1993). One of the more compelling applications of landscape in recent years has been in the areas of global, intercultural, eco-political, and postcolonial performance. Critics in these fields have theorized how the construction of landscape mediates humanity's relationship with its natural, social and cultural environments, whether focusing on scenography (Aronson 2007), spectacle (Cosgrove 2008), site-specificity (Kaye 2000), place and memory (Carlson 2003; Roach 1996), or other aspects of performance. Consideration of landscape's role in tourism and eco-tourism—for example, from Coco Fusco and Guillermo Gómez-Peña's *Two Undiscovered Amerindians* (1992) to Rachel Rosenthal's radical environmentalist solo-performance—has also gained focus.

Such examples offer evidence for the argument that, whether theorized as a genre or a discourse, landscape is as germane to an analysis of performance as it is to that of visual studies or agricultural science, suggesting a myriad of possibilities for future applications and definitions of the term in our discipline.

### *Further reading*

Bowers (1991); Chaudhuri and Fuchs (2002).

### *References*


Aronson, Arnold. 2007. *Looking into the Abyss: Essays on Scenography*. Ann Arbor, MN: University of Michigan Press.

Bowers, Jane Palatini.1991. *They Watch Me As They Watch This: Gertrude Stein's Metadrama.* Philadelphia, PA: University of Pennsylvania Press.

Carlson, Marvin. 2003. *The Haunted Stage: The Theatre as Memory Machine.* Ann Arbor, MI: The University of Michigan Press.

Chaudhuri, Una. 1996. *Staging Place: The Geography of Modern Drama.* Ann Arbor, MI: University of Michigan Press.

Chaudhuri, Una and Elinor Fuchs. 2002. *Land/scape/theater.* Ann Arbor, MN: University of Michigan Press.

Clark, Kenneth. 1949. *Landscape Into Art.* Reprint, New York: Harper & Row, 1979.

Cosgrove, Denis. 2008. *Geography and Vision: Seeing, Imagining and Representing the World.* London: I. B. Tauris & Co.

Fuchs, Elinor. 1996. "The Death of Character: Perspectives on Theater After Modernism." In *Drama and Performance Studies,* edited by Timothy Wiles. Bloomington, IN: Indiana University Press.

Gombrich, E.H. 1961. *Art and Illusion: A Study in the Psychology of Pictorial Representation.* Princeton, NJ: Princeton University Press.

Kaye, Nick. 2000. *Site-Specific Art: Performance, Place and Documentation.* London: Routledge.

Marranca, Bonnie. 1977. *The Theatre of Images.* New York: Drama Book Specialists.

Mitchell, W.J.T. 1994. *Landscape and Power.* Chicago, IL: University of Chicago.

Roach, Joseph. 1996. *Cities of the Dead: Circum-Atlantic Performance.* New York: Columbia University Press.

Schafer, R. Murray. 1993. *The Soundscape.* Rochester, VT: Destiny Books.

Stein, Gertrude. 1935b. "Play as Landscape." In *Lectures in America.* Boston: Beacon Press.


### *Cross references*

"**Celebrity**" by Nayar; "**The Ecodramaturgy of Anna Halprin, Eeo Stubblefield, and Rachel Rosenthal**" by Thomas; "**Environmental Theater**" by Alker; "**Liminality**" by Levine; "**New Genre Public Art**" by Irish; "**Scenario**" by Taylor; "**Theatre of Images**" by Marranca; "**Virtual Reality**" by Auslander.

## Mise-en-scène

Kimberly Jannarone

The term in French means "the placing or the setting of the scene," or "putting into theatrical action, language, or arrangement." Its closest English equivalents would be "staging" or, more generally, "setting." Theatrically, mise-en-scène signifies all the elements and techniques involved in arranging a performance, including scenic effects, costuming, props, lighting, and all that occurs in time and space, including music and sound, blocking and choreography, and the production's overall rhythm and tempo. In film, mise-en-scène refers to that which happens before a camera (acting, costume, make-up, lighting, setting) and can also include diagetic sound and the camera's placement, movement, and framing. (In French, the director in both theatre and film is called the "*metteur en scène*".) Mise-en-scène also, in its largest sense, signifies the setting or backdrop of any event or action, such as that of a public appearance or a work of fiction.

Patrice Pavis describes mise-en-scène "not as an empirical object, but as an abstract system, an organized ensemble of events" (2003, 9). Mise-en-scène can signify the overall correlation and organization of the elements of a performance, including such things as sounds and silences, correspondences between actor's interpretations and design elements, and the relationship between the performance and the audience. In this regard, Pavis suggests mise-en-scène can be understood as a process of "vectorization": "signs or moments in performance exist in relations of tension, interconnected through networks of meaning that make the dynamic interaction of the signs relevant" (2003, 17–18).

André Veinstein distinguishes between a narrow and a broad definition of mise-en-scène in the theatre (1955). In the narrow sense, mise-en-scène describes the theatrical arrangements that bring a dramatic text to life on a stage. In a broader sense, the term refers to the totality of a staging as a complete work itself, whether or not it has been created in the service of interpreting a text. Mise-en-scène first came into use in the early nineteenth century, but the term became particularly important in the latter half of that century, answering a need to discuss productions in terms of the overall event and the unifying creative work of a single artist or director. Artists particularly crucial to the development of the use and understanding of mise-en-scène include "total theater" artists and stage directors. Total theater artists, beginning with Wagner, strove to create a unified art work whose impact would be brought about not only through the development of plot, character, and poetic language, but also, crucially, through the synthetic organization of music, movement, gesture, and design. As stage directors gained more power in the unfolding of the theatrical event in the late nineteenth century and as the text lost some of its authority, mise-en-scène emerged as the way to organize and unify various performance elements into one coherent artwork.

The early twentieth-century writings of Edward Gordon Craig and Adolphe Appia contributed to a shift away from the prevailing assumption that staging elucidated the meaning of a written text and toward the idea that mise-en-scène—particularly in its shape, tempo, light, and atmosphere—could create and contain meaning itself. Antonin Artaud wrote in 1938 that the stage needed to find a "pure theatrical language" and called for the elevation of the mise-en-scène as a "physical language" that "consists of everything that occupies the stage, everything that can be manifested and expressed materially on a stage and that is addressed first of all to the senses instead of being addressed primarily to the mind, as is the language of words" (1958, 38). This sense of the term has become particularly useful in describing non-text-based performance, such as dance or devised performance, and in discussing the work of auteurs such as Robert Wilson, for whom mise-en-scène is the creative work's primary substance and organizational principle.

### Further reading

Artaud (1958); Pavis (2003).

### References

Artaud, Antonin. 1958. *The Theater and Its Double*. Trans. Mary Caroline Ruchards. New York: Grove Press Inc.

Pavis, Patrice. 2003. *Analyzing Performance: Theater, Dance, and Film*. Translated by David Williams. Ann Arbor, MA: University of Michigan Press.

Veinstein, André. 1955. *La mise en scène théâtrale et sa condition esthétique*. Paris: Flammarion.

### Cross references

"**Broad-spectrum approach**" by Schechner;

"**Circus**" and "**Emotions**" by Tait; "**Environmental theater**" by Alker; "**Installation art**" by Haidu; "**Disciplines in Performance**" by Morrison; "**Post-linearity**" by Bay-Cheng; "**Postdramatic theatre**" by Fuchs.

## Prison culture

Kathleen Ryan

At the beginning of the twenty-first century, Americans live in a prison culture. Over two million people are locked in cages. The imprisoned are disproportionately African American, American Indian, and Latino/a. Most have been convicted of nonviolent crimes. Women are the fastest growing population. The rate of incarceration surpasses 700 per 100,000 people, a percentage, as Loïc Wacquant notes, "about 40 per cent higher than South Africa's at the height of the armed struggle against apartheid" (2005). Torture at Abu Ghraib and the rise of supermaximums in other countries testify to the exportation of the US American model—"the prison nation abroad," to borrow from Michelle Brown (2005, 973).

The vital intersection between prison studies and performance studies emerges from a determination to make scholarship, practice, and teaching relevant to struggles for justice. Prison culture applies to realities on both sides of the walls—to governments that spend more money to incarcerate citizens than to educate them, and to locked-down lives. In the United States, prison culture is inextricable from a history of slavery and convict leasing. This fact is well documented by Douglas Blackmun, David Oshinsky, Angela Davis, and H. Bruce Franklin. The Thirteenth Amendment (1865) famously abolished slavery "except as a punishment for crime whereof the party shall have been duly convicted". Davis has organized for decades to end the prison industrial complex, the profitable merger of corporations, government, and punitive punishment. Franklin, who published a 1978 study of prison literature and a 1998 anthology of incarcerated writers, argues that "if we teach modern American literature without reference to the American prison and its literature, we are behaving like those who failed to see, hear, or speak about slavery and its literature." (2000, online)

Performance analysis can help to intervene in the roles scripted by a prison culture. Dwight Conquergood's essay, "Lethal Theatre," tracks the political staging of capital punishment from colonial public hangings to the lethal poisoning of Timothy McVeigh on closed-circuit TV. Conquergood suggests that the "death penalty cannot be understood simply as a matter of public policy debate or an aspect of criminology, apart from what it pre-eminently is: performance" (2002, 342). In addition to revealing how cultural stages can obscure the realities of imprisonment and executions, performance studies also look to plays, street demonstrations, radio, and other kinds of performance to illuminate what is often hidden from public view. Because prison creates a hidden, authoritarian space, the "theater of imprisonment attempts to rectify this invisibility by putting the prison experience into a palpable and confined space (on stage) with real people (actors)" (Fahy and King 2003, 1). Victoria Brittain and Gillian Slovo's play, *Guantánomo* (2004), is a recent example.

Performances are also created behind the barbed wire. In *Imagining Medea* (2001), Rena Fraden documents her theatre work with women in prison, and Jonathan Shailor's anthology *Performing New Lives: Prison Theatre* (2010) analyzes international prison-related efforts. The Prison Creative Arts Project, directed by William Alexander, enables imprisoned adults and young people to create theatre, and the program *Changing Lives through Literature* offers the study of literature as an alternative to traditional sentencing. Organized efforts to resist mass imprisonment and abolish the death penalty continue to build, and performance remains a critical part of this struggle.

### *Further reading*

Fahy and King (2003); Fraden (2001).

*References*

Brown, Michelle. 2005. "'Setting the Conditions' for Abu Ghraib: The Prison Nation Abroad." *American Quarterly* 57.3: 973–997.

Conquergood, Dwight. 2002. "Lethal Theatre: Performance, Punishment, and the Death Penalty." *Theatre Journal*, 54.3: 339–367.

Fahy, Thomas and Kimball King, eds. 2003. *Captive Audience: Prison and Captivity in Contemporary Theater*. New York: Routledge.

Fraden, Rena. 2001. *Imagining Medea: Rhodessa Jones & Theater for Incarcerated Women*. Chapel Hill, NC: University of North Carolina Press.

Franklin, H. Bruce. 1978. *The Victim as Criminal and Artist*. Oxford: Oxford University Press.

Franklin, H. Bruce, ed. 1998 *Prison Writing in 20th-Century America*. New York: Penguin.

Franklin, H. Bruce. 2000. "From Plantation to Penitentiary to the Prison-Industrial Complex: Literature of the American Prison." Paper delivered at the Modern Language Association Convention, December. Accessed June 14, 2015. http://andromeda.rutgers.edu/~hbf/MLABLACK.htm

Shailor, Jonathan, ed. 2010. *Performing New Lives: Prison Theatre*. London: Jessica Kingsley Publishers.

Wacquant, Loic. 2005. "The Great Leap Backward: Imprisonment in America from Nixon to Clinton." In *The New Punitiveness: Trends, Theories, Perspectives*, edited by John Pratt, David Brown, Mark Brown, Simon Hallsworth, and Wayne Morrison, 3–26. London: Willan.

*Cross references*

"**Ai Weiwei's transnational public spheres**" by Zheng; "**Global censorship**" by Shea; "**Hierarchy**" by Luber; "**Identity politics**" by Adewunmi; "**Intervention**" by Olivares; "**Performing surveillance camera art**" by Nayar; "**Racialization**" and "**War**" by Sell.

## Proxemics

Gabrielle H. Cody

Edward T. Hall is most closely associated with the study of human use of space in culture, and the application of this concept to cross-cultural communication. Hall argues in *The Hidden Dimension* (1966) that our use and perception of space are culturally determined. His analysis has elucidated and measured both our quotidian use of space (we stand closer to those we know well) and the proxemics of urban life such as street patterns, neighborhoods, and city plans.

Proxemics in a theatrical setting "analyzes the cultural coding of spatial relations between individuals" (Pavis 2003, 153). To consider the role of proxemics as it relates to performance is to focus on the relational space between performers, between performers and spectators, and between spectators. For Anne Ubersfeld, "there is no one spectator; rather there is a multiplicity of spectators who react to each other" (1999, 23). As she remarks: "[i]t is the spectators, much more than the director, who create the spectacle [...] Brecht did not invent the concept of the creative role of the spectator, but he did discover the fundamental law of theater whereby the spectator is a participant, an important actor [...]" (1999, 23).

The tensions inherent in audience proxemics have tremendous value to performance studies since they reveal the performative and hierarchical dimensions of embodied spaces. Numerous theorists and practitioners as disparate as Jarry, Eisenstein, Meyerhold, Artaud, Brecht, Bausch, The Living Theater, Schechner, Foreman, Gómez-Peña, Finley, and Sprinkle have problematized and incorporated proxemics into their work through their radical emphasis on the audience as the true locus of their performance's most productive intentions. When Annie Sprinkle invites her audience to pick up a flashlight and look into her cervix, and when the majority of those in line turn out to be men, the politics of gender and sexuality become part of her performance; when Gómez-Peña rhetorically asks his audience if they are "fully documented," the unspoken and naturalized aspects of whiteness are exposed. When Pina Bausch has her dancers address the audience and ask for change, the unequal pay-for-service transactions of all spectator/artist relationships are dis-covered. When Karen Finley interrupts her show to address and berate a latecomer, or throws candy to unsuspecting spectators, the audience's comfortable anonymity is broken. In each of these cases, the most compelling, complex and efficacious performance (performance as critique) remains the one the artist has ignited *between* audience members.

*Further reading*

Pavis (2003); Ubersfeld (1999).

*References*

Hall, Edward T. 1966. *The Hidden Dimension.* Garden City, NY: Doubleday.

Pavis, Patrice. 2003. *Analyzing Performance: Theater, Dance, and Film.* Translated by David Williams. Ann Arbor, MA: University of Michigan Press.

Ubersfeld, Anne. 1999. *Reading Theater.* Translated by Frank Collins. Toronto: University of Toronto Press.

*Cross references*

"**Ai Weiwei's transnational public spheres**" by Zheng; "**Audience**" by Cody; "**Hierarchy**" by Luber; "**Multicentricity**" by Cheng; "**The Muslim performative**" by Barlas; "**Sisters of Survival Signal S.O.S.**" by Gaulke; "**Transnationalism**" by Yang.

## Fifteen principles of Black Market International

Michaël La Chance

The performances of BMI (*Black Market International*) are exercises in derision and concentration, sacralization and effacement. The performer tries to take life seriously while revealing that it is worth very little, that it is held together by a gesture. That is the work of BMI: create fundamental moments. This article samples solo BMI performances through 15 basic principles.

1. The privilege of encounter. The art of encounter (*Begegnung*) becomes a politics of *communitas*. There is never the limitation of a common theme; the work is done according to a principle of open cooperation, on the rare occasions in which they can be produced collectively. The title "Black Market" (1985) does not designate a group, but ideas at work.

   Lee Wen, sitting on a blue stool, makes visual contact with the public. He begins a mortifying ritual in which he takes small stones and bounces them on his head. He then starts to chew a handful of chili peppers, leaving the audience in awe, our throats knotted in organic empathy. Through this excess, Lee Wen wants to denounce our tendency to "spice" things, especially in the media and entertainment.
2. The diversity of initial impulses. The performer is a vehicle for experimentation. Elvira Santamaria wants to get on a bus without paying, trying to negotiate the fare. She offers a small cutout of a duck, asking the driver to be her accomplice. The impulse is accentuated by the resistance provoked in the driver, and by the prospect of eventual negotiations.
3. The parallelism of the performances. We can imagine many actors on the same stage, each performing his/her own play! Each one unraveling the continuous thread of his/her own (real or illusory) existence. There is no common ground between Alastair MacLennan nailing fish on the wall and Roi Vaara writing a spiral of words on the ground. One thing is certain: we must not try to find a narrative link between the interventions because it would reduce them to "episodes."
4. BMI is only an artistic idea, a creative hypothesis that cannot be established on certainties. Our familiar world, or our certainties are made up of a tight web of conventional links. Performance destabilizes these certainties and requires a disconnection of people and objects; it is a silent heresy (*de-ligere*) manifested through the body and through gesture.

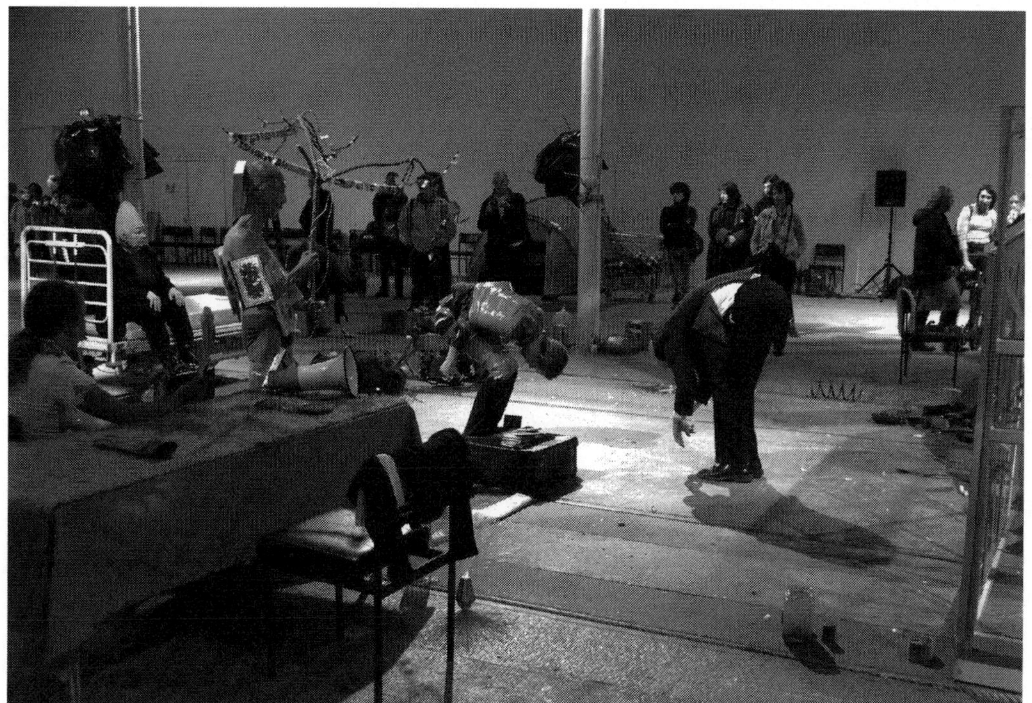

**Figure 4** A performance scene from Black Market International, in Glasgow 2007. Photo by Naranja. The artists present in the image are: Helge Meyer, Elvira Sanatmaria, Julie Andrée T, Alastair MacLennan, Boris Nieslony, Lee Wen.

In Helge Meyer's relation with his public, an unstated contract is circulated: "All the clothes I wear are the result of an exchange (in a past festival in the Philippines) and I must exchange them all with you today!" Meyer's mechanism is one link in an international transmission chain: the group from Quebec bonds with the Philippines group. The spectators are not only people who are asked to be there; they participate in an action and become performers. Helge Meyer can go to his next festival with a bunch of Québécois clothes.

5. The artist must adjust to the way s/he feels in the space, and to the way s/he creates duration in time through actions. Roi Vaara, elegant in his tuxedo, starts his performance by putting an alarm clock on the floor. Then he writes a series of words on the floor in a spiral. He swirls around and falls. He lights a cigarette and gets up, follows the spiral in the other direction, canceling the words and replacing them by others. The words in brackets replace the original words: money (life), power (sensitivity), competition (collaboration), disposables (recyclables), pollution (composting), Bush (bushman), Jesus Christ (Mickey Mouse), gross national product (welfare) etc. ...
6. The whole process must not end in a synthesis; the event's indetermination must be maintained. BMI is an event without terms, produced within events that leave us waiting for something to follow, awakening the sense of community in the hope of a better world. Performance must give the most tangible manifestation of hope, must make hope stream like energy flowing out of immateriality.

Boris Nieslony, almost nude, rolls on the gravel holding a stone to his breast. He underlines his nakedness in a poetical action close to the definition that Cage gave to poetry: a "celebration of the fact that we own nothing." His acts transform the gravel of a parking lot into something as precious as the Ryoanji Zen garden in Kyoto.

7. Time is the basis of the event. In it, we become conscious of others; we get closer to each other, but we also practice exclusion. In the flux of time, objects and living people are all temporal actors; inert objects can become useful actors, performers of equal value as the live ones.
8. BMI is the exploration of ethnic and cultural dimensions that are neglected in the usual tracking of ethno-cultural markings. Alastair MacLennan's performance deals with objects whose connotation is specific to certain regions: in Northern Ireland, an individual with a nylon stocking on his head who nails mackerels to the wall, doesn't give the same impression as in, say Italy. MacLennan presents an installation: three small plastic ducks, three mackerels on the wall, and assorted objects on the floor require an interpretation, just like the door through which he finally disappears.
9. Performance investigates different forms of attention, from the reflective or meditative attention to a purely instinctive attention. This instinct enables us to instantly recognize the natural traveling of time. But we are not familiar with the logic of the event; we cannot narrate its course–it stems from an inner knowledge of the structural unity of the world.
10. Art must occur in life. Art must be founded in life and merge with life so that in return life can lean on art: aesthetics must open the road of ethics.
11. It is in the heart of total solitude that we can find the greatest concentration and accomplish being-entity. We think of Lee Wen's solitude holding on to his stool to absorb the shock of his peppers, Nieslony's solitude when he realizes that the stone is his ally.
12. Maintaining performance in an ontological paradox: the ambivalence of being and non-being, of visible and invisible–trying to give form to a third element, that of a differed existence, of a constantly imminent emergence. A lot of our experiences and perceptions don't seem to contribute to our positivistic view of the world. However we must recognize these experiences as sketches of another world: as dreams dreaming themselves.
13. Performativity. Performance, as seen by BMI, is not the pursuit of a greater technical or utilitarian efficiency or a challenge to the great tales of modernity. It is the performativity of a direct transmission, where saying is doing and doing is saying. Indirect performativity–as in "direct provocation"–discourse and action merge: a thought or a word surfaces from the action, and thought or words must become action.
14. We must stay away from common language; we must practice a game of non-communicative provocations, a deficit of interpretation, a hearing hindrance. Pro-vocation: *provocare*, "call (*vocare*) out," place the voice outside, towards the outside. It is rather an *ante-vocation*, a call from inside. This concerns first of all the performer who is carrying out a scenic activity disjointed from the reactions and participation of the public.
15. All is possible. This simple fact during a performance means inciting shock. It puts us in touch with the weight (*Sto*–the blow, the jolt) of the immensity of reality.

## Scenography

Matthew Smith

Scenography is the collection of spatial signs—including stage scenery, stage machines, stage lighting, and stage architecture—that creates a stage setting. Costuming is sometimes included in the definition, but generally not included are sounds, gestures, and words.

The range and variation of world scenography defies brief summary. Generally speaking, stage design has not been as central to non-Western performance as it has been for the theater of the post-Renaissance West. And yet exceedingly complex scenographic traditions are found in numerous non-Western theatrical genres, such as the Chinese *zaju* performances of the Yuan (1260–1368) and Ming (1368–1644) Dynasties, in the *jingju* ("Peking Opera") performances of the Qing Dynasty (1644–1911), and in the Japanese No and Bunraku theatres, to name but a few. The Japanese Kabuki theatre particularly relies upon scenic spectacle, and makes extensive use of devices such as revolving stages, wagon platforms, trap-lifts, and curtains.

Many of the most influential innovations in Western scenography were developed in Renaissance and Baroque Italy, where innovations in stage design closely mirrored those in painting. Among these were the use of geometrical perspective in stage sets (introduced around 1500), the invention of the "carriage-and-frame" method of rapidly changing flats (invented in the 1640s), and the introduction of angled perspective around 1700. The modern break with the legacy of the Baroque is particularly indebted to the work of Henry Irving, Adolphe Appia, and Edward Gordon Craig between 1880 and 1920. In 1881, Irving embraced the three-dimensionality of the stage by introducing the "free plantation" system, in which scenery could be placed anywhere on stage. In subsequent decades, Appia and Craig adapted Irving's free plantation system to radicalize non-illusionistic stage designs, ultimately severing the connection between theater and painting.

In the first half of the twentieth century, numerous theatre artists took up the gauntlet thrown by Irving, Appia, and Craig. Bauhaus artists Oskar Schlemmer and László Moholy-Nagy radically imagined three-dimensional, hyper-kinetic, non-mimetic stage spaces in which machine and organism would be fused into a moving, theatrical totality. In the Soviet Union, director Vsevolod Meyerhold constructed "biomechanical" stage spaces such as that for *The Magnanimous Cuckold* (1922), which merged acrobatic actors to Liubov Popova's set design of moving windmills, wheels, ramps, beams, and chutes. Many of these experiments in radically kinetic stage design would, by mid-century, be incorporated into the enormously influential work of Josef Svoboda at the Laterna Magika in Prague. Beginning with the first Laterna Magika production at the Brussels Expo in 1958 and continuing to his death in 2002, Svoboda relentlessly experimented with new technologies, pioneering the use of modern hydraulic and lighting systems as well as lasers and holograms. His work combines a Baroque passion for mechanical stage illusion with a more Romantic desire for an organically unified theatre, and his extension of Appia and Craig's innovations has shaped scenography worldwide.

### Further reading

Aronson (2007); Baugh (2005); Oenslager (1975).

### References

Aronson, Arnold. 2007. *Looking into the Abyss: Essays on Scenography*. Ann Arbor, MN: University of Michigan Press.

Baugh, Christoper. 2005. *Theater, Performance, and Technology: The Development of Scenography in the Twentieth Century*. New York: Palgrave Macmillan.

Oenslager, Donald. 1975. *Stage Design: Four Centuries of Scenic Invention*. New York: Viking.

### Cross references

"**Circus**" by Tait; "**Environmental Theatre**" by Alker; "**Expanded cinema**" by Jarosi; "**Installation art**" by Haidu; "**Mediaturgy**" and "**Theatre of images**" by Marranca; "**Wang Wei's *Temporary Space***" by Tinari.

## Surveillance

Elise Morrison

Surveillance means "watching from above," "oversight," or "supervision"—it connotes a hierarchical relationship in which the watcher holds power and control overs the watched. Surveillance is significant to performance studies as a socio-political practice in contemporary everyday life, as a theoretical concept through which to analyze structures of discipline and power in formal and informal performance situations, and as a representational tool with which theatre and performance artists and activists critique and reimagine contemporary society.

Panoptic surveillance was developed by social theorist Jeremy Bentham in 1791 in the form of a prison design, and then famously theorized by Michel Foucault in *Discipline and Punish* (1977) as the ür-model for modern surveillance practices. Bentham's design produced an efficient and self-sustaining form of disciplinary power through a visible but unverifiable authoritarian gaze, located in a central tower (Foucault 1977, 201). The subject of panoptic surveillance, realizing any infraction might be punished if observed by the seemingly ever-present surveilling gaze (be it a prison guard or a CCTV camera), would internalize the authoritarian aims and ideology and begin to discipline him or herself. The panoptic model has continued to influence modern systems of surveillance, as evidenced by the continued expansion of CCTV cameras in monitoring public and private spaces; at the same time, contemporary surveillance technologies and practices have expanded beyond visual surveillance of discrete bodies and spaces to focus on the capture, storage, and circulation of virtual information (dataveillance) and biological guarantors of identity (biometrics) by and between state and corporate entities (Deleuze 1990; Lyon 2001).

As in panoptic surveillance, theatrical representation, particularly in the Western realist tradition, has depended upon a strategic balance between visibility and invisibility, watcher and watched: audiences members (economically or socially privileged viewers) sit in the dark, viewing highly visible actors, sets, and props, which are themselves undergirded by invisible systems of directorship and stage-craft (Morrison 2012, 130–131). Performance theorist John McGrath has likened director-dominated avant-garde theatre groups in the twentieth century, such as those of Bertolt Brecht, Robert Wilson, Jerzy Grotowski, Anne Bogart, and Liz LeCompte, to hierarchies of socio-political surveillance, arguing that "the dominant cultural fantasies of surveillance—the protecting eye or controlling Big Brother—equate in many ways with the fetishized figure of the twentieth-century theatre director, controlling events from which he or she is absent through the creation of a structure that necessitates and depends upon continued obedience" (McGrath 2004, 3).

Contemporary surveillance systems have also provided new platforms and tools for cultural performance: Facebook, Twitter, personal blogs, and reality TV, which have been theorized as manifestations of participatory, social surveillance (Andrejevic 2004), function as experimental stages for what Erving Goffman termed "the presentation of self in everyday life" (1959, 30), as well as forums for marginalized voices seeking to express political criticism or organize protests (as in the Arab Spring and Occupy Wall Street movements of 2011). As part of the mixed media genre of "digital performance" (Dixon 2007), which is characterized by the "remediation" of emergent technologies within theatrical frames of performance (Bolter and Grusin 2000, 54), a growing number of artists and activists have employed drones, CCTV cameras, GPS tracking systems, medical surveillance equipment, and a host of other commercially available surveillance technologies as representational tools with which to critique and reimagine the social and political landscape of contemporary surveillance (Morrison 2013). Examples of surveillance art and performance include Steve Mann's "sousveillance" technologies that reverse the disciplinary gaze of surveillance by arming everyday users with performative tools to "watch from below" (Mann 2003); the Surveillance Camera Players' street performances for publicly installed CCTV cameras in New York City (1999-ongoing); Jill Magid's installations *Surveillance Shoe* (2000), *System Azure* (2003-ongoing) and *Evidence Locker* (2004), which explore the gendered gaze of surveillance; and theatre productions that stage socio-political impacts of surveillance on contemporary life, such as The Builders Association's *SuperVision* (2006), Shunt Collective's *Contains Violence* (2008), and

George Brandt's *Grounded* (2013). By reframing the use-value of surveillance technologies within formal and informal performance spaces, surveillance artists employ what Jill Dolan—writing about a determining "male gaze" in dominant forms of visual culture—identified as materialist performance tactics that "denaturalize the psychological identification processes implicit in representation," so that, "when the representational apparatus is foregrounded, its once mystified ideology becomes clear" (Dolan 1988, 14–15). In so doing, surveillance art works encourage a critical spectatorship towards the disciplinary gaze of dominant surveillance.

### Further reading

Andrejevic (2004); Foucault (1977); Lyon (2001).

### References


Andrejevic, Mark. 2004. *Reality TV: The Work of Being Watched*. New York and London: Rowman and Littlefield, Inc.

Bentham, Jeremy. 1791. "Panopticon, or the Inspection House." In *The Panopticon Writings*, edited by Miran Bozovic. Reprint, London: Verso, 1995.

Bolter, Jay David and Richard Grusin. 2000. *Remediation: Understanding New Media*. Cambridge, MA: MIT Press.

Deleuze, Gilles. 1990. "Societies of Control." *L'autre journal* 1 (May 1990): 3–7.

Dixon, Steve. 2007. *Digital Performance*. Cambridge, MA: MIT Press.

Dolan, Jill. 1988. *Feminist Spectator as Critic*. Ann Arbor, MI: University of MichiganPress.

Foucault, Michel. 1977. *Discipline and Punish: The Birth of the Prison*. Translated by Alan Sheridan. New York: Vintage.

Lyon, David. 2001. *Surveillance Society: Monitoring Everyday Life*. New York: Open University Press.

Mann, Steve. 2003. "Existential Technology: Wearable Computing is Not the Real Issue!" *Leonardo*, 36.1: 19–25.

McGrath, John Edward. 2004. *Loving Big Brother: Performance, Privacy, and Surveillance Space*. London: Routledge.

Morrison, Elise. 2012. "Witness Protection: Surveillance Technologies in Theatrical Performance." In *Bastard or Playmate? Adapting Theatre, Mutating Media and Contemporary Performing Art*, edited by Robrecht Vanderbeeken, Boris Debackere, David Depestel, and Christel Stalpaert. Amsterdam: University of Amsterdam Press.

Morrison, Elise. 2013. "User-*un*friendly: Surveillance Art as Participatory Performance." *Theatre Magazine*, 43.3: 4–23.


### Cross references

**"Environmental theater"** by Alker; **"Invisible theatre"** by Cody; **"Liveness"** by Auslander; **"Performing surveillance camera art"** and **"Posthumanism"** by Nayar.

## Performing Surveillance Camera Art

Pramod K. Nayar

Surveillance is the organizing principle of our lives, whether it occurs in the form of Close Circuit Television or Loyalty Cards, biometric identification, or the voluntary sharing of information on social media. Surveillance is a structural condition in which a whole new form of subjectivity–my consciousness of who I am, the appropriateness of my behavior in public spaces, and of course my responsibility as a good citizen in keeping my neighborhood safe by participating in Neighborhood Watch programs - emerges. The surveilled subject is the newest form of citizenship itself (see Nayar, 2015).

New York Performing Surveillance Camera Art (hereafter SCP, videos may be viewed on YouTube) call attention to not only the nature of surveillance–now increasingly omniscient and ambient, seamlessly merged into our environs, documenting us as we pass by—but the nature of our *performance of being surveilled*. The classic model of this performance is an enactment of Orwell's *1984* (http://www.youtube.com/watch?v=RILTl8mxEnE). Julia and Winston meet, are assigned identities ("4224 DOE J." and "6079 SMITH W."). As the performance progresses, Winston is tortured until he accepts with a sign, "I love Big Brother." Ominously we also see cops—not players—real ones, at the edge of the screen, trying to find out what is going on. What is important is that other people using the subway do not pay any attention to the players performing in front of the camera. This itself is part of the performance where most of the general populace sees the "performance" of the players as just play-acting, while they, going about their business under the camera, are doing something more real. Thus, the SCP draw attention to the normalizing of surveillance and our acquiescence to being monitored, so that nothing except the critique of the surveillance seems out of the ordinary. Further, the "performance" includes not the players alone but the "normal" people who ignore the camera, its intrusion and movements. The world is literally the stage where all the people who pass in front of the camera are "merely players."

In other performances, the surveillance camera records the players' enactment of Edgar Allan Poe's "The Raven" and Samuel Beckett's *Waiting for Godot* (http://www.youtube.com/watch?v=TUxQQGXQZVs). Even as the performance is being filmed by the surveillance camera of the U.S. government, the players' camera periodically focuses on this surveillance camera, resulting in an information loop which is a part of the performance. The government is being watched and recorded as it watches and records, thus suggesting an endless, *ad nauseum* process of surveillance where we consciously watch to see who is watching us. Some scenes show people in the station watching the TV monitors that are showing the SCP performance. Even though the state's camera has no role in the original tale, we are forced to concede that the performance of art is a suspicious act in and of itself; hence, we might as well perform for the state's eyes. The texts chosen are also symbolic: the "nevermore" from Poe (a placard held up by a player in the act) and the now-classic "nothing happens, nobody comes, nobody goes" motif of Beckett's play together convey a powerful critique of surveillance. Even when nothing happens, the cameras are on. The camera records non-activity too, and, as the SCP performance suggests, the recording is an end in itself. The absence of activity does not make the camera obsolete, because the camera's sentinel role is the performance of state power. SCP's plays present surveillance as potential: even when "nothing happens, nobody comes, nobody goes," the camera is in anticipation of something happening. The camera symbolizes a potential performance of something. The camera *is the stage* itself, anticipating a performance, any performance.

Where surveillance once targeted individuals (Finn 2009), it now targets entire populations. SCP shows in its performances that where once the individuals going about their daily lives constituted the public space of a city, this public space is one which is constructed through surveillance acts: SCP draws attention to a contemporary social condition which is built on the assumption that anything public must be monitored for the public to stay a public. If, as Andrea Brighenti has proposed, "visibility [...] contributed to the demarcation of the public domain" (2010, 58), then SCP enacts this demarcation through visibility. My being a member of the public is testified when I perform routine chores in front of the CCTV, and my trust in the safety of the remaining occupants of this public space is the result of their being similarly monitored. Hence, in SCP's performances, the players' cameras record not just the intentional performers, but the passers-by and the bystanders. My belongingness, like that of the others, is determined by my "doing my thing" unconsciously conscious that it is being recorded. This is the rise of surveillance citizenship itself.

Finally, SCP's performances draw attention to the construction of us as witnesses *to* others. Witnessing implies subjectivity (Oliver 2001). When the SCP players record *others* watching them, the camera watching *all*, and this "all" also noting the impersonal camera (we do not know who, or what, is watching the state's cameras) in the information loop described above, SCP posits a new cultural practice where we move from surveillance citizenship to witness citizenship. Watching random strangers and people we may know via cameras and their documentary archive constitutes our participation in not just the public space but in a whole new system of social relations. Distant others are made proximate when SCP's cameras record, for themselves, for the state's camera, and for *us* watching them both, a public "performance." The suddenly proximate Other is now a member of my consciousness as the video is archived. Surveillance cameras mediate my interaction with the Other, producing a form of intersubjective subjectivity because the Other is within my "frame".

In this light, SCP's contribution highlights not only the surveillance but also the subjectivities that emerge within the structure of surveillance.

References

Brighenti, Andrea Mubi. 2010. "Democracy and Surveillance." *Surveillance and Democracy*, edited by Kevin D. Haggerty and Minas Samatas, 51-68. Abingdon, Oxon: Routledge.

Finn, Jonathan. 2009. *Capturing the Criminal Image: From Mug Shot to Surveillance Society*. Minneapolis, MN and London: University of Minnesota Press.

Oliver, Kelly. 2001. *Witnessing: Beyond Recognition*. Minneapolis, MN and London: University of Minnesota Press.

Nayar, Pramod K. 2015. *Citizenship and Identity in the Age of Surveillance*. Cambridge: Cambridge University Press.

Surveillance Camera Players. 2006. "1984." https://www.youtube.com/watch?v=RILTI8mxEnE

Surveillance Camera Players. 2008. "The Raven." / "Waiting for Godot." / "Ubu Roi." https://www.youtube.com/watch?v=TUxQQGXQZVs

## Virtual reality

Philip Auslander

In everyday use, the word "virtual" means "almost," as in "She's a virtual genius." The context in which one most commonly finds the word today probably is the expression "virtual reality" (VR), which refers to immersive, computer-based simulations of self-contained environments. Taking the two meanings together, we might say that VR environments are intended to seem *almost* real. It is important to note that VR is no longer confined to special circumstances but is part of many people's daily lives. The desktop metaphor employed by the operating systems of personal computers, for example, involves our use of a virtual desktop, virtual documents, virtual files, and so on. Each of these things functions similarly enough to their "real world" counterparts to be familiar while also functioning in ways that have no real-world correlatives (manila folders generally do not snap open to devour documents, for instance).

That VR seems almost, but not fully real, is important. As Gabriella Giannachi observes in *Virtual Theatres: An Introduction*, VR "is in a paradoxical relationship to the real," in part because "it has to be constructed as different from the real in order to be perceived as separate from it" (2004, 123). In order to be useful, a flight simulator used to train pilots must offer an experience as close as possible to the actual experience of flying, while asserting that since it is an educational environment, it is allowable, even valuable, for pilots to make errors that would have disastrous consequences in the real world.

This complicated and ambiguous relationship between VR and RL (real life) underlies both the freedom sometimes claimed for VR and the moral panics surrounding it. On the one hand, people have the freedom to construct and perform whatever identities they wish in VR, whether by building avatars to represent themselves in online games, selectively presenting aspects of themselves on social networking sites, or fabricating identities from whole cloth (e.g., men online masquerading as women and vice versa). Because performances of identity do not clearly have the same consequences in VR as in RL, and it is also not entirely clear the degree to which each bleeds into the other, there is concern that the freedoms offered by VR may sometimes lead to unforeseen dangers.

From the disciplinary perspective of performance studies, it is worth noting that virtuality is a concept that bridges the performance paradigms outlined by Jon McKenzie in *Perform or Else: From Discipline to Performance* (2001). Virtuality manifests itself across the entire range of cultural performances, from the use of virtual images and performers in theatre and performance art to the incursion of virtuality into ritual—the first wedding in cyberspace took place in 1996. VR simulations are essential tools in organizational and technological performance, of which VR is, of course, itself a manifestation.

### *Further reading*

Giannachi (2004); McKenzie (2001); Parker-Starbuck (2014).

### *References*

Giannachi, Gabriella. 2004. *Virtual Theatres: An Introduction*. London: Routledge.

McKenzie, Jon. 2001. *Perform or Else: From Discipline to Performance*. New York: Routledge.

Parker-Starbuck, Jennifer. 2014. *Cyborg Theatre: Corporeal/Technological Intersections in Multimedia Performance*. New York: Palgrave Macmillan.

### *Cross references*

"**Becoming *Kinocognophore***" by Bucher and Zeeb, with Cheng; "**The Internet**" and "**Performance in the digital age**" by Auslander; "**Liminality**" by Levine; "**Postdramatic theatre**" by Fuchs; "**Scenario**" by Taylor.

# Action

## Appropriation

Winnie Wong

In the cultural critique of capitalism, appropriation is a vision of labor, one that is vividly tied to the Marxist notion of alienation. The political theorist Bertell Ollman has given an influential account of its central place in Marx's conception of man. Ollman writes, "In its most general sense, 'appropriation' means to utilize constructively, to build by incorporating; the subject, whether stated or implied, is man's essential powers. For Marx, the individual appropriates the nature he perceives and has become oriented to by making it in some way a part of himself with whatever effect this has on his senses and future orientation" (Ollman 1971, 89). Under capitalism, however, appropriation takes the form of estrangement and alienation. As Ollman notes, Marx's concept of appropriation is implicitly envisioned in the figure of the artist; for example, Marx likens full and personal appropriation to the painter's appropriation of a sunset (Ollman 1971, 23). Thus the artist is compellingly envisioned as a full, self-conscious, self-expressive and authentically productive individual, the artist and his appropriation of the material world contrasts with alienated labor, and this is one of theoretical pillars around which the "work" of artists has been understood throughout the twentieth century.

In contemporary practice and theory, appropriation in art is rarely distinguishable from the longstanding artistic practices of reference, imitation and citation. Indeed, despite modernist claims to *ex nihilo* creation, the formal, stylistic or conceptual reference to prior sources is simply integral to the recognizability of a work of "art" as such. Nevertheless, in the post-WWII era, the renewed reception of Marcel Duchamp's readymades, the use of mass media and popular visual culture by Andy Warhol, Robert Rauschenberg, Roy Lichtenstein, and the rise of appropriation artists such as Barbara Kruger, Jeff Koons, Sherry Levine, Hans Haacke, Cindy Sherman, and Richard Prince, gave rise to a new and influential American artistic legacy of "appropriation" with broad effects across many genres, areas and disciplines of cultural practice. With reference to this recent history, appropriation has come to signify nearly any *re*use of objects, images, gestures, forms, ideas, works and intellectual properties from any pre-existing artistic, political, institutional or commercial source. Moreover, appropriation is considered a performative act, a tactic, or a gesture assumed to *intentionally* mount a critique of the institutions, corporations and values crucial to the Western valorization of originality and individual property.

Concentrated heavily in the legacy of post-WWII American art, and targeted primarily at the critique of American institutions, copyright law, and consumer culture, the discourse of artistic appropriation in the 2000s merged with popular activist movements, which arose from the digital revolution and opposed the expansion of the American intellectual property legal regime. This popular ethos combined the valorization of appropriation with the argument that technological innovation requires a free and accessible "creative commons." Appropriations were applied to consumer and popular activities that parodied or ironized corporate logos, trademarks, copyrights, high fashion, recorded music, or any public or private property. Such "cultural appropriations" were likewise assumed to express the anti-capitalist and anti-authoritarian cultural politics of its American artistic and activist legacies, even in non-Western contexts in which such politics were neither central nor relevant. As global differences in political, legal and cultural regimes become more distinct and nationally competitive, champions of the creative commons and the creative rights of anyone—including non-Westerners—to appropriate (or "steal"), have begun to re-evaluate the universality of these earlier claims.

In the US legal context, an intellectual conundrum has developed around the appropriation artists emerging in the 1980s who have become celebrated authors and whose appropriation works were the subject of high-profile copyright lawsuits. These lawsuits allege that their "appropriation" amounted to copyright violations and the theft of other artist's property. In these disputes, defenders of appropriation art often argue for artworks made from appropriation as original and innovative. Such a defense, grounded in the art historical value of artistic appropriation, thus effectively robs appropriation works of their original intention to challenge (if not, undo) these very constructs of ownership and authorship undergirding intellectual property law. These disputes demonstrate how the law can be moved to reincorporate "appropriation" within the powerful regimes of property, despite—or precisely because of—the commercial and critical "success" of such works, returning us, as Marx described, to a situation in which estranged labor appears as appropriation, and appropriation as estranged labor.

The double irony of appropriation for contemporary art is that it now contains two countervailing assumptions: on the one hand, appropriation derives its implicit individual intentionality from the Marxist critique of labor under capital, as an opposing force to the alienation that is so anathema to the artist. On the other hand, validations of appropriation as a critique of authorship and ownership appear to depend upon prevailing professional hierarchies with undeniable market effects. It is notable, for example, that the string of US copyright cases brought against 1980s appropriation artists tends to pit these artists with high-value sales and powerful institutional backing against unrecognized photographers whose work they appropriated without acknowledgement (as in the legal disputes pitting Jeff Koons against Art Rogers and Andrea Blanch, Shepard Fairey against Mannie Garcia, and Richard Prince against Patrick Cairou). Such disputes raise the question of whether appropriation as fair use under the American legal regime has become a special privilege afforded only to a certain class of artists, and only for certain kinds of activities deemed artistic.

### *Further reading*

Ollman (1971); Wong (2014).

### *References*

Ollman, Bertell. 1971. "Alienation: Marx's Conception of Man in Capitalist Society". In *Cambridge Studies in the History and Theory of Politics*, edited by Maurice Cowling, G.R. Elton, E. Kedourie, J.G.A. Pocock, J.R. Pole, and Walter Ullman. Cambridge: Cambridge University Press.

Wong, Winnie. 2014. *Van Gogh On Demand: China and the Readymade.* Chicago, IL: University of Chicago Press.

*Cross references*

"**Cindy Sherman's Real Fakery**" by Schneider; "**Cultural production**" by Colleran; "**Heather Cassils' indeterminate body**" by Jones; "**Paradox**" by Fabião; "**Prosthetic performance**" by Gass; "**Readymade**" by Hoefer; "**Reproduction**" by Bay-Cheng; "**Sampling**" by Hodges Persley.

## Circus

Peta Tait

Circus is artistic, body-based, acrobatic performance with apparatus. Semiotic analysis (Bouissac 1976; Carmeli 1990), along with cultural and gender theory (Stoddart 2000; Davis 2002; Tait 2005) have expanded the literature on this subject (Toole-Stott 1962). A metaphoric idea of circus co-opted by culture encapsulates notions of disrupted social order, chaos and danger, although, paradoxically, circus arts are presented by highly trained bodies doing disciplined athletic action. The technical knowledge of movement on the ground and in the air, and of balancing, tumbling, juggling, and object manipulation has passed down through lineages of performers who create displays of dexterity and gracefulness. In this popular live entertainment, performers strive for physical records, and their exciting death-defying feats make anxiety-provoking, but pleasurable viewing.

Circus skills are practiced world-wide, but most commonly recognized in acts programmed into the "traditional" circus, the "new" or "contemporary" post-1970s animal-free circus (Albrecht 1995), and in community-activist "social" circus. Paul Bouissac (1976) discerns how the socially marginalized circus is symbolically central to culture. The close-knit, itinerant lifestyle of the tenting circus evokes cultural fascination, pervasively across the arts and literature, and circus skills feature in over 1,000 films. The body phenomenology created by a muscular circus performer can traverse categories of gender, sexuality, ethnicity, race and even species to seem fluid and malleable in its performative identity (Tait 2005).

Circus became conflated with sideshows (Goodall 2002), as an enticing site of transgression and the carnivalesque grotesque (Russo 1994). Historically, each circus skill, such as rope-walking and clowning, long predates its inclusion in Astley's equestrian shows in London, which founded the European-American circus after 1768 (e.g. Speaight 1980; Assael 2005), and which then proliferated absorbing Chinese, Japanese and Middle Eastern acrobatic traditions. This traditional circus as an institution travelled globally, influencing major social innovations: from equipment invention to transportation, marketing promotion to national spectacles, and physical education to superheroes. Circus spectacles became grandiose, as individual artists invented apparatus and created artistic and skills innovations; flying trapeze action was invented by Léotard in 1859, with females like Leona Dare the leading flyers by 1880. Trained wild animals were controversially added to the ring during the 1890s (Joys 1983).

From graduates of national schools to family dynasties in well-established and newer circuses like Australia's Circus Oz and Canada's Cirque du Soleil, circus and its analysis continues to evolve in the twenty-first century.

*Further reading*

Bouissac (1976); Tait (2005).

*References*


Assael, Brenda.2005. *The Circus and Victorian Society*. Charlottesville, VA: The University of Virginia Press.

Albrecht, E.J. 1995. *The New American Circus*. Gainesville, FL: University of Florida Press.

Bouissac, Paul. 1976. *Circus and Culture*. Bloomington, IN: Indiana University Press.

Carmeli, Yoram S. 1990. "Performing the 'Real' and 'Impossible' in the British Traveling Circus." *Semiotica* 80 (34): 193–220.

Davis, Janet M. 2002. *The Circus Age: Culture and Society under the American Big Top*. Durham, NC: The University of North Carolina Press.

Goodall, Jane. 2002. *Performance and Evolution in the Age of Darwin.* London: Routledge.
Russo, Mary. 1994. *The Female Grotesque: Risk, Excess and Modernity.* London and New York: Routledge.
Joys, Joanne Carol. 1983. *The Wild Animal Trainer in America,* Boulder, CO: Pruett Publishing Co.
Speaight, George. 1980. *A History of the Circus.* London: Tantivy Press.
Stoddart, Helen. 2000. *Rings of Desire: Circus History and Representation.* Manchester: Manchester University Press.
Tait, Peta. 2005. *Circus Bodies: Cultural Identity in Aerial Performance.* London: Routledge.
Toole-Stott, Raymond.1962. *A Bibliography of Books on the Circus in English from 1773 to 1964.* Cheltenham: Harpur and Sons.

*Cross references*

"**Animal Studies**" by Chaudhuri; "**Animalworks**" and "**Extreme performance**" by Cheng; "**Choreography**" by Lepecki; "**Intercultural performance**" by Alker; "**Performing body modifications**" by Henkes; "**Play**" by Schechner; "**Puppet and object performance**" by Bell.

## Experimental music

Andrew J. Henkes

Music is experimental if it purposefully interrogates or transgresses the definitive limits of music genres or music generally. According to John Cage, "the word 'experimental' is apt [for music], providing it is understood not as descriptive of an act to be later judged in terms of success and failure, but simply as an act the outcome of which is unknown" (1961, 13). Music that seeks this innovation often transcends commoditization, critical judgment, and even audience enjoyment.

Avant-garde rebels like Cage who produced the earliest experimental music challenged Western composition's traditions of harmony, structure and practice. American innovators incorporated popular music into classical composition (e.g., Charles Ives), explored dissonance (Charles Seeger), and played instruments in unorthodox ways (Henry Cowell), rejecting European musical axioms in favor of a distinctly American art of individualist approaches and pioneering experiments. Italian Futurists found inspiration in machinery. Luigi Russolo, for example, asserted in the "Art of Noises" (1913) that mechanical clanks, whistles and hums represented the future of music. Cage came to be the century's most influential voice in music with his revolutionary explorations of randomness, electronic music, and noise. In the first public performance of Cage's most famous piece, *4'33"* (1952), pianist David Tudor merely closed and opened the keyboard lid three times to mark respectively the beginning and end of each movement, but he did not play a single key for the titular duration. The spectators thus became the performers as the sounds of their bodies joined with the room's ambient noises to create the music.

In subsequent decades, *musique concrete* and *elektronische Musik* experimented with non-acoustic sources including electronic synthesizers and recorded sounds. Yoko Ono derived a vocal style of dissonant tonalities, moans and spoken-word elements from Asian and Western roots. In *Duets on Ice* (1974), an early experiment in multimedia performance, Laurie Anderson accompanied recordings of herself with her violin until the ice blocks she stood upon melted. In popular music, Grand Wizard Theodore introduced the iconic thumping and screeches of record scratching to Hip-hop, and buzzing feedback became a staple of rock. The future of music might be found in current experiments with computer-produced compositions and noise rock that pushes static and volume to the limits of human comprehension. By calling attention to alternative techniques and sounds, experimental music challenges the boundaries that delineate music from noise, speech, silence, and other art forms, and thus opens up new potentialities for musicians and audiences alike.

*Further reading*

Cage (1961); Holmes (2002); Nyman (1999).

*References*

Cage, John. 1961. *Silence: Lectures and Writings*. Middletown, CT: Wesleyan University Press.

Holmes, Thomas B. 2002. *Electronic and Experimental Music: Pioneers in Technology and Composition*. New York: Routledge.

Nyman, Michael. 1999. *Experimental Music: Cage and Beyond*. Cambridge: Cambridge University Press.

Russolo, Luigi. 1913. "The Art of Noises Futurist Manifesto." In *The Art of Noises* (1916), translated by Barclay Brown. Reprint, New York: Pendragon Press, 1986.

*Cross references*

"**Feminist hip-hop fusion**" by Hodges Persley; "**Grace notes: Meredith Monk's *Songs of Ascension***" by Marranca; "**Modernism**" by Albright, Pearl, and Speca; "**Post-linearity**" by Bay-Cheng; "**Sampling**" by Hodges Persley.

## Grace notes: Meredith Monk's *Songs of Ascension*

Bonnie Marranca

For half a century Meredith Monk has been creating a unique form of performance, bringing together music, movement, image, text, and sound, whether in chamber pieces, site-specific projects, opera, film or video. In recent years, music has more often become the prominent artistic element in her work, though as a composer and singer it was always foundational in the operas and musical pieces she has created. Now, after her compositions for the St. Louis and New World symphonies, there is a strong sense of Monk pushing the music into multiple performance situations, resulting in new forms of music theatre and expanded musical settings. Indeed, her recent *Songs of Ascension* (2008) and *On Behalf of Nature* (2013) have no text at all. Music, especially the human voice–in solo or group configurations–is foregrounded in exquisite song settings that shape an entire performance. Monk is known for the "extended vocal technique" that she has developed over the decades.

*Songs of Ascension* grew from a conversation with a Zen mentor of Monk who told her of psalms people sang or recited as they ascended a mountain with their offerings of a harvest. The German poet Paul Celan had written of them. Around the same time as hearing this story Ann Hamilton invited Monk to sing at the opening of her eight-story cement *Tower*, created for a private ranch in Geyerserville, California. The work was performed in a concert version with the Elysian String Quartet, performing in daylight, in the Great Hall of Dartington College of Arts, in Devon, England, and then with the British musicians replaced by the Todd Reynolds Quartet for its world premiere at Stanford University before coming to the Next Wave Festival at the Brooklyn Academy in 2009. That same year Monk created *Ascension Variations*, a site-specific performance for 130 performers in the rotunda of the Solomon R. Guggenheim Museum in New York.

During the process of development, Ann Hamilton had begun to collaborate with Monk on *Songs of Ascension*. She devised turntables to throw video images along the walls of the darkened theatre, generating an immersive experience for the audience. Monk claims that she and Hamilton from the start thought of the video as "weather" (Marranca 2009, 19). Images such as a horse, a bird, a ship, and faces were used abstractly, and not to illustrate the work. The effect was particularly striking against the peeling reddish-brown walls of BAM's Harvey Theatre, as if they were pictographs or ancient cave images, thrown from projectors on the ceiling and floor of the theatre.

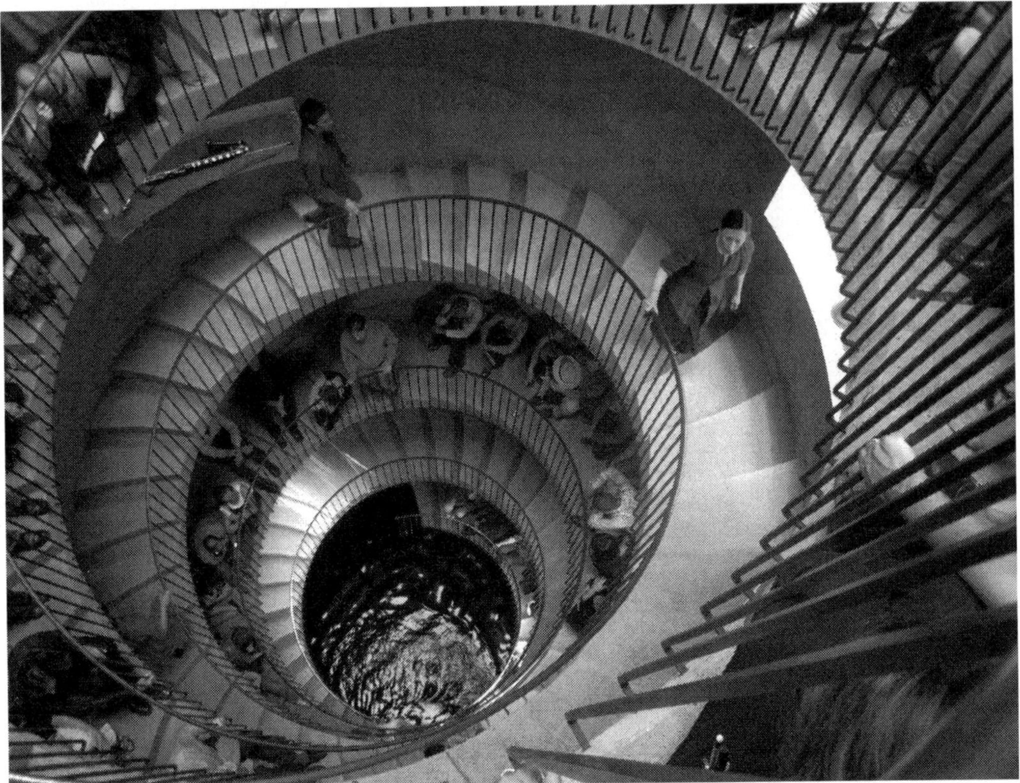

**Figure 5** Meredith Monk, *Songs of Ascension* (2008), performed inside the *Tower - Oliver Ranch* (2007), designed by Ann Hamilton. Courtesy of the artist.

Lasting slightly over an hour, *Songs of Ascension* opens with the wide sweeping movements of long-time ensemble performer Ellen Fisher, her white dress punctuating the darkness of the stage as she traverses it. Stretching outward, emphatically using the shoulders and arms, was characteristic of movement solos by Monk and Ching Gonzalez, too. As in other recent pieces, the singers–featuring Katie Geissinger, who often appears with Monk in vocal concerts–and musicians of both the regular company under the direction of Allison Sniffin and the Reynolds group, at times performed as they intermingled in the same space. The highly individualized expressivity of each of the twelve performers is valued in the performance. While some executed movements, others sang, and still others played instruments simultaneously, giving a strong sense of *presentness* in the elaboration of the process of the work. It could be at one moment melancholic and at another joyful. Besides the superb musicianship and musical arrangements, the effect is that of spatial "composition," in the sense of the stage picture the performers delineated. Movement and singing and playing instruments are what happens. There is no narrative, no spoken language. Costume designs, by Yoshio Yabara, emphasize strong reds, black and gray, or white. The stage is always dark, with a performer spotlighted to establish focus.

Other elements of the piece that reflect Monk's vocabulary are the procession form in group movements and the use of the periphery of the space where performers at times sit and watch others perform or play music. For a long time now it has seemed that the performers in a Monk piece are not cast members but rather individuals of a community who have their own way of moving, singing and playing instruments. They frequently engage in harmonic group singing, accompanied by the poignant sounds of a violin. The music is sometimes melancholic and at other times joyful. Sitting on the floor, Monk plays a harmonium-style Indian instrument called a shruti. A unique feature of *Songs of Ascension* is that at the end of the work the musicians lie down on the floor with their instruments on top of them, among other recumbent performers. Members of the Stonewall Chorale line the edge of the upper balcony, creating a full sound that envelops the theatre.

The overall effect of this work is a deep feeling of meditative calm, emanating from the artist's long-time Buddhist practice, which has characterized other recent pieces such as *mercy* (2002) and *Impermanence* (2008). Monk has said of *Songs of Ascension*: "I am striving for theatre as a transformational experience and also as offering" (Marranca 2009, 30). Indeed the spectators are less an audience than a congregation. There is an atmosphere of quietude and mindfulness that infuse the work with a spiritual dimension. For Monk creating art is a spiritual practice.

In recent years, besides Meredith Monk, a number of artists here and abroad–as disparate as Heiner Goebbels, Kirsten Denholm, Peter Sellars, Joan Jonas, Anne Teresa De Keersmaeker–have brought music into their various performance forms, inspiring a level of emotional intensity that stands apart from much of the real-time theatre prevalent today. Monk's own achievement in *Songs of Ascension* can be measured by its grace, stillness, and clarity of vocal expression–elements of performance that are also an ethics.

*References*

Marranca, Bonnie. 2009. "Performance and the Spiritual Life: Meredith Monk in Conversation with Bonnie Marranca." *PAJ: A Journal of Performance and Art*, 31.1: 16-36.

## Extreme performance

Meiling Cheng

Extreme performance is not a specialized term. It does not name a live art genre, nor does it identify a particular group of performance practitioners. Unlike, for example, Arte Povera, an Italian art movement initiated in 1967 by Germano Celant, who promulgated an innovative engagement with wide-ranging art materials and processes (Christov-Bakargiev 2005), extreme performance has neither a specific historical inception, nor a visionary theorist to define its contemporaneous contexts, stylistic priorities, or characteristic preoccupations. Generally used by critics as a floating signifier, extreme performance articulates an art action's push against its medium's preexisting limits. Extreme performance exposes a sensibility verging on the scandalous, even as the artist/performer absorbs the risk of a transgression.

As an adjective, "extreme" denotes the outermost edge that extends far beyond the norm. Semantically, the qualifier may be linked with various nouns to suggest the intensity of affect generated by what the compound phrase specifies—such as "extreme sports," so-called for their excessive speeds, extraordinary technical demands, and a likelihood of danger during practice. While, in common perceptions, the extreme, like heroism or martyrdom, has always enjoyed a mixed appeal, the concept becomes highly suspect in the post-9/11, anti-terrorist Euro-American world, contaminated as it were by the fanaticism linked with its etymological relative, extremism. Ironically, the term has also gained some fashionable currency in popular cultures, as witnessed by "extreme makeover."

More an indicator of degree than of kind, extreme performance exists as a methodological possibility for all contemporary performative and performing art genres, from theatre, dance, music, to installation, conceptual photography, electronic, multimedia, and performance art. An extreme performance disrupts the inertia within its medium by violating the conventional boundaries guarding its constituent elements. If a performance artwork is composed of a dynamic *time-space-action-performer-audience* matrix (Cheng 2002), then an extreme performance may pit each of these interlinked irreducible elements against its minimal or maximal potentials: by turning *time* into the brevity of an explosive collision (e.g. Chris Burden's *Shoot*, 1971) or an endurance duration too protracted and tedious to be witnessed in its entirety (Tehching Hsieh and Linda Montano's one-year performance, 1983–84); by making *space* as miniscule as the DNA laboratory within a molecule (Eduardo Kac's transgenic *GFP Bunny*, 2000) or as expansive as the solar system and beyond (Cai Guo-Qiang's *Project for Extraterrestrials* series, 1989–1999); by stilling *action* into a wordless energetic exchange between the artist and a spectator (Marina Abramovic's *The House with the Ocean View*, 2002) or enlarging it to include the planting of 7,000 trees and columnar basalt stones (Joseph Beuys's social sculpture *7,000 Oaks*, 1982–1987); by zeroing in on *performer* as a blanched and bleeding male body (Franko B., *I Miss You!*, 2003) or as an involuntary mass of smelly, writhing, and dying maritime animals (Peng Yu's *Curtain*, 1999); by abstracting the audience to be the eye of a camera lens (Cindy Sherman, *Untitled Film Stills*, 1977–1980) or entrusting it with the process of creating the very performance it experiences (John Cage, *4'33"*, 1952).

Far from a formalistic artifact, an extreme performance becomes embroiled within its sociocultural, political, economic, and spiritual contexts through its confrontation with loaded or taboo issues, its inquisition into the globalized institution of art, and its exposure of the normative assumptions regarding the production, transmission, and documentation of ephemeral performances. Controversial themes from zoophilia, transsexuality, to pornography, from immigration, terrorism, asylum-seeking, to ethnic cleansing and genocide, from cannibalism, animal torture, self-mutilation, to necrophilia, from child labor, organ trafficking, addiction, epidemic, to bio-technology jointly enliven the proper of extreme performances. In extreme performances, an artist's body and that of a non-human animal may become entangled, symbolically merged to be a unit of enactment (Kira O'Reilly, *inthewrongplaceness*, 2006); an internet-circuited performing body may partially surrender itself to the kinetic manipulation of remote viewers/collaborators (Stelarc, *Fractal Flesh*, 1995); a sculptor of corporeal collage may question her own complicity and ambivalence by partnering with cosmetic surgeons (Orlan, *The Reincarnation of Saint Orlan*, 1990–1993); a feminist artist may legally designate her various bodily organs for postmortem sales (Suzanne Lacy, *Body Contract*, 1974); a messianic body artist may transport his erotic-painful body to the religious iconography of St. Sebastian in martyrdom (Ron Athey, *Sebastian Suspended*, 1999). Precisely through its protean guises, extreme performance transmutes the delirium of an indiscretion into an ethical conundrum-in-motion.

### *Further reading*

Cheng (2005, 2006, 2013); Miglietti (2003).

### *References*

Cheng, Meiling. 2005. "Violent Capital; Zhu Yu on File." *TDR: The Drama* Review, 49.3: 58–77.

Cheng, Meiling. 2002. *In Other Los Angeleses: Multicentric Performance Art*. Berkeley, CA: University of California Press.

Cheng, Meiling. 2006. "Extreme Performance and Installation from China." *TheatreForum*, 29 (Summer 2006): 88–96.

Cheng, Meiling. 2013. *Beijing Xingwei: Contemporary Chinese Time-Based Art*. London, New York, Calcutta: Seagull Books.

Christov-Bakargiev, Carolyn. 2005. *Arte Povera (Themes and Movements)*. London: Phaidon Press.

Miglietti, Francesca Alfano. 2003. *Extreme Bodies: The Use and Abuse of the Body in Art*. Translated by Antony Shugaar. Milan: Skira.

*Cross references*

**"35 Years of Living Art (Excerpts from Linda Mary Montano's blog, Thursday, December 6, 2012)"** by Montano; **"Bodies in action"** by Stiles and O'Dell; **"Body Art Still Image Action: *OFFERING*"** by Caranza, with Darsalia and Cheng; **"Endurance performance"** by Klein; **"Explicit body performance"** by McGinley; **"Goat Island's *The Sea and Poison*"** by Garoian and Gaudelius; **"Marina Abramovic's durational opus"** by Carr; **"Performing body modifications"** by Henkes; **"*Weights*: An excerpt"** by Manning.

## He Yunchang's limit acts

Meiling Cheng

In broad daylight, a naked man walked into the upper streams of Niagara Falls, slicing through the rapid currents to move toward the falls. He swam across a small creek and stood among the low bushes mid-stream. He paused, pulling at a rope attached to his waist that stretched from a boulder on the bank across the water. Shivering in the chill that dips below 35°F, he threw the rope's loose end forward. He was surprised when the rope sank under the water and dismayed when he failed to dislodge the rope after repeated tugging. He turned around and retraced the rope back to the bank, hoping to get a razor to cut loose the stuck end. Several policemen were waiting for him on the bank. They glanced at the man's drenched body–blue from the cold and raw from a multitude of flesh wounds–handcuffed him, wrapped him up in a blanket and rushed him off to a hospital in Buffalo.

The man was Beijing-based artist He Yunchang (何云昌), enacting a self-sponsored bodywork during his first U.S. visit to participate in *The Wall: Reshaping Contemporary Chinese Art*, a large-scale exhibition curated by Gao Minglu at the Albright-Knox Art Gallery in Buffalo, New York. The evening before his plunge into Niagara Falls, He performed *The General's Command* (21 October 2005) outside behind the Albright-Knox as part of the opening events for *The Wall* (Gaasch, 2005). With just a coating of grease on the skin, He climbed into a transparent Plexiglas cube (70 inches in length and width, 1 foot and 40 inches in height) to execute *The General's Command*. He seated himself down on a chair inside the cube, tied his ankles to the chair, and asked assistants to activate a churning cement-mixer, which began pouring concrete into the cube. Within minutes, He's body was buried up to his shoulders in a solid damp mass. After about 30 minutes, when several attempts at intervention by the gallery staff were met with the artist's refusal, a woman in the audience yelled, "Make the decision for him!" (Fedyszyn 2006). But He, while revealing distress by repeatedly banging his head backward against the Plexiglas surface, endured his physical suffering in self-internment. After an hour, the artist finally consented to being rescued from his concrete encasement. The cement paste slid off the artist's body when assistants removed the Plexiglas walls. Acidic traces of concrete, however, had seared He's skin, leaving around 2,000 blackened scars on his torso and limbs.

Less than 20 hours later, He walked into the dazzling waterscape of Niagara Falls, attempting to enact *A Rock in Niagara Falls* (2005). He's proposal for this extreme performance on the aquatic border between the United States and Canada was deceptively simple: he would find a rock in Niagara Falls and stay there for 24 hours. The water's low temperature forced the artist to revise the project's duration to an hour, but his arrest after only about 20 minutes aborted the performance. A tourist who spotted He's action called a suicide alert to the police. The artist was eventually tried and convicted on misdemeanor counts of "inappropriate behavior in public" and "indecent bodily exposure" (He 2006). He was fined, as were the two students who had helped him film the performance onsite. The gallery that sponsored He's visit suffered no legal liability, because it had explicitly rejected the artist's site-specific proposal for *A Rock in Niagara Falls* in favor of his alternative

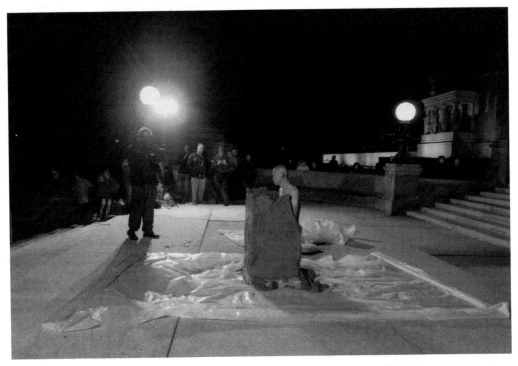

**Figure 6** He Yunchang performing *The General's Command*, 21 October 2005, at the Albright-Knox Art Gallery in Buffalo, New York. Image courtesy of the artist.

scheme, carried out as *The General's Command*. Though without official endorsement, the artist considered the propinquity of a spectacular natural site an invitation for action.

Both *The General's Command* and *A Rock in Niagara Falls* dramatize the head-on collision between mortal flesh and external force, be it natural or manufactured. The chance for the human individual to survive the inhuman onslaught seemed so slim that observers read them as scenes of senseless danger. The woman yelling "make the decision for him" during *The General's Command* and the tourist who helped stop *A Rock in Niagara Falls* probably did not mean to censor an art performance; instead, they responded to a dangerous slippage between art and life occasioned by He's limit acts. Although the woman in the gallery knew she was viewing a live art event, the artist's seemingly irrational doggedness in placing himself in harm's way invalidated his artistic license, making her ethically responsible to intervene. The gallery staff members who sought to shorten the performance likely shared her view, but their ultimate ethical obligation as guardians of art compelled them to support the artist's freedom of expression. The Niagara Falls tourist did not see art but rather suicidal behavior, which amounted to a life-and-death emergency demanding an immediate call to 911. According to the misdemeanor counts with which He was charged, the U.S. court adjudicates the artist's "harm condition" (Ellis 1984, 3) not on the legal ground of individual rights (e.g. to criminalize He for a suicide attempt, reckless body art, etc.) but on that of public interest (for offenses like inappropriate behavior and nakedness in public).

"The body is the place in which a series of relationships of power converge and tend to transform it into a territory of experimentation," writes Francesca Alfano Miglietti, referring to Michel Foucault's influential theory of biopolitics for her study of European bodyworks (2003, 30). The diverse responses from a range of U.S. citizenry to a Chinese artist's extreme performances demonstrate the converging political and ethical forces that claim control over the artist's body. As He Yunchang's public behaviors push toward the edge of fatality, their perceived irreversible consequences render his artistic intention suspect to his witnesses and jurors alike, simultaneously exposing the artist's and his spectators' preexisting assumptions regarding individual agency. To follow Miglietti's metaphor, we may take He's body in thrall to his self-determined limit acts as a living laboratory in which the test items include certain randomly gathered civilian subjects' conflicting ethical judgments, sociopolitical habits, legal expectations, and enculturated reactions–all made acute by the artist's vulnerability within supra-human circumstances.

He Yunchang's two bodyworks staged in Buffalo, NY, invite contemplation of the purpose of extreme performance in an era when live art products are frequently consumed by volitional or accidental viewers in a transcultural, glocalized context. His pieces bring into relief a paradox of extreme bodyworks: when artists disregard the normative boundary safeguarding their own bodies' physical integrity, they effectively surrender their private flesh to public ownership, activating their observers' species-centered, hence implicitly proprietary, engagement.

### References

Ellis, Anthony. 1984. "Offense and the Liberal Conception of the Law." *Philosophy and Public Affairs*, 13.1: 3–23.

Fedyszyn, Joan. 2006. "The Concrete Wall: What Happened?" *Buffalo Pundit.com*. http://www.buffalorising.com/home/archives/001653php

Gaasch, Cynnie. 2005. "Permanence and Change." *ARTVOICE* 4.44. Accessed June 14, 2015. http://artvoice.com/issues/v4n44/permanence_and_change

He Yunchang. 2006. Author's phone interview with the artist, from Los Angeles to Beijing. 31 January.

Miglietti, Francesca Alfano. 2003. *Extreme Bodies: The Use and Abuse of the Body in Art*. Translated by Antony Shugaar. Milan: Skira.

## Happenings

Mariellen Sandford

This late-20th-century performance genre got its name from one of the first Happenings, *18 Happenings in 6 Parts*, staged by Allan Kaprow in 1959 at the Reuben Gallery in New York. Perceived by many as spontaneous anti-art, Happenings were from the beginning scripted works conceived with aesthetic considerations. Michael Kirby noted in 1965 that the common misconception regarding Happenings is that they "just happen" and offered a more rigorous definition: "A performance using a variety of materials (films, dance, readings, music, etc.) in a compartmented structure, and making use of essentially nonmatrixed performance, is a Happening" (1965a: 29). The "multiple compartments," cites Kirby, differentiate Happenings from Events, which comprise the works performed by contemporaneous Fluxus artists (1965a, 27). "Happening" was not used in print in relation to an artistic performance until 1959; Kirby refers to a subtitle of sorts for the performance text of *The Demiurge* by Kaprow published in *The Anthologist*, a Rutgers University literary journal (1965, 53). Kaprow, who began his career as a painter, has become synonymous with Happenings, although he worked toward "un-arting" (Kaprow 2001, xxix).

Kirby retrospectively refers to *Theatre Piece No. 1* by John Cage—performed at Black Mountain College in the summer of 1952 with Robert Rauschenberg, Merce Cunningham, and others—as a Happening, and in the Happenings issue of *TDR* he refers to Cage as the "touchstone" of "The New Theatre" (1965b, 41). In response to the *TDR* issue, Kaprow questions the emphasis on Cage as a "germinal influence," stressing the importance of early 20th-century avant-garde predecessors from the Futurist, Dada, and Surrealist movements, which

Kirby also relates to Happenings. Happenings, Fluxus, postmodern dance, visual theatre, experimental theater, new music theater, and the various permutations of performance art—"live art" (Goldberg 1979)—all trace their lineage back to the experiments of the historical avant-garde. Besides Cage, Kaprow credits artists of many genres who were at the same moment in the late 1950s and early '60s blurring the boundaries of painting, sculpture, theater, music, dance, and the performance of everyday life to move beyond the historically defined limits of their art forms. He tracks his own influences back, before Cage, to Jackson Pollock, whose action painting led "not to more painting, but to *more action*" (Kaprow 1966a, 282).

Although Happenings are often discussed in relation to US artists, Kaprow notes that there were many artists in Europe, Latin America, and Asia breaking boundaries. Günter Berghaus traces the antecedents of Happenings-related work in Europe through Pop Art to New Realism; the First Festival of New Realism in July 1961 included activities performed by artists that, unlike ephemeral Happenings, were intended to produce a "tangible trace" (Restany and Von Saurma 1996, 314). In Asia, the Gutai group in Japan is referred to by Kaprow (1961, 16) and others in relation to Happenings.

### *Further reading*

Kaprow. (1966a, 1966b); Sandford (1995).

### *References*

Goldberg, Roselee. 1979. *Performance: Live Art, 1909 to the Present*. New York: Harry N. Abrams, Inc.

Kaprow, Allan. 1961. *Essays on the Blurring of Art and Life*. Reprint, Berkeley, CA: University of California Press, 1993.

Kaprow, Allan. 1966a. *Some Recent Happenings.* New York: Something Else Press.

Kaprow, Allan. 1966b. "Letter to the editor." *Tulane Drama Review*, 10.4: 281–283.

Kaprow, Allan. 2001. "Preface to the Expanded Edition: On the Way to Un-Art." In *Essays on the Blurring of Art and Life*, Berkeley, CA: University of California Press.

Kirby, Michael. 1965a. *Happenings*. New York: E.P. Dutton & Co., Inc.

Kirby, Michael. 1965b. "The New Theatre." *Tulane Drama Review*, 10.2: 23–43.

Restany, Pierre and Sara Von Saurma. 1996. *Le Monde De L'art En 1995 = The World of Art in 1995*. Paris: UNESCO

Sandford, Mariellen R., ed. 1995. *Happenings and Other Acts*. London: Routledge.

### *Cross references*

"**Anti-art**" and "**Fluxus**" by Stiles; "**Experimental music**" by Henkes; "**Installation art**" by Haidu; "**Performance, postmodernism, and beyond**" by Davidson.

## Historicity

Jeanne Colleran

"Always historicize," Fredric Jameson's admonition in *The Political Unconscious* (1981, 9), could well serve as the credo of the "turn to history" movement in 1980s' North American critical theory, a movement that complicated both notions of historical research and literary appraisal. But such a motto would be quickly rebutted with questions about the methods of historical understanding and historical writing. Examining the act of historical analysis raised new concerns: arguments that history is not directly accessible, that history is itself textual, and that any reconstruction of the past entails an account of how power and containment are exercised via cultural as well as political means; hence, traceable in cultural products. All these arguments have diminished faith in historical objectivity and completeness.

At the same time, these ideas extended and invigorated newer disciplinary practices, including the self-reflexivity of historiography, the emergence of new historicism—born, in part, of significant reappraisals of Renaissance literature, especially

Shakespeare—and the politically committed historical critiques that have exposed exclusion and bias. The term "historicity" itself has been used primarily to refer to distinctions between the real/authentic and the fictitious/mythic, while privileging the former. Yet, because the term also suggests the placement of a person, society, or incident within an historical context, it also alludes to the process of historicization, suggesting that understanding history as primarily an idea ("revolution") or an event ("the execution of Charles I") understates its contemporaneous shaping. Contemporary criticism seems at times to mourn the loss of historicity and at others to harbor deep reservations about the objectivity of the historical archive and the uses to which it is put. History, historicism, historicity—each remains a vexed term in critical theory, not least because of Derrida's description of deconstruction as a "jetty" that is intimately bound to history in order to destabilize it.

The contested status of history is also on display in contemporary performance and theatre. The historians' dedication to the accumulation of evidence—and to the recovery of lost or muted voices—is reprised in documentary theatre such as the Tribunal Plays—including *Guantanamo: Honor Bound to Defend Freedom* (2005); *The Color of Justice* (1996); and *Bloody Sunday* (2005)—produced at London's Tricycle Theatre. Anna Deavere Smith's ethnographic work interrogates social events (the Crown Heights and Los Angeles riots) through multiple interviews assembled into a one-woman performance. Similarly, David Hare examines the Israeli–Palestinian conflict through interviews he conducted and then performed in *Via Doloroso* (1998). Smith and Hare's form of evidentiary drama enacts multiple and contradictory perspectives even while they highlight the ineluctability of personal bias—and the possibility of empathic understanding—by choosing the single-actor format.

Undertaking an examination of national identity—the subject of Shakespeare's Histories—continues explicitly or as an undercurrent in the work of many British playwrights, and increasingly so in the U.S., especially in works by Tony Kushner and August Wilson. Plays like Michael Frayn's *Copenhagen* (1998), Tom Stoppard's *Coast of Utopia* (2002), David Edgar's *Albert Speer* (2000), among many others, trace the implications of key scientific discoveries, political philosophies, or historical personalities on contemporary social life. Re-staging the historical past in order to amend exclusion and depict subjectivities developed under the strain of institutionalized oppression remains central to much post-colonial and globalized theatre.

### Further reading

Krieger (1987); Jameson (1981).

### References

Krieger, Murray, ed. 1987. *The Aims of Representation: Subject/Text/History*. New York: Columbia University Press.

Jameson, Fredric. 1981. *The Political Unconscious: Narrative as a Socially Symbolic Act*. Ithaca, NY: Cornell University Press.

### Cross references

"**Archive and repertoire**" by Taylor; "**Historiography**" by Fabião; "**Performing the archive**" by Nyong'o; "**Reenactment**" by Bay-Cheng; "**Remains**" by Morrison; "**Through the Eyes of Rachel Marker**" by Roth.

## Intervention

Lissette Olivares

Intervention is an interdisciplinary and conceptual form of art practice characterized by critical inquiry and political commitment. Intervention's mode of operation encourages art as activism, foregrounding the art of everyday life and the social sphere as sites of subversion, resistance, disruption and provocation. Interventionists generally attempt to engage a public sphere beyond traditional sites of artistic reception, though interventionists can and do take place within traditional art institutions (i.e. galleries, museums, arts magazines). To mobilize the act of intervention is to emphasize the degree of transgression in each scenario, where transgression can be defined as the capacity for symbolic inversion.

The Soviet Constructivists (1913–1930) are often cited as an early interventionist art movement because of their assault on the boundary between art and life, and their interest in "developing an art that would be useful for the advancement of an unprecedented revolutionary society" (Sholette 2004, 34). The constructivists reframe artists as proletarians, echoing the Marxist idea that it is the capitalist division of labor that constructs the artist as an entity separate from the masses (Sholette 2004, 34). The constructivists are distinguished from contemporary interventionists because of historical shifts in political determinism. Whereas the constructivists aspired to improve a national political agenda inspired by a revolutionary telos, contemporary interventionists are often skeptical about traditional political representation. Interventionists approach art as an instrument for revealing institutional, political and historical power so that audiences can develop their own politics (Sholette 2004, 139). Glenn Harper argues that contemporary interventionists are "post-utopian" because they have "lost the early twentieth century's faith in radical transformations and transcendental ideals," focusing instead on the transfiguration of an audience through a momentary or liminal experience (1998, viii).

Symbolic and skeptical, interventionist practice is historically informed by Guy Debord's *The Society of Spectacle*, which argues that modern conditions of capitalist production have transformed all aspects of everyday life into spectacle, where the spectacle is "the stage at which the commodity has succeeded in *totally* colonizing social life," transforming social actors into passive spectators (1967, 2). As a response to this commodification of culture, and in the hope of creating active situations (as opposed to passive spectatorship), the Situationist International art movement (1957–1972) developed two important estrangement tactics that are often adopted by interventionists. These tactics are: "detournement," which rearranges popular sign systems in order to produce new meanings, and "dérive," "a technique of transient passage through varied ambiances," which emphasizes "psychogeographical" awareness and which proposes a politics of being in physical space (Debord 1956, 50).

The concept of the "tactic" recurs in interventionist practice, and was developed by theorist Michel De Certeau, who explains that in contrast to strategies, tactics are "calculated action determined by the absence of a proper place" (1980, 5). Tactics can be understood as episodes of micro activism within everyday life, which "operate blow by blow," and depend on momentary possibilities (De Certeau 1980, 5). Interventionist tactics occur in concrete geographies (from cartographies of the body to urban areas) and are increasingly available in virtual space.

### *Further reading*

Debord (1967); Thompson and Sholette (2004).

### *References*

De Certeau, Michel. 1980. "On the Oppositional Practices of Everyday Life." *Social Text* Vol. 3, translated by Frederic Jameson and Carl Lovitt, 3–43.

Debord, Guy. 1956. "Theory of the Dérive." *Situationist International Anthology*, edited and translated by Ken Knabb. California: Bureau of Public Secrets. http://www.bopsecrets.org/SI/2.derive.htm

Debord, Guy. 1967. *The Society of Spectacle*. New York: Zone.

Harper, Glenn, ed. 1998. *Interventions and Provocations: Conversations on Art, Culture and Resistance*. New York: SUNY University Press.

Sholette, Gregory. 2004. "Interventionism and the historical uncanny, or: can there be revolutionary art without the revolution?" In *Interventionists: User's Guide for the Creative Disruption of Everyday Life*, edited by Nato Thompson and Gregory Sholette. North Adams, MA: MASS MoCA Publications.

Thompson, Nato and Gregory Sholette. 2004. *Interventionists: User's Guide for the Creative Disruption of Everyday Life*. North Adams, MA: MASS MoCA Publications.

*Cross references*

**"The d/Deaf Performative"** by Pendgraft; **"Destruction art"** by Stiles; **"Double-coding"** by Bial; **"Excerpts from *Prostitution Notes* (1974)"** by Lacy; **"He Yunchang's limit acts"** by Cheng; **"Memoirs of Björk-Geisha"** by Takemoto; **"New genre public art"** by Irish; **"Performance in the digital age"** by Auslander; ***"Reality Ends Here"*** by Watson.

## Sisters Of Survival Signal S.O.S.

Cheri Gaulke

> It was through S.O.S. and others of their contemporaries that I came to understand that there is a difference between "political art" - art *about* political issues - and art that actually is political: art made in and with communities of people at risk that truly aims to make a difference.
>
> Linda Frye Burnham
> (Allyn, Gauldin, Gaulke, Maberry 2011, 2)

It all clicked in the grocery store, when a skeleton peered out at me from the cover of *Time* magazine (November 30, 1981). It was 1981 and the painted skeletal face was a European activist, one of millions demanding an end to the arms race between the U.S. and the U.S.S.R. They chanted "Wir Wollen Kein Euro Shima," fearing European soil would be the battleground for a nuclear war between the two juggernauts–a war that would surely destroy the continent and possibly the world.

During the previous weeks, members of two feminist performance art groups, Feminist Art Workers and The Waitresses, had been meeting to strategize a performance tour of Europe. The women who made up the two groups had met at The Woman's Building in Los Angeles as participants in the Feminist Studio Workshop, a post-graduate, independent, feminist art school founded in 1973. Feminist Art Workers (FAW) was formed in 1976 by Nancy Angelo, Candace Compton, Cheri Gaulke and Laurel Klick to infuse feminist education techniques into participatory performance art experiences. The following year, Jerri Allyn and Anne Gauldin formed The Waitresses, utilizing the image of the waitress as a metaphor for women in society. Both groups were early innovators in collaboration, following a new feminist aesthetic that I have called 1+1=3 (Gaulke 2011, 20). Both groups created art that moved into non-art environments (restaurants, buses, etc.) and pursued the democratization of art through audience participation. Our art addressed so-called "women's issues" of nurturance, sexual violence, and pay equity. We were grappling with what our combined theme should be, as we took our feminist art to Europe. It was *Time* that gave us the answer. Europeans taking to the streets landed the skeleton face on the cover of *Time*. We heard their cry and now it was our turn to respond. We were determined to be artist ambassadors of peace, bypassing official media and government channels, and, through our people-to-people civic engagement, helping to bring an end to this nuclear madness.

### Visual Identity–S.O.S.

Our first tactic was to create a visual identity that would in and of itself express our message. Inspired by a dream image of Nancy Angelo's, we clothed ourselves in rainbow-hued nuns' habits and dubbed ourselves Sisters Of Survival. In addition to Angelo, the newly formed group included Jerri Allyn, Anne Gauldin, Cheri Gaulke and Sue Maberry. We

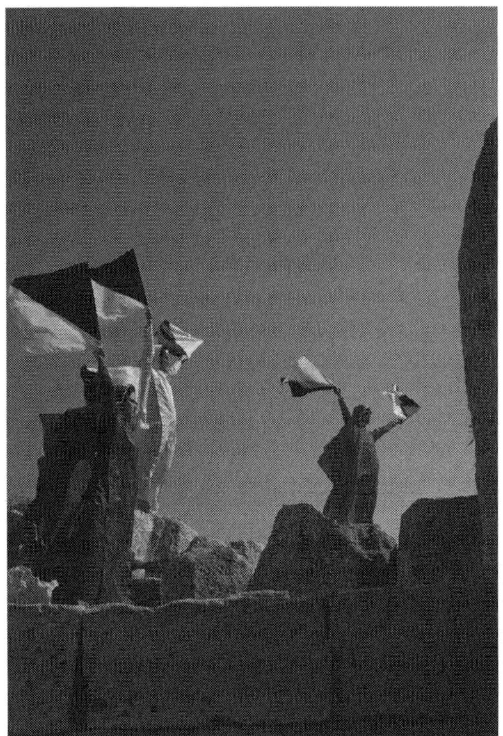

**Figure 7** *Sisters Of Survival Signaling S.O.S.–Save Our Ship / Planet Earth*, 1982, Los Angeles, CA, Copyright: Sisters Of Survival–Jerri Allyn, Nancy Angelo, Anne Gauldin, Cheri Gaulke, Sue Maberry; photographer: Daniel J. Martinez. Image courtesy of the artists.

were indeed a sisterhood, ordered around nuclear disarmament and world peace, signaling an S.O.S. for the planet. At a time when Catholic nuns were trying to get away from the dour pre-re-Vatican II black and white nun image, our rainbow sisters' outfits functioned as a visual metaphor for diversity, humor and hope. Confronting global nuclear annihilation was so epic as to be absurdist: gallows humor, irony and a dose of gentleness were in order. Our strategy of visual branding was more out of the advertising world than the art world. It included custom-made costumes, publicity photos, graphics (brochure, postcards, buttons, stationery), and a logo of nuns signaling S.O.S. with semaphore flags.

## Performance art structure

Suzanne Lacy coined the phrase "performance art structure," in which a period of time or a series of activities might all be considered one art performance. It was a way of putting a frame around an extended art project. We conceived of our work as a single conceptual performance "to network artists and activists in North America and Western Europe around the nuclear threat" (Gaulke 1981). We published a brochure that articulated our three-part plan called *End of the Rainbow*. Part One included educating ourselves about our own government policies by staging a media performance (*Shovel Defense*), creating a participatory activity (*Fold a Crane for Peace*), gathering anti-nuclear North American art, and collecting messages from peace groups to take to Europe. Part Two was a performance and lecture tour of Western Europe and Part Three was a culminating exhibition.

## Media performance–Shovel Defense

On the front lawn of Los Angeles City Hall, nuns in multicolored habits passed through a shovel graveyard in choreographed movements inspired by solemn religious processionals, Cold War-era duck-and-cover exercises, and the haunting movements of Japanese Atomic bomb survivors, walking with burned arms outstretched, as depicted in drawings from 1945. The piece satirized a Reagan administration official who said Americans could survive a nuclear war if there were enough shovels to go around. Political cartoonist Paul Conrad responded by drawing shovels as crosses arranged as a graveyard (*Los Angeles Times* 1982). Sculptor and Woman's Building colleague Marguerite Elliot brought his cartoon to life and invited S.O.S. to collaborate with her on a media performance and installation. Inspired by the media performance strategy of Suzanne Lacy and Leslie Labowitz-Starus, we carefully crafted *Shovel Defense* for the mainstream media with all the accoutrements of a press conference. A banner with our words "Civil Defense: A Grave Mistake" ensured that our message would get through no matter from which angle it was photographed. The performance received national TV and print media coverage.

## Community workshops–Fold a Crane for Peace

For *Target LA: Anti-Nuclear Music and Arts Festival*, S.O.S. collaborated with two Asian American peace groups–AAND (Asian Americans for Nuclear Disarmament and APANA (Asian Pacific Americans for Nuclear Awareness)–to facilitate children and adults to fold thousands of origami cranes. An instructional graphic we designed taught people the story of Sadako Sasaki, a young victim of Hiroshima who attempted to fold 1000 origami cranes before succumbing to radiation sickness. The simple and poignant crane-folding tradition in Japan signifies a hope for peace; we used it as a community-based, symbolic art-making activity to teach about the issues. We invited audience members to participate everywhere we went, including during our Western European Tour.

## Networking and sharing artworks

As we contacted sponsors in Europe and designed our tour for Part Two, we invited North American artists to give us 8.5 x 11-inch anti-nuclear artworks or documentation that we could share with people in Europe. These were mostly presented as a slide lecture at various locations ranging from a feminist coffeehouse in The Netherlands, an Artists for Peace (*Kunstler fur den Frieden*) festival in West Berlin, cultural centers and a school in Malta, among others. Sharing this work across continents was a crucial component of our networking; in this pre-internet and social media era, artists and activists did not know of each others' efforts.

Part Three of *End of the Rainbow* culminated in an exhibition that included the over 300 artworks that we collected from North Americans and Western European artists. The uniform 8.5 x 11-inch format made everyone's work and voice equal as it was presented within a grid-like installation. Like the female tradition of quilt-making (with many squares that make up a quilt), the grid was a feminist art strategy to use one's own art as a context for others' expression.

## Public spectacle–Twist, Signal, Float

Just showing up at peace demonstrations as nuns in rainbow-hued habits was a spectacle, but we also created three public spectacle performances. *Twist for Life Habit* employed 25 rainbow sisters (women and some bearded men!) and two go-go nuns marching down the streets of New York City as part of a massive demonstration for the United Nations Special Session on Disarmament in 1982. At the largest U.S. demonstration to date, our strategy was to use humor to counter the sometimes heavy-handed, ghoulish imagery. In contrast to a narrative that is continuously about war, death and destruction, we wanted to interject a celebration of life as we gyrated to the infectious beat of Chubby Checker's music.

We performed our second public spectacle, *Public Action*, throughout our Western European tour. We invited art and peace groups we knew in Los Angeles and New York to give us messages they would like to communicate to Europeans. We translated these messages into pictographs and drew them on flags, creating a universal language of peace. We hung the flags in various locations from war memorials to city squares. The Sisters' hanging ceremony was solemn and included signaling S.O.S. with the semaphore flags. Once the message flags were installed, we came out of performance character and had open conversations with passers-by. We also distributed flyers with the flags' messages translated into the local language. As we traveled, we collected new messages and created new flags adding to the overall scale of our public installations. All of the message flags were presented in the culminating *End of the Rainbow* traveling exhibition that also showcased the 8.5 x 11-inch artworks from both continents.

The final spectacle, a participatory performance called *Toro Nagashi*, took place at the opening of our final exhibition. It was based on a Japanese tradition in which people float lanterns down rivers at the anniversary of a loved one's death. On the anniversaries of the Hiroshima and Nagasaki bombings, rivers in Japan are glutted with lanterns. A procession of Sisters led the audience to the nearby Venice canals where people wrote messages on luminaria and floated them onto the water. Two barges emerged, one with a giant origami crane and the other with the members of S.O.S. singing an African American spiritual "Wade in the Water," whose words had been changed to reflect a peace message. The performance was a moving ceremony that tapped into the deep tragedy of loss from war.

References

Allyn, Jerry, Anne Gauldin, Cheri Gaulke, and Sue Maberry. 2011. *Sisters Of Survival*. Los Angeles, CA: Otis College of Art and Design.

Gaulke, Cheri. 1981. *Sisters Of Survival: End of the Rainbow*. Los Angeles, CA: Self published.

Gaulke, Cheri. 2011. *Doin' It in Public: Feminism and Art at the Woman's Building*. Los Angeles, CA: Otis College of Art and Design.

## Mediaturgy

Bonnie Marranca

Bonnie Marranca first used the concept of mediaturgy in a 2006 interview with Marianne Weems, artistic director of The Builders Association, in reference to Weems's use of text and image, live and virtual performers, in *Super Vision* (Weems 2008, 189–206). The production demonstrated that thematic material could be carried in digital media, which previously would have been presented to the audience through dialogue or action. *Super Vision* embedded media in the performance event rather than simply using it as illustration or decoration. Media evolved as a language, not merely an event—it had its own DNA. In terms of the theatrical, this is a contemporary distinction on the order of what Jean Cocteau once defined as the difference between poetry *in* the theatre and poetry *of* the theatre. In the work of The Builders Association, narrative is designed.

Subsequently, mediaturgy was further elaborated in Marranca's essay on *Firefall*, the computer-generated work with live performers by John Jesurun (2010, 16–24). The term suggests a deliberate departure from the familiar "dramaturgy," which has historical ties to drama. In contrast, mediaturgy foregrounds the digital—the image—in the artistic process. *Firefall* elaborated radical new compositional strategies for theatre in its split-screen projections of Web pages that functioned as a "character" whose articulation took the form of an audio-visual language. Performance space was translated into cyber space.

Mediaturgy presents a further development from Intermedia (an interdisciplinary poetics) and the Theatre of Images (where the human figure in real time and real space prevails). A mediaturgy for today requires of the viewer the comprehension of an event that takes place in physical space and virtual space, while offering no fixed perspective—only altered modes of perceiving space and time, image and text, bodies and their disappearance.

The exploratory ground for contemporary performance and media is in a range of forms that now alternate between human presence and electronic presence, between the actor performing live and the actor acting for the camera, with both conditions at times evident in the same scene. The resulting performance is revealed as staging the tensions of "liveness." Looking at such works in the context of their mediaturgy suggests new critical modes of experiencing and writing about them.

Mediaturgy acknowledges no hierarchy between text and image as languages of an artwork. In fact, it moves towards resolution of the conflict between text and image that has played out over a century of performance practices. A wide diversity of theatre artists can be set in the context of mediaturgy, including The Wooster Group, Meredith Monk, Laurie Anderson, Gob Squad, and Societas Raffaello Sanzio. Likewise, application of the idea extends to visual artists as it encompasses image, storytelling, video, and photography, in the examples of Joan

Jonas, Martha Rosler, Andrea Fraser, Akram Zaatari, Gary Hill, and William Kentridge.

Mediaturgy can be understood as the construction of narrative inseparable from image-making in the work process. It is both concept and method. If narrative is challenged by the rhetoric of the image, so also are body, character, and scene. The task of the viewer is not merely to turn back and forth between media, but to comprehend the live (or virtual) performer and the mediated image as an integrated experience. This manner of looking reflects the complexity of spectatorship in the contemporary age.

### *Further reading*

Bay-Cheng (2001); Dixon (2007); Parker-Starbuck (2011, 2014).

### *References*


Bay-Cheng, Sarah. 2001. "An Illogical Stab of Doubt: Avant-Garde Drama, Cinema, and Queerness." *Studies in the Humanities*, 28.1–2: 1–12.

Dixon, Steve. 2007. *Digital Performance*. Cambridge, MA: MIT Press.

Marranca, Bonnie. 2010. "Performance as Design: The Mediaturgy of John Jesurun's *Firefall*." *PAJ: A Journal of Performance and Art*, 32.3: 16–24.

Parker-Starbuck, Jennifer. 2011. "Cyborg Theatre: Corporeal/Technological Intersections in Multimedia Performance." In *Performance Interventions*, edited by Elaine Aston and Bryan Reynolds. Hampshire: Palgrave Macmillan.

Parker-Starbuck, Jennifer. 2014. *Cyborg Theatre: Corporeal/Technological Intersections in Multimedia Performance.* New York: Macmillan.

Weems, Marianne. 2008. "SuperVision." SuperVision. http://www.superv.org


### *Cross references*

"**Cybernetics**" and "**Performance in the digital age**" by Auslander; "**New Media Art**" by Cicchini; "**Reception theory**" by Mee; "**The Wooster Group's *TO YOU, THE BIRDIE! (Phèdre)***"" by Cody.

## Romeo Castellucci's *Hey Girl!*

Daniel Sack

Dense fog occupies the hollowed shell of the Eglise Des Celestins, a 14th-century church emptied of all ecclesiastical trappings whose nave is now a theatre housing Romeo Castellucci's *Hey Girl!* at the 2006 Festival d'Avignon. A dim fluorescent light steadies its flicker to overlook a table where something troubles itself: a mass of flesh heaves across the metallic surface, the slow churning of skin beginning to drape to the ground in swathes of matter. Joints articulate themselves, fingers, then an arm or leg, or several—organs without a body, too loose for form. Then somehow there she is, in the midst, rising up to sit facing away from us. The girl lifts a butcher knife and runs the blade down her slight back, scraping away the other skins still gathering below this operating table, this butcher's block. She is sculpting herself out of the chaos of creation.

*Hey Girl!* is also the portrait of a girl waking from oneiric pre-subjectivity to face the daily world: we watch an adolescent rise from rest, watch her dress herself, watch as a crowd of men/boys harass her. A beam of light will extend like the finger of some divine director out of the thick history of occidental representation, indexically revealing this towel, this mirror, this sword. Each object illuminated belongs to the iconography of either female sainthood or contemporary quotidian femininity. In keeping with the director's "theatre of iconoclasm," where representation swells as if from the pressure of an internal tumor (those many skins flaking off some cancerous reproduction) or collapses endlessly on its own negation, *Hey Girl!* simultaneously profanes the sacred and elevates the banal. The girl takes up a bottle of Chanel N°5 and, kneeling before the burning sword of Joan of Arc, dabs herself in a gesture that raises the cosmetic to the sanctified register of ceremonial tincture or holy water. When she pours the liquid on the smoldering blade, its hissing evaporation sends forth a thin plume of smoke, a foul-smelling incense. The iconographic Chanel N°5 was the first perfume to rely strictly on synthetic floral aldehydes to construct its scent. As Coco Chanel famously said upon its commercial release in 1921: "I want to give women an artificial perfume. Yes, I really do mean artificial, like a dress, something that has been made" (2009).

*Hey Girl!* stages the process by which a life becomes an artificial, synthetic *character* in relation to the cultural objects (material and linguistic) that surround her. Each object calls out the eponymous "Hey Girl!" to place her as an identity determined to perform a part in relation to a history of roles and representations. It recalls the scene through which Louis Althusser illustrates interpellation: a policeman "hails" the individual on some anonymous street corner, crying "Hey, you!" to subjectify one within a system of authority. Dramaturg Claudia Castellucci writes: "That which seems to be the portrait of a young woman is rather the portrait of the objects around the young woman" (Castellucci 2006). Each dialogue between girl and object invokes a distinct set of ritualized behaviors akin to a stations of the cross, all threatening an inevitable martyrdom before representation. Deprived of ceremonial props and set, each object in the Eglise des Celestins becomes a surrogate for the absent altar. Could we not say the same of the theatre *qua* theatre, that space with an indefinite heart, where all objects are substitutes for the altar that once stood at the center of the tragic theatre of Dionysus and where everything is a double of the absent Logos?

*Hey Girl!* explicitly implicates the theatre—more specifically the spectator—in this theological system of representation. Juliet's speech about the "rose by any other name" from *Romeo and Juliet*, perhaps the most famous theatrical rumination on the arbitrariness of the signifier, hangs projected over one scene. Another "station" ties the hailing of the object to the logic of the stage direction: high on one side of the stage, a square red light emblazoned with the letter "R" is illuminated

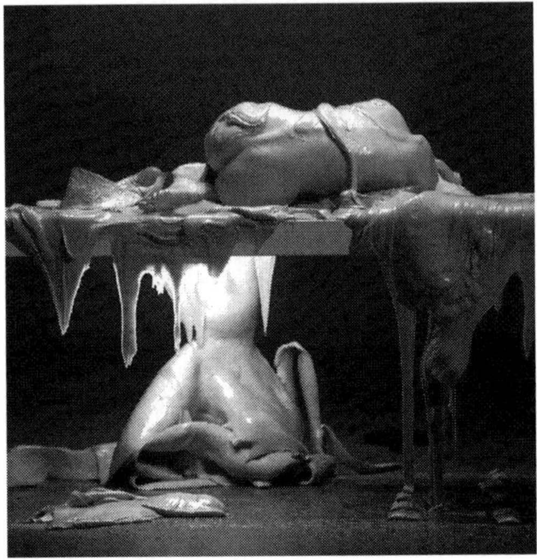

**Figure 8** Romeo Castellucci's *Hey Girl!* Credit: Manninger/Steirischerherbst-Graz. Image courtesy of the artist.

and draws the girl to it. A square of white light with the letter "L" alights on the opposite side of the stage. She walks over and contemplates it in turn. Then the red again, then the white, back and forth, calling the girl in an increasingly frenzied course. Stage directions embodied—"stage left" and "stage right"—they refer to our orientation, not her own.

In the final span of the performance, the spotlight intensifies into a blinding stroke of light—a laser—"gracing" the Girl's brow with near radioactive force. The needle of light resembles the epiphany of *becoming saintly* depicted in any number of Classical paintings, but here the finger of god is accompanied by a sound that also seems to drill through the air. A torrent of words flash a nearly indiscernable dictionary of names and parts across the back wall—the whole of language boring into the Girl.

One might bristle at Castellucci's presumption to speak on behalf of this young woman, but the final image suggests it is the director himself caught in this *mise en abyme*. Only just visible in the slow fade to black at the performance's end, a massive reproduction of Jan van Eyck's 1433 portrait *Man with a Turban* is revealed standing upside down, a decapitated onlooker.

Art historians, uncertain about the identity of the sitter, often refer to the Flemish painting as a self-portrait. Castellucci, too, has claimed that–following Flaubert's description of his constructed female protagonist, Madame Bovary–"Hey Girl c'est moi [Hey Girl is me]." In interviews Castellucci has imagined someday staging a *Hey Boy!* to create a diptych of portraits, but the inverted portrait that concludes *Hey Girl!* suggests that such a double is already contained within the original work as a mirror image. As darkness descends the painted portrait topples face down on the stage. Blinded and asking to be trod upon, it underscores the perspective that informs all action on its boards: this is not the portrait of a Girl, but the director calling himself out into the open.

References

Castellucci, Romeo. 2006. "Après: Changer Dans L'inertie," Press Packet for the Avignon Production of Hey Girl!, 2006." http://www.festival-avignon.com/en/Archive/Artist/2013/227

"Chanel: Fragrances–No 5 History." Chanel website, accessed July 21, 2009. http://uma.live.chanel.com/fragrances/n05-history.php

## Mimicry

Jessica Applebaum

Biology defines mimicry as an organism's ability to closely resemble the external characteristics of an animal, plant or inanimate object—in other words—to camouflage. Transported to the field of social science, mimicry and its relationship to the external allow theorists and performers the ability to expose both everyday habits and highly choreographed behaviors. Mimicry provides a space in which traditional epistemologies of subjectivity can be re-thought, re-performed and re-claimed.

Whereas mimesis poses truthful relations between referent and sign, model and copy, role and performer, mimicry calls attention to itself as representation, continually exposing difference, making visible the subject and its double—revealing the process of depiction through a double articulation of the referent. Within this space the impossibility for a direct correlation between sign and referent – what Homi Bhabha articulates as the point of being "almost the same, but not quite"—is demonstrated (1984, 127). In positing the relationship "almost the same, but not quite," mimicry draws attention to the impossibilities for hierarchical distinctions of difference to be defined as truth. Or, as Rebecca Schneider states, mimicry challenges our "habitual modalities of vision which buttress socio-cultural assumptions about relationships between subject and object" (1997, 2).

In his performance of Christine Jorgensen in his one-man show *Christine Jorgensen Reveals,* Bradford Louryk employs the concept of counter-mimicry. Louryk re-performs a famous interview between Jorgensen (America's first celebrated transsexual) and Mr. R. Russell (later to become the prominent comedian Nipsey Russell). It is Louryk's ability to re-double the representation of Jorgensen, to viscerally connect her recorded words with the acute repetitions of her gestures, that makes Louryk's body the ultimate scrim upon which the multiple layers of how Jorgensen defined herself are shown. Louryk disrupts the dominant, hetero-authority of the gaze, re-doubling the representation of Jorgensen, opening the boundaries of and dialogues for subjectivity.

As we move into yet to be defined modes of academic thought—no longer postmodern—the next phase of rethinking our post-colonial, queer, feminist, and performative epistemologies will be in counter-mimicry, an act upon which the referent is doubled back upon itself. It is there that we will find future means to give voice to and empower the multiple subjectivities with which we choose to define ourselves.

*Further reading*

Bhabha (1984); Diamond (1997); Irigaray (1985); Schneider (1997); Taussig (1993).

*References*

Bhabha, Homi K. 1984. "Of Mimicry and Man: The Ambivalence of Colonial Discourse." *October*, 28.1: 125–133.

Diamond, Elin. 1997. *Unmaking Mimesis: Essays on Feminism and Theatre*, New York: Routledge.

Irigaray, Luce. 1985a. *Speculum of the Other Woman*. Translated by Gillian C. Gill. Ithaca: Cornell University Press.

Irigaray, Luce. 1985b. *This Sex Which Is Not One*. Translated by Catherine Porter and Carolyn Burke. Ithaca: Cornell University Press.

Schneider, Rebecca. 1997. *The Explicit Body in Performance*. New York and London: Routledge.

Taussig, Michael. 1993. *Mimesis and Alterity: A Particular History of the Senses*. London: Routledge.

*Cross references*

"**Appropriation**" by Wong; "**Cindy Sherman's Real Fakery**" by Schneider; "**Mimesis**" by Diamond; "**Paradox**" by Fabião; "**Performativity**" by Pendgraft; "**Reenactment**" by Bay-Cheng; "**Rhetoric**" by Morrison; "**Simulacrum**" by Cesare Schotzko.

## Montage

T. Nikki Cesare Schotzko

In the "Montage of Attractions," Sergei Eisenstein wrote, "the spectator himself constitutes the basic material of the theatre [...] An attraction [...] is any aggressive aspect of the theatre [...] that subjects the spectator to a sensual or psychological impact" (1974, 78). Combining the "molecular" units of performance, and juxtaposing otherwise unrelated images as visual signifiers, Eisenstein, like the avant-gardists before him, employed montage to free theatre from the "weight of the 'illusory imitativeness' and 'representationality'" (1974, 79).

Inspired by the popular arts after the 1917 Russian Revolution (subject of his film, *Oktyabr* [*October*, 1924]) that drew on clowning and music hall performance in opposition to bourgeois theatre, Eisenstein's work in theatre and film developed from the "eccentric" within 1920s Soviet theatre practice—itself adopted from circus aesthetic—in which, "the occurrences appear as though displaced from their usual positions and receive unexpected shifted meanings" so as to "expose their hidden truth" (Gerould 1974, 297). In Eisenstein's use, montage creates imagistic metaphors that shock the spectator into a (usually political) engagement. Referencing in turn an avant-garde aesthetic practiced by such artists as Picasso (in an aesthetic sense) and John Heartfield (in a sociopolitical sense), montage, in Peter Burger's consideration, "presupposes the fragmentation of reality and describes the phase of the constitution of the work" (1984, 73). Montage also refers to a postmodern performative practice that becomes, as Rebecca Schneider writes, "representation about representation" (2002, 293). In this sense, montage in contemporary art and performance might as easily examine the "politics of quotation" (Schneider 2002, 293) than serve as a purely aesthetic device as it often does in photomontage and collage.

*Further reading*

Burger (1984); Gerould (1974); Schneider (2002).

*References*

Burger, Peter. 1984. *Theory of the Avant-Garde*. Translated by Michael Shaw. Minneapolis, MN: University of Minnesota Press.

Eisenstein, Sergei. 1974. "The Montage of Attractions." *TDR: The Drama Review*, translated by Daniel Gerould, 18.1: 77–85. Originally published in *LEF* (1923).

Gerould, Daniel. 1974. "Eisenstein's *Wiseman.*" *TDR: The Drama Review*, 18.1: 71–85.
Schneider, Rebecca. 2002. *The Explicit Body in Performance*. London: Taylor & Francis.

*Cross references*

"**Circus**" by Tait; "**Elevator Girls Return: Miwa Yanagi's Border Crossing between Photography and Theatre**" by Yoshimoto; "**Installation art**" by Haidu; "**Photography and performance**" by Auslander; "**Precariousness**" by Fabião; "**Quotation**" by Garrett.

## New genre public art

Sharon Irish

"New genre public art" is a phrase introduced by artist and theorist Suzanne Lacy. Initially used to describe "City Sites," a series of events organized by Lacy in 1989 in Oakland, California, Lacy then formalized the term in her 1995 edited volume, *Mapping the Terrain: New Genre Public Art*. "New genre public art" is, in her words, "visual art that uses both traditional and nontraditional media to communicate and interact with a broad and diversified audience about issues directly relevant to their lives [ ... ]" (1995, 19). With a history in earlier artistic and political critique, including Russian constructivism, suffragists' tableaux, pro-union pageants, interventions by Greenpeace activists, conceptual art, and happenings, new genre public art has served as a bridge between past collective actions and current artistic efforts.

Lacy's feminism suffuses new genre public art; at least in theory, if not always in practice, her artistic projects and other work she champions prioritize collaboration, challenge existing power structures, and aim to amplify previously unheard voices. Like feminism, new genre public art has evolved in content and context as art practices change. Critics have grappled with appropriately naming these evolving practices that have ranged from large-scale, multi-year participatory projects to brief exchanges with a single artist in a gallery setting. Nicolas Bourriaud (2002), for example, coined "relational aesthetics" to describe physical interactions with and offerings from artists to audience members, characterizing exchanges that keep creative agency firmly within the artist's grasp. Lacy, in contrast, remains committed to the risky "broken middle" (Rose 1992), in often unpredictable public projects that value reciprocity among disparate ideas, emotions, and bodies.

"New genre public art" involves participants in the development and integration of aesthetic ideas, generating artistic experimentation and social interactions, which emerge from what curators Paul O'Neill and Mick Wilson call a "durational dialogical process" (2010, 13). In this process, as Meiling Cheng has noted, the artist's self "becomes reiterated, fragmented, multiplied, and transformed by [ ... ] others [ ... ]." (2002, 129–130). As Cheng described, new genre public art "multiplies" in time and space often through networks established among the originating artist(s) and participants. The audience shares the "responsibility for the creation as well as the reception" of an artwork (Irish 2010, 84).

Recognizing that what is "new" changes over time and that different "genres"—video, performance, text, sound, photography, tableaux, or staged conversation, for example—necessarily address different audiences and issues, new genre public art keeps its critical edge by emphasizing the transformative potential of creative processes for everyone involved. A recent manifestation of new genre public art is the collaborative book and website, *A Guidebook of Alternative Nows* (Hickey 2012). One of the 34 alternatives featured is the Watts House Project, an artist-facilitated neighborhood development effort. The project pairs designers with resident families, not only to improve existing housing but also to reimagine the urban area of Los Angeles through partnerships, plants, and programs. This guidebook offers strategies to create change within "a cacophony of realities and potentialities" (Hickey 2012, 3; http://alternativenows.net/).

*Further reading*

Hickey (2012); Irish (2010).

*References*

Bourriaud, Nicolas. 2002. *Relational Aesthetics*. Dijon: Leses Du Réel.

Cheng, Meiling. 2002. *In Other Los Angeleses: Multicentric Performance Art*. Berkeley, CA: University of California Press.

Hickey, Amber, ed. 2012. *A Guidebook of Alternative Nows*. Los Angeles, CA: The Journal of Aesthetics and Protest Press.

Irish, Sharon. 2010. *Suzanne Lacy: Spaces Between*. Minneapolis, MN: University of Minnesota Press.

Lacy, Suzanne, ed. 1995. *Mapping the Terrain: New Genre Public Art*. Seattle, WA: Bay Press.

O'Neill, Paul and Mick Wilson, eds. 2010. *Curating and the Educational Turn*. London: Open Editions.

Rose, Gillian. 1992. *The Broken Middle: Out of Our Ancient Society*. Oxford: Wiley-Blackwell.

*Cross references*

"**Anti-art**" by Stiles; "**Happenings**" by Sandford; "**Intermediality**" by Auslander; "**Landscape theatre**" by Holzapfel; "**Multicentricity**" by Cheng; "**Paratheatre**" by Olivares; "**Precariousness**" by Fabião; "**Play**" by Schechner.

**Excerpts from *Prostitution Notes* (1974)**

Suzanne Lacy

Early spring, 1974:

I decided to do a project on prostitution. I wondered who they were, these women whose lives were such powerful icons for my gender. I didn't want to put myself inside their shoes, walk the streets as an "art performance," or dress up like a prostitute to flirt with their reality. I didn't even want to tell their stories, except as these were told to me along my journey. Rather, I thought to locate the work in my own experience, to record my entry into an *understanding* of "The Life." I began simply and found it within my own networks; there were friends who had "tricked," or knew firsthand someone who had. "The Life" wasn't far from mine. Just below the surface, if you knew where to look, the street corners, restaurants, and bars of Los Angeles took on a new appearance.

So the performance was a frame drawn round my life and investigation: I performed myself as I learned. Over a period of several months I recorded several of my encounters on large crudely drawn maps of Los Angeles, Baja California, and San Francisco:

May 14, Cappuccino with Margo

I meet top whore Margo St. James in San Francisco. She takes me to see Kitty at a bar where she is talking to some British guy. He asks if I do the same thing Kitty does. He has bad breath and tells me he makes a lot of money. Kitty works in a massage parlor, and three gentlemen came in who turned out to be cops. Now she's depressed: It was her first bust, and on top of that, she's got the clap. Margo is going to make a test case out of it. People in this game are always talking about cases and courts. At the airport I use my illegal ticket, obtained from a friend's credit card and under someone else's name, to get a flight home. Fortunately they don't ask for ID at airport. (Note about 1974: plane travel was so lax that I got my travel agent to buy discounted tickets and traveled under her name.)

*The Fast Track–"The Life" "The Game" "The Pimp-Ho Scene"*
*Fast Talking and Free Movement.*
*Where Are We Going?*

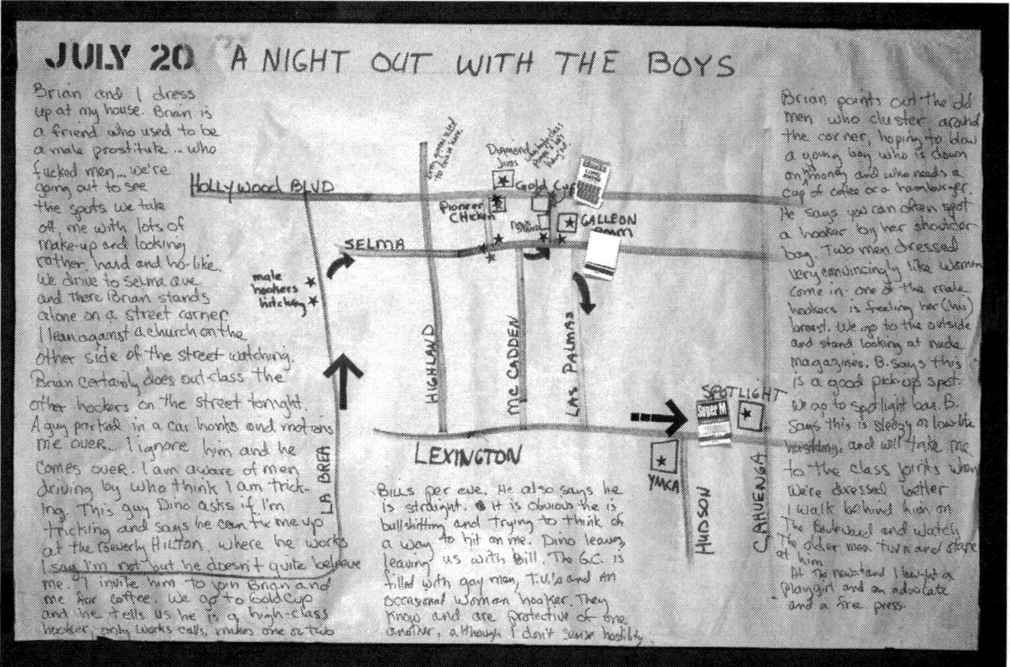


**Figure 9** Excerpt from *Prostitution Notes* (1974). Image courtesy of the artist.

June 29, Trip to Mexico

In Baja I stay in a lovely room overlooking the ocean paid for by my lover and read all day about pimps and whores: *All Women* are ho's (whores) and *All Men* are pimps or tricks. The pimp appeals to a woman's natural instincts. He accepts her "ho-nature." He gives her the guidance and control over her life she naturally needs. She tricks the man for him. She exchanges sex for the trick's money. The pimp in turn "tricks" her. He exchanges *his* sex and illusions for *her* money. Everyone gets their sex and their illusion, except the pimp, who gets money, which is power. I give my lover the books to read when he arrives. He starts gaming with me. After awhile it gets obnoxious, so I use various strategies to counter his pimp behavior. He loves it.

July 12, Saturday lunch with the girls

Lunch at the Hyatt Regency. I have shrimp salad. This is where hookers and pimps hang out, but not this afternoon. Only one in the coffee shop. Hookers are tolerated by the hotel, which is frequented by show-business types.

> *Note: How To Get Into "The Life"?*
> *Movement across large surfaces as a function of life in L.A. (freeways)*
> *Movement Is the Form of "The Life"*

What is the form for this artwork? I am getting a sense the project may be about arranging appointments, scheduling time, drawing maps in my datebook. My investigations have begun over coffee or lunch. My appointment book is riddled with instructions for getting there, time, names, etc. I record my journey, my questions, what I'm eating. I collect matchbook covers and draw diagrams. When bored, I affix decals and stars to them.

July 20, Night out with the boys

Brian (my best friend's gay lover) and I take off—me with lots of makeup and looking rather hard and ho-like. We drive to Selma Avenue and Brian stands on a street

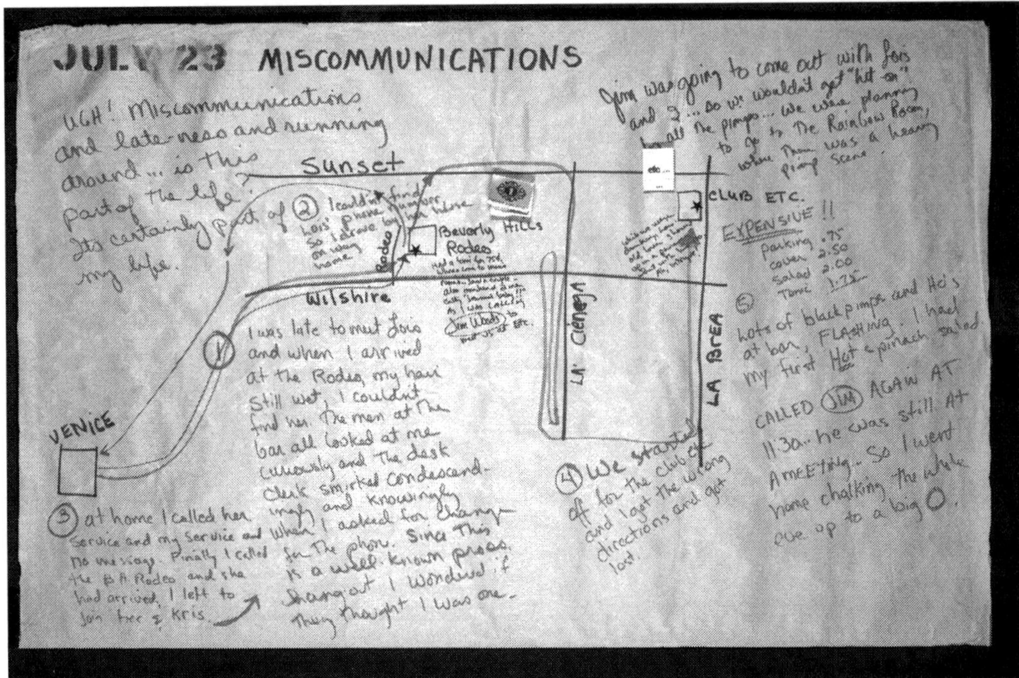


**Figure 10** Excerpt from *Prostitution Notes* (1974). Image courtesy of the artist.

corner where he—an ex-hooker—outclasses the other boys. Dino asks if I'm tricking and says he can fix me up at the Beverly Hilton. I say no but he doesn't believe me. He joins us at the Gold Cup but it is impossible to eat—greasy grilled cheese and BLTs. Dino tells us he makes one or two bills hooking, but also says he is straight. It is obvious he is trying to think of a way to hit on me. He takes off, leaving us with the bill. Brian points out the old men who cluster near the corner, hoping to blow a young boy down on his luck and needing a hamburger.

## July 23, Miscommunications

I am late to meet Lois at the "pross" hang out, the Rodeo Hotel. My hair's still wet; she isn't there. The men at the bar all look at me curiously and the desk clerk smirks condescendingly, or so it seems, when I ask for change for the phone. I can't find her phone number in information—naturally she's not listed—so I drive by her house. No luck. At home I call her service and mine but no message. Finally I call the Rodeo and she has arrived. We leave there in separate cars for the Rainbow Room and I get lost. Call Jim (James Woods, a Black artist and entrepreneur who built housing in Watts) again at 11:30 pm. He is still at a "meeting" he says. I wonder if he is pimping me then decide to go home, chalking the whole evening up to a big, expensive O.

## August 27, Peter the John

*Men seem to find whores even in strange cities.*

At the motels on Sunset and Highland a man says he is from Florida, here on business.

I mention the hookers here, as an opening, and he says he was just talking to one. I ask if he himself goes to hookers. He says yes, he likes the looks on their faces when they see the size of his dick, which is big around though not so long. To provoke him, I ask him if he knew that some hookers dislike men, and he says vaguely, yeah, lots of them were bisexual and, not to be distracted, he asks me if I am one?

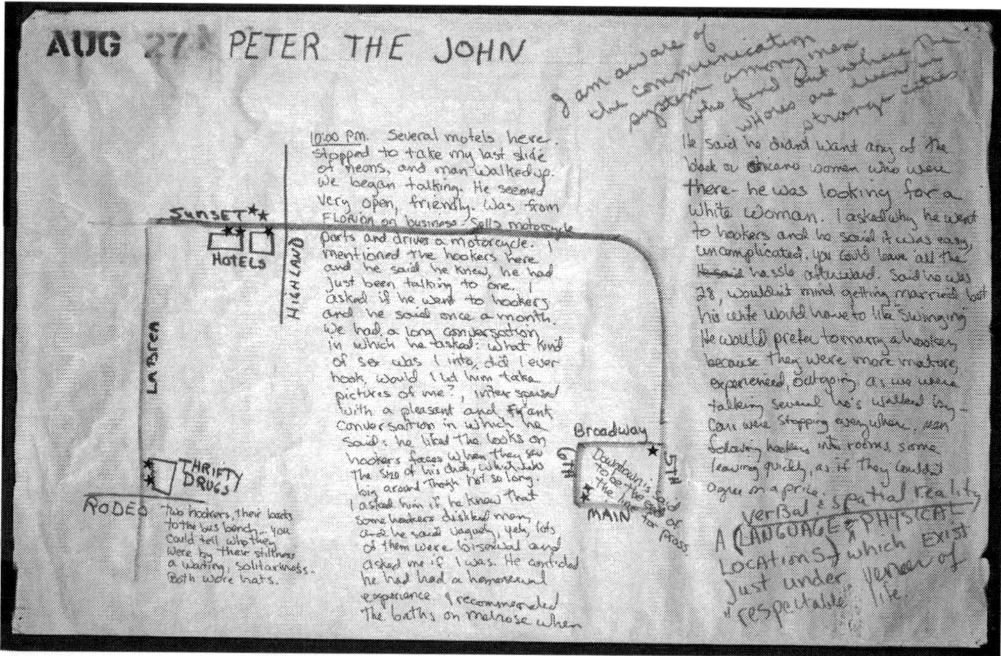


**Figure 11** Excerpt from *Prostitution Notes* (1974). Image courtesy of the artist.

*A language of physical spaces that exist just under veneer of "respectable" life.*
*A code of sexual signification between men and women just under casual conversation.*

Early spring, 2014:

It's been 40 years since this project took place and it still holds up for me. As social practices and research become visual arts methodologies, this conceptual work (which I framed as a performance although it was documented on paper) clearly anticipated issues of ethics, relationality and identity that are still discussed today. What is the spatial "shape" of a time-based work? What is the responsible position from which an artist speaks? How deeply is an artist implicated in the "subject" of the work? At the time, prostitution was becoming visible in popular culture, with films like *Klute* (Jane Fonda and Donald Southerland, 1971) where the frame of raunchy glamour fitted in with the *Playboy* revolution. Some women and men performance artists experimented with placing themselves in situations of prostitution or pornography. I was interested in a differentiated and clearly articulated subject position that did not presume to take on a different persona but rather to explore empathy and implicatedness on an intimate level.

## Paradox

Eleonora Fabião

In the fields of linguistics, mathematics or logics, paradox's most common implications are absurdity, inconsistency, and impossibility. In the realm of performance, however, paradox's dubiousness is a major epistemological force both dramaturgically cultivated and critically reinforced. The paradox is often the only "logic" able to address performance's multilayered sense, that is, the complexities of its simultaneous temporal and spatial equations and its permanent state of mobility by never reaching resolution or synthesis. As Richard Schechner

(2003) theorizes, performance (whether in the performing arts, rituals, sports, or everyday life) suspends unitary meanings and absolute forms of behavior.

Paradox's poetics and ethics disturb the *doxa*, that is, good sense's straightness and common sense's fixity (*para* = distinct from; *doxa* = common sense and good sense; *para-doxa* = what "escapes" from common sense and good sense). The paradox's drive—regarded neither as contradiction nor as nonsense but as an intertwinement of simultaneous meanings in motion (including nonsensical and contradictory ones)—points to the extreme condition of vulnerability, relativity, and precariousness so crucial to performance. A theatrical performance, for example, is and is not fictive: the actor is actually experiencing the reality of theatrical representation while acting a role. In a more extreme vein, a piece of performance art may position itself as being both art and not art. The energetics of the paradox dismantles such strict dichotomies by forcing representation towards unpredictable extremes (see Deleuze 1969). Thus, Allan Kaprow must declare regarding his "lifelike art" project: "Anything less than a paradox would be simplistic" (1993, 222). Performance, as a paradoxical practice, is neither searching for definitions nor producing neat classifications but rather proposing modes of creating and experiencing always provisional meanings.

Philosopher José Gil identifies a decisive relation between body and paradox and maps its performative resonances: "The body is such a paradoxical instance that we can consider it the source of all kinds of paradoxes. [...] The paradoxical body is the virtual and latent body in all kinds of empiric bodies that form and inhabit us. It is through it that dance and art in general are possible" (2006). The performative body, a body that intensifies paradoxes, evokes, traverses, and crosses several other bodies—existing and nonexistent, phantasmatic and palpable, imaginary and mnemonic, individual and collective, present, past and future.

*Further reading*

Deleuze (1969); Gil (2006); Kaprow (1993).

*References*

Deleuze, Gilles. 1969. *The Logic of Sense*. Translated by Mark Lester and Charles Stivale. Reprint, New York: Columbia University Press, 1990.
Gil, José. 2006. "Paradoxical Body." *TDR: The Drama Review*, 50.4: 21–35.
Kaprow, Allan. 1993. *Essays on the Blurring of Art and Life*. Berkeley, CA: University of California Press.
Schechner, Richard. 2003. *Performance Theory* Routledge Classics. London: Routledge

*Cross references*

"**Actor**" by Mee; "**Boychild**" by Halberstam; "**Extreme performance**" by Cheng; "**Liveness**" by Auslander; "**Mimesis**" by Diamond; "**Play**" by Schechner; "**Precariouness**" by Fabião.

## Paratheatre

Lissette Olivares

"Paratheatre" is a term coined by Polish theatre director Jerzy Grotowski to describe a series of performance experiments that were developed by the "Theatre Laboratory" between 1969 and 1978 (Schechner 1997, 207). The root "para" implies a set of codes and conventions that are superseded by emergent concepts but which nonetheless are informed by historical traditions of theatre. Paratheatre, also known as "Theatre of Participation," involves a process of disarmament that alters the conventional structure of dramatic performance by trying to erase the boundary between performer and spectator, leading to "meetings" that emphasize introspection and a "live communion" amongst all participants (Wolford 1997, 9–10).

The foundations of paratheatrical exploration are enunciated in Grotowski's book, *The Poor*

*Theatre* (1968), in which the author describes his theatrical work as an experimental laboratory used to develop methodologies that concentrate on the "personal and scenic technique of the actor as the core of theatre"(1968, 15). Grotowski proposes "poor theatre" as a practice that rejects the "synthetic" elements in theatrical composition (i.e. costumes, sets, lighting, etc.) and focuses on the actor's body and craft using a method called "via negativa," which "eradicates the actor's blocks" through a series of rigorous physical and vocal techniques drawn from a range of actor training methods (1968, 15–25).

Actions pertinent to paratheatre include self-confrontation and the elimination of the spectator or audience through a process of incorporation referred to as "meetings" (Schechner 1997, 207). Paratheatrical "meetings" often took place in pastoral settings and welcomed anyone who could act on their desire to become "open" (Schechner 1997, 211). Through group sessions, experienced work-leaders from the Theatre Laboratory "attempted to create concrete and authentic instances of communion among co-actants engaged in spontaneous activity..." (1997, 10). As paratheatre developed, the people participating in its experiments grew from a few dozen to thousands, culminating in Worclaw's month long "University of Research," of the Theatre of Nations in which over 4,500 people participated (1997, 212). Other paratheatrical events conducted by the Theatre Laboratory include: *Jerzy Grotowski's Special Project* (1972), *Vigil* (1976–1977), *The Mountain of Flame* (1977) and *Tree of People* (1979). Grotowski's own reflections on paratheatre are found in *Holiday* (1972), a text composed of his excerpted statements.

Paratheatre has been compared to Antonin Artaud's Theatre of Cruelty based on its rejection of the mimetic aspects of performance and its attempt to create events that fall outside of the realm of representation (Schechner 1997, 10). Grotowski, who admired Artaud's vision for the theatre, claimed that his practice was distinct because of his emphasis on methodology, a facet that Artaud never developed (1968, 24). Despite Grotowski's reticence, many scholars believe that the principles of the *Theatre of Cruelty*, especially those developed by Jacques Derrida (1978) and Herbert Blau (1990) can help to explore the dynamics of paratheatre (Schechner 1997, 10).

### *Further reading*

Derrida (1978); Schechner (1997).

### *References*

Blau, Herbert, 1990. *The Audience*. Baltimore, MD: Johns Hopkins University Press.

Derrida, Jacques. 1978. *Writing and Difference*. Translated by Alan Bass. Chicago, IL: The University of Chicago Press.

Grotowski, Jerzy. 1968. *The Poor Theater*. New York: Simon and Schuster.

Schechner, Richard. 1997. "Paratheater, 1969–78, and Theater of Sources, 1976–82: Introduction." In *The Grotowski Sourcebook*, edited by Richard Schechner and Lisa Wolford. New York: Routledge.

Wolford, Lisa. 1997. "General Introduction: Ariadne's Thread." In *The Grotowski Sourcebook*, edited by Richard Schechner and Lisa Wolford. New York: Routledge.

### *Cross references*

"**Audience**" and "**Proxemics**" by Cody; "**Excerpts from *Prostitution Notes* (1974)**" by Lacy; "**Intervention**" by Olivares; "**New genre public art**" by Irish; "**Performing surveillance camera art**" by Nayar; "**Pornography**" by Shea; "***Reality Ends Here***" by Watson; "**Surveillance**" by Morrison.

### Feminist blogging as activism and pedagogy

Jill Dolan

I've maintained my blog, *The Feminist Spectator*, since 2005, as an outlet for my own insights about and ruminations on theatre, performance, and popular culture. When I found myself itching to return to the topical, short-form criticism with which I'd begun my career in the late 1970s and early '80s, I considered approaching local newspaper editors for reviewing assignments. But I quickly realized I didn't want to be beholden to someone else's judgments about which performances were important enough to assign for review, or about how many words would be worthwhile. "Blogger" had just begun as an online platform; with very little technical expertise, I created a template and began *The Feminist Spectator*.

Although I sometimes wish I wrote more frequent, punchy posts, I'm drawn to longer, more reflective writing, which the blog format forgives. The activist gesture in this writing comes from lending my own time, expertise, and attention to work that often doesn't get discussed in detail elsewhere, or to popular culture that doesn't receive the feminist engagement I think it demands. The blog, then, serves an advocacy, as well as an activist, function, neither of which I find inconsistent with feminist pedagogy. As a teacher, one of my most important commitments is to make visible work by women and people of color that conventional theatre canons continue to ignore. I try to make work visible that's too often overlooked, and I try to comment on work that's celebrated in mainstream forums but frequently without consideration of its sometimes sexist, heterosexist, or racist presumptions. For example, my post on director David Fincher's film, *The Social Network*, the story of the founding of Facebook, received more comments than any other on my blog, mostly because I took issue with the general critical acclaim for the film (including its Academy Award nomination for Best Picture) by pointing out what I found to be blatant visual and narrative exploitation of women, including its nasty portrait of an Asian American woman character as a stereotypical Chinese "dragon lady".

At the same time, one of the blog's pedagogical gestures comes from my commitment to the pleasure of what I call "critical generosity." I tell my students that engaging with the popular culture we love doesn't have to detract from our pleasure but can in fact enhance it, by making us more aware of how and why it works to produce the effects we so enjoy. And I try to write about performances, independent films, and other work struggling to receive a public hearing with an emphasis on what's good about it: how it works, why it's pleasurable, and why it's important, instead of spending my words and my critical time tallying up its faults or missteps. As a committed reader of public arts criticism, I'm tired of powerful critics' easy dismissals and disparagements. Blogging, and the infinite space of the internet, allows me to be generous partly because my words aren't limited by an editor's count or by the expectation that I tell readers how to spend their leisure dollars.

In addition, being critically generous lets me engage culture and representation with an eye toward stories that aren't as frequently heard or seen. I'll approach an independent film made by someone marginalized by identity or power from the Hollywood mainstream, for example, with an appreciation for its limited budget and other resources, and with an understanding of the scramble required to find actors, crew, and the rest of the creative team. My engagement with Madeleine Olnek's *Codependent Lesbian Space Alien Seeks Same* (2011), for example, appreciates its community-based approach to filmmaking, its WOW Café-inspired narrative and genre quirks, and the zany affection with which it treats its characters. Considering this queer indie through the same lens as *The Social Network* (or even *The Kids are Alright*, a bigger budget Hollywood film about a lesbian family) wouldn't make sense, according to the ethics of critical generosity.

I hope that *The Feminist Spectator* also demonstrates that writing itself is an activist project. Too often, students interested in the arts overlook the importance of critical commentary as a venue for their own talents and insights. My blog proselytizes by example for arts journalism and critical engagement in general, and I hope the commitment of my own words and thought demonstrates the necessity that we talk publicly about the culture we consume and create. Art demands discussion. Teaching our students to be articulate–when they speak and when they write–about their own creative work and about the performance and culture they engage strikes me as a politically and artistically necessary. Otherwise, the discourse about the arts in America will become increasingly puerile and vapid. And an impoverished arts discourse means it will be too easy for those speaking the loudest against the arts to end its already paltry public funding.

Neither *The Feminist Spectator* nor any other feminist blog about theatre or popular culture save our public arts discourse by themselves. But I've long held that one of my responsibilities as a educator is to impress on my students a commitment to enriching and extending the project of art-making. Since the arts are embattled and too often denigrated in public discourse in the U.S., I believe it is incumbent on those of us who teach to help our students be clear and persuasive arts advocates. Because of its public reach and easy accessibility, blogging offers a method for enlivening that discourse. The internet is no longer a privileged site with limited reach. Diverse voices stake their claim to web sites and blogs, on computers that can be freely accessed at public libraries. Web-based sites for collective cultural consideration have a better chance of reaching more diverse constituencies than conventional subscription-based or paid publications. And the increasing ubiquity of inexpensive cell phones and their web-browsing technology will continue to open possibilities for cultural exchange.

Blogging, then, gives me hope. *The Feminist Spectator* might not be the loudest voice in the public cultural landscape, but it's one site at which an alternative view of culture can be promoted. Feminists, progressives, and people without access to mainstream publicity machines can see their work engaged with hope for its ability to transform however small a part of the social landscape. That's why I keep writing.

## Propaganda

Matthew Smith

Propaganda is a systematic, intentional effort to influence or manipulate the beliefs of an audience. While many performances seek to shape public opinion, the term "propaganda" is usually reserved for works that do so in an unusually forceful way. This forcefulness, however, need not be explicit. While some forms of propaganda trumpet their political intentions (by means of banners, anthems, and so on), other forms attempt to hide their aims, and the most effective forms of propaganda generally involve a combination of exposed and subliminal messages.

The use of propaganda is as old as civilization, but the term itself derives from the Congregatio de Propaganda Fide (Congregation for Propagation of the Faith), a Roman Catholic missionary organization founded in 1622. While long a term of neutral and even positive connotations, the term has acquired particularly negative overtones in the twentieth century, in part due to the activities of agencies such as the Third Reich's Ministry of Pubic Enlightenment and Propaganda.

In order to disseminate propaganda, modern regimes have learned to connect performances across a broad spectrum of live, recorded, and broadcast media. In the case of the Nazi state, performances such as rallies, musical concerts, radio broadcasts, film, and dance were often developed in collaboration with one another, the common aim being a single, totalizing impression. The mass rally at Nuremberg in 1934, for example, was planned and directed by the architect Albert Speer in collaboration with the film director Leni Riefenstahl, whose film *Triumph of the Will* then brought the message of the rally to an even wider public. In such a case, the "live" event of the rally and the recorded event of the film are inseparable. A similar interconnection may be found in a propaganda event such as a US presidential nominating convention, in which live performance and televised broadcast have become symbiotic.

While the term's modern usage generally has negative connotations, a very different conception of "propaganda" exists among some revolutionary socialists. In his pamphlet *What Is to Be Done?* (1902), Lenin defined "propaganda" as the rational presentation of an integrated system of political and historical truths to a relatively small audience. He juxtaposed the term to "agitation," which exhorts the masses with a single, easily grasped idea. Lenin considered both strategies necessary to revolution, but held that propaganda relies more on the printed word, and agitation more on speech.

With the foundation of the Department of Agitation and Propaganda in the USSR in 1920, these two terms were collapsed into a neologism: "agitprop." The Department sponsored numerous agitprop performances, the most influential being the Blue Blouse theatrical movement. Formed in 1923 and active across the Soviet Union, Blue Blouse troupes combined documentary-style theatre with folk forms of dance and song. They were strongly influenced by the work of Meyerhold and Eisenstein, and subsequently influenced theatre movements throughout the world. The Living Newspaper unit of the Federal Theatre Project, for example, owed a debt to Soviet agitprop, as did the work of Bertolt Brecht. In the revolutionary atmosphere of the late 1960s and early 70s the form reawakened in Europe and North America, and increasingly inspired performers in the global South.

### *Further reading*

Jackall (1995); Mayhew (1997).

### *References*

Jackall, Robert, ed. 1995. "Propaganda." In *Main Trends of the Modern World Series*, edited by Arthur J. Vidich and Robert Jackall. New York: NYU Press.

Lenin, Vladimir. 1902. "What Is to Be Done? Burning Questions of our Movement." *Marxists Internet Archive*. https://www.marxists.org/archive/lenin/works/1901/witbd/

Mayhew, Leon H. 1997. "The New Public: Professional Communication and the Means of Social Influence." In *Cambridge Cultural Social Studies*, edited by Jeffrey C. Alexander and Steven Seidman. Cambridge: Cambridge University Press.

### *Cross references*

"**Audience**" by Cody; "**Double-coding**" by Bial; "**Modernism**" by Albright, Pearl, and Speca; "**Reception theory**" by Mee; "**Terrorism and performance**" by Colleran; "**War**" by Sell.

## Quotation

Shawn-Marie Garrett

Quotation is usually considered as a rhetorical strategy involving reference in speech or text to the speech, writing, or thought of another. In the performing arts, quotations may take the form of, for example, textual or gestural references enacted by characters; movement or dance sequences transposed from one context to another; imitated musical phrases or stylings. Such quotations are usually though not necessarily recognizable (at least to the cognoscenti) and are commonly assumed to be intentional on the part of the artist. Quotation makes a performance "intertextual," positioning it in relation to a prior text or performance, inviting comparison, and acknowledging its own representational status. Conventional theatre performance itself can be thought of as "quotation from a script" (Marsh 1993, 447).

In *Republic* III, Plato considers direct quotation in Homeric performance (when the poet speaks as Chryses, but not when he speaks in the first person) as a form of acting or mimesis. At the same time, mimesis is quotation: performances and even everyday behaviors consist in reiterations of actions, discourses, gestures, and habits learned and adopted consciously and unconsciously from previous models. For Plato's doctrinal purposes, the character of the performance quoted is crucial, for "dramatic and similar representations, if indulgence in them is prolonged into adult life, establish habits of physical poise, intonation and thought which become second nature" (2003, 89).

The affective, behavioral relations Plato recognizes among quotation, mimesis, habit, and human nature, or rather "second nature," are of particular interest to contemporary performance theorists. In his philosophy of linguistics, Jacques Derrida argued that all text is citation and duplication, i.e. quotation (1982). Many now seek to understand how performances, social and otherwise, are quotations, and to answer such questions as: How do the relations between mimesis and quotation affect our understanding of, for example, authenticity, originality, gender, race, ethnicity, the self? How do the practices of everyday quotation contribute to the formation of behaviors, ideas, individual and institutional practices?

### *Further reading*

Banes (2006); Barber (1999); Diamond (1997).

### *References*

Banes, Sally. 2006. *Before, Between, and Beyond: Three Decades of Dance Writing.* Madison, WI: University of Wisconsin Press.

Barber, Karin. 1999. "Quotation in the Constitution of Yoruba Oral Texts." *Research in African Literatures*, 30.2: 17–41.

Derrida, Jacques (1982). *Margins of Philosophy.* Chicago, IL: The University of Chicago Press.

Diamond, Elin. 1997. *Unmaking Mimesis: Essays on Feminism and Theatre*, New York: Routledge.

Marsh, Anne. 1993. *Body and Self: Performance Art in Australia 1969–92*, Melbourne: Oxford University Press.

Plato. 2003. *The Republic.* Translated by Lee, D. 2nd edn. London: Penguin.

### *Cross references*

"**Cindy Sherman's Real Fakery**" by Schneider; "**Hierarchy**" by Luber; "**Mimesis**" by Diamond; "**Montage**" by Cesare Schotzko; "**Reenactment**" by Bay-Cheng; "**Rhetoric**" by Morrison; "**Whiteness**" by Jones.

## Reenactment

Sarah Bay-Cheng

Literally meaning to act again, reenactments have often been associated with historical reenactments, in which participants recreate past events. These performances may attempt historical authenticity, as in American Civil War reenactments that use only materials available in the 19th century and follow battle plans outlined in historical documents; or, such reenactments may be more interpretative, as in the biographical performances of famous people (e.g., Harriett Tubman, Abraham Lincoln) that occur in national, state, and amusement parks, particularly in the US. Suzan-Lori Parks addresses this fascination in her *The America Play* (1993), whose central character finds his vocation performing Abraham Lincoln at the moment of his assassination.

In addition to historically based performances, contemporary media art and performance have become significant sites for reenactments, particularly of iconic performance works. This trend toward reenactment may be, in part, a compensation for the inherent loss suffered by time-based art, which exists temporarily and cannot be experienced again (if at all) except in mediated reproductions. Such strategies of reenactment fundamentally challenge notions of authenticity and originality within performance. As Robert Blackson suggests, performance reenactments reassign "the authorial agency of the (re)performed works" (2007, 39). Major recent examples of such work include Marina Abramovic's highly contested repetition of famous performance works at the Guggenheim as part of the Performa Biennial 2005. Her *Seven Easy Pieces* (2005) included redoing Vito Acconci's masturbation piece *Seedbed* (1972) and her own *Lips of Thomas* (1975) in which Abramovic carves a star into her body with a razor and performs other acts of self-mutilation. In the wake of her reenactments, art students began requesting permission to re-perform Abramovic's pieces.

New media performance domains, such as Second Life, have opened up further possibilities for reenactment. In 2007, artists Eva and Franco Mattes, also known as 0100101110101101.org, began staging "Synthetic Performances" in the virtual social environment Second Life. Using their avatars and virtual environments, the Matteses reenact iconic performance art pieces, including, among others, Acconci's *Seedbed* and Chris Burden's *Shoot* (1971). These simulations challenge authority and authenticity, but by performing in a virtual context, they further question whether physical presence and material bodies are essential elements of body-based performance art.

### Further reading

Blackson (2007); Lütticken (2005); Weick (1979).

### References

Blackson, Robert. 2007. "Once More ... with Feeling: Reenactment in Contemporary Art and Culture." *Art Journal*, 66.1: 28–40.

Lütticken, Sven, ed. 2005. *Life, Once More: Forms Of Reenactment In Contemporary Art (Performance Art)*, with Jennifer Allen, Peggy Phelan, and Eran Schaerf. Rotterdam, Netherlands: Witte de With Center for Contemporary Art.

Weick, Karl E. 1979. "The Social Psychology of Organizing." In *Topics in Social Psychology Series*. New York: McGraw Hill Publishing.

### Cross references

"**Dance or we are lost: The Tanztheater of Pina Bausch**" by Birringer; "**Mimesis**" by Diamond; "**Performing the archive**" by Nyong'o; "**Quotation**" by Garrett; "**Reproduction**" by Bay-Cheng; "**Sampling**" by Hodges Persley; "**The Wooster Group's *TO YOU, THE BIRDIE! (Phèdre)***" by Cody.

## Heather Cassils' indeterminate body

Amelia Jones

In the early 1970s feminist artists–usually identified as straight, white, and middle-class–valiantly interrogated norms of female embodiment and sexuality in Euro-American mainstream culture. Two key projects in this opening of art to performance and aligning of female subjectivity with agency were Eleanor Antin's conceptual body art work entitled *Carving: A Traditional Sculpture* (1972) and Lynda Benglis's *Artforum* advertisement (1974). For *Carving*, Antin had herself photographed daily (from four vantage points) as she went on a rigorous diet over a 45-day period. The resulting work is a grid of the 180 photographs in which Antin theatricalizes the act of weight loss as well as takes on the role of both "sculptor" and "sculpture," literally "carving" her body down from its original shape. In a complementary move, Benglis, notoriously, posed for the 1974 advertisement completely naked and with sunglasses; her skin greased, she holds an impossibly large double-ended dildo erect from her pubic area.

Putting their bodies on the line, feminist artists from the 1960s and 1970s thus strategically redefined gender as a performative while simultaneously using the specific modes, styles, and bodily interventions incisively to critique normative ideals of feminine embodiment, behavior, and comportment. Since the 1970s, partly due to such incisive and brave strategies, gender roles and sexual identifications have radically changed both within and beyond the art world. Thanks to the advances of feminism, the LGBTQ movements, and queer theory (historically intertwined with performance theory in the work of scholars such as Eve Sedgwick and Judith Butler), and to the tireless labors of queers and feminists of color to redefine performative sexual and gender identities

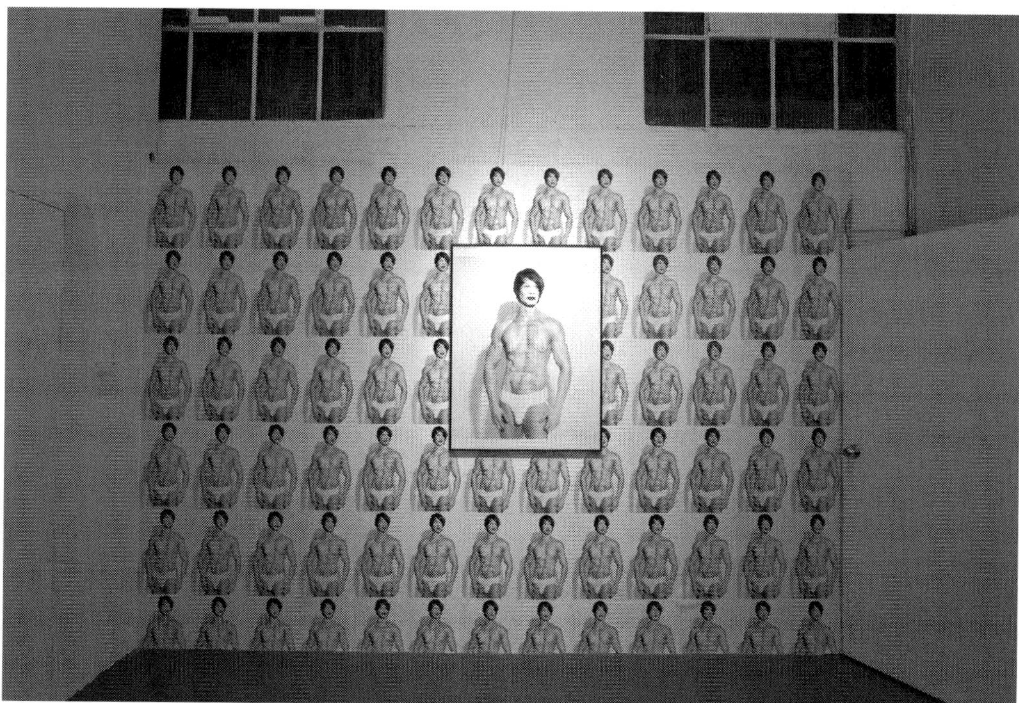

**Figure 12** Heather Cassils, Installation image of *Advertisement (Homage to Benglis)* (2011). Photograph and Xerox copies; Key art: 30 x 40 inches, and tabloid-sized Xerox: 11 x 17 inches. Key image © Heather Cassils and Robin Black 2011. Wall installation © Heather Cassils 2011.

beyond whiteness, we can no longer pretend to posit a singular "feminine ideal" (presumptively white and slim, heteronormative, and thus available for male delectation) for the female body.

Canadian artist Heather Cassils, who currently works in Los Angeles, has produced a range of recent performance projects that exemplify the productive rethinking–reperforming and retheorizing–of earlier models for articulating sexual difference and for empowering feminists as the creative agents of art and of their own appearance and identifications. Cassils (a transgender multimedia artist who is her/himself also a body builder and personal trainer) most notably produced reworked versions of the Antin and Benglis classics in two works–*Cuts: A Traditional Sculpture* and *Homage to Benglis*–commissioned for the 2011 Los Angeles Contemporary Exhibitions (LACE) event "Los Angeles Goes Live: Performance Art in Southern California 1970-1983." For *Cuts* Cassils worked with a body building coach and a nutritionist as well as, for a brief part of the training, taking low-level steroids in order to *build up* rather than "carve" away her/his body. Just as Antin had done, Cassils documented his/her changing body, taking four photos a day from four vantage points. Rather than producing a grid of still photos (a classic format for conceptual art in the late 1960s and early 1970s), s/he produced instead *Fast Twitch/Slow Twitch*, a time-lapsed two channel video of her/his shifting bodily contours as viewed from the front, juxtaposing this footage with slow motion scenes of her/his simultaneously buff and sensual, masculine/feminine body posing as an odalisque in a jock strap and wig, straining and bursting the seams of her/his shirt, and otherwise perverting expectations of the fetishized body. The slowed-down images force our desire to fetishize to *drag* out through time; by languorously delaying the movements of Cassils' reshaped body through slow motion and simultaneously making the cross-gender codes more evident, the videos destroy the possibility of fetishism; in process rather than frozen, ambiguously sexed and gendered, her/his body cannot serve as "phallus" to allay anxieties about sexual difference.

Cassils' *Homage to Benglis* is a photographic portrait of the artist naked except for a jock strap, her/his muscular chest and arms and short hair countered by her/his brilliantly red lipstick. To make the image and others relating to this part of the project, the artist collaborated with Robin Black, known for her commercial images of gay male bodies in magazines such as *Butt*. The photographs, one of them repeated over the walls of the gallery like Warhol's *Cow Wallpaper* (serving as another homage, in this case to a key figure in the articulation of non-normative sexualities in the art world), became as well the center of Cassils' and Black's collaborative zine of soft-core pinups; entitled *LADY FACE // MAN BODY*, the zine is available for purchase over the internet, where the image of the zine's cover has taken on a life of its own. Cassils has described this project in relation to her/his desire "to show my body as I have always wanted to be seen [...] Substituting my ripped masculine physique for [Benglis's...] double ended phallus, the [...] zine signals the shift in our cultural landscape and the role of artists like Benglis in bringing about those changes."

Cassils could be said to queer feminist strategies of visual critique with this multi-part *Cuts* project. As Cassils suggests, the world has changed since the mid-1970s and the reversal in performative sculpting, from paring away to *adding on*, as well as the shift away from a binary notion of gender to a polymorphous and openly trans- approach to queering the gendered body signals a changed perspective from the frameworks defining Antin's *Carving* and Benglis's *Artforum* advertisement. These radical shifts point both to broader social and cultural views of gender and sexual identification as well as to Cassils' stated individual relationship to the conventional notions of "femininity" or "masculinity," which s/he reworks beyond what would have been recognized as a "woman's" or a "man's" body in the 1970s. While Antin and Benglis both retained a relationship to heteronormative images of the (white, middle-class) feminine body—albeit in Antin's case also an avowedly Jewish one—Cassils performs gender across norms and sexual identifications. Cassils experiences and thus produces an explicitly sexualized yet also explicitly transgendered body.

Ultimately Cassils found her/himself exploring not only the limits of her/his body in enacting extraordinary feats in the weight room ("I felt disoriented" by the effects of the steroids, "ungrounded and in flux"), but the limits of a society that is supposedly vastly more "hip" to gender permutations in accepting a masculinized "female" or just plain gender-fluid body: "When my body crossed over from socially acceptable ripped chick to freaky androgyny, it was noticeable for me in my day-to-day interactions. [...] I had achieved a confusing body that ruptured expectation" (Cassils 2013). Deploying a range of representational techniques, the *Cuts* project also "ruptures expectation" by enacting this in-between transgendered body across different contemporary modes of visuality. Thus, while Antin used the format of the artwork in the gallery (a classic conceptualist grid structure to emphasize the quality of her body image as repetitive, rationalized "information"), and Benglis that of *Artforum* (to perform herself as "pin-up," but within an art magazine context), Cassils updates our access to her deliberately excessive bodily transformation by producing a zine, time-lapse video footage, and images that are circulated and made available through the web (for example, she launched the Benglis homage images on *homotography.tumblr.com*, a website of homoerotic images oriented towards a gay male viewership).

Antin and Benglis clearly understood themselves as "women artists" (implicitly imagined, whether accurately or not, as white, middle-class, and heterosexually identified) and performatively enacted their critiques within this framework, producing more or less final objects or works to be viewed in the future. Cassils, in contrast, produces a performative body that will never be aligned in any simple way with femininity or the role of the "woman artist." Both pin-up, overtly responsible for her/his own collaborative objectification, and manipulator of her/his own bodily gender habitus–as picture and as physical and muscular embodied subject–Cassils asks us to rethink the crucial ideas Antin and Benglis set forth about femininity, fetishism, and the agency of women artists and women as embodied subjects. Antin and Benglis laid the groundwork, as Cassils acknowledges, and Cassils uses various new media to take the gendered body to a space of radical indeterminacy.

References

Cassils, Heather. 2011. "LadyFace // ManBody." *LadyFace // ManBody*. http://www.ladyfacemanbody.com/?zx=e95d696671a03bb6

Cassils, Heather. 2013. "Bashing Binaries - Along with 2,000 Pounds of Clay." *The Huffington Post*, September 7. http://www.huffingtonpost.com/heather/bashing- binaries-along-with-2000-pounds-of-clay_b_3861322.html

## Scenario

Diana Taylor

Scenario, a term originally used in theatre studies, reflects the unstable oscillation between place (stage-Latin *scaena)* and action (the *scena* or scene as an element of plot). Commedia dell'arte players used to follow a scenario, an outline of performance action and plot pinned to the back of the scenery. Within these established parameters, actors played on the broad range of audience assumptions and expectations. Improvisations embellishing the general plot line allowed for variations and surprises. Contemporary events could easily be folded into the plot, and actors could adapt to audience response. While the actors could test the limits of the scenario, suggesting alternate possibilities and outcomes, at the end of the play they returned to the conventional endings and assumed worldview. Only in their playful improvisations could they outstrip the reigning conventions. The usefulness of the term far outreaches its 16th-century origins.

Scenarios, as frameworks for thinking, have become the privileged site for modeling a wide range of practices—the theatrical "as if" simulation of catastrophic events such as nuclear war, to hypothetical "what if" set-ups such as the ticking bomb, to acts of torture ("scenarios designed to convince the detainee that death or severely painful consequences are imminent" (Lukes 2006, 6)), to scenarios that aim to heal victims by working through trauma (simulations such as "Virtual Iraq" help veterans with P.T.S.D. (Halpern 2008, 31–37)), to conflict resolution preparation, such as *Virtual Peace,* developed by Tim Lenoir, which trains peacekeepers in an "immersive, multi-sensory game-based environment that simulates real disaster relief and conflict resolution" (Lenoir 2008). The basic idea—that people learn, experience, and come to terms with past/future behaviors by physically *doing* them, trying them on, acting them through and acting them out—is the underlying theory of ritual, older than Aristotle's theory of mimesis, and as new as theories of "mirror neurons" that explore how empathy and understandings of human relationality and intersubjectivity are vital for human survival (Gallese 2001, 33–50). Scenarios are not necessarily, or even primarily, mimetic. While the paradigm allows for a continuity of cultural myths and assumptions, it usually works through reactivation rather than duplication. Rather than a copy, the scenario constitutes a once-againness.

Scenarios reveal our fantasies not only of "what if" but of causality, "if this, then that." While not predictive in function, scenarios tempt participants to extrapolate that what *is* determines what *will be.* Participants can play out the multiple variables in search for "likely" outcomes. As in theatre, groups can offer interpretations and make decisions based on what they perceive as other forces/players' motivation, disposition, character, past behaviors, and present conditions. When thinking of competitors (be they business or political actors), they put themselves in the (imagined) place of the other—so and so will do or say the following. The relationship is agonistic—who holds the better cards? Whose move will trump ours? Participants read gestures and signs for effect (will competitors tough it out?), even as they rehearse face-saving maneuvers. The more persuasive the scenarios put forth, the more likely participants will buy into them as a viable way of making sense of the world. As in commedia dell'arte, scenario thinking often ends up affirming the conventional ending and the given worldview. Nonetheless, scenarios function as the framework within which thinking takes place. Neither inherently good nor bad, they can simultaneously prepare us for and/or blind us to what is going on. We might go so far as to suggest that they are what's going on. They reveal cultural imaginaries, ways societies envision themselves, their conflicts, and possible dénouements.

Because scenarios say more about the "us" envisioning them than about the other they try to model, they are fundamental to the ways societies understand themselves. They make visible, yet again, what is already there—the ghosts, the images, the stereotypes that haunt our present and resuscitate and reactivate old dramas. And because scenarios are about "us," we need to factor ourselves in the picture—as participants, spectators or witnesses we need to "be there," part of the act of transfer. Thus, the scenario precludes a certain kind of distancing, and places spectators within its frame, implicating "us" in its ethics and politics. The better informed the participants, the better the outcomes. Bad scenarios blind us—they're all about percepticide—or self-blinding (Taylor 1997). Good scenarios heighten our awareness and encourage best behaviors. Rather than allow scenarios to be used as weapons against us, perhaps we need to fight for the ability to see ourselves acting, to compose and rehearse different scenarios, to enact different futures, and more liberating denouements.

*Further reading*

Gallese (2001); Hayles (2012); Taylor (1997).

*References*


Gallese, Vittorio. 2001. "The 'Shared Manifold' Hypothesis: From Mirror Neurons To Empathy." *Journal of Consciousness Studies*, 8.5–7: 33–50. http://www.unipr.it/arpa/mirror/pubs/pdffiles/Gallese/Gallese%202001.pdf

Halpern, Sue. 2008. "Virtual Iraq." *The New Yorker* (May 19). Accessed June 14, 2015. http://www.newyorker.com/magazine/2008/05/19/virtual-iraq

Hayles, N. Katherine. 2012. *How We Think: Digital Media and Contemporary Technogenesis*. Chicago, IL: University of Chicago Press.

Lenoir, Timothy. 2008. "Recycling the Military Entertainment Complex." *Virtual Peace*. http://www.virtualpeace.org/whitepaper.php

Lukes, Steven (2006). "Liberal Democratic Torture." *British Journal of Political Science*, 36.1: 1–16.

Taylor, Diana. 1997. *Disappearing Acts: Spectacles of Gender and Nationalism in Argentina's "Dirty War."* Durham, NC: Duke University Press.


*Cross references*

"**Performance Studies**" by Joy; "**Play**" by Schechner; "**Proxemics**" and "**Invisible theatre**" by Cody; "**Reception theory**" by Mee; "**Simulacrum**" by Cesare Schotzko; "**Virtual reality**" by Auslander.

## Simulacrum

T. Nikki Cesare Schotzko

Derived from the Latin *simulare*, "simulacrum," the stand-in representation, image, or counterfeit of a real object, indicates a specifically material manifestation of a thing or person. Jean Baudrillard popularizes the term in critical theory through his deconstructionist work, most notably in *Simulacra and Simulation* (1981). By carefully deconstructing conventional Marxist utopian binaries, such as subject-object, infrastructure-superstructure, and exploitation-alienation, Baudrillard claims that the "real" has been subsumed by the simulacrum through the collapse of value and, hence, meaning. The result is what he terms "hyperreality," where signs of the real substitute for the real itself, a continuous looping that leads to "*the radical negation of the sign as value*" (Baudrillard 1994, 6).

The collapse of discernible binaries results in a social impetus to reverse the privileging of the real, epitomized for Baudrillard by Disneyland, which "is presented as imaginary in order to make us believe that the rest is real, whereas all of Los Angeles and the America that surrounds it are no longer real, but belong to the hyperreal order and to the order of simulation" (1994, 4). The collapse of signification reinforces the cycle by which ultimately the simulation is entirely independent of any reference to the real, the process that Baudrillard refers to as the "precession of simulacra" (1994, 4).

As Walter Benjamin suggests in "The Work of Art in the Age of Mechanical Reproduction" (1936), the simulacrum not only troubles the relationship of the copy to the original, as in Andy Warhol's work, but also complicates distinctions between the live and the mediated. This is a central debate within performance studies, which emerged in part from Peggy Phelan's seminal essay "The Ontology of Performance: Representation without Reproduction" in *Unmarked* (1993) and from Philip Auslander's response in *Liveness* (1999). This particular debate becomes further complicated with regard to digital media technologies in performance, as in the work of companies emerging on the cusp of the twenty-first century, like Big Art Group, Gob Squad, or Ars Mechanica. The term simulacrum is widely used to describe multi- and intermedial productions, such as the Wooster Group's performance of *Poor Theatre* (2004), subtitled "a series of simulacra." In this piece, the group exposed their mechanism of task-based acting in their strictly physical re-performance of the recording of Jerzy Grotowski's *Akropolis* (1964), a documentary about artist Max Ernst, and a lecture by choreographer William Forsythe.

### *Further reading*

Benjamin (2008); Clausen (2007); Deleuze (1990).

### *References*


Auslander, Philip. 1999. *Liveness: Performance in a Mediatized Culture*. London and New York: Routledge.

Baudrillard, Jean. 1994. *Simulacra and Simulation*. Ann Arbor, MI: University of Michigan.

Benjamin, Walter. 1936. "The Work of Art in the Age of Mechanical Reproduction." In *Illuminations: Essays and Reflections*, edited by Hannah Arendt and translated by Harry Zohn. New York: Schocken.

Benjamin, Walter. 2008. *The Work of Art in the Age of its Technological Reproducibility, and Other Writings on Media*, edited by Michael William Jennings,

Clausen, Barbara. 2007. *After the Act: The (Re) presentation of Performance Art*. Wien: MUMOK Museum Moderner Kunst Stiftung Ludwig

Deleuze, Gilles. 1990. "Societies of Control." *L'autre journal* 1 (May 1990): 3–7.

Phelan, Peggy. 1993. *Unmarked: The Politics of Performance*. New York: Routledge.


### *Cross references*

"**Cindy Sherman's Real Fakery**" by Schneider; "**Cultural production**" by Colleran; "**Liminality**" by Levine; "**Liveness**" by Auslander; "**Mimicry**" by Applebaum; "**Montage**" by Cesare Schotzko; "**Scenario**" by Taylor.

## War

Mike Sell

War and performance are related conceptually, instrumentally, and culturally.

Conceptualizing war as performance is common. "Theatre of war" and "theatre of operations" name the space in which military actions occur; the terms may derive from the violent spectacles staged at the Roman coliseum two millennia ago. At the First Battle of Bull Run (July 21, 1861), citizens picnicked on the hillsides above Manassas, Virginia, wrongly anticipating an easy and entertaining victory for Union forces. Their children enjoyed the Wild West spectacles of Buffalo Bill Cody, which staged thrilling battles between Native Americans and U.S. soldiers. In the 1930s and 40s, the Nazis used theatre, spectacle, and mass ritual to promote a national commitment to "total war" (Berghaus 1996). The annual rallies held in Nuremberg assembled hundreds of thousands of party members and citizens to celebrate the divinity of Adolf Hitler, the manifest destiny of the Nazi party, and the organizational might of the German nation.

The instrumental use of performance is typified by such conventional strategies as camouflage and diversionary tactics. The military doctrine of "shock and awe" (a.k.a. "rapid dominance") was developed by Harlan K. Ullman and James P. Wade to exploit the sensory impact of warfare. The dazzling bombardment of Baghdad that signaled the 2003 U.S. invasion of Iraq is exemplary, but "shock and awe" has precedents in the Roman legions, Sun Tzu's *Art of War*, the Nazi blitzkrieg, and the nuclear bombing of Hiroshima and Nagasaki (Ullman and Wade 1996). The "military-industrial-entertainment complex" deploys sitcoms, sporting events, and war itself to ensure assent and distraction. To counter this tendency, French avant-garde group the Situationist International developed insurgent performance practices that were based in a theory of cultural civil war (Debord 1997 and 2005). Michel Foucault (1975) demonstrated the foundational role of theatre in the development of the modern military; the precise gestures and movements of soldiers that we associate with the modern military were developed in a "theatrical forum" in which individuals and groups were observed and corrected. Currently, University of Pittsburgh sports medicine researchers are working with Navy SEALs to improve the physical training of the soldier, fine-tune their movement strategies, and extend their "operational service life".

The dynamic between war and culture is an old one. Rituals of victory have been with us since prehistoric times; Roman generals celebrated their victories with "triumphs," a combination civil ceremony and religious ritual that displayed the spoils of war to citizens and civil authorities. The uniforms of elite troops and leaders visually impress and intimidate, and military parades demonstrate might to citizens and enemies without the expense of actual battle. Theatrical entertainments are common in the camps of soldiers, free and prisoner alike. No stranger to prison stages is drag performance. The ability of performance to raise morale is clear, too. The United Service Organizations, Inc., a private, not-for-profit operation, has provided entertainment to U.S. soldiers since the 1940s.

The tradition of radical art known as the avant-garde takes its name from a military strategy—the advance force of an army—and is, more generally, a response to "the central reality of war" in the modern era (Calinescu 1987, 100). Avant-gardes tend to favor aggressive, violent, even terroristic forms of aesthetic action, as well as the language of war and terrorism—intervention, tactical engagement, attack, etc. War has been a catalyst on both the ideological and technical-formal levels of the avant-garde, as demonstrated by such diverse performance-centered vanguards as Dada, Italian Futurism, the Blue Blouse Troupes, the Living Theatre, Las Madres de la Plaza de Mayo, and others (Sell 2009).

Twenty-four hour broad- and webcast news, on-delivery video, and ubiquitous phones and video recorders have introduced a new kind of war performativity. On the one hand, there is the "masquerade of information" used by superpowers in the age of supercomputers, satellites, and the internet (Baudrillard 1995, 40); on the other, video recordings and oral histories of military operations have provided material to those challenging power. Conceptually, culturally, instrumentally, and in the avant-garde, the relationship between war and performance continues to evolve and conquer.

### Further reading

Sell (2009); Turkle (1997).

### References

Baudrillard, Jean. 1995. *The Gulf War Did Not Take Place.* Translated by Paul Patton. Bloomington, IN: Indiana University Press.

Berghaus, Günter, ed. 1996. *Fascism and Theatre: Comparative Studies on the Aesthetics and Politics of Performance in Europe, 1925–1945*, New York: Berghahn Books.

Calinescu, Adriana. 1987. *Of Gods and Mortals: Ancient Art from the V.G. Simkhovitch Collection; Indiana Art Museum, Sept. 16–Dec. 20, 1987.* Bloomington, IN: Indiana University Press.

Debord, Guy. 1997 "The Game of War." In *Guy Debord: Revolutionary*, by Len Bracken. Venice, CA: Feral House.

Debord, Guy. 2005 *The Society of Spectacle.* Translated by Ken Knabb. Oakland, CA: AK Press.

Foucault, Michel. 1975. *Discipline & Punish.* New York: Random House, Inc.

Sell, Mike. 2009. *The Avant-Garde: Race Religion War.* Kolkota: Seagull Books.

Turkle, Sherry. 1997. *Life on the Screen: Identity in the Age of the Internet.* New York: Touchstone.

Ullman, K. Harlan, and James P. Wade. 1996. *Shock and Awe: Achieving Rapid Dominance.* Washington, DC: National Defense University Press.

### Cross references

"**Ai Weiwei's transnational public spheres**" by Zheng; "**Global censorship**" by Shea; "**Media**" and "**Terrorism and performance**" by Colleran; "**Prison culture**" by Ryan; "**Propaganda**" by Smith; "**Sisters of Survival Signal S.O.S.**" by Gaulke.

# Performer

## Active Analysis

Sharon Carnicke

Active Analysis (*Deistvennyi analiz*) is a flexible rehearsal technique that melds intellectual processes of analysis with embodied, hence active, analysis of performance texts. The ensemble works collectively through a series of études (improvisations), like drafts, with each successive étude coming progressively closer to the desired performance. Études are planned, using a systematic approach to storytelling that envisions performance as a *chain of events*, each of which occurs when an impelling *action* encounters a *counteraction* that alters its trajectory and causes the performers' circumstances to change, inducing the need for a new action. This map of *action-counteraction-event* focuses the ensemble's work and demands that individual actors choose and perform specific active verbs to pursue their actions and counteractions. Études are performed silently or verbally—using the actors' or author's words, or paraphrases of written texts (Carnicke 2009, 194–206, 212).

The Russian actor and director, Konstantin Stanislavsky, developed Active Analysis as part of his lifelong investigation into acting as an independent art. He honed its principles in his last Studio, the Opera-Dramatic (1934–1938), using a variety of performance styles and genres: (1) verse drama; (2) opera; and (3) devised performances. He worked from his home, while internally exiled by Stalin for artistic ideas that violated Soviet policies on Socialist Realism. The Soviets promoted sanitized versions of Stanislavsky's training generally and Active Analysis in particular, calling it the Method of Physical Actions in order to bring his artistry into compliance with Marxist materialism (Carnicke 2009, 183–194). With the so-called Soviet "thaw" during the 1960s, one of his assistants at the Opera-Dramatic Studio, Maria Knebel, revealed the fuller version in her teaching and books, giving it the more apt descriptor of Active Analysis (Carnicke 2010, 99–116). While widely used in contemporary Russia, it is known in the West primarily through the work of scholar/artists including Sharon Carnicke in the US, Bella Merlin from the UK, and Egil Kipste in Australia. Directors who have adapted its techniques include Georgy Tovstongov and his followers in St. Petersburg (Russia), the Russian émigré Vasily Vasiliev (France), and Declan Donnellan (UK).

Cognitive scientists are proving Stanislavsky's prescience. When he insists that actors create "filmstrips" of mental images through sensory-based visualizations (1989, 130), he anticipates

Antonio Damasio's investigation into the "problem of consciousness [which] is the problem of how we get a 'movie-in-the-brain,' provided we realize that in this rough metaphor the movie has as many sensory tracks as our nervous system has sensory portals" (1999, 9). When Stanislavsky uses études to investigate the dynamics of performance before asking actors to memorize anything, he anticipates the findings of Helga and Tony Noice, who found that actors memorize text through a tacit process of "active experiencing" that employs "all the physical, mental and emotional channels to communicate the meaning of material to another person" (2006, 14–15). The Noices' description closely mirrors the theory behind Active Analysis. Stanislavsky's mapping of performative dynamics also anticipates Patrice Pavis' proposition that scholars examine "a performance's lines of force," its "vectorization" (2003, 16–17). Sharon Carnicke's research, conducted with scientists at the University of Southern California, has shown the value of using Active Analysis in cinematic motion capture technology to study the ways in which human movement communicates emotion (2012, 321–338).

*Further reading*

Carnicke (2009, 2012); Damasio (1999).

*References*


Carnicke. Sharon. 2009. *Stanislavsky in Focus: An Acting Master for the Twenty-first Century.* London: Routledge.

Carnicke. Sharon. 2010. "The Knebel Technique: Active Analysis in Practice." In *Actor Training,* edited by Alison Hodge, 99–116. London: Routledge.

Carnicke. Sharon. 2012. "Emotional Expressivity in Motion Picture Capture Technology." In *Acting and Performance in Moving Image Culture: Bodies, Screens, Renderings,* edited by Joerg Sternagel, Deborah Levitt, and Dieter Mersch, 321–338. Berlin: Verlag für Kommunikation, Kultur und soziale Praxis.

Damasio, Antonio. 1999. *The Feeling of What Happens in the Body: Body and Emotionin the Making of Consciousness.* New York: Harcourt.

Noice, Helga and Tony Noice. 2006. "What Studies of Actors and Acting Can Tell Us About Memory and Cognitive Function." *Current Directions on Psychological Science,* 15.1: 14–18.

Pavis, Patrice. 2003. *Analyzing Performance: Theater, Dance, and Film.* Translated by David Williams. Ann Arbor, MA: University of Michigan Press.

Stanislavskii, K. S. 1989. *Sobranie sochinenii,* vol. 2, Moscow: Iskusstvo.


*Cross references*

"**Animalworks**" by Cheng; "**Audience**" by Cody; "**Broad spectrum approach**" and "**Play**" by Schechner; "**Choreography**" by Lepecki; "**Dance or we are lost: The Tanztheater of Pina Bausch**" by Birringer.

## Actor

Erin Mee

People perform social roles such as lawyer, teacher, mother, uncle, child, woman, or man all the time. As Richard Schechner suggests, "Each of these [roles], in every culture, comes equipped with ways of behaving and interacting" (2002, 208) and phrases such as "act your age" and "you need to be more managerial" reveal the "not-so-hidden social scripts" for these performances (2002, 209). The scripts—and methods of "actor training"—for these roles are found in parenting books, faculty handbooks, etiquette manuals, management workshops, schools, and casual comments made by friends, colleagues, and parents. Thus people learn and perform social roles all the time, although they may be more or less conscious of themselves as performers, and are more or less aware of the effects of their performances on others.

Nevertheless, as Schechner points out, "all actors are performers, but not all performers are actors" (2002, 208). An actor is someone who performs an act or action. In the theatre, an actor is someone who performs a role, usually of a character. The Greek word for actor means "one who interprets" the role. Becoming a character is a profound act of empathy, of putting oneself in another's place, seeing what it is like to be another person, and seeing the world from another's perspective. However, not all definitions of acting or systems of actor training require the actor to become the character. For example, director Kavalam Narayana Panikkar refers to the actor as a *katha patram* (*katha* means story, and *patram* means vessel or pot), whose job is to be a vessel through which the rasa of the play is carried to and shared with the spectator. Rasa is the aesthetic flavor or sentiment tasted in and through performance: the *Natyashastra*, the Sanskrit treatise on aesthetics, tells us that when foods and spices are mixed together in different ways, they create different tastes. Similarly, the mixing of different basic emotions arising from different situations, when expressed through the performer, gives rise to an emotional experience or "taste" in the spectator, which is rasa (Bharata 1996, 55). The Sanskrit term for acting, *abhinaya*, literally means "to carry forward"; it is "that which takes the [rasa of the] performance to the audience" (Gupt 1994, 181–182). The goal of the actor is to create a rasic experience for the partaker, and the actor does not need to become the character to do so (Mee 2009).

Different systems of actor training have been developed based on particular ideas about the role of the actor in performance. For example, the director and acting teacher Konstantin Stanislavsky believed that theatre is "the art of reflecting life" (1989). He developed a method of physical actions to bridge the gap between fiction and reality, and the actor's job was to "become the character" in order to be believable as the character. Actor/director Vsevolod Meyerhold believed that theatre is a means of transforming society by revealing, or making visible the political truths hidden under the surface of everyday life. He developed a system of actor training called biomechanics, which trains the actor to bring the subtext to the surface and give it physical form. Director Anne Bogart feels she lives in a mediated world; for her, theatre is a way of making connections between people. She has developed a practice of actor training that teaches the actor to make immediate and unmediated connections to each other and to the audience. Thus, each of these systems of actor training expresses particular philosophies about theatre and its relationship to the world, and therefore defines and shapes it.

### Further reading

Mee (2009); Schechner (2002).

### References

Bharata. 1996. *Bharata: The Natyashastra*, edited by Kapila Vatsyayan. New Delhi: Sahitya Academy.

Gupt, Bharat. 1994. *Dramatic Concepts Greek and Indian*. Delhi: D.K. Printworld.

Mee, Erin. 2009. *Theatre of Roots: Redirecting the Modern Indian Stage*. Kolkata: Seagull Books.

Schechner, Richard. 2002. *Performance Studies: An Introduction*. London: Routledge.

Stanislavsky, Constantine. 1989. *Creating a Role*, London: Routledge.

### Cross references

"**Active analysis**" by Carnicke; "**Becoming *Kinocognophore***" by Bucher; "**Emotions**" by Tait; "**Explicit body performance**" by McGinley; "**Liminality**" by Levine; "**Scenario**" by Taylor.

## Animalworks

Meiling Cheng

The term "animalworks", first proposed by Meiling Cheng in her article, "Animalworks in China" (2007, 63–91), specifies performances and installations that use animals as materials and/

or performers in art. Being the plural name for an emergent genre, animalworks both identify those durational artworks that bring into play the figure and presence of animals and evoke another time-based genre, "bodyworks" (1975), as their counterparts in performance art.

Characteristically, a bodywork treats the artist's body as the basis, perimeter, material, subject, and object of a performance action. An animalwork, in contrast, involves the artist's interaction with or manipulation of another body, that of an animal in its various guises as a concept, a somatic mass, a sensorial stimulus, a material symbol, and an alien spectacle. Bodyworks and animalworks have a common interest in the intersection between corporeality and temporality—that is, in the nature and attributes of a mortal body. Both genres tend to challenge normative sensibilities and thrive on the violence of the unexpected, the grotesque, or the extremely visceral. Bodyworks and animalworks nevertheless energize the performance medium from almost opposite standpoints. The potential danger associated with a bodywork comes from a predetermined stable element: the artist's willingness to subject his/her own body to an endurance task, which includes self-harm. Conversely, an animalwork often derives its thrill from a relatively uncontrollable risky element: the strength, volition, motility, and aggression of a body other than that of the artist. Whereas a bodywork questions an individual's right to unrestricted corporeal self-control, an animalwork foregrounds a self's ethical interrelations with an other, human or otherwise (see Cheng 2013, 234–301).

*Further reading*

Cheng (2007, 2013); Parker-Starbuck (2014); Warr (2012); Wolfe (2003).

*References*


Cheng, Meiling. 2007. "Animalworks in China." *TDR: The Drama* Review, 51.1: 63–91.

Cheng, Meiling. 2013. *Beijing Xingwei: Contemporary Chinese Time-based Art.* Greenford: Seagull London.

Museum of Contemporary Art, Chicago. 1975. *Bodyworks* (Exhibition). Curated by Ira Licht. Exhibition Catalogue. 8 March–27 April.

Parker-Starbuck, Jennifer. 2014. *Cyborg Theatre: Corporeal/Technological Intersections in Multimedia Performance.* New York: Palgrave Macmillan.

Warr, Tracey, ed. 2012. *The Artist's Body.* Expanded Edition. London: Phaidon.

Wolfe, Cary. 2003. *Animal Rites: Animal Culture, the Discourse of Species, and Posthumanist Theory.* Chicago, IL: University of Chicago Press.


*Cross references*

"**Animal Studies**" and "**Knowing animals now: *The unreliable bestiary*, a multi-part, ongoing performance project by Deke Weaver**" by Chaudhuri; "**Carolee Schneemann's *CatScan (New Nightmares/Ancient History)***" by Rundle; "**Circus**" by Tait; "**Extreme performance**" by Cheng; "**Posthumanism**" by Nayar.

## Body Art Still Image Action: *OFFERING*

Mariel Carranza, with Svetlana Darsalia and Meiling Cheng

> Never try to convey your idea to the audience, it is a thankless and senseless task. Show them life, and they'll find within themselves the means to assess and appreciate it.
>
> Andrei Tarkovsky, Russian filmmaker (2006)

*OFFERING*, a single performance piece in a series of Mariel Carranza's durational performances, was presented at the *Depicting Action* (September 2006) international exhibition of time-based art, curated by

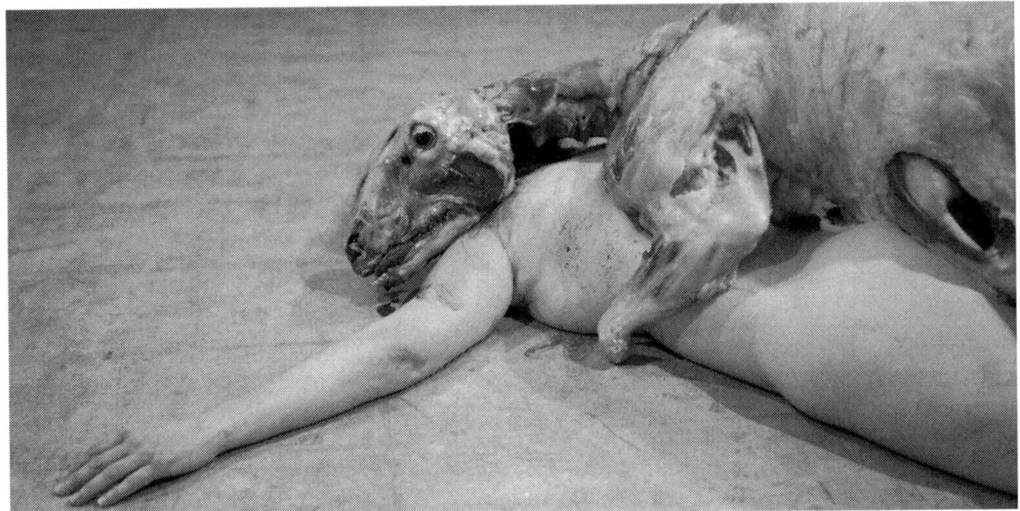

**Figure 13** Mariel Carranza performing *OFFERING* (2006) in *Depicting Action*, curated by Jamie McMurry, at 18th Street Art Center in Santa Monica. Image courtesy of the artist.

Jamie McMurry at the 18th Street Art Center in Santa Monica, California. This performance was distinguished by a sculpture-like stillness in composition, incorporating the artist's body. This technique of borrowing sculptural properties for live body art performance challenges conventional sculpture and may be termed "Body Art Still Image Action."

The sculptural element in Carranza's art performances derives conceptually from the *Living Matter* series of liquid sculptures, Carranza´s ongoing project since 1994. In this series, liquid organic matter, applied to canvas over a long period of time, hardens, acquiring either controlled or accidental form, while fresh liquid matter continues to be added to the canvas, creating new layers. Over time the living matter goes through the aging process, gradually changing its appearance. Carranza began exploring sculptural properties in the medium of performance by first incorporating her body into a large-scale installation (e.g. a durational performance, *Drum*, 1989, Wight Gallery, University of California, Los Angeles). The performance presented a large wooden drum with the artist's body suspended inside by means of a swinging harness, allowing her to hit the walls with her hands and feet to produce the sound of the drum. In her later durational performances, Carranza turned her body contour, dimension, and flesh into an actual still-life sculpture.

Stillness in Carranza's sculptural body art performances often displays a serene, meditative quality, even when the artist's idea involves a physical challenge with a degree of endurance, as in *I Am/Ja Jesam,* the performance that took place in Stanglinec, Croatia, June 2011. During this performance, the artist's body was immobilized, her hands and feet tied by ropes to large rocks buried in the ground. For four hours, the artist endured sudden weather changes and was helpless to insects and other natural phenomena.

The stillness of the created image over a durational time frame allows the artist to distance herself from the event she produces, while enduring various physical challenges. Silence and seeming non-action for the duration of the performance heighten the visceral immediacy in the viewer and can elicit strong emotional responses (anxiety, consternation, awe, etc.).

In *OFFERING*, Carranza expresses her intense psychological reaction to the idea and act of "sacrifice," as well as her philosophical approach to spiritual and physical aspects of violence. As a Body Art Still Image Action, *OFFERING* displays a powerful image of two apparently inert bodies: a newly slaughtered, 65-pound sheep corpse weighing upon the artist's prostrate nude body. Taking *OFFERING* as a case study allows us to understand certain mechanisms in Carranza's thought process during the preparation and execution of its concept. Carranza's work is largely intuitive and analytical, reflecting on her emotional responses to situations and events in her personal life, while the mystery of the images she creates lies in the metaphorical way they are expressed. By showing life through the still image of live performance, Carranza lets her embodied metaphor speak for itself.

The idea for the performance came to Carranza after her conversation with a friend of Eastern European origin about the custom of "animal sacrifice" (mostly sheep) as a ritual offering to God to ensure good fortune. To the artist, practicing animal sacrifice in the contemporary United States seemed foreign and barbaric. The custom's supposed ritualistic efficacy disturbed her deeply and flooded her with an onslaught of images from another time and culture. Having been a vegetarian for several years, Carranza felt repulsed at merely the thought of touching or smelling raw meat, let alone participating in a ritualistic feast. But the subject matter of animal sacrifice continued to fascinate her. She was appalled and intrigued by the realization that animal sacrifice was still being practiced today, reminding her of familiar biblical stories from her Catholic convent school in Peru and of recent debates regarding the morality of any form of sacrifice and the ethical problem of animal cruelty. This preoccupation evolved into a deeper consideration of the violence associated with the Hamas political party's victory in the 2006 election, which jeopardized the possibility of peace in Gaza. Even though Carranza refrained from working in an explicitly political mind-frame, the idea for the performance manifested itself in a visual language as both a means of solving her personal dilemma and a metaphor for the concepts of sacrifice, offering, suffering, and larger forms of punishment.

Carranza's initial idea for *OFFERING* was to be suspended from the ceiling next to a hanging sheep carcass. When the artist realized that it was physically impossible for her to maintain this position for an extended durational performance, she chose to have the sheep carcass placed on top of her nude body, thus achieving several objectives at once. She would have to physically bear the weight of the sacrificed animal's body and emotionally deal with the guilt of causing the animal's unjustified death for the sake of art, all the while allowing herself to experience and comprehend on a gut level what this innocent animal represents through its offering: sacrifice or propitiation?

With the still warm carcass of the dead sheep on top of her nude body, Carranza lay face-down on the cold concrete floor of the gallery space with the sheep's dangling head next to her own face, forcing her to look into the sheep's glassy eyes. When she tried to close her own eyes, she saw the dead bodies of animals. The longer her eyes were closed, the more bodies piled up in her minds' eye, although she knew in reality that the gallery was mostly empty. She smelled the sheep's breath; she even tasted its blood when thick drops touched her lips. As the carcass got cold, so did the artist and she began to shiver. With the animal's body still jerking on top of her, the artist was aware that the sheep's smothering weight was crushing her. Gradually she felt as if her heart was carrying the sheep's dead weight and she sensed how the breathing movements of her chest gave the animal's stagnant flesh the appearance of life.

Perhaps unconsciously, the artist turned her experience into a metaphor for the complex philosophical and moral questions that prompted her to create this multi-layered performance. *OFFERING* was also a means of addressing personal issues, like meditation on letting go. As in a Buddhist Vipassana meditation, the truth came in the acknowledgement of "letting go": by causing pain she let go of pain and with it centuries of human injustice, violence, and cruelty toward animals and other vulnerable beings. She realized the cause of her suffering, and in the course of this realization, her identity as a contemporary female artist came forth and she felt the whole experience as a violation. Her memories made her feel at one with the animal, whose body was able to lift her own pain away. At the instant when she became conscious of the heavy, and violent load of guilt on her shoulders, it had transformed into a shared agony of death and compassion: she let it go.

## Reference

Tarkovsky, Andrey A. and Giovanni Chiaramonte, eds. 2006. *Instant Light: Tarkovsky Polaroids*. London: Thames & Hudson.

## Archive and repertoire

Diana Taylor

"Archival" memory exists as documents, maps, literary texts, letters, archaeological remains, bones, videos, films, CDs—all those items supposedly resistant to change. Archive, from the Greek, etymologically refers to "a public building," to "a place where records are kept" (Skeat 1980, 24). From *arkhe*, it also means a beginning, the first place, the government. The archival, from the beginning, sustains power. Archival memory works across distance, over time and space—researchers can go back to reexamine an ancient manuscript; letters find their addresses through time and place, and computer discs can cough up lost files with the right software. What changes over time is the value, relevance, or meaning of the archive, how the items it contains are interpreted, even embodied. Bones might remain the same while their story may change—depending on the paleontologist or forensic anthropologist who examines them. *Antigone* might be performed in multiple ways, while the preserved text assures a stable signifier. Written texts allow scholars to trace literary traditions, sources, and influences.

Insofar as it constitutes materials that seem to endure, the archive exceeds the "live". Several myths surround the "archive." One is that it is unmediated—that objects located there might mean something outside the framing of the archival impetus itself. But what makes an object archival is the process whereby it is selected for analysis. Another falsehood is that the archive resists change, corruptibility, and political manipulation. Yet individual objects—books, DNA evidence, photo IDs—might mysteriously appear in or disappear from the archive.

The repertoire, on the other hand, enacts embodied memory through performances, gestures, orality, movement, dance, singing—in short, all those acts usually thought of as ephemeral, non-reproducible knowledge. Repertoire, etymologically "a treasury, an inventory," also allows for individual agency, referring also to "the finder, discoverer," and meaning "to find out" (Skeat 1980, 30). The repertoire requires presence—people participate in the production and reproduction of knowledge by being there, being a part of the transmission. As opposed to the supposedly stable objects in the archive, the actions that are the repertoire do not remain the same. The repertoire both keeps and transforms choreographies of meaning. Sports enthusiasts might claim that soccer has remained unchanged for the past hundred years, even though players and fans from different countries have appropriated the event in diverse ways. Dances change over time, even though generations of dancers (or even individual dancers) swear they're always the same. While the embodiment changes, the meaning might very well remain the same.

The repertoire too, then, allows scholars to trace traditions and influences. Many kinds of performances have traveled throughout the Americas, leaving their mark as they move. Scholar Richard Flores (1995), for example, maps out the way *pastorelas* or shepherds' plays moved from Spain, to central Mexico, to Mexico's Northwest and then to what is now the Southwest of the U.S. The different versions permit him to distinguish among various routes. Max Harris (2000) has traced the practice of a specific mock battle, *moros y cristianos*, from pre-conquest Spain to 16th-century Mexico, and into the present. The repertoire allows for alternative perspective on historical processes of transnational contact, and invites a re-mapping of the Americas, this time by following traditions of embodied practice.

Certainly it is true that individual instances of performances disappear from the repertoire. This happens to a lesser degree in the archive. The question of disappearance in relation to the archive and the repertoire is one of kind as well as degree. The "live" performance can never be captured or transmitted through the archive. A video of a performance is not a performance, though it often comes to replace the performance as a *thing* in itself (the video is part of the archive; what it represents is part of the repertoire). Embodied memory, because it is "live," exceeds the archive's ability to capture it. But that does not mean that performance—as ritualized, formalized, or reiterative behavior—disappears. Performances also replicate themselves through their own structures and codes. This means that the repertoire, like the archive, is mediated. The process of selection, memorization or internalization, and transmission takes place within (and in turn helps constitute) specific systems of re-presentation. Multiple forms of embodied acts are always present, though in a constant state of again-ness. They reconstitute themselves—transmitting communal memories, histories, and values from one group/generation to the next. Embodied and performed acts generate, record, and transmit knowledge.

The relationship between the archive and the repertoire is certainly not sequential (the former ascending to prominence after the disappearance of the latter). While it seems intuitive that the live event associated with the repertoire would precede the documentation of the archive, this is not necessarily the case. An original "live" theatre performance might well interpret an ancient text. Or, to give a very different kind of example, obituaries of famous people are usually written before they die, so that the media immediately has the materials when the time comes. Nor is it "true" versus "false," mediated versus unmediated, primordial versus modern. Nor is it a straightforward binary—with the written and archival constituting hegemonic power and the repertoire providing the anti-hegemonic challenge. The modes of storing and transmitting knowledge are many and mixed and embodied performances have often contributed to the maintenance of a repressive social order. We need only look to the broad range of political practices in the Americas exercised on human bodies from pre-conquest human sacrifices, to Inquisitorial burnings at the stake, to the lynchings of African Americans, to contemporary acts of state-sponsored torture and "disappearances." We need not polarize the relationship between these different kinds of knowledge to acknowledge that they have often proved antagonistic in the struggle for cultural survival or supremacy.

### *Further reading*

De Certeau (1988); Taylor (2003).

### *References*

Michel de Certeau. 1988. *The Practice of Everyday Life*, translated by Steven Randall, London: University of California Press.

Skeat, Walter W. 1980. *A Concise Etymological Dictionary of the English Language*. New York: A Perigee Book.

Taylor, Diana. 2003. "Bush's Happy Performative." *TDR: The Drama Review*, 47.3: 5–8.

### *Cross references*

"**Excerpts from *Prostitution Notes* (1974)**" by Lacy; "**Historicity**" by Colleran; "**Performing the archive**" by Nyong'o; "**Prosthetic performance**" by Gass; "**Quotation**" by Garrett.

---

**35 Years of Living Art (excerpts from Linda Mary Montano's blog, Thursday, December 6, 2012)**

Linda Mary Montano

Dear Reader,
With all due respect to time and memory, I will regress to 1984 and tell you about *14 YEARS OF LIVING ART*, my chakra endurance piece. I will also share a few journal entries from each year. You can go to my webpage, www.lindamontano.com, for images from this endurance. Look for the entry: CHAKRA STORY and ART/LIFE STORY.

Backstory 1:

Let's begin at the beginning. I was raised a very strict Roman Catholic and became enamored of transformation via spiritual rituals/visions/incense/

chanting and intense mysteries. I even entered a convent to continue this research, but left after 2 years to become a full fledged hippie artist and wild tantrica.

Backstory 2:

In 1971 I met my husband-to-be, photographer Mitchell Payne, and my spiritual guru, Dr. RS Mishra. The ecstasy of knowing that I was loved by my husband and spiritually nourished by both of these beauties, opened my creative floodgates. I began an intense yoga practice that infused/inspired my performances. I am forever grateful to both of these heart teachers/friends.

Backstory 3:

During my 5 years daily association with Dr Mishra's ashram, I was learning Hindu theology. Gurugi told us that there are 7 powerful and mystical centers inside the body and each had a color, sound association, and bija mantra. I became so intoxicated with this knowledge that I wanted to understand it more deeply.

Backstory 4:

Mitchell and I divorced. A year and a half later he was murdered. I moved to a Zen center for two years and then came out in the early 1980s to make art that would engulf me in its passion. The healing that I was receiving from Eastern theologies, and the martial arts (karate high green belt) catapulted me into wanting to hide and heal inside the monastery of my own art/life.

This is what I created:

*7 YEARS OF LIVING ART 12/8/84-12/8/91*

*AN EXPERIENCE BASED ON THE 7 ENERGY CENTERS OF THE BODY*

*PART A. INNER: ART/LIFE INSTITUTE*

*Daily for 7 years I will:*

1. *Stay in a colored space (minimum 3 hours)*
2. *Listen to one pitch (minimum 7 hours)*
3. *Speak in an accent (except with family)*
4. *Wear one-color clothes associated with the color of the chakra*

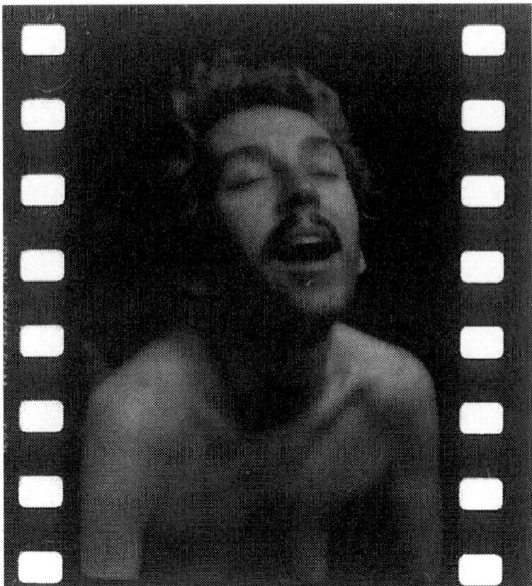

**Figure 14** Linda Montano in the persona of Bob Dylan. Photo by Annie Sprinkle. Image courtesy of the artist and photographer.

*PART B: OUTER: THE NEW MUSEUM*

1. *Once a month for 7 years, I will sit in a window installation at the New Museum and talk about art/life with individuals who join me.*

*PART C: OTHERS: INTERNATIONAL*

1. *Once a year for 16 days, a collaborator will live with me.*
2. *Others can collaborate in their own way wherever they are.*

THE CHAKRAS, QUALITIES AND PARTICULAR DISCIPLINES OUTLINED: 1984-91

FIRST CENTER: sex, red, B pitch, tip of coccyx, 1984-85
SECOND CENTER: security, orange, C pitch, pelvis, nun accent, 1985-86
THIRD CENTER: courage, yellow, G pitch, navel, jazz accent, 1986-87
FOURTH CENTER: compassion, green, D pitch, heart, country western accent, 1987-88
FIFTH CENTER: communication, blue, A pitch, throat, British accent, 1988-89

SIXTH CENTER: intuition, purple, E pitch, third eye, Slavic accent, 1989-90
SEVENTH CENTER: peace, white, F pitch, top of head, normal accent, 1990-91

++++++++++++++++++++++++++++++++++++++++++++
FROM 1991-1998, I CONTINUED THIS PROCESS BUT WENT FROM WHITE TO RED
++++++++++++++++++++++++++++++++++++++++++++

Journals

Red year: 1984-85

The sex chakra is eliciting sex! I am drawing people but more important am feeling "sex" myself. I want it; they want it. It's inevitable. That's what this chakra is about. I need protection and hope that I won't be pushed in the wrong way.

The piece is portable. I string my red cloth like a tent (vow to stay in a red room 3 hours a day), duplicating my upstate red room, which I painted. The sound (from a hand-held oscillator that I listen to 7 hours a day) especially travels well (it is small and portable). I wear earphones in the city and walk jubilantly down the streets listening to B, watching trucks drown it out, and listening to its return, wondering what everyone else is listening to

My clothes get dirty and there are just so many red things in my repertoire. I have not broken the dress code yet and always wear red even if I am cold (and don't have a red winter coat).

I felt last night that if I didn't get out of bed immediately that I would get so overstimulated and sick from the red room, red clothes, red sound that I would fall apart. I considered calling FAMILY (phone counseling hotline)! I am beginning to worry about the consequences (of this piece). Will I go crazy?

Red attracts bulls. It is vitality, roots, Chinese weddings. It is passion, energy. I wear a uniform again like a nun.

Orange year: 1985-86

Eleanor (my aunt) lived and died half way through the second chakra. I did the sex center (death) and security with her ... thought that I had actually "created" a lump on my uterus and breast that year ... realizing that when you work on the chakras, you attract many things and symptoms as you clean out the body/mind debris, conditioning and belief systems. Taking care of E. for 9 months during this performance has been a trip! Caregiver Chakra Art!

So Eleanor was a good guide for me also, someone who had worked all of her life (physical security), had a house (financial security), and was dying (lack of security).

The piece is about forgiveness and about my inability to keep commitments ... It is a psychological ploy that I had unconsciously set up to cure myself of guilt, which I had let the church (self)impose on me as a child.

I danced mightily to Celia Cruz records, made believe that I was Latin and guilt free and in general lost my breath at the beauty of the orange.

Yellow year: 1986-87

Physically I resemble Doris Day in drag, Dinah Shore after a chicken commercial, or Cory Aquino giving a tour of Manila. Dressed entirely in yellow, I and all viewers are forced to smile, respond, see me, comment. I am clean-cut looking (nobody wearing all yellow can be that bad). I am the sun, I am radiance, I am summer days.

Green year: 1987-88

I and my heart are opened by default. Everything shifted in 1988 and because I intended to "open the heart," I asked life to send me everything I needed in order to do just that. I stripped down the piece to those basic elements of intentionality (open the heart) and I reminded myself of the intention by keeping my vows (green clothes, colored room, ART/LIFE COUNSELING, listening to one pitch, speaking in an accent).

My brother-in-law, my dog, and my mother died in the green year. My heart opened.

Blue year: 1988-89

I am beginning to gain a perspective on the project and see it all as a giant experiment in re-programming and re-parenting. ... that I am giving myself time and a structure and a chance and an invitation to fill in the blanks and iron out the wrinkles of my past.

I asked how else I can open the throat and communicate when the idea to go to the Newman Center (Catholic center on university campuses) and talk to a priest about how I felt betrayed by the Catholic Church came into my mind and I did it and opened my throat center ...

And when I felt it was a perfect time for singing lessons, I took them and opened my throat center ... And when I thought that I should have a doctor look at my throat, I did that ...

At the ashram (Ananda Ashram, Monroe NY) I start blossoming creatively and Guruji (Dr. Mishra) has me read a lot (spiritual hubris) and my voice comes from the earth. I find that I can call the spiritual authors into myself, become them (usually) and channel the information as them even though I'm reading. A trick I call: getting out of my own way.

DREAM: I'm in front of Guruji and a big wad of phlegm comes out of my nose and mouth. I am healed and scream in the dream.

## Purple year: 1989–90

Severe headache as if some vein or artery or nerve is damaged. It travels from the back of my eye to the top of my head on the left side. I am alarmed, go to an internist, who counsels me on my personal life and says that I am in need of right living.

I see that the body is impermanent and changes: menopause, physical changes, wrinkles, cellulite, fibroids are alarming.

I see that I need communal life for a while, that living alone is detrimental, so I invest in living at the ashram for 2 years.

I see that I can receive and need nurturing and reparent with an Indiana couple, 2 ayurvedic doctors living at the ashram during the summer.

## White year: 1990–91

No entry.......About 10 years ago I burned 70 journals. All records lost.

## Another 7 years of living art: 1991–98

Reader,
After the first seven years was completed, I could hardly stop the process. I kept going and did it again with the same colors but starting from the head (white) and going down to the first center (red).

This time, I appeared once a month ***ASTRALLY OR REALLY*** at the United Nations Chagall Chapel and let myself be, let myself feel and was taught by the chakras. I stopped pushing for success, I stopped wanting to do, DO, DO!

My will was broken. My need for superwoman actions was depleted. My art was becoming more life-like and human. I taught for 7 years at University of Texas, Austin.

When that growth spurt of loyalty and vow to the 7 chakras was over and I didn't get tenure, I was concurrently hearing a voice inside saying: *GO AND BE WITH YOUR FATHER!!!!!!!!!!!!!!!*

That meant that I would leave Texas and come back to Upstate New York to take care of my father for 7 years. That was reality and life but it became so incredibly intense and complicated emotionally (he had a stroke and needed 24/7 care) that I called it DAD ART, hiding behind my video camera because the fire of intensity, watching my Dad dissolve, was too much for life.

Art became my veil once again.

I was also back in the real world, wanted to "teach," so I created my own UNIVERSITY, SCHOOL, ASHRAM under the auspices of THE ART/LIFE INSTITUTE. It is free of rules, regulations, grades, faculty meetings and salaries.

In 2019, **ANOTHER 21 YEARS OF LIVING ART** will complete a 35-year cycle of paying attention to art as life via the chakras (now translated as glands).

## Camp

Ann Pellegrini

Camp has a long history of association with gay men and, especially, with gay male practices of female impersonation. In a kind of transfer of properties, camp is equally associated with the larger than life divas (such as Mae West, Bette Davis, Judy Garland), whom female impersonators have emulated and parodied. Camp names an aesthetic sensibility and performative style characterized by a kind of extravagant impersonation of the real. This extravagance blurs boundaries between true and false, depth and surface, masculine and feminine, and other binaries key to a metaphysics of substance.

The most influential critical analysis of the camp sensibility is Susan Sontag's 1964 essay, "Notes on 'Camp.'" In it, Sontag captures well the way camp sidles up to reality and sets it "in quotation marks. It's not a lamp, but a 'lamp'; not a woman, but a 'woman'" (1964, 275–292). To perceive Camp in objects and persons is to understand Being-as-Playing-a-Role. It is the farthest extension, in sensibility, of the metaphor of "life as theatre." For all its bravura stagings, Sontag's analysis remains controversial both for its minimization of the homosexual specificity of camp and for her characterization of camp as "apolitical" (1964, 275–292). For some queer cultural commentators—among them Michael Bronski, David M. Halperin, Esther Newton, and Moe Meyer—what is or might be political in camp emerges precisely in relation to its emergence out of gay lifeworlds. In her path-breaking anthropological study of pre-Stonewall drag culture, *Mother Camp: Female Impersonators in America* (1979), Newton analyzes camp as a performance practice that is also a survival strategy for lessening the stigma of homosexual identity.

Extrapolating from Newton's analysis of the scene and "seen" of female impersonation, Judith Butler theorizes all gender as an imitative practice whose performance fabricates its origins and passes them off as natural ground. Camp here emerges not just as the exception that "outs" the rule; it can also function as a strategy for critically up-ending gender norms. If gender is a citational performance—an imitation with no original—then "man" and "woman" are always already in quotation marks. By putting quotation marks between quotation marks, Camp throws into dizzying relief the everyday processes whereby gender—and the sexual norms propped up by the fiction of essential (hetero)sexual difference—are done and redone.

Now nearly five decades on from Stonewall and well into the commodified camp of *Queer Eye for the Straight Guy* and the homonormativity of same-sex marriage, the politics, possibilities, and performances of camp are hardly settled matters. Lesbian critics, feminist scholars, and queer critics of color have put pressure on the whiteness and maleness of camp, asking what happens to the politics and punch of camp when we make space for other camp styles and camp proximities: lesbian (Case 1993; Davy 1994; Roberston 1993), Jewish (Ockman 2005; Pellegrini 2007), Latino/a (Muñoz 1999), or African American (Nyong'o 2002). These questions, far from undermining some one and true version of camp, seem utterly in keeping with camp's own arch refusal of origins and the claims of the real.

### *Further reading*

Pellegrini (2007); Sontag (1964).

### *References*

Case, Sue-Ellen. 1993. *Performing Feminisms: Feminism and Critical Theory and Theatre*, Baltimore, MD: Johns Hopkins University Press.

Davy, Kate. 1994. *The Politics and Poetics of Camp*, London: Routledge

Muñoz, José Estaban. 1999. *Disidentifications: Queers of Color and the Performance of Politics*. Minneapolis, MN: University of Minnesota Press.

Newton, Esther. 1979. *Mother Camp: Female Impersonators in America*. Chicago, IL: University of Chicago Press.

Nyong'o, Tavia. 2002. "I Feel Love: Racial Kitsch and Black Performance" *Yale Journal of*

*Criticism* 12.2: 371–391.
Ockman, Carol and Kenneth Silver. 2005. *Sarah Bernhardt: The Art of High Drama,* New Haven, CT: Yale University Press.
Pellegrini, Ann. 2007. "After Sontag: Future Notes on Camp." In *A Companion to Lesbian, Gay, Bisexual, Transgender, and Queer Studies,* edited by George E. Haggerty and Molly McGarry. Oxford: Blackwell.
Robertson, Pamela. 1996. *Guilty Pleasures: Feminist Camp from Mae West to Madonna,* Durham, NC: Duke University Press.
Sontag, Susan. 1964. *Against Interpretation and Other Essays,* New York: Farrar, Straus and Giroux, 1964. (Reprinted many times)

*Cross references*

"**Boychild**" and "**Gaga Feminism**" by Halberstam; "**Drag**" by Edgecomb; "**Ethnic drag**" by Herrera; "**Guillermo Gómez-Peña attempts to explain performance art to people who may have never heard of it**" by Gómez-Peña; "**Identification/dis-identification**" by Muñoz; "**Memoirs of Björk-Geisha**" by Takemoto.

## Celebrity

Pramod K. Nayar

A celebrity is one who is always in a performance, and whose performance is always a spectacle. Celebrities are individuals whose achievements in any domain—sports, film, television, science, finance, business—sets them apart from other individuals. Unlike fame (Braudy 1986), celebrityhood depends on media spectacle.

Celebrityhood, in contrast to fame, requires a visual presence before the eyes of the beholder. Ancient kings and emperors, in an age without portraiture and photography (not to mention impression management via Facebook), relied on hearsay, praise, songs, and such to be "known," although eventually, recognizing the need for a visual supplement to their renown, they began carving their visages into coins and currency.

Celebrity performance demands a constant corporeality—the tweet, the email, the fan appearance, and the screen—that foregrounds the individual's looks and body, whether as portraits and engravings in an earlier age or posters, photographs, public, and screen appearances today. The attention to clothing—carried very often to dramatic extremes such as Lady Gaga's costumes—makeup, gestures, and diction is part of celebrity corporeal performance.

This visual dimension of celebrity performance ensures the recognizability of the face of the celebrity. Celebrities are brands and therefore instantly recognizable. A brand (Frow 2002; Lury 2012) is at once unique and iterable: it can be repeated across contexts and still remains the same. Serena Williams, Bill Clinton, and Justin Beiber are recognizable outside their domains (sport, politics, and music respectively) because, having become brands, their meanings can be performed in any context. A celebrity is one who can move across contexts, genres, formats, and domains because their celebrityhood functions independent of their "original" domains.

Celebrity performance demands iterability and iconicity. Celebrities functioning as icons enable the forging of social bonds because they come to represent something other than and more than themselves. Celebrity humanitarianism, embodied in Angelina Jolie, Princess Diana, Aishwarya Rai Bachchan and, in an earlier era, Audrey Hepburn, is a performance that reinforces the iconicity of the celebrity in an entirely different domain. The celebrity establishes social bonds across peoples, nations, and cultures by focusing on the toiling, sympathetic, and activist body of the celebrity embedded in contexts —AIDS, poverty, child-abuse, war victims, natural disasters —completely different from Hollywood, Wimbledon, the White House, or the fashion industry. The celebrity internalizes social anguish (Littler 2008) as a part of her/his celebrityhood. An icon generates a distinctive semiotic economy that lends itself to forging social bonds (Ghosh 2010). Such a performance ensures that the celebrity is located at the intersection of a financial and a cultural economy (Nayar 2009).

Individuals acquire celebrityhood, according to Chris Rojek, when we as a public begin to take an interest in their private lives (Rojek 2001). Celebrity performance is the orchestrated but occasionally unintended circulation of information about the individual in her/his public and private realms. Their marriages, divorces, children, eating disorders, love affairs, and substance abuse become a part of celebrity performance when these are made public through the gossip columns, interviews, or scoops. Thus information is central to the celebrity's performance whether this takes the form of a public disaster —Nigella Lawson being slapped by her ex-husband in a restaurant in 2013, for example, or Lance Armstrong's failed dope test— the celebrity continues to be a media spectacle through the availability of information about private conditions, battles, and tensions.

Very often celebrity performance through the circulation of information takes the form of revelation of actions and behavior that are socially unacceptable. If celebrities are engaged in a parasocial relationship (Turner 2004), they are also icons that imbue themselves with the aspirations, ideals, norms and prejudices of their society and culture. Scandals are instances when celebrity performance varies from the social norms and belief systems into which they have inserted themselves over the years through iterative acts. Thus Lance Armstrong, who had embodied the perfectibility of the human body and spirit—and therefore the embodiment of human aspirations itself—fell from grace upon the circulation of information about his doping. Armstrong's scandal was less about his personal misdemeanor than a betrayal of the collective aspirations of a people for whom he had performed every year for decades on his bicycle. Scandal here is the performance of a betrayal, an erosion of the parasocial relationship and the disavowal of the symbolic value of a celebrity's body and action.

*Further reading*

Ghosh (2010); Lury (2012); Nayar (2009).

*References*

Braudy, Leo. 1986. *The Frenzy of Renown: Fame and its History*. New York: Oxford University Press, Inc.

Frow, J. 2002. "Signature and Brand." In *High-Pop: Making Culture into Public Entertainment*, edited by Jim Collins, 56–74. Malden: Blackwell.

Ghosh, Bishnupriya. 2010. "Looking through Coca-Cola: Global Icons and the Popular." *Public Culture*, 22.2: 333–368.

Littler, Jo. 2008. "'I Feel your Pain': Cosmopolitan Charity and the Public Fashioning of the Celebrity Soul." *Social Semiotics*, 18.2: 237–251.

Lury, Celia. 2012. "Bringing the World into the World: The Material Semiotics of Contemporary Culture." *Distinktion*, 13.3: 247–260.

Nayar, Pramod K. 2009. *Seeing Stars: Spectacle, Society, Celebrity Culture*. New Delhi: Sage.

Rojek, Chris. 2001. *Celebrity*. London: Reaktion.

Turner, G. 2004. *Understanding Celebrity*. London: Sage.

*Cross references*

"**Actor**" by Mee; "**Cindy Sherman's Real Fakery**" by Schneider; "**Cultural production**" and "**Media**" by Colleran; "**Feminist hip-hop fusion,**" by Hodges Persley; "**Identification/dis-identification**" by Muñoz.

## Cultural production

Jeanne Colleran

The study of cultural production involves an investigation into the processes by which products (goods, artifacts, art forms, visual and experiential objects, related services) are created, diffused, and used as part of the constitution of consumer culture. Because the culture industry has so affected everyday life that it is no longer possible to think of "art" and "life" as separate from each other, cultural products become sites and occasions through which questions of identity, power, and significance are raised.

For Walter Benjamin, writing in 1936, the possibilities for art that could be mechanically reproduced and widely disseminated—film and photography were his key examples—were deeply liberatory. While the artwork's "aura" of originality would diminish, the gain in public accessibility would compensate, reversing the "total function of art." "Instead of being based on ritual," Benjamin wrote, art would be "based on another practice—politics" (1936, 23–25). Against this view, Theodor Adorno and Max Horkheimer's mid-1940s essay, "The Culture Industry" (Horkheimer and Adorno, 2007), voiced the counter argument: that mass culture would always serve the market economy, and aesthetic ideals would be subsumed by materialism. This early twentieth-century disagreement marks contentions that still inform current debates over culture and defines the field of cultural studies—of which the issue of cultural production is a major component. How cultural products are coded and how these values are disseminated (and contested) in order to encourage consumption is inherently performative.

As Fredric Jameson (1981) and Jean-Francois Lyotard (1984) have observed, launching a critique from outside late-capitalist consumer culture is impossible. However, it is not necessary to think of cultural production (or for some, a second stage, cultural *reproduction*) in the direst terms: that it always serves the interests of the ruling class or that it is always consumed passively by audiences increasingly alienated, and disempowered. Rather, as Michel Foucault maintains, power may also be thought of as both productive *and* restrictive; as open to contest *and* resistant to change (1980). With the wide access provided by the internet, modes of cultural production are less easily categorized as dominant or resistant, mainstream or alternative.

A study of cultural production, then, raises questions such as: Who are the producers? Who are the consumers? How is desire for products managed via symbols and images, and how, in turn, is ideological meaning attached to particular symbols and images? What is the relationship of cultural products to a macro-political sphere, such as national identity? How have aesthetics been politicized and politics aestheticized? How is cultural production implicated in debates about representation and appropriation?

The category of the performative is an especially valuable heuristic for understanding this implicitly ideological struggle over meaning. Interdisciplinary investigations in the social sciences—anthropology, sociology, ethnography—might examine the creation and dissemination of cultural products as a key to local knowledge. Thus, "wearing a burkha" signifies differently in Dubai than in Detroit. The performance of these identities becomes an opportunity for understanding cultural affiliations, cultural differences, and cultural hybridity—and how these might be "translated" across cultures or "collapsed" by globalizing trends. Recently, business-oriented scholarship has examined performative strategies not only as a means of increasing market gains but also because "selling experience"—selling lifestyles, from the ideal family vacation to the best wedding—has blurred the distinction between product and process. The contemporary political scene is an especially rich area for examining how performance as both cultural product and cultural process positions ideology. These investigations lead back to the anxieties voiced in the earliest debates about the cultural industry: that mass mediated images will always swamp critical judgment and resistance. One solace proffered by performance theorists, however, is that performance has the potential to demystify cultural meanings attached to cultural products and maintain a space for more self-reflexive critical judgment.

## Further reading

Horkheimer and Adorno (2007); Benjamin (1936); Jameson (1981).

## References

Benjamin, Walter. 1936. "The Work of Art in the Age of Mechanical Reproduction." In *Illuminations: Essays and Reflections*, edited by

Hannah Arendt and translated by Harry Zohn. New York: Schocken.

Foucault, Michel. 1980. *Power/Knowledge: Selected Interviews and Other Writings 1972–1977*, edited by Colin Gordon and translated by Colin Gordon, Leo Marshall, John Mepham and Kate Soper. New York: Pantheon.

Horkheimer, Max and Theodor W. Adorno. 2007. *Dialectic of Enlightenment*, Edited by Gunzelin Schmid Noerr, Translated by Edmund Jephcott. Stanford, CA: Stanford University Press.

Jameson, Fredric. 1981. *The Political Unconscious: Narrative as a Socially Symbolic Act*. Ithaca, NY: Cornell University Press.

Lyotard, Jean-François. 1984. *The Postmodern Condition: A Report on Knowledge*. Translated by Geoff Bennington and Brian Massumi. Minneapolis, MN: University of Minnesota Press.

*Cross references*

"**Global censorship**" by Shea; "**Media**" by Colleran; "**Mediaturgy**" by Marranca; "**Modernism**" by Albright, Pearl, and Speca; "**Performance in the digital age**" by Auslander.

## Drag

Sean Edgecomb

According to Laurence Senelick, the term "drag" originated as "homosexual slang" (2000, 302) in the eighteenth century, connoting the physical "drag of a gown with train." Partridge dates "go on the drag" (1953, 239) to 1850, meaning the donning of women's clothing by men who were soliciting sex. It is unclear when the term connoting gender bending was first applied to theatrical performance, though it has been used widely in the twentieth century. Drawing upon Foucaultian discourse, Butler (1988) provides a discursive feminist (re)definition of drag to include the intentional donning of any socialized garment wherein drag becomes a symbol of fluid gender as performance.

Although the etymology of "drag" is of modern origin, the practice of wearing clothes of the opposite gender is nearly as old as civilization itself. Since ancient times, tribal religions have included performative rites and rituals dependent on transvestitism, such as shamanic magic. In male-dominated societies (Classical Athens, Medieval Europe, and Elizabethan England) where women shared few social privileges and were subjugated by codes of social decency, men in women's garments played female roles in public performance. Similarly, traditional Asian theatrical forms necessitated all-male acting troupes to use transvestitism as a heightened artistic practice. These include the *onnegata* of Japanese Kabuki or the *dan* of *jingju* (Peking Opera), both forms which depend on a channeling of an idealized femininity communicated by the male performer through skills perfected over years of training.

The use of drag as a comic convention also predates modernity. The manipulative and often vulgar disguise of men as women is found both in Euripides and Aristophanes. This appropriation of drag to incite laughter became the backbone of low comedy, burlesque, and minstrelsy. Bakhtin's theory of the carnivalesque (1984) also supports a subversion of socially imposed gender norms through drag practice, whereby with costumes and masks an individual creates a new identity that replaces the old within the temporal frame of carnival.

Revolutionary progress in civil rights in the latter half of the twentieth century promulgated the dissolution of prescribed gender codes inspiring new forms of drag. The "drag queen" and other forms of drag royalty replaced male and female impersonators as performance artists who created personas based on satiric wordplay, hyperbolic extravagance, or cultural significance. Unlike a transvestite, it is not the drag queen's intention to pass as female. Postmodernist drag artists have taken this to the next level, often employing extremist and "gender-fuck" performance. Gender-fuck, or literally a self-conscious "fucking" with gender, developed out of a freedom of exploration that coincided with advancements in civil rights. The Cockettes, a San Francisco drag troupe, is credited with introducing the concept in the late 1960s.

*Further reading*

Butler (1988); Partridge (1953); Pellegrini (2007); Senelick (2000).

*References*

Bakhtin, Mikhail. 1984. *Problems of Dostoevsky's Poetics*, edited and translated by Caryl Emerson. Vol. 8 of *Theory and History of Literature*, edited by Wlad Godzich and Jochen Schulte-Sasse. Minneapolis, MN: University of Minnesota Press.

Butler, Judith. 1988. "Performative Acts and Gender Constitution: An Essay in Phenomenology and Feminist Theory." *Theatre Journal*, 40.4: 519–531.

Partridge, Eric. 1953. *From Sanskrit to Brazil; Vignettes and Essays upon Languages*. London: Hamilton.

Pellegrini, Ann. 2007. "After Sontag: Future Notes on Camp." In *A Companion to Lesbian, Gay, Bisexual, Transgender, and Queer Studies*, edited by George E. Haggerty and Molly McGarry. Oxford: Blackwell.

Senelick, Laurence. 2000. *The Changing Room: Sex, Drag, and Theatre*. New York: Routledge.

*Cross references*

"**Boychild**" by Halberstam; "**Camp**" by Pellegrini; "**Ethnic drag**" by Herrera; "**Explicit body performance**" by McGinley; "**Heather Cassils' indeterminate body**" by Jones; "**Romeo Castellucci's Hey Girl!**" by Sack.

## Ethnic drag

Brian Herrera

The term "ethnic drag" delineates performance strategies that amplify attributes of racial and ethnic distinction in order to highlight the poignancy, absurdity, artifice, and/or politics of a particular culture's history of racialized difference. The concept elaborates upon theories of race as a social construction always in formation (Omi and Winant 1994) and notions of parodic performativity (Butler 1990) to rehearse a heightened critical awareness regarding the operation of race and ethnicity in performance for both audiences and practitioners alike. As Katrin Sieg contends in *Ethnic Drag: Performing Race, Nation, Sexuality in West Germany*, "ethnic drag includes not only cross-racial casting on the stage, but, more generally, the performance of 'race' as masquerade" (2002, 2).

Ethnic drag underscores how the performative accoutrements of ethnic or racial distinction—things like accents, costumes, physical gestures and postures, as well as conventionalized social or character types—are utilized within performance to configure racial or ethnic difference. Ethnic drag sometimes revels in the spectacle of ethnic or racial surrogation, as when solo performers like Anna Deavere-Smith, Danny Hoch, and Sarah Jones "quick change" through scores of ethnically and racially distinct characters, or when Henry Higgins schools Eliza Doolittle's transformation in Shaw's *Pygmalion* (1913) and in Lerner and Loewe's *My Fair Lady* (1956). At other times, ethnic drag might be less obvious, as when a Mexican American student in the U.S. Southwest adopts an accent to portray a Puerto Rican character in a college production of *West Side Story* (1957) or dons "native costume" in order to perform in a *Ballet Folklorico* troupe. The most conspicuous examples of ethnic drag, however, are those performances wherein the racial masquerade becomes a centerpiece of the performance itself, as when television sketch comedians Eddie Murphy or Dave Chappelle perform characters in "white face," or when performance artists Coco Fusco and Guillermo Gómez-Peña simultaneously inhabit and critique performance tropes of indigeneity in their installation *Two Undiscovered Amerindians* (1992). Yet, whether offered as a critique or as a celebration, ethnic drag exploits the performance event to highlight the theatrical and aesthetic conventions that construct race and/or ethnicity within a given culture.

*Further reading*

Omi and Winant (1994); Sieg (2002).

*References*

Butler, Judith. 1990. *Gender Trouble: Feminism and the Subversion of Identity.* Reprint, New York: Routledge 1999.
Omi, Michael and Howard Winant. 1994. *Racial Formation in the United States: From the 1960s to the 1990s.* New York: Routledge.
Sieg, Katrin. 2002. *Ethnic Drag: Performing Race, Nation, Sexuality in West Germany.* Ann Arbor, MI: University of Michigan Press.

*Cross references*

"**Guillermo Gómez-Peña attempts to explain performance art to people who may have never heard of it**" by Gómez-Peña; "**Intercultural performance**" by Alker; "**Memoirs of Bjork-Geisha**" by Takemoto; "**Racialization**" by Sell; "**Transnationalism**" by Yang; "**Whiteness**" by Jones.

**Memoirs of Björk-Geisha**

Tina Takemoto

21 June 2006: Outside the San Francisco Museum of Modern Art, a crowd lines up around the building waiting for the much anticipated opening of the *Matthew Barney: Drawing Restraint* exhibition featuring Barney and his wife Björk as "Occidental guests" on a whaling ship in Japan. Rumor has it that Barney and Björk are already inside mingling among VIP members. Their fans are eager to catch a glimpse of this dynamic artstar couple.

Two heavily costumed characters arrive on the scene. Björk-Geisha wears an elaborate DIY kimono adorned with numerous flayed stuffed-animal sharks, whales, lobsters, and harp seals. Barney-Whaler dons a furry mammal suit made of synthetic human wigs, mountain climbing gear, and a small speaker set strapped to his chest. Their four-minute drag performance features lip syncing, fan dancing, and samurai whaling choreographed to Björk's song "Big Time Sensuality." For the climax, Björk-Geisha erotically sharpens chopsticks in a pencil sharpener inside her geisha wig and plunges them, harakiri-style, into a whale attached to her obi. Her death aria is followed by her "rebirth" as a dancing whale while Barney-Whaler struts to the sound of the beat.

Artist Jennifer Parker and I envisioned our guerrilla appearances as Barney-Whaler and Björk-Geisha, respectively, as an "opening interruptus" of *Drawing Restraint*. The goals of our piece were two-fold: first, to call attention to the absurd Orientalist storyline in which Westerners go to Japan to drink tea, fall in love, and turn into whales; second, to parody Björk's and Barney's cross-cultural code-switching, ethnic drag, and Art World Orientalism. We managed to perform our live piece in the grand atrium, the women's restroom, and numerous locations within the upper-level galleries. Our intervention would not have been possible without the extravagance of the opening itself. Amid the loud experimental music and Zen-themed cocktails, it was difficult for viewers and the gallery guards to determine whether we were part of the hired entertainment or not. One woman, who was clearly enamored by Barney's unique perspective on Japan, told me that I looked "absolutely beautiful" as a geisha.

This project left me with two questions. First, if a guerrilla performance takes place but it is not "legible" as an intervention until it appears on YouTube, does it still function as a guerrilla intervention? Second, was it more disappointing to make my drag debut dressed as a geisha or to be complimented for looking "beautiful" while doing it? As interventionist artists, we knew that our guerrilla tactics hovered between "protest" and "entertainment." Rather than picketing the museum or lecturing viewers, we presented short blasts of performance designed to amuse, confuse, and raise questions for the viewers. On the one hand, this strategy increased our ability to circulate among the public and perform throughout the museum. On the other hand, our performance was not fully legible as a critique during the opening itself. While Parker and I reveled in the subversive pleasure of getting away with our performance, we also learned that SFMOMA press photographers published our image in their promotional membership pamphlet. It was stunning, though not surprising, to witness how quickly our intervention could be reappropriated by the museum for its own publicity and marketing. Months later, a person from SFMOMA's education department proudly informed me that we inspired the museum to create their own drag spectacles for their Frida Kahlo and Cindy Sherman's Real Fakery exhibition openings.

The second question forces me to take a closer look at the role of Björk-Geisha and my personal experience of performing Orientalist drag. Björk-Geisha's over-the-top costuming, flamboyant expressions, and exaggerated death aria were all intended to signal humor, satire, and artifice. I wondered how anyone could have perceived this disarray of Orientalist stereotypes as an "absolutely beautiful" geisha. Couldn't this viewer see that I was using José Muñoz's strategy of "disidentification" to work within and against the language of Orientalist stereotypes in order to expose their racist and imperialist implications (Muñoz 1999, 31)? Yet, what linger for me are the more complicated feelings of outrage, complicity, and grief that I now associate with performing Orientalist drag.

The "misreading" of Björk-Geisha speaks to the instability of interventionist art practices and the risk that racial disidentification can also be read as reinforcing the stereotypes that are under scrutiny. This predicament reminds me of Spike Lee's film *Bamboozled* featuring a minstrel show in which African Americans wear blackface as a critique only to find the public enthusiastically enjoying the show. While the film clearly condemns American racism, it also shows the corrosive and debilitating effect of performing toxic racial representations. One heart-wrenching scene in the film shows the actors applying burnt cork to their faces in preparation for their minstrel roles. The application of blackface "erases" their identities and leaves one performer weeping as he repeats his stage name "Sleep 'n' Eat" in the mirror. Zeinabu Irene Davis asserts that the "actors are forced into recreating and becoming the hurtful stereotypes that eventually erode their psyche and sense of self ..." (Davis 2001, 17).

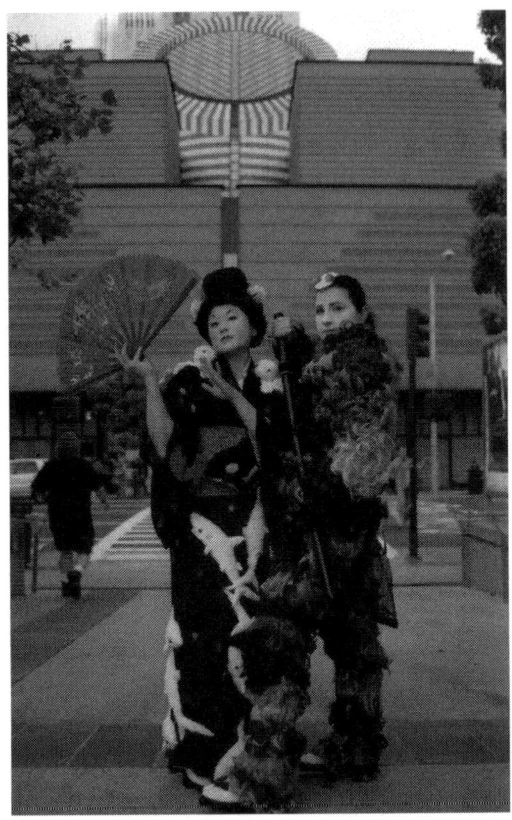

**Figure 15** Jennifer Parker and Tina Takemoto, *Drawing Complaint: Memoirs of Björk-Geisha*, performance documentation, San Francisco Museum of Modern Art, June 21, 2006. Photo by Rebecca Bausher. © Jennifer Parker and Tina Takemoto. Courtesy of the artists.

For me, performing Björk-Geisha required putting on yellowface by applying white geisha make up. The act of covering over my genderqueer self in order to embody this exaggerated stereotype of Asian femininity was more painful than I had anticipated. Unlike other personas I have taken on for performance art, this role tapped into my deepest personal struggles with Asian American femininity and forced me to recall grim moments of racial and sexual misrecognition. I do believe that our intervention was successful in terms of its ability to open up discussions on art world Orientalism. But, its playful and pleasurable mode of critique cannot erase the grief caused by embodying my own racial abjection. This sorrow reveals the fine line between the outrage over racist Orientalist fantasies and the experience of racial anguish and despair that is part of the daily lives of so many people of color in America. In "Big Time Sensuality," Björk sings out, "It takes courage to enjoy it." I wonder what future acts of courage will be required to interrupt, resist, and transform dominant representations of race and the cultural climate of art world Orientalism.

References

Davis, Zeinabu Irene. 2001. "'Beautiful-Ugly' Blackface: An Esthetic Appreciation of *Bamboozled*." *Cineaste*, 26.2: 16–17.

Muñoz, José Esteban. 1999. *Disidentifications: Queers of Color and the Performance of Politics*. Minneapolis, MN: University of Minnesota Press.

## Explicit body performance

Paige McGinley

Rebecca Schneider's wide-ranging and provocative book, *The Explicit Body in Performance* (1997), brought feminist and queer theory, Frankfurt School materialism, and critical race theory into conversation with feminist performance from the 1960s to the 1990s. Schneider investigates how and why various artists, among them "Post Porn Modernist" Annie Sprinkle, painter and filmmaker Carolee Schneemann, and the Native American company Spiderwoman, made their bodies stages upon which gendered, raced, and classed representations could be displayed, replayed, and critiqued. Such exploration of historically marked bodies and their relation to habits of viewing, Schneider suggests, makes visible not an essentialized female body, but the "sedimented layers of signification themselves" (1997, 2). Building upon Teresa De Lauretis' argument that "woman is unrepresentable except as representation," Schneider argues that explicit body performers "summon the ghosts" of historical representations in order to make visible their machinations (1997, 22). Though much of the book focuses on artistic works of the late-twentieth century, Schneider also demonstrates how feminist performance has been deeply entangled with histories of modernism and the historical avant-garde. Explicit body performance is haunted by histories of modernist primitivism, a nostalgia for the "noble savage" that the historical avant-garde located in non-white, non-Western, and female bodies. Explicit body artists "wrestle with primitivization" and its legacies, both invoking its ghost and revising its claims (Schneider 1997, 151).

Much of the explicit body performance that Schneider explores grew out of the culture wars of the 1980s and early 1990s; this period in the United States was characterized by a backlash against feminist, queer, and sex-positive art. Distinctions between art and pornography were parsed in the courts, in feminist debates, and by organizations such as the National Endowment for the Arts. The works of Sprinkle, Ann Magnuson, Schneemann, and Karen Finley underscored the paradoxes at the heart of this parsing, particularly the "binary terror" of the nude female in art and pornography (Schneider 1997, 13). Feminist artists made the body explicit, then, not only to interrogate the supposed distinctions between art and porn, but as a strategic defamiliarization of, for example, the classical female nude. Drawing upon the feminist scholarship of Luce Irigaray, Elin Diamond, and others, Schneider argues that artists of the explicit body staged themselves as both objects of a fetishizing male gaze, *as well as* the agents in this creation. With their "objectified" status destabilized by their authorship of the scene, many of these artists situated themselves in the interstices between pornography and art, highlighting the undecidability that arises when women are both commodity fetish and authors who reconstruct spectacles of desire.

*Further reading*

Cheng (1998); Diamond (1997); Dolan (1988); Jones (1998).

*References*

Cheng, Meiling. 1998. "*Les Demoiselles d/L.A.:* Sacred Naked Nature Girls' *Untitled Flesh.*" *TDR: The Drama Review,* 42.2: 70–97.

Diamond, Elin. 1997. *Unmaking Mimesis: Essays on Feminism and Theatre,* New York: Routledge.

Dolan, Jill. 1988. *Feminist Spectator as Critic.* Ann Arbor, MI: University of Michigan Press.

Jones, Amelia. 1998. *Body Art/Performing the Subject.* Minneapolis, MN: University of Minnesota Press.

Schneider, Rebecca. 1997. *The Explicit Body in Performance.* New York and London: Routledge.

*Cross references*

"**Bodies in action**" by Stiles and O'Dell; "**Boychild**" and "**Gaga Feminism**" by Halberstam; "**Cindy Sherman's Real Fakery**" by Schneider; "**Masochism**" by O'Dell; "**Performing body modifications**" by Henkes; "**Pornography**" by Shea.

## Gestus

Henry Bial

In its modern usage, the term "gestus" is usually attributed to the German playwright Bertolt Brecht, referring to a gesture, phrase, image, or sound used in performance to indicate a particular idea and attitude. Though it is rooted in the Latin word meaning "gesture," Brecht theorized gestus as something both more specific and more wide-ranging than that word usually implies. As an acting technique, gestus (sometimes translated as "gest") is a key component of Brecht's desired *verfremdungseffekt* (alienation or estrangement effect), in which the actor does not wholly subsume his or her identity into that of the character, but mediates between the character and the audience, encouraging the latter to think critically about the actions of the former.

Though a gestus can take various forms (spoken, written, musical, physical, or some combination of these), it is characterized by its brief duration and reflexive quality. Combining, in the words of John Willett, "both gist and gesture" (1964, 42), a gestus conveys elements of both story and context, both action and commentary on that action. "These expressions of [gestus]," writes Brecht, "are usually highly complicated and contradictory, so that they cannot be rendered in a single word and the actor must take care that in giving his image the necessary emphasis he does not lose anything, but emphasizes the entire complex" (1964, 198).

Subsequent theorists and directors have frequently interpreted the gestus as a kind of performative citation, a way of representing behavior "in quotation marks." As in Brecht's Epic Theatre, the goal of such a gestus is to indicate rather than imitate, foregrounding the role of the performer as interlocutor between the spectator and the character or event to which the gestus refers. Such gestic revisioning of the theatrical event is often undertaken for political purposes. As Elin Diamond writes: "because the Gestus is effected by a historical actor/subject, what the spectator sees is not a mere miming of social relationship, but a *reading* of it, an interpretation by a historical subject who supplements (rather than disappears into) the production of meaning" (1988, 90).

This type of gestus may also be seen in the work of many performance artists, especially those who take on multiple roles in a single performance (Anna Deavere Smith and Eric Bogosian) and those who emphasize narrative storytelling (Spalding Gray and Holly Hughes). The use of gestus as a performance technique allows such artists to quickly establish character changes, to communicate distanced, critical, or ironic attitudes about the characters they are portraying, and to shift their performance to a heightened, less realistic mode of acting.

Because gestus combines multiple elements of mise-en-scène into a discrete moment or action, it has often attracted the attention from scholars interested in semiotic analyses of performance, including most notably Patrice Pavis and Keir Elam. Further, because gestus is often non-verbal, many scholars use it as an example of the need to supplement text-based histories and critiques of theatre with performance-based analysis.

### Further reading

Brecht (1964); Pavis (1982).

### References

Brecht, Bertolt. 1964. *Brecht on Theatre*. Translated by John Willett. New York: Hill & Wang.

Diamond, Elin. 1988. "Brechtian Theory/Feminist Theory: Toward a Gestic Feminist Criticism." *TDR: The Drama Review*, 32.1: 82–94.

Willett, John. 1964. *The Theatre of Bertolt Brecht: A Study from Eight Aspects*. London: Methuen.

### Cross references

"**Broad spectrum approach**" by Schechner; "**Camp**" by Pellegrini; "**Mise-en-scène**" by Jannarone; "**Performativity**" by Pendgraft; "**Quotation**" by Garrett; "**Semiotics/semiology**" by Scheie.

## Glossolalia

Chelsea Adewunmi

Also known as speaking in tongues, "glossolalia" is the vocal eruption of long strings of phonemes into a spontaneously formed, neologistic language. Glossolalic performances are part of religious performance, ritualistic performance (especially those involving healing and magic), and pathologic performance, as well as experimental and avant-garde performance, such as the theatre of Antonin Artaud and the experimental music of John Cage and Meredith Monk.

In religious contexts, glossolalia complicates the boundaries between audience and performer by the addition of a third player, the divine source which has possessed the tongue, and often the entire body of the speaker as well. Believed to be a sign of the chosen people in several Christian cosmologies, the "gift of tongues" has notably been the means for women to gain power in the gendered hierarchies of the Church: it was Hildegard von Bingen's *Lingua Franca*, a complex language that came to her glossolalically which she recorded and translated, that allowed her to counsel Pope Anastasius, and it is the embodiment and intimacy with the divine in glossolalic performance that allows African American women to establish spiritual leadership in Holiness-Pentecostal churches today.

Glossolalia is also an important site for using performance critique in literary analysis, due to the glossolalic aesthetics of Dada, language poetry, and sound poetry, particularly the polyphonic sound poetry of Kurt Schwitters ("Ursonata," 1923; see Blonk 2009), lyrical compositions of Gregory Whitehead ("Everything I Know About Glossolalia," 2012), the disintegrative poetics of John Cage ("Empty Words," 1979), or even the "mumbo jumbo" of the novels of Ishmael Reed (1966). Practices of vocal improvisation such as the jazz scat or the nonsense choruses of children's songs could also be considered performance practices derived from glossolalia, for their open phonemes and a liveness aesthetic which exists in its own time.

### Further reading

Cage (1957); de Certeau (1996).

### References

Blonk, Jaap. 2009. "Some Words to Kurt Schwitters' URSONATE." In *Kurt Schwitters in Norway*. (Exhibition Catalogue), www.jaapblonk.com/Texts/ursonatewords.html.

Cage, John. 1957. "Experimental Music." Lecture, Convention of the Music Teachers National Association. Chicago.

Cage, John. 1979. *Empty Words: Writings '73–'78*. Middletown, CT: Wesleyan University Press.

De Certeau, Michel. 1996. "Vocal Utopias: Glossolalias." Translated by Daniel Rosenberg. *Representations*, 56: 29–47.

Reed, Ishnael. 1996. *Mumbo Jumbo*. New York: Scribner.

Whitehead, Gregory. 2012. "Everything I Know About Glossolalia," http://gregorywhitehead.net/2012/06/07/everything-i-know-about-glossolalia/.

### Cross references

"**Communitas**" and "**Liminality**" by Levine; "**Experimental music**" by Henkes; "**Grace notes: Meredith Monk's Songs of Ascension**" by Marranca; "**Multicentricity**" by Cheng; "**Proxemics**" by Cody; "**Rhetoric**" by Morrison; "**Transcontextual**" by Garoian and Gaudelius.

## Identity politics

Chelsea Adewunmi

First used in the Combahee River Collective's manifesto (1974), "identity politics" came to dominate critical theoretical understandings of subjectivity and personhood in the 1980s and early 1990s. Since then, much of the criticism around identity politics has fallen around issues of essentialism and authenticity, calling instead for more nuanced epistemologies of what defines group membership and the political strategies of marginalized individuals. Performances such as Coco Fusco and Guillermo Gómez-Peña's *Two Undiscovered Amerindians Visit ...* (1992), Stew's *Passing Strange* (2006), and Annie Sprinkle and Elizabeth Stephens' *Love Art Lab* (2003) all redefine the workings of identity within dominant institutions (such as museums and the church). Adrian Piper's *Cornered* (1988) critiques the visual epistemology of perceived identity, Greg Tate's *Black Rock Coalition* (1985) redefines performances of aural blackness, and the Third World Gay Revolution resists the "we" of homonormative agendas for a more inclusive queer utopic politics (Muñoz 1999, 20).

Sites of performance inquiry into identity politics include minstrelsy, passing, Afro-futurism, hybridity, affect, non-traditional casting, queer futurity and utopias, intersectional feminisms, gender identity, and psychoanalytic theory. Judith Butler's work on the performativity of gender, Eve Sedgwick's founding theories on queer sexuality, and José Muñoz' theories of disidentification and queer utopia have proved invaluable for understanding the history and future of identity in performance theory. More recently, identity politics has also come to include post-identity studies. Stemming from Thelma Golden's exhibit *Freestyle* (2001), post-black art and performance is not without or after race; rather, it resists the idea of authentic or essential Black art, in favor of a more expansive and individually focused definition.

### Further reading

Anzaldúa (1987); Muñoz (1999).

### References

Anzaldúa, Gloria. 1987. *Borderlands, La Frontera: The New Mestiza*. San Francisco: Aunt Lute Press.

Combahee River Collective. 1974. "The Combahee River Collective Statement." http://circuitous.org/scraps/combahee.html

Muñoz, José Esteban. 1999. *Disidentifications: Queers of Color and the Performance of Politics*. Minneapolis, MN: University of Minnesota Press.

### Cross references

"**The d/Deaf Performative**" by Pendgraft; "**Ethnic drag**" by Herrera; "**Guillermo Gómez-Peña attempts to explain performance art to people who may have never heard of it**" by Gómez-Peña; "**Identification/dis-identification**" by Muñoz; "**Memoirs of Björk-Geisha**" by Takemoto; "**The Muslim performative**" by Barlas; "**Postcolonial performance inquiry**" by Chatterjee.

## *Weights*–an excerpt

Lynn Manning

Preface:

The following excerpt is taken from Lynn Manning's autobiographical solo performance piece, *Weights* (2001), which he composed after he was shot and blinded at the age of 23 by a stranger in a Hollywood bar in 1978. As a front-page article in *Los Angeles Times* puts it, "Thirty-six years after the shooting, Manning is a vital part of Los Angeles' cultural landscape: a poet, actor and playwright whose work leans on sharp perception and unflinching social commentary" (Streeter 2014). Manning's artistic work demonstrates the expressive agility of "self performance" (Cheng 2001) in facilitating an artist's identify-formation. It also illustrates how a creative agent's so-called "disability" often initiates a performative process of acquiring alternative abilities. A performer who shares these alternative abilities with a witnessing public further reveals that art-making is always already a communal project, as Carrie Sandahl vividly recalls her experience as an audience member in a production of *Weights* at the Kennedy Center's Millennium Stage on 14 June 2003:

> While even the most bare-bones solo performances rely on some collaboration with others, they tend to downplay or hide their support structures. Manning's piece, though, made visible a whole network of people needed to perform a "one-man" show, even before the performer set foot on stage. On that night, the audience of about four hundred people included at least one hundred fifty from the disability community, with its variety of accessibility needs. Downstage right, an American Sign Language (ASL) interpreter perched on a stool, waiting. At the edge of downstage left was a long rectangular screen ready to display real-time captioning of Manning's words for the hard of hearing. In an elevated box seat situated house left was an audio describer, a person wearing a headset and ready to describe the visual aspects of the performance for those with visual impairments [...] Neat rows of chairs with clearly delineated empty spaces meant for wheelchair users morphed into hodge-podge clusters as the audience rearrange chairs to fit the bodily configurations of particular social groupings. Aisles were adjusted to make room for crutches, canes, large power wheelchairs, and service dogs.
> [ ... ] It was a fire marshal's nightmare.
>
> (2004, 579-580)

The morning after the shooting, I awake in the Los Angeles County USC Medical Center. My left eye is heavily bandaged. That's where the bullet entered. My right eye is bruised blue/black and feels about to pop from its socket. The right side of my face and head are swollen and cramped with pain, but there's no bullet exit wound. This is a source of real distress for the doctors. It's why they keep having me squeeze their fingers–they're testing for brain damage. It's also why they REFUSE [to give] me anything for the pain.

I slowly become aware that something's terribly wrong. There's this nebulous fog of colors swirling before my eyes. Whenever someone enters the room, a reddish silhouette appears amidst the fog. If more people enter, more silhouettes appear. No matter what the people in the room are doing, these silhouettes stand stark still. If I lie back in bed, they remain before my eyes. When I squeeze my eyes shut, the apparitions are still visible. It's not until the last visitor leaves the room that they slowly dissolve into the fog. I'm both fascinated and terrified by these visions, but I don't tell a soul about them.

After surgery comes the medicine. Alone in my room and cruising on painkillers, I discover I can manipulate the colors in my mental canvas. I quickly progress from childlike finger paintings in primary colors to near photographic renderings of places and faces. It's a pleasurable distraction, but is this blindness or madness?

You see, as far back as I can remember, it's been my dream to be a freelance artist–ultimately, an expatriate painter in Paris.

I had even taken high school French toward that end.

[...]

I was also a firm believer in Murphy's Law: "Anything that can go wrong, will go wrong." So, back when I was 18, I had asked myself, "What's the worse possible thing that could happen to you?" My answer had been, "To go blind." Now, I had heard of blind people doing some pretty incredible things, but painting was definitely not one of them. Since the literary arts had always been my second love, I decided, if I was ever forced to throw away the paintbrush and charcoal stick, I would fearlessly pick up the pen.

I had also prepared for blindness in another way. I began secretly doing everyday tasks in the dark or with my eyes closed: dialing the phone, tying my shoes, washing the dishes. Now, sitting in this hospital bed, in a constant state of hallucination, I am terrified that my blindness is hysterical. Am I subconsciously fulfilling my own morbid prophecy?

My surgeon, Dr. White, finally gets around to delivering a medical verdict.

(As Dr. White)

"Mr. Manning, we removed what remained of your left eye. We were also able to eliminate the possibility of brain damage. Regarding your right eye, well, the bullet totally severed the optic nerve. There's nothing we can do to re-attach it."

Something akin to joy surges through me. It must be obvious because Dr. White asks, "You do understand what I'm telling you Mr. Manning?"

[...]

(Lynn)

"Well, at least I'll still have my good looks."

While Dr. White was delivering what was supposed to be devastating news, my sister, Dorothy, and my mother, Moms, were waiting in the hallway. Dorothy told me later that the doctor told them that my behavior was abnormal and I'd bear close watching for a while.

Dr. White isn't the only person to plant such concerns. The hospital's psychiatric social worker strongly suggests to my visitors—right in front of me—that I not be left alone once released from the hospital. This kind of talk gets everyone around me so anxious and depressed that I spend most of their visits trying to cheer them up.

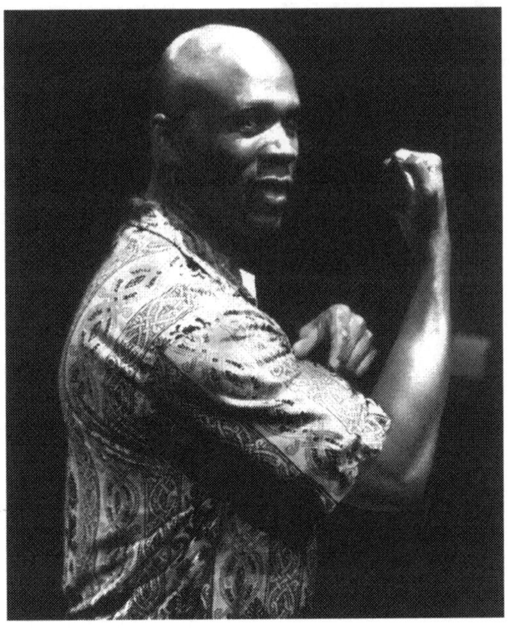

**Figure 16** From Center Theatre Group's 2001 production of *Weights* at The Actors' Gang, Hollywood. Photo by Craig Schwartz. Image courtesy of the artist.

[...]

Past experiences with family and foster homes had made me leery of being dependent on anyone but myself, so, I set out to reclaim my independence as quickly as possible. Toward that end there was much bureaucratic boogaloo: plenty of crowded waiting rooms, much paper work, and several "initial denials of service."

Moms, Mandy, Mandy's two kids and I eventually find ourselves in the offices of the State Department of Rehabilitation. After inviting Moms and me into her office, Mrs. Hereford, my rehab counselor, says,

(As Mrs. Hereford)

"I'm really surprised to see you here so soon after your accident, Mr. Manning. It's only been, what? Three weeks?!"

(Lynn)

"I want to take control of my life as quickly as possible."

(Hereford)

"Mr. Manning, after a loss such as yours, there's a grieving process that occurs. With some people it takes years."

(Lynn)

"I don't need to grieve the loss of my sight. I already accept it. That's why I'm here."

(Hereford)

"Look, Mr. Manning, I'm legally blind, myself. I know the challenges you have to face out there."

[...]

(Hereford)

"You may not want to believe me, Mr. Manning, but the grieving process is real. You *will* go through it; if not now, then a year from now. Then all that we'll have invested in you will go to waste."

Back at the apartment Moms says,

(As Moms)

"You really should slow down, Honey. You should be takin' it easy like that rehab counselor said."

(Lynn)

"Screw Mrs. Hereford. If you don't fit their little cookie cutter profile, they can't do a damn thing for you. Who's spoze to take care of business while I'm takin' it easy? I gotta do for my damned self."

[...]

I storm into my bedroom to do some private bitching about how some people can't be satisfied until you "hulk-out" on their asses. I hear Moms out there on the phone, telling Dorothy it's finally happened.

A laugh tries to well up out of me. I think, "Maybe this little outburst will satisfy the nay sayers. Maybe now, Moms and whoever she tells about this will sweep up these damned eggshells."

[LIGHT AND SOUND TRANSITION INTO POEM, *WEIGHTS*]

Yesterday, she said,

"I couldn't be so strong if it happened to me."

"You have to lift weights," I quipped.

She laughed, and tapped me on the bicep.

[...]

[TRANSITION TO STORY LIGHT]

My experience at the Braille Institute was completely different from the Department of Rehabilitation. [...] My first classes would be Braille reading, Braille writing, and Techniques of daily living. This last covered: how to differentiate money, label clothing–that kind of stuff. I couldn't wait to get started!

Late in January I received the most priceless service the Braille Institute has to offer: Orientation and Mobility instruction.

[...]

My O. and M. instructor was Tom Rotuno. The first time he came out to the apartment, he brought with him my official white traveling cane.

(Lynn retrieves a folded white cane.)

For three months, I hadn't been anywhere without my hand on somebody's shoulder. I was more than ready to walk alone.

[SOUND CUE: VOICE OVER]

Out on the street, Tom shows me the basic cane technique.

*(Demonstrates as he speaks)*

The trick is to extend the cane out in front of me, centered with my body–like this. Grip the handle, not too tightly, palm up, elbow out-like this. Now, with just the movement of my hand and wrist, tap the cane from side to side–like this. The intent is to check or clear the space in front of me as I walk. [...] Now I've got to add this strange rhythm to my walk. I'm supposed to tap left, when I step with my right foot; and tap right, when I step with my left. Like this: tap left, step right. Tap right, step left. Tap left, step right. Tap right, step left. It feels a little dorky at first, but I catch on. I've got natural rhythm. I'll figure a way to make it look cool later.

Tom says, "Ok, let's walk to the corner."

I take off and hit something immediately. "Damn." I make an adjustment and take of again. I hit something to the other side of the sidewalk. "Double damn." I repeat this several times and I'm getting pissed. "Why the hell can't I walk straight?" I stop.

*(Exhales, frustrated)*

Tom's been following, a few steps behind. He catches up, saying, "What's wrong, Lynn?"

"I can't walk straight. I keep hitting things with the cane."

Tom says, "That's what the cane is for. When you hit something, you know where it is."

[END OF VOICE OVER]

I made wondrous discoveries every time out. A whole new way of knowing the world was opening up to me, and I couldn't absorb it fast enough: through my ears, through my nose, through my feet, through my pores! Light and shadow took on physical dimensions, became solid bands of heat and coolness that swiped at me as I passed. As cars cruised by, I began to appreciate the Doppler effect of sound: the way it swells when near, and diminishes to a vanishing point in the distance. And the smells! Good God! The smells! Who knew such sensory lushness existed in this, more immediate realm. Blind people knew. Blind people had to have known all along.

[LIGHT AND SOUND TRANSITION TO POETRY LIGHT]

(Poem: THE MAGIC WAND)

Quick-change artist extraordinaire,
I whip out my folded cane
and change from black man to blind man
with a flick of my wrist.
It is a profound metamorphosis–
From God gifted wizard of roundball
dominating backboards across America,
To God-gifted idiot savant
pounding out chart-busters on a cockeyed whim;
From sociopathic gangbanger with death for eyes
to all-seeing soul with saintly spirit;
From rape deranged misogynist
to poor motherless child;
From welfare-rich pimp
to disability-rich gimp;
And from "white man's burden"
to every man's burden.
It is always a profound metamorphosis.
Whether from cursed by man to cursed by God;
or from scripture condemned to God ordained,
My final form is never of my choosing;
I only wield the wand;
You are the magicians.

References

Cheng, Meiling. 2001. "Highways, L.A.: Multiple Communities in a Heterolocus." *Theatre Journal*, 53.3: 429–454.

Sandahl, Carrie. 2004. "Black Man, Blind Man: Disability Identity Politics and Performance." *Theatre Journal*, 56.4: 579–602.

Streeter, Kurt. 2014. "Tragedy Shapes a South L.A. Playwright's Artistic Life." *LA Times*, November 14. http://www.latimes.com/local/great-reads/la-me-c1-lynn-manning-20141114-story.html#page=1

## Identification/dis-identification

José Esteban Muñoz

In their invaluable reference source book for the discourse of psychoanalysis J. Laplanche and J.-B. Pontalis offer a useful definition of what the term identification meant for Sigmund Freud: "In Freud's work the concept of identification comes little by little to have the central importance which makes it, not simply one psychical mechanism among others, but the operation itself whereby the human subject is constituted" (Laplanche and Pontalis 1973, 206). Identification is much more than a process known as spectatorship. Instead, it is about how the reception of the world outside the self is ultimately self-constituting. After Freud there were various adjustments to the term in the work of other prominent psychoanalytic theorists, such as Melanie Klein and W.R. Bion. Klein offers a notion of projective identification, while Bion further refines her mode of emphatic projective identification. Michel Pêcheux, a linguist/philosopher inspired by the work of Louis Althusser, pioneered the concept of "disidentification." Althusser's term describes what a subject does through language to counter dominant ideology.

In performance studies, the term "disidentification" has been useful to describe minoritarian or subaltern identity constitution. This alternative form of engagement can be characterized as performing a distinctly queer subject position in its anti-normative, innovative erotics. In *Disidentifcations: Queers of Color and the Performance of Politics*, José Esteban Muñoz describes "the work of disidentification" *queerness' labor*: the imaging and enactment of a mode different from the material conditions of the present (1999). Disidentification is a utopian endeavor that allows us to redeploy the past for the purposes of critiquing the present and imagining queer futurity. *Disidentifications* recognizes work that attempts to neither identify nor reject material and psychic sites within dominant culture. Disidentification simultaneously works on, with, and against dominant ideological structures. This work happens on various levels. Most importantly this occurs on the level of everyday life. The process of disidentification denotes the multiple ways in which people of color, queers and other minoritarian subjects negotiate and survive hostile environments.

*Further reading*

Freud (1933); Muñoz (1999).

*References*

Freud, Sigmund. 1933. *New Introductory Lectures on Psycho-analysis*. New York: W.W. Norton.

Laplanche, Jean and Jean-Bertrand Pontalis. 1973. *The Language of Psycho-analysis*. London: Hogarth.

Muñoz, José Estaban. 1999. *Disidentifications: Queers of Color and the Performance of Politics*. Minneapolis, MN: University of Minnesota Press.

*Cross references*

"**Boychild**" by Halberstam; "**Ethnic drag**" by Herrera; "**Gyrl grip**" by Máire and Newman; "**Identity politics**" by Adewunmi; "**Intercultural performance**" by Alker; "**Memoirs of Björk-Geisha**" by Takemoto; "**Performativity**" by Pendgraft; "**Postcolonial performance inquiry**" by Chatterjee; "**Reception theory**" by Mee.

## Masochism

Kathy O'Dell

When, in the nineteenth century, Léopold von Sacher-Masoch wrote erotic novels that were thinly disguised accounts of his relationships with women who agreed to inflict sexually arousing pain upon him, he did not anticipate that his name would become the root for the word "masochism," a term first used as underground code among its practitioners (Cutler 2003, 100). Psychologist Richard von Krafft-Ebing codified masochism as a "general pathology" in his *Pyschopathia Sexualis* (1886/1894, 89), and by 1905, Sigmund Freud had theorized that a pain-pleasure symbiosis fueled both masochism and sadism (1905). Freud's convincing theories and analytic methodologies linking pain and pleasure, often imagined in equal measure, rose to near-truth over subsequent decades.

During World War II, psychoanalyst Theodor Reik problematized such thinking in "Masochism in Modern Man" (1941), positing the key elements of masochism as fantasy, suspense, demonstration, and provocation. Reik concluded that masochism "undoubtedly constitutes a cultural step ahead when the masochist, faced with the necessity to choose, prefers to be hit rather than to hit" (1984, 366). In 1967, Gilles Deleuze further defined the type of agreement that facilitated masochism in Sacher-Masoch's own relationships and those of his characters, including Severin and Wanda in *Venus in Furs*: it was the contract (1967). In citing the contract as central to masochism, Deleuze extended Reik's social and moral approach to the subject to include its legal and ethical dimensions, thereby enabling historians of masochism in performance—works by artists who took their bodies to extreme physical and psychical limits—to consider such actions from new perspectives. This development was especially timely, as body art crested in the early to mid-1970s, the same period that witnessed the first translation of Deleuze's 1967 book into English in 1971; Grant Gilmore's 1974 book *The Death of Contract*, in which he observed a shift in courtrooms from "what was said" in legal agreements to "what was meant" (1974, 41); and the protracted crisis of the sadistic war in Vietnam, in which the distance between media representation and truth proved to be vast.

Deleuze's useful phrase "masochistic contract," considered in the historical contexts of war, semantic shifts in legalese, and traditions of psychoanalysis, helps to analyze extreme performances of the period: Gina Pane's stamping out flames with her bare feet (*Nourriture, actualités télévisées, feu*, 1971); Chris Burden's inhaling water (*Velvet Water*, 1974); and Ulay's sewing his mouth shut as Marina Abramović answered viewers' questions (*Talking about Similarity*, 1976). Such examples are less about shock and more about the bond between artist and viewer, who together instigate and allow the self-infliction of pain to occur. These pieces hold viewers—even at today's historical remove—tacitly responsible for the actions performed (O'Dell 1998). The same holds true for contemporary masochistic performance. The work of artists like Ron Athey and others shows how the phenomenon of pain in the masochistic contract unveils the strongest, most confounding, ethical and even spiritual bonds among those who enter into its agreement. The ebbs and flows of masochism in performance often parallel the tempos of socio-political tensions in the world, exposing webs of agreement that make pain possible, and require its ontology to be explored.

### Further reading

Cutler (2003); O'Dell (1998).

### References

Cutler, Bert. 2003. "Partner Selection, Power Dynamics, and Sexual Bargaining in Self-Defined BDSM Couples." PhD diss., The Institute for Advanced Study of Human Sexuality.

Deleuze, G. 1971. *Masochism: An Interpretation of Coldness and Cruelty*. Translated by Jean McNeil. New York: Braziller, Originally published 1967 as *Présentation de Sacher-Masoch*. Paris: Editions Minuit.

Freud, Sigmund. 1905. "Three Contributions to the Theory of Sex." In *The Basic Writings of Sigmund Freud*, ed. A.A. Brill. Reprint, New York: Modern Library, 1938.

Gilmore, Grant. 1974. *The Death of Contract*. Columbus, OH: Ohio State University Press.

Krafft-Ebing, Richard Von. 1886. *Psychopathia Sexualis*. Translated by Charles Gilbert Chaddock. Reprint, Philadelphia, NJ: F.A. Davis Co., 1894.

O'Dell, Kathy. 1998. *Contract with the Skin: Masochism, Performance Art, and the 1970's*. Minneapolis, MN: University of Minnesota Press.

Reik, Theodor. 1941. *Masochism in Modern Man*. Translated by Margaret H. Beigel and Gertrud M. Kurth. New York: Farrar & Rinehart.

Reik, Theodor. 1984. "Masochism in Modern Man." In *Of Love and Lust: On the Psychoanalysis of Romantic and Sexual Emotions*. New York: Farrar, Straus & Giroux.

### Cross references

"**Destruction art**" by Stiles; "**Endurance performance**" by Klein; "**Explicit body performance**" by McGinley; "**He Yunchang's limit acts**" by Cheng; "**Marina Abramovic's durational opus**" by Carr; "**Performing body modifications**" by Henkes.

## Performing body modifications

Andrew J. Henkes

On the evening of 29 June 2013, spectators descended past rows of empty seats to a small theatre stage at Stanford University for Ron Athey's third installment of the *Incorruptible Flesh* series: *Messianic Remains.* In the center of the stage, they found Athey lying naked and unmoving upon a slatted steel table. Saline injections had swollen his scrotum to the size of a grapefruit, and screws secured a black Pharaonic beard made of wood or plastic to the flesh of his chin. A silver baseball bat protruding from between the slats and into his anus locked his body into place, while hooks that penetrated his cheeks and eyebrows pulled his facial skin upwards toward a metal bar behind his head. The spectators, now participants, gathered around his form, bearing witness to his Christ-like suffering. Accepting the white latex gloves and petroleum jelly offered by the two attendants, many stroked and comforted him, ultimately causing his skin, crisscrossed with tattoos of geometric patterns and mystic symbols, to glisten under the stage lights.

Performing without moving, Athey relies upon his body modifications to tell the story of the titular messianic remains. His body calmly endures pain that seems beyond what mortals can handle, and cites symbols of divinity: super-virility in his enlarged manhood, and eternal vigilance in his unblinking gaze (achieved with the hooks). The pharaoh's beard and tattoos complemented the body's larger-than-life elements with symbols of mystical traditions, evoking the Holy Land, ancient sarcophagi, and even a royal corpse in state. He performed multiple liminal dualities in those minutes: living flesh and bodily remains, mortal subject and divine object. Through this ritual of suffering, Athey invited the audience to ponder the intersection of the sacred and the profane, as well as the relationship between the performance of martyrdom and the revelation of wisdom.

Athey is one of many body artists whose work interrogates the social and physical limits of the flesh. Body artists challenge theatrical conventions by

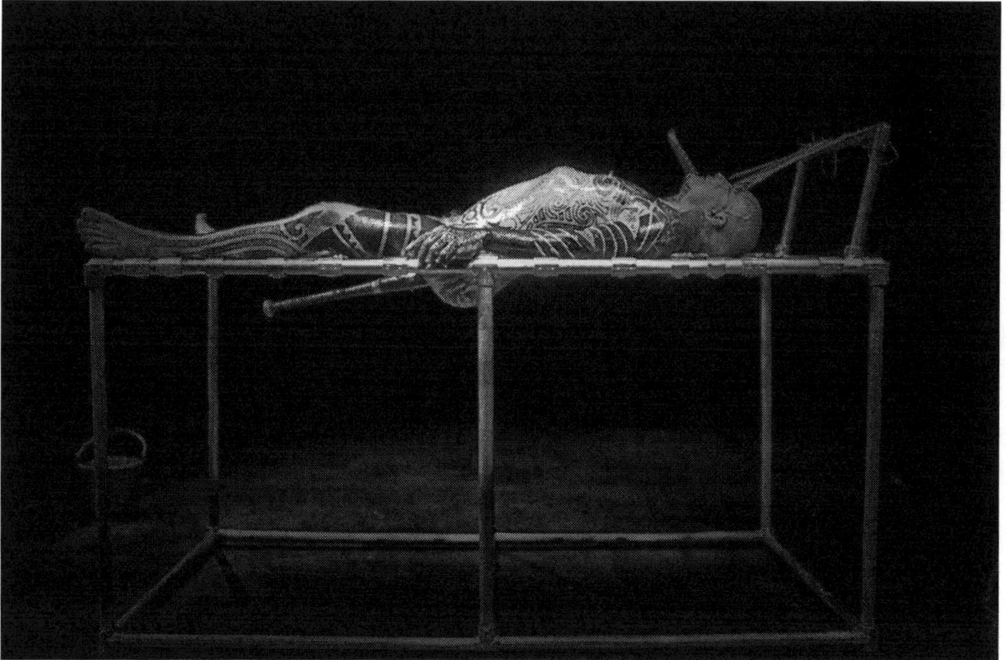

**Figure 17** Ron Athey in *Messianic Remains* (2013). Photo Credit: Jamie Lyons. Courtesy of the photographer.

eschewing illusion in favor of actuality–in body art the blood is real and pain truly is felt. Athey literally goes deeper in realizing his messianic role by puncturing and enflaming his flesh rather than simply decorating the surface, compelling stronger emotional (and even physical) responses from his spectators by denying them the comfort of knowing his suffering to be feigned. His performances transgress and challenge normative stigmas against penetrating the skin, especially in the age of AIDS. These artists confront their audiences in Artaudian spectacles of violence not only with blood normally hidden inside, but also with pain that, as Elaine Scarry argues, cannot be verbalized.

While Athey portrays characters in theatrically demarcated spaces, French artist Orlan blurs the line between art and life through the transformation of her own face in *The Reincarnation of Saint Orlan*. Through nine cosmetic surgeries starting in 1991 over the course of five years, Orlan acquired the individual facial features of the women of famous European paintings, such as Venus' chin from Botticelli's *The Birth of Venus* and Mona Lisa's forehead in Da Vinci's portrait. Orlan staged her surgeries as titillating shows that she broadcasted live to museums and galleries. She played both the conductor and lead actor of each performance, reciting poetry and music in colorful costumes with her supporting cast of physicians performing their work on her body in the operating theatre. While the initial phase of her "carnal art" ended in the hospitals, the overall performance continues today as the artist has permanently *become* Saint Orlan, the character and actor now inseparable from one another.

Australian artist Stelarc also has made his body the locus of ongoing body modification in his interrogation of postmodern humanity's collision with technology. From swallowing robotic probes to enabling distant spectators to contract his muscles through connected electrodes, Stelarc sees technology's penetration and control of the body as inevitable. In his most ambitious project, *Ear on Arm*, he has created a flesh prosthetic grafted to his left forearm. In successive surgeries, he aims to achieve an ear made from his own flesh that will incorporate technology to enable it to "hear." The ear will automatically connect to available Wi-Fi and transmit sounds around the artist to online spectators. Moreover, through a connected receiver in his mouth working with the ear's transmitter, Stelarc hopes to be able to hear distant people in his head, his two organs thus operating in tandem as a corporeal phone (and, as his ear might hear for others, so too might his mouth speak for others). Stelarc reconstitutes the body as an object that can be rearranged and augmented through technology–as a human agent, he decides how many ears to have, and where to put them.

Body modifications serve non-artistic purposes as well. In the 1980s and 1990s, the modern primitive movement arose, with body modification experimentalist Fakir Musafar as its most vocal advocate. They embraced the scarification, tattoos and skin-stretching traditions of non-Western peoples and adopted fetish fashions such as corsets that reshaped the body. Previously, with the exception of pierced ears, body modifications had been déclassé except for sailors, prostitutes and punks. While some were body artists (e.g. Athey), most modern primitives used body modifications for self-expression–what Rufus Camphausen calls making "the invisible self visible"–seeking an individual fashion distinct from mass-produced commodities (1997, 79). Modern primitives saw modifications as tools for syncretic spiritual practices as well, mimicking rituals such as the pierced dancing of the Indian Taipusham festival to stimulate ecstatic or trance states through pain. Indeed, the ritual frame distinguished the modern primitives' practices from similar performances. For example, while both Musafar and Stelarc have pierced and suspended their bodies with steel hooks, the former overtly imitates Native American rituals while the latter uses no such cultural trappings. Thus, while body artists deploy modifications to challenge audiences' understandings of the human body, many others perform modifications as a means of elucidating the self, both probing the nature of their own flesh and as an aesthetic statement to the world.

## Reference

Camphausen, Rufus. 1997. *Return of the Tribal: A Celebration of Body Adornment*. Rochester, VT: Inner Traditions/Bear.

## Media

Jeanne Colleran

Media coverage once meant transmitting news images about significant public events. Now it has come to signify a new kind of instantaneous and ubiquitous reportage, one with unprecedented global reach and an ability to assemble a large audience not because of the importance of the event itself but because of such highly developed technologies of speed and visibility. The generation of many new media forms—from cable channels to internet sites—blurs distinctions between information, entertainment, and marketing. Within this highly performative, image-saturated public environment, theatre practitioners have sought to critique and to employ the new media, in part to understand their social determinations, in part to expand artistic resources. Thus, in Suzan-Lori Parks' *The America Play*, when the character Brazil combs through a blighted landscape looking for evidence of the father who deserted him to make his fortune as a Lincoln impersonator, he never uncovers his father's body but instead digs up a television set with his father's face filling the screen. The absent father has become a disembodied image, a media spectacle flattening familial and national history into a recorded talking head.

Parks' image of a television found amid so much social and personal detritus aptly evokes the postmodern scene envisioned by Jean Baudrillard as an "excremental" culture of "pure simulation" (1994), or by Gilles Deleuze and Felix Guattari as a mediascape of a "body without organs" (1983) Their descriptions amplify Marshall McLuhan's famous observation, "the medium is the message," (1977) by gesturing toward the influence of media on the production of knowledge, the quality of the public sphere, on social organization, global politics, subjectivity, and identity. Other aphorisms McLuhan coined, such as "if it works, it's obsolete" or "the price of eternal vigilance is indifference," give voice to some of the anxieties about a media-driven symbolic economy that is virtual, ephemeral, and performative.

These anxieties include a deep concern about access to fact and truth, about diminishing possibilities for agency and intervention, and about media's colonizing capacities. The production of desires, felt as necessities, by images connected to commodities, is an instance of the latter. Guy Debord's *Society of the Spectacle* (1967) suggests that the transaction of "pseudo-needs" is the logical effect of a public realm dominated by media. Baudrillard's provocative essays on subjects from Watergate to the Gulf War go further to posit that reality has been displaced by the hypperreal. While simulation, in effect a copy without an original, is everywhere visible in America from Disneyworld to Las Vegas, Baudrillard's darker suggestion is that simulations constitute everyday life. Hence, even the mundane becomes the emulation of an artificially produced ideal, and politics play out according to already scripted scenarios for disaster. For Paul Virilio, technology developed in disparate spheres, such as the military or biotechnology, enter the social order with largely destructive results. Virilio's emphasis on the negative impact of the technology of acceleration is part of a larger fear about how media atomizes social life, isolates individual subjects, overexposes and disperses information to the point of meaninglessness, and so blurs distinctions between the real and the apparent to such an extent that authenticity has been replaced by contrivance. In this view of media, all action is performance that is then spun into a re-performance. The prevailing mode is parody where objectivity and transparency have devolved into superficial enactments of sincerity.

Alternatively, Pierre Bourdieu acknowledges that the media are a factor of depoliticization, but maintains that a "moment of resistance" can splinter media hegemony (1993). Others emphasize the interconnectivity that new technologies enable, the access to alternative forms of information they provide, and the possibility, according to Henry Jenkins, of creating a populist participatory culture (1992). The availability of easily usable technologies, from digital technology to the Web, has made media production an amateur as well as commercial undertaking. For

N. Katherine Hayles, understanding the cultural constructions attached to virtual reality offers an important opportunity to re-think our definitions of embodiment and the posthuman (1999). For Mark Poster, discussions around emergent technologies must envisage how the new media is making deep changes in culture by restructuring social community and offering opportunities for greater self-construction (1995). Sue-Ellen Case has argued that writing on a computer screen is a performative act (2003).

Historically, multimedia performances may be traced to the optimistic view of technology associated with Italian Futurism and other avant-garde movements in the early twentieth century. Incorporating linear technologies into theatre (such as tape recordings in Beckett's *Krapp's Last Tape*) have yielded to digitalized and interactive performances. Major figures associated with multimedia performance include Robert Wilson, Robert Le Page, and the Wooster Group, and a growing number of experimental theater labs, such as the Gertrude Stein Repertory Theater, the Institute for the Exploration in Virtual Realities, and the Interactive Performance Laboratory (Saltz 2001). As these hybrid art forms continue to emerge, melding virtual, electronic, and live performances, theorists will need to rethink how to make critical and aesthetic appraisals of the new "cybrids."

### Further reading

Debord (1967); Poster (1995).

### References

Bourdieu, Pierre. 1993. *The Field of Cultural Production*. New York: Columbia University Press.

Case, Sue-Ellen. 2003. *The Domain-Matric: Performing the Lesbian at the End of Print Culture*. Indianapolis, IN: University of Indiana Press.

Debord, Guy. 1967. *The Society of the Spectacle*. New York: Zone.

Deleuze, Gilles and Felix Guattari. 1983. *Anti-Oedipus: Capitalism and Schizophrenia*. Minneapolis, MN: University of Minnesota Press.

Hayles, N. Katherine. 1999. *How We Became Posthuman: Virtual Bodies in Cybernetics, Literature, and Informatics*, Chicago and London: The University of Chicago Press.

Jenkins, Henry. 1992. *Textual Poachers: Television Fans and Participatory Culture*. New York: Routledge.

McLuhan, Marshall. 1977. "The Medium is the Message." ABC Radio National Network, Australia, June 27. https://www.youtube.com/watch?v=ImaH51F4HBw>/

Poster, Mark. 1995. *The Second Media Age*. Cambridge: Blackwell Publishers Inc.

Saltz, David Z. 2001. "Live Media: Interactive Technology and Theatre." *Theatre Topics*, 11.2: 107–130.

### Cross references

"**Celebrity**" by Nayar; "**Expanded cinema**" by Jarosi; "**Liveness**" and "**Virtual reality**" by Auslander; "**Mediaturgy**" by Marranca.

## New Media Art

Emily Ball Cicchini

The term "New Media" emerged in the 1960s with the advent of the personal computer to distinguish the new possibilities of interactive two-way mixed media apart from the one-way broadcasts of radio, television, and hard media distribution of recorded film and music. The difference was that instead of dots and dashes of the early days of the telegraph, we could now send not only characters, but eventually, sound, images, and, most recently, moving images via digital video back and forth to each other. During this time, artists began to adopt these technological tools as modes of self-expression, with labels that have included Digital art, Computer art, Multimedia art, Interactive art, Electronic art, Robotic art, Video art, Transmission art, Experimental Film, and Genomic art, and are still evolving today. Mark Tribe, whose book on the subject helped define the term, even wonders if "New Media Art" has already "run its course" as a specific artistic movement (Tribe, Reena, and Grosenick 2006). Often, scholars consider the term "media" for the social conventions that have developed around the use of mass media for non-transformative information purposes, such as news reporting and journalism. But media is also a term used by an artist to create a work, including pens, paint, chalk, metal, wood, film, video, musical instruments, and the human body. As computer devices are becoming capable of transmitting and receiving words, sound, and images with greater distance, resolution, fluency and frequency, it only makes sense for "new media" to remain a part of an artist's possible set of tools.

The pioneering video artist Nam June Paik, who incorporated video displays into his sculptures and projected moving images onto objects such as clothing in performance installations, perhaps explained it best: "Our life is half natural and half technological. Half-and-half is good. You cannot deny that high-tech is progress. We need it for jobs. Yet if you make only high-tech, you make war. So we must have a strong human element to keep modesty and natural life" (McGill 1986). This call to balance humanity with technology, and vice versa, is a charge uniquely suited for the boundary-crossing artistic pursuits.

While it is hard to put firm boundaries around New Media Art, one way to think of its possibilities is through the elements that can be created, recorded, presented and interact within a digital format: text, images, audio, video, and actions (clicks, taps, swipes, and even fuller ranges of physical human motion through sensory capture devices); then, to consider how these elements can be recombined, as single elements, or as a range of elements, and as asynchronous recorded or synchronous live display, in a confined space to a confined subscription audience, or to an open audience that ostensibly includes the entire networked world. The digital can be blended with live performance; and the presentation of material on a dynamic website presents itself as performative, as it happens uniquely for the observer at a specific time. Tribe points out that the artists that embraced early New Media Art were often influenced by Dadaism and other counterculture traditions, and included themes of corporate parody, activism, and social interventions. Along with the larger cyberculture, themes of openness, collaboration, identity masking and creation, and appropriation often appear in the work of artists who use digital media. As technology becomes more mobile and ubiquitous, the use of the digital has become part of mainstream art. The adoption of "Transmedia" techniques by the entertainment industry, such as releasing a film, video game, graphic novel, and social media scavenger hunt around a specific time and setting and set of fictional characters, points towards a different future are contemporary examples where mainstream art is fully co-opted by the for-profit entertainment culture (Scolari 2009).

Some interactive websites that exemplify the online performance experience include *Born Magazine*, *We Feel Fine*, or *Jackson Pollock*. These are sites that alter the perspectives, capture deep attention, and illuminate the human condition in a way that mimics live performance for the viewer/user (Cicchini 2013). Blurring the boundaries of real and digital life, artists such as Laurie Frick explore the notion of "Quantified Self," using the data that can be collected about bodily functions and daily activities to create collages of self-identity (Dunne 2013). Whatever the label, the range of human concepts expressible through media creatively is boundless, if contingent upon technological advances.

### *Further reading*

Cicchini (2013); Dunne (2013); Tribe, Reena, and Grosenick (2006).

### *References*

Cicchini, Emily. 2013. "New Media as Performance." *HowlRound A Journal of Theatre*

*Commons*, January 18. http://howlround.com/new-media-as-performance

Dunne, Susan. 2013. "'Making Tracks' by Laurie Frick at Real Art Ways." *Hartford Courant*, January 8. http://articles.courant.com/2013-01-08/entertainment/hc-artweek-0110-20130108_1_real-art-ways-activity-data

McGill, Douglas. 1986. "Art People." *The New York Times*, October 3. http://www.nytimes.com/1986/10/03/arts/art-people.html

Scolari, Carlos A. 2009. "Transmedia storytelling: Implicit consumers, narrative worlds, and branding in contemporary media production." *International Journal of Communication*, 3.4: 586–606.

Tribe, Mark, Reena Jana, and Uta Grosenick. 2006. "New media art." In *Taschen Basic Art Series*. Cologne: Taschen.

*Cross references*

"**Extreme performance**" by Cheng; "**Media**" by Colleran; "**Performance in the digital age**" by Auslander; "**Posthumanism**" by Nayar; "**Virtual reality**" by Auslander; "**Fluxus**" by Stiles.

## Performance in the digital age

Philip Auslander

Our daily lives are now increasingly defined by our use of digital technology, which has become a shaping force, a cultural dominant. Some uses of digital technology in performance enhance and amplify the possibilities of traditional theatrical technologies, including computer-controlled lighting systems and digital scenographic projections. However, digital technology also opens up new possibilities for performance, such as the use of telematic systems that unite performers in different locations. The United Kingdom's Station House Opera has pioneered such work. In *What's Wrong with the World* (2008), for example, performers and settings in Brazil and the United Kingdom were fused together into a single performance that took place simultaneously in both locations.

The use of digital technology in performance also has the potential to re-open fundamental questions about performance, including just what counts (or should count) as a performer and what kinds of experience constitute spectatorship. Performing robots and technological agents possessed of AI (Artificial Intelligence) are now possible, as are other kinds of virtual performers. Violinist and composer Mari Kimura has performed her piece *GuitarBotana* (2004) with GuitarBot, a robotic musical instrument created by Eric Singer. Kimura programmed the robot both to play her score and to improvise at certain points in the piece; at these moments, she responds improvisationally to what the robot plays. Inasmuch as GuitarBot behaves as an improvising musician, it can be considered a performer rather than an instrument or a piece of musical technology. Not surprisingly, there is resistance to thinking of technological agents as performers. Despite the prevalence of computer-generated (CGI) performances in film, for example, the Academy of Motion Picture Arts and Sciences has refused to consider such performances in films like *The Lord of the Rings* or *Avatar* for Oscars. Deciding whether or not a device such as GuitarBot or CGI-enhanced characters should be regarded as performers invites careful consideration of just what we understand performers and performance to be as well as of what they may be becoming.

Social theorist Alan Kirby argues in his book, *Digmodernism* (2009), that there are no longer spectators in the traditional sense because now everyone has the opportunity to create and publish their own texts and films online as well as the ability to reshape existing materials, as in mash-ups. To an increasing extent, people bring the expectation of being able to intervene actively and substantively in their experiences to bear on all cultural forms. One response has been the incorporation of audience interaction techniques resembling the voting practices of television programs such as *American Idol* and *Big Brother*, which enable the audience to determine the direction of the narrative, into live performances of dance and music. Audience members are provided with an app for their smartphones which they can use collectively to determine aspects of the productions: the lighting in the case of choreographer Jonah Bokaer's *FILTER* (2011), the placement of a rock guitarist's sound in the performance space in another case, and even the sounds being performed in still other cases. Such innovations point toward a new understanding of the audience in the digital age: as collaborators in the performance rather than just recipients of it.

### *Further reading*

Auslander (2006a, 2006b); Dixon (2007); Kirby (2009); Parker-Starbuck (2014).

### *References*

Auslander, Philip. 2006a. "The Performativity of Performance Documentation." *PAJ: Performing Arts Journal*, 28.3: 1–10.

Auslander, Philip. 2006b. "Humanoid Boogie: Reflections on Robotic Performance." In *Staging Philosophy: Intersections of Theatre, Performance and* Philosophy, edited by David Krasner and David Saltz, 87–103. Ann Arbor, MI: University of Michigan Press.

Dixon, Steve. 2007. *Digital Performance.* Cambridge, MA: MIT Press.

Kirby, Alan. 2009. *Digimodernism: How New Technologies Dismantle the Postmodern and Reconfigure Our Culture.* New York: The Continuum International

Parker-Starbuck, Jennifer. 2014. *Cyborg Theatre: Corporeal/Technological Intersections in Multimedia Performance.* New York: Palgrave Macmillan.

### *Cross references*

"**Cybernetics**", "**The Internet**" and "**Liveness**" by Auslander; "**Expanded cinema**" by Jarosi; "**Performance, postmodernism, and beyond**" by Chin Davidson; "**Posthumanism**" by Nayar.

## Performativity

Tylar Pendgraft

In a series of lectures given in 1955, J. L. Austin describes how words not only have the constative power to convey meaning, but the power to perform action as well. The most commonly cited example of Austin's is the power of the statement "I do" in a wedding ceremony: the words constitute a speech-act, carrying sufficient force to actually marry a couple rather than simply report the action (1975, 12–13).

Austin's idea of performatives depends on a set of rules that would make the action felicitous, namely a marriage of intent and context. He calls the performative that doesn't conform to these rules "unhappy," meaning that, in the context of the speech-act, the performer was insincere or the circumstances for performance would invalidate the act in some way. He uses theatre as an example of an unhappy performative, parasitic due to its citational nature. To Austin, theatre may possess context, but it lacks purity of intention.

French philosopher Jacques Derrida questions Austin's force and context binary, arguing instead that all performatives may possess a measure of citational quality because they reference pre-established meanings (1982, 326). Alternatively, Derrida proffers the idea of iterability, suggesting that the performative can break from its prior context in order to formulate new meaning, separate from its original intention. Derrida's proposal of iterability offers a means for understanding all language as performance.

As Derrida's argument exemplifies, Austin's theory of the performative becomes increasingly complicated in terms of phenomenology, queer theory and gender studies. Feminist theorist Judith Butler weighs each of these critical theories in her examination of identity construction by expanding Derrida's commentary on performative iterability from the linguistic into a paralingustic domain. Butler articulates performativity as the continuous acculturation of heteronormative ideology across the body and psyche that dictates the manner by which gender is performed. By pointing out gender as a belief separate from the facticity of sex, Butler aligns her argument with queer theory. She references the acceptability of transgender performance on-stage and unacceptability of the same performance off-stage as evidence of heteronormative indoctrination; behavioral violations are met with corrective cues meant to act as a panacea for the "other."

Andrew Parker and Eve Sedgwick further link the notion of alterity to performativity by examining what they refer to as the "mutual perversion," or queering, of performative reference and performative act (1995, 3). Building on Derrida's analysis of performative iterability as a response to Austin's introduction of the sick performative, Parker and Sedgwick investigate the "nature of the perversion" (1995, 4). Exposing Austin's heteronormative bias in his initial discussion of the sick performative, Parker and Sedgwick argue that the measure of a performative's perversion depends largely, if not entirely, on how it is received.

Parker and Sedgwick's question of what occurs on the "hither" side of the performative presupposes the presence of an audience. It is within the audience space that the perversion takes place as meaning is deconstructed and re-interpreted by those on the receiving end of the speech-act. Identity is reified through performative authority, as Parker and Sedgwick demonstrate in their analysis of "Don't Ask Don't Tell" policy hearings. The hearing itself, rather than the policy, is an active and exposed example of the ways in which the heteronormative ethos links speech to act and act to identity, reaffirming Butler's hypothesis of the performative. Within the audience space of the hearings, however, the words that link speech to identity becomes open to radical interpretation, raising more questions in regards to meaning than answering them. If the performer exerts force to re-establish uncontested performative authority, then the audience possesses the power to deny the performer authorial power of the performative. As a result the audience may radically alter the geopolitical, social and linguistic space where meaning is performed, opening new avenues for the ways identity is constituted and understood.

### *Further reading*

Austin (1975); Butler (1999); Parker and Sedgwick (1995).

### *References*

Austin, J.L. 1975. *How to Do Things with Words: The William James Lectures Delivered in 1955.* Cambridge, MA: Harvard University Press.

Butler, Judith. 1989. *Gender Trouble: Feminism and the Subversion of Identity.* London: Routledge.

Derrida, Jacques. 1982. *Margins of Philosophy.* Chicago, IL: University of Chicago Press.

Parker, Andrew and Eve Sedgwick. 1995. "Introduction." In *Performativity and Performance*, edited by Andrew Parker and Eve Sedgwick, 1–18. New York: Routledge.

### *Cross references*

"**The d/Deaf Performative**" by Pendgraft; "**Double-coding**" by Bial; "**Glossolalia**" by Adewunmi; "**Rhetoric**" by Morrison; "**Semiotics/semiology**" by Scheie; "***Weights*: An excerpt**" by Manning.

## Pornography

Megan Shea

The term "pornography" traditionally invokes literature and images intended to promote sexual arousal, but in the late twentieth century the definition widened for the purpose of censorship. Andrea Dworkin and Catherine MacKinnon have formed a "feminist" anti-porn alliance that has sought to condemn and outlaw all sexual pictures and even nude pictures of women because, according to MacKinnon, all pornography is "forced sex" that participates with "rape and prostitution" in reifying "the sexuality of male supremacy" (Dworkin and MacKinnon 1984,

325). Dworkin and MacKinnon's censorious re-envisioning of the term not only serves the interests of conservative/religious groups who wish to monitor sexual images (particularly those including homosexual acts and women), but also contradicts the work of feminist and queer performance artists who employ nudity and sex in their work to critique patriarchal representations of women.

In defense of feminist performance and against the claims of MacKinnon and Dworkin, scholars like Rebecca Schneider have made distinctions between pornography that demeans women and performance art that resists these misogynist depictions of women. Schneider does not rely on content but rather on frame to make the distinction between pornography and art: "Thus, historically, the demarcation between art and porn has not been concerned with the explicit sexual body itself, but rather with its agency, which is to say with *who gets to make what explicit where and for whom*" (1997, 20). To counter misogynist pornography and free the body from a capitalist gaze, performance artists redeploy images and language that have been used to suppress women.

Performance artist Annie Sprinkle, for example, has worked as a prostitute and a porn star in the past. In the late 1980s and early 1990s, Sprinkle transferred her sex work to performance art (Cody and Sprinkle 2001). In a variety of performances, she projected her previous pornographic films, inserted a speculum in her vagina and invited the audience to look her cervix; she brought herself to orgasm onstage and recreated oral sex on a wall of dildos. While certainly Sprinkle's work could be labeled as pornographic, how she frames her work alters the perspective from which it is viewed. Sprinkle's aim, in part, is to critique the patriarchal suppression of the sexual body by reclaiming her body in a pornographic context. It is Sprinkle's choice to make her body explicit, and she does so with control over how she is viewed.

Performance artists, especially queer and feminist performance artists, use their bodies to push back against the culture that critiques them; resistance relies on re-presenting the body, especially when that re-presentation of the body may generate controversy over whether the image is pornography. The legal parameters for what counts as pornography fall under obscenity laws. Originally, the legal litmus test for discerning hardcore, and therefore censored, pornography was, as Justice Potter Stewart famously stated in a Supreme Court brief, "I know it when I see it" (*Jacobellis* v. *Ohio*, 1964). While obscenity laws no longer restrict pornography on this basis, they have expanded the legal definition of pornography to include artistic work. Under the new obscenity laws, performance artists, such as Annie Sprinkle, Karen Finley, Holly Hughes, Tim Miller, John Fleck, Rachel Rosenthal, Veronica Vera, Carolee Schneeman, and Robbie McCauley have all used their bodies in performances that could somehow be labeled either obscene or pornographic. Exploring the binary between art and pornography opens up the discourse on the limitations of what should be construed as pornographic.

### Further reading

Cody and Sprinkle (2001); Schneider (1997).

### References

Cody, Gabrielle H. and Annie Sprinkle. 2001. *Hardcore from the Heart: The Pleasures, Profits and Politics of Sex in Performance*. London and New York: Continuum.

Dworkin, Andrea and Catherine A. MacKinnon. 1984. *Pornography and Civil Rights: A New Day for Women's Equality*. Minneapolis, MN: Organizing Against Pornography.

Schneider, Rebecca. 1997. *The Explicit Body in Performance*. New York and London: Routledge.

### Cross references

"**Bodies in action**" by Stiles and O'Dell; "**Drag**" by Edgecomb; "**Ethnic drag**" by Herrera; "**Explicit body performance**" by McGinley; "**Masochism**" by O'Dell.

# Audience

## Audience

Gabrielle H. Cody

If, as Herbert Blau reminds us, there is theory in the act of seeing, there is also theory in the role of spectating. The theatrical audience is an entity whose *competence* depends on, as Keir Elam puts it, "the ability to recognize the performance as such" (1980, 87). This competence is achieved through the creation of a frame, or the "cognitive division, and symbolic spatial or temporal boundaries" between performers and spectators (Elam 1980, 87–88). While Jerzy Grotowski famously declared that "at least one spectator is needed to make it a performance," (1968, 32), there is little disagreement that live performance "produces two way communication" (Whitmore 1994, 61) between stage and audience. But another crucial exchange of energy takes place through audience proxemics, the relations between spectating individuals.

As Blau suggests, an audience does not "exist before the play," but rather is "*initiated*, or *precipitated* by it" (1990, 25). As he recounts, when Lee Breuer and Ruth Malezcheck (the founders of Mabou Mines) were asked if they were "interested in moving an audience," Malezcheck replied, "Yes, from one place to another" (1990, 27). This answer perfectly embodies the tension between the two main audience paradigms: the Aristotelian thrust toward cathartic identification, where the audience generally remains stationary, and the anti-Aristotelian thrust away from emotional involvement in which the audience may be encouraged to take a critical, and sometimes physical stance. These two philosophies of spectatorship have defined much of western theatre history. Certainly, the theatre—and performance in general—depends on audience reception as a carefully structured event, one that is shaped by the particular ideology and dramatic or political requirements of a text, author, or auteur. In some cases, the intention is to unify an audience such that it undergoes a collective, shared experience. In other cases, audiences are intentionally fractured, and asked to accept the solitude of self-presence. In all cases, however, Blau's contention that "[g]athered in the audience [...] are issues of representation, repression, otherness, the politics of the unconscious, ideology and power" (1990, 26) elucidates the invisible psychic anatomy of the audience's outward body.

The ancient Greek *theatron*, or "place for viewing," was an outdoor amphitheatre that could hold up to 14,000 (most likely) male spectators during yearly, state-sponsored festivals (Bennett 1990/1997, 3). We know that these festivals played an important role in the development of Athenian civic life, but if women were present, they would have witnessed a mise-en-scène of iconic female characters played by men: mimesis without a gendered referent. Similarly, while the Athenian theatre was a privileged locus of speech and debate, and its audience was invited to participate through their engagement as citizens in the emergence of a democratic state, that state was also highly restrictive and exclusionary. Equally complicated were the proxemics of the Elizabethan audience, which mirrored the strong erotic and libidinal drives of theatre itself. While transvestitism still prevailed on stage, and spectators interacted sometimes boisterously with the actors while eating or drinking, strict economic hierarchies were embedded into theatre architectonics, identifying space with social rank, the "stinkards" with the pit, the nobility with the gallery.

In the West, it was only after the advent of late nineteenth-century Naturalism and the enshrining of the fourth wall that anonymity and silence, and a formal dramaturgy of appropriate behavior (such as intermittent applause) became normative for "legitimate theatre" audiences. This code of social conduct has prevailed until now in mainstream theatre, though early in the 20th century, audience passivity was disrupted by the provocative and anarchic experiments of the avant-garde. Later, the theatricalist anti-illusionistic theories of Meyerhold, Piscator, Brecht, and Boal helped to shatter the fictional stage world and re-complicate the boundaries between stage and auditorium. Much site-specific, environmental or performance art work in which the audience is asked to participate requires us to engage those around us in ways that radically disrupt conventional spectatorship. As Richard Schechner asks in the "participation" section of *Environmental Theater*: "Audience participation expands the field of what a performance is, because audience participation takes place precisely at the point where the performance breaks down and becomes a social event" (1973, 40).

Postmodern audiences are confronted with self-reflexive auteur-theatre—a theatre "about itself" as Elinor Fuchs puts it, which often disrupts an audience's cognitive process (Yamomo 2007). Here, the social, the existential and the theatrical converge (such as in Richard Foreman's phenomenological fables about the theatre of self/consciousness or Pina Bausch's painful body-parables) and an audience must "make" meaning for itself through an intensely interpretive spectatorship. Post-organic theatre (virtual, digital, mediated performance, in which the body is no longer an "organic" entity) inaugurates yet another fraught model of audience participation. Here, ontology is no longer predicated on the guarantee of bodily presence, and message maker and recipient are separated in time and space. In digital technologies that feature avatars and virtual environments, the audience may nevertheless have a significant impact on the way a performance unfolds; such a disembodied mise-en-scène creates a kind of hybrid spectator, or spectactor, a performer/spectator. Virtual theatres are increasingly popular in commercial applications (game environments and computer-generated images in film and military ventures) where they thrive on the anonymity of audience participation. Perhaps more important in relation to the meaning of performance itself is the disappearance of the human body from any frame of signification.

### *Further reading*

Bennett (1990); Blau (1990); Chaudhuri (1984).

### *References*

Bennett, Susan, ed. 1990. *Theatre Audiences: A Theory of Production and Reception*. Reprint, London and New York: Routledge, 1997.

Blau, Herbert, 1990. *The Audience*. Baltimore, MD: Johns Hopkins University Press.

Chaudhuri, Una. 1984. "The Spectator in Drama/Drama in the Spectator." *Modern Drama*, 27.3: 281–298.

Elam, Keir. 1980. *The Semiotics of Theater and Drama*. London: Routledge.

Schechner, Richard. 1973. *Environmental Theater: An Expanded New Edition including "Six Axioms for Environmental Theater."* Reprint, New York: Applause, 1994.

Whitmore, Jon. 1994. "Directing Postmodern Theater: Shaping Signification in Performance." In *Theatre – Theory, Text, Performance,* edited by David Krasner and Rebecca Schneider. Ann Arbor, MN: University of Michigan Press.

Yamomo, MeLê. 2007. "PostModern Theatre in today's world." *Theater Port,* October. http://www.theatreport.com/modules/soapbox/print.php?articleID=22

*Cross references*

"**Invisible theatre**" and "**Proxemics**" by Cody; "**Liveness**" by Auslander; "**Precarity**" by Fabião; "**Prosthetic performance**" by Gass; "**Surveillance**" by Morrison.

## Global censorship

Megan Shea

Censorship attempts to silence an individual or group who speaks, writes, acts, or creates a work critiquing a dominant regime. Censorship, therefore, is an act of discipline, in the Foucauldian sense, where discipline "dissociates power from the body," producing "subjected and practised bodies, 'docile' bodies" (Foucault 1991, 138). Censorship is also an act of performance. Through censorship, individuals are suppressed and lose the support of their audience; by making an example of the loudest nonconformist, a dominant regime may control the actions of many.

The point of censorship is to suppress opposing political consciousness inspired by activism and art. Those in power utilize taxes/fines, coercion, imprisonment, or assassination to silence the performers or those associated with them. But if the act of censorship fails to create dissociate power from the body of the person being censored, how is his/her consciousness affected? After the educational activist Malala Yousafzai gained global attention for her advocacy of women's education in the Swat Valley portion of Pakistan, the Taliban sought to silence her through assassination. A gunman boarded her school bus and shot her in the head at close range (Bryant 2013). Remarkably, she survived the assassination attempt, and the incident increased awareness of her political actions. In 2014, she became a global figure and the youngest recipient of the Nobel Peace Prize. The more her fame increased, the less those from the Swat valley, where she was shot, desired affiliation with her, because they feared the Taliban might come back into power in the region and take revenge against those supporting her (Masgood and Walsh 2013). Globally, this act of censorship failed, making those around the world more aware of Yousafzai's fight and the Taliban's suppressive force; locally, the act of censorship instilled a deep fear among the residents of the Swat valley, yielding a public receptive to Taliban politics, even if that "receptiveness" stems from intimidation.

Oftentimes moves to control an individual through intimidation provoke public rebellion. On 21 February 2012, five members of the all-female Russian punk group Pussy Riot aspired to perform in a prominent Moscow cathedral to expose the relationship between the Russian Orthodox Church and Vladimir Putin's regime. The women barely had the chance to begin their song denouncing Putin before being chased off and/or arrested (Schuler 2013, 10–11). Their defiance led to a harsh sentence: two years in a prison work camp for public hooliganism motivated by religious hatred. Their theatricality in court, however, inspired protests both within Russia and outside, garnering worldwide support for their plight (*Pussy Riot: A Punk Prayer* 2013). In this case, Russia's attempt at censorship served only to expose the realities of Putin's regime, painting Putin as the dictator Pussy Riot claimed that he was (though he eventually released the imprisoned members as part of an amnesty law established to soften Russia's image before the Sochi Olympics) (Herszenhorn 2013). Censorship does not always yield the docile bodies it attempts to create. It can mutate into an exposed fallacy, inspiring awareness of a government's attempts to restrict the art and freedom of its own people.

The Pussy Riot case is a clear-cut instance of a subcultural movement using aesthetic power to expose the regime's practices. Regimes too recognize aesthetic power and exploit it, creating a kind of implicit censorship—sponsoring artists whose work serves their politics. Thus, for a government regime, an artist can be a representation of its power. Ai Weiwei was the lead architectural consultant of China's iconic Bird's Nest Stadium, designed by the Swiss firm Herzog and de Meuron and constructed for the 2008 Beijing Olympics (Andelman 2012, 15). Ai initially represented the power of Chinese artistry, but that changed when he became critical of his involvement with the Bird's Nest, writing an article for *The Guardian* lambasting the Chinese government for driving migrant workers from Beijing during the Olympics (Ai 2008). He was further compelled to voice his critique of the government after 5,000 students died in the 2008 Sichuan Earthquake because of poorly constructed school buildings (Block 2013). Ai sought out and posted the names of the students on his blog, and China recast him as a threat (Cheng 2011, 10), shutting down the blog they originally granted him. Surveillance followed restriction, but Ai found innovative methods of resistance, highlighting the invasiveness of his surveillance by installing "his own web-cams so anyone could watch him day and night" (Andelman 2012, 15). Intent upon penalizing the outspoken artist, the Chinese government charged him with tax evasion, submitting a bill to him for 15 million yuan ($2.4 million U.S.). This act too did not dispel his fans, as he points out, "within one week, we received more than 9 million yuan {1.4 million} from 30,000 young people on the Internet" (Ai 2012, 17). While the government intended to enforce these acts of censorship as a warning to other would-be activists that unacceptable forms of art or action would receive punishment, the acts, along with Ai's brazen theatricality, transformed into opportunities that inspired others to counter with social action.

Yousafzai, Pussy Riot, and Ai all were censored by institutions notorious for restricting the freedoms of their people, but they prevailed in getting their message across locally and globally. Yet democracy can become a pretext for censorship too, as artists in the U.S. have discovered. When the House of Un-American Activities Committee started its investigations into the film industry in the late 1940s, it began to alter the consciousness of communist sympathizers in the U.S. through semantics, vowing to investigate those "unfriendly" to democracy, particularly those who wielded aesthetic power. "Friendlies," on the other hand, individuals such as Ronald Reagan and Ayn Rand, were called upon to identify the communist infiltrators in Hollywood. Ten "unfriendly" movie producers, writers, and directors appeared before the committee in 1947 and refused to answer questions about their communist affiliations. Subsequently blacklisted by the rest of the industry, the group eventually became known as the Hollywood Ten, those whose careers were halted under the guise of supporting "freedom" (Houchin 2003, 157–158). While some members of the Hollywood Ten never worked in the industry again, many of the screenwriters continued working, using others as fronts for their screenplays. When the politics of the film industry shifted in the 1960s, the Hollywood Ten were recognized by the industry and many penned memoirs of their experience that reversed the semantic values established by HUAC (Eckstein 2004, 424–425). The very act of censorship can cause dominant forces to lose their audience as politics shift—especially in an ever-changing democracy.

These cases are felicitous in that those censored exposed how dominating regimes control social practices. But the problem with any historical, epistemological, or categorical account of censorship is that our understanding of the term solely depends on voices that have survived censorship. What is tragically missing from this account (and others) is an understanding of those whose resistant voices cannot be traced or documented and remain forever silent.

### Further reading

Ai Weiwei (2012b); Cheng (2013); Reinelt (2007).

### References

Ai, Weiwei. 2008. "Happiness Can't Be Faked." *The Guardian,* August 18. http://www.theguardian.com/commentisfree/2008/aug/18/china.chinathemedia

Ai, Weiwei. 2012b. *Ai Weiwei: New York Photographs 1983–1993,* edited by Mao Weidong, Stephanie Tung, and Christophe Mao. Beijing: Three Shadows Press.

Andelman, David. 2012. "The Art of Dissent: A Chat with Ai Weiwei." *World Policy Journal,* 29: 15–21.

Block, Melissa. 2013. "In 'According To What?' Ai Weiwei Makes Mourning Subversive." *All Things Considered.* NPR, January 23. http://www.npr.org/2013/01/23/169973843/in-according-to-what-ai-weiwei-makes-mourning-subversive

Bryant, Ben. 2013. "Malala Yousafzai Recounts Moment She Was Shot in the Head By Taliban." *The Telegraph,* October 13. http://www.telegraph.co.uk/news/worldnews/asia/Pakistan/10375633/Malala-Yousafzai-recounts-moment-she-was- shot-in-the-head-by-Taliban.html

Cheng, Meiling. 2011. "Ai Weiwei: Acting is Believing." *TDR: The Drama Review,* 55.4: 7–13.

Cheng, Meiling. 2013. *Beijing Xingwei: Contemporary Chinese Time-based Art.* Greenford: Seagull London.

Eckstein, Arthur. 2004. "The Hollywood Ten in History and Memory." *Film History,* 16.4: 424–436.

Foucault, Michel. 1991. *Discipline and Punish: The Birth of the Prison.* Translated by Alan Sheridan. New York: Vintage Books.

Herszenhorn, D.M. 2013. "Released Punk Rockers Keep Up Criticism of Putin." *New York Times,* December 23. http://www.nytimes.com/2013/12/24/world/europe/member-of-russian-punk-band-reed-under-amnesty-law.html

Houchin, John H. 2003. *Censorship of the American Theatre in the 20th Century.* Cambridge and New York: Cambridge University Press.

Masgood, Salman, and Declan Walsh. 2013. "Pakistani Girl, a Global Heroine After an Attack, Has Critics at Home." *New York Times,* October 11. http://www.nytimescom/2013/10/12/world/asia/pakistanis-cant-decide-is-malala-yousafzai-a-heroine-or

Reinelt, Janelle. 2007. "The Limits of Censorship." *Theatre Research International,* 32.1: 3–15.

Schuler, Catherine. 2013. "Reinventing the Show Trial: Putin and Pussy Riot." *TDR: The Drama Review,* 57.1: 7–17.

### Cross references

"**Ai Weiwei's transnational public spheres**" by Zheng; "**Audience**" by Cody; "**Intervention**" by Olivares; "**Pornography**" by Shea; "**Surveillance**" by Morrison; "**Terrorism and performance**" by Colleran; "**Transnationalism**" by Yang.

**Ai Weiwei's transnational public spheres**

Bo Zheng

Labeling Ai Weiwei as a Chinese artist is not completely accurate. It is perhaps more productive to regard him as an international artist, who works trans-nationally–that is, across nation-states, between cultural spheres. For example, when looking at his performative photograph humorously titled *Study of Perspective–Tiananmen Square,* one would not be able to grasp the provocativeness of the work if one did not understand the hand gesture to mean "fuck you"–a western vernacular–or if one did not recognize Tiananmen, the Gate of Heavenly Peace, as the symbol of the centralized power of the Chinese state.

Ai was born in Beijing in 1957, and spent most of his youth in the remote Xinjiang Uyghur Autonomous

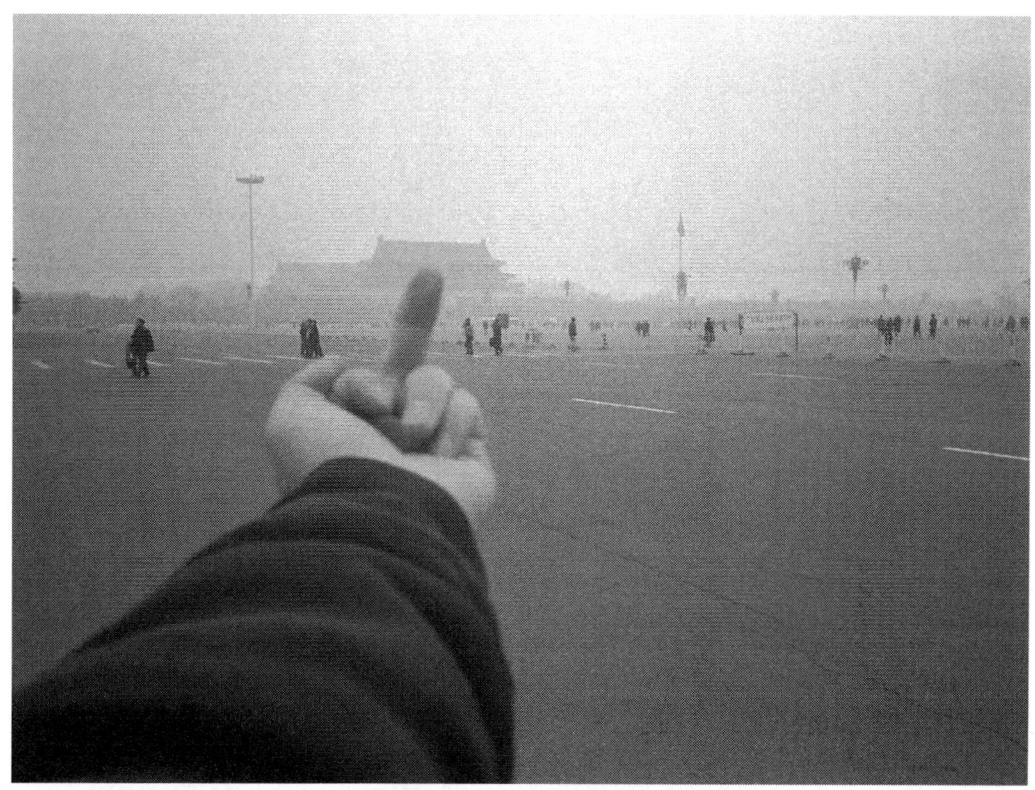

**Figure 18** Ai Weiwei, *Study in Perspective: Tiananmen* (1994). Image courtesy of the artist.

Region, where his father, renowned poet Ai Qing, was banished for "betraying" the Communist Party. Ai Weiwei came back to Beijing in 1976–after Mao died and the Cultural Revolution ended–just in time to join the burgeoning avant-garde art movement that culminated in the Stars exhibitions in 1979 and 1980 (Zheng 2012). Two years later Ai immigrated to New York, where he led a Bohemian life, photographed friends and events around him (Ai 2012b), made some installations, but never developed a distinct line of work. He returned to Beijing in 1993 and devoted himself mainly to improving the art ecology. He self-published three books on experimental art (*Black Cover Book*, *White Cover Book*, and *Grey Cover Book*, edited with Xu Bing and others), co-founded (with Hans Van Dijk and Frank Uytterhaegen) China Art Archives and Warehouse–and co-curated (with Feng Boyi) the controversial exhibition *Fuck Off* (2000) to challenge the official Shanghai Biennale.

Ai's work and life took dramatic turns in the 2000s. By 2011, he would become an enemy of the state within China, and a superstar abroad. First, Ai found his medium: the internet. He started blogging in October 2005 and published more than 2,700 entries before the blog was shut down by Chinese authorities in 2009 (Ai 2011). Initially he wrote mostly about art and architecture, and shared pictures of his cats. Realizing that the internet afforded him a following beyond the art circle, he soon migrated to politics–not the complex political issues which dominated elite debates, but dramatic events that attracted popular attention. He criticized the way that the Chinese government exploited the Olympics for nationalism, dug up materials on the Yang Jia case–Yang killed six policemen in Shanghai as retaliation for wrongful detention and physical abuse, and was sentenced to death after a closed-door trial–and called for a "Citizen Investigation" after learning

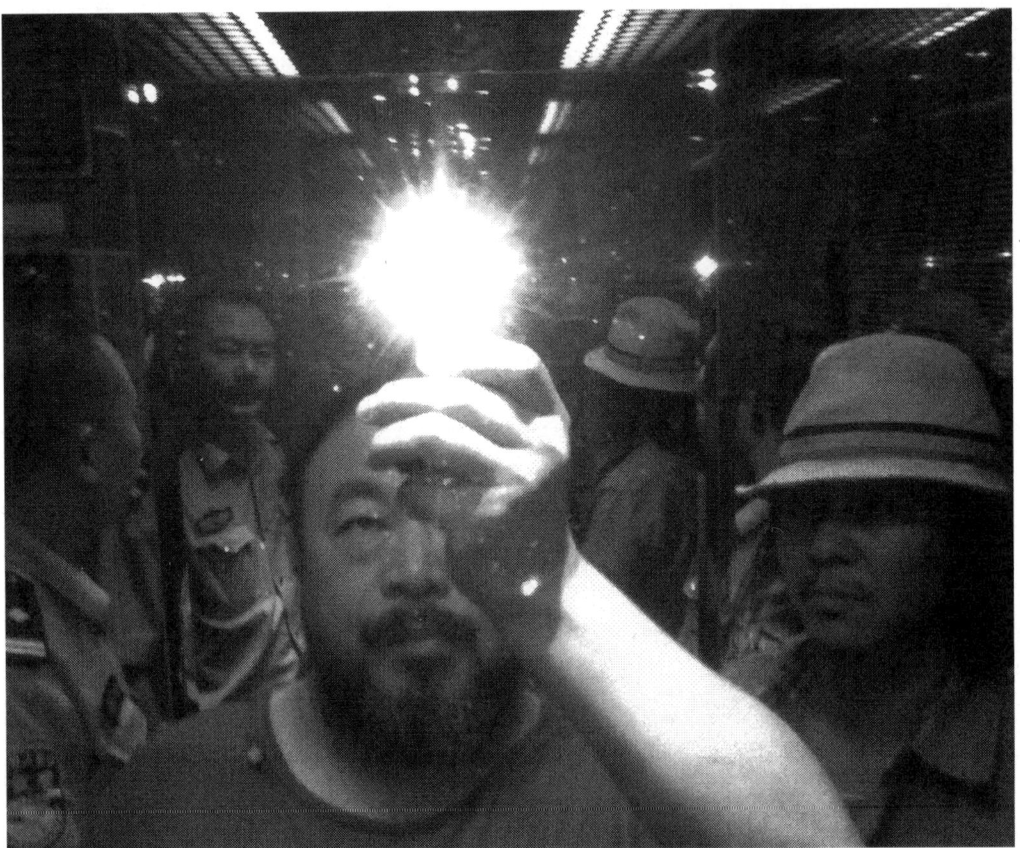

**Figure 19** Ai Weiwei and Zuoxiao Zuzhou (a rock musician) with two policemen in the Anyi Hotel elevator, Chengdu, August 12, 2009. Image courtesy of the artist.

that thousands of students were killed in the Sichuan Earthquake in 2008 as the result of shoddy construction. Unlike investigative journalists who would write up long articles at the end of extensive research, Ai reported findings as they emerged and provided brief analysis and commentaries, effectively turning his blog into live broadcasting. He wrote inflammatory pieces, attacking a wide range of evils condoned by the Chinese state, from organ harvesting to official corruption, from cultural censorship to political suppression. While other Chinese artists addressed sociopolitical issues in their practice, Ai was the only one to become an open critic and agitator.

The internet played a pivotal role in the series of actions Ai orchestrated in "Citizen Investigation," serving as both an information conduit and an organizing platform. He called upon other citizens to join him "seek out the names of each departed child" through his blog on 20 March 2009. As volunteers travelled to Sichuan to find information, Ai published their diaries detailing interactions between parents and teachers and harassment from local police. The names of the students were posted online. Although the authorities could delete Ai's blog entries, they could not completely erase information once it got online. In 2010, on the second anniversary of the Sichuan Earthquake, Ai invited people to read the students' names and email the recordings to him. Within a week, around two thousand emails were received. His assistants edited the recordings into one

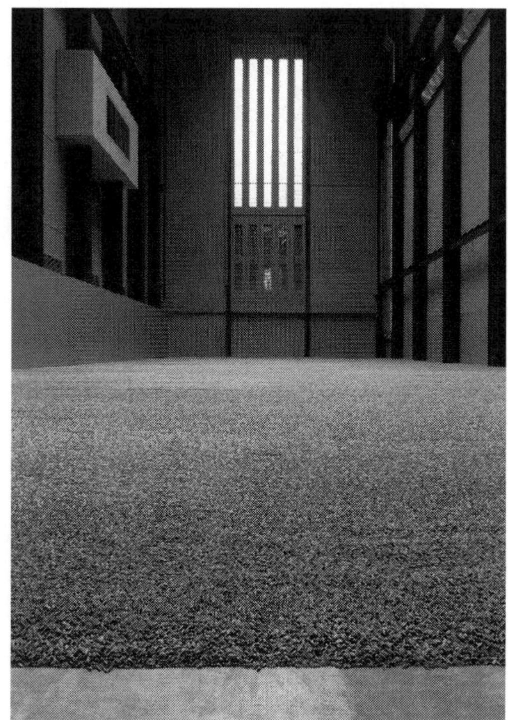

**Figure 20** Ai Weiwei, *Sunflower Seeds* (2010), installation view, Turbine Hall, Tate Modern, in The Unilever Series: Ai Weiwei (2010-2011). Tate Photography. Image courtesy of the artist.

sound file, lasting 3 hours and 41 minutes, and posted it online. This collectively-sourced sound piece was given the title *Nian*, meaning both "to read" and "to commemorate" (Zheng 2012).

Ai's media life also manifested in the form of constant visual documentation. He was often accompanied by an entourage of assistants with cameras and camcorders, and when alone, he was happy to take lots of "selfies." The most famous one was of himself in a Chengdu hotel elevator at 5am on 12 August 2009, when local police came to stop him from testifying for Tan Zuoren, another activist who accused the government of hiding information regarding the cause of student deaths (see page 142). Photos and videos served as palpable evidence of Ai's courage and defiance, and helped to transform his image–puffy eyes, short hair, long beard, casual t-shirt–into a widely recognized icon, like Warhol half a century ago. On the surface Ai resembled a peasant rebel; intellectually, he conversed like a cosmopolitan. Besides challenging state power, he also took humorous photos featuring his naked body, smashed a Han Dynasty urn, reassembled traditional furniture into geometric sculptures, and frequently used profanities. His contempt for authority, tradition, and cultural taboos was highly unusual for a man in his fifties and made him popular among rebellious youths and foreign journalists.

As the Arab Spring unfolded in the Middle East in early 2011, the Chinese government became wary of any social unrest. More than thirty activists, lawyers, and bloggers were arrested. Ai was taken away by the police on April 3. Artists and curators in the West responded immediately and vehemently, signing petitions and staging protests. Ai was released on June 22, after 81 days in detention.

In China his voice was silenced, his movements confined, and his influence curtailed. In the West, Ai gained enormous popularity. How can this disparity and the Ai Weiwei phenomenon tell us about art and performance in a physical-digital age? We tend to imagine contemporary art as a globalized field where ideas, artworks, and discussions–like the internet–circulate freely around the world, but the reality is far more complex. Although Ai lived and worked in Caochangdi, a village in the northeast suburb of Beijing, he had much more access to and presence in the West, in terms of media, art, and ideological freedom. In China, he had to resort to the internet to voice his opinions, and even this outlet was gradually taken away; in Europe, his essays and interviews were published in major newspapers. In China, he never achieved the status of a leading artist, due to both artistic and political reasons; in Europe, he was invited to participate in the prestigious Documenta exhibition in 2007, to mount a huge solo exhibition at Munich's Haus der Kunst, and in London, to create an enormous installation (*Sunflower Seeds*) in Tate Modern's Turbine Hall–both in 2010. Ideologically his relentless focus on human rights and freedom of speech aligned with the political culture in the West, but did not resonate strongly with the majority of the Chinese public, who are much more concerned with economic development than political freedom. As the Cold War ideology lingers in the China-West divide, the more Ai is suppressed in China, the more celebrated he becomes in the West.

A disturbing and contradictory aspect of Ai's practice lies in his non-media-based work: massive sculptural installations like the 1001 Qing Dynasty wooden chairs in *Fairytale* (2007), 9000 backpacks in *Remembering* (2010), and 100 million porcelain seeds–weighing over 150 metric tons–in *Sunflower Seeds* (2010). These pieces were funded by Western capital, but mass-produced in China, and shipped to the West for exhibition. Like other industrial goods made in China, they depend on cheap labor and weak environmental control. This operational condition–a defining feature of global capitalism–is integral to the same Chinese sociopolitical order Ai has so passionately criticized.

The case of Ai Weiwei suggests the urgency of transnational public spheres, in which critical engagement can help us to reflect on issues beyond the borders of nation-states. This is essential for both art and activism in the age of global capitalism.

### References

Ai, Weiwei. 2011. *Ai Weiwei's Blog: Writings, Interviews, and Digital Rants, 2006-2009*, edited and translated by Lee Ambrozy. Cambridge: MIT Press.

Zheng, Bo. 2012. "From *Gongren* to *Gongmin*: A Comparative Analysis of Ai Weiwei's *Sunflower Seeds* and *Nian*." *Journal of Visual Art Practice*, 11. 117-123

## Double-coding

Henry Bial

The term "double-coding" refers to the phenomenon whereby a performance can carry one meaning for a certain portion of its audience, while bearing a distinct (though not necessarily contradictory) meaning for another portion of the audience. Though this term was used by Charles Jencks as early as 1977 to describe postmodern architecture, its application to performance is attributable to Henry Bial's *Acting Jewish* (2005), which explores how Jewish identity may be communicated through performances which have little or no explicit Jewish content.

As a concept, double-coding draws on the postmodern recognition that meanings in performance are multiple and contested, but suggests that spectators' ethnic and cultural backgrounds significantly shape the parameters of their interpretation. "While theoretically there are as many variant readings of the performance as there are spectators," writes Bial, "in practice readings tend to coalesce around certain culturally informed subject positions: a 'Jewish' [in-group] reading, and a non-Jewish or 'gentile' [general public] reading" (2005, 16). Drawing on shared cultural knowledge between artists and audience, double-coding offers the minoritarian spectator an opportunity for self-recognition that does not preclude other audience members from similarly identifying with the performance.

In this way, the concept of double-coding is distinct from the phenomenon of double-consciousness, as articulated by W.E.B. Du Bois with respect to African-American identity. For Du Bois, the "sense of always looking at one's self through the eyes of others," limited freedom of expression for oppressed peoples, forcing African-American performers of his era to encode their resistant messages in techniques such as parody and "signifying" (1903, 8). While such performances did carry multiple, culturally specific meanings, the white audience was neither encouraged nor able to identify with the performers. Thus while Bial's model of double-coding is potentially applicable to any *identity* group, it is perhaps more useful when analyzing performances of identities whose difference from the norm is less readily visible (e.g. Irish or queer identity), as it helps explain why some performances that minoritarian audiences feel speak uniquely to their own experience are nevertheless hailed as "universal" by the general public.

*Further reading*

Bial (2005); Krasner (1997).

*References*

Bial, Henry. 2005. *Acting Jewish: Negotiating Ethnicity on the American Stage and Screen*. Ann Arbor, MI: University of Michigan Press.
Krasner, David. 1997. *Resistance, Parody and Double Consciousness in African American Theatre, 1895–1910*. New York: Palgrave Macmillan.
Du Bois, W.E.B. 1903. *The Souls of Black Folk*. Reprint, New York: Dover Publications, 1994.

*Cross references*

"**Identity politics**" by Adewunmi; "**Memoirs of Björk-Geisha**" by Takemoto; "**Propaganda**" by Smith; "**Reception theory**" by Mee; "**Sampling**" by Hodges Persley; "**Transcontextual**" by Garoian and Gaudelius.

## Dramaturgy

Kimberly Jannarone

Dramaturgy has its origin in the Greek *dramatourgia*, meaning the composition, making, or doing of drama. Since the 18th century, the word has designated: 1. the act of writing a play (largely outmoded in English); 2. the specific profession of dramaturgy (discussed below); and 3. the craft and techniques that factor into the creation of a performance event—the "dramaturgy" of a performance understood as its composition, structure, or fabric.

The history of dramaturgy in the second sense stems from the work of Gotthold Ephraim Lessing, a prominent mid-eighteenth-century German intellectual, playwright, and critic, whose essays of performance criticism and dramatic theory written while serving as the in-house critic for the Hamburg National Theatre (1767–1769) were collected in the influential *Hamburg Dramaturgy*. After Lessing, artists such as Bertolt Brecht, Otto Brahm, Ludwig Tieck, and Henrik Ibsen took up the profession, combining the study, criticism, and practice of theatre-making while remaining especially alert to its artistic and social contexts. The role arrived in the United States in the 1960s, notably when the O'Neill Theater Center organized a group of critics, scholars, and playwrights to "dramaturg"; i.e., to comment on new works, suggest strategies for development, and lead post-production discussions. The institutionalization of dramaturgy as a profession was crystallized in the 1970s with the creation of graduate programs for dramaturgy, such as the one at the Yale School of Drama, which combined scholarship, criticism, and collaboration on new productions.

On a production, the dramaturg is "that artist who functions in a multifacted manner helping the director and other artists to interpret and shape [a work's] sociological, textual, acting, directing, and design values" (Bly 1996); a dramaturg contributes to the "texture of thought" of a production (Rafalowicz 1997, 159–164). This contribution is made by collaboration with the director and company before and during the rehearsal process. The dramaturg draws on a wide knowledge base of the history, theory, and practice of performance and produces new research on all aspects of the artistic world of the production at hand.

In the most general sense, dramaturgy refers to, in Eugenio Barba's words, the "weaving together" of a performance's varied elements, including text, language, "sounds, lights, [and] changes in the space" (1985, 75–78). It provides a way of conceptualizing the multidimensional nature of a performance event and its creation, equally apropos of devised performance, dance, and traditional and experimental theatre.

*Further reading*

Jonas, Proehl and Lupu (1997); Turner and Behrndt (2008).

*References*

Barba, Eugenio. 1985. "The Nature of Dramaturgy: Describing Actions at Work." *New Theatre Quarterly*, 1: 75–78.

Bly, Mark, ed. 1996. *Theatre in Process*. Vol. 1 of *The Production Notebooks*. New York: Theatre Communications Group.

Jonas, Susan S., Geoffrey S. Proehl, and Michael Lupu, eds. 1997. *Dramaturgy in American Theater: A Scource Book*. Fort Worth, TX: Harcourt Brace and Company.

Rafalowicz, Mira. 1997. "Dramaturg in Collaboration with Joseph Chaikin" in *Dramaturgy in American Theater: A Source Book*, edited by Susan S. Jonas, Geoffrey S. Proehl, and Michael Lupu. Fort Worth, TX: Harcourt Brace and Company.

Turner, Cathy and Synne Behrndt. 2008. "Dramaturgy and Performance." In *Theatre and Performance Practices*, edited by Graham Ley and Jane Milling. Hampshire: Palgrave Macmillan.

*Cross references*

"**Ecodramaturgy**" by Thomas; "**Historiography**" by Fabião; "**Mediaturgy**" by Marranca; "**Semiotics/semiology**" by Scheie; "**Transcontextual**" by Garoian and Gaudelius.

## Emotions

Peta Tait

Love, hate, and anger energize performance everywhere. But performed emotions do much more as they influence as well as reflect social and cultural values, and they change historically (Roach 1985). Performance seeks to selectively induce feeling, and recent science reveals its physiological potential (Hurley 2010; Damasio 2003). But, as Denis Diderot (1957) explains, the paradox of emotional feelings in theatre is that feeling can be absent from an actor's experience while interpreted by spectators. An actor's delivery of emotional expression cannot simply be assumed to transmit feeling (Konijn 2000), and especially since acted emotion is surrounded by the textual effects of the *mis-en-scène* and/or music.

While philosophical perspectives on emotions originate with Aristotle on pity and fear in tragedy, the rejection of the emotion vs. reason binary, and the questioning of whether subjective emotional feeling can be known by another, challenge beliefs in universal intrinsic sameness and authenticity. Moreover, performance corresponds with ideas of cultural construction because artistic intention shapes emotions. Current arguments for affect suggest how mood, impersonal feeling, and emotional engagement between performer and audience might be theorized (e.g. Gregg and Seigworth 2010). But their existence remains speculative, unfolding as fluid, performative conditions within embodied spaces (Tait 2002). In performance, emotions materialize as and are communicated in culturally meaningful ways through speech, vocal cues, facial expression, and bodily gesture; their interpretations are shaped by variables from genre to ideology, from gender and race identity to sexuality and personal experience. Because theatre, drama, and performance work with and within socially interpretative languages of emotions, theatrical knowledge can be aligned with understandings from anthropology, psychology, and sociology (e.g. Ekman and Davidson 1994; Williams 2001; Parkinson, Fischer, Manstead 2005). Performance confirms the politics of embodied emotions in society (Ahmed 2004).

*Further reading*

Ahmed (2004); Damasio (2003); Roach (1985); Tait (2002).

*References*

Ahmed, Sara. 2004. *The Cultural Politics of Emotion*. New York: Routledge.

Damasio, Antonio. 2003. *Looking for Spinoza: Joy, Sorrow and the Feeling Brain*. Orlando, FL: Harcourt Inc.

Diderot, Denis. 1957. *The Paradox of Acting*. New York: Hill and Wang.
Ekman, Paul and Richard J. Davidson. 1994. *The Nature of Emotion: Fundamental Questions,* Oxford: Oxford University Press.
Hurley, Erin. 2010. *Theatre & Feeling*. Basingstoke: Palgrave Macmillan.
Gregg, Mellisa and Gregory J. Seigworth. 2010. *The Affect Theory Reader*, Durham, NC: Duke University Press.
Konijn, E.A. 2000. *Acting Emotions: Shaping Emotions on Stage*. Amsterdam: Amsterdam University Press.
Parkinson, Brian, Agneta Fischer, and A. S. R. Manstead. 2005. *Emotions in Social Relations: Cultural, Group, and Interpersonal Processes,* London: Taylor and Francis.
Roach, Joseph. 1985. *The Player's Passion*. Newark, DE: The University of Delaware Press.
Tait, Peta. 2002. *Performing Emotions: Gender, Bodies, Spaces in Chekhov's Drama and Stanislavski's Theater*. Aldershot: Ashgate.
Williams, Simon. 2001. *Emotion and Social Theory: Corporal Reflections on the Rational*. London: Sage Publications.

### *Cross references*

"**Active analysis**" by Carnicke; "**Actor**" by Mee; "**Communitas**" and "**Liminality**" by Levine; "**Mimesis**" by Diamond; "**Remains**" by Morrison.

## Framing

Matthew Smith

Theories of framing date back to Gregory Bateson's "A Theory of Play and Fantasy" (1955, 177–193), which describes play as a paradoxical zone in which messages are simultaneously real and unreal, meant and not meant. Bateson identifies processes by which people frame certain messages as "play," and compares the framing processes of play and psychotherapy. Bateson's insights strongly influenced Erving Goffman, whose *Frame Analysis* (1974), among other works, introduced a number of key terms. These include "frame breaking" (an act that temporarily breaks down the frame; e.g., spectators disrupting a performance by heckling an actor), "keying" (the set of conventions by which a given activity is shifted from one frame to another, e.g., a translation of a work, or a satirical version of an earlier work), and "fabricated frames" in which frames are deceitfully manipulated, as in the activity of a con-artist or propagandist.

In performance theory, a frame is a collection of explicit or implicit messages that show how messages within the frame are meant to be received. The process of framing involves identifying a particular set of messages as distinct from the rest of experience. A frame is therefore metacommunicative; that is, it is a type of communication that structures and makes meaningful other forms of communication. The theory is partly inspired by Wittgenstein's notion of "language games," and framing can be seen as the boundary conditions of a given language game (see Binkley 2012, 64). A frame may convey the rules of a language game to participants and spectators, identify when the game begins and ends, and show where it is to be played and where it is not, and so on.

To know the meaning of, say, a man blowing a whistle, we must first know the frame. If the frame involves messages such as a referee's uniform and a space marked off as a football field, the whistle may indicate "foul!" If the frame involves a carnival outfit and a brass band, the whistle may indicate "hurray!" Issues of framing become far more complex when one turns to forms such as irony and humor, to zones of activity where the line between play and reality is blurred, or to performances of gender, race, or status.

### *Further reading*

Bateson (1955); Goffman (1974); Turner and Bruner(1986).

### *References*

Bateson, Gregory. 1955. *A Theory of Play and Fantasy: A Report on Theoretical Aspects of The project for Study of the Role of the Paradoxes of Abstraction in Communication.* Indianapolis, IN: Bobbs-Merill.

Binkley, Timothy. 2012. *Wittgenstein's Language.* New York: Springer Science & Business Media.

Goffman, Erving. 1974. *Frame Analysis.* Cambridge, MA: Harvard University Press.

Turner, Victor and Edward M. Bruner, eds. 1986. *The Anthropology of Experience.* Urbana, IL: University of Illinois Press.

*Cross references*

"**Happenings**" by Sandford; "**Invisible theatre**" by Cody; "**Liminality**" by Levine; "**Performance Studies**" by Joy; "**Scenario**" by Taylor; "**Virtual reality**" by Auslander.

## Historiography

Eleonora Fabião

As defined in the *Oxford American Dictionary,* historiography means the "writing of history," with "history" classically defined as "the study of past events." "Historiography" stresses both the fact of writing (and therefore the existence of a writer, a historiographer) and the linguistic/graphic character of history. The term makes explicit some determinant factors related to the "study of past events," including the living/transforming condition of language and meaning, the psychophysical existence of a writer, and the performance of writing itself. These factors—because they incorporate elements such as movement, action, corporeity and presence—imply a performative approach to "the study of past events." This performative perspective questions the idea that historiography's meaning and purpose is to present the past "the way it really was" (von Ranke 1965, 255) in order to preserve it.

Historiography, understood as a performative practice, assumes and explores its linguistic representational condition, its corporeal and experiential dimension, and the relativity of "past events" in order to compose dynamic systems of historical meaning. This performative understanding is not only based on the idea that narratives are relative to their historiographers, their very concrete means of production and contexts, but also that the layers of representation concerning the historiographic task must be displayed in the text. However, to acknowledge the performativity of the historiographic act certainly does not mean to dilute the facticity of past events or the actuality of archives. The goal is to investigate the multiplicity and mobility of apparently singular and static facts, to explore how these singularly plural events exist in and as relational circuits, to propose that "historical facts" are not absolutes but as multifaceted as their narrators and readers, or, that there will always already be, within the very "singularity" of the event, a multiplicity of simultaneous facts already taking place.

To approximate performance and history in search of a performative historiography is also a matter of considering the temporal field generated by the historiographic act: an action in the present about a past event envisioning the creation of a future (Fabião 2006 and 2012). In his unfinished *Arcades Project,* Walter Benjamin suggests, "Say something about the method of composition itself: how everything one is thinking at a specific moment in time must at all costs be incorporated into the project then at hand" (1999, 456). Benjamin's methodological suggestion also indicates a question: has the past to be historiographed really already passed? Or, is the performance of researching and writing, of linguistically moving the past, an evidence that it has not exactly "passed"? In a performative sense, "the past" also continues passing and coming as archival presence, research agency, writing and reading experience. "The past" is not a monolithic block waiting to be moved by omnipresent, omniscient, and omnipotent historians as if they were demiurgic recording machines; "the present," as well, is not a static and neutral receptacle ready to didactically accommodate the historical lesson. As Gilles Deleuze clarifies, "A scar is the sign not of a past wound but of the 'present fact of having been wounded'" (1994, 77). In the performative sense, the historiographer is not a mere collector of data but a producer of affects and effects. The archive, reciprocally, is not a mere collection of data but a producer of affects and effects, a source of historical experience.

*Further reading*

Benjamin (1999); Deleuze (1994); Fabião (2006 and 2012); Jones and Heathfield (2012).

*References*

Benjamin, Walter. 1999. *The Arcades Project*, edited by Rolf Tiedemann. Cambridge, MA: Belknap Press of Harvard University Press.

Deleuze, Gilles. 1994. *Difference and Repetition*. New York: Columbia University Press.

Fabião, Eleonora. 2006. *Precarious, Precarious, Precarious: Performative Historiography and the Energetics of the Paradox*. New York: New York University Press.

Fabião, Eleonora. 2012. "History and Precariousness: In Search of a Performative Historiography." In *Perform, Repeat, Record: Live Art in History*, edited by Amelia Jones and Adrian Heathfield. Bristol: Intellect.

Jones, Amelia and Adrian Heathfield. 2012. *Perform, Repeat, Record: Live Art in History*. Bristol: Intellect.

Von Ranke, Leopold. 1965. *Leopold Ranke, the Formative Years*. Ann Arbor, MI: University Microfilms.

*Cross references*

"**Archive and repertoire**" by Taylor; "**Dramaturgy**" by Jannarone; "**Historicity**" by Colleran; "**Performance, postmodernism, and beyond**" by Davidson; "**Performing the archive**" by Nyong'o; "**Prosthetic performance**" by Gass.

**Through the Eyes of Rachel Marker**

Moira Roth

In 2001, while in Berlin, I began "Through the Eyes of Rachel Marker," a fragmented narrative about a fictional Czech Jew, a singer, poet, and playwright who witnesses many significant moments of European history in the last century. It is a history that I too have partially encountered; I was born in England in 1933 and brought up in a town outside London, where we lived with Jewish refugees during World War II.

I worked on this narrative while visiting Europe–staying in Berlin, Prague, and Paris, and traveling in Spain and Greece, writing by hand mostly in local cafés. It has slowly evolved through a range of media, including published texts (Roth 2001, 2003, 2006a, 2006b), performances and readings in Germany, Hawaii and California, handwritten letters and journals, photographs of shadows, and now (2013) a "literary installation."

In 1916, during World War I, Rachel Marker appears in neutral Zurich. Here, she encounters the exiled Vladimir Lenin in the Café Odeon and attends the first night of the Cabaret Voltaire, meeting many of its young Dadaists. She also meets two other fictional characters (with whom she corresponds periodically): Maria Sanchez, a Spaniard with whom she will visit Guernica in 1937, and Rachel Spiegel, a German activist who will witness the October Revolution in 1917 Russia, and later become involved in Erwin Piscator's theatre projects in Berlin.

On June 12, 1924, the day after Franz Kafka's funeral in Prague, Rachel Marker writes a letter to him for the first time. "You once said that 'writing is a form of prayer. Even if no redemption comes, I still want to be worthy of it every moment.' ... I, too, brood on such things and I know that is why I am so drawn to you, and why I have made the resolution to write to you every day until I die."

She gives these letters, which she writes in a café, to a waiter, who accumulates them in a trunk that once belonged to Kafka. Over the years, she writes to

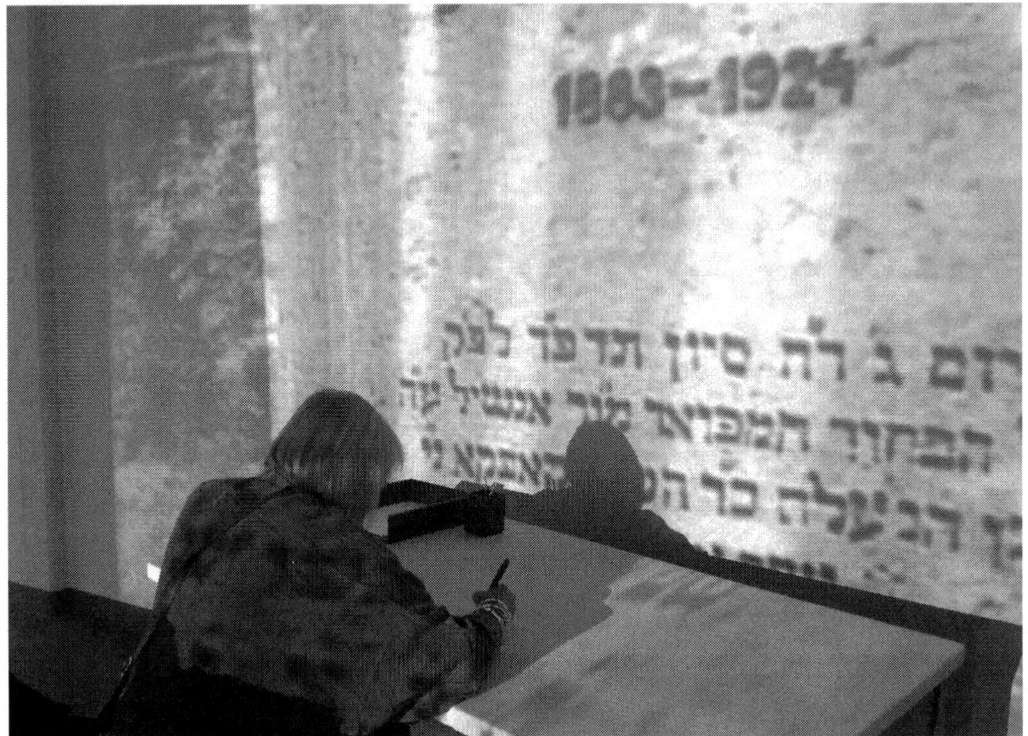


**Figure 21** Griselda Pollock writing a letter to Rachel Marker in the Magnes Collection of Jewish Art and Life gallery, Berkeley, California. Photo by Moira Roth.

Kafka about the rise of Fascism and the Spanish Civil War, about alchemy and astronomy, and about her own experiments in writing. Then, in 1939, Rachel Marker leaves Prague for Paris at the beginning of World War II. After the Nazi troops occupy France, almost nothing is known about what happens to her until the 1989 Fall of the Berlin Wall. It is in Berlin, no longer divided into West and East, that she regains her pre-war memory while standing in front of Bertolt Brecht's grave, and then begins to take daily photographs of the city's shadows.

In addition to her daily letters to Kafka, Rachel Marker begins to write a series of plays for the Mute Players. She meets them in 1924 in a Prague café, where they give her a note that reads: "We are four young actors. Will you write a play for us, taking into account that we are all mute?" The next day she gives them the script of *365 Days of Silent Acts*. In June of 1940, now in Paris, she finds on Charles Baudelaire's grave a letter addressed to her from the Mute Players, saying, "We think it is time that you wrote us another play." Again, within a day, she creates *Letters to the Dead*, to be performed for one hundred years in cemeteries around the world. Each year the Players are to choose a series of words significant to them and each day lay out a single letter from one of these words on a grave.

In May 2013, Alla Efimova curated "Through the Eyes of Rachel Marker: A Literary Installation" at the Magnes Collection of Jewish Art and Life in Berkeley, California. This multimedia exhibition interwove material by and about Rachel Marker with publications and photographs about two extraordinary, real Jewish women who had profoundly influenced my narrative. They were Rose Hacker, a British activist and my unofficially adopted mother, who died in London at age 101 in 2008, and Alice Herz-Sommer, her friend, a well-known Czech pianist, and a survivor of the Theresienstadt concentration camp, who, in 2013, lived in London. [She died at age 110 in 2014.]

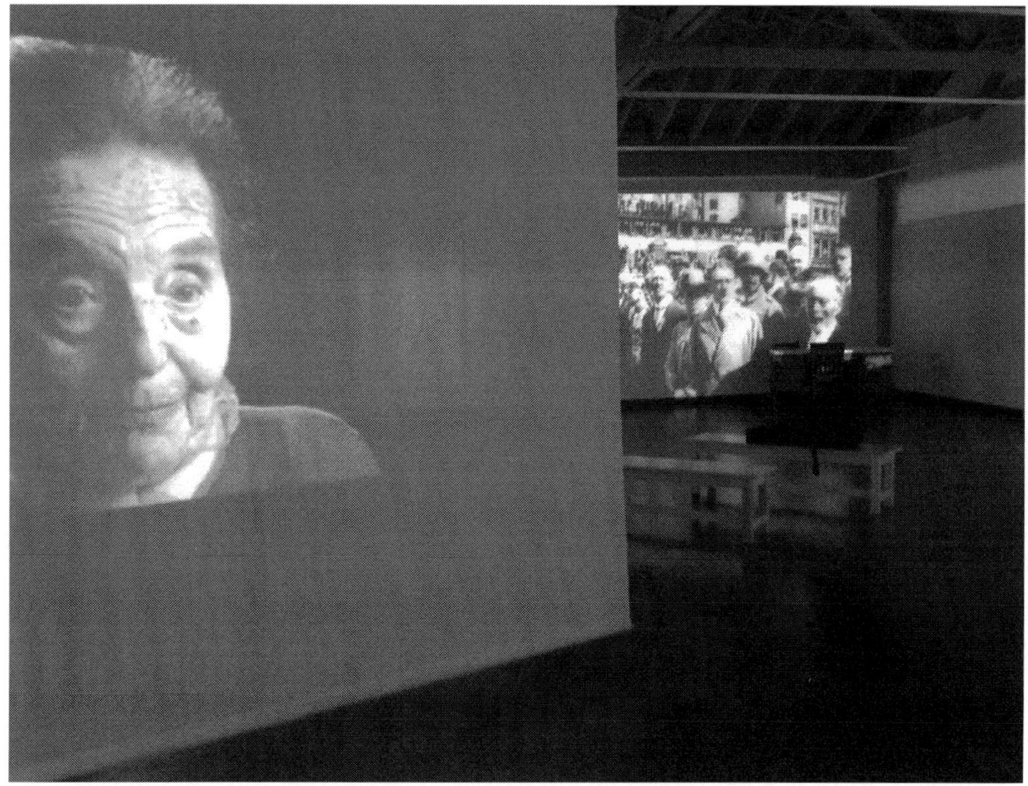

**Figure 22** Installation (with video of Alice Herz-Sommer on left), "Through the Eyes of Rachel Marker: A Literary Installation," The Magnes Collection of Jewish Art and Life, The Bancroft Library, University of California Berkeley, 2013. Photo by Alla Efimova. Image courtesy of The Magnes Collection.

In the Magnes gallery, visitors could compose handwritten letters to Rachel Marker at a desk over which documentary footage of 20th-century European history is was projected. At the same time they heard the soundtrack of a one-hour film about Alice Herz-Sommer, shown at the other side of the gallery. These letters, including one from Griselda Pollock, the English art historian and theorist, were then pinned up on a nearby bulletin corkboard.

Just before the Magnes exhibition opening, Rachel Marker received the first of a series of handwritten letters, sent in the regular mail, from "John" (John Alan Farmer, an art historian, attorney and close friend of mine). In one he writes: "One of the defining events of your life was the war. One of the defining events of mine was the great plague that reached its crescendo when I was a young man living in New York." Rachel Marker responds by telling him that the Mute Players are now in Paris, planning a ceremony about French gay culture and "the great plague" of AIDS in the city's Père Lachaise Cemetery. She dreams that the Mute Players will invite Farmer and his partner to participate "in whatever way you want."

John Farmer and his partner, Mike Ly, visited Paris at the end of March, and found a box on Charles Baudelaire's grave in which the Mute Players had put together a number of items (including a tiny 1924 French almanac, old photographs, and a handwritten collection of texts) that Rachel Marker had left with them for safekeeping when she fled from Paris in 1940. Following instructions, they carried the box unopened to the Père Lachaise Cemetery–which contains the graves of Oscar Wilde, Marcel Proust, and a number of prominent gay writers, filmmakers, performers, and activists who died of AIDS. Here they opened the box, and discovered a note from the Mute Players addressed to Rachel Marker with instructions for the prelude of a future performance called "Letters to the Living" that they ask her to write for them. It will take place in the future in gardens around the world.

The journal of Rachel Marker, Saturday, November 8, 2014, Nabolom Café

I sit musing about the European history that I have encountered in the course of my long life.

In the newspaper today I read an article about Spain: "Rallying Catalans to the Separatist Cause"–about Carme Forcadell, a street activist in Barcelona and president of the Catalan National Assembly.

I look out of the café window and think about my visit to Barcelona in 1936 at the start of the Spanish civil war.

I turn back to read another article: "How the Berlin Wall Really Fell" and find out that, according to its author, "the fall of the wall came about because of the complex interplay among Soviet reforms, East Berlin's incompetence and, crucially, rising opposition from everyday Germans."

Again I stare out of the window, remembering my stay in what used to be East Berlin after the fall of the Berlin Wall on November 9, 1989–25 years ago this Sunday. And how, shortly after that, leaving my Book of Shadows there, I left my home in the Mitte, and over the next years slowly wended my way to live in Northern California.

References

Roth, Moira. 2001. "Rachel Marker and the City of Maps, Berlin, Summer 2001." *X-tra*, 4.3. http://x-traonline.org/article/rachel-marker-and-the-city-of-maps-berlin-summer-2001/

Roth, Moira. 2003. "Rachel Marker and Her Book of Shadows." *Art Journal*, 62.3: 66-73.

Roth, Moira. 2006a. "Through the Eyes of Rachel Marker." *Camerawork: A Journal of Photographic Arts*, 33.1: 30-37.

Roth, Moira. 2006b. "Rachel Marker, Franz Kafka and Alice Sommer, adapted from a theatre piece in three acts," *Paradoxa*, 17: 19-29.

## Invisible Theatre

Gabrielle H. Cody

Most often associated with the theatre work and pedagogy of Brazilian theorist Augusto Boal in the early 1970s—but with antecedents in Marc Estrin's American Playground in Washington, DC, in the late 1960s, and already anticipated by "planned actions" during the last years of the Weimar republic (Kohtes 1993)—"Invisible Theatre" is a para-theatrical form of clandestine activism in which the audience is unwittingly made to assume an active social role in a non-theatrical space. This theatre is invisible *as* theatre to the onlookers, who see the occurrence as spontaneous, though it has been scripted in advance. A rich but controversial form, Invisible Theatre is ideologically aligned with the strategies of Marxism, and in the theatre, with Brecht's teaching plays, or *Lehrstücke.*

If Boal could not dismantle the brutal military regimes and entrenched power structures of his native Brazil, his hope was that using theatre as a tool for social change might disrupt the "cop in the head" passivity of internalized political oppression. Profoundly influenced by Critical Pedagogy educator Paulo Freire, whose *Pedagogy of the Oppressed* (1970) was a clear precursor to his own *The Theater of the Oppressed* (1979), Boal primarily intended for his practice to give representational power back to citizen "spec*tactors.*" Nevertheless, involuntary participants in Invisible Theatre often accused Boal of deception, after the fact (Boal 1979). He maintained that his practice exposed systemic class conflicts that recur repeatedly over time and across continents, though he may not always have been present to help sort out the complicated after-effects of these social experiments.

Boal and his work continue to influence a variety of offshoot practices, including the infiltration of Shopping Malls (Gray 1993), events at Occupy encampments (*Occupy* 2011), invisible choreographies in restaurants in "transparent large-scale urban dioramas" (http://www.guardian.co.uk/stage/theaterblog/2009/), and in media activism as well. The Yes Men—founded in 1999—have had as their target multinational corporations and government organizations. By registering website domains that closely mimic those of large corporations, they pose as official actors and expose corporate agendas. During the 20th anniversary of the 1984 Union Carbide disaster in Bhopal, India—in which over 20,000 people died, and 120,000 continued to suffer from severe medical and economic repercussions—the BBC sent an email to what they believed was the official Dow Chemical site. This prompted the Yes Men to stage a live interview broadcast on BBC World in which one member disguised as "Jude Finisterra," a fictitious Dow Chemical spokesman, offered compensation of $12 billion dollars to the victims of the disaster. In the hours it took for the Yes Men's hoax to be discovered, their statements reached the Bhopal victims, "reproduce[ing] the rhetoric of hegemony" (Wiegmink 2008).

Based on his paradigm of the Invisible Theatre, Boal might have defended the Yes Men for having—however briefly—exposed, through invisible performance, the ethical response Dow Chemical and other corporations programmatically foreclose. The "real" Dow Chemical website, for sure, did not mention Bhopal on the 20th anniversary of the disaster. The purpose of Invisible (Theatre) interventions is to generate critical consciousness. But, as shown in the case of the Yes Men, this may not always lead to protagonistic agency.

### *Further reading*

Boal (1979); Wiegmink (2008).

### *References*

Boal, Augusto. 1979. *Theater of the Oppressed*. New York: Urizen Books.

Freire, Paulo. 1970. *Pedagogy of the Oppressed*, London: Bloomsbury Academic.

Gray, John, ed. 1993. *Action Art: A Bibliography of Artists' Performance from Futurism to Fluxus and Beyond*. Westport, CT: Greenwood Press.

Kohtes, Martin Maria. 1993. "Invisible Theatre: Reflections on an Overlooked Form." *New Theatre Quarterly*, 9: 85–89.

Wiegmink, Pia. 2008. "Performing Resistance: Contemporary American Performance-Activism." *COPAS: Current Objectives of Postgraduate American Studies* 7. http://copas.uni-regensburg.de/article/view/86/110

### *Cross references*

"**Happenings**" by Sandford; "**Intervention**" and "**Paratheatre**" by Olivares; "**Performing surveillance camera art**" by Nayar; "**Terrorism and performance**" by Colleran; "**War**" by Sell.

## Liveness

Philip Auslander

Theatre and performance studies have always tacitly assumed that their objects of inquiry are live performances, understood broadly as events that unfold in real time and involve performers and spectators who are physically co-present to one another. Considering how fundamental to performance live exchange is presumed to be, it is surprising to discover that the term "liveness" actually comes from television studies rather than performance studies.

In the context of television studies, liveness refers to the quality of immediacy possessed by television broadcasts, whether live or not, a quality rooted in television's history as the first audiovisual medium able to convey events as they occur to a distant audience. Although television programming is no longer made up primarily of live broadcasts, the medium arguably retains that sense of immediacy in the cultural imaginary. In this context, liveness refers to an affective experience that may or may not be grounded in a live event.

The concept of liveness invites one to consider the idea of the live not simply as an ontological given of performance but as a problematic one as well. This discussion is inseparable from the context established by mass media, since it is within that context that the liveness of performance has become an issue. Arguably, what counts as a live experience is continually redefined in relation to technological change. Whereas, classically, only situations involving the physical and temporal co-presence of performers and spectators could be considered live performances, broadcasts in which the audience observes what is happening in real time but is not physically present at the event are routinely called "live," thus expanding the concept's referents (Auslander 1999).

The question of liveness in performance has been reframed recently by the dominance of digital technologies. When a website is made available to users, it is said to "go live." This suggests an understanding of liveness that focuses primarily on the audience's affective experience: to the degree that technological artifacts such as websites, bots, and avatars engage with us, and respond to us, in real time, we may have the sense of interacting with a live agent, regardless of whether there is a person "behind" the technology. The discussion of liveness thus intersects with posthumanist theory to suggest not only that liveness may be an aspect of events that are not live performances in the traditional sense, but also that non-human agents may be capable of live performance.

*Further reading*

Auslander (1999, 2008); Blau (1982).

*References*

Auslander, Philip. 1999. *Liveness: Performance in a Mediatized Culture*. London and New York: Routledge.

Auslander, Philip. 2008. "Live and Technologically Mediated Performance." In *The Cambridge Companion to Performance Studies*, edited by Tracy C. Davis. Cambridge: Cambridge University Press.

Blau, Herbert. 1982. *Take Up the Bodies: Theater at the Vanishing Point*, Urbana, IL: University of Illinois Press.

*Cross references*

"**Media**" by Colleran; "**New Media Art**" by Cicchini; "**Performance in the digital age**" and "**Virtual reality**" by Auslander; "**Performing surveillance camera art**" by Nayar; "**Precariousness**" by Fabião.

## Prosthetic performance

Arianna Gass

The word "prosthetic" comes from Greek, meaning an addition or attachment. Usually, a prosthetic (such as a prosthetic limb) is used to enhance or extend the capabilities of something that is perceived as lacking. In a literal interpretation of the phrase, "prosthetic performance" can describe the use of mechanical and medical prosthesis in performance art. In a metaphorical sense, the phrase addresses the afterlife of performances and how they can be experienced after-the-fact.

Between 1980 and 1988, Stelarc, an Australian performance artist, performed *Third Hand*. In this piece, Stelarc controlled a mechanical replica of his right hand with electric signals transmitted from muscles in his legs and abdomen to electrodes, which were then fed through a computer, and relayed back to his third hand. In a world polluted by mass media, rapid technological advances, and ever-shrinking time-scales, Stelarc's technological prostheses are not a "sign of lack, but rather a symptom of excess" (Stelarc 1988). Stelarc upends the traditional understanding of "prosthesis," pointing towards a posthuman world in which human life augments technology, rather than technology supplementing human life.

In a different interpretation of the concept, as proposed by Meiling Cheng (2002), "prosthetic performance" brings to light how most audience members (off-site viewers, students, other artists, laypeople) experience performance art: after-the-fact. An understanding of "prosthetic performance" relies upon the idea that every performance is unique and irreplaceable. Each instance of performance lives and dies the moment it is born. To confront performance's ephemerality, prostheses have been developed to extend the life of a performance for future viewers. These prostheses range from video and audio recordings, photographs, to firsthand accounts, artist's scores, scripts, to critical commentaries. Such documents breathe life into the perishing performance, itself becoming "a surrogate that replaces and extends its lost origin" (Cheng 2002, xxv). By consuming the documents surrounding a performance, a person experiences the piece as a prosthetic performance while simultaneously proliferating more prosthetic performances in response to the lost source of performance. These prosthetic performances are related to but also different from their now-vanished precursor.

Prosthetic performance evokes Alison Landsberg's concept of "prosthetic memory," or memories that do not "come from a person's lived experience in any strict sense," but are produced and assimilated as one's own through the consumption and synthesis of media (1996, 175). These prosthetic memories usually come in the form of stories "remembered" about one's childhood based on a picture, or events taken from movies or books that are remembered as part of the watcher or reader's life. As Landsberg argues, these appropriated memories suggest that one's memories are "less about authenticating the past, than about generating possible courses of action in the present" (1996, 183).

In *Beijing Xingwei* (2013), Meiling Cheng further analyzes prosthetic performance in relationship to a viewer's composite memories enabled by performance documentation. Cheng questions the distinction between the source and prosthetic performances by demonstrating that in certain performances, such as Qui Zhijie's "calli-photographic" series entitled *The Shape of Time* (2007), the source performance can only be experienced by third-parties through its prosthetic traces. In *The Shape of Time,* Qui inserts "his body into a chosen site, in front of his tripod-mounted camera, and [uses] a flashlight to inscribe in reverse calligraphy a linguistic phrase, illuminating his momentary poetic act" (Cheng 2013, 397). The resulting performance is captured by the camera as illuminated Chinese or English phrases in the air, the performer's body barely visible. These images record Qiu's performance and serve as simultaneous documentation. As documents, they spawn other prosthetic performances in the minds of viewers.

The concept of prosthetic performance relaxes the time-bound and place-bound understanding of performance art. It gives performance a life outside of the moment in which it happens, but also works towards a multicentric understanding of performance. In the Information Age, the intention of the artist(s) and the qualities of the work are just as vital as the documentation and afterlife of the performance.

### *Further reading*

Cheng (2002; 2013), Stelarc (2013).

### *References*


Cheng, Meiling. 2002. *In Other Los Angeleses: Multicentric Performance Art*. Berkeley, CA: University of California Press.

Cheng, Meiling. 2013. *Beijing Xingwei: Contemporary Chinese Time-based Art*. London, New York, Calcutta: Seagull Books.

Landsberg, Alison. 1996. "Prosthetic Memory: *Total Recall* and *Blade Runner*." In *Cyberspace/ Cyberbodies/Cyberpunk: Cultures of Technological Embodiment*, edited by Mike Featherstone and Roger Burrows, 175–

189. London, Thousand Oaks, CA, New Delhi: Sage Publications.

Stelarc. 1988. Artist's Statement in "The Function in Art and Culture Today," *High Performance* 11 (Spring/Summer): 70.

Stelarc. 2013. "stelarc // Third Hand." http://stelarc.org/?catID=20265

*Cross references*

"**Active analysis**" by Carnicke; "**Appropriation**" by Wong; "**Audience**" by Cody; "**Historiography**" by Fabião; "**Performance Studies**" by Joy; "**Readymade**" by Hoefer; "**Transcontextual**" by Garoian and Gaudelius.

## Gyrl grip

Llewyn Máire and Lisa Newman

The gyrl grip is the intimate live art collaboration of 2 gyrlz founders: Lisa Newman and Llewyn Máire.

Our work is driven by the desire to reveal and de-veil challenging issues of gender, violence, and the politics of intimacy through video projection, spoken word, live actions, and sound sculpture. Our goal is not to provide answers, but to expose the difficult questions hidden behind cultural taboos and media spectacle, and to provide a forum for dialogue (internal and external) through the performative act.

Although we began making work in 2001, our largest performance series, *Surgemony,* commenced in 2004, following Llewyn's orchiectomy (gonad removal) as part of hyr ongoing evolution of body and gender. The surgery was performed "off-the-grid" in a converted manger by transgendered surgeons sympathetic with transpeople and who offered the procedure and care for an affordable fee. Llewyn asked Lisa to document the surgical process in video. The resulting hour-long video became the primary visual component of the five-part *Surgemony* series, performed at various locations and events in the US, Canada, and Europe between 2005 and 2010.

### *Surgemony I: Loving the Alien*

The series began with a multi-faceted piece including the video of the surgery footage, a text performed by Lisa, and a series of actions by Llewyn, who engaged in feminization rituals of removing facial hair, applying make-up, and intermuscular injections of estrogen. The piece ends with Llewyn serenading Lisa with an adapted version of Elton John's *Your Song.*

*Loving the Alien* aims to identify the universality of change in committed relationships, as well as the uncertainty that change brings. The piece responds to the anxieties and confusion surrounding the dynamics of our relationship post-surgery. We ask both ourselves and the audience: What happens when the body that you are learning to love changes into something new? What happens then when the seemingly consistent elements of who we are change into something–which, culturally–we have no language for? How would you define yourself if you were in a relationship with someone who was neither male nor female? How would you refer them to others–your friends, your family, and on federal documents?

By presenting these questions, we intend to find ways to show a unity in our desire to find the right words–the right code–to be able to truly know each other on an intimate level.

We performed *Loving the Alien* at the Gender Symposium at Lewis and Clark University in Portland, Oregon in 2005, and again that year at the annual Performance Studies international (PSi) conference at Brown University in Rhode Island, where transgender performance artist and author, Kate Bornstein, acted as respondent for audience discussion.

### *Surgemony II: Segue*

*Segue* explored discovering intimacy again within the post-surgery relationship. In this installation, the surgery video was projected onto our bodies and the performance space, enveloping us in the images of flesh, blood, and metallic flashes of the scalpel. Through barely perceptible micro-movements, we slowly found each others' bodies through touch. In the duration of an hour, we evolved from separation to tight embrace.

We performed *Segue* only once in 2006, at the Lewis and Clark University annual Gender Symposium.

*Surgemony III: Here With You*

In this action, we wanted to acknowledge other transpeople and their partners by reading their names aloud, followed by a toast to their love. We prerecorded our reading of the names, which Llewyn manipulated to slowly fill the sonic space with repetition. By the end, the names of 44 couples, with an accompanying ringing of a glass to announce the toast, became cacophonous. The surgery footage was subdued, appearing within the video footage of *Segue* projected above our heads.

With each name and indicating ring, Llewyn and Lisa raised and drained a glass of wine. Mid-way through the performance, we both vomited, but we continued drinking until the last of the names had been read. At the Harta Monza festival in Italy, we provided the audience with glasses of wine, which they raised along with us.

Polish artist, Jan Swidinski, commented that it was nice to see that "love is not always about sex."

*Surgemony IV: Honey Is Home*

In his book, *Lover's Discourse: Fragments*, Roland Barthes theorizes that in the act of longing, it is the

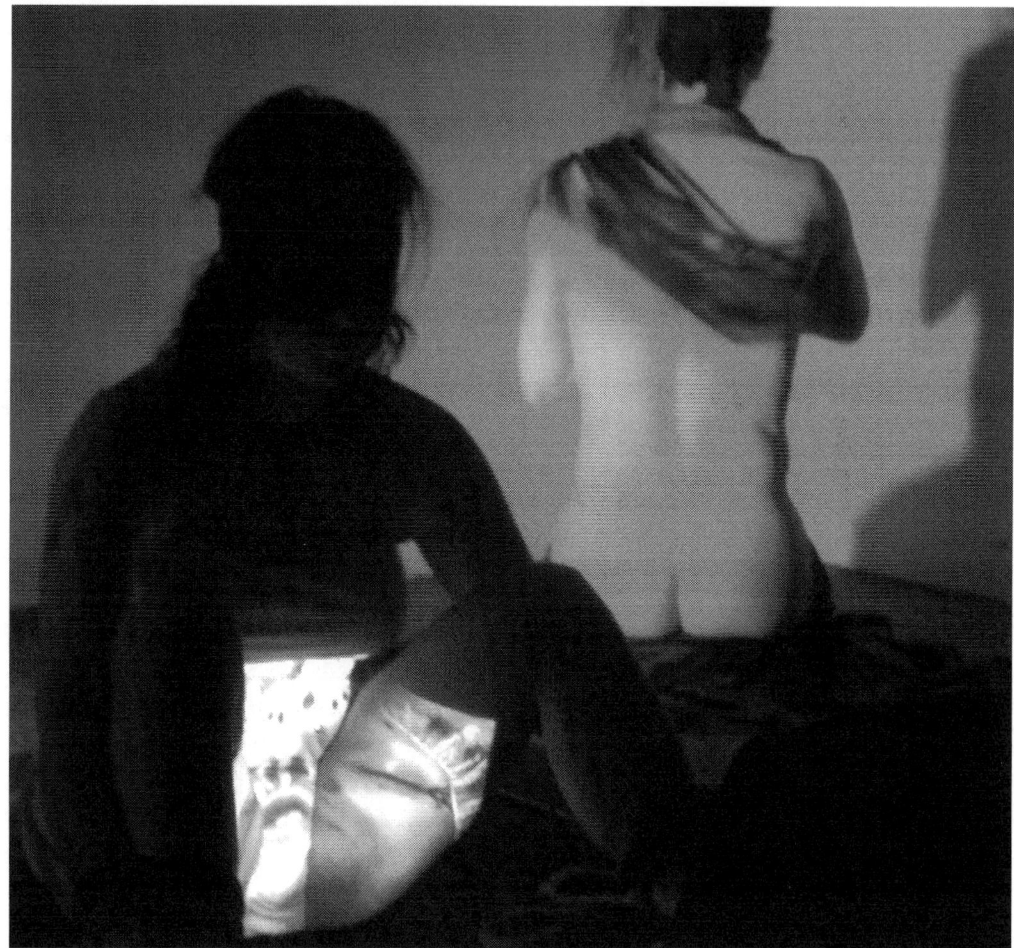

**Figure 23** *Surgemony V: seemefeelmetouchmehealme* (2009) Gender Symposium Lewis and Clark College. Portland, Oregon. Photo credit: J. DeKom for gyrl grip. Image courtesy of the artists.

woman who waits and the man who leaves. A man waiting, in a passive role, becomes feminized, and vice versa. Our performance challenges this theory by blurring our gender roles—who is male, who is female, or do we become a new gender? Who is waiting? Who is the one who will return?

In Part One, we perform in separate spaces, linked by a live video feed showing Llewyn in a state of "waiting," at the Hotel Pupik residency in Austria in 2007. Lisa, as the one who "leaves," uses the video image to reconstruct a portrait of Llewyn made from honey, which also drips onto Llewyn's face. The piece's soundtrack comes from a Percy Sledge album, which consists of an hour-long hymn to longing for love.

In Part Two, we are reunited physically and dance together to the Sledge soundtrack as honey drips down on us through a sieve from above. Though we are together, there is still a sense of longing for a uniting of selves; as if our bodies have become a barrier from our true unification. The honey stings our eyes and forms an adherent between our skin and clothing, causing bruising as our flesh tears when we pull away from one another.

We danced in the centre of a crossroads, flanked by four video monitors showing, respectively: the surgery footage; the *Segue* performance; a video of Lisa, in drag, under a honey drip; and a montage of mass media's depictions of violent attacks against transpeople; this last video was used in our 2004 performance called *Boot Camp*. The audience was invited to walk through the space and around us, viewing different temporal points in the *Surgemony* journey.

We presented Part Two in England, Oregon, Victoria BC, and Denmark during 2007-2008.

*Surgemony V: seemefeelmetouchmehealme*

This final piece in the *Surgemony* series builds on the idea of longing while the lovers are united. In the performance, Llewyn flogs hyrself while Lisa sits blindfolded and bound by ropes with her legs apart; the surgery footage is projected onto her genitals. The image depicts both self-destruction and frustration, and a scene of sexual S/M play that has become apathetic, with each partner oblivious to the internal processes and struggles of the other.

We performed *seemefeelmetouchmehealme* in 2009 in the Lewis and Clark Gender Symposium, at a conference on collaboration at the University of Calgary, Canada, and in 2010 in Plymouth, UK as part of the Red Ape festival in conjunction with Marina Abramovic's *Pigs of Today are the Hams of Tomorrow* symposium.

*Current works*

Since 2011, our new works address the conundrums surrounding the preservation and historicization of performance art, and the apparent disregard for the artist body in favor of the replaceable surrogate in reenactment performance. In *The Artist is Preserved* (a play on Marina Abramovic's 2010 MoMA retrospective and performance, *The Artist is Present*), we exhibited ourselves as generic examples of the "feminist" and "neo-avant garde" performance bodies as catalogued in the museum collection. Additionally, we compiled a slideshow of documentation of reenacted iconic performance works, accompanied with the text "Now You Were There." The slideshow speaks to the issue of presence in performance, historicization, and the document.

## Reception theory

Erin Mee

Reception theory developed in the 1970s out of reader-response theory, which reminds us that the meanings of a text are "neither manifested in the printed text, nor produced solely by the reader's imagination" (Iser 1978, 135), but generated from a synthesis between the two. This dispels the notion that there is a single, timeless, objective, sui generis, or independent meaning of a text and introduces the notion of reader agency: the notion that a reader actively negotiates and interprets rather than passively receives a text.

Stanley Fish subverted the authority of the text by pointing out that readers bring interpretive strategies to a text which exist "prior to the act of reading and therefore determine the shape of what is read" rather than the other way around (1980, 171).

Fish and Iser focused on responses of the individual reader, which led to the idea that there are as many readings of a text as there are readers, and consequently that all readings are subjective and arbitrary. Attempting to locate the reader in history, Hans Robert Jauss pointed out that the reception of a text is neither arbitrary nor subjective but "a process of directed perception" that is shaped by a "horizon of expectations" (1982, 23). A reader's cultural background, aesthetic expectations, personal experiences, class, gender, sexuality, political motivations, and the historical moment in which they live all determine the horizon of expectations.

Locating the reader response in time, as a reflection of a particular historical moment, allows theorists to examine the various ways a single text has been understood over time. Classicists have used reception theory to understand the force and power of classical material in the modern world. As one of the leading reception theorists in classics notes: "reception is and always has been a field for the practice and study of contest about values and their relationship to knowledge and power" (Hardwick 2003, 11).

Feminists have made use of reception theory to formulate a critical feminist reader response. In *The Resisting Reader*, Judith Fetterly argues that the unmarked "universal" view of the world is male, rendering the female reader powerless. She notes that, "at its best, feminist criticism [here she positions the reader as critic] is a political act whose aim is not simply to interpret the world but to change it" (1978, viii). Fetterly calls for a feminist reader who would function as "a resisting rather than an assenting reader" (1978, xxii) in the same way that, in *The Feminist Spectator as Critic* (1998), Jill Dolan calls for a resisting rather than assenting feminist spectator.

Although "the text" is now widely used to refer more generally to creative work in numerous media, reception theory reflects its origins in studies of written text, and has limited application to performance, an inherently multimedia and multidisciplinary genre requiring multiple strategies for making meaning. In her study of theatre audiences, Susan Bennett notes that "interest in a semiotic approach to theatre studies emerged in the 1970s as an attack on the text-centred criticism of traditional dramatic writing" (1997, 68). In a critique of reception theory, Robert Holub (1994) points out that it has developed in isolation from other theories such as semiotics and poststructuralism, but Bennett goes further to note that "the omission of social, economic, and political relations is surely more serious" (1997, 54)

By introducing a "spectator-oriented criticism," Una Chaudhuri has pointed out one way that performance studies can formulate its own mode of reception theory: "The description of how a play works on a spectator—rather than of what it means—can supply the terms our criticism needs in order to erase the gap between theory and its object" (1984, 296). Research into fan culture (most notably *Textual Poachers: Television Fans and Participatory Culture* by Henry Jenkins (1992) and *Interacting with Babylon 5: Fan Performances in a Media Universe* by Kurt Lancaster (2001)) focuses not on how people understand (for example) *Star Trek*, but on how they put it to use, which is another way to generate an analysis of performance reception. Feminist ethnography (which locates the researcher in the research), cognitive psychology (which analyzes how we perceive and process information), and the linguistics of sign language (as a specific example of how we interpret body language) are three other areas in which performance theorists might begin to find a non-text-based analysis of response.

### *Further reading*

Dolan (1988); Holub (1984); Jenkins (1992).

## References

Bennett, Susan, ed. 1990. *Theatre Audiences: A Theory of Production and Reception*. Reprint, 1997. London and New York: Routledge.

Chaudhuri, Una. 1984. "The Spectator in Drama/ Drama in the Spectator." *Modern Drama*, 27.3 (Fall): 281–298.

Dolan, Jill. 1988. *Feminist Spectator as Critic*. Ann Arbor, MI: University of Michigan Press.

Fetterly, Judith. 1978. *The Resisting Reader*. Bloomington, IN: Indiana University Press.

Fish, Stanley. 1980. *Is There a Text in This Class?* Cambridge, MA: Harvard University Press.

Holub, Robert C. 1984. *Reception Theory: A Critical Edition*. New York: Routledge.

Hardwick, Lorna. 2003. *Reception Studies*. Oxford: Oxford University Press.

Iser, Wolfgang. 1978. *The Act of Reading: A Theory of Aesthetic Response*. Baltimore, MD and London: Johns Hopkins University Press.

Jauss, Hans. 1982. *Toward an Aesthetic of Reception*. Vol. 2 of *Theory and History of Literature*, edited by Wlad Godzich and Jochen Schulte-Sasse. Minneapolis, MN: University of Minnesota Press.

Jenkins, Henry. 1992. *Textual Poachers: Television Fans and Participatory Culture*. New York: Routledge.

Lancaster, Kurt. 2001. *Interacting with Babylon 5: Fan Performances in a Media Universe*. Austin, TX: University of Texas Press.

## Cross references

"**Active analysis**" by Carnicke; "**Disciplines in performance**" by Morrison; "**Feminist blogging as activism and pedagogy**" by Dolan; "**Performance Studies**" by Joy; "**Postdramatic theatre**" by Fuchs; "**Prosthetic performance**" by Gass; "**Semiotics/semiology**" by Scheie.

# Concept entries and paired case studies bibliography


Adorno, Theodore W. 2001. *The Culture Industry: Selected Essays on Mass Culture*, edited by J.M. Bernstein. New York: Routledge.

Ahmed, Sara. 2004. *The Cultural Politics of Emotion*. New York: Routledge.

Ai, Weiwei. 2008. "Happiness Can't Be Faked." *The Guardian*, August 18. http://www.theguardian.com/commentisfree/2008/aug/18/china.chinathemedia

Ai, Weiwei. 2011. *Ai Weiwei's Blog: Writings, Interviews, and Digital Rants, 2006–2009*, edited and translated by Lee Ambrozy. Cambridge: MIT Press.

Ai, Weiwei. 2012a. *Ai Weiwei: Never Sorry*. Documentary. Directed by Alison Klayman.

Ai, Weiwei. 2012b. *Ai Weiwei: New York Photographs 1983–1993*, edited by Mao Weidong, Stephanie Tung, and Christophe Mao. Beijing: Three Shadows Press.

Albrecht, E.J. 1995. *The New American Circus*. Gainesville, FL: University of Florida Press.

Allyn, Jerry, Anne Gauldin, Cheri Gaulke, and Sue Maberry. 2011. *Sisters Of Survival*. Los Angeles, CA: Otis College of Art and Design.

Andelman, David. 2012. "The Art of Dissent: A Chat with Ai Weiwei." *World Policy Journal*, 29: 15–21.

Andrejevic, Mark. 2004. *Reality TV: The Work of Being Watched*. New York and London: Rowman and Littlefield, Inc.

Anzaldúa, Gloria. 1987. *Borderlands, La Frontera: The New Mestiza*. San Francisco: Aunt Lute Press.

Aronson, Arnold. 2007. *Looking into the Abyss: Essays on Scenography*. Ann Arbor, MN: University of Michigan Press.

Artaud, Antonin. 1958. *The Theater and Its Double*. Trans. Mary Caroline Richards. New York: Grove Press Inc.

Aspling, Fredrik. 2011. "The Private and the Public in Online Presentations of the Self: A Critical Development of Goffman's Dramaturgical Perspective." Thesis, Stockholms Universitet. http://www.diva-portal.org/smash/get/diva2:431462/FULLTEXT01.pdf

Auslander, Philip. 1999. *Liveness: Performance in a Mediatized Culture*. London and New York: Routledge.

Auslander, Philip. 2001. "Cyberspace as a Performance Art Venue." *Performance Research*, 38.2: 123–126.

Auslander, Philip. 2006a. "The Performativity of Performance Documentation." *PAJ: Performing Arts Journal*, 28.3: 1–10.

Auslander, Philip. 2006b. "Humanoid Boogie: Reflections on Robotic Performance." In *Staging Philosophy: Intersections of Theatre, Performance and Philosophy,* edited by David Krasner and David Saltz, 87–103. Ann Arbor, MI: University of Michigan Press.

Auslander, Philip. 2008. "Live and Technologically Mediated Performance." In *The Cambridge Companion to Performance Studies,* edited by Tracy C. Davis. Cambridge: Cambridge University Press.

Auslander, Philip. 2012. "Digital Liveness: A Historico-Philosophical Perspective." *PAJ: A Journal of Performance and Art,* 34.3: 3–11.

Austin, J.L. 1975. *How to Do Things with Words: The William James Lectures Delivered in 1955.* Cambridge, MA: Harvard University Press.

Badiou, Alain. 2005. *Being and Event.* Translated by Oliver Feltham. London and New York: Continuum.

Banes, Sally. 2006. *Before, Between, and Beyond: Three Decades of Dance Writing.* Madison, WI: University of Wisconsin Press.

Bakhtin, Mikhail. 1984. *Problems of Dostoevsky's Poetics,* edited and translated by Caryl Emerson. Vol. 8 of *Theory and History of Literature,* edited by Wlad Godzich and Jochen Schulte-Sasse. Minneapolis, MN: University of Minnesota Press.

Barba, Eugenio. 1985. "The Nature of Dramaturgy: Describing Actions at Work." *New Theatre Quarterly,* 1: 75–78.

Barber, Karin. 1999. "Quotation in the Constitution of Yoruba Oral Texts." *Research in African Literatures,* 30.2: 17–41.

Bateson, Gregory. 1955. *A Theory of Play and Fantasy: A Report on Theoretical Aspects of The project for Study of the Role of the Paradoxes of Abstraction in Communication.* Indianapolis, IN: Bobbs-Merill.

Baudrillard, Jean. 1983. *Simulations.* Los Angeles, CA: Semiotext(e).

Baudrillard, Jean. 1994. *Simulacra and Simulation.* Ann Arbor, MI: University of Michigan.

Baudrillard, Jean. 1995. *The Gulf War Did Not Take Place.* Translated by Paul Patton. Bloomington, IN: Indiana University Press.

Baugh, Christoper. 2005. *Theater, Performance, and Technology: The Development of Scenography in the Twentieth Century.* New York: Palgrave Macmillan.

Bay-Cheng, Sarah. 2001. "An Illogical Stab of Doubt: Avant-Garde Drama, Cinema, and Queerness." *Studies in the Humanities,* 28.1–2: 1–12.

Beckett, Samuel. 1961. *Happy Days: A Play in Two Acts.* New York: Grove Press.

Benjamin, Walter. 1936. "The Work of Art in the Age of Mechanical Reproduction." In *Illuminations: Essays and Reflections,* edited by Hannah Arendt and translated by Harry Zohn. New York: Schocken.

Benjamin, Walter. 1999. *The Arcades Project,* edited by Rolf Tiedemann. Cambridge, MA: Belknap Press of Harvard University Press.

Benjamin, Walter. 2008. *The Work of Art in the Age of its Technological Reproducibility, and Other Writings on Media,* edited by Michael William Jennings, Brigid Doherty, Thomas Y. Levin and Edmund Jephcott. Cambridge, MA: Belknap Press of Harvard University Press.

Bennett, Susan, ed. 1990. *Theatre Audiences: A Theory of Production and Reception.* Reprint, 1997. London and New York: Routledge.

Bensaïd, Daniel. 2004. "Alain Badiou and the Miracle of the Event." In *Think Again, Alain Badiou and the Future of Philosophy,* edited by Peter Hallward. London and New York: Continuum.

Bentham, Jeremy. 1791. "Panopticon, or the Inspection House." In *The Panopticon Writings,* edited by Miran Bozovic. Reprint, London: Verso, 1995.

Berghaus, Günter, ed. 1996. *Fascism and Theatre: Comparative Studies on the Aesthetics and Politics of Performance in Europe, 1925–1945,* New York: Berghahn Books.

Bhabha, Homi K. 1984. "Of Mimicry and Man: The Ambivalence of Colonial Discourse." *October,* 28.1: 125–133.

Bharata. 1996. *Bharata: The Natyashastra*, edited by Kapila Vatsyayan. New Delhi: Sahitya Academy.

Bial, Henry. 2005. *Acting Jewish: Negotiating Ethnicity on the American Stage and Screen.* Ann Arbor, MI: University of Michigan Press.

Blackson, Robert. 2007. "Once More ... with Feeling: Reenactment in Contemporary Art and Culture." *Art Journal*, 66.1: 28–40.

Blau, Herbert. 1982. *Take Up the Bodies: Theater at the Vanishing Point*, Urbana, IL: University of Illinois Press.

Blau, Herbert, 1990. *The Audience.* Baltimore, MD: Johns Hopkins University Press.

Block, Melissa. 2013. "In 'According To What?' Ai Weiwei Makes Mourning Subversive." *All Things Considered.* NPR, January 23. http://www.npr.org/2013/01/23/169973843/in-according-to-what-ai-weiwei-makes-mourning-subversive

Bly, Mark, ed. 1996. *Theatre in Process.* Vol. 1 of *The Production Notebooks.* New York: Theatre Communications Group.

Boal, Augusto. 1979. *Theater of the Oppressed.* New York: Urizen Books.

Boal, Augusto. 1990. "Invisible Theater." In *Re:Direction,* edited by Rebecca Schneider and Gabrielle H. Cody. London: Routledge.

Bolter, Jay David and Richard Grusin. 2000. *Remediation: Understanding New Media.* Cambridge, MA: MIT Press.

Bourdieu, Pierre. 1993. *The Field of Cultural Production.* New York: Columbia University Press.

Bouissac, Paul. 1976. *Circus and Culture.* Bloomington, IN: Indiana University Press.

Bourriaud, Nicolas. 2002. *Relational Aesthetics.* Dijon: Leses Du Réel.

Braudy, Leo. 1986. *The Frenzy of Renown: Fame and its History.* New York: Oxford University Press, Inc.

Brecht, Bertolt. 1964. *Brecht on Theatre.* Translated by John Willett. New York: Hill & Wang.

Brighenti, Andrea Mubi. 2010. "Democracy and Surveillance." *Surveillance and Democracy,* edited by Kevin D. Haggerty and Minas Samatas, 51–68. Abingdon, Oxon: Routledge.

Broadhurst, Susan. 1999. *Liminal Acts: A Critical Overview of Contemporary Performance and Theory.* London and New York: Cassell.

Bryant, Ben. 2013. "Malala Yousafzai Recounts Moment She Was Shot in the Head By Taliban." *The Telegraph,* October 13. http://www.telegraph.co.uk/news/worldnews/asia/Pakistan/10375633/Malala-Yousafzai-recounts-moment-she-was- shot-in-the-head-by-Taliban.html

Büchner, Georg. 1836. *Woyzeck.* London: Eyre Methuen.

Burger, Peter. 1984. *Theory of the Avant-Garde.* Translated by Michael Shaw. Minneapolis, MN: University of Minnesota Press.

Butler, Judith. 1988. "Performative Acts and Gender Constitution: An Essay in Phenomenology and Feminist Theory." *Theatre Journal,* 40.4: 519–531.

Butler, Judith. 1990. *Gender Trouble: Feminism and the Subversion of Identity.* Reprint, New York: Routledge 1999.

Cage, John. 1957. "Experimental Music." Lecture, Convention of the Music Teachers National Association. Chicago.

Cage, John. 1961. *Silence: Lectures and Writings.* Middletown, CT: Wesleyan University Press.

Calinescu, Adriana. 1987. *Of Gods and Mortals: Ancient Art from the V.G. Simkhovitch Collection; Indiana Art Museum, Sept. 16–Dec. 20, 1987.* Bloomington, IN: Indiana University Press.

Camphausen, Rufus. 1997. *Return of the Tribal: A Celebration of Body Adornment.* Rochester, VT: Inner Traditions/Bear.

Carlson, Marvin. 2003. *The Haunted Stage: The Theatre as Memory Machine.* Ann Arbor, MI: The University of Michigan Press.

Carmeli, Yoram S. 1990. "Performing the 'Real' and 'Impossible' in the British Traveling Circus." *Semiotica* 80 (3-4): 193–220.

Carnicke. Sharon. 2009. *Stanislavsky in Focus: An Acting Master for the Twenty-first Century.* London: Routledge.

Carnicke. Sharon. 2010. "The Knebel Technique: Active Analysis in Practice." In *Actor Training*, edited by Alison Hodge, 99–116. London: Routledge.

Carnicke. Sharon. 2012. "Emotional Expressivity in Motion Picture Capture Technology." In *Acting and Performance in Moving Image Culture: Bodies, Screens, Renderings*, edited by Joerg Sternagel, Deborah Levitt, and Dieter Mersch, 321–338. Berlin: Verlag für Kommunikation, Kultur und soziale Praxis.

Case, Sue-Ellen. 2003. *The Domain-Matrix: Performing the Lesbian at the End of Print Culture.* Indianapolis, IN: University of Indiana Press.

Cassils, Heather. 2011. "LadyFace // ManBody." *LadyFace // ManBody*. http://www.ladyfacemanbody.com/?zx=e95d696671a03bb6

Cassils, Heather. 2013. "Bashing Binaries – Along with 2,000 Pounds of Clay." *The Huffington Post*, September 7. http://www.huffingtonpost.com/heather/bashing- binaries-along-with-2000-pounds-of-clay_b_3861322.html

Castellucci, Romeo. 2006. "Après: Changer Dans L'inertie," Press Packet for the Avignon Production of Hey Girl!, 2006." http://www.festival-avignon.com/en/Archive/Artist/2013/227

"Chanel: Fragrances-No. 5 History." Chanel website, accessed July 21, 2009. http://uma.live.chanel.com/fragrances/n05-history.php

Chaudhuri, Una. 1984. "The Spectator in Drama/Drama in the Spectator." *Modern Drama*, 27.3: 281–298.

Chaudhuri, Una. 1996. *Staging Place: The Geography of Modern Drama*. Ann Arbor, MI: University of Michigan Press.

Chaudhuri, Una and Elinor Fuchs. 2002. *Land/scape/theater*. Ann Arbor, MN: University of Michigan Press.

Cheng, Meiling. 1998. "*Les Demoiselles d/L.A.*: Sacred Naked Nature Girls' *Untitled Flesh*." *TDR: The Drama Review*, 42.2: 70–97.

Cheng, Meiling. 2001. "Highways, L.A.: Multiple Communities in a Heterolocus." *Theatre Journal*, 53.3: 429–454.

Cheng, Meiling. 2002. *In Other Los Angeleses: Multicentric Performance Art*. Berkeley, CA: University of California Press.

Cheng, Meiling. 2005. "Violent Capital; Zhu Yu on File." *TDR: The Drama Review*, 49.3: 58–77.

Cheng, Meiling. 2006. "Extreme Performance and Installation from China." *TheatreForum*, 29 (Summer 2006): 88–96.

Cheng, Meiling. 2007. "Animalworks in China." *TDR: The Drama* Review, 51.1: 63–91.

Cheng, Meiling. 2011. "Ai Weiwei: Acting is Believing." *TDR: The Drama Review*, 55.4: 7–13.

Cheng, Meiling. 2013. *Beijing Xingwei: Contemporary Chinese Time-Based Art*. London, New York, Calcutta: Seagull Books.

Christov-Bakargiev, Carolyn. 2005. *Arte Povera (Themes and Movements)*. London: Phaidon Press.

Cicchini, Emily. 2013. "New Media as Performance." *HowlRound A Journal of Theatre Commons*, January 18. http://howlround.com/new-media-as-performance

Clark, Kenneth. 1949. *Landscape Into Art*. Reprint, New York: Harper & Row, 1979.

Clark, Lygia. 1997. *Lygia Clark*. Reprint, Barcelona: Fundació Antoni Tàpies, 1998.

Clausen, Barbara. 2007. *After the Act: The (Re) presentation of Performance Art*. Wien: MUMOK Museum Moderner Kunst Stiftung Ludwig.

Cody, Gabrielle H. and Annie Sprinkle. 2001. *Hardcore from the Heart: The Pleasures, Profits and Politics of Sex in Performance*. London and New York: Continuum.

Combahee River Collective. 1974. "The Combahee River Collective Statement." http://circuitous.org/scraps/combahee.html

Conquergood, Dwight. 2002. "Lethal Theatre: Performance, Punishment, and the Death Penalty." *Theatre Journal*, 54.3: 339–367.

Cosgrove, Denis. 2008. *Geography and Vision: Seeing, Imagining and Representing the World*. London: I. B. Tauris & Co.

Cutler, Bert. 2003. "Partner Selection, Power Dynamics, and Sexual Bargaining in Self-

Defined BDSM Couples." PhD diss., The Institute for Advanced Study of Human Sexuality.

Damasio, Antonio. 1999. *The Feeling of What Happens in the Body: Body and Emotion in the Making of Consciousness*. New York: Harcourt.

Damasio, Antonio. 2003. *Looking for Spinoza: Joy, Sorrow and the Feeling Brain*. Orlando, FL: Harcourt Inc.

Davis, Zeinabu Irene. 2001. "'Beautiful-Ugly' Blackface: An Esthetic Appreciation of *Bamboozled*." *Cineaste*, 26.2: 16–17.

De Certeau, Michel. 1980. "On the Oppositional Practices of Everyday Life." *Social Text* Vol. 3, translated by Frederic Jameson and Carl Lovitt, 3–43.

De Certeau, Michel. 1996. "Vocal Utopias: Glossolalias." Translated by Daniel Rosenberg. *Representations*, 56: 29–47.

Debord, Guy. 1956. "Theory of the Dérive." *Situationist International Anthology*, edited and translated by Ken Knabb. California: Bureau of Public Secrets. http://www.bopsecrets.org/SI/2.derive.htm

Debord, Guy. 1967. *The Society of the Spectacle*. New York: Zone.

Debord, Guy. 1971. *Masochism: An Interpretation of Coldness and Cruelty*. Translated by Jean McNeil, 1971. New York: Braziller. Originally published as *Présentation de Sacher-Masoch*. Paris: Editions Minuit, 1967.

Debord, Guy. 1997 "The Game of War." In *Guy Debord: Revolutionary*, by Len Bracken. Venice, CA: Feral House.

Debord, Guy. 2005 *The Society of Spectacle*. Translated by Ken Knabb. Oakland, CA: AK Press.

Deleuze, Gilles. 1969. *The Logic of Sense*. Translated by Mark Lester and Charles Stivale. Reprint, New York: Columbia University Press, 1990.

Deleuze, Gilles. 1990. "Societies of Control." *L'autre journal* 1 (May 1990): 3–7.

Deleuze, Gilles. 1994. *Difference and Repetition*. New York: Columbia University Press.

Derrida, Jacques. 1978. *Writing and Difference*. Translated by Alan Bass. Chicago, IL: The University of Chicago Press.

Derrida, Jacques. 1982. *Margins of Philosophy*. Chicago, IL: University of Chicago Press.

Derrida, Jacques. 1994. *Specters of Marx: The State of the Debt, the Work of Mourning, and the New International*. New York: Routledge.

Diamond, Elin. 1988. "Brechtian Theory/Feminist Theory: Toward a Gestic Feminist Criticism." *TDR: The Drama Review*, 32.1: 82–94.

Diamond, Elin. 1997. *Unmaking Mimesis: Essays on Feminism and Theatre*, New York: Routledge.

Diderot, Denis. 1957. *The Paradox of Acting*. New York: Hill and Wang.

Dixon, Steve. 2007. *Digital Performance*. Cambridge, MA: MIT Press.

Dolan, Jill. 1988. *Feminist Spectator as Critic*. Ann Arbor, MI: University of Michigan Press.

Dolan, Jill. 2005. *Utopia in Performance: Finding Hope at the Theatre*. Ann Arbor, MI: University of Michigan Press.

Dolan, Jill. 2013. *The Feminist Spectator in Action: Feminist Criticism for the Stage and Screen*. New York: Palgrave Macmillan.

Dolan, Jill. 2014. "Critical Generosity." *Public: A Journal of Imagining America* 1. http://public.imaginingamerica.org/blog/article/critical-generosity-2/

Douglas, Mary. 2004. *Purity and Danger: An Analysis of Concept of Pollution and Taboo*. London and New York: Routledge.

Du Bois, W.E.B. 1903. *The Souls of Black Folk*. Reprint, New York: Dover Publications, 1994.

Dunne, Susan. 2013. "'Making Tracks' by Laurie Frick at Real Art Ways." *Hartford Courant*, January 8. http://articles.courant.com/2013-01-08/entertainment/hc-artweek-0110-20130108_1_real-art-ways-activity-data

Dworkin, Andrea and Catherine A. MacKinnon. 1984. *Pornography and Civil Rights: A New Day for Women's Equality*. Minneapolis, MN: Organizing Against Pornography.

Eckstein, Arthur. 2004. "The Hollywood Ten in History and Memory." *Film History*, 16.4: 424–436.

Eisenstein, Sergei. 1974. "The Montage of Attractions." *TDR: The Drama Review*, translated by Daniel Gerould, 18.1: 77–85. Originally published in *LEF* (1923).

Elam, Keir. 1980. *The Semiotics of Theater and Drama*. London: Routledge.

Ellis, Anthony. 1984. "Offense and the Liberal Conception of the Law." *Philosophy and Public Affairs*, 13.1: 3–23.

Fabião, Eleonora. 2006. *Precarious, Precarious, Precarious: Performative Historiography and the Energetics of the Paradox*. New York: New York University Press.

Fabião, Eleonora. 2012. "History and Precariousness: In Search of a Performative Historiography." In *Perform, Repeat, Record: Live Art in History*, edited by Amelia Jones and Adrian Heathfield. Bristol: Intellect.

Fabião, Eleonora. 2014. "The Making of a Body: Lygia Clark's Anthropofagic Slobber." In *Lygia Clark: The Abandonment of Art*, edited by Cornelia Butler and Luis Pérez-Oramas. New York: The Museum of Modern Art.

Fahy, Thomas and Kimball King, eds. 2003. *Captive Audience: Prison and Captivity in Contemporary Theater*. New York: Routledge.

Fedyszyn, Joan. 2006. "The Concrete Wall: What Happened?" *Buffalo Pundit.com*. http://www.buffalorising.com/home/archives/001653php

Fetterly, Judith. 1978. *The Resisting Reader*. Bloomington, IN: Indiana University Press.

Finn, Jonathan. 2009. *Capturing the Criminal Image: From Mug Shot to Surveillance Society*. Minneapolis, MN and London: University of Minnesota Press.

Fish, Stanley. 1980. *Is There a Text in This Class?* Cambridge, MA: Harvard University Press.

Foucault, Michel. 1966. *The Order of Things: An Archaeology of the Human Sciences*. Reprint, London: Tavistock Publication, 1970.

Foucault, Michel. 1971. "The Discourse of Knowledge" In *The Archaeology of Knowledge*, translated A.M. Sheridan Smith, 215–237. New York: Pantheon.

Foucault, Michel. 1975. *Discipline & Punish*. New York: Random House, Inc.

Foucault, Michel. 1977. *Discipline and Punish: The Birth of the Prison*. Translated by Alan Sheridan. New York: Vintage.

Foucault, Michel. 1980. *Power/Knowledge: Selected Interviews and Other Writings 1972–1977*, edited by Colin Gordon and translated by Colin Gordon, Leo Marshall, John Mepham and Kate Soper. New York: Pantheon.

Foucault, Michel. 1991. *Discipline and Punish: The Birth of the Prison*. Translated by Alan Sheridan. New York: Vintage Books.

Fraden, Rena. 2001. *Imagining Medea: Rhodessa Jones & Theater for Incarcerated Women*. Chapel Hill, NC: University of North Carolina Press.

Franklin, H. Bruce. 1978. *The Victim as Criminal and Artist*. Oxford: Oxford University Press.

Franklin, H. Bruce, ed. 1998 *Prison Writing in 20th-Century America*. New York: Penguin.

Freud, Sigmund. 1905. "Three Contributions to the Theory of Sex." In *The Basic Writings of Sigmund Freud*, ed. A.A. Brill. Reprint, New York: Modern Library, 1938.

Freud, Sigmund. 1933. *New Introductory Lectures on Psycho-analysis*. New York: W.W. Norton.

Frow, J. 2002. "Signature and Brand." In *High-Pop: Making Culture into Public Entertainment*, edited by Jim Collins, 56–74. Malden: Blackwell.

Fuchs, Elinor. 1996. "The Death of Character: Perspectives on Theater After Modernism." In *Drama and Performance Studies*, edited by Timothy Wiles. Bloomington, IN: Indiana University Press.

Fuentes, Marcela. 2015. "Performance Constellations: Memory and Event in Digitally Mediated Protest in the Americas." *Text and Performance Quarterly*, 35.1: 24–42.

Gallese, Vittorio. 2001. "The 'Shared Manifold' Hypothesis: From Mirror Neurons To Empathy." *Journal of Consciousness* Studies, 8.5–7: 33–50. http://www.unipr.it/arpa/

mirror/pubs/pdffiles/Gallese/Gallese%20 2001.pdf

Gaulke, Cheri. 1981. *Sisters Of Survival: End of the Rainbow*. Los Angeles, CA: Self-published.

Gaulke, Cheri. 2011. *Doin' It in Public: Feminism and Art at the Woman's Building*. Los Angeles, CA: Otis College of Art and Design.

Gerould, Daniel. 1974. "Eisenstein's *Wiseman*." *TDR: The Drama Review*, 18.1: 71–85.

Ghosh, Bishnupriya. 2010. "Looking through Coca-Cola: Global Icons and the Popular." *Public Culture*, 22.2: 333–368.

Giannachi, Gabriella. 2004. *Virtual Theatres: An Introduction*. London: Routledge.

Gil, José. 2006. "Paradoxical Body." *TDR: The Drama Review*, 50.4: 21–35.

Gilmore, Grant. 1974. *The Death of Contract*. Columbus, OH: Ohio State University Press.

Goffman, Erving. 1959. *The Presentation of Self in Everyday Life*. New York: Anchor.

Goffman, Erving. 1974. *Frame Analysis*. Cambridge, MA: Harvard University Press.

Goldberg, Roselee. 1979. *Performance: Live Art, 1909 to the Present*. New York: Harry N. Abrams, Inc.

Gombrich, E.H. 1961. *Art and Illusion: A Study in the Psychology of Pictorial Representation*. Princeton, NJ: Princeton University Press.

Gonzales Rice, Karen. 2010. "Enduring Belief: Performance, Trauma, Religion." Dissertation, Duke University. http://hdl.handle.net/10161/2988

Goodall, Jane. 2002. *Performance and Evolution in the Age of Darwin*. London: Routledge.

Goodman, Lizbeth and Jane deGay, eds. 1998. *The Routledge Reader in Gender and Performance*. New York: Routledge.

Gray, John, ed. 1993. *Action Art: A Bibliography of Artists' Performance from Futurism to Fluxus and Beyond*. Westport, CT: Greenwood Press.

Grotowski, Jerzy. 1968. *The Poor Theater*. New York: Simon and Schuster.

Gupt, Bharat. 1994. *Dramatic Concepts Greek and Indian*. Delhi: D.K. Printworld.

Haidu, Rachel. 2010. *The Absence of Work: Marcel Broodthaers, 1964–1976*. Cambridge, MA: MIT Press.

Hall, Edward T. 1966. *The Hidden Dimension*. Garden City, NY: Doubleday.

Hall, Stuart. 1993. "Cultural Identity and Diaspora." In *Colonial Discourse and Post-Colonial Theory. A Reader*, edited by Patrick Williams and Laura Chrisman, 392–403. New York: Harvester Wheatsheaf.

Hardwick, Lorna. 2003. *Reception Studies*. Oxford: Oxford University Press

Harper, Glenn, ed. 1998. *Interventions and Provocations: Conversations on Art, Culture and Resistance*. New York: SUNY University Press.

Hayles, N. Katherine. 2012. *How We Think: Digital Media and Contemporary Technogenesis*. Chicago, IL: University of Chicago Press.

Heathfield, Adrian, ed. 2004. *Live: Art and Performance*. New York: Routledge.

Heathfield, Adrian and Tehching Hsieh. 2009. *Out of Now: The Lifeworks of Tehching Hsieh*. London: Live Art Development Agency.

Herszenhorn, D.M. 2013. "Released Punk Rockers Keep Up Criticism of Putin." *New York Times*, December 23. http://www.nytimes.com/2013/12/24/world/europe/member-of-russian-punk-band-reed-under-amnesty-law.html

Hickey, Amber, ed. 2012. *A Guidebook of Alternative Nows*. Los Angeles, CA: The Journal of Aesthetics and Protest Press.

Holm, Jean and John Bowker, eds. 1994. *Rites of Passage*. London: Continuum International Publishing Group.

Holmes, Thomas B. 2002. *Electronic and Experimental Music: Pioneers in Technology and Composition*. New York: Routledge.

Holub, Robert C. 1984. *Reception Theory: A Critical Edition*. New York: Routledge.

Houchin, John H. 2003. *Censorship of the American Theatre in the 20th Century*. Cambridge and New York: Cambridge University Press.

Hurley, Erin. 2010. *Theatre & Feeling*. In *Theatre &* Series, edited by Jen Harvie and Dan Rebellato. Basingstoke: Palgrave Macmillan.

Irigaray, Luce. 1985a. *Speculum of the Other Woman*. Translated by Gillian C. Gill. Ithaca: Cornell University Press.

Irigaray, Luce. 1985b. *This Sex Which Is Not One*. Translated by Catherine Porter and Carolyn Burke. Ithaca: Cornell University Press.

Irish, Sharon. 2010. *Suzanne Lacy: Spaces Between*. Minneapolis, MN: University of Minnesota Press.

Iser, Wolfgang. 1978. *The Act of Reading: A Theory of Aesthetic Response*. Baltimore, MD and London: Johns Hopkins University Press.

Jackall, Robert, ed. 1995. "Propaganda". In *Main Trends of the Modern World Series*, edited by Arthur J. Vidich and Robert Jackall. New York: NYU Press.

Jameson, Fredric. 1981. *The Political Unconscious: Narrative as a Socially Symbolic Act*. Ithaca, NY: Cornell University Press.

Jakovljevic, Branislav. 2009. *Daniil Kharms: Writing and the Event*. Evanston, IL: Northwestern University Press.

Jauss, Hans. 1982. *Toward an Aesthetic of Reception*. Vol. 2 of *Theory and History of Literature*, edited by Wlad Godzich and Jochen Schulte-Sasse. Minneapolis, MN: University of Minnesota Press.

Jenkins, Henry. 1992. *Textual Poachers: Television Fans and Participatory Culture*. New York: Routledge.

Joys, Joanne Carol. 1983. *The Wild Animal Trainer in America*, Boulder, CO: Pruett Publishing Co.

Jonas, Susan S., Geoffrey S. Proehl, and Michael Lupu, eds. 1997. *Dramaturgy in American Theater: A Scource Book*. Fort Worth, TX: Harcourt Brace and Company.

Jones, Amelia. 1998. *Body Art/Performing the Subject*. Minneapolis, MN: University of Minnesota Press.

Jones, Amelia and Adrian Heathfield. 2012. *Perform, Repeat, Record: Live Art in History*. Bristol: Intellect.

Kafka, Franz. 1971. *The Complete Stories*. Translated by Willa and Edwin Muir. New York: Schocken Books.

Kaprow, Allan. 1961. *Essays on the Blurring of Art and Life*. Reprint, Berkeley: University of California Press, 1993.

Kaprow, Allan. 1966a. *Some Recent Happenings*. New York: Something Else Press.

Kaprow, Allan. 1966b. "Letter to the editor." *Tulane Drama Review*, 10.4: 281–283.

Kaprow, Allan. 1993. *Essays on the Blurring of Art and Life*. Berkeley, CA: University of California Press.

Kaprow, Allan. 2001. "Preface to the Expanded Edition: On the Way to Un-Art." In *Essays on the Blurring of Art and Life*, Berkeley, CA: University of California Press.

Kaye, Nick. 2000. *Site-Specific Art: Performance, Place and Documentation*. London: Routledge.

Kirby, Alan. 2009. *Digimodernism: How New Technologies Dismantle the Postmodern and Reconfigure Our Culture*. New York: The Continuum International Publishing Group Inc.

Kirby, Michael. 1965a. *Happenings*. New York: E.P. Dutton & Co., Inc.

Kirby, Michael. 1965b. "The New Theatre." *Tulane Drama Review*, 10.2: 23–43.

Kirshenblatt-Gimblett, Barbara. 1998. *Destination Culture: Tourism, Museums, and Heritage*. Berkeley, CA: University of California Press.

Kohtes, Martin Maria. 1993. "Invisible Theatre: Reflections on an Overlooked Form." *New Theatre Quarterly*, 9: 85–89.

Konijn, E.A. 2000. *Acting Emotions: Shaping Emotions on Stage*. Amsterdam: Amsterdam University Press.

Krafft-Ebing, Richard Von. 1886. *Psychopathia Sexualis*. Translated by Charles Gilbert Chaddock. Reprint, Philadelphia, NJ: F.A. Davis Co., 1894.

Krasner, David. 1997. *Resistance, Parody and Double Consciousness in African American Theatre, 1895–1910*. New York: Palgrave Macmillan.

Krieger, Murray, ed. 1987. *The Aims of Representation: Subject/Text/History*. New York: Columbia University Press.

Lacy, Suzanne, ed. 1995. *Mapping the Terrain: New Genre Public Art*. Seattle, WA: Bay Press.

Lancaster, Kurt. 2001. *Interacting with Babylon 5: Fan Performances in a Media Universe*. Austin, TX: University of Texas Press.

Landsberg, Alison. 1996. "Prosthetic Memory: *Total Recall* and *Blade Runner*." In *Cyberspace/ Cyberbodies/Cyberpunk: Cultures of Technological Embodiment*, edited by Mike Featherstone and Roger Burrows, 175–89. London, Thousand Oaks, CA, New Delhi: Sage Publications.

Laplanche, Jean and Jean-Bertrand Pontalis. 1973. *The Language of Psycho-analysis*. London: Hogarth.

Lenin, Vladimir. 1902. "What Is to Be Done? Burning Questions of our Movement." *Marxists Internet Archive*. https://www.marxists.org/archive/lenin/works/1901/witbd/

Lenoir, Timothy. 2008. "Recycling the Military Entertainment Complex." *Virtual Peace*. http://www.virtualpeace.org/whitepaper.php

Littler, Jo. 2008. "'I Feel your Pain': Cosmopolitan Charity and the Public Fashioning of the Celebrity Soul." *Social Semiotics*, 18.2: 237–251.

Lury, Celia. 2012. "Bringing the World into the World: The Material Semiotics of Contemporary Culture." *Distinktion*, 13.3: 247–260.

Lütticken, Sven, ed. 2005. *Life, Once More: Forms Of Reenactment In Contemporary Art (Performance Art)*, with Jennifer Allen, Peggy Phelan, and Eran Schaerf. Rotterdam, Netherlands: Witte de With Center for Contemporary Art.

Lyon, David. 2001. *Surveillance Society: Monitoring Everyday Life*. New York: Open University Press.

Mann, Steve. 2003. "Existential Technology: Wearable Computing is Not the Real Issue!" *Leonardo*, 36.1: 19–25.

Marranca, Bonnie. 1977. *The Theatre of Images*. New York: Drama Book Specialists.

Marranca, Bonnie. 2009. "Performance and the Spiritual Life: Meredith Monk in Conversation with Bonnie Marranca." *PAJ: A Journal of Performance and Art*, 31.1: 16–36.

Marranca, Bonnie. 2010. "Performance as Design: The Mediaturgy of John Jesurun's *Firefall*." In *PAJ: A Journal of Performance and Art*, 32.3: 16–24.

Marsh, Anne. 1993. *Body and Self: Performance Art in Australia 1969–92*, Melbourne: Oxford University Press.

Masgood, Salman, and Declan Walsh. 2013. "Pakistani Girl, a Global Heroine After an Attack, Has Critics at Home." *New York Times*, October 11. http://www.nytimescom/2013/10/12/world/asia/pakistanis-cant-decide-is-malala-yousafzai-a-heroine-or-western-stooge.html?module=Search&mabReward=relbias%3Ar

Mayhew, Leon H. 1997. "The New Public: Professional Communication and the Means of Social Influence". In *Cambridge Cultural Social Studies*, edited by Jeffrey C. Alexander and Steven Seidman. Cambridge: Cambridge University Press.

McGill, Douglas. 1986. "Art People." *The New York Times*, October 3. http://www.nytimes.com/1986/10/03/arts/art-people.html

McGrath, John Edward. 2004. *Loving Big Brother: Performance, Privacy, and Surveillance Space*. London: Routledge.

McKenzie, Jon. 2001. *Perform or Else: From Discipline to Performance*. New York: Routledge.

McLuhan, Marshall. 1977. "The Medium is the Message." ABC Radio National Network, Australia, June 27. https://www.youtube.com/watch?v=ImaH51F4HBw>/

Mee, Erin. 2009. *Theatre of Roots: Redirecting the Modern Indian Stage*. Kolkata: Seagull Books.

Miglietti, Francesca Alfano. 2003. *Extreme Bodies: The Use and Abuse of the Body in Art*. Translated by Antony Shugaar. Milan: Skira.

Mitchell, W.J.T. 1994. *Landscape and Power*. Chicago, IL: University of Chicago.

Morrison, Elise. 2012. "Witness Protection: Surveillance Technologies in Theatrical Performance." In *Bastard or Playmate? Adapting Theatre, Mutating Media and Contemporary Performing Art*, edited by Robrecht Vanderbeeken, Boris Debackere, David

Depestel, and Christel Stalpaert. Amsterdam: University of Amsterdam Press.

Morrison, Elise. 2013. "User-*unfriendly*: Surveillance Art as Participatory Performance." *Theatre Magazine*, 43.3: 4–23.

Muñoz, José Esteban. 1999. *Disidentifications: Queers of Color and the Performance of Politics.* Minneapolis, MN: University of Minnesota Press.

Nancy, Jean Luc. 1991. *The Inoperative Community.* Minneapolis, MN: University of Minnesota Press.

Nayar, Pramod K. 2009. *Seeing Stars: Spectacle, Society, Celebrity Culture.* New Delhi: Sage.

Newton, Esther. 1979. *Mother Camp: Female Impersonators in America.* Chicago, IL: University of Chicago Press.

Noice, Helga and Tony Noice. 2006. "What Studies of Actors and Acting Can Tell Us About Memory and Cognitive Function." *Current Directions on Psychological Science*, 15.1: 14–18.

Nyman, Michael. 1999. *Experimental Music: Cage and Beyond.* Cambridge: Cambridge University Press.

O'Dell, Kathy. 1998. *Contract with the Skin: Masochism, Performance Art, and the 1970s.* Minneapolis, MN: University of Minnesota Press.

Oenslager, Donald. 1975. *Stage Design: Four Centuries of Scenic Invention.* New York: Viking.

Oliver, Kelly. 2001. *Witnessing: Beyond Recognition.* Minneapolis, MN and London: University of Minnesota Press.

Ollman, Bertell. 1971. "Alienation: Marx's Conception of Man in Capitalist Society". In *Cambridge Studies in the History and Theory of Politics*, edited by Maurice Cowling, G.R. Elton, E. Kedourie, J.G.A. Pocock, J.R. Pole, and Walter Ullman. Cambridge: Cambridge University Press.

Omi, Michael and Howard Winant. 1994. *Racial Formation in the United States: From the 1960s to the 1990s.* New York: Routledge.

O'Neill, Paul and Mick Wilson, eds. 2010. *Curating and the Educational Turn.* London: Open Editions.

Parker, Andrew and Eve Sedgwick. 1995. "Introduction." In *Performativity and Performance*, edited by Andrew Parker and Eve Sedgwick, 1–18. New York: Routledge.

Parker-Starbuck, Jennifer. 2011. "Cyborg Theatre: Corporeal/Technological Intersections in Multimedia Performance". In *Performance Interventions*, edited by Elaine Aston and Bryan Reynolds. Hampshire: Palgrave Macmillan.

Parker-Starbuck, Jennifer. 2014. *Cyborg Theatre: Corporeal/Technological Intersections in Multimedia Performance.* New York: Palgrave Macmillan.

Partridge, Eric. 1953. *From Sanskrit to Brazil; Vignettes and Essays upon Languages.* London: Hamilton.

Pavis, Patrice. 2003. *Analyzing Performance: Theater, Dance, and Film.* Translated by David Williams. Ann Arbor, MA: University of Michigan Press.

Pellegrini, Ann. 2007. "After Sontag: Future Notes on Camp." In *A Companion to Lesbian, Gay, Bisexual, Transgender, and Queer Studies*, edited by George E. Haggerty and Molly McGarry. Oxford: Blackwell.

Phelan, Peggy. 1993. *Unmarked: The Politics of Performance.* New York: Routledge.

Plato. 2003. *The Republic.* Translated by Lee, D. 2nd edn. London: Penguin.

Poster, Mark. 1995. *The Second Media Age.* Cambridge: Blackwell Publishers Inc.

Rafalowicz, Mira. 1997. "Dramaturg in Collaboration with Joseph Chaikin" in *Dramaturgy in American Theater: A Source Book*, edited by Susan S. Jonas, Geoffrey S. Proehl, and Michael Lupu. Fort Worth, TX: Harcourt Brace and Company.

Reinelt, Janelle. 2007. "The Limits of Censorship." *Theatre Research International*, 32.1: 3–15.

Restany, Pierre and Sara Von Saurma. 1996. *Le Monde De L'art En 1995 = The World of Art in 1995.* Paris: UNESCO

Roach, Joseph. 1985. *The Player's Passion.* Newark, DE: The University of Delaware Press.

Roach, Joseph. 1996. *Cities of the Dead: Circum-Atlantic Performance.* New York: Columbia University Press.

Rojek, Chris. 2001. *Celebrity*. London: Reaktion.

Roth, Moira. 2001. "Rachel Marker and the City of Maps, Berlin, Summer 2001." *X-tra*, 4.3. http://x-traonline.org/article/rachel-marker-and-the-city-of-maps-berlin-summer-2001/

Roth, Moira. 2003. "Rachel Marker and Her Book of Shadows." *Art Journal*, 62.3: 66–73.

Roth, Moira. 2006a. "Through the Eyes of Rachel Marker." *Camerawork: A Journal of Photographic Arts*, 33.1: 30–37.

Roth, Moira. 2006b. "Rachel Marker, Franz Kafka and Alice Sommer, adapted from a theatre piece in three acts," *n. Paradoxa*, 17: 19–29.

Rose, Gillian. 1992. *The Broken Middle: Out of Our Ancient Society*. Oxford: Wiley-Blackwell.

Russo, Mary. 1994. *The Female Grotesque: Risk, Excess and Modernity*. London and New York: Routledge.

Russolo, Luigi. 1913. "The Art of Noises Futurist Manifesto." In *The Art of Noises* (1916), translated by Barclay Brown. Reprint, New York: Pendragon Press, 1986.

Saltz, David Z. 2001. "Live Media: Interactive Technology and Theatre." *Theatre Topics*, 11.2: 107–130.

Sandahl, Carrie. 2004. "Black Man, Blind Man: Disability Identity Politics and Performance." *Theatre Journal*, 56.4: 579–602.

Schafer, R. Murray. 1993. *The Soundscape*. Rochester, VT: Destiny Books.

Schechner, Richard. 1973. *Environmental Theater: An Expanded New Edition including "Six Axioms for Environmental Theater."* Reprint, New York: Applause, 1994.

Schechner, Richard. 1997. "Paratheater, 1969–78, and Theater of Sources, 1976–82: Introduction." In *The Grotowski Sourcebook*, edited by Richard Schechner and Lisa Wolford. New York: Routledge.

Schechner, Richard. 2001. "What is Performance Studies?" Interview with Diana Taylor. November 27. http://hidvl.nyu.edu/video/003305515.html

Schechner, Richard. 2002. *Performance Studies: An Introduction*. London: Routledge.

Schechner, Richard. 2006. *Performance Studies: An Introduction*. New York: Routledge.

Schechner, Richard and Willa Appel, eds. 1990. *By Means of Performance: Intercultural Studies of Theatre and Ritual*. Cambridge: Cambridge University Press.

Schneider, Rebecca. 1997. *The Explicit Body in Performance*. New York and London: Routledge.

Schneider, Rebecca. 2001. "Performance Remains." In *Performing Remains: Art and War in times of Theatrical Reenactment*, 100–108. Reprint, Abingdon, Oxon: Routledge, 2011.

Schneider, Rebecca and Gabrielle H. Cody, eds. 2002. *Re:direction: A Theoretical and Practical Guide*, London and New York: Routledge.

Schuler, Catherine. 2013. "Reinventing the Show Trial: Putin and Pussy Riot." *TDR: The Drama Review*, 57.1: 7–17.

Scolari, Carlos A. 2009. "Transmedia storytelling: Implicit consumers, narrative worlds, and branding in contemporary media production." *International Journal of Communication*, 3.4: 586–606.

Shalson, Lara. 2012. "On the Endurance of Theatre in Live Art." *Contemporary Theatre Review*, 22.1: 106–119.

Sell, Mike. 2009. *The Avant-Garde: Race Religion War*. Kolkota: Seagull Books.

Senelick, Laurence. 2000. *The Changing Room: Sex, Drag, and Theatre*. New York: Routledge.

Sholette, Gregory. 2004. "Interventionism and the historical uncanny, or: can there be revolutionary art without the revolution?" In *Interventionists: User's Guide for the Creative Disruption of Everyday Life*, edited by Nato Thompson and Gregory Sholette. North Adams, MA: MASS MoCA Publications.

Sieg, Katrin. 2002. *Ethnic Drag: Performing Race, Nation, Sexuality in West Germany*. Ann Arbor, MI: University of Michigan Press.

Skeat, Walter W. 1980. *A Concise Etymological Dictionary of the English Language*. New York: A Perigee Book.

Stein, Gertrude. 1935a. *Lectures in America*. New York: Random House.

Stein, Gertrude. 1935b. "Play as Landscape." In *Lectures in America*. Boston: Beacon Press.

Stelarc. 2013. "*stelarc // Third Hand*." http://stelarc.org/?catID=20265

Streeter, Kurt. 2014. "Tragedy Shapes a South L.A. Playwright's Artistic Life." *LA Times*, November 14. http://www.latimes.com/local/great-reads/la-me-c1-lynn- manning-20141114-story.html#page=1

Surveillance Camera Players. 2006. "1984." https://www.youtube.com/watch?v=RILTl8mxEnE

Surveillance Camera Players. 2008. "The Raven." / "Waiting for Godot." / "Ubu Roi." https://www.youtube.com/watch?v=TUxQQGXQZVs

Tait, Peta. 2002. *Performing Emotions: Gender, Bodies, Spaces in Chekhov's Drama and Stanislavski's Theater*. Aldershot: Ashgate.

Tait, Peta. 2005. *Circus Bodies: Cultural Identity in Aerial Performance*. London: Routledge.

Tarkovsky, Andrey A. and Giovanni Chiaramonte, eds. 2006. *Instant Light: Tarkovsky Polaroids*. London: Thames & Hudson.

Taussig, Michael. 1993. *Mimesis and Alterity: A Particular History of the Senses*. London: Routledge.

Taylor, Diana. 1997. *Disappearing Acts: Spectacles of Gender and Nationalism in Argentina's "Dirty War."* Durham, NC: Duke University Press.

Taylor, Diana. 2003. "Bush's Happy Performative." *TDR: The Drama Review*, 47.3: 5–8.

Thompson, Nato and Gregory Sholette. 2004. *Interventionists: User's Guide for the Creative Disruption of Everyday Life*. North Adams, MA: MASS MoCA Publications.

Tribe, Mark, Reena Jana, and Uta Grosenick. 2006. *New media art*. Taschen Basic Art Series. Cologne: Taschen.

Turkle, Sherry. 1997. *Life on the Screen: Identity in the Age of the Internet*. New York: Touchstone.

Turner, Cathy and Synne Behrndt. 2008. "Dramaturgy and Performance." In *Theatre and Performance Practices*, edited by Graham Ley and Jane Milling. Hampshire: Palgrave Macmillan.

Turner, Victor. 1974. "Liminal to Liminoid, in Play, Flow, and Ritual: An Essay in Comparative Symbology." *The Rice University Studies*, 60.3: 53–92.

Turner, Victor. 1987. *The Anthropology of Performance*. New York: PAJ.

Turner, Victor and Edward M. Bruner, eds. 1986. *The Anthropology of Experience*. Urbana, IL: University of Illinois Press.

Ubersfeld, Anne. 1999. *Reading Theater*. Translated by Frank Collins. Toronto: University of Toronto Press.

Ullman, K. Harlan, and James P. Wade. 1996. *Shock and Awe: Achieving Rapid Dominance*. Washington, DC: National Defense University Press.

Van Gennep, Arnold. 1909. *The Rites of Passage*. Chicago, IL: University of Chicago Press.

Veinstein, André. 1955. *La mise en scène théâtrale et sa condition esthétique*. Paris: Flammarion.

Veloso, Caetano. 1991. *Fora da Ordem*. Circuladô: Nonesuch.

Vergine, Lea. 1974. *The Body as Language: "Body Art" and Performance*. Reprint, 2001. Milan: Skira.

Von Ranke, Leopold. 1965. *Leopold Ranke, the Formative Years*. Ann Arbor, MI: University Microfilms.

Wacquant, Loic. 2005. "The Great Leap Backward: Imprisonment in America from Nixon to Clinton." In *The New Punitiveness: Trends, Theories, Perspectives*, edited by John Pratt, David Brown, Mark Brown, Simon Hallsworth, and Wayne Morrison, 3–26. London: Willan.

Warr, Tracy and Amelia Jones. 2000. *The Artist's Body (Themes and Movements)*. Reprint, 2102. London: Phaidon Press.

Watson, Gray. 2003. "Alastair MacLennan: A Poetic Invitation." In *Alastair MacLennan Knot Naught*. Belfast: Ormeau Baths Gallery.

Weems, Marianne. 2008. "SuperVision." *Super Vision*. http://www.superv.org

Weick, Karl E. 1979. *The Social Psychology of Organizing*. In *Topics in Social Psychology Series*. New York: McGraw Hill Publishing.

Weisgerber, Corinne. 2011. "Negotiating Multiple Identities on the Social Web: Goffman, Fragmentation, and the Multiverse." Keynote Address, WebCom Montréal from Montréal, 2011. http://academic.stedwards.edu/socialmedia/blog/2011/11/16/negotiating-multiple-identities-on-the-social-web-goffman-fragmentation-and-the-multiverse/

Welchman, John. 2003. *Art After Appropriation: Essays on Art in the 1990s*. London: Gordon & Breach.

Whitmore, Jon. 1994. "Directing Postmodern Theater: Shaping Signification in Performance." In *Theatre – Theory, Text, Performance*, edited by David Krasner and Rebecca Schneider. Ann Arbor, MI: University of Michigan Press.

Wiegmink, Pia. 2008. "Performing Resistance: Contemporary American Performance-Activism." *COPAS: Current Objectives of Postgraduate American Studies* 7.

Willett, John. 1964. *The Theatre of Bertolt Brecht: A Study from Eight Aspects*. London: Methuen.

Williams, Raymond. 1977. *Marxism and Literature*. Oxford: Oxford University Press.

Wolford, Lisa. 1997. "General Introduction: Ariadne's Thread." In *The Grotowski Sourcebook*, edited by Richard Schechner and Lisa Wolford. New York: Routledge.

Wolfe, Cary. 2003. *Animal Rites: Animal Culture, the Discourse of Species, and Posthumanist Theory*. Chicago, IL: University of Chicago Press.

Wong, Winnie. 2014. *Van Gogh On Demand: China and the Readymade*. Chicago, IL: University of Chicago Press.

Yamomo, MeLê. 2007. "PostModern Theatre in today's world." *Theater Port*, October. http://www.theatreport.com/modules/soapbox/print.php?articleID=22

Zheng, Bo. 2012. "From *Gongren* to *Gongmin*: A Comparative Analysis of Ai Weiwei's *Sunflower Seeds* and *Nian*." *Journal of Visual Art Practice*, 11: 117–133.

# Part III

# Methodologies/ turning points and paired case studies

## Aging

Cynthia Port

Race, class, gender, and sexuality have been at the center of artistic production and criticism for decades, whereas the significance of age as a category of identity and difference has been slower to gain widespread recognition. In 2004, Margaret Morganroth Gullette made the case that aging is a cultural as well as a biological phenomenon; Gullette has identified the cultural assumptions that unconsciously structure attitudes about aging as "age ideology" (2004, 28).

The dominant age ideology in the United States constructs youth and old age as opposing categories rather than parts of an interconnected spectrum. Mainstream culture equates youth with beauty and opportunity and old age with loss, decline, and decrepitude. Obsessed with the future and fetishizing the new and the young, American cultural rhetoric positions older people as obsolete burdens on younger generations. Art by or about older people can mitigate the invisibility and disempowerment of the old and help resituate aging in the cultural hierarchy. However, artists and performers should be aware of the risk of reasserting stereotypes of old age—even those that highlight positive traits. Too often, as Kathleen Woodward argues, older age is "deemed a matter for comedy or sentimental compassion" (2006, 164). Also damaging is the tendency to celebrate "successful" aging, while further marginalizing the disabled, frail, or cognitively impaired old. Rather than "prescribing what it means to be old," performance can aim to illuminate "a range of possibilities of what aging can be" (Basting 1991/1998, 145).

Anne Basting was the first to theorize extensively the relation between aging and performance. In *The Stages of Age* (1991/1998), she examines a variety of performance idioms including senior theatre, feminist performance art, and a Broadway musical. In one chapter, Basting analyzes the dance *Water Lilies* by the eighty-seven-year-old choreographer Kazuo Ohno, in which Ohno and his son embody a fluid, non-linear mix of genders, ages, and cultures, revealing "the inseparability of life stages" in what Basting calls a "depth model of aging" (1998, 141, 148). More recently, Basting has worked directly with nursing home residents with cognitive challenges, as well as nursing home staff, family members, actors, and students to develop a collaborative ensemble performance (thepenelopeproject.com).

Basting and others have adapted Judith Butler's notion of gender performativity to the recognition that age is, in part, constituted by the repeated iteration of gestures and social scripts by bodies and selves that are constantly, incrementally, changing over time (Basting 1998; Lipscomb 2004: Lipscomb and Marshall 2010; Swinnen and Stotesbury 2012). Staged performance therefore entails a "slippery and complex interplay between an actor's and character's chronological ages and such behavioral norms as the performance challenges or reproduces" (Moore 2014). An age dynamic emerges among performer, character, and audience member, often inflected by "the youthful structure of the look," which Kathleen Woodward defines as the culturally induced tendency of a spectator to self-identify as younger than a character who is thereby "reduced ... to the prejudicial category of old age" (2006, 164). What Woodward elsewhere calls a "masquerade of youthfulness" is often deployed, especially by women, to mask the physical effects of aging and thereby delay its social implications (1991, 147–166).

Some methods of resisting limiting age norms include "age bending," the parodic transgression of age categories (Swinnen and Stotesbury 2012, 8), and intergenerational collaboration (Basting 1998; Berson, 2010), though such methods carry the risk of further marginalizing rather than effectively integrating the old. Works might also explore the intersectionality of age with other categories of difference that compound the discriminatory effects of ageism. Whereas both "decline narratives" and "progress narratives" can produce reductive, limited visions of the life course (Gullette 2004; Port 2012), temporal experimentation might suggest ways to highlight the multiple "age-selves" that we often experience simultaneously or nonlinearly (Cristofovici 1999). With thoughtful attention to age as a category, performance has the potential, as Anne Basting tells us, to "unsettle existing definitions of aging and put forth an image of age as a heterogeneous blend of mental, physical, and spiritual growth and loss" (1991, 81).

### Further reading

Basting (1991/1998); Lipscomb and Marshall (2010).

### References


Basting, Anne Davis. 1991. *The Stages of Age: Performing Age in Contemporary American Culture*. Reprint, 1998. Ann Arbor, MN: University of Michigan Press.

Berson, Jessica. 2010. "Old Dogs, New Tricks: Intergenerational Dance." In *Staging Age: The Performance of Age in Theatre, Dance, and Film*, edited by Leni Marshall and Valerie Barnes Lipscomb, 164–189. New York: Palgrave Macmillan.

Cristofovici, Anca. 1999. "Touching Surfaces: Photography, Aging, and an Aesthetics of Change." In *Figuring Age: Women Bodies, Generations*, edited by Kathleen Woodward, 268–293. Bloomington, IN: Indiana University Press.

Gullette, Margaret Morganroth. 2004. *Aged by Culture*. Chicago, IL: University of Chicago Press.

Lipscomb, Valerie Barnes. 2004. *Act Your Age: The Performance of Age in Modern and Postmodern Drama*. PhD diss., University of South Florida, Tampa, FL.

Lipscomb, Valerie Barnes and Leni Marshall, eds. 2010. *Staging Age: The Performance of Age in Theatre, Dance, and Film*. New York: Palgrave.

Moore, Bridie. 2014. "Depth, Significance, and Absence: Age-Effects in New British Theatre." *Age, Culture, Humanities: An Interdisciplinary* Journal, 1. http://ageculturehumanities.org/WP/depth-significance-and-absence-age-effects- in-new-british-theatre/

Port, Cynthia. 2012. "No Future? Aging, Temporality, History, and Reverse Chronologies." *Occasion: Interdisciplinary Studies in the Humanities*, 4 : 1–19.

Swinnen, Aagje and John A. Stotesbury, eds. 2012. *Aging, Performance, and Stardom: Doing Age on the Stage of Consumerist Culture*. Berlin: Lit.

Woodward, Kathleen. 1991. *Aging and its Discontents: Freud and Other Fictions*. Bloomington, IN: Indiana University Press.

Woodward, Kathleen. 2006. "Performing Age, Performing Gender." In *NWSA Journal*, 18.1: 162–189.


### Cross references

"**Actor**" by Mee; "**The ecodramaturgy of Anna Halprin, Eeo Stubblefield, and Rachel Rosenthal**" by Thomas; "**Emotion**" by Tait; "**Ethnic drag**" by Herrera; "**Explicit body performance**" by McGinley; "**Racialization**" by Sell.

## The ecodramaturgy of Anna Halprin, Eeo Stubblefield, and Rachel Rosenthal

Arden Thomas

In the photograph titled *Old Woman Series #31* from Eeo Stubblefield's photographic series *Still Dance with Anna Halprin*, we witness a striking image: a craggy, grey old woman kneeling on moss-covered rocks near a rushing stream. The deep creases and wrinkles on her chest, arms, and shoulders crack the clay and mud that unevenly coats her body as her breasts droop toward the rocks. Dried grass wildly protrudes from her muddied hair. Her hands are clasped together as she hunches towards a small patch of bright green grass springing up from the rock. She seems particularly attuned to that sprite of grass as the water rushes behind her.

In another image, we see the same woman. Covered in mud, slime, and leeches, she wallows in the muck. Her arms arch over her head and she holds clumps of mud that splatter down onto her body. We see the deep wrinkles on her shoulder and back as she lifts her torso and dances in the mud.

Between 1998 and 2002, when she was in her late 70s and early 80s, dancer Anna Halprin participated with performance artist Eeo Stubblefield in site-specific pieces in nature, a genre that Stubblefield developed and coined *Still Dance*. For Stubblefield's *Still Dance with Anna Halprin* series, Halprin performed in twenty-eight locations selected by Stubblefield, who coated Halprin's body with mud, sand, grass, straw, clay, bark, body paint, molasses, plants, twigs, or dirt. As Halprin improvised each of her dances, Stubblefield encouraged her to slow down and find a place of stillness in the performance. Stubblefield then photographed the "still point" of the dance. Allowing the elemental rhythms of nature to touch her body and influence her movements, Halprin and Stubblefield resist dance's historic imperative to assert its choreographic authority through mobility, mapping the dancer's body onto the land. Instead, in the stillness and the slowness of the breath, Halprin listens to and is receptive to the natural world, discovering points of connection and responsiveness.

Through stillness, Stubblefield and Halprin's pieces offer the dance partners–the performer and nature–a chance to assert agency and interconnectivity. By discovering the still, sensual moments between humans and nature, these dances refuse to objectify nature, and instead invite a relationship with nature based on mutuality and connection. The slowing down of temporal flow allows witnesses and participants to directly experience an empathy for the natural world, to reflect on this kinship with the earth. It is Halprin and Stubblefield's hope that this work will move spectators to move out into social actions that help protect the earth.

Too often a call for ecological change can seem romantic or naïve, beckoning aestheticized ideals of

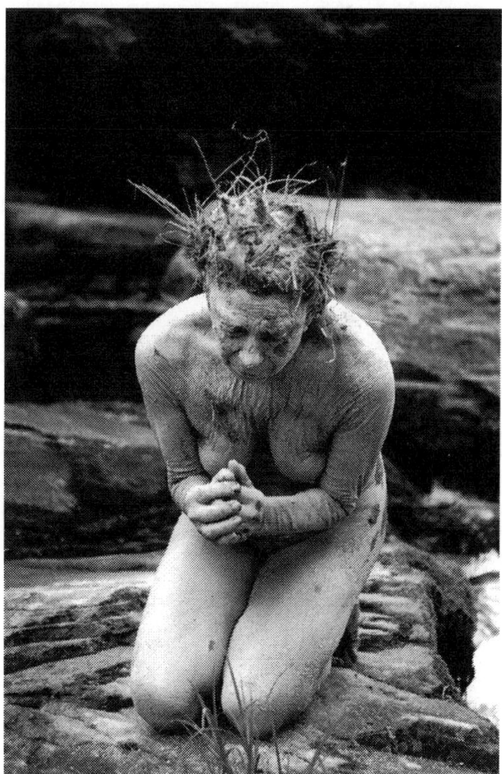

**Figure 24** *Still Dance with Anna Halprin, Old Woman Series* #31. 20 x 24 Color C-Print © Eeo Stubblefield, 1999. Photo courtesy Eeo Stubblefield.

nature far removed from the realities of need and survival related to environmental destruction. Halprin's and Stubblefield's dances in nature, however, are connected to their desire for ecological healing. As Halprin argues, "I believe if more of us could contact the natural world in a directly experiential way, this would alter the way we treat our environment, ourselves and one another." Because of this fundamental commitment to agency, mutuality, and reciprocity with the natural world, these dances offer a politics of equality that acknowledges human beings, nature, animals, and species as co-performers and partners in life.

Like Halprin, performance artist Rachel Rosenthal—performing into her 70s during the 1980s and 1990s—also foregrounds her own aging body as a site for ecological inquiries. Unlike Halprin who embraces duration and sensual moments in the natural world, however, Rosenthal is unruly and excessive, disruptive and angry, registering a deep, passionate, and provocative empathy with the Earth. As she performs *L.O.W. in Gaia*, for example, she chants and raves, dances and bellows, howls and snarls, creating a brutally embodied, mesmerizing performance in which she sets up a correlation between the Earth's body, pain, and passions, and her own:

> I am a loner. All that love, all that lust, all that passion.
> Buried deep. Does it fester inside, does it grow toxic? ...
> I can feel it now.
> In every caged animal.
> Every trapped paw.
> In the tortured lab rat.
> In the rabbits in stocks, their eyes burned out with cosmetic testing.
> In the deep injection of toxic wastes into the Mother.
> In the ignoble plan to plant electrodes in her body and vitrify nuclear waste and mummify it for all eternity.
> I am ill with unquenched vengeance!
> Gaia, my beauty, my lovely, my adored one!
> My core melts with love for you. And compassion.
> And tenderness.

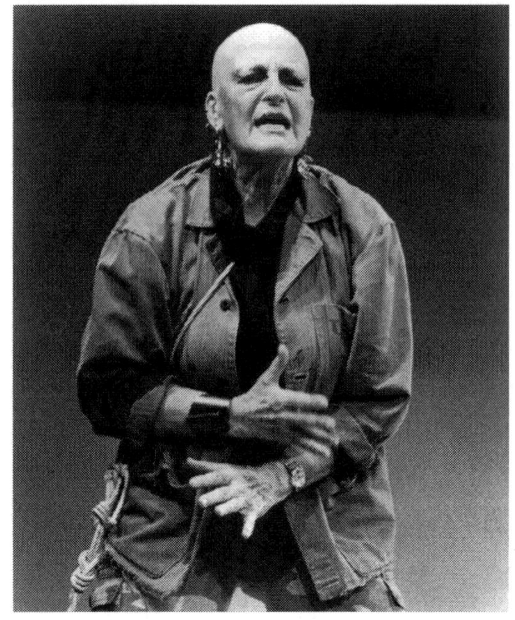

**Figure 25** Rachel Rosenthal, *L.O.W. in Gaia*, performed at the Laguna Museum of Art, 1986. Photo by Jan Deen. Image courtesy of the artist.

> But not calm. Not peaceful.
> (*She bellows*) I could kill!
>
> (*She sobs, picks up the candle, and pours the hot wax on her head.*) [2001: *L.O.W. in Gaia* 108]

In this stunning moment in her performance, Rosenthal holds the audience spellbound, scalding her bald head with hot wax as a means of identifying intimately with the pain felt by animals and the Earth, a pain caused by humans in a culture that uses non-human others as a commodity to be consumed for the sake of technological advancement. Moments of deep love and quiet tenderness rub up against chthonic howls of great anger, betrayal, and violence.

Similarly, in *Pangaean Dreams* she wails, "I will live my allotted time torn apart by my duality, kicking and screaming all the way. With the violent love of Gaia. With fear and trembling, and tender care. With the Pangaean dinosaur ensconced in my brain. In the Earth. Of the Earth. In the world, of the world. Eating and shitting and dreaming and loving, whole or broken (hey, nobody's perfect), until I die!" (2001, 195). Rather than offering a sensual communion with the earth as Halprin does, Rosenthal presents the audience with toxic wastes, the crunching of broken bones, volcanic lava, poisoned soils, the grinding of crustal plates, monsters, dinosaurs, flames, the "gaping fissures that swallow you alive" (2001, 110), erosion, evolution, "sea wind, foam, minor and major tsunami, the leaping of giant turtles and the Antarctic gale" (2001, 189), chaos, and extinction.

Rosenthal argues that ecological citizenship requires a keen, knife-sharp awareness of issues of globalization, pollution, cruelty towards other sentient beings, global warming, and technology. Though Rosenthal embraces a broad, almost mythological sense of the earth and the cosmos ("Gaia" and "Pangaea" play significant roles in her work, for example), at the same time she remains doggedly unwilling to idealize the "natural" world, filling her performances with scientific data, meticulous research into environmental history, pointed comments about modernity and globalization, and methodical enumerations of climate change.

These feelings of anger, melancholia, and disgust put Rosenthal in a dialectic relationship with a toxic, poisoned, radiated environment. Staging a being here, now, in this grief, passion, destruction, and catastrophic ecological moment, Rosenthal snarls and growls, ultimately embracing damage with love.

*References*

*Pangaean Dreams: A Shamanic Journey*, DVD. 2001. Directed by Rachel Rosenthal. Rachel Rosenthal Company.

Rosenthal, Rachel. 2001. *Rachel's Brain and Other Storms. Rachel Rosenthal: Performance Texts*, edited by Una Chaudhuri. London: Continuum.

## Animal Studies

Una Chaudhuri

Animal Studies seeks to extend rigorous study of animals, and of human–animal relationships, far beyond the disciplinary niche in the sciences to which it has traditionally been confined. A programmatically interdisciplinary field, Animal Studies brings the perspectives and methodologies of the humanities and social sciences to what an influential anthology calls "the question of the animal" (Wolfe 2003, xiii)—a question that the field conceives of in the broadest possible ethical, aesthetic, historical, cultural and political terms.

The title of a seminal essay by John Berger, "Why Look at Animals?" indicates one aspect of the field's relevance to studies of performance. Berger argues that modernity organizes a transformation of animal presence in social life, from actual to virtual, or simulated, as exemplified most poignantly by zoo animals, who are "living monument," writes Berger, "to their own disappearance" (1980, 26). A related theorization of the animal in modernity is offered by Akira Lippit in the figure of "the electric animal" (2000, 112), produced within psychoanalysis and cinema as a rethinking of animality, animation, and wildness.

Beyond its capacity to enrich historical accounts of modernity and other periods (the early modern and Victorian periods have also begun to be viewed through this lens (Fudge 2000; Rivto 1987)), it is as a radical rethinking of the fundamental assumptions of humanism that Animal Studies holds greatest promise. The tangled ideological roots of the human-animal binary have engaged contemporary philosophers like Jacques Derrida, Gilles Deleuze, Felix Guattari, and Giorgio Agamben, each of whom has contributed influential concepts to Animal Studies (respectively: "carno-phallologocentrism" (Derrida 1991, 280), "becoming-animal" (Deleuze 1972, 232), and "the anthropological machine" (Agamben 2004, 33), while a sustained literary engagement with the subject is found in the novels of J.M. Coetzee). The most explicit of Coetzee's animal texts, *The Lives of the Animals* (1999), provides multiple connections to performance:

itself originally a performance (delivered as the Tanner Lectures at Princeton) and consisting largely of the description of a performance (fictional lectures at a fictional college), the book's protagonist is urgently concerned with the question of ethical and efficacious animal representation. Though her inquiry concludes with a type of poetry, the criteria she enunciates suggest that it is in fact performance, the embodied practice of imagination, which might best renew the currently impoverished relationship between human and non-human animals.

Special Issues of two performance studies journals, *Performance Research* and *TDR*, guest-edited respectively by Alan Read and Una Chaudhuri, have initiated discussion of the many contemporary performance practitioners, companies, and playwrights like Romeo Castelluci, Forced Entertainment, Rachel Rosenthal, Caryl Churchill, Edward Albee, Sam Shepard, and Zingaro, who have all, in recent years, updated a theatrical tradition reaching back at least as far as Greek "tragedy" (etymologically, "goat-song") and, in terms of ritual performance, to the dawn of religion. This work joins that of countless artists working in various media, worldwide, in envisioning a "postmodern animal" (Baker 2000, 52) whose disturbed and disturbing form is an invitation to imagine living ethically in a "more-than-human world" (Abram 1996, 256).

### Further reading

Chaudhuri and Hughes (2014a); Orozco (2013); Parker-Starbuck (2014); Wolfe (2003).

### References

Abram, David. 1996. *The Spell of the Sensuous: Perception and Language in a More- than-Human World.* New York: Pantheon Books.

Agamben, Giorgio. 2004. *The Open: Man and Animal.* Stanford, CA: Stanford University Press.

Baker, Steve. 2000. *The Postmodern Animal.* London: Reaktion.

Berger, John. 1980. "Why Look at Animals?" In *About Looking.* New York: Pantheon.

Chaudhuri, Una and Holly Hughes, eds. 2014a. *Animal Acts: Performing Species Today.* Ann Arbor, MN: University of Michigan Press.

Coetzee, J.M. 1999. *The Lives of Animals.* Princeton, NJ: Princeton University Press.

Derrida, Jacques. 1991. *Who Comes after the Subject?*, edited by Eduardo Cadava, Peter Connor, and Jean-Luc Nancy. New York: Routledge.

Guattari, Felix and Gilles Deleuze. 1972. *Anti-Oedipus: Capitalism and Schizophrenia,* London: A&C Black.

Fudge, Erica. 2000. *Perceiving Animals: Humans and Beasts in Early Modern English Culture.* New York: Basingstoke.

Lippit, Akira Mizuta. 2000. *Electric Animal: Toward a Rhetoric of Wildlife.* Minneapolis, MN: University of Minnesota Press.

Orozco, Lourdes. 2015. *Theatre and Animals.* Basingstoke: Palgrave Macmillan.

Parker-Starbuck, Jennifer. 2014. *Cyborg Theatre: Corporeal/Technological Intersections in Multimedia Performance.* New York: Palgrave Macmillan.

Read, Alan, ed. 2000. "On Animals." *Performance Research,* Vol. 5.2, special issue.

Ritvo, Harriet. 1987. *The Animal Estate: The English and Other Creatures in the Victorian Age.* Cambridge, MA: Harvard University Press.

Wolfe, Cary. 2003. *Animal Rites: Animal Culture, the Discourse of Species, and Posthumanist Theory.* Chicago, IL: University of Chicago Press.

### Cross references

"**Animalworks**" by Cheng; "**Body Art Still Image Action: Offering**" by Caranza, with Darsalia and Cheng; "**Broad spectrum approach**" by Schechner; "**Carolee Schnemann's *CatScan (New Nightmares/Ancient History)***" by Rundle; "**Ecodramaturgy**" by Thomas.

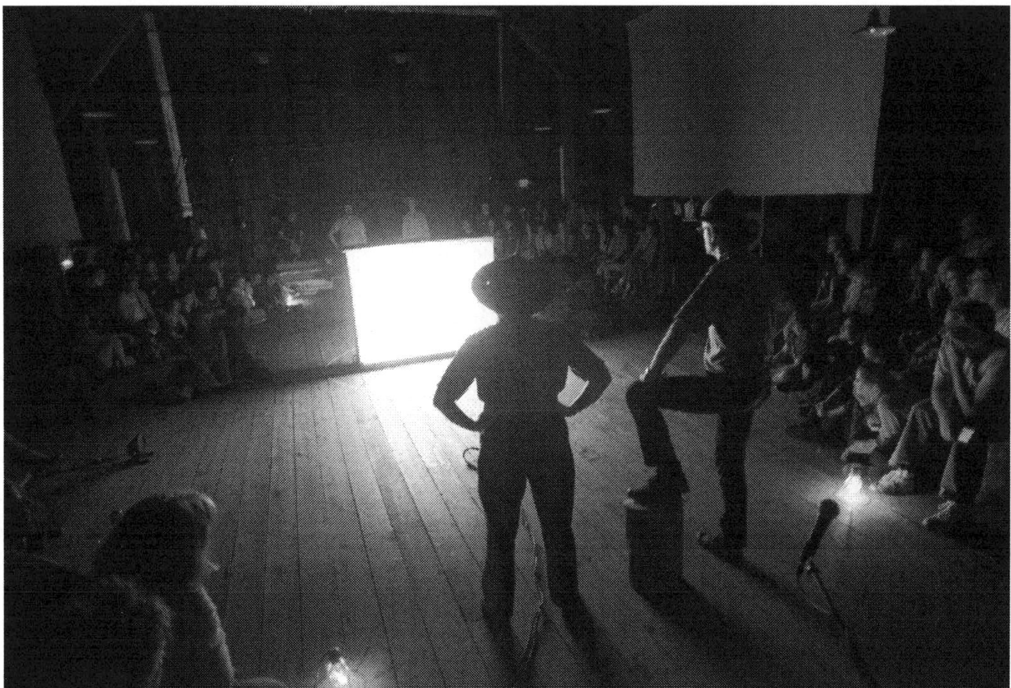

**Figure 26** *Wolf* by Deke Weaver. Image credit Valerine Oliveiro. Image courtesy of the photographer.

## Knowing animals now: *The Unreliable Bestiary*, a multi-part, ongoing performance project by Deke Weaver

Una Chaudhuri

We're welcomed on board the bus by a uniformed Forest Ranger, a genial fellow who gives us a sort of orientation to the unusual place we'll be visiting for this performance (in truth, of course, the performance of *The Unreliable Bestiary* has begun). Along with details about the forest we're going to–an "island" of forest among the monocultural Illinois farmlands–he mentions "The Energy," and promises us an intense experience of it. His presentation includes video clips of wolf experts, wolf stories from world mythology, and drawings of wolf faces in various emotional states–aggression, fear–expressions he gets us to try out on each other. He also leads us in a sing-along of "Home on the Range," and gets another "Ranger" to give a rendition of "The Biologist's Lullaby," an achingly tender song intended to calm the wolves being sedated from scientific reasons, as well as to remind the scientist about the order in which the drugs are to be administered.

We arrive at and walk through the moonlit forest, toward the mysterious sounds of "The Energy" coming from deep within it. At one point we have to skirt a red cape abandoned on the path ("We had an incident here earlier today; the faint of heart should look away," remarks the Ranger); at another point there's a wolf lying on the side of the path, and the Ranger whispers to us about how the wolf has been trapped and sedated in order to be studied by those who are monitoring the fragile wolf population in the forest preserve. The wolf suddenly gets up on two feet and darts off. "Wow!" says the Ranger, "That's very unusual. Wow!" Giggling happily, we proceed to a glorious barn for the rest of the show.

*Wolf* is the third part of an ongoing project by performance artist/storyteller Deke Weaver and his artistic collaborators. *The Unreliable Bestiary* is a series of multi-media performances, one for each letter of the alphabet, each representing an endangered species or habitat. The first letter performed was M, for Monkey, followed by E, for Elephant. That Weaver is now on W tells us something about his unconcern with alphabetic "order." His concern, rather, is with the traumatic *disorder* into which modernity has plunged so many species and landscapes, and with the attitudes of mind and habits of life that are responsible. These ways of thinking are as much Weaver's topic as are the animals he studies and presents, and the underlying principle of *The Unreliable Bestiary* is that live, embodied performance can reveal and perhaps revise the ideological mechanisms that have allowed human beings to bring so many other species to the brink of extinction.

Like most contemporary thought and art that takes animals seriously (DeGrazia 1996), Weaver's attention to other species unfolds within a keen recognition of their incalculable value to our own–a value that extends far beyond the material or utilitarian spheres: "By 2050 climate change and our exploding population will push half the species on the planet into extinction. The lions and tigers and bears of our ancient stories will be long gone. Central to our myths, embedded in our language, rooted in our imaginations–what will we do when our dreams disappear?" *The Unreliable Bestiary* defies that unthinkable disappearance by reactivating as many modes of animal knowledge as human beings have at their disposal, to "reveal the connections between science, behavioral observations, economics, politics, spirituality, myth, and imagination."

Gathering and aligning disparate discourses on animals is no easy task. For one thing, it runs smack into the deep-seated prejudices people harbor about the legitimacy of different disciplines with regard to animals. Indeed, the new field of animal studies is precisely a disciplinary intervention, insisting that rigorous study of animals be extended beyond the science to the humanities and social sciences. But Weaver goes further than that. It is the knowledge contained in myths, fairytales, superstitions that he wants to take seriously, knowing full well that as science and technology improve, many things that artists and poets and old-wives-telling-tales have always known or intuited are being "scientifically proven." And, suddenly, the experience is removed from the "New Age Bullshit" category and enshrined in the "Validated by Science" category. Until then, if you want to keep speaking to most scientists and academics, you keep your mouth shut about visions and dreams and hunches and coincidences and trances.

*The Unreliable Bestiary* opens a space in which the most fantastic flights of the animalized imagination can have heated debates and animated encounters with the often more fantastic facts discovered by animal science. In addition to mixing discourses, genres, and epistemologies, Weaver mingles a variety of artistic media and styles in his performances. Live performance–in many styles: story telling, dialogue, puppetry, and dance–is accompanied by video works of many kinds–landscapes, animation, claymation–as well as by old filmclips, documentary footage, photographs, drawings, maps, diagrams, and graphs. This richly textured material frames the artist's voice and vision, which balances his commitment to first-hand knowledge (his preparation for the pieces has included things like attending wolf-management workshops and mahout training camps) with his profound respect for animal mystery and otherness. Relinquishing any hopes of "'accurate' and 'truthful' representations," he involves us instead in the drama of "the failure of [animal] representation, as a way to point out the absence of the real animal."

*The Unreliable Bestiary* pits the powers of live performance against the increasing absence–and impending total absence–of real animals from our world. If zoo animals, as John Berger (1980) influentially argued, are monuments to their own disappearance in modernity, the animals of *The Unreliable Bestiary* are something more complicated: both moving memorials of a lost relation and hopeful harbingers of a richer, happier, healthier, and more genuinely reciprocal one in the future.

## *References*

Berger, John. 1980. "Why Look at Animals?" In *About Looking*. New York: Pantheon.

DeGrazia, David. 1996. *Taking Animals Seriously: Mental Life and Moral Status*. Cambridge: Cambridge University Press.

## Anti-art

Kristine Stiles

Opinions divide on how to define anti-art. The concept has become a multipurpose signifier for the denunciation of art, rejection of aesthetic norms, ridicule of art institutions, repudiation of art markets, and is even sometimes confused with iconoclasm. Initially the word identified extreme manifestations of the modernist avant-garde's effort to transform and break with cultural convention, refute bourgeois society and its values, and align with radical politics, from nihilism to anarchism. Despite the prodigious aesthetic productivity of Dada and Futurist artists, both movements have been described as anti-art: Dada for its inclusion of non-aesthetic materials, and resistance to World War I; and, ironically, Futurism for its celebration of war and violence. The subtitle to Hans Richter book *Dada: Art and Anti-Art* (1964) is instrumental in associating Dada with anti-art. Richter may have misappropriated the term from Hannah Höch's collage, *Cut with the Kitchen Knife through the Beer-Belly of the Weimar Republic* (1919), in which the words "Die anti dada ists" appear in its upper right-hand corner. Rather than a reference to the Dadaists' attitudes toward art, the text identifies the caricaturized figures immediately below it of several German generals and Kaiser Wilhelm II, who led Germany into World War I. Richter also identified the readymade as anti-art, regardless of the fact that Duchamp made it clear that he was "against the word 'anti'" for its association with the "atheist [who is] as much a religious man as the believer is" (Schwarz 1969, 33). Anti-art offered a pretext for Surrealists to appropriate the Freudian unconscious as authentic art material. Yet, in 1958 after musing on Werner Heisenberg's Uncertainty Principle (1926) and its relation to the nuclear age, Salvador Dalí wrote "Anti-material Manifesto," turning away from Freud's "iconography of the interior world" to the indeterminacy of physics and "the exterior world [in order] to transport my works into anti-matter" (Dalí 1958, n.p.).

Although Jean Dubuffet would lecture on "Anticultural Positions" in 1951, he deftly avoided "anti-art." Nevertheless, Dubuffet's *L'Art brut* is widely associated with the term for his embrace of untrained artists and non-elite objects; use of organic and supposed non-aesthetic materials; and refusal to accept either the term "beautiful" or "ugly" as a judgment of either art or life. Some scholars have considered Fluxus and its alleged "anti-commercial aesthetic" as "anti-art," even though Fluxus-associated artists created a profusion of objects explicitly for George Maciunas to sell, and Maciunas was an early investor in New York real estate that led to the gentrification of SoHo. Moreover, the often neglected subtitle of the renowned proto-Fluxus publication, *An Anthology of Chance Operations* (1963), compiled and edited by Jackson Mac Low and La Monte Young, attests to how the artworks and the ideas about art in the book are linked to the rhetoric of anti-art: "concept art anti-art indeterminacy improvisation meaningless work natural disasters plans of action stories diagrams music poetry essays dance constructions mathematics compositions." In addition, the deployment of destruction as a creative means in the mid-1960s continues to be routinely considered anti-art, despite the growing value of such works. As late as 2005, Thomas McEvilley asserted that conceptual and performance art constitute "anti-art" for being hybrid, an opinion reified in his book's title: *The Triumph of Anti-Art: Conceptual and Performance Art in the Formation of Post-Modernism*. These paradoxical examples evince the logical fallacy of the term itself. For "anti-art" defines—as not art—the very thing that it is: art.

It is further noteworthy that the term "anti-psychiatry," associated with Franz Fanon, R.D. Laing, Féliz Guattari, Gilles Deleuze, and others involved in poststructuralism and deconstruction, derives from many of the same anti-philosophical roots as does so-called anti-art, and has fostered both mental health and "knowledge production" consumerism in the same measure that anti-art has become coveted, protected, and highly commercial. Anti-philosophy, Boris Groys explains, traces its long history at least from Søren Kierkegaard to Jacques Derrida, but equally originates in Richard Wagner's theory of *Gesamtkunstwerk*, which emphasized "the people [as] the only true artist" (2012, 201). Thus does the "genealogy of participatory art" (from Dada to the present) owe a debt to Wagner's demand that artists surrender art and their identity to collective action, the resulting deliberate excess and scandal marshaled toward a singular goal, "to instruct us to change our mind" (Groys 2012, xiv). Despite this utopian proposition, the interconnected epistemologies of anti-art, anti-philosophy, and anti-psychiatry are inextricably intertwined in the "extreme violence" and "radical cruelty" of the nineteenth and twentieth centuries (Badiou 2005/2011, 114), and fascination with the insidious affect of the concept of "anti-art" continues to draw the crisis of negation into the twenty-first century.

### *Further reading*

Badiou (2005/2011); Dalí (1958).

### *References*


Badiou, Alain. 2005. *The Century.* Reprint, Cambridge, England and Malden, Massachusetts: Polity, 2011. Originally published as *Le Siècle*, Paris: Éditions du Seuil, 2005.

Dalí, Salvador. 1958. *Anti-Material Manifesto*. New York: Carstairs Gallery.

Dubuffet, Jean. 1951. "Anticultural Positions." Lecture at The Arts Club of Chicago, Chicago, IL, December 20.

Groys, Boris. 2012. *Introduction to Antiphilosophy.* London and New York: Verson.

Mac Low, Jackson and La Monte Young, eds. 1963. *An Anthology of Chance Operations*, USA: Jackson Mac Low.

McEvilley, Thomas. 2005. *The Triumph of Anti-Art: Conceptual and Performance Art in the Formation of Post-Modernism.* New York: McPherson & Co.

Richter, Hans. 1964. *Dada: Art and Anti-Art.* Reprint, New York: Thames and Hudson Inc., 1985.

Schwarz, Arturo. 1969. *The Complete Works of Marcel Duchamp.* London: Thames and Hudson Inc.


### *Cross references*

"**Appropriation**" by Wong; "**Fluxus**" by Stiles; "**Modernism**" by Albright, Pearl, and Speca; "**Performance, postmodernism, and beyond**" by Chin Davidson; "**Postdramatic theatre**" by Fuchs; "**Readymade**" by Hoefer; "**Sampling**" by Hodges Persley; "**Simulacrum**" by Cesare Schotzko.

## Broad-spectrum approach

Richard Schechner

Taking the broad-spectrum approach to performance means studying the whole range of performative behaviors, non-human as well as human. Performances among insects, reptiles, birds, and mammals—particularly primates, dolphins, and whales—feature complex interactions of play and ritual involving sophisticated techniques and displays. Cultures, defined as learned-invented rather than genetically encoded behaviors and systems, exist in both human and non-human animals. Of course, in performance inquiry, most of the attention is on human behavior. But one must never forget that humans operate as part of an extremely complex system of life forms interacting with each other locally and within larger global and even more comprehensive solar, stellar, and galactic systems.

Among humans, the broad spectrum ranges from ritual, play, and the arts, to popular entertainments of all kinds, the performances of everyday life including but not limited to what happens in politics, medicine, economics ... and more: the range could be extended indefinitely. Adopting such a comprehensive approach is based on the assumption that everything and anything can be studied "as performance" (Schechner 2006). But what is performance?

Performances mark identities, bend time, reshape and adorn bodies, tell stories.

Performances are "restored behaviors," "twice-behaved behaviors," actions that are re-arranged, rehearsed, repeated, and further developed in an ongoing system of transformations. This is clear in the arts. But everyday life also involves years of training and practice wherein a person learns specific bits of behavior adjusting the performance of life roles in relation to ever-changing circumstances. All the activities of life—both private/personal and public/social—are performances. In Erving Goffman's definition: "A performance may be defined as all the activity of a given participant on a given occasion which serves to influence in any way any of the other participants" (1959, 15).

Taking the broad-spectrum approach means never losing sight of the fact that performance is an over-arching, comprehensive concept. The consequence of this approach is a recognition of the ongoing, dynamic, interactive, and transformative quality of performance. Although every performance takes place within a specific performative region, and can be assigned to a specific performative category (art, everyday life, professional life, etc.), what happens in one region affects and is affected by what happens in other regions—and may redefine one or more categories. The broad spectrum is not fixed, final, static, or stable, but dynamic and processual.

### *Further reading*

Goffman (1959); Schechner (2006).

### *References*

Goffman, Erving. 1959. *The Presentation of Self in Everyday Life*. New York: Anchor.

Schechner, Richard. 2006. *Performance Studies: An Introduction*. New York: Routledge.

### *Cross references*

"**Animalworks**" by Cheng; "**Animal Studies**" by Chaudhuri; "**Ecodramaturgy**" by Thomas; "**Fifteen principles of Black Market International**" by La Chance; "**Global censorship**" by Shea; "**Glossolalia**" by Adewunmi; "**Intercultural performance**" by Alker; "**Media**" by Colleran; "**Mimesis**" by Diamond; "**Performance Studies**" by Joy; "**Paratheatre**" by Olivares; "**Proxemics**" by Cody.

## Choreography

André Lepecki

In 1589, Thoinot Arbeau published *Orchesography*, a book written as a platonic dialogue between a master and his student and where it became necessary for movement descriptions to be written down in order for dances to survive. Here a fundamental element anticipates the affective drive behind the Western choreographic impulse: a melancholic lament to dance's ephemerality, and the necessity of re-directing dance's temporal condition through paperly representation.

The term "choreography" made its first appearance in Raoul-Auger Feuillet's dance manual *Chorégraphie, ou l'art de décrire la danse par caracteres, figures et signes demonstratifs* (Choreography, or the art of describing dance with letters, figures and signs) published in France in 1700. As the composite neologism clearly indicates, choreography is concerned with a very specific mode of translation—that between the physical performance of danced movements, and the representation of these movements as written descriptions (*décrire*). In the case of Feuillet's book, this writing down took place not through the means of words, but through very abstract "figures and signs" which, once traced on the page, took the form of complex floor patterns. Dance historian Susan L. Foster has noted (2010) a very intriguing mirroring in Feuillet's method: page and dance stage are isomorphic, as if there were no gap between paperly representation and spatial-corporeal performance.

But, if choreography is, as suggested, a translation—and particularly, a trans-semiotic translation—then, as Walter Benjamin reminds us, its translatability has produced all sorts of unexpected results. Indeed, one could say that since movement and writing were fused into one new word (orchesography; choreography), this fusion has created not only a new semantic and behavioral field but a force producing much more than the mere sum of each part. Movement and writing, fused into one word, reflect and refract each other in an endless game of mirrors where each term is a *mise-en-abime* (heightening) of the other.

Indeed, movement assumes an ever-increasing centrality in philosophical, scientific, political, economic, and aesthetic practices and discourses that have indeed shaped the project of modernity. Peter Sloterdijk reminds us, historically and ontologically, how movement can be seen as that (physical and metaphoric) force that both grounds and propels the hyper-mobilization of all living that constitutes modernity *as* mobilization. In modernity's spectacle of agitation, geo-political and bio-political questions become essentially choreographic ones: to decide *who* is able or allowed to move; to decide *where* one is allowed to move to; to define which bodies can *choose* full mobility and which bodies are *forced* into displacement. The end result of this politics of mobility is that of transforming the *right* for free and ample circulation into a *privilege*, and then turn that privilege into a prized subjectivity.

As for writing, the issues this term opens for performance theories and dance practices have been on the foreground since Derrida's, Judith Butler's and Shoshana Felman's revision of J.L. Austin's notions of performativity (1962). Most obviously, the concept and practice of writing in performance and dance theory—from Peggy Phelan's famous articulation of the tensions existing between performance's "only life" and its reproducible documents (1993) to Fred Moten's proposition that there is no performance without documentation (2003)—troubles any stable dichotomy between writing and performing. Besides these more recent authors, we may also invoke Heidegger's and Merleau-Ponty's phenomenologies and the whole psychoanalytic project, where we find an increasing consensus that writing is something profoundly more dynamic, active, fluid, and indeed mobile *and* ephemeral *and* uncontainable than it is usually perceived as being. Double mobility then: the mobility of and in movement; the mobility of and in writing. Both multiply their effects in the choreographic.

Corporeally, choreography was invented in order to structure a system of command to which bodies have to subject themselves into the system's wills and whims. Thus, choreography also names the need to pedagogically and biologically (re) produce bodies capable of carrying out certain movement imperatives. Choreography is therefore akin to an apparatus of capture (Deleuze and Guattari) or to a body-snatcher (Franz Anton Cramer) that seizes bodies in order to make them into other(ed) bodies—highly trained (physically, but also emotionally, artistically, and intellectually) variations of what Foucault once called "docile bodies." No wonder the dancers in the French *corps-de-ballet* are called *sujets*—this is the appropriate naming of those freely falling into the apparatus of capture called choreography. Known but seldom theorized is how dancers must subjugate themselves to choreographic or para-choreographic imperatives—from dieting to gender or racial stereotypes; from strict physical discipline to the precise enactment of positions, attitudes, steps, gestures, but also words, all for the sake of exact repetition.

It is no surprise then that "choreography" appears crucial to the works of some key figures that have concerned themselves with destabilizing notions of self-conscious authorship in performance, and emphasized the sovereignty of the performative act as force. The strict choreographic notations of Allan Kaprow for *18 Happenings in 6 Parts* (1959), written down before being actually executed by his performers; or the strict and repetitive choreographic exercises by Bruce Nauman in his studio, where action mirrors simple instruction-titles that operate as so many order-words, as imperative commands with immediate corporeal manifestations, clearly reveal how choreography is first and foremost a structure of command that has to be reckoned with. This structure can be brutal, but it can also be responded to out of profound love, the commitment and responsibility involved in surrendering to the demands or commands of a voice, of another's desire, of another's whims to whom we carefully listen, and whose wishes we willingly fulfill.

### *Further reading*

Foster (2010); Moten (2003).

### *References*

Arbeau, Thoinot. 1589. *Orchesography*. Translated by Mary Stewart Evans. Reprint 2012, The Noverre Press.

Austin, J.L. 1962. *How To Do Things With Words*. Oxford and New York: Oxford University Press.

Feuillet, Raoul-Auger. 1700. *Chorégraphie, ou l'art de décrire la danse par caracteres, figures et signes demonstratifs*, Paris: Self-published.

Foster, Susan Leigh. 2010. *Choreographing Empathy: Kinesthesia in Performance*. New York: Routledge.

Phelan, Peggy. 1993. *Unmarked: The Politics of Performance*. New York: Routledge.

Moten, Fred. 2003. *In the Break: The Aesthetics of the Black Radical Tradition*. Minneapolis, MN: University of Minnesota Press.

### *Cross references*

"**Bodies in action**" by Stiles and O'Dell; "**Boychild**" by Halberstam; "**Circus**" by Tait; "**Dance or we are lost: The Tanztheater of Pina Bausch**" by Birringer; "**Gestus**" by Bial; "**Goat Island's *The Sea and Poison***" by Garoian and Gaudelius; "**Happenings**" by Sandford; "**Marina Abramovic's durational opus**" by Carr; "**Puppet and object performance**" by Bell.

## Dance or we are lost: The Tanztheater of Pina Bausch

Johannes Birringer

When Wim Wenders's film on Pina Bausch and Tanztheater Wuppertal was released in 2011, it had become a tribute to the late choreographer who did not live to see this visually opulent 3-D documentary of her work. The German director had known Bausch for some years, and both had developed a plan for a film focusing on some of her most well-known works. But days before the shoot was due to start, in June 2009, Bausch died suddenly, shortly after being diagnosed with cancer. When this unimaginable event occurred, the project was cancelled, since Wenders had projected Bausch as the central figure. He would have followed her into rehearsals where she used to pose questions to the dancers. Wenders also had planned to go on tour with her to Asia and South America, perhaps dreaming of the peculiar kind of road movies for which he had become known (*Paris, Texas; Until the End of the World*).

Yet eventually, filming went ahead, and while footage of Bausch's dance works performed on stage was still to be a main element, Wenders shifted the focus onto her dancers, letting them speak and remember, making them her voice, turning her own method of constantly asking her dancers questions into the method of the film. But Bausch's earliest works did not come out of this Socratic method. At the beginning of her directorship of the Tanztheater Wuppertal, the company Bausch founded in 1973, works such as her 1974 *Iphigenie auf Tauris*, and her 1975 *Orpheus und Eurydike* or *Le Sacre du Printemps*, were large-scale choreographies still based on through-composed music and influenced by her ballet and modern dance training (at Folkwang Schule in Essen, and in New York). When I first saw her work in 1978, nothing was the same anymore. All concepts people had had of stage dance seemed to be breaking down with *Er nimmt sie an der Hand und führt sie in das Schloss, die andern folgen* (1978), a turbulent psychotic nightmare of guilt and obsessive denial, inspired by a forgotten stage direction in *Macbeth* and acted out in a cluttered space gradually

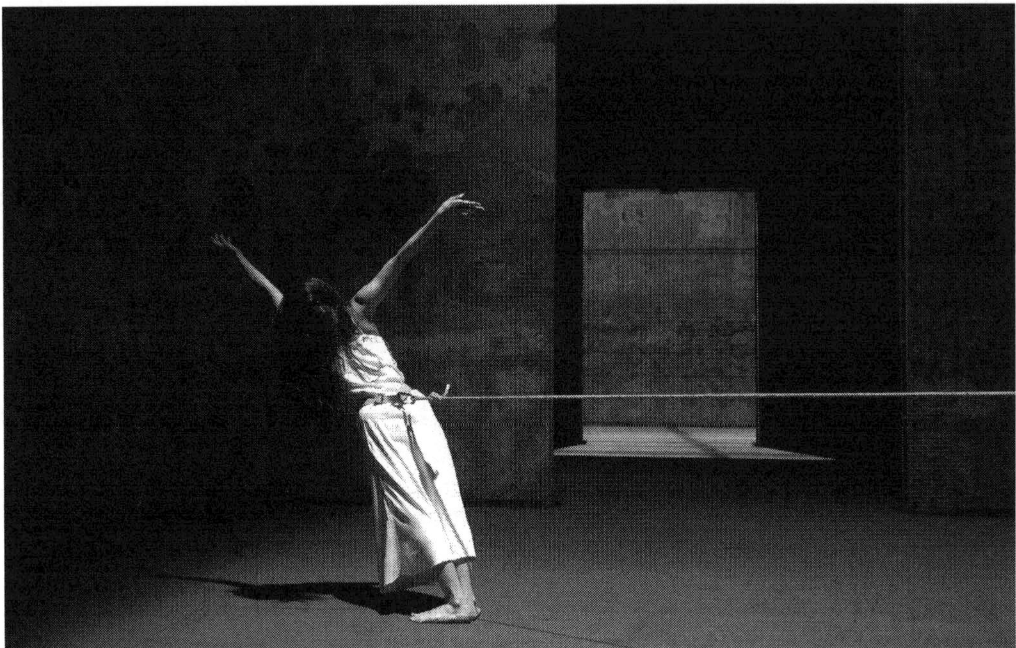

**Figure 27** Tsai-Chin Yu, solo from "...Como el Musgulto en la Piedra, ay si, si, si..." (2009), Cooking Plant, Zollverein Coal Mine, Essen, 2010 © Donata Wenders / New Road Movies.

filling with water. More than half of the infuriated audience had left before the end.

The provincial Westphalia town of Wuppertal commissioned Bausch to work for both the opera and municipal theatre. What could not have been expected was the raw emotional and sheer relentless unraveling that Bausch's *Stücke* (pieces)–often unnamed yet on the night of the premiere–precipitated. The unraveling was psychological, with the dancers' body language, gestures, and stories crashing through the surface realism into a stark, almost bottomless series of excavations, an unpeeling of the many protective layers we all know to exist in our everyday lives, hiding our intimate desires and fears, our longing for love and acceptance, envy of others or aggression turned against those others and our own damaged selves, insecurities, obsessive denials, vanities and suppressed hopes. Bausch's *tanztheater* asserts its intensities in ways that are like a physical assault on our senses. She abandons the decorum of theatrical form; her collages expose ruptured subjectivities in flailing bodies. Role-playing is turned inside out. Little tricks become threatening gestures; technique turns into travesty. Men and women wrestle with each other, women drop out of their clothes, men don women's costumes or prostitute themselves, in disheveled tutus, like body builders in a seedy world of debased freak-shows, parading "gender performativity" in an increasingly wide range of acute observations about traumatized masochistic or sadistic behavior. This is performativity on the edge. The scandal she produced was undoubtedly a kind of cultural violence. (And the term performativity had not even entered academic discourse on gender trouble yet.)

In *1980*, a lone male dancer opens the piece on a platform, eating spoonfuls of soup, recounting the voice of a cajoling parent. Later a woman skips around the stage, waving a white scarf, persistently chanting "I'm tir-ed, I'm tir-ed" in a sing-song child-like rhythm until she begins to falter, out of breath. The word-actions exhaust, literally. With this dance, spoken language firmly enters into the social choreographies Bausch constructs through her collage method, interlacing revue-like sketches, overlapping story vignettes, strange confessions ("I'll keep my lips really wet just in case someone's behind me ..."), and absurd questions ("What comes to mind when I say 'dinosaur'?") with larger ensemble polonaises, small gestural solos, and slowly evolving stage images, like *1980*'s exaggerated sun-bathing scene to Judy Garland's broken voice in "Over the Rainbow." The assemblage resembles a Felliniesque, surrealist dream cinematography. In *1980*, many of the dissonant verbal cacophonies revolve around dancers each excitedly telling the audience about their personal fears, how they cope or how they pretend not to be afraid in the dark.

By the mid-1980s, I had seen most of the early Bausch works after an extensive retrospective at Venice (Italy); her vision seemed so dark and unforgivingly pessimistic that the shocked reactions during her first US tours in 1984/85 hardly came as a surprise (see Birringer 1986; Servos and Weigelt 1984; Hanraths and Winkels 1984). It is not easy to re-live the excitement of those early experiences as an audience member captivated by the work's brutal honesty, poetic strength and bitter irony, by this daring living theatre of no pretence but a relentless willingness to test how far a gesture and a physical-mental attitude can be pushed to reveal something, to alienate our conceptions of kitsch, banality and truth, sincerity and uncomfortable humor, straddling the porous line between anger and shame, the fear of violence and need for compassion. The famous love trio of forced/failed embraces in *Café Müller*, enacted by Dominique Mercy, Malou Airaudo and Jan Minarik, has been disseminated in countless video clips on YouTube. It is a microcosm of Bausch's ability to analyze human behavior, stretch it literally until it becomes dissonant by building a deadpan scene of insistent accelerated repetition. Something goes irreparably wrong, when Mercy cannot carry out the embrace and a kiss with Airaudo, but needs to be forced into it by the third dancer who enacts the gestures for both male and female partner, enfolds and instructs them, so to speak, until they reach the point where they repeat the embrace/kiss automatically, interrupted by failure and the attempt to try again/fail again. Bausch's bleak existentialism, going beyond Beckett's, focuses on the potential of the bodies' gestures to hang on to a peculiar, often riveting stubbornness which can turn painfulness into the opposite of despair.

This extraordinary social ritual falls into place with hundreds of similar scenes Bausch created with the dancers who often tell us directly, or show us, something of their actual life stories, their injuries, pregnancies, and hang-ups, their insecurities, unfulfilled needs and cravings, thus transforming what we had known as dance into performances of the subjective, private and public role of bodies and bodily composures, with their barely veiled psychic and emotional constrictions and anxieties on the line. Bausch's *tanztheater* also has an ecstatic dimension: we hold our breath when we recognize the banal logic of conventions and the absurd reproduction of power or sexual relations tied into the habitus of cultural behavior.

For many years Bausch worked with the same core ensemble of dancers whose personalities imprinted themselves onto the movement qualities for which the Wuppertal company became known throughout the world once they started regular and massive touring around the globe from the 1980s onward (see Bentivoglio and Carbone 2003; Briginshaw and Burt 2009; Climenhaga 2008, 2012; Coates 2010; Cody 1998; Fernandes 2005; Goldberg 1989; Manning 1986; Schmidt 2002). The earlier impression of Bausch's virulently probing and taboo-breaking style of physical realism was later modulated. The company began to receive numerous invitations to develop and coproduce new pieces on location in different cities (Palermo, Rio de Janeiro, Tokyo, Los Angeles, Hong Kong, Lisbon, etc.), and Bausch's transcultural road work often tended to resort to a more poetically acquiescent, and even melancholic mood in her late work, as if her harsher outlook on life had become filtered through a more forgiving lens, or a desperate persistence to dance over unresolved and back-breaking contradictions. Her music collages, though still full of surprising contrasts, as well tended to become more consoling in her late work, tango and Japanese drumming, Billie Holiday and Purcell, waltz and bagpipe music entering into strange mixes encompassing an increasingly beautiful if haunted loneliness on stage where we now see a younger generation of newly cast dancers taking on recognized roles. This generational change in fact is reflected well in Wenders's film, sometimes to stunning effect as in the scenes where he intercuts the current production of *Café Müller*, by a younger cast, with archival footage from the early version, after Mercy and Airaudo peek into a small maquette of the stage set, reminiscing over how all the chairs got piled in there and then had to be flung out of the dancers' paths by a dancer. The archival footage features Bausch herself, moving upstage with eyes wide shut, in the only stage performance she continued to enact for many years. Helena Pikon confesses that she froze when Bausch eventually asked her to take over the role, and that she is haunted by her absent ghost.

The interviews are done indirectly. We hear the dancers dubbed over their silent, contemplative faces, which tends to be awkward at times because the younger members often appear shy and inarticulate, prone to expressing banalities or speaking of their fear of Pina's power as Übermutter: "I was lost, and had to pull myself up by my hair." We then see a dancer, filmed in a swimming pool, pulling herself up by her hair. Another speaks simply of missing Bausch, not just as a choreographer and guide but as a presence: "Pina, I still haven't dreamed about you," she says plainly. "Please visit me in my dreams." These ponderous statements mystify, rather than explain, choreographic labor, compositional process, and the ideas that drove the work. But the interviews with the dancers thus point to an underlying, fascinating question that also accompanied the trajectory of Tanztheater Wuppertal, especially during recent revivals of *Kontakthof* (two production-projects cast with senior citizens over 65 and with teenagers, here splendidly fused and intercut as we watch the professional and amateur dancers enact the same scenes)—namely whether the charisma of the company is not owed to the unique personalities of the dancers who originally worked with Bausch for many years and sustained the roles they had created collaboratively with the choreographer. Back in 1980 it seemed as if only these particular dancers had enabled Bausch to push the borders of dance and theatre, and Bausch herself told me once that she imagined them to grow old on stage, along with her. Some of them did, indeed.

The emotional artistry of this company and its search for a theatrical exposure of human fragility and strength in life thus also formulates a utopian project, dancing on to resist the cliché of ephemeral live art or the brutal laws of the industry requiring quick turn-overs of beauty and youth, building a sustainable aesthetic intensity of exacting cruelty directed at questions about life and the expressive energy with which we must venture to experience our corporeality as social subjects, as volatile and hysterical members of the societies into which we were born or into which we move. Bausch's ensemble, from the beginning, has been completely international; the critical perception of German *angst* in the work is a prejudice that would need to be parsed more carefully, and Wenders unfortunately plays too much on the idea of fear himself as he keeps eliciting hushed comments from the younger members rather than letting us thrive on the superb, Buster Keaton-like comedic skills and surrealist fantasies the dancers act out in the outdoor urban locations: there is an amazing "Japanese" robot sound performance by Regina Advento on the Wuppertal overhead tram; in another scene, a woman walks around a derelict pond with a 10-foot tree in her backpack.

On the one hand, then, Wenders's film does not address the presumed *angst* nor capture the collaborative creation process, nor offer a closer insight into the socio-political contexts reflected in Bausch's insistence on particular themes in her fragmented revue form of aesthetic and social dance. Bausch's broken syntax of modern dance vocabulary and of the chorus, her subversion of gender roles, and her rendering absurd of the fetishization of female beauty or male possessiveness—along with her relentless exposure of physical vulnerability and the clumsiness of social intercourse—has left a major impact on the performing arts, both conceptually and formally. Later emergences of physical theatre, Konzepttanz and performance art in Europe are unthinkable without Bausch's cutting open the anatomy of the body and its psychic predispositions, and one would like to see the film probe the deeper layers of Bausch's existentialism and her attack on post-war compensatory sublimations (the era of "normalization" after the Holocaust). Wenders tries hard with his 3-D film to evoke the depth and sculptural quality of Bausch's stagings, and some of the scenes from *Sacre de Printemps* and *Café Müller* are breathtakingly rendered, while other scenes, staged outside around the environs of Bausch's home base of Wuppertal on traffic islands, in front of industrial backdrops or on top of a quarry, fail to tell us anything Bausch had not already done in *Die Klage der Kaiserin* (in fact Wenders imitates that film's internal structure).

On the other hand, even if constricted by this sense of a pious homage to the late Bausch, Wenders's camera succeeds in the last twenty minutes to grip the viewer in a mesmerizing crescendo of dancing, on and around the rock and the water surfaces of *Vollmond*, a piece in which Bausch's younger cast goes full out to release an untrammelled energy of immersion, inhabiting the elements to the point of self-abandon. Drenched to the skin, they dance and dance. As a counterpoint to the opening ritual of *Sacre de Printemps*, and framed by the opening and closing promenade from *Nelken* performed by the older cast in understated ironic fashion (this polonaise offers an ironic comment on the cycle of the seasons), the over-dance of *Vollmond* succeeds in imprinting a sense of exuberant defiance within this dangerous slippery landscape, as if for a moment the thought of mortality could be plotted out and transformed into an unspeakable poetic sensory rewilding, in excess of any fear.

The anxiety of forgetting is the insurmountable challenge, after all, for any company that survives their founding choreographer, facing the question of how to continue (see http://www.pinabausch.org/).

## *References*


Bentivoglio Leonetta, and Francesco Carbone. 2003. *Pina Bausch vous appelle*. Reprint, L'Arche, 2007.

Birringer, Johannes. 1986. "Pina Bausch: Dancing Across Borders," *TDR* 30:2, 85-97. Reprinted in *Theatre, Theory, Postmodernism*. Bloomington: Indiana University Press, 1989, pp. 132-145.

Briginshaw, Valerie A. and Ramsay Burt. 2009. *Writing Dancing Together*. Basingstoke: Palgrave Macmillan.

Climenhaga, Royd. 2008. "Pina Bausch". In *Routledge Performance Practitioners*, edited by Franc Chamberlain. New York: Routledge.

Climenhaga, Royd, ed., 2012. *The Pina Bausch Sourcebook: The Making of Tanztheater*. London: Routledge.

Coates, Emily. 2010. "Beyond the Visible: The Legacies of Merce Cunningham and Pina Bausch." *PAJ: A Journal of Performance and Art*, 32.2: 1-7.

Cody, Gabrielle H.. 1998. "Woman, Man, Dog, Tree: Two Decades of Intimate and Monumental Bodies in Pina Bausch's Tanztheater." *TDR: The Drama Review*, 42.2: 115-131.

Fernandes, Ciane. 2005. *Pina Bausch and the Wuppertal Dance Theatre: The Aesthetics of Repetition and Transformation*. New York: Peter Lang.

Goldberg, Marianne. 1989. "Artifice and Authenticity: Gender Scenarios in Pina Bausch's Dance Theatre." *Women & Performance: A Journal of Feminist* Theory, 4.2: 104-117.

Hanraths, Ulrike, and Winkels, Herbert, eds., 1984. *Tanzlegenden*. Frankfurt: Tende Verlag.

Manning, Susan. 1986. "An American Perspective on Tanztheater." *TDR: The Drama Review*, 30.2: 57-79.

Servos, Norbert and Gert Weigelt (photography). 1984. *Pina Bausch-Wuppertal Dance Theater, or, The Art of Training a Goldfish: Excursion into Dance*. Translated from the German by Patricia Stadie. Koln: Ballett-Bühnen-Verlag.

Schmidt, Jochen. 2002. *Pina Bausch: Tanzen gegen die Angst*. Munich: Econ

Wenders, Wim (dir). 2011. *Pina: tanzt, tanzt sonst sind wir verloren (Pina: Dance, dance otherwise we are lost)*, 103 mins.

## Cybernetics

Philip Auslander

A term coined by the mathematician Norbert Wiener around 1947, cybernetics describes a new interdisciplinary field of research, anchored in mathematics and engineering, created to explore "the entire field of control and communication in the animal or machine," as Wiener put it in his definitive book (1961, 147). The term derives from the Greek *cybernos*, or helmsman, the figure vested with the responsibility for assessing seafaring conditions and making the necessary adjustments to keep the vessel on course. The choice of name reflects the field's particular emphasis on feedback, a general term for the processes by which information is used to keep a system functioning smoothly. The circulatory system of a living being is an example of such as self-regulating system, as is an artificially intelligent robot that "learns" from and responds to the information it receives from its environment. Theories developed under the umbrella of cybernetics have proved crucial to systems theory, information theory, management, and artificial intelligence, among other fields. Sociologist Erving Goffman, in *The Presentation of Self in Everyday Life* (1959) and other work, theorized everyday social interaction as a form of cybernetic performance in which social actors design and adjust their self-presentations on the basis of information, communication, and feedback.

The cultural legacy of cybernetics resides not only in the impact of the field itself but also in its effect on the popular lexicon, since it is from the term "cybernetics" that we get the popular prefix *cyber-*, as in cyberspace (an alternative term for the Internet), cybersex, cyborg (a contraction of cybernetic organism), cyberpunk, cyberculture, etc. This prefix, which became popular in the 1980s with the rise of personal computing and the Internet, indicates a cultural connection to computer technology or virtual reality. Cyberpunk, for example, is a genre of science fiction in which the stories frequently center on a conflict over control of technology waged between a dominant corporate or governmental power and technologically adept resistance fighters. Cybersex refers to the practice of having sexual relations in virtual environments, such as chat rooms.

Cybernetics provides a useful framework for analyzing new media performances and installations, particularly with regard to the nature of interaction in them. In Marie Sester's installation *ACCESS* (2003), for example, a bright theatrical spotlight follows a visitor around the exhibition space while a voice exhorts the subject to behave in certain ways. Users of the work's website choose which visitors to pursue; past that point, however, the mechanism controlling the spotlight takes over and tracks the visitor automatically. Some visitors-turned-performers relish their moment in the spotlight; others seek to escape, while still others play with the light by trying to out-run or out-maneuver it. Being in the spotlight prompts the visitor's initial response, which determines the spotlight's movements, which, in turn, prompt further action on the visitor's part, thus creating a cybernetic feedback loop.

By contrast, the information flow in Stelarc's *Ping Body* (1996) performance was quite different. Stelarc initiated the work by "pinging" (sending a signal to) multiple web domains. The speed at which signals echoed back from the domains controlled Stelarc's movement through muscle-stimulating electrodes. In this case, the continued pinging elicited a flow of controlling signals, but Stelarc's movements were the end product of this system—they did not feed back into the circuit of information. In this respect, *Ping Body* replicated a traditional choreographic model, in which the dancer does the choreographer's bidding, albeit with digital information replacing the human agent. *ACCESS* is similar to *Ping Body* in that the performer's primary engagement is with an information system and only indirectly with other human beings. Whereas *Ping Body* models a relationship with technology in which the human subject surrenders control to the system, *ACCESS* leaves open the subject's response to the spotlight—and, implicitly, the fact of surveillance—and suggests that the subject has a measure of agency. Just as people react differently to the levels of surveillance to which we are subjected in contemporary societies, some visitors may shun the spotlight while others treat it matter-of-factly and others still play with it or treat it as an opportunity to show off.

### Further reading

Stelarc (1996); Wiener (1961).

### References

Goffman, Erving. 1959. *The Presentation of Self in Everyday Life*. New York: Anchor.

Stelarc. 1996. "Ping Body." http://v2.nl/events/ping-bod

Wiener, Norbert. 1961. *Cybernetics, or Control and Communication in the Animal and the Machine*. Cambridge, MA: MIT Press.

### Cross references

"**Audience**" by Cody; "**New Media Art**" by Cicchini; "**Performance in the digital age**" and "**Virtual reality**" by Auslander; "**Performing surveillance camera art**" and "**Posthumanism**" by Nayar; ***"Reality Ends Here"*** by Watson.

## The d/Deaf Performative

Tylar Pendgraft

The term "d/Deaf," utilizing lowercase and capital "D," can refer to someone who is both physiologically deaf and culturally Deaf. The term itself indicates a division in the collective consciousness of Deaf culture between those who fit into the broader deaf culture and those who do not. This distinction is fundamental to understanding the formulation of a d/Deaf culture within a phonocentric ethos that denies the collective and individual deaf body agency.

Deaf Cultural Studies is a relatively new field, bolstered by the advent of film and digital technology as a medium by which d/Deaf culture (i.e. TTY services, personal narratives, video blogs) can be recorded and transmitted on a national and cross-cultural stage (Humphries 2007). Patty Ladd calls attention to how d/Deaf individuals' language and cultural formation have been colonized over time by a hearing majority (2007). In the 19th and early 20th centuries, sign languages were systematically eliminated by a hearing majority bent on instilling the superiority of phonocentricity in the minds of d/Deaf individuals. Today, the push for phonocentricity is more closely aligned with technology as well, particularly with the advent of cochlear implants and strategies for bioengineering the body to eliminate hearing impairments. Ladd posits that, as cultural minorities, d/Deaf individuals have had to contend with the enculturation of the self into two separate cultures: that of the hearing majority and the d/Deaf minority. What Ladd points to on a broader ontological level is the d/Deaf performative.

When Michael Davidson proposes the existence of a deaf performative (little "d" intentional), he defines it as "a form of speech that enacts or performs rather than describes" (2008, 80). The result is, as Davidson submits, a kind of scandal of speech (2008, 80), one in which the deaf individual consciously attempts to reclaim ownership of their identity from a hearing performative. As Tom Humphries argues, the formulation of a d/Deaf culture has been long fraught with a need to define what d/Deaf culture actually is, calling for literature and art to present the relevance of d/Deaf culture (2007). In order for Deaf Cultural Studies to obtain validity, many Deaf scholars had to defer to the demands of a foundationally heteronormative and phonocentric university learning system. Deaf scholars had to consider what it meant to be culturally d/Deaf within the confines of a deaf-hearing binary. In order to "transcend the relationship with the other," Humphries (2007) proposes for the future of d/Deaf Cultural Studies to welcome literary and artistic criticism. Humphries' proposal implies that d/Deaf Culture must build an identity that breaks its binary relationship with phonocentricity.

In contrast to the deaf performative, the hearing performative is the manner in which hearing individuals construct and perpetuate phonocentric modes of thought and being. This performative is much more pervasive and goes unnoticed arguably because the performance (or the action) of hearing has been naturalized as inseparable from the physiological ability to hear and speak. Bauman refers to this phenomenon as the phonocentric blind spot (2007, 128), unrecognized until confronted by the existence of the other. The d/Deaf performative itself is still in the process of formation: the ways in which one becomes a part of Deaf culture extend beyond strict considerations of physiological deafness as it becomes more inclusive in its definition of cultural Deafness. The awareness of historic colonization of the d/Deaf consciousness and body also allows for the collective majority to respond by creating new modes of understanding as to how identity is continuously formed and re-formed.

As d/Deaf culture more clearly defines itself as one with independent linguistic and cultural integrity, a number of artists are employing the hearing performative to call attention to its exclusionary nature and the privilege it perpetuates. The Deaf artistic movement began in the 1960s with such poets as Clayton Valli and Ella Mae Lentz demonstrating the ways in which sign language not only inscribes itself culturally in the body, but also creates new understandings of paralinguistic performance. Contemporary artist Christine Sun Kim, deaf from birth, denies the sound ownership and etiquette by using vibrations to translate noise into the visual. Perhaps more critical of the hearing performative, Darrin Martin works with the concepts of synesthesia and perception to demonstrate that the body is not an either-or binary, as the hearing performative would suggest, but an organism constantly in transition. If this is the case, we must begin to re-evaluate how ableness is defined on a deeper physiological and ontological level. By focusing on the hearing performative as a social construct, these artists create spaces where one can reclaim language by rejecting phonocentric hegemony in favor of other modes of communication, supporting a more inclusive and wide-ranging d/Deaf performative.

### Further reading

Kuppers (2003); Sandahl and Auslander (2005).

### References

Bauman, H.-Dirksen L. 2007. "On The Disconstruction of (Sign) Language in Western Tradition: A Deaf Reading of Plato's *Cratylus*." In *Open Your Eyes: Deaf Studies Talking*, edited by H.-Dirksen L. Bauman, 127–166. Minneapolis, MN: University of Minnesota Press.

Davidson, Michael. 2008. "Hearing Things: The Scandal of Speech in Deaf Performance." In *Concerto for the Left Hand: Disability and the Defamiliar Body*. Ann Arbor, MN: University of Michigan Press.

Humphries, Tom. 2007. "Talking Culture and Culture Talking." In *Open Your Eyes: Deaf Studies Talking*, edited by H.-Dirksen L. Bauman, 35–41. Minneapolis, MN: University of Minnesota Press.

Kuppers, Petra. 2003. *Disability and Contemporary Performance: Bodies on Edge*. New York: Routledge.

Ladd, Patty. 2007. "Colonialism and Resistance: A Brief History of Deafhood." In *Open Your Eyes: Deaf Studies Talking*, edited by H.-Dirksen L. Bauman, 42–59. Minneapolis, MN: University of Minnesota Press.

Sandahl, Carrie and Philip Auslander, eds. 2005. *Bodies in Commotion: Disability and Performance*. Ann Arbor, MN: University of Michigan Press.

### Cross references

"**Aging**" by Port; "**Gestus**" by Bial; "**Identity politics**" by Adewunmi; "**Intermediality**" by Auslander; "**Performativity**" by Pendgraft; "**The Muslim performative**" by Barlas; "***Weights:* An excerpt**" by Manning; "**Whiteness**" by Jones.

## Destruction art

Kristine Stiles

Destruction *in* art is not destruction *of* art, but rather an aesthetic technique for creating new forms of perception and knowledge related to violence in society, war and trauma, trafficking in bodies, economic crisis, environmental contamination, natural disaster, and especially the aftermath of World War II, the Shoah, and the use of the atomic bomb (Stiles 1987). The Japanese artist Saburo Murakami ran through and broke open wall-size paper screens in 1955 at the "1st Gutai Art Exhibition" in Tokyo, an action symbolizing an attack on and destruction of traditional Japanese culture. In 1959, Gustav Metzger, a Polish-German Holocaust survivor, published "Auto-Destructive Art," a manifesto describing site-specific, self-destructing civic monuments that required collaboration between artists and scientists to link destruction to science and technology, and that would implode anytime from twenty seconds to twenty years with the aid of internal computerized devices (Metzger 1959). The Swiss artist Jean Tinguely built *Homage to New York* in 1960, a large kinetic assemblage that partially destroyed itself in the sculpture garden of the Museum of Modern Art in New York when an unintended fire broke out in one of its mechanical parts. In 1961, the American artist Niki de Saint Phalle created *Tirs*, in which she fired a gun at her own figurative assemblages, the same year that the Argentinian Arte Destructivo group, led by the artist Kenneth Kemble, exhibited destroyed objects in Buenos Aires. Then in 1962, NBC commissioned and televised Tinguely's *Study for an End of the World No. 2*, a kinetic sculpture that exploded on the Nevada desert near the US nuclear tests grounds. 1962 also saw the Puerto Rican American artist Raphael Montañez Ortiz's "Destructivism: A Manifesto," which described artists as "destroyers, materialists and sensualists dealing with process directly" (1962, 52). Soon Yoko Ono would perform *Cut Piece* (1964), sitting silently on a stage while the audience cut off her clothing, according to her instructions.

Both Ortiz and Ono participated in the 1966 Destruction in Art Symposium (DIAS), a month-long series of events and a three-day symposium organized by Metzger in London, and devoted to destruction in culture, society, and politics. Over fifty artists and poets from some fifteen countries participated in DIAS, many of whom were the pioneers of happenings, action art, and Concrete Poetry. They demonstrated how certain types of presentational art evinces "a predisposition for and an ability to convey the ontological effects of the technology, phenomenology, and epistemology of destruction [ ... ] in the center of the question of destruction and survival," and how "individuals and the collective negotiate the resulting crises" (Stiles 1992, 75). Such works emphasized process and concept over product and aesthetics, using the body as material together with destruction as method, to challenge time-honored beliefs that art must be an intrinsically stable aesthetic object, under the protection and preservation of art institutions, and to prove that philosophical aesthetic thought and experience can be conveyed through ephemeral means. It is not coincidental that between 1968 and 1972, the French mathematician René Frédéric Thom developed an aspect of singularity theory called "catastrophe theory," which explained how dynamical systems degenerate at critical points, or "folds," that initiate the unfolding of a whole. Thom's theory informed Gilles Deleuze's theories in *Fold: Leibniz and the Baroque* (1988), whose effect, akin to destruction art, has had considerable impact on much contemporary art.

Destruction art shares no unified aesthetic or technique and is purely an indexical device for identifying global tendencies in a wide field of very different types of practices that have, from the 1950s to the present, continued to emerge worldwide. Never systematically organized or methodically publicized, destruction art resists classification for lack of a manageable identity, and is often culturally undetectable, obscure in a way that permits artists to undertake opposition to abuses of power and to infiltrate social and political spheres without being co-opted by the market. At the same time, concealment within culture makes destruction art vulnerable to mystification, neglect, and invisibility.

### Further reading

Metzger (1959); Ortiz (1962); Stiles (1987, 1992).

### References

Deleuze, Gilles. 1988. *Fold: Leibniz and the Baroque*. Minneapolis, MN: University of Minnesota Press.

Metzger, Gustav. 1959. "Auto-Destructive Art." Radical Art. Accessed February 4, 2015. http://radicalart.info/destruction/metzger.html

Ortiz, Rafael Montañez. 1962. "Destructivism: A Manifesto." In *Rafael Montañez Ortiz: Years of the Warrior, Years of the Psyche, 1960–1988* by Kristine Stiles, 52. New York: El Museo del Barrio, 1988.

Stiles, Kristine. 1987. "Synopsis of The Destruction in Art Symposium (DIAS) and Its Theoretical Significance." *The Act*, 1 (Spring 1987): 22–31.

Stiles, Kristine. 1992. "Survival Ethos and Destruction Art." *Discourse: Journal for Theoretical Studies in Media and Culture*, 14.2: 74–102.

### Cross references

"**Anti-art**" by Stiles; "**Invisible theatre**" by Cody; "**Masochism**" by O'Dell; "**Precariousness**" by Fabião; "**Terrorism and performance**" by Colleran; "**Wang Wei's *Temporary Space***" by Tinari.

## Disciplines in performance

Elise Morrison

The concept of discipline has a complex status within performance studies, since performance scholars have historically defined the field as a methodology practiced in the interstices, overlaps, and liminal spaces between established, traditional academic disciplines, declaring it variously as inter-disciplinary, post-disciplinary, and anti-disciplinary (see Taylor 2003; Schechner 2002). In a Rockefeller Foundation report (1999), Barbara Kirshenblatt-Gimblett described performance studies as "a provisional coalescence on the move," a field that through its inclusionary practices resists the division of artistic mediums into distinct disciplines and confounds the categorization of traditional medias, genres and cultural traditions (Schechner 2002, 3). Disciplinary points of contact that have invigorated performance disciplines include theoretical and practical collaborations between theatre studies, anthropology, oral interpretation/rhetoric, dance research, feminist theory, critical race theory, psychoanalysis, Marxist philosophy, digital media, and animal studies, among an ever-growing network of others. Even as its scholars have resisted the disciplinary effects of institutionalization, performance disciplines have been characterized by a commitment to working between multiple knowledge formations and across disciplinary boundaries (see Carlson 2001; Conquergood 2002; Jackson 2004; Schechner 1985; Turner 1987). Perhaps because of the field's interdisciplinary origins and practices, the term "discipline" itself also has multivalent applications within performance scholarships, figuring prominently in studies of the role of performance in social and political identity, gender construction, visual culture, and everyday life.

The French philosopher Michel Foucault notably analyzed discipline as the dominant tool of power and control in modernity through his writings on the development and processes of institutions and networks of surveillance (1977). Foucault distinguished discipline from punishment, which functioned in the early modern era as public, fear-inducing spectacle. In contrast, discipline functioned through the rise of modern social and political institutions such as prisons, asylums, hospitals, and schools that divide social subjects into controlled segments in order to instruct, regulate, and normalize behavior to be compatible with capitalist ideology. In his essay "Ideology and Ideological State Apparatuses" (1971), Foucault's mentor Luis Althusser coined the term "interpellation" to describe the process by which individual social subjects are hailed into the social order by a figure of discipline (for him a policeman; for us perhaps a surveillance camera). In *Perform or Else* (2001), Jon McKenzie updated the Foucauldian understanding of discipline by arguing that "performance" ontologically replaces "discipline" in 20th and 21st century matrices of power and knowledge. Performance, like discipline, McKenzie argues, produces a new subject of knowledge, one who more effectively embodies the processes of socio-technical systems in the digital age.

The concept of discipline has also figured significantly in gender studies, feminist theory, and visual culture studies. According to Laura Mulvey (1975), male and female spectators alike internalize habits of representation and reception in film and performance that discipline the spectatorial gaze to assume a patriarchal logic or male subject position. Many feminist performance theorists have consequently argued that these normalized habits of visual representation can be radically reformulated and critiqued through feminist performance strategies, highlighting the embedded patriarchal ideology and disciplinary operations, while simultaneously counter-disciplining spectators and performers to adopt critical feminist viewpoints and subject positions (see Cheng 1998; De Lauretis 1984; Diamond 1997; Doane 1982; Dolan 1988; Silverman 1996).

Gender theorist Judith Butler has more broadly analyzed the ways in which subjects are always already conditioned and disciplined by social processes of gender; her various works argue that gender is performed and simultaneously performative: one's gender is constructed by and through repetition and iterability. While Butler's work advocates for insubordination within the disciplined performance of gender, like Foucault, she simultaneously contests the degree of agency inherent in subjects whose identities are reflexively imbricated in powerful social systems and institutions that discipline them (see Butler 1990, 1993).

### Further reading

Butler (1990, 1993); Diamond (1997).

### References

Althusser, Louis. 1971. *Lenin and Philosophy and Other Essays.* Reprint, New York: Monthly Review Press, 2001.

Butler, Judith. 1990. *Gender Trouble: Feminism and the Subversion of Identity*. New York: Routledge.

Butler, Judith. 1993a. *Bodies that Matter*. Routledge: New York.

Butler, Judith. 1993b. "Imitation and Gender Insubordination." In *The Lesbian and Gay Studies Reader*, edited by Henry Abelove, Michele Aina Barale, and David M. Halperin, 307–320. New York: Routledge.

Carlson, Marvin A. 2001. *The Haunted Stage: The Theatre as Memory Machine*. Ann Arbor, MN: University of Michigan Press.

Cheng, Meiling. 1998. "*Les Demoiselles d/L.A.*: Sacred Naked Nature Girls' *Untitled Flesh*." *TDR: The Drama Review*, 42.2: 70–97.

De Lauretis, Teresa. 1984. *Alice Doesn't: Feminism, Semiotics, Cinema.* Bloomington, IN: Indiana University Press.

Diamond, Elin. 1997. *Unmaking Mimesis: Essays on Feminism and Theatre*, New York: Routledge.

Doane, Mary Anne. 1982. "Film and the Masquerade: Theorizing the Female Spectator." In *Writing on the Body: Female Embodiment and Feminist Theory*, edited by Katie Conboy, Nadia Medina, and Sarah Stanbury. New York: Columbia University Press.

Dolan Jill. 1988. *Feminist Spectator as Critic.* Ann Arbor, MN: University of Michigan Press.

Foucault, Michel. 1977. *Discipline and Punish: The Birth of the Prison*. Translated by Alan Sheridan. New York: Vintage.

Jackson, Shannon. 2004. *Professing Performance: Theatre in the Academy from Philology to*

*Performativity*. Cambridge: Cambridge University Press.
Kirshenblatt-Gimblett, Barbara. 1999. "Performance Studies." Rockefeller Foundation: Culture and Creativity, September.
McKenzie, Jon. 2001. *Perform or Else: From Discipline to Performance*. New York: Routledge.
Mulvey, Laura. 1975. "Visual Pleasure and Narrative Cinema." *Screen*, 16.3: 6–18.
Schechner, Richard. 1985. *Between Theatre and Anthropology*. Philadelphia, NJ: University of Pennsylvania Press.
Schechner, Richard. 2002. *Performance Studies: An Introduction*. London: Routledge.
Silverman, Kaja. 1996. *The Threshold of the Visible World*. New York: Routledge.
Turner, Victor W. 1987. *The Anthropology of Performance*. New York: PAJ.

*Cross references*

"**Active analysis**" by Carnicke; "**Broad Spectrum Approach**" by Schechner; "**Hierarchy**" by Luber; "**Identity politics**" by Adewunmi; "**Performance in the digital age**" by Auslander; "**Prison culture**" by Ryan; "**Surveillance**" by Morrison.

## Ecodramaturgy

Arden Thomas

Coined by theatre scholar Theresa May in 2007, the term "ecodramaturgy" refers to the burgeoning field of studies that critically applies an ecological perspective to performance. In her pioneering essay "Beyond Bambi: Toward a Dangerous Ecocriticism," May makes a convincing case for performance's particularly unique position as an embodied art form that can, and should, accept the urgent call of twenty-first century ecological issues to "flesh out the way in which the human imagination participates in, and is integral to, our ecological 'situatedness'" (2007, 95). Ecodramaturgical scholars have mapped out conversations between studies in environmental history, literary ecocriticism, postcolonial studies, gender studies, phenomenology, environmental justice, cultural geography, and performance to generate compelling questions regarding our embeddedness in the ecomaterial world.

Ecodramaturgy includes both critical and creative practices, and theorizes the intersections between performance studies and ecocriticism. Ecodramaturgy analyzes ecological performance-making, and studies the material-ecological implications of cultural performances. Ecodramaturgy also examines the presentation and representation of nonhuman animals in performance, and fleshes out various and wide-ranging ecological and performance-based connections. Such links vary, but can include drawing complex connections between global warming, environmental justice, food security, globalization, watershed democracy, and the natural resources that go into theater-making. Ecodramaturgy refers also to "theatre and performance making that puts ecological reciprocity and community at the center of its theatrical and thematic intent" (Arons and May 2012, 4).

Ecodramaturgy's attention to the materiality and multiplicity of the subject also calls for a rigorous re-thinking about the non-human animal. Una Chaudhuri, who laid the theoretical groundwork for a "responsible ecological theater" (1994, 25), terms the intersections between ecodramaturgy, performance studies, and animal studies "zooësis." Chaudhuri defines zooësis as "the myriad performance and semiotic elements involved in and around the vast field of cultural animal practices [ ... ] Comprising both our actual and our imaginative interactions with non-human animals, zooësis is the discourse of animality in human life, and its effects permeate our social, psychological, and material existence" (2003, 647). Zooësis provides a valuable field for ecodramaturgy, which refuses to take for granted that the subject is always already human.

Examples of an ecodramaturgical practice are diverse in form and theme: Cherríe Moraga's play *Heroes and Saints* (1992) is about environmental injustices in California's farmland, whereas E.M. Lewis's play *Song of Extinction* (2008) deals with species extinction. Wu Mali's *Trekking the Plum Street Project* (2010–2012) is a collaboration in which the artist works with community members both to revitalize the polluted Plum Street Stream in Tamsui, Taiwan, and to change their lifestyles. Chantal Bilodeau's play *Sila* (2012) discusses climate change and its consequences for humans and animals living in Canada's Inuit territory, while Rachel Rosenthal's passionate performance art pieces like *filename: FUTURFAX* (1992) and *Pangaean Dreams* (1990) examine ecocatastrophes and human-animal relations. Marc Bamuthi Joseph's multi-media hip-hop performance *red, black & GREEN: a blues* (2012) enlarges the ecocritical language of sustainability to include living and thriving in urban centers. Eiko and Koma's evocative dance pieces such as *Hunger* (2008), *Raven* (2010), *Wind* (1993), *River* (1995), and *Land* (1991) explore images associated with hunger and food scarcity, water, and the relationships between humans, the earth, and living creatures. Yin Xiuzhen's performance-installation piece *Washing the River* (1995) invites passers-by to scrub dirty blocks of ice made from the polluted water of a river in Chengdu, Sichuan Province, China.

By stirring the collective imagination towards a deeper sense of our material embeddedness in and accountability for the ecomaterial world, ecodramaturgical practices are poised to shift the paradigms of human-nature relations and to change audience perceptions of themselves. With its insistent emphasis on embodied connectivity, performance practices are crucial sites of investigation into the networks of exchange between culture, the environment, and animals.

### Further reading

Arons and May (2012); Besel and Blau (2013).

### References


Arons, Wendy and Theresa J. May, eds. 2012. *Readings in Performance and Ecology*. New York: Palgrave Macmillan.

Besel, Richard D., and Jnan A. Blau, eds. 2013. *Performance on Behalf of the Environment*. New York: Rowen and Littlefield Publishing Group.

Chaudhuri, Una. 1994. "'There Must Be a Lot of Fish in That Lake': Toward an Ecological Theater." *Theater*, 25.1: 23–31.

Chaudhuri, Una. 2003. "Animal Geographies: Zooësis and the Space of Modern Drama." *Modern Drama*, 46.4: 646–662.

May, Theresa J. 2007. "Beyond Bambi: Toward a Dangerous Ecocriticism in Theater Studies." *Theatre Topics*, 17.2: 95–110.


### Cross references

"**Animalworks**" by Cheng; "**Animal Studies**" and "**Knowing animals now: *The Unreliable Bestiary*, a multi-part, ongoing performance project by Deke Weaver**" by Chaudhuri; "**Becoming *Kinocognophore***" by Bucher; "**The ecodramaturgy of Anna Halprin, Eeo Stubblefield, and Rachel Rosenthal**" by Thomas; "**Environmental Theatre**" by Alker; "**Expanded cinema**" by Jarosi; "**Goat Island's *The Sea and Poison***" by Garoian and Gaudelius.

## Expanded cinema

Susan Jarosi

The term "expanded cinema" originates from the selfsame title of Gene Youngblood's 1970 book, which examines the conjunction of cybernetics, communication theory, commercial entertainment, and art in the "Paleocybernetic Age" (1970, 41). Expanded cinema translates most succinctly to "expanded consciousness," which Youngblood elaborates as a "process of becoming, [of] man's ongoing historical drive to manifest his consciousness outside of his mind, in front of his eyes" (1970, 41). The proposed expansion of cinema does not promote a formalist telos of medium specificity, nor privilege visual technologies per se; however, it does involve novel methods of image-making including the conjunction of art and technology that "promise to extend man's communicative capacities beyond his most extravagant visions" (1970, 41). Gender issues aside, the "beyond" of cinema imagined by Youngblood is a utopic condition where "cinema will be one with the life of the mind, and humanity's consciousness will become increasingly metaphysical" (1970, 43). The realization of expanded cinema means no less than "the beginning of creative living for all mankind and thus a solution to the so-called leisure problem" (1970, 43).

Process and experience; ontological awareness and expanded consciousness; the yoking of art and life—the methodological directives central to Youngblood's concerns are also the cornerstones of performance art. They link expanded cinema to a number of influential performance forms and practitioners, including Happenings (Allan Kaprow, *Hello*, 1969), Fluxus Events (Nam June Paik and Charlotte Moorman, *TV Bra for Living Sculpture*, 1969), Viennese Actionism (Valie Export, *Tap and Touch Cinema*, 1968–1971), Kinetic Theater (Carolee Schneemann, *Illinois Central*, 1968), Destructivism (Raphael Montañez Ortiz, *Self-Destruction*, 1966), and Relation Works (Marina Abramovic and Ulay, *Relation in Time*, 1977). Expanded cinema and performance also share a specific investment in theories of intermedia. When Fluxus artist Dick Higgins penned his essay entitled "Intermedia" (2007), a fair portion was devoted to a critique of traditional proscenium theatre and the obsolete social order that it represents. In its stead, Higgins described the bourgeoning interest (his own included) in new forms of theatre that rejected linear sequence altogether "by systematically replacing [time and sequence] as structural elements with change" (1984, 22). Intermedia works in theatre, visual arts, and music most often exploring the terrain "in between" art forms, such as the intermedia between music and theatre ("action music") or the intermedia between sculpture and poetry ("constructed poems"). Higgins also described the more rare, and perhaps more provocative, possibility of intermedia works that lie in the field between established art media and life media, citing the hypothetical example of "work which has consciously been placed in the intermedium between painting and shoes" (1984, 20).

Youngblood's advocacy of intermedia echoed its antecedent in Fluxus. He defined "intermedia theater," for example, as a form that draws individually from theatre and cinema—being cognizant of their distinctions but unconcerned with protecting the purity of either—all the while orchestrating media divisions "as harmonic opposites in an overall synaesthetic experience" (Youngblood 1970, 365). These objectives should be understood in two ways: as contributing a set of generative parameters for the creation of intermedia performance, and as proposing a model of art whose object—both in regard to materials and outcome—is the transformation of the spatial environment as such.

Expanded cinema's emphasis on art as environment extends more broadly to include an engagement with environmental*ism*, placing it at the forefront of historical and theoretical formulations of ecological art (Jarosi 2012). In fact, Youngblood was the first to suggest the "artist as ecologist," by which he meant one who comprehends the "totality of relations between organisms and their environment" and who, like a scientist, "rearranges the environment to the advantage of society" (1970, 346). The aesthetic and social values of expanded cinema thus connect the concept to a major facet of contemporary performance practice and, given the increasing urgency surrounding the effects of global climate change, constitute one of its most significant legacies. Although expanded cinema may have been superseded in current clinical discourse by more modish terms such as site-specific work, multimedia installation, relational aesthetics, and social practice, nonetheless it demonstrates clear affinities with them. Indeed, the continued relevance of expanded cinema can be located in its commitment to the most persistent, compelling, and embedded ideas at the core of performative modes. This is confirmed by the fact that the most influential works of performance continue to circle around many of the same concerns, problems, and even fantasies that were once associated with expanded cinema.

*Further reading*

Hatfield (2003); Mekas (1972).

*References*

Hatfield, Jackie. 2003. "Expanded Cinema and Its Relationship to the Avant-Garde: Some Reasons for a Review of the Avant-Garde Debates Around Narrativity." *Millennium Film Journal*, 39/40: 50–65.

Higgins, Dick. 1984. *Horizons, the Poetics and Theory of the Intermedia*. Carbondale, IL: Southern Illinois University Press.

Higgins, Dick. 2007. "Intermedia" (1965). In *Horizons*, 21–31. n.p.: /ubu Editions.. Accessed 7 July 2015. http://www.scribd.com/doc/38186653/Higgins-Horizons#scribd

Jarosi, Susan. 2012. "Recycled Cinema as Material Ecology: Raphael Montanez Ortiz's Found-footage Films and Computer-Laser-Videos." *Screen*, 53.3: 228–245.

Mekas, Jonas. 1972. *Movie Journal: The Rise of a New American Cinema, 1959–1971*. New York: Macmillan.

Youngblood, Gene. 1970. *Expanded Cinema*. New York: Dutton.

*Cross references*

"**Cybernetics**" and "**Intermediality**" by Auslander; "**Dance or we are lost: The Tanztheater of Pina Bausch**" by Birringer; "**Ecodramaturgy**" by Thomas; "**Environmental Theatre**" by Alker; "**Fluxus**" by Stiles; "**Installation art**" by Haidu.

## Carolee Schneemann's *Cat Scan (New Nightmares/Ancient History)*

Erika Rundle

A rough pyramid of small televisions, their screens lit by the forward projection of a Super-8 film, sits in the center of a white rectangular space. We can just make out, playing over the uneven surfaces of this precarious sculpture, the image of a fish, its glistening flesh pierced by a needle trailing red thread. A whistle is blown, and four performers, clad in colorful sportswear, burst from a single door in the back wall. They carry with them a wooden crate, suitcase, stool, and mop, which they drop hastily on the floor amidst the now disrupted TVs. A soundtrack of police sirens, cat cries, and cricket chirps accompanies the actors as they exit the stage in a frenzy, returning with a grocery cart, hula-hoop, and other ordinary objects, which replace the items in the existing assemblage. These, in turn, are hurriedly transported offstage, triggering yet another cycle of purposeful exchange.

This frantic activity continues until the performers take to the floor in pairs, studiously embracing ladders, chairs, or tabletops to form improbable threesomes. Four prerecorded voices recite common animal metaphors ("there are many ways to skin a cat"; "look what the cat dragged in"; "the cat's meow"; "stop pussyfooting around") as the pliant idiom of human limbs and the angled geometry of manufactured shapes intertwine with slow, uncanny tenderness. When the interlude exhausts itself, the performers stand up and move about as in a trance, each carrying a single object. Occasionally they trade with one another, and in one particularly jarring event, a platter of eggs is thrust onto someone's chest; we watch the cascade of crushed shells and viscous liquid, but discover no reason for or reaction to it. Finally gathering at the former site of the pyramid, the actors pile their bodies atop one another in communal release. Projected onto them in a dissolve, at the effective center of the work, we glimpse the burial ceremony of Carolee Schneemann's cat, Cluny.

This image cues a new series of concurrent slides and stage actions, narrated by alternating male and female voices whose lines bring the charged specificities of dream logic into dialogue with authoritative accounts of Egyptian mythological history and religious practices. These vocal tracks–

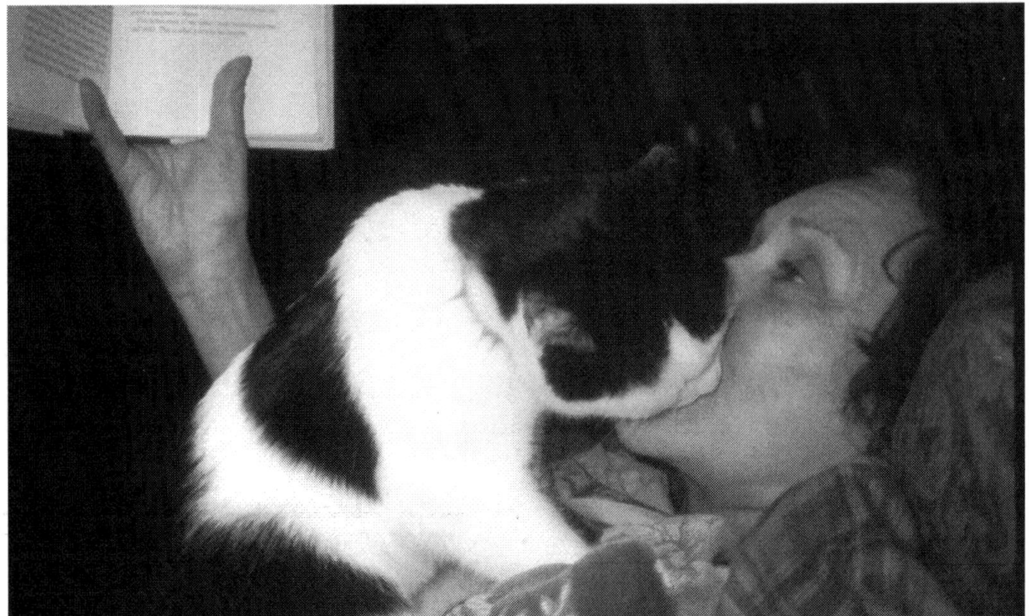

**Figure 28** Carolee Schneemann performing with her cat in *Infinity Kisses II*, 1990–1998, self-shot 35mm photographs from the *Infinity Kisses* Series Photos. Courtesy of the artist.

set against a series of related images–inaugurate Schneemann's entrance onto the stage, clad in green and gold, and blindfolded. The other performers disperse and ascend a high platform stage left, taking with them the long ropes that have been hanging from the rafters throughout the show's preamble, and attach them to their waists. Schneemann tethers the end of a long strip of red fabric wrapped around her torso to the rear wall, and then, with a Walkman hanging from her neck, begins a gentle circular dance to samples of Marvin Gaye's "Sexual Healing," unraveling further with every revolution, like a mummy freed from her bandages. Schneemann's moving shadow–visible against a projected close-up of she and Cluny locked in a kiss–flickers across the provocative scene as the divergent scripts steadily veer toward one another, meeting, finally, in parallel tales of death and reincarnation. The story of Cluny's demise from a rat bite and his return in the form of another cat, Wicca, is matched by a vision of the Egyptian afterworld, where immortality is granted via the Lion Goddess's "breath of life."

Schneemann–a feather hanging from her mouth–and the chorus (who are now all seated) lift their right hands, elbows bent at a 45-degree angle, to their hearts and then back down to their laps. They repeat this gesture with veneration as they return once more to circle the stage, and then, kneeling, raise up their offerings of fish and silver bowls of milk. On the back wall of the performance space, we see a fragment from an Egyptian relief, in which a regal human and large feline gaze at one another while touching noses. The image of this ancient carving (a relic from the pyramids at Dahshur) joins the modern photograph of woman and cat to create a double portrait. (These same images, doubled yet again, form the apex of *Infinity Kisses I*, Schneemann's self-shot photo grid of close-up kisses with Cluny, from 1981 to 1987.) Amidst the plaintive return of meows, chirps, and sirens, the performers resume their silent gestures, and, as the lights slowly fade to black, Schneemann recites "Aphrodite Drained of Her Waters," a poetic lament of the violent psychosexual, environmental, and geopolitical degradation and collapse evoked by the play's foreboding subtitle.

First shown in 1987, *Cat Scan* is exemplary of the groundbreaking, multidisciplinary work Schneemann has produced over the past half-century. From the ecstatic comingling of flesh in *Meat Joy* (1964) to the caretaking rituals of *Kitch's Last Meal* (1973-76) and the immersive mourning in *Vesper's Pool* (1999-2000), a profound interspecies alliance flows through much of her work, from conception to execution. The impetus for *Cat Scan* arose from Schneemann's chance encounter with a stray cat; petting its fur, memories of a "dream instruction" from the recently deceased Cluny came flooding back, causing her to rediscover a sketch she had made of an outstretched paw, which she now recognized as Cluny's. The action suggested by the drawing–a hand rising to meet the heart–inspired the repetitive movement that would become the central *gestus* of the piece. Cluny's message, transmitted via sensual contact and mediated by Schneemann's own artistic hand, became a subject of embodied research for her "kinetic theatre" ensemble, who divined its connection to Egyptian belief in the spiritual continuity of life and death, and the transformative power of animal gods–many of whom possessed a feline aspect.

This transcendent duality is signaled by *Cat Scan*'s multivalent title, which links an acronym ("CAT" stands for Computer Assisted Tomography) with its familiar homonym, bringing two seemingly opposed entities–machine and animal–together in a realm that is at once technical and biological, digital and organic. Like the penetrating waves produced by CAT scans, which map internal realms hidden from the naked eye, *Cat Scan* seeks to render visible, in banal yet vivid detail, the affective experiences of loss and reanimation. By the end of the show, the recuperative procedures of performance have also revealed "new nightmares"–the vampiric reality of a neoliberal body politic expressed in Schneemann's poem–rising from the tombs of "ancient history."

## Fluxus

Kristine Stiles

Fluxus is an international movement of artists, poets, composers, and individuals formally untrained in art, producing objects, installations, performances, collective festivals, celebrations, exhibitions, publications, mail art, editions, and multiples. Often characterized by its lack of pretension, playfulness, and humor, Fluxus is also noted for its philosophical acceptance of life's fluidity and ephemerality. George Brecht distinguished Fluxus artists as those who understand that "the bounds of art are much wider than they have conventionally seemed," and who "never ... attempt to agree on aims or methods" (1964, 111). Some Fluxus artists also pioneered queer sexual politics and aesthetics, including George Maciunas, the self-appointed titular head of Fluxus. Jon Hendricks, curator of the Gilbert and Lila Silverman Fluxus Collection, which the Silvermans donated to the Museum of Modern Art in New York in 2009, considers Maciunas "the father" of Fluxus and only what Maciunas "put forward" as constituting authentic Fluxus works (2002, 14, 20). Hendricks also dates the end of Fluxus to Maciunas' death in 1978, despite the many artists who identify with and continue to exhibit under the Fluxus moniker. Others agree with Ina Bloom that, "The history of Fluxus [...] demonstrates the difficulty of speaking of Fluxus as *one* phenomenon, movement or artistic identity," and that to assert this "does not mean [...] that Fluxus is essentially inclusive and endlessly pluralist" or that it "def[ies] definition" (2002, 49).

Such views suggest how contested the history of Fluxus remains. Nonetheless, Fluxus officially began with fourteen "concerts," billed as "Fluxus International Festival of New Music," in Wiesbaden, Germany, September 1–23, 1962. Robert Filliou, Wolf Vostell, Arthur Køpcke, Nam June Paik, Dick Higgins, Alison Knowles, Emmett Williams, and Maciunas participated, performing their own and a plethora of other artists' works. The list documents the initial inclusive eclecticism of Fluxus, which also involved more women and people of color than most avant-garde movements. Critical antecedents of Fluxus include John Cage's class on experimental composition at the New School for Social Research in New York (1956–1958), which inspired George Brecht's "Event Scores," texts calling for reflection and/or performance. Yoko Ono also produced "Instructions" during this period, which functioned much like event scores and were performed in the Wiesbaden "concerts." Three additional events in 1961 anticipated Fluxus: the composer La Monte Young organized a series of performances at Ono's Manhattan loft; Maciunas presented similar events at his AG Gallery; and Young and the poet Jackson Mac Low began editing the proto-Fluxus publication *An Anthology* (1963), which Maciunas designed.

While Maciunas described Fluxus as "anti-art," his source for such hyperbole was the Marxist-Leninist artist Henry Flynt, who gave public lectures (between 1961 and 1964) railing against European "serious culture," among a host of other notorious actions (Flynt 1975). Indeed, Maciunas' language in his 1963 "Manifesto"—such as "PURGE THE WORLD OF 'EUROPANISM'!", "PROMOTE ... NON ART REALITY," and "FUSE the cadres of cultural, social & political revolutionaries into united front & action" derives directly from Flynt's thinking and writings. Already in April of 1963, following the distribution of Maciunas' *Fluxus Newsletter* No. 6, or "Policy Letter," Mac Low, Brecht, and Higgins rejected Maciunas' suggestions for acts of cultural sabotage, and cautioned him to cease following Flynt's radical politics or they would disassociate from Fluxus. The representation of Fluxus as anti-art faded among those associated with it, but was kept alive primarily by art historians, and Maciunas began concentrating on marketing Fluxus products, organizing events, and purchasing property in lower Manhattan to turn into artists' lofts.

In 1965, Higgins, a co-founder of Fluxus, coined the term "intermedia" to describe artists' activities operating between aesthetic and disciplinary categories (1969, 11–29). Higgins' concept of intermedia is associated with Fluxus, de facto, and the open mandate of intermedia continues to represent the most generous interpretation, if not the legacy, of Fluxus.

### Further reading

Brecht (1964); Flynt (1975).

### References

Bloom, Ina. 2002. "Shifting Affiliations & Conflicting Visions: A Short Note on Fluxus in Scandinavia." In *Q que é Fluxus? O que Não é! O porqué. What's Fluxus? What's Not? Why*, edited by Jon Hendricks, 111–112. Rio de Janeiro and Detroit: Centro Cultural Banco do Brasil and The Gilbert and Lila Silverman Fluxus Collection Foundation.

Brecht, George. 1964/2002. Something About Fluxus. In Jon Hendricks (ed) *Q que é Fluxus? O que Não é! O porqué. What's Fluxus? What's Not? Why.* Reprint, 46–49. Rio de Janeiro and Detroit: Centro Cultural Banco do Brasil and The Gilbert and Lila Silverman Fluxus Collection Foundation.

Flynt, Henry. 1975. *Blueprint for a Higher Civilization.* Milano: Multhipla Edizioni.

Hendricks, Jon, ed. 2002. *Q que é Fluxus? O que Não é! O porqué. What's Fluxus? What's Not? Why.* Rio de Janeiro and Detroit: Centro Cultural Banco do Brasil and The Gilbert and Lila Silverman Fluxus Collection Foundation.

Flynt, Henry. 1975. *Blueprint for a Higher Civilization.* Milano: Multhipla Edizioni.

Higgins, Dick. 1969. *Foew & Ombwhnw: A Grammar of the Mind and a Phenomenology of Love and a Science of the Arts as Seen by a Stalker of the Wild Mushroom.* New York: Something Else Press.

Mac Low, Jackson and La Monte Young, eds. 1963. *An Anthology of Chance Operations,* USA: Jackson Mac Low.

### Cross references

"**Anti-art**" by Stiles; "**Experimental music**" by Henkes; "**Happenings**" by Sandford; "**Intermediality**" by Auslander; "**New genre public art**" by Irish; "**Performance, postmodernism, and beyond**" by Chin Davidson.

## Gaga Feminism

Jack Halberstam

The "existing conditions" under which the building blocks of human identity were imagined and cemented in the last century—what we call gender, sex, race, and class—have changed so radically that new life can be glimpsed ahead. The existence of sperm banks, artificial reproduction of life, surrogacy, gay marriage, and new arrangements of kinship and households—and not to mention the high rates of divorce—give evidence that the revolutionary conditions for gender transformation have arrived.

A new era of theory has recently emerged—we might call it "wild theory"—within which thinkers, scholars, and artists take a break from orthodoxy and experiment with knowledge, art, and the imagination, even as they remain all too aware of the constraints under which all three operate. In some ways, wild theory is failed disciplinary knowledge. The cultivation of such alternatives occurs in a variety of cultural sites: low and high culture, museum culture, and street culture. This takes the form of participatory art, ephemeral parties, and imaginative forms of recycling and different relations to objects, economies, and the environment. Jack Halberstam seeks openings in this new era for different formulations of kinship, pleasure, and power, and calls these "Gaga Feminism" (2012).

A brilliant rendition of the elemental struggle between, on one side, wild thought and wild practices, and on the other side, the canny force of institutionalization, can be found in *Wildness* (2012), a documentary film by Los Angeles-based artist Wu Tsang (co-written with Roya Rastega). The film presents the story of "Wildness," a short-lived party hosted by Tsang and his collaborator Ashland Mines, which took place on Tuesday nights at a club called The Silver Platter in the Rampart neighborhood of Los Angeles. On other nights, the club was home to a community of mostly Mexican and Central American gay men and transgender women. When "Wildness" begins to take over and brings unwanted publicity to The Silver Platter, both communities are forced to reckon with the ways in which the competing subcultural spaces cannot coexist, and with the possibility that one will swallow the other.

The utopia that *Wildness* sets out to document can be understood in the terms that José E. Muñoz lays out for queer potentiality in *Cruising Utopia: The Then and There of Queer Futurity*. Muñoz articulates utopia not as a place but as a "horizon," as a "mode of possibility," a queer future that is "not an end but an opening" (1999, 91, 99), and, referencing Ernst Bloch, as an event that is "not yet here" (1999, 32). This sense of a queer community that is not yet here makes the project of "Wildness" legible.

In an extraordinary body of work, Berlin-based artist Kerstin Drechsel explores the sexual entropy of the everyday and the chaos inherent to capitalism. Drechsel refuses the neat division between a chaotic world ordered by capitalist modes of production and the chaos of anarchy that capitalism supposedly holds at bay. Drechsel's work recognizes that capitalism too is chaotic and disordered, that the world we live in tends towards breakdown, and that the state simply manages and marshals chaos for capital accumulation and biopower. Anarchy is thus no more oriented to chaos than capitalism. In the series *Unser Haus*, Drechsel confronts messiness directly in paintings of explicitly junky domestic interiors. In some spaces, the books and the paper overwhelm the spaces that should contain them; in others, the materials we use to clean away the traces of dirt—toilet paper, for instance—become waste itself. The paintings of messy interiors taunt the collector and liken the collecting of art to the collecting of things, useless things, *stuff*. They menace and snarl; they refuse to be the accent on a minimal interior; they promise to sow disorder and shove any environment firmly in the direction of anarchy.

Wes Anderson's animated genius, *Fantastic Mr. Fox* (2009), when watched closely, gives us clues and hints about revolt, riot, fugitivity, and its relation to charm and theft. The film tells a simple story about a fox who gets sick of his upwardly mobile lifestyle and goes back to his roots. He lives a respectable life with his wife and his queer son by day, but by night he steals chickens from the farmers down the hill. When the farmers come for him, Mr. Fox asks his motley woodland crew of foxes, beavers, raccoons, and possums to retreat with him to the maze of tunnels that make up the forest underground. And in scenes that could be right out of *The Battle of Algiers*, the creatures go down to rise up: they thwart the farmers, the policemen, the firemen, and all the officials who come to drive them from their homes and occupy their land.

But the most poignant scene comes in the form of a quiet encounter with the *wild* at the end of the film. In this scene, Mr. Fox is on his way home after escaping from the farmers once again. As he and his merry band of creatures turn the corner on their motorbike with sidecar, they come upon a spectral figure loping into their path. Mr. Fox pulls up and they all stand in awe. They watch as a lone wolf turns and stares back at them. Mr. Fox, ever the diplomat, declares his phobia of wolves and yet tries to communicate with the wolf in three languages. When nothing works, he tries gestures. With tears in his eyes, Mr. Fox raises a fist to the wolf on the hill and stares transfixed as the wolf understands the universal sign of solidarity and raises his own fist in response, before drifting off into the forest. This exchange, silent and profound, brings tears to Mr. Fox's eyes precisely because it puts him face to face with the wildness he fears and the wildness he harbors within himself.

The *wild* here is a space that opens up when we step outside of the conventional realms of political action and confront our fears; it rhymes with Muñoz's sense of queer utopia and manifests what Fred Moten and Stefano Harney call the power of the "the undercommons" (2013). The wild and the fantastic enter the frame of visibility in the form of an encounter between the semi-domesticated and the unknown, speech and silence, motion and stillness. Ultimately, the revolutionary is a wild space where temporality is uncertain, relation is improvised, and futurity is on hold. Into this "any instant whatsoever" (Deleuze) walks a figure that we cannot classify, that refuses to engage us in conventional terms, but speaks instead in the gestural language of solidarity, connection, and insurrection.

The *wild* archive that I have gathered here is made up of the improbable, impossible, and unlikely visions of a queer world to come. Change involves giving and risking everything for a cause that is uncertain, a trajectory that is unclear, and a mission that may well fail. Fail well, fail wildly.

### Further reading

Halberstam (1998, 2012); Muñoz (2009).

### References

*Fantastic Mr. Fox*, film. 2009. Directed by Wes Anderson. Performed by George Clooney, Meryl Streep, Bill Murray. Screenplay by Wes Anderson and Noah Baumbach. Twentieth Century Fox, Indian Paintbrush, Regency Enterprises.

Halberstam, J. Jack. 2012. *Gaga Feminism: Sex, Gender, and the End of Normal.* Boston, MA: Beacon Press.

Halberstam, Judith. 1998. *Female Masculinity.* Durham and London: Duke University Press.

Harney, Stefano, and Fred Moten. 2013. *The Undercommons: Fugitive Planning & Black Study.* New York: Autonomedia.

Muñoz, José Esteban. 1999. *Disidentifications: Queers of Color and the Performance of Politics.* Minneapolis, MN: University of Minnesota Press.

Muñoz, José Esteban. 2009. *Cruising Utopia: The Then and There of Queer Futurity.* New York: New York University Press.

*Wildness*, documentary. 2012. Directed by Wu Tsang. Screenplay by Wu Tsang and Roya Rastegar.

### Cross references

"**Boychild**" by Halberstam; "**Cultural production**" by Colleran; "**Drag**" by Edgecomb; "**Emotion**" by Tait; "**Feminist hip-hop fusion**" by Hodges Persley; "**Memoir of Björk-Geisha**" by Takemoto; "**Performing body modification**" by Henkes; "**Romeo Castellucci's *Hey Girl!***" by Sack; "**The Wooster Group's *TO YOU, THE BIRDIE! (Phèdre)***" by Cody.

## Boychild

Jack Halberstam

"Rage," June Jordan once declared, "has gone out of style." This was in the 1990s and while it was true then, in the early years of a post-Cold War era of total capitalism, rage, on the other side of total capitalism's boom/bust cycle, is making a come back. Rage directed at bankers on the rampage, pillaging and looting from their clients and rage at new theocratic orders that bully their congregations into docility, seems to be expressing itself in a wide variety of social scripts, political choreographies and environmental mayhem; but this current expression of anger does not necessarily feel gendered in a way that would make sense of a descriptor like "Angry Women." So, let's dismantle this epithet to understand both what is meant by "anger" and what the term "women" may signify.

The original *Angry Women* book from 1999 was interested in rage as a potent source of creativity, as a mode of political mobilization and as an appropriate response to what was already in the 1990s being experienced as the ruination of the earth, the environment and the planet. With the high stakes of survival in play, *Angry Women* wondered whether any response but anger is even appropriate to the patriarchal hubris that has brought the earth to the edge of collapse. Defining performance art as the creative channeling of rage, the two editors Andrea Juno and V. Vale showcased a brace of female-bodied theorists who variously challenged the stasis of a gender politics that assigned agitation, rage and anger to men and sullenness, apathy and depression to women.

Anger and rage are affective responses, in other words, they cannot lead to strategies for containment or to practical projects and programs. Indeed, the list of things that may make people angry at this particular historical juncture is long and varied, but there are also forms of anger that come without justification because

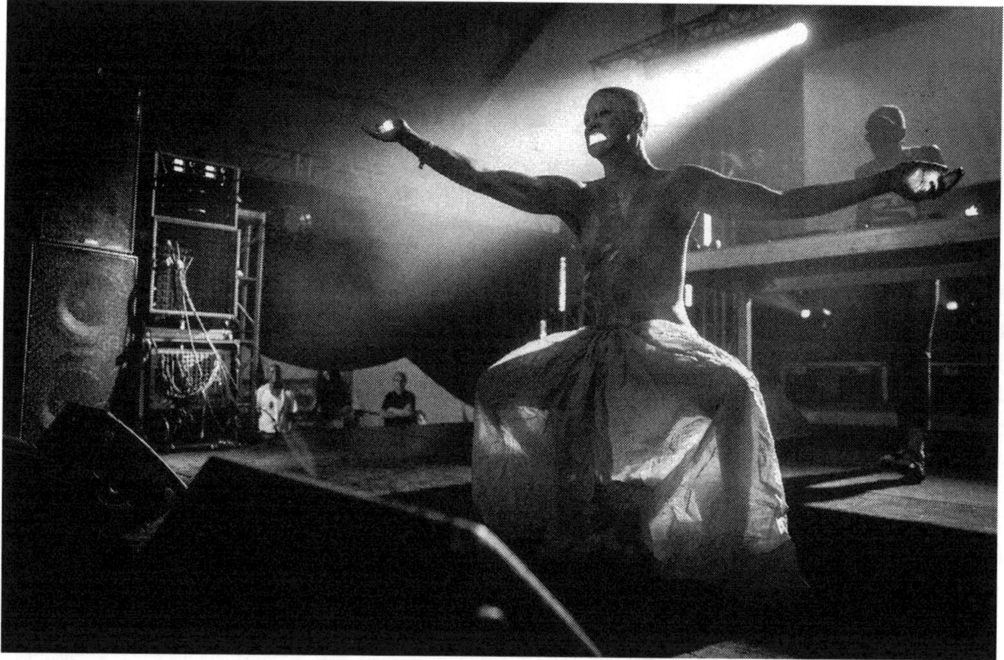

**Figure 29** The American performance artist Boychild pictured live on stage at her show for *Off Festival* 2013. Photo by Malthe Ivarsson. Image courtesy of the photographer.

they are existential; they exist because inequality and injustice exists. These forms of anger play out dramas of possession in dispossession. They occupy and pre-occupy us and they lead to various forms of outrage, rudeness, incivility, violence and excess. We could use the term "angry women" as Juno and Vale did to define anger that wholly possesses and takes over the body. In such a context, "women" are not simply females but rather they represent the force, place and shape of dispossession. We might also name this force "blackness" or "the colonized" and indeed this is exactly the terminology that has been used for other genres of anger by theorists of anti-colonial rage. According to this logic, *anger* is not the expression of individuals who are upset about this or that event; anger is the collective expression of those classes of people who have been systematically rendered disposable, dispensable, foreign, criminal. Needless to say, not all women are angry, not all angry women are female, and not all females are women.

Anger can express itself in and through different bodies, with or without intent, before and after the event or setting that creates it. Anger, we might say, is less a form of expression and more of a mode of being possessed by dispossession. The angry body is charged, wild, anguished. But it is also gripped, tormented and moved. If we begin to think of anger as less of a form of communication within which an embittered and tormented person—call her "woman"—rages against a world that has marked her as the cause and the origin of chaos, disorder and ruin; and we come to see anger as a force that ripples across bodies, that contorts the face, makes the body rigid and then releases it to a kind of shattered collapse, then we come close to the meaning of "Angry Women."

But what does anger express? We live in a world of polite exchange, manners and civility and we know that these forms of social conduct actually mask vast reservoirs of violence, cruelty and destruction. And so, the US government tortures prisoners but calls it security; people abuse their children and call it discipline; lovers beat each other and call it desire. Anger expressed singularly is just that, one person's sense of injustice or frustration. But anger expressed across a crowd, within a mob or through an iconic figure is a mode of politics that seeks to unmake the world and undo the forms of being that it has mandated.

Anger is a particular kind of choreography. It grips and shakes the body, sometimes in a blaze of fury and sometimes in a cold and dark expression of rage. The performance of anger can mesmerize or repel, seduce or induce revulsion; but anger can also spark. While other forms of high emotional intensity do not necessarily create a mirrored response, anger tends to inspire anger. What happens when an artist traps and distils anger, or at least when an artist enters the dramatic space of anger and inhabits it?

Boychild, a gender-ambiguous performer in San Francisco, performs dramatic possession in short, inventive sequences that begin in the genre of club scene drag acts and end in a highly idiosyncratic form of the avant-garde practice of *Butoh*. Boychild has made a series of performances in clubs, art galleries and other venues and has in a very short period of time, come to be recognized as a new and startling performance artist. With their highly ambiguous appearance and their inventive bodily practice that combines dance, installation art and intervention art, Boychild is redefining the drag, queer performance and dance all at once.

A nightclub, late, drag acts sweep on and off the stage. The lights go down and when they come back up they reveal a lone figure high on a pedestal, bare from the chest up, powdered, muscled, enigmatic. As the music begins, the performer begins to weave around the song and she opens her mouth to reveal a burning, ecstatic light, a flame that is working its way from inside to out, from the lyric to the mouth. The body looks unnaturally pale, racially illegible, freaky and wondrous and the dance that issues forth, like the light that flashes between the teeth, combines sinewy motions that ripple through the form with convulsive, rhythmic gestures.

What we see and hear in Boychild's charming and mesmerizing performance is an ecstatic mode of drag where, instead of re-performing an act in a cross-gender mode, the artist becomes a vessel for a performance that moves through her and disorders her in the process. Given the performer's name, "Boychild" and the fact that she has taken Rihanna's song "Rude Boy" and slowed down the vocal tracks so that it sounds like a male-ish voice, there are all kinds of gender wildness in the recreation of the song. Boychild seems to be channeling something, she literally becomes a conduit for the song and in doing so the song becomes something else—not just a sexy come-on to the rude boy but a new embodiment of "boy" altogether. The light sticks in the mouth give the performer a kind of terrifying presence—like she is filled with fire or glowing with the words/song/music. In this sense, Boychild resembles a kind of deity, an alien presence whose language burns brightly and whose gestural language is less about enacting the song and more about taking it apart.

As if to acknowledge the racial quality of the wildness she channels, Boychild smears black polish around on her body in a parody of blacking up and in the process, she makes blackness into something messy and vibrant rather than something factual and fetishized. Blackness moves around on her rather than representing a fixed form of being. Blackness is also however a performance repertoire that she channels in movement and in the ecstatic loss of control that the song's lyrics seem to hold at bay but that Boychild herself brings into being.

The movements that Boychild channels and performs are reminiscent of Butoh, a Japanese dance form that emerged in post-war Japan in the 1960s, partly as a rejection of western dance forms and partly as an expression of the dark, damaged, and diseased legacy of Hiroshima and Nagasaki. Student protests voiced the outrage of a new generation both against their parent's legacy of war and death and against the US military nuclear action that had devastated the country. In the midst of this turmoil, a "dance of darkness" or Ankoku Butoh emerged. Pioneered by Tatsumi Hijikata and his partner Kazuo Ohno, Butoh became a dance form, an art, a practice and a discipline. It combined slow, almost grotesque movements with ghostly and spectral appearances to give the affect of the living dead. The dance movements were supposed to be unconscious, channeling repressed emotions that bubble up from the depths of the dancer and spill out into both surreal and organic forms of expression.

What do we make then of this eruption of some queer version of the Butoh form in a subcultural queer performance? Boychild in no way sets out to perform Butoh, rather she is possessed by some of the same animating conditions that inspires Butoh. Boychild, born of a generation that has inherited a spoiled earth, a broken economy, a selfish social system and a hypocritical religious order, transforms his gender queer embodiment into a platform for a wildly emotional, deeply moving choreography. While the "Rude Boy" piece speaks directly and immediately to the combination of racial and gendered ambiguity that Boychild wears and performs, other images of Boychild play on the boundary between the living and the dead.

In a gorgeous piece titled *DLIHCYOB* and recorded for MOCAtv by Mitch Moore, ethereal electronic music plays in the background while a spectral Boychild glows in some kind of infra red light. Her hair, eyes, nose and mouth seem to emit a ghostly light while her body shimmers and shines through x-ray like optics. Boychild's tattoos, one in large block capitals that reads "BLISS" on the neck and another in the form of small script of the same letters on her right shoulder, pulse through a kind of post nuclear haze and then the body starts to move. Unlike the slow, twisting, anguished movements of her "Rude Boy" performance, in *DLIHCYOB*, Boychild twitches like a body in electro-shock treatment, or like a cyborg coming to life. The cinematography brings out the beauty of the movements, allowing each to leave a shadow into which the next gesture steps. Half way through the performance, Boychild stops moving for a moment and then the close up shows him struggling, struggling to do what we don't know, but struggling for life, for breath, for survival. The video ends with Boychild's startled movements, animal-like small gestures of confusion, physical chaos and, possibly, death.

We end then in an apocalyptic state; the fury of a body trying to survive, the pathos of an organism beginning to die. Boychild gives us access to beginnings and ends—he births new forms of being through his unique and carefully choreographed movements of struggle. We don't know, after watching

Boychild, if there is any way to survive the decaying universe implied by his performances; we don't know if his struggle will end in rebirth, monstrous mutation or something else entirely. But we do know, that this struggle is ongoing and desperate and that it leads equally to bliss and oblivion. Boychild's performances are elemental, savage and sweet, a kind of visitation not from the future but from some other concept of temporal sequencing altogether. And while time itself is rearranged in the braiding of bliss and body that she enacts, space also opens and closes in her wake. Be she in a club or a gallery, a museum or a theatre, when the dance is done, Boychild leaves us all stranded in the wilderness of our own making.

## Hybridity

Erin Mee

The term "hybrid" was originally used in biology to describe the mixing of two species into a third, as in the combination of two varieties of rose to create a new rose. In performance theory "hybridity" is associated with the emergence of postcolonial responses to colonial cultural superiority and narratives of cultural imperialism. Homi Bhabha defines hybridity as a space/place where "denied" knowledge enters "the dominant discourse and estrange[s] the basis of [colonial] authority" (1994, 114). The "interstitial passage between fixed identifications opens up the possibility of a cultural hybridity that entertains difference without an assumed or imposed hierarchy" (Bhabha 1994, 4). Hybridity denies racial and cultural essentialisms.

After India's Independence in 1947, practitioners searched for a theatre that could reflect the complex historical, political, social, and cultural realities faced by the new nation. In 1971, Girish Karnad wrote *Hayavadana* (*The One with the Horse's Head*, arguably the most influential play of the Indian post-Independence era) to address the divided self of the post-colonial subject. In *Hayavadana*, hybridity was not just the subject of the play, but its structural strategy. Karnad employed a linear narrative structure, the proscenium stage, the fourth wall, and human characters, strategically placing them in a play with a structure of concentric circles, nonhuman characters, an acting style that breaks the fourth wall, and a way of seeing that challenged the frame of the proscenium. By weaving together structures, aesthetics, and techniques inherited from the playwright-initiated, text-based, and plot-driven colonial theatre with structures, aesthetics, and techniques from *Yakshagana*, a well-known genre of dance-drama performed in his native state of Karnataka, Karnad created a play that is neither "Western" nor "Indian" but both: a new theatre that is both more than and different from the sum of its parts. Karnad consciously created a hybrid play that challenges the authority of colonial culture not by rejecting "Western" theatre or by giving center stage to theatrical practices and aesthetics denied by the dominant colonial theatrical discourse, but by challenging the binary terms on which colonial cultural authority was constructed. Hybridity is useful because it does not resolve "the tension between two cultures," but "creates a crisis for any concept of [cultural] authority" by disrupting the production of cultural differentiation (Bhabha 1994, 113–114).

Critics have argued that hybridity theory relies on false essentialisms, and that its articulation is often homogenizing. Ella Shohat has pointed out the need "to discriminate between the diverse modalities of hybridity, for example forced assimilation, internalized self-rejection, political co-optation, social conformism, cultural mimicry, and creative transcendence" (1993, 110). Other critics point out that numerous anti-colonialists have generatively appropriated and mobilized the notion of a binary opposition in order to create a "national" identity, a position that seems antithetical to notions of hybridity. As

Neil ten Kortenaar points out, however, "*neither* authenticity nor creolization has ontological validity; both are valid as metaphors that permit collective self-fashioning" (1995, 40–41).

Hybridity has been employed in theorizing identity, racism, postcolonialism, and more recently, globalization and glocalization. For example, Marwan Kraidy sees hybridity as an effect of globalization in that the "cultural logic" of globalization "entails that traces of other cultures exist in every culture, thus offering foreign media and marketers transcultural wedges for forging affective links between their commodities and local communities" (2005, 148).

### Further reading

Kapchan (1999); Loomba (2007); Robertson (1995).

### *References*

Bhabha, Homi K. 1994. *The Location of Culture*. London: Routledge.

Kapchan, Deborah A. 1999. *Theorizing the Hybrid*. Arlington, VA: American Folklore Society.

Karnad, Girish, 1971. *Hayavadana*. In *Collected Plays, Volume I*. Reprint, New Delhi: Oxford University Press, 2005.

Kortenaar, Neil Ten. 1995. "Beyond Authenticity and Creolization: Reading Achebe Writing Culture." *PMLA*, 110.1: 30–42.

Kraidy, Marwan M. 2005. *Hybridity: Or the Cultural Logic of Globalization*. Philadelphia, NJ: Temple University Press.

Loomba, Ania. 2007. *Colonialism/Postcolonialism*. London and New York: Routledge.

Robertson, Roland. 1995. "Glocalization: Time-Space and Homogeneity-Heterogeneity." In *Global Modernities*, edited by Mike Featherstone, Scott M. Lash and Roland Robertson, 25–44. London: Sage Publication Ltd.

Shohat, Ella and Robert Stam. 1993. *Unthinking Eurocentrism: Multiculturalism and the Media*. London and New York: Routledge.

### *Cross references*

"**Boychild**" and "**Gaga Feminism**" by Halberstam; "**Ethnic drag**" by Herrera; "**Guillermo Gómez-Peña attempts to explain performance art to people who may have never heard of it**" by Gómez-Peña; "**Identification/dis-identification**" by Muñoz; "**Memoirs of Björk-Geisha**" by Takemoto; "**Postcolonial performance inquiry**" by Chatterjee.

## Intercultural performance

Gwendolyn Alker

The Latin prefix "inter-" in the term "intercultural," meaning between or among, suggests a value-free melding of differing cultural traditions. Patrice Pavis, in his edited volume on intercultural performance, presents myriad definitions of culture, beginning with the idea of human culture as a "system of significations which allows a society or a group to understand itself in its relationship with the world" (1996, 2). Culture, then, is always already intercultural. The central discussion of intercultural performance interrogates how cultures interact and what the reception of ensuing enactments signifies.

In the broadest sense, any performance that is crafted with an awareness of and focus on the meeting of disparate cultures could be seen as intercultural. Historical examples range from the Nahua-Christian liturgical dramas of the sixteenth century, to the introduction of spoken drama in Chinese performance during the early twentieth century, from Peter Brook's restaging of the *Mahabharata* in the mid-1970s, to the border art of Guillermo Gómez-Peña in the late 1990s. Gómez-Peña, as both an artist and a theorist, has exposed the possibilities and pitfalls of intercultural performance. In *Warrior for Gringostroika* (1993), he notes the ways that conscious and subconscious racist attitudes, stereotypes and a culture of fear over-determine any cultural dialogue between North Americans and Latin (or Latino) Americans. For Gómez-

Peña, a true -dialogue would depend upon a "two-way, ongoing communication between peoples and communities that enjoy equal negotiating powers" (1993, 48). Therefore, engaging in work that crosses geographic, aesthetic, and cultural borders is necessarily political.

According to Schechner, the term "intercultural" arose from the shift away from nationalistic theatre models. Its related noun, "interculturalism," was established in the early 1970s to refer to an emergent performance genre, when Richard Schechner and others began celebrating the idea of a cultural hybridity in the U.S. and European avant-garde. Peter Brook's work fell into this category, as did the work and influence of Jerzy Grotowski, Eugenio Barba, Lee Breuer, Ariane Mnouchkine, John Cage and Schechner himself. "Intercultural performance," as defined by Pavis, suggests the voluntary and conscious melding of two distinct cultural forms in order to create a new work in which the original influences may no longer be traceable (1996, 8).

The connection between Pavis' utopian idea and the specificity of the borrowed cultures in an intercultural performance mark two poles in the contentious debate that has ensued regarding the political realities of this genre. Rather than creating a reciprocal dialogue, many would argue that intercultural theatre is too often propagated by European or U.S. artists borrowing, or even un-self-consciously stealing, performance traditions from Asian, Latin American, African or other cultures that are politically and/or economically less privileged. In one of the most avid critiques of the use of Indian performance traditions in the West, Rustom Bharucha notes that "this 'two-way street' could be more accurately described as a 'dead end'" (1992, 2). In *Theatre and the World*, Bharucha harshly criticizes Brook's *Mahabharata* as a central example in which "a particular *kind* or western representation [...] negates the non-western context of its borrowing" (1992, 98). As a result, debates around interculturalism have often been tied to this one production, and indeed Brook's adaptation of this Hindu epic can be seen as an exemplary case study of the pros and cons of intercultural performance. Bharucha's criticism of a Western influence over intercultural performance can also be seen as energizing his own political views and artistic endeavors, such as his intercultural staging of Franz Xaver Kroetz's silent piece, *Request Concert* in Calcutta, Mumbai (Bombay), and Madras.

A more inclusive narrative of the history of intercultural performance might extend back to Antonin Artaud's Occidentalist idealizations of Balinese dance and Mexican landscapes. The influence of these cross-cultural experiences were central to his formulations of the "Theatre of Cruelty," (1938/1958) which, in turn, have influenced those who have subsequently read and utilized Artaud. Over the last thirty years, the U.S./Mexican border has provided the location and inspiration for much intercultural performance: from the mid-1980s with the Border Art Work Shop/Taller de Arte Fronterizo, to the turn of the twenty-first century with the work of Gómez-Peña as he reworks the idea of interculturalism. The increase in globalization and technologies will make intercultural research and production more accessible, perhaps at the risk of masking the persistent inequalities that often plague intercultural practices.

### Further reading

Bharucha (1992); Pavis (1996).

### References

Artaud, Antonin. 1958. *The Theater and Its Double.* Translated from the 1938 French edition by Mary Caroline Richards. New York: Grove Press.

Bharucha, Rustom. 1992. *Theatre and the World: Essays on Performance and Politics of Culture.* New Delhi: Manohar Publishers.

Gómez-Peña, Guillermo. 1993. *Warrior for Gringostroika: Essays, Performance Texts, and Poetry.* St. Paul, MN: Graywolf Press.

Pavis, Patrice, ed. 1996. *Intercultural Performance Reader.* New York: Routledge.

*Cross references*

"**Communitas**" by Levine; "**The d/Deaf Performative**" by Pendgraft; "**Ethnic drag**" by Herrera; "**Guillermo Gómez-Peña attempts to explain performance art to people who may have never heard of it**" by Gómez-Peña; "**Marc Bamuthi Joseph's *red, black, & GREEN: a blues***" by Thomas; "**Memoirs of Björk-Geisha**" by Takemoto; "**Transnationalism**" by Yang.

## Guillermo Gómez-Peña attempts to explain performance art to people who may have never heard of it

Guillermo Gómez-Peña

*I Explaining to a nurse what I do*

Performance memory #267 stored in my liver.

I've been hospitalized in Mexico City for 2 weeks. I won't discuss my illness tonight for I've already done so in another script. I'm trying to explain what I do to a nurse; I mean, I'm trying to explain to a nurse what I do. But I'm not getting anywhere.

She asks me for the 10th time, "Perdone, what did you say you were? A per-for-man-que?"

A contra-dic-tion in terms–I say. A wrestler without a ring, a rocker without a band, a cyber-pirate without "access," a theorist without methodology, a dervish without a mountain top, a poet who writes his metaphors on his body/her body; siete locos, seven, locked inside an empty room. This one! It's my mind, not theirs, not yours ...

Remember, I'm still trying to explain to a nurse what I do.

She looks at me with a combination of tenderness and fear and says: "No entiendo nada ... del arte ... moderno, pero, señor Guillermo, la verdad, los artistas me caen bien."

I make a final attempt to explain to her the substance of my work:

"I'm an artist who sells ideas, not objects, not images, not skills, a per-for-man-ce artist, which means that ... I write letters with my own blood; I wrestle with historical ghosts & postcolonial demons; I research the possibilities of silence & darkness."

She looks at me in complete disbelief as I continue to anthologize my work in an attempt to recapture my sense of self: "I set my hair on fire just to make a point. I cross the border without documents just to make a point & when I am pissed I tend to speak in tongues."

The nurse changes the page of the script for me. She finally gets it. "Ahh"–she says

*"Es como vivir en un mundo paralelo. Es algo hermoso pero inútil."*

Translation please?

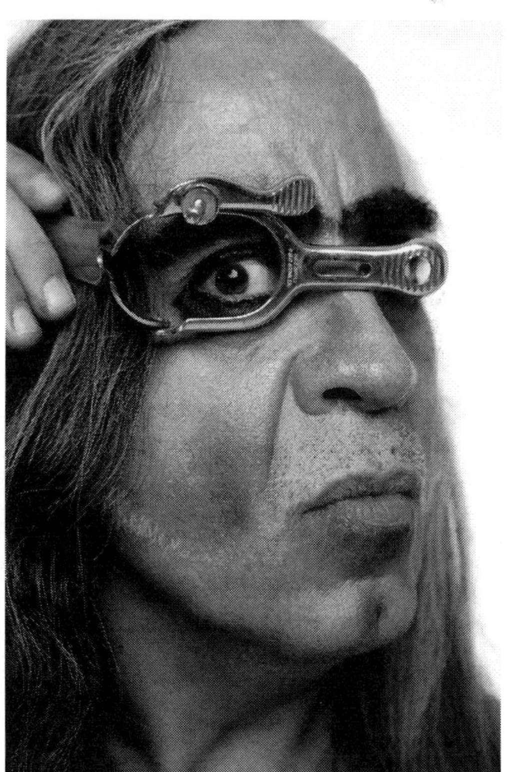

**Figure 30** Guillermo Gómez-Peña photographed by Zach Gross, 2010. Image courtesy of the artist.

You know, I agree with the creators of *South Park*. We've already lost the main battle: Politicians have highjacked our imagination and replaced it with fear. And that may be worse than losing our civil rights que no?

*II Flagrantly stupid acts of transgression*

Damas y caballeros,

I've got 45 scars accounted for—half of them produced by art & this is not a metaphor. I just can't get disability insurance.

My artistic obsession has led me to carry out some flagrantly stupid acts of transgression including: living inside a cage as a Mexican Frankenstein; crucifying myself as a mariachi to protest immigration policy; crashing Ellis Island & the Met as El Mad Mex being led on a leash by a Spanish dominatrix. I mean, you want me to be more specific than, say, drinking Mr. Clean to exorcise my colonial demons or handing a dagger to an audience member & offering her my abdomen?

"Here ... my colonized body," I said. "My solar plexus ... your moon-like madness," I said. And she went for it, inflicting on me my 45th scar, right here on my soul.

*(I show my scar to the audience)*

She was only 20, boricua & did not know the difference between performance, rock & roll & street life. Bad phrase, delete ... Script change. Memory #1280.

*III Dwelling in unnecessary wounds*

Marina Abramovic tells this painful joke: Question: How many performance artists does it take to change a light bulb? Answer: I have no idea. I left after 3 hours.

Ay, but if only I was a good actor, the bastard son of Klaus Kinski and Sophia Loren, or the border twin of Nicolas Cage, none of this would have ever happened.

If only good performance art equaled bad acting, misdirected acting or vice versa, as mediocre theatre directors tend to believe, this performance would have never taken place. Que weird thought!

If only I was a furious rocker, a trendy painter, a cutting edge comedian? Maybe? Not really. Performance & comedy don't mix very well. The result is a joke that no one understands.

Pero, if only I had had the guts to join the Zapatistas for good, the guts to fight the border patrol in situ, with my bare hands, the guts to tell my family I am truly sorry for all the pain my sudden departure caused them 25 years ago, when I was young & handsome & still had no audience whatsoever.

But I was a coward. I ended up making a 30-year-long performance piece to justify my original departure, *el pecado original*.

Pero if only I had never left in the first place, what would have become of my life?

It would be considerably simpler. I'd be less loco, perhaps, less angry, perhaps; less ... Chicano. Awkward phrase, insensitive, delete!

Pero ... if only I didn't have to worry about my audience; entertaining you with Aztec glam, high heels and weird jokes; making art to pay my bills, to avoid prison, deportation and mental hospitals, to justify intellectually my anti-social tendencies.

If only I didn't have to perform to exercise my freedoms, for I could do it every day, everywhere—but that's the subject matter of an essay not a performance. Besides, you did not come here to witness a radical political mind at work.

Or did you?

## Intermediality

Philip Auslander

The Fluxus artist and theorist Dick Higgins is often credited with having popularized the term "intermedia" in a 1965 essay. Higgins used the term to describe works of art that could be related to traditional artistic genres but could not be assimilated to any single genre or seen as an amalgamation of genres. In that sense, they were inter-media, new forms that lay *between* disparate media. Higgins drew some of his main examples from performance, with which he was involved as an artist. Allan Kaprow's *Happenings* exemplified intermedia for Higgins because they explored "an uncharted land that lies between collage, music and the theater" (2007, 25). Artists who made Happenings were therefore not subject to the rules governing any of these traditional media but had to discover the new form's conventions.

Higgins explicitly distinguished intermedia from "mixed media," "a venerable term from art criticism, which covers works executed in more than one medium, such as oil color and gouache " (2007, 27–28). Higgins described opera as a mixed medium because it incorporates both music and libretto. It does not qualify as an intermedium, however, because the different media are clearly distinguishable and there is no attempt to chart new territory.

Over time, the term intermedia has lost much of its specificity and tends now to be used interchangeably with "multimedia" to refer to artistic or cultural forms that bring different media together on the same platform, a development prompted in part by the capacity of digital technology to combine sound, video, graphics, animation, and other media in a single artifact. Nevertheless, the term continues to be used critically in a more precise way to focus on the ideas of "between-ness" and undecideablity it connotes, particularly in discussions of mixed-media performances and adaptations of a work from one medium to another.

Perhaps intermediality is best understood not as a characteristic of certain forms or works but as a critical choice of how to perceive or describe them. For example, one could argue that screen dance, the practice of making dances on film or video that cannot be performed live, is not an intermedium because its products are, in the end, films or videos, and the experience they provide is that of watching a screened image. On the other hand, one could insist that screen dance is an intermedium because its works lie *between* film/video and dance in a way that problematizes the boundary between the forms. On this view, the screenic and choreographic aspects of screen dance are inseparable: because the dances have no autonomous existence apart from the films, the films are not simply recordings of dance events.

Peter M. Boenisch defines the intermediality of theatre (pace Higgins) as a mode of spectatorship. For Boenisch, the idea that things on stage exist simultaneously on two different levels (a table on stage, for example, is both a table and a representation of a table in a particular dramatic context) opens up the possibility that the spectator can perceive the theatrical production as operating in the interstices between the two levels rather than as a seamless fusion of them (Boenisch 2006). The intermediality of theatre, in this view, is not on the stage but in the minds of the audience—it is a mode of perception that dismantles theatrical illusion to reveal the workings of mediation within theatrical representation.

### *Further reading*

Boenisch (2006); Higgins (1965).

### *References*

Boenisch, Peter M. 2006. "Aesthetic Art to Aisthetic Act: Theatre, Media, Intermedial Performance." In *Intermediality in Theatre and Performance*, edited by Freda Chapple and Chiel Kattenbelt. Amsterdam: Editions Rodopi B.V.

Higgins, Dick. 2007. "Intermedia" (1965). In *Horizons*, 21–31. n.p.: /ubu Editions.. Accessed 7 July 2015. http://www.scribd.com/doc/38186653/Higgins-Horizons#scribd

### *Cross references*

"**Audience**" by Cody; "**Cindy Sherman's Real Fakery**" by Schneider; "**Elevator Girls Return: Miwa Yanagi's Border Crossing between Photography and Theatre**" by Yoshimoto; "**Expanded cinema**" by Jarosi; "**Fluxus**" by Stiles; "**Mediaturgy**" by Marranca; "**Performance in the digital age**" by Auslander.

**Elevator girls return: Miwa Yanagi's border crossing between photography and theatre**

Midori Yoshimoto

The Japanese artist Miwa Yanagi is primarily a photographer, but not in the traditional sense. She does not seek to capture real life but creates fictitious and elaborately detailed worlds, complete with special makeups and advanced computer graphic manipulations, mostly revolving around women's lives. An undeniable degree of theatricality permeates Yanagi's entire oeuvre. Her earliest series, *Elevator Girls* (1993-1999), featured the impeccably uniformed young Japanese women who usually greet customers in department stores and guide them to the elevators, which will whisk them away to different floors. Most photographs in this series are panoramic, some of them consisting of triptychs. They emphasize the emptiness of the space by showing repetitive shop windows and department store façades, illuminating them by mysterious lights. Cut off from the rest of the world, seemingly in fatigue or contemplation, elevator girls are trapped in these surreal spaces. There is an aura of science fiction to the series, as if the girls represented survivors of an apocalypse.

This photographic series stemmed from Yanagi's first solo exhibition (1993) at a rental gallery, Art Space Niji in Kyoto, where she used live models dressed in elevator-girl attire as part of her installation. The following year, at the Hyogo Prefectural Museum of Art, she expanded the work and hired fourteen "elevator girls," who, like docents, would explain the artworks in the museum's collection to the audience (Yanagi 2006). The performance subverted the typically passive role of uniformed women guards in the galleries of Japanese museums and simultaneously critiqued the Japanese consumer culture that often objectifies young female bodies. Although not widely known, these performances seem to have formed the core essence of Yanagi's art—evolving into such major photographic series as *My Grandmothers* and *Fairy Tale* in the late 1990s and the 2000s.

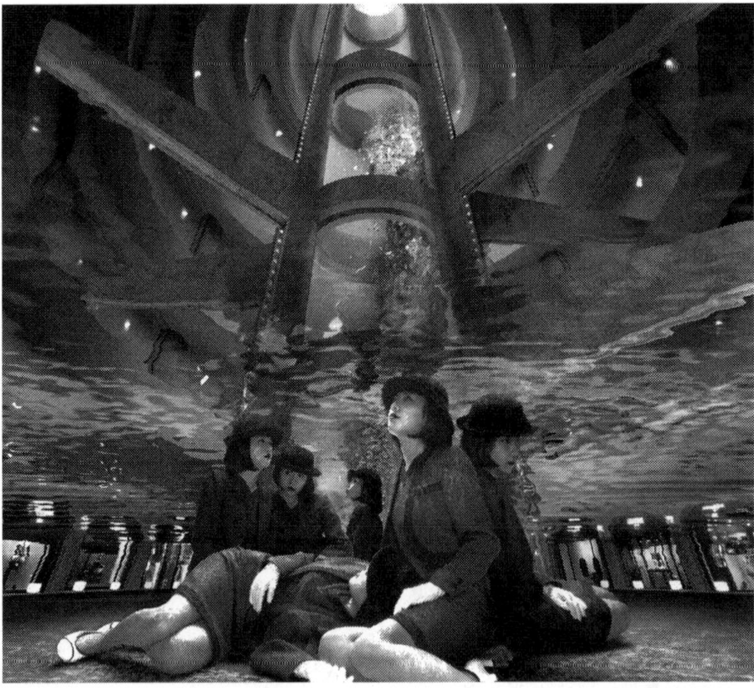

**Figure 31** Miwa Yanagi, *Elevator Girl House B4* (1994) C-print, 200 x 240cm. Image courtesy the artist.

Consisting of over twenty-six photographs, *My Grandmothers* (1999–ongoing) presents the imagined possible futures of various sitters, primarily women in their twenties (with the exception of a few men and an eleven-year-old girl). Yanagi would interview her subjects in a very detailed manner, asking them how they imagine themselves to be in fifty years, both in their appearances and life situations. Then, the sitters would be transformed through special make-up, wigs, and costumes, into their own versions of "grandmothers" in the various settings they specified (Niwa 2009, 57). Accompanied by the statements of the models, photographic outcomes read as fictitious visual narratives in which individuals' fantasies are enacted by themselves. Each of the photographs possesses a cinematic depth, with the past and present embodied simultaneously.

While the *My Grandmothers* series was widely shown overseas and established Yanagi's fame as a photographer, she returned to performance in 2010, and developed an impressive theatrical trilogy in 2011-2012. One of her 2010 performances was *Café Rottenmeier*, presented during the Festival Tokyo in November. In it, a dozen Japanese women of various ages were made up and dressed to look like the middle-aged, conservative governess character, Mrs. Rottenmeier, from the 1970s anime classic, *Heidi*, based on the Swiss novel. These women would then serve customers drinks, food, and provide entertainment in what was clearly a critique of the popular "maid cafés" in Tokyo, where young women dress in blue and white French maid uniforms to serve their mostly male clientele. Drawing from her multi-year commitment to visualizing aging in *My Grandmothers*, Yanagi became more vocal about the discrimination that Japanese society practices towards older women and presented *Café Rottenmeier* as a parody.

The experience in realizing two small performances in 2010 gave Yanagi a springboard to venture into a major theatrical production. In conjunction with the exhibitions of two modern artists, László Moholy-Nagi

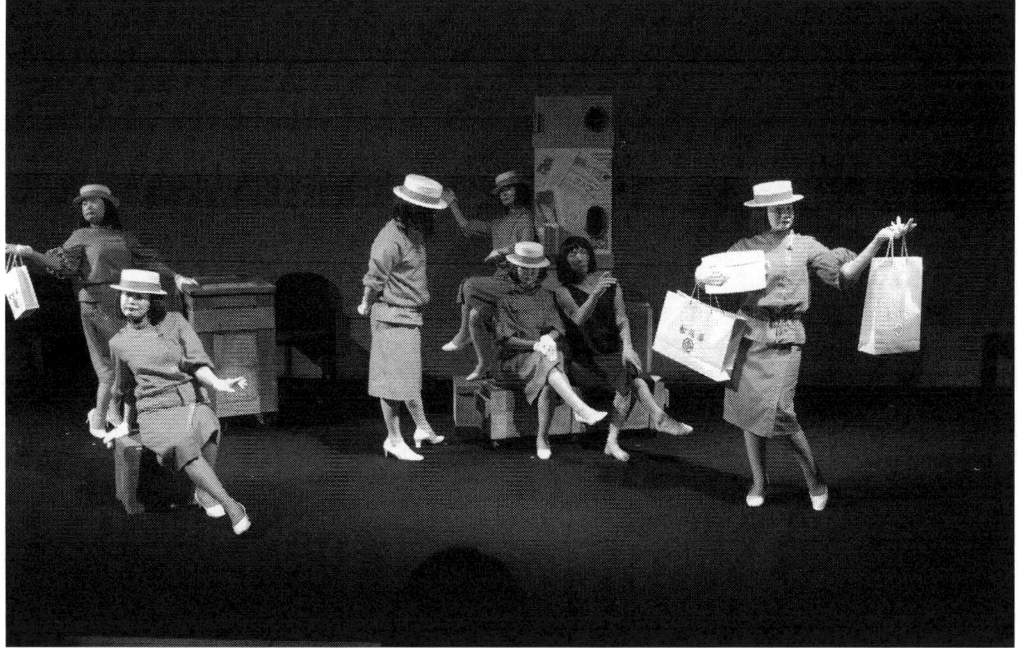

**Figure 32** Miwa Yanagi, Theater Project, *1924 Machine Man*, performed at Takamatsu City Museum of Art, June 9-10, 2012. Performers include Manabu Masuda and Maki Yamamoto. Photo: Sansei Kimura. Courtesy of the artist.

and Tomoyoshi Murayama, who was the leader of the Japanese avant-garde art group MAVO, to be held at the Kyoto Prefectural Museum of Modern Art, Yanagi conceived a theatrical trilogy entitled *1924*. It consisted of the works *Tokyo-Berlin*, *Sea Battle*, and *Machine Man*. She formed her own theatre group and presented the trilogy at various museum venues in Kyoto, Takamatsu, and Tokyo. Throughout the trilogy, women dressed up as "elevator girls" wearing identical masks and uniform, and served as guides. They passed headsets to the audience members who could only listen to girls' electronically altered voices through the apparatus. Some parts of the plays took place inside the gallery, where these women provided explanations of artworks on display. Then, the audience was led to a theatre space temporarily set up within a museum. In the finale of the last play, the elevator girls guided the audience to the freight elevator and demonstrated the transport of Murayama, played by a live actor, in a display case back into storage, as if to connote that the artist himself was turned into an artifact. Although the series was based on Yanagi's close study of Murayama's life and work from the 1920s, as well as the avant-garde theatre movement, the presence and interventional actions of elevator girls undoubtedly brought the audience back to the world in the twenty-first century. The girls served as mediators between different worlds; the past and present, fiction and reality, theatre and museum. They simultaneously constructed and deconstructed a theatrical narrative by revealing the constructedness of the whole situation in which the audience took part.

Thus, elevator girls have symbolically presided over Yanagi's border crossing between the worlds of photography (visual art) and theatre, museum and everyday life. It is not known how long the artist will devote herself to theatrical ventures and if she will return to photography at some point. Perhaps she will create a hybrid art form that questions presumed boundaries of photography, performance, and theatre, as separate genres.

*References*

Niwa, Harumi. 2009. "My Grandmothers: The Resonance of Memory." *Miwa Yanagi*. Tokyo: Tokyo Metropolitan Museum of Photography.

Yanagi, Miwa. 2006. *Elevator Girls*. Art Space Niji, Kyoto.

## Mimesis

Elin Diamond

Any discussion of a performance's or an artwork's relation to the world outside itself will be shadowed by the long and vexed history of mimesis. Probably derived from *mimos*, meaning both actor and actor's performance, mimesis is almost impossible to pin down. Its meanings run the gamut from the deprecatory—mimesis is *mere* copying, imitation, mimicry, fakery, reproduction—to the profoundly significant—mimesis is a faculty, a magical system of resemblance and correspondence, a fundamental component of human behavior.

Plato's *Republic* (380 BCE) is responsible for the low valuation of mimesis. By defining art as mirror image of, and thus inferior to, something real or true, Plato sets the terms for debates on dramatic and pictorial art for the next two millennia. Plato's Socrates will repeatedly condemn mimesis as mere appearance or a copy of an ideal form, and he deplores the mimetic behavior of poet-performers whose affecting impersonations not only excite the young guardians of the republic to imitate unseemly behavior, but also taint the selfhood and masculine authority of the impersonator (see Books 2, 3, and 10). But Socrates protests too much. By making mimesis the enemy of reason and the state, he embeds mimesis in the deepest structures of human thought and action. By showing how images and impersonation can be taken for real conditions (the allegory of the cave in Book 7), he reveals the power of mimesis to manipulate public opinion and the stability of the state.

Aristotle's *Poetics* (360–320 BCE) rebuts his teacher Plato on many key matters. While Plato grouped all the arts under the rubric of mimesis, Aristotle distinguishes among the arts, positing materials and ends unique to each, thus changing the emphasis from the poet as liar to the poet as maker of potentially significant fictions. While Plato prefers to banish mimesis rather than expose children to bad models, Aristotle affirms the pleasure for children and adults of learning about the world through mimetic activity (see *Poetics*, Chapter 4). Most importantly, in defining tragedy as, principally, a "mimesis of human action" (Halliwell 1987, 77) and structuring that action in a coherent plot (*mythos*) in which a character's choices (*ethos*) produce significant consequences, Aristotle endows dramatic art with a philosophical *gravitas* that undergirds, rather than undermines, human reason (Potolsky 2006, 32–43).

Yet beyond antiquity a tension remains between understanding mimesis as a mirror of nature or as a powerfully generative means of producing new truths, new knowledge in a rapidly changing world (Turner 1987, 1–14). Renaissance critics distinguished between imitation (*imitare*) and copying (*ritrarre*) or portraiture, the former emphasizing the artist's distinctive embellishments of a model, the latter dedicated to reproducing it (Black 1984, 117; Diamond 1997, iv). Denis Diderot insisted "the painter's sun is not that of the universe and could not be" (1857/1957). Yet critic Tzvetan Todorov, in a review of neoclassical and romantic concepts of mimesis, finds a recurrent slippage between imitation as representation or staging, and imitation as production of an object that resembles its model" (Todorov 1983, 117; Diamond 1997, iv). We might say that such hesitation reflects the double origin of mimesis itself. *Mimos* refers *both* to the performer and to what is performed; to the embodied activity of representing (and improvising) and to a representation of an already existing idea, model, or truth (Diamond 1997, 768).

Avant-garde performance at the beginning of the twentieth century, with its loud condemnation of bourgeois realism, its rejection of Plato's truth-illusion matrix and Aristotle's logical plotting, might have signaled an end to mimesis, but instead both interest and concept have burgeoned. For example, while Freud rejected hysterical mimicry as foundational to hysteria, he named identification, or an unconscious imitation of an internalized model, as the source of ego development. While identity politics suggests that a person's identity can be contested and changed, Freudian identification is an *involuntary* mimesis, a phantasmatic assimilation not responsive to political ethics, in fact quite likely to be politically *in*correct. Writing at the end of the twentieth century, Richard Dawkins goes even further in imagining an involuntary mimesis, one centered on the *meme* or "unit of imitation." Like the self-replicating human gene, a meme replicates itself in the form of "tunes, ideas, catch-phrases, clothes, fashions [ ... ]." For Dawkins, humans function as hosts for memes, which leap "from brain to brain" producing new variations of (post)human culture (1989, 192).

In James Frazer's *The Golden Bough* (1890/1922), mimesis is a select means to a very human end. Using what Frazer called "imitative magic," the magician "infers that he can produce any effect he desires" (Frazer 1922, 12; Potolsky 2006, 138). Frazer assumed that magical thinking—the belief in the power of imitation to affect real world conditions—would vanish with modern science. But for sociologist Marcel Mauss, magical mimesis implied "a network of reciprocal sympathies [instead of a] hierarchical ladder of rational forms" (Potolsky 2006, 139). Frankfurt School theorists Theodor Adorno and Max Horkheimer offered a bio-anthropological, anti-Enlightenment account of mimesis based in adaptive mimicry and magic which they saw as a persistent, if suppressed, feature of modernity. Walter Benjamin extended the bio-anthropological argument, positing a "mimetic *faculty*," the innate compulsion to become and behave like something else. Echoing Aristotle but excluding his rationalist framework, the mimetic faculty is pleasurably expressed in children imitating windmills or, past childhood, in our ability to produce or recognize, in the world or in language, "nonsenuous" or nonidentical similarities and correspondences (Benjamin 1936, 334–335). While no longer robust, this faculty enables us as alienated subjects to experience others and the world differently.

Feminist theory has subverted mimesis in several ways. In "Plato's Hystera", Luce Irigaray parodies Plato's allegory of the cave by transforming the cave into a female womb. Her version of *mimétisme* or mimicry is figured as a kind of embodied womb-theatre practice, replete with mirrors, fetishes, voices, "the whole stage set-up" which upends Plato's truth-illusion matrix by issuing "fake offspring" (Irigaray 1985, 243; Diamond 1997, x–xii). More recently Drucilla Cornell takes up Adorno's [and Benjamin's] notion of the nonidentical similar to posit "the mimetic capacity as an attempt at an ethical relationship to otherness" (Cornell 1995, 149). Cornell calls the potential for such a relationship the "hope" of mimesis (1995, 147). T. Minh-Ha Trinh offers a distinctly hopeful version of Walter Benjamin's nonidentical similar in the title of her article, "Not You/Like You: Post-Colonial Women and the Interlocking Questions of Identity and Difference" (Trinh 1997, 415–419). Trinh suggests that an imagined relation between and among post-colonial women could be one of nonidentical similarity in which no one would play model or copy or possess a single truth.

Perhaps the "hope" of mimesis lies in our emphasis on an inventive recreation of social life, on the actor or doer, who, in her behavior and actions, may be able to assume an ethical posture, a not you/like you relation to others. In any case theorists of mimesis from Plato and Aristotle onward suggest that we cannot escape mimetic activity: it generates the stories and performances that express and explain our lives; in the guise of identification it makes us who we are, expressed as a meme it tells us that we are individually irrelevant; as a feminist trope of complex relatedness it may just save the world.

### Further reading

Benjamin (1986); Diamond (1997).

### *References*


Aristotle. 1987. *The Poetics of Aristotle: Translation and Commentary*, edited by Stephen Halliwell. Chapel Hill, NC: University of North Carolina Press.

Benjamin, Walter. 1936. "The Work of Art in the Age of Mechanical Reproduction." In *Illuminations: Essays and Reflections*, edited by Hannah Arendt and translated by Harry Zohn. Reprint, New York: Schocken, 1969.

Benjamin, Walter. 1986. *Reflections: Essays, Aphorisms, Autobiographical Writings*, edited by Peter Demetz. New York: Schocken Books.

Black, Joel. 1984. "Idolology: The Model in Artistic Practice and Critical Theory." In *The Literary and Philosophical Debate*. Vol. 1 in *Mimesis in Contemporary Theory*, edited by Mihal Spariosu. Philadelphia, NJ: John Benjamins.

Cornell, Drucilla. 1995. *The Imaginary Domain: Abortion, Pornography and Sexual Harassment*. New York: Routledge.

Dawkins, Richard. 1989. *The Selfish Gene*. Oxford: Oxford University Press.

Diamond, Elin. 1997. *Unmaking Mimesis: Essays on Feminism and Theatre*, New York: Routledge.

Diderot, Denis. 1857/1957. *The Paradox of Acting*. New York: Hill and Wang.

Frazer, James George. 1890/1922. *The Golden Bough*. New York: Macmillan.

Halliwell, Stephen. 1987. *The Poetics of Aristotle: Translation and Commentary*. Chapel Hill, NC: University of Muñoz North Carolina Press.

Irigaray, Luce. 1985. *Speculum of the Other Woman*. Translated by Gillian C. Gill. Ithaca: Cornell University Press.

Plato. 2003. *The Republic*. Translated by Desmond Lee. 2nd edn. London: Penguin.

Potolsky, Matthew. 2006. *Mimesis*. New York and London: Routledge.

Todorov, Tzvetan. 1983. *Theories of the Symbol*. Translated by C. Porter. Ithaca: Cornell University Press.

Trinh, T. Minh-Ha, 1997. "Not You/Like You: Post-Colonial Women and the Interlocking Questions of Identity and Difference." In

*Dangerous Liaisons: Gender, Nation, and Postcolonial Perspectives*, edited by Anne McClintock, Aamir Mufti and Ella Shohat, 415–419. Minneapolis, MN: University of Minnesota Press.

Turner, Victor W. 1987. *The Anthropology of Performance.* New York: PAJ.

*Cross references*

"**Actor**" by Mee; "**Appropriation**" by Wong; "**Camp**" by Pellegrini; "**Cindy Sherman's Real Fakery**" by Schneider; "**Mimicry**" by Applebaum; "**Photography and performance**" by Auslander; "**Readymade**" by Hoefer; "**Reenactment**" by Bay-Cheng; "**Scenario**" by Taylor.

## Minimalism

André Lepecki

Minimalism names an art movement, particularly relevant in sculpture, whose early developments took place during the second half of the 1960s. Major exponents of minimalism in the visual arts include Robert Morris, Donald Judd, Frank Stella and Sol LeWitt; while in the performing arts, minimalism has been mostly associated with the choreography of Yvonne Rainer in the 1960s, particularly her masterpiece *Trio A*—even though we can identify the influence on Robert Morris' minimalism coming from the work in the early 1960s of the choreographer Simone Forti, particularly her *Dance Constructions*. Trisha Brown's *Equipment Pieces* of the late 1960s and early 1970s are another example of choreographic minimalism.

The characteristics of this kind of minimalist dance were most explicitly articulated in Rainer's famous manifesto "A Quasi Survey of some 'minimalist' tendencies in the quantitatively minimal dance activity midst the plethora, or an analysis of *Trio A.*" There, Rainer notes how "the display of technical virtuosity and the display of the dancer's specialized body no longer make any sense" and thus she advocates "for a more matter-of-fact, more concrete, more banal quality of physical being in performance" (1999, 33). Rainer's words echo John Perreault's 1967 essay for *The Village Voice*, where he clarified: "what is minimal about Minimal Art, or appears to be when contrasted with Abstract Expressionism of Pop Art, is the *means*, not the ends" (Perreault 1967, 260).

What are these means? Mostly they are means of reduction, including the situation where it is placed (the environment treated as a non-neutral space, a non-neutral framing for the work). By refusing the art object (be it a sculpture, a painting, or a dance) as a mechanism for the display of representational functions, minimal art asserts the concrete qualities of the object's constitutive materiality. This mode of reduction entailed a refusal of any spectacularization of the object, and a refusal of superfluous details superimposed on the object. As Robert Morris wrote in his influential "Notes on Sculpture," "the most important sculptural value" was to be "*shape*" (1964, 223). Art critic and historian James Meyer comments that if, for Morris, "shape was desirable, detail was not, for detail made the shape difficult to see" (2004, 158). Against Clement Greenberg's emphasis on modernist art as the realm of the optical, visual arts' Minimalism refused the optical as ground for the aesthetic object. Instead, the emphasis fell on creating "shapes" where the concreteness of the object would confront the viewer. Through this aesthetic operation, an inevitable social effect would result: a very different and literal grounding would emerge for the minimal art object: "The ground plane, not the wall, is the necessary support for the maximum awareness of the object" (Meyer 2004, 156). This common ground, where sculpture and audience would now share approximated stature with postmodern dance in a very physical and specific way: aesthetic object and their viewers now shared the same floor and the same gravitational pull.

For art historian and critic Michael Fried, the grounding of the object in the concreteness of its physical situation *and* on its very concrete material conditions produced an effect of co-presence that he identified as being essentially "theatrical." As a result, the artwork was no longer self-contained and autonomous (as in modernist art) but depended on (1) a situation of its "installation"; and (2) the co-presence of a viewer. Moreover, for Fried, these two conditions initiated a kind of temporality that he thought particularly non-aesthetic: the temporality of duration, of a shared time that is endless. Hence the paradox of minimalism: the more it takes from the aesthetic object, the more it multiplies and expands in time. Fried perceives all minimalist objects as secreting temporality in a social situation. This multiplying excess, which Fried explicitly associated with a kind of "presence" that he named "theatricality," is what becomes so unbearable to minimalism's critics. Fried would see in minimalism art's final step towards its degeneration. As he famously put it: "art degenerates as it approaches the condition of theater" (Fried 1998, 164).

Performance theorist Fred Moten followed Fried's argument to the end, and re-framed it with the help of the work of visual artist Adrian Piper. Moten basically agrees with Fried's evaluation of minimalism's effects (i.e., co-presence; theatricality). Nevertheless, he points out the disturbing political project in Fried's dismissal of minimalism's mode of presence. "Fried writes from the position of a subject who, in the very fullness of a presence that could never admit its own psycho-political ephemerality, is not there: [...] the viewer from nowhere" (Moten 2003, 237). This ideal(ized) "viewer from nowhere" is above and beyond any plane constituted by concrete social, political, historical, racial, and gendered forces.

Moten's insight confirms that Fried advocates not only a viewer from nowhere, but an art from nowhere. In fact, minimalism refuses both the viewer and the object as being above and beyond the social. That Minimalism could re-frame radically the field of presence, and in such ways as to identify in the object a kind of performative force, and a kind of co-presence, even a kind of subjectivity, is its greatest legacy to a contemporary political theory of performance.

*Further reading*

Fried (1998); Moten (2003).

*References*

Fried, Michael. 1998. *Art and Objecthood: Essays and Reviews*. Chicago, IL: University of Chicago Press.

Meyer, James. 2004. *Minimalism: Art and Polemics in the Sixties*. New Haven, CT: Yale University Press.

Morris, Robert. 1964. "Notes on Sculpture." *Artforum*, 4.6: 223.

Moten, Fred. 2003. *In the Break: The Aesthetics of the Black Radical Tradition*. Minneapolis, MN: University of Minnesota Press.

Perreault, John. 1967. "Minimal Abstracts." *The Village Voice*, 260.

Rainer, Yvonne. 1999. *A Quasi Survey of Some "Minimalist" Tendencies in the Quantitatively Minimal Dance Activity Midst the Plethora, or an Analysis of Trio A*. Baltimore, MA: Johns Hopkins University Press.

*Cross references*

"**Choreography**" by Lepecki; "**Dance or we are lost: The Tanztheater of Pina Bausch**" by Birringer; "**Installation art**" by Haidu; "**Mise-en-scène**" by Jannarone; "**Modernism**" by Albright, Pearl, and Speca; "**Performance, postmodernism, and beyond,**" by Chin Davidson; "**Surveillance**" by Morrison.

## Modernism

Daniel Albright, Allison Pearl, and Kelly Speca

In the time period punctuated by two world wars and the industrial revolution, Modernism began in Europe as more than just an artistic movement—it was a radical rupture from the past. Romanticism, representationalism, linearity, and narrative—all those conventions associated with the past—were broken. The old, tired systems of thinking and representation, even language itself, were no longer considered an adequate means to measure and express an individual's experience of the world. Reflecting on this urgent struggle in his writing, Ezra Pound recycled the Chinese scholar Chu Hsi's saying "Make it new!" to fit the current sentiment of the changing world he was living in. This call to creativity became a kind of slogan of Modernism for many other artists and writers.

At the same time, new methods of reproduction and the far-reaching effects of the printed page jeopardized the old standards of value in the art world, the consequences of which Walter Benjamin addresses in his seminal essay, "Art in the Age of Mechanical Reproduction" (1936). Benjamin writes that new methods of mass reproduction and the far-reaching effects of the printed page jeopardized the old standards of value in the art world. Technological advancements such as transportation and weaponry and the rise of the new social class also heavily influenced Modernism and changed how people viewed the world and themselves within it. As the concept of self and identity became increasingly muddled, the context of Modernism and other social theories, such as those of Darwin and Freud, complicated the portrayals of "protagonists" in dramatic writings. How people perceived themselves became a central question for Modernist thinkers—a question tackled with techniques such as stream-of-consciousness in literature, Cubism in visual art, or Symbolism in theatre. Artists began to question what could be deemed a work of art and what could not, who had the authority to define art, and what the purpose of art should be, given the massive political, social, economic, and cultural shifts that were occurring internationally in this time period.

Modernism developed alongside and in conflict with the idea of modernity, and this complex relationship manifested in modernist artwork that did not operate upon an assumed reliability of reality. It challenged the basic elements of human experience in order to probe and question contemporary historical events and the changing world around them. Theatre artists such as Jean Cocteau and Bertolt Brecht faced similar questions as the artists of literature, visual art, architecture, and other disciplines, but they were also reflecting on the specific legacy of the theatre of the past as they endeavored to define and ultimately explode theatre's role in modern society.

## Modernism in the theatre

### *1. Problems in value*

The first specifically Modernist theatre was probably the Symbolist theatre, and the Symbolist theatre begins with Richard Wagner—in fact one of the first great Symbolist plays, Auguste Villiers d'Isle-Adam's *Axël* (1890) is, more or less, the music of Wagner's *Tristan und Isolde* (1865) set to words. The Symbolist theatre is Nietzschean (even before Nietzsche's time, in some cases) in that it concerns transvaluation of all values—especially the fragility of all valuations, regular, trans-, over-, or under-, because a physical object can only be a temporary placeholder for the immaterial supreme essence that the Symbolist seeks. An example in Wagner's work is the ring in *Der Ring des Nibelungen* (1850–1876): forged from a lump of gold at the bottom of the Rhine by a dwarf who renounces Love in order to gain Power, it supposedly affords its owner mastery of the universe—all characters are agreed on this point; but it actually gives no one mastery over anything. The emptiest of stage props, it moves by theft or fraud or whim from one hand to the next, until Valhalla and all the gods catch on fire and the ring plops back into the Rhine. Wagner gave musical motives to the Ring and to other talismans of power (Spear, Sword, Tarnhelm, and so forth), but these musical motives retain their semantic force only by extreme over-insistence, and eventually dissolve back into the sound-matrix from which they were laboriously quarried—just as the physical props, such as Spear and Sword, are shattered and made impotent by the events of the drama.

In later Symbolist plays, we see a similar rhythm of overvaluation followed by devaluation. In Maurice Maeterlinck's *Alladine et Palomides* (1894), the lovers find themselves in a castle's dark foundation-space and embrace in desperate wonder. The lovers imagine that they are in a heaven of roses and smiling jewels, surrounded by water so blue that it seems a distillate of sky. But when the sunlight at last streams in, they see that the grotto is actually all fungus and rock and rot—the glamour is in some sense real, but its reality is not of this world. In William Butler Yeats's *The King's Threshold* (1903), a poet, on hunger strike because the king has abolished some ancient privileges of the poet, announces that the king's gold would have no value without the services of poets:

> Cry out that the King's money would not buy,
> Nor the high circle consecrate his head,
> If poets had never christened gold, and even
> The moon's poor daughter, that most whey-
> faced metal,
> Precious ...

For Yeats, Wallace Stevens' allegation is literally true: money is poetry. The playwright who seems the last of the great Symbolists, Samuel Beckett, fills his plays with shriveled carcasses or abortions of symbols, such as, in *Waiting for Godot* (1953), the Tree and the Stone (or Mound), completing the deflation, detumescence, of the swollen prop that had begun long ago.

### *2. Loss of agency*

In the older theatre, whether *Everyman* or *Macbeth*, the hero has to make decisions—has to choose between two or more courses of action. So a king is an attractive protagonist: the field of choice is large, and the field of constraint is small. But in the Modernist theatre the protagonists' range of action is often limited: they often have to adjust their behavior to survive at all, for they are low men on low totem poles. They rarely lack all freedom of movement, but they must husband their resources of volition for mass action, since singly they can accomplish little. The great playwright of this sort is Bertolt Brecht, who attacked the very notion of character: in 1926 he told an interviewer, "when a character behaves by contradiction that's only because nobody can be identically the same at two unidentical moments. Changes in his exterior continually lead to an inner reshuffling. The continuity of the ego is a myth. A man is an atom that perpetually breaks up and forms anew" (Albright 2000, 123). And in 1954, Brecht warned an actress, "One should never start out on the basis of a figure's character because a person has no character" (Albright 2000, 123). In the absence of character, an individual is simply the occupant of an ecological niche: if the shape of the niche changes, the shape of the occupant will change commensurately. In *Mann ist Mann* (1926—the title could be translated *Man is man,* in German a homophone of *Man eats man*), Brecht shows that a humble bumbling porter can be transformed into a soldier of amazing ferocity if circumstances require it; as one character remarks, if you toss a man into a pool he will soon develop webbed fingers. The human self, even the human body, can be disassembled and reassembled in any way you like; we all of us consist of interchangeable parts.

Because Brecht's stage has no fixed elements—the characters in his plays are always taking apart the décor and putting it back together in odd ways, so that the furniture in a bar suddenly becomes a ship bound for Alaska—there is a remarkable indeterminacy about his theatre. He even wrote an alternative text to his play *Der Jasager* (*The Yes-sayer,* 1930) called *Der Neinsager* (*The No-sayer*), in which the all-important decision the hero makes at the end of the play is reversed: it's as if Shakespeare himself wrote the happy end to *King Lear* (fabricated by Nahum Tate) in which Cordelia survives and marries Edgar, and then allowed directors to choose whichever ending they liked.

### *3. Dramatizing technology*

The new technology of the twentieth century gave playwrights the opportunity to de-emphasize or re-emphasize the standard components of theatre: Plot, Character, Diction, Thought, Music, and Scenery, as Aristotle classifies them. Brecht dismissed Character, but made Thought (*dianoia,* general ideas not bound to the specific circumstances on stage) central, partly by means of placards and projections and other ways of underscoring his mottoes. Gertrude Stein dismissed Plot, but made Diction almost the entire substance of her plays—games with grammar, games with substitution of letters. Many of the old humane elements of theatre were studied and in some cases abolished, as when in 1917 the Futurist painter Giacomo Balla made a sort of ballet out of Igor Stravinsky's four-minute-long orchestral piece *Fireworks* on a stage with no human beings, only abstract geometrical designs lit up by lights flashing in a carefully contrived sequence: all Scenery and Music, none of the other four Aristotelian aspects.

Jean Cocteau's *Les mariés de la Tour Eiffel* (*The Wedding Party at the Eiffel Tower*, 1921) is the most impressive of all dramatizations of technology. In some sense it's Walter Benjamin's dream play: the work of art in the age of mechanical reproduction has enfolded into itself, in magnified form, the apparatus of mechanical reproduction. On each side of the stage, enormous acoustic gramophone horns poke out, inside each of which a speaker, like a Greek chorus, reads his lines, narrating the action and reciting all the dialogue; on one side, there is a huge camera, large enough that the characters can pass through its "lens" and enter or exit the stage down its vast bellows. Technology can dehumanize, or technology can preserve what is precious in our lives: the tape recorder in Beckett's *Krapp's Last Tape* (1958) seems to do both at once. All Modernist love of technology can be seen as the triumph of the stage—the actual physical environment—over the actors that inhabit it; for the Modernists, space can be personified, just as people can be environmentalized.

### Further reading

Albright (2000, 2003, 2004); Berghaus (2005).

### References

Albright, Daniel. 2000. *Untwisting the Serpent: Modernism in Music, Literature, and Other Arts.* Chicago, IL: University of Chicago Press.

Albright, Daniel. 2003. *Beckett and Aesthetics.* Cambridge: Cambridge University Press.

Albright, Daniel. 2004. *Modernism and Music: An Anthology of Sources.* Chicago, IL: University of Chicago Press.

Berghaus, Günter. 2005. *Theatre, Performance, and the Historical Avant-garde.* New York: Palgrave Macmillan.

Benjamin, Walter. 1936. "The Work of Art in the Age of Mechanical Reproduction." In *Illuminations: Essays and Reflections*, edited by Hannah Arendt and translated by Harry Zohn. Reprint, New York: Schocken 1969.

### Cross references

"**Dramaturgy**" by Jannarone; "**Experimental music**" by Henkes; "**Historicity**" by Colleran; "**Performance, postmodernism, and beyond**" by Chin Davidson; "**Simulacrum**" by Cesare Schotzko.

## Multicentricity

Meiling Cheng

"Multicentricity" first appeared in Cheatle and Cutler's book, *Tumors of the Breast* (1931), which details the authors' pathological studies of whole-organ sections of mastectomy specimens. The term is still widely used in oncologic research to indicate multiple foci of carcinomas found in distinctly different bodily regions. The concept became current in performance studies when Guillermo Gómez-Peña promulgated "a multicentric perspective" in his seminal collective document, "The Multicultural Paradigm: An Open Letter to the National Arts Community" (1989, 49). Since Gómez-Peña links the adjective specifically with the composition of alternative histories by variously disenfranchised groups, multicentricity—as a dynamic individual outlook—contrasts with "multiculturalism," which originated in the 1970s as a redressive educational policy to promote an antiracist social and cultural life (see Gordon and Newfield 1996).

Inspired by Gómez-Peña and by the centrifugal urban geography of Los Angeles, Meiling Cheng explored multicentricity as an analytical angle in her book, *In Other Los Angeleses: Multicentric Performance Art* (2002). Cheng posits multicentricity as a descriptive methodology rather than a prescriptive politics (hence, explicitly differentiating it from multiculturalism) and exposes its linkage with the idea of centricity (thus, implicitly challenging the poststructuralist notion of decentering). Taking "center" both literally as a converging point and metaphorically as a sentient unit, Cheng further theorizes multicentricity (i.e., multiple centers) along three postulates: "(1) the inevitability of perceptual centricity, (2) the coexistence of multiple (and multiscaled) centers, and (3) the fundamental inadequacy of any one center" (2002, xix). The first postulate references the condition of human perception; the second delineates the phenomena of terrestrial and cosmic existence; the third reveals the perceptual, cognitive, and experiential limits of any finite being among multitudes. These propositions, in their embryonic states, hint at theories of subjectivity, cosmology, and epistemology.

More relevant to performance inquiry, Cheng argues that multicentricity elucidates the conceptual basis of performance art, for this intermedial "live/life art" (2002, xxiii) thrives on the tacit contract and mnemonic co-agency between the artist/self (a singular center) and the onsite or remote viewers/others (multiple centers). Performance art's tendency to remain open to interpretations allows its conceptual ownership to be dispersed and shared among spectatorial others, thereby offering incentives for its experiential shareholders—those touched by the work's presence or traces—to disseminate its efficacy and impact. By surrendering its centricity and acknowledging its radical insufficiency, performance art, though impermanent, engenders its own posthumous return as re-tapped cultural reservoirs for posterity. Multicentricity is then a survival tactic evolved by performance art, which propagates its historical significance by ever issuing creative licenses to all interested spectatorial others.

### Further reading

Cheng (2002, 2013); Jones and Stephenson (1999); Phelan and Lane (1998).

### References

Cheatle, G.L. and M. Cutler. 1931. *Tumors of the Breast: Their Pathology, Symptoms, Diagnosis and Treatment*. Philadelphia, PA: Harper & Row.

Cheng, Meiling. 2002. *In Other Los Angeleses: Multicentric Performance Art*. Berkeley, CA: University of California Press.

Cheng, Meiling. 2013. *Beijing Xingwei: Contemporary Chinese Time-based Art*. Greenford: Seagull London.

Gómez-Peña, Guillermo. 1989. "The Multicultural Paradigm: An Open Letter to the National Arts Community." *High Performance*, 12.3: 18–27.

Gordon, Avery F. and Christoper Newfield, eds. 1996. *Mapping Multiculturalism*. Minneapolis, MN: University of Minnesota Press.

Jones, Amelia and Andrew Stephenson, eds. 1999. *Performing the Body/Performing the Text*. London and New York: Routledge.

Phelan, Peggy and Jill Lane, eds. 1998. *The Ends of Performance*. New York: New York University Press.

### Cross references

"**Guillermo Gómez-Peña attempts to explain performance art to people who may have never heard of it**" by Gómez-Peña; "**Historiography**" by Fabião; "**Intercultural performance**" by Alker; "**The Muslim performative**" by Barlas; "**Performance Studies**" by Joy; "**Prosthetic performance**" by Gass; "**Readymade**" by Hoefer; "**Sampling**" by Hodges Persley; "**Semiotics/semiology**" by Scheie.

## Performing the archive

Tavia Nyong'o

The archive is the source of historical authority, and all modern forms of historicism depend on it. But the archive, as a collection of texts, objects, practices, and the institutional topography into which they are embedded, is also an enigma, one that perpetually displaces and defers the certainty we seek in its confines. Given the ephemerality of the evidences of performance, a painstaking and meticulous scrutiny of what limited archive is available to study is often required. At the same time, the idiosyncratic rites of access through which archives choreograph their authority in relation to other sources of meaning—such as collective memory—are too fascinating and too relevant in their own right to entirely ignore.

Performance history is both the history of performance and the performance of history. But what do we mean by "the performance of history"? Beyond identifying history-making as a cultural practice of the present—which we see in various modes from public history to historical reenactment—is it not also the case that the processes, as well as the products, of historical research, are performative? This question animates much study and theorization of the archive. The foundational archive of performance inquiry is the archive of intercultural encounter. This archive finds its emblem in the "fetish," an object that performs in the very space between difference-as-incommensurability and difference-as-exchange.

Originally a Eurocentric means of dismissing the theories of causation of racialized others, the discourse of the fetish was developed by Karl Marx and then Sigmund Freud into a reflexive critique of European culture. In his theory of commodity fetishism, Marx turned anthropology around to assert that it was modern capitalist behavior that was fetishistic, because it attributed to commodities powers that mystified actual class relations. Freud in turn inverted the modernist superiority complex over the so-called savage mind, making the sexual fetishes of neurotics emblematic of a society divorced from a direct contact with the reality of its senses. The field which grew up after the 1960s, in the wake of decolonization and counter-cultural ferment, and which valorized intercultural performance as a response to Eurocentric theatre history, drew on these Freudian and Marxist critical archives of fetishistic exchange in launching its own versions of performed cultural critique.

The archive is a focal point of interest in performance inquiry. Walter Benjamin's historical notes and essays remain touchstones for addressing the archive, calling attention to the performativity of archival objects. Benjamin's theory of the dialectical image has proved adaptable to performance contexts, inspiring theorists to reveal the tension and contradiction in seemingly stable objects of historical evidence. Benjamin offers an approach to the objects of the past that is post-fetishistic, rejecting the easy equation of historical and cultural alterity—the past as "another country," the past "as it really was"—in favor of a dialectical insistence on our continual and contradictory notions of history (1936). Perhaps the best-known theorist of the post-fetishistic archive is Michel Foucault. Foucault led historians to question the transparency of the archive. Foucault's skepticism was buttressed with an archival praxis. He frequently turned to performance metaphors—drama, masking, and the carnivalesque body—as a means of describing what he was trying to accomplish. Foucault's archaeology of knowledge (1969) can be thought of as an updated cultural critique of the Western faith in its own fetishes of a stable grid of historical and cultural knowledge. Once such a perspective was displaced, and the Eurocentric grid of knowledge that produced it overthrown, what remained, Foucault thought, was pure theatre.

### *Further reading*

Benjamin (1936); Foucault (1969).

### *References*

Benjamin, Walter. 1936. "The Work of Art in the Age of Mechanical Reproduction." In

*Illuminations: Essays and Reflections*, edited by Hannah Arendt and translated by Harry Zohn. Reprint, New York: Schocken 1969.

Foucault, Michel. 1969. *The Archaeology of Knowledge*. Translated by A.M. Sheridan Smith. London: Routledge.

*Cross references*

"**Archive and repertoire**" by Taylor; "**Heather Cassils' indeterminate body**" by Jones; "**Historiography**" by Fabião; "**Performance Studies**" by Joy; "**Prosthetic performance**" by Gass; "**Semiotics/semiology**" by Scheie; "**Through the Eyes of Rachel Marker**" by Roth.

## Performance, postmodernism, and beyond

Jane Chin Davidson

Performance provides a unifying concept for postmodernism as a mode of activity that affects far more than theatre and dance, impacting the visual, aural, plastic, media, architectural arts, literature, and philosophy. The terms "postmodernism," "postmodernity," and "post-Modernist" correspond closely to the meaning of such terms as "modernism," "modernity," and "Modernist"—the latter being a specific artistic movement. Postmodernism relates to the epochal shift after World War II that is characterized by the "logic of late capitalism," which Fredric Jameson defines as the "political stance on the nature of multinational capitalism" affecting "every position [of] Postmodernism in culture" (1991, 3). Aesthetic production in late capitalism was considered as indiscernible from commodity production, and performative strategies in the visual arts would either critique or support this idea. For instance, Lucy Lippard in 1968 explained how performance attitudes toward painting and sculpture contributed to the dematerialization of the arts as a method of rejecting the commodification of the art object (Lippard and Chandler 1968). Allan Kaprow in 1961 stated that "Happenings cannot be sold and taken home; they can only be supported" (1961, 25). By 1984, Andreas Huyssen introduced his essay "Mapping the Postmodern" with the example of Joseph Beuys's artwork, *7000 Planting Stones*, enlisting the performance of citizens of Kassel, Germany to plant trees at the exhibition site of Documenta 7.

Artists demonstrated the break from modernism through their critiques of modernist beliefs in such ideals as master narratives, authorial identity, myths of originality/authenticity, and conventions for viewing art. Jean-Francois Lyotard's 1984 critique of master narratives challenged the legitimacy of "universal" truth and knowledge. Yvonne Rainer, in her piece *This is the Story of a Woman Who …* (1973), transformed narrative structure in dance in order to express secular myths and personal stories. The breakdown of narrative time and space in postmodern theatre, ascribed to artists such as the Wooster Group, Heiner Müller and Robert Wilson, represents the "death" of dramaturgy, a concept that also includes the critique of the authority of the modernist author/subject.

Postmodernism's "crisis of cultural authority," as explained by Craig Owens, was a liberating concept based on relinquishing "the authority vested in Western European culture and its institutions" (1983, 57). European modernism was the domain of "high art" and its original, one-of-a-kind, authentic/real art object, as distinguished from "low art" and its commodity copy. Jean Baudrillard, however, defined the unoriginal and inauthentic as the simulacral "sign" of postmodernism. His "hyper-realism" was exemplified by the inclusion of television on the theatrical sets of Müller's *Hamletmachine* (1977) and Lee Breuer's *Hajj: A Performance* (1983). The critique of originality extended to the "purity" of individual art media—a critique based on the traditional understanding of painting and sculpture as the fulfillment of high Modernist art. The intermedia practices espoused by Dick Higgins and John Cage further contributed to the shift in emphasis on the viewer/beholder in place of the art object.

Michael Fried in 1967 criticized this shift as the negation of art, while others viewed it as a new performative engagement. Minimalist works such as Tony Smith's *Die* (1962), a six by six foot fabricated steel cube, was made to reflect, confront, or stand-in for the body of the viewer rather than follow the aesthetic function of Modernist sculpture, the latter conveying the genius of the heroic and transcendent Modernist (male) artist. Amelia Jones argues that body art and performance can be defined as "constitutive of postmodernism," because performance potentially subverts modernism's fixed modes of identification (1998, 21). Twyla Tharp's dance choreography, which diversified the bodies onstage, incorporating different genders, ages, ethnicities, and sexualities, demonstrated this break from modernist exclusions. But, as Owens states, because the Modern was specifically European in origin, "art" dance was treated differently from "ethnic" and "black" dance, similarly to the way in which intercultural theatre was classified separately from postmodern drama.

The reconstrual of 1990s performance under "relational aesthetics" as the new focus on art's social engagement initiated the de-politicizing of postmodernism's feminist and civil rights influences. For instance, Vanessa Beecroft's *VB 35* (1998) performance, featuring lined-up, scantily dressed women, was presented unproblematically as a "social encounter" without addressing female objectification. In the "post-political" of relational aesthetics, the precluding of identity issues was considered a return to modernism. According to Coco Fusco, the eschewing of politics in art (after the Iraq war and the 2008 economic crisis) was caused by the "backlash of the 1990s" in the "so-called 'return to beauty'" and the "unstoppable growth of the art market" (2008, 57). The return to modernist ideals can be seen in many post-postmodern theories such as Raoul Eshelman's "performatism," a new aesthetic of unification through the "return of the phallus as a positive enabling force in culture" (2001, 6).

But discourses on modernism, postmodernism and post-variations have always overlapped, including the pronouncement of the "death of postmodernism," which came as early as 1977 in reference to the outdated period of postmodern art. The declaration that "postmodernism is over" comprises the context of the Tate Museum's 2009 triennial titled *Altermodern,* a term that describes the new modernity and universalism that characterizes a twenty-first-century global culture. An example from the exhibition is Navin Rawanchaikul's video/installation *Hong Rub Khaek (Visitors Welcome)* (2008), a performative work that invites the viewer to share in the universal migrant experience as expressed by the émigré from India to Thailand. The most significant of the post-postmodernist concepts might be "digimodernism," as acknowledged by the 2012 *The Art of the Video Games* exhibition at the Smithsonian's Museum of American Art. Modernism's previous passive spectator of mass-culture spectacles has been replaced by interactive participants, performing with thumbs and fingers online on Facebook, Twitter, American Idol, and Big Brother. Performativity via digimodernism's web interfacing establishes the shift to digitized textuality with its multiple anonymous authors, such as the Wikipedia entry. The digital revolution shows a clear transformation of Lyotard's postmodernist critique of technological progress that fuels the consumerism of late capitalism.

### *Further reading*

Eshelman (2001); Groys (2012).

### *References*

Eshelman, Raoul. 2001. "Performatism, or the End of Postmodernism." *Anthropoetics* 6.2. http://www.anthropoetics.ucla.edu/ap0602/perform.htm

Fried, Michael. 1967. "Art and Objecthood." In *Art and Objecthood: Essays and Reviews.* Chicago, IL: University of Chicago Press, 1998.

Fusco, Coco. 2008. *A Field Guide for Female Interrogators.* New York: Seven Stories Press.

Groys, Boris. 2012. *Introduction to Antiphilosophy.* London and New York: Verson.

Gullette, Margaret Morganroth. 2004. *Aged by Culture.* Chicago, IL: University of Chicago Press.

Huyssen, Andreas. 1984. "Mapping the Postmodern." *New German Critique*, 33: 5–52.

Jameson, Frederic. 1991. *Postmodernism, Or, The Cultural Logic of Late Capitalism*. Durham: Duke University Press.

Jones, Amelia. 1998. *Body Art/performing the Subject*. Minneapolis, MN: University of Minnesota Press.

Kaprow, Allan. 1961. *Essays on the Blurring of Art and Life*. Reprint, Berkeley, CA: University of California Press, 1993.

Lippard, Lucy R. and John Chandler. 1968. "The Dematerialization of Art." *Art International*, 12:2: 31–36.

Lyotard, Jean-François. 1984. *The Postmodern Condition: A Report on Knowledge*. Minneapolis, MN: University of Minnesota Press.

Owens, Craig. 1983. "The Discourse of Others: Feminists and Postmodernism." *The Anti-Aesthetic: Essays on Postmodern Culture*. Seattle, WA: Bay Press.

*Cross references*

"**Intermediality**" and "**The Internet**" by Auslander; "**Minimalism**" by Lepecki; "**Modernism**" by Albright, Pearl, and Speca; "**Post-linearity**" by Bay-Cheng; "**Postdramatic theatre**" by Fuchs; "**Transnationalism**" by Yang; "**Whiteness**" by Jones.

## Performance Studies

Jenn Joy

Performance Studies is a discipline that resists any single definition, as can be attested to by its many narratives, pedagogical, methodological, and discursive effects. Described alternatively as a "post-discipline," a "trans-discipline," and an "anti-discipline," performance studies takes performance as its object of analysis and simultaneously engages performance, itself a "contested" object (Carlson 1996), to problematize what analysis means and what it can do. Drawing from social sciences, ethnography, anthropology, cultural studies, theatre studies, dance studies, visual culture, linguistics, semiotics, psychoanalysis, philosophy, feminist theory, queer theory, race theory, and post-colonial studies, performance studies maps a conjunctive constellation of disparate theoretical and critical projects: Gilles Deleuze invites Pina Bausch to dance and Karl Marx tunes into improvised jazz.

To attempt to define performance studies requires an attention not only to its diverse and at times contradictory histories and challenges, but also to how these intellectual and artistic epistemologies translate into a discipline. Scholars including John MacAloon, Jon McKenzie, and Richard Schechner locate the incipient theoretical trajectories of Performance Studies in the emergence of cultural performance scholarship in the 1950s, aligning Victor Turner's experiential conception of "social drama," "Milton Singer's 'cultural performance', Kenneth Burke's 'dramatistic pentad' and Erving Goffman's 'social psychology of everyday life'" with Gregory Bateson's and Roger Callois' theories of play and Schechner's theory of "restored behavior" (McKenzie 2009, 33–34; Schechner 2002, 10). These encounters—as anthropology embraced theatre and ethnography conversed with quotidian ritual—opened up new intellectual, disciplinary, and pedagogical relationships that pressured traditional institutional delineations of subject and discipline. In 1980 these interdisciplinary dilemmas produced—or as Peggy Phelan describes the meeting of Turner and Schechner—"gave birth to," the first institutionalized Performance Studies Department at New York University (Phelan and Lane 1998).

Another distinct disciplinary formation also occurred during the 1980s at Northwestern University as Performance Studies emerged from the department of Oral Interpretation, "a subfield within Speech Communication, and/or Rhetoric" (Jackson 2004, 9). Rather than breaking from a theatre tradition, the Northwestern department evolved from a tradition of oral performance and poetry, the arts of elocution as professed by Wallace Bacon among others, and the "analysis and dissemination of cultural texts," and media (Jackson 2004, 9). As articulated by Dwight Conquergood, the department aspired to the alliterative challenge of "artistry, analysis, activism" through "creativity, critique, and community," explicitly tying the work of social justice to artistic and theoretical innovation and thus dissolving the academic hierarchies that previously divided these projects (2002, 152).

Yet these oft-cited narratives still render an incomplete history of Performance Studies as it evolved not only in the U.S. context, but also in the U.K., Europe, Australia, and beyond. Taking these histories to task, Shannon Jackson turns to Michel Foucault's conception of genealogy to pressure the coherent logics of such narratives and to argue instead for an "embrace of the awkwardness of emergence" that accompanies these discursive ruptures (2004, 2). To borrow the title of the 2005 Performance Studies international (PSi) conference held at Brown University, this would mean embracing "becoming uncomfortable" as an ontological effect of Performance Studies.

Tracing the multiple debates around concepts including, to cite just a few, embodiment, liveness, agency, performativity, theatricality, textuality through a broader geographic and institutional dramaturgy reveals yet another disciplinary genealogy. One way of locating these debates is through the shifting locations, affiliations, and thematic organizations of recent PSi conferences. Performance Studies' anxious relationship to its own contingent and "discontinuous history" (1995) and its ways of performing history was highlighted in the first annual PS conference "The Future of the Field" (1995) organized by the department at New York University. Challenging linear temporality with a future-oriented thinking, the conference looked at the ways in which desire, death, and colonial gaze not only inflect the work of historiography, but also open up ways of thinking about the new (Phelan 1998). This re-thinking of futurity also animated PSi 13, "Happening, Performance, Event" (2007), again hosted by NYU. The conference proposed a dialectical tension between a historical conception of the avant-garde event and a radical philosophy of the event along the lines of Alain Badiou: here the present acts as rupture of thought and practice.

While perhaps always implicit, the explicit positioning of the political in terms of performance studies structured PSi 10, "Perform: State: Interrogate" (2004) in Singapore—a conference that focused on power as an imperative and defining force, not only of the state, but also of theory, performance, artistic, and academic labor. Questioning the political efficacy of performance as a practice of social justice, PSi 11, "Performing Rights" (2005) at Queen Mary University of London proposed a mutual challenge to performance by human rights work and human rights work by performance artists and scholars. Questions of exception raised during "Performing Rights" resurfaced in PSi 14, "Interregnum: In Between States" (2008) in Copenhagen, shifting from a terminology of liminality to a thinking of between as an exceptional hermeneutic.

Gesturing toward J.L. Austin's foundational theory of speech-acts and its critique and extensions by scholars including Judith Butler and Homi Bhabha, PSi 15, "Misperformance: Misfiring, Misfitting, Misreading" in Zagreb (2009) takes seriously the failures of performance, its confusions, dysfunctions, and stalls. In this context, failure becomes a productive reiteration of the shifting artistic, theoretical, cultural, and historical blindspots of Performance Studies, and hopefully pointing again toward something and somewhere else as the 2015 conference "Fluid States" takes as its mission. Untethered from any single site or ritual academic gathering, these events take place in Bosnia, Greenland, the Bahamas, and beyond. Stay tuned ...

### *Further reading*

Berlant (2011); Lepecki (2006); Muñoz (2009).

### *References*

Berlant, Lauren. 2011. *Cruel Optimism.* Durham: Duke University Press.

Carlson, Marvin A. 1996. *Performance: A Critical Introduction*. New York: Routledge.

Conquergood, Dwight. 2002. "Performance studies: Interventions and Radical Research." *TDR: The Drama Review*, 46.2: 145–153.

Jackson, Shannon. 2004. *Professing Performance: Theatre in the Academy from Philology to Performativity*. Cambridge: Cambridge University Press.

Lepecki, André. 2006. *Exhausting Dance: Performance and the Politics of Movement*. New York: Routledge.

McKenzie, Jon. 2009. "Counter-Perfomatives: Economic Meltdowns, Techno-Snafus, and Beyond." In *Performance Studies International*, 15: Misperformance: Misfiring, Misfitting, Misreading.

Muñoz, José Esteban. 2009. *Cruising Utopia: The Then and There of Queer Futurity*. New York: New York University Press.

Phelan, Peggy. 1988. "Feminist Theory, Poststructuralism, and Performance." *TDR: The Drama* Review, 32.1: 107–127.

Phelan Peggy and Jill Lane. 1998. *The Ends of Performance*, London: Routledge.

Schechner, Richard. 2002. *Performance Studies: An Introduction*. London: Routledge.

*Cross references*

"**Broad Spectrum Approach**" and "**Play**" by Schechner; "**Choreography**" by Lepecki; "**Disciplines in performance**" and "**Rhetoric**" by Morrison; "**Guillermo Gómez-Peña attempts to explain performance art to people who may have never heard of it**" by Gómez-Peña; "**Multicentricity**" by Cheng.

## Photography and performance

Philip Auslander

The relationships between photography and performance may be plotted along a number of vectors, including performance documentation, the artistic genre known as "performed photography," and the possibility of theorizing photography itself as performative. One fundamental question that emerges from looking at the relationship between performance and photography is whether we perceive a given photograph as a transparent record of an event that existed apart from the photograph, whether the photograph and the event are co-extensive, or whether the photograph brings the event into being.

Photographers have been shooting theatre and dance since the late 1850s. Initially, they focused on creating portraits of actors and dancers, sometimes in character but always shot in the studio. It was not until after 1901 that the practice of photographing scenes from plays emerged, though these scenes were not shot during performances but restaged for the camera at special photo calls, a procedure that persists to this day. The photographic practice known as performance documentation began in the 1950s and developed alongside the evolution of performance art from Happenings on. Although theatre, dance, and performance art works are now regularly captured on video, still photography remains the predominant form of performance documentation. This practice has given rise to both theoretical speculation and practical concern about how best to document performances, not least because still photography seems incompatible with time-based forms, and also because seeking to capture performance at all seems to some to betray performance's intrinsic ephemerality.

Nevertheless, the existence of images that provide an impression of how past performances looked and what relationships with audiences they entailed enhances the possibility of writing the history of performance. Performance artists in particular, whose works are often performed a limited number of times and witnessed by relatively small audiences, have become increasingly conscious of the fact that their historical standing depends on their performances being documented and therefore ensure that their work is recorded for posterity. The theoretical discourse around performance documentation has been preoccupied with the ontological connection between the event and its representations. It is arguable, however, that over time, the photographic record replaces the original event and becomes the historical truth of the performance. Ultimately, the connection between the photograph and the original live performance may be less important than the ways viewers experience the performance from photographs. In this way, photographs originally intended to document an absent event become what theorist Michael Kirby called "surrogate performances" in themselves, performances that take place in the viewers' present tense when they experience the performance in the photograph.

Jennifer Blessing, a curator at the Guggenheim Museum, coined the phrase "performed photography" in 1997 to describe work for which artists create characters and stage performances solely to photograph them. Photographic space is thus the only space in which these performances take place for their audiences. Practitioners of performed photography include Marcel Duchamp, who took photos of himself in drag as Rrose Selavy in the early 1920s, and Yves Klein, whose *Leap Into the Void* (1960) shows Klein flying off the window of a building without a safety net, an event that took place only in the photograph itself. Contemporary artists who work in performed photography include Cindy Sherman, who photographs herself, usually heavily disguised, in portraits that resemble such cultural genres as film stills, fashion images, or old master paintings. Nikki S. Lee also uses herself as her own subject, but she remains generally recognizable as she inserts herself into staged recreations of real social interactions. In her series of wedding photographs (2005), for example, she appears as the Asian bride in a Jewish wedding celebration. Unlike Sherman and Lee, Gregory Crewdson does not appear in his own photographs of otherworldly scenes anchored in the mundanity of suburban life, but stages them like film shoots with elaborate sets, lighting, and costumed performers.

While a conventional analysis might suggest that documentary photographs are clearly different from performed ones because the former show things that "really happened" while the latter do not, this distinction is not nearly so clear-cut. For one thing, it is not always possible to distinguish them visually, and performed photographs are often mistaken for documentary ones. Klein created this confusion intentionally by removing the safety net he used from some versions of the photograph. Whether or not it was his intention, Rudolf Schwarzkogler's mid-1960s images of a man (not himself) with an apparently dissected penis, were taken to document an actual physical action but actually were entirely staged fictions (see Stiles 1990). The fact that events such as those staged by Klein and Schwarzkokler exist only in the photographs that depict them has not prevented them from achieving landmark status in the history of performance.

Another case goes beyond the issue of misrecognition. Between 1935 and 1941, the dancer Martha Graham collaborated with the photographer Barbara Morgan on a series of images eventually published in 1941 as a book titled *Martha Graham: Sixteen Dances in Photographs*. Morgan did not photograph full performances; rather, Graham repeated specific movements from her choreography in Morgan's studio until Morgan felt that she had achieved the images she wanted. Morgan's images do document Graham's dancing, but Morgan conceived of her images not as means by which a viewer might experience Graham's performance but as distilling the spiritual truth of Graham's dancing, implicitly suggesting that her carefully posed images could get closer to that truth than photographs of actual performances. Morgan's images are documentary in the sense that they do provide factual information about Graham's dancing. Nevertheless, they are not images of performances but of recreations of performance carefully staged in a photographer's studio to convey a sense of Graham's dancing intended to transcend factual information about it.

Paul Jeff suggests that photography is intrinsically performative in the sense that it creates the reality it depicts by emphasizing "the inherent act of performance implicit in all photography" (2006) and pointing out that photographs are inevitably staged, if only through the photographer's formal choices. Drawing on speech act theory, David Green and Joanna Lowry argue that photographs do not simply record the reality that presented itself to the camera but should be seen as performative gestures on the part of the photographer that indicate or point to, rather than reproduce, the real and thus draw "our attention to the ways in which notions of the real are discursively produced." If all photographs are understood "to designate the real, rather than to represent it" (Green and Lowry 2006) the distinction between documentary and performed photography becomes less meaningful, since in both cases the performances in the photographs come into existence through the performative act of photographing them.

### *Further reading*

Blessing and Spector (1997); Butler (1993).

### *References*

Blessing, Jennifer and Nancy Spector. 1997. *Rrose is a Rrose is a Rrose: Gender Performance in Photography*. New York: The Solomon R. Guggenheim Foundation.

Butler, Judith. 1993a. *Bodies that Matter*. Routledge: New York.

Butler, Judith. 1993b. "Imitation and Gender Insubordination." In *The Lesbian and Gay Studies Reader*, edited by Henry Abelove, Michele Aina Barale, and David M. Halperin, 307–320. New York: Routledge.

Green, David and Joanna Lowry. 2006. *Stillness and Time: Photography and the Moving Image*. Brighton: Photoworks/Photoforum.

Jeff, Paul. 2006. "Performed Photography: The Map is not the Terrain." Paper presented at the Land/Water Symposium, Plymouth, University of Plymouth, June.

Morgan, Barbara. 1941. *Martha Graham; Sixteen Dances in Photographs*. New York: Duell, Sloan & Pearce.

Stiles, Kristine. 1990. "Notes on Rudolf Schwarzkogler's Images of Healing." *WhiteWalls: A Magazine of Writings by Artists*. Chicago, IL: White Walls.

### *Cross references*

"**Cindy Sherman's Real Fakery**" by Schneider; "**Elevator Girls Return: Miwa Yanagi's Border Crossing between photography and theatre**" by Yoshimoto; "**Expanded cinema**" by Jarosi; "**Fluxus**" by Stiles; "**Historicity**" by Colleran; "**Intermediality**" by Auslander; "**Prosthetic performance**" by Gass.

## **Cindy Sherman's real fakery**

Rebecca Schneider

I attended Cindy Sherman's recent retrospective at New York's Museum of Modern Art in 2012. This is what happened: Entering the exhibition I am struck by the sheer volume of the hordes in attendance. There are lines around the block to buy tickets, lines to check bags, lines to use the ladies room. It is "as if" MoMA is a kind of Disneyland, a kind of *Lion King*, Caesar's Palace, Madame Tussaud's, the Tower of London, or a massive All-You-Can-Eat buffet at some Art World Hooters where, ironically, feminist art is being served up on mile high platters in the shape of aging socialites ... Indeed, I am amazed. It almost makes sense, but not quite! If art museums are modernity's temples, this temple, with Sherman's transubstantiations in the house, is massively popular, touching a nerve that runs between the falsities of gender, class, race, age. It is not insignificant, after all, that it was Madonna who sponsored Sherman's first exhibition at MoMA in 1997–an artist riding the same arguably feminist wave of making overt mimesis work for women. In any case, navigating the crowds,

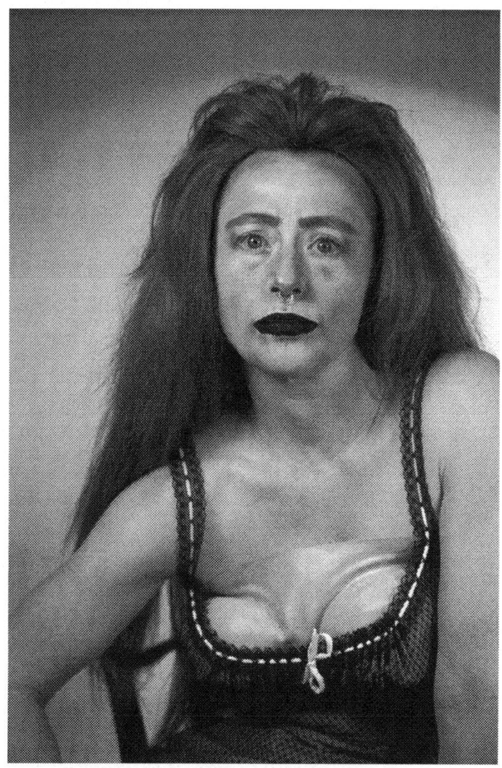

**Figure 33** Cindy Sherman. *Untitled* (2000) Chromogenic color print (image) 27 x 18 inches. (frame) 37 x 28 x 1 1/2 inches. Edition of 6. (MP# CS-352). Courtesy of the artist and Metro Pictures.

I find myself standing at the gallery entrance of the Sherman exhibition where one is greeted by a crowd of Sherman images, each about 15 feet tall, standing in multiple at the gate like 21st-century Syllas and Charybdises.

Lingering at the entrance to rest a bit after battling the lines, I notice a young woman preoccupied with her phone. She is diligently taking pictures of herself between two of the massive Shermans. I watch her surreptitiously, pretending to be admiring the monumental Cindys at her back. She sucks in her cheeks and widens her eyes. Apparently, she wants to appear to be appearing. With Sherman behind her, looking tacky and just plain ugly in her enormities, I wondered: Was this art-goer using photography as documentary evidence for the instantaneous Facebook upload, proving, like a tourist, that "she was almost there"? Or did her affected facial expressions before her own camera suggests something else? Did her own face mime the very real aspect of fakery, the fake aspect of realery, that Sherman was so talented at marking as daily way back in the 1970s? Perhaps Sherman's young spectator accepts the mantra, a truism both realized and spoofed by Sherman herself, that we appear as women and men in the 21st century only to the degree that we underscore our appearance theatrically or compose ourselves to be recognized via misrecognition.

At MoMA's opening doors, Cindy Sherman stands larger than life. And life, like a big broad joke, becomes larger than any singular Cindy Sherman who multiplies herself across the bodies and body parts of many others, crossing gender, time, media, age, and race in photographs that are overtly and exuberantly theatrical. In fact, after almost forty years of art making, Sherman's campy portraits are by now each distinctly recognizable as *a* "Cindy Sherman," even if, in each one, Cindy Sherman is not Cindy Sherman. Not Cindy Sherman, not not Cindy Sherman, not not not Cindy Sherman—the disarticulations seem as endless as the proscenial vanishing point on a baroque stage set.

Following the spectator photographer through the massive Shermans into her exhibition, I caught myself looking at more than one image with awe. I look at Sherman's re-do of Carravagio's 1593 "Sick Bacchus" ("Untitled 224," 1990). The grapes Sherman-Bacchus holds are obviously plastic, as are the ivy leaves that grace Dionysus's brow. The muscles on "his" arm are clearly made with theatrical body paint. But the look of irony and the undecidability in the god of theatre's smile seems to me to twist the pile of errors into something quite right. To recognize oneself misrecognizing is a great and theatrical pleasure.

Looking at the body of her work across time—as thousands of art patrons were able to do as the MoMA exhibition traveled to the San Francisco Museum of Modern Art and the Walker in Minneapolis—one is struck not only by the consistency of theatricality, but by the accumulative force in the affective, gut-wrenching punch of spoof. In pose work from the mid-1970s to her most current aging socialites series of untitled prints from 2008, it is in the uncertain space between the joke and the truth that Sherman's uncanny portraiture lives and breathes a kind of undead power where the fake comes back to haunt the real only to find the real deeply–*really*–fake.

From its invention in the 1830s until the threshold of the digital age, photography has been considered the medium of reality. Anything captured by photography was, it could be claimed, definitely there, with the photograph as testament to the reality of the imaged. Photography, through what Roland Barthes called its "that was there" aspect, was linked more to the documentary real more than it was to the vicissitudes of fakery (Barthes 1981). Fakery was far more content to live in theatre–the most anti-photographic, and even anti-artistic of art forms. Precedents to Sherman–artists who made highly theatrical photographs such as the self-portraiture of Claude Cahun or the tableaux of Lady Clementina Hawarden–were, if not anti-artists, certainly engaged in a gender and/or identity play that marked women (who could not be recognized as artists anyway) as always engaged in silly masquerade. Since the mid-1970s, Cindy Sherman has deployed that theatricality at a fevered whirlpool pitch until her photographs seem to have tipped the "documentary" meter, breaking the dividing line between real and fake, and ultimately requiring a different means to gage the work at all. For, through the looking glass of Sherman's work, real and fake have become the same thing.

Why is "theatrical" an apt descriptor for Sherman's art photography? Theatricality refers to a theatre-like appearance as evident in the art of posing, feigning, appearing "as if," miming, dissimulating, masquerading, or acting. Most often, theatricalilty is evident to a viewer. That which can be seen as theatrical is that which does not quite pass–at least on second or third or nth look–something is slightly or even overtly amok. Something (such as an exaggerated gesture or an error of affect or an anachronism of some kind) gives the "act" away as, precisely, an act. The irony in much of Sherman's work is that her poses attempt to capture the energy of the pass itself. Her "characters" (if they can be called that) can each be seen to labor to some degree at their show, making the labor of the show part and parcel of the point of the work itself. Sherman thus exposes a base-line theatricality in any pose, an effort that we might articulate as Sherman's ironic attempt to pass *as theatrical*, not to pass as real, in order to show the theatrical underpinnings of social life, and especially gendered social life,. Attempting to capture the real of a theatrical pose, and the theatricality in a real pose is a conundrum–a knot of nots exposing the entanglements of mimesis in the social worlds of our interactions not only with others, but with our own self images.

On my way out of the museum, I pass again a docent at the gallery entrance. She is an aging socialite dressed as a museum employee. The lines of plastic surgery make it difficult for her to smile. But she does. And I smile back. Glad, then, to step out of line.

References

Barthes, Roland. 1981. *Camera Lucida: Reflections on Photography*. Translated by Richard Howard. New York: Hill and Wang.

## Play

Richard Schechner

Playing is one of the two fundamental processes of human behavior, performing rituals being the other. Everyone plays and most people enjoy watching others play—either formally as in sports or casually as in "people watching." Play can challenge the powers-that-be as during carnival or by means of parody. Play can also be amoral, cruel, irrational—what Shakespeare's Gloucester meant when he cried out, "As flies are to wanton boys, are we to the gods, / They kill us for their sport" (*King Lear* 4.1, 38–39).

Performance may be defined as ritualized behavior permeated by play. While rituals are most often fixed or at least regularized, playing is "free." Of course, games (sports, cards, chess, and so on) are possible only if the players adhere to agreed-upon rules. Gaming involves understanding the rules in order to gain an advantage. Cheating is possible only within the framework of rule-bound behavior, which the cheater intentionally and surreptitiously subverts or violates. Child-play is different from adult-play. Children spend a great amount of time and energy in exploratory playing while adults spend most of their playtime in games. However, experimenting—in science as well as art—is a mode of "playing around," close to child-play: except that scientists and artists keep records of their playing, developing theories, and art works, systematically.

Play is very hard to pin-down and define. Aside from being a set of activities, it is a mood, a spontaneous eruption or disruption; a pleasurable disturbance; a dash of chaos peppering the orderliness of social life. In Western thought, from the 18th to the 20th centuries, a strong effort was made to marginalize and control play, to reign-in its anarchic expression channeling it into rule-bound, site-and-calendar-specific activities. The success of industrialization depended upon containing play and regularizing and expanding the domain of work. But play is not easily contained. Even in the midst of seriousness, play erupts to disturb the status quo with drunkenness, gambling, sex, truancy, and myriad other behaviors.

Friedrich Nietzsche was the first modern philosopher to restore play to its place as a powerful human category of thought and action. After Nietzsche came notions of the unconscious in psychology and literature, theories of relativity and indeterminacy in physics, and game theory in mathematics and economics. In the arts, painters began playing around with representation and abstraction; Konstantin Stanislavsky taught how to actualize the "as if" (or make-believe) in theatre; musicians such as Erik Satie and John Cage practiced absurd and chance music; many dancers took up the playful challenges of contact improvisation.

Both child and adult play involve exploration, learning, and risk with a payoff in the pleasurable experience of "flow" or total involvement in an activity for its own sake. Playing creates its own realities: playing is full of world-making, truth-telling and lying, illusion and actuality, sincerity and deceit. Playing can be physically and emotionally dangerous. The perils of play are masked by asserting that playing is fun, voluntary, ephemeral, a leisure activity. But Clifford Geertz, building on an idea of Jeremy Bentham's, showed how people involved themselves in "deep play," playing over their heads, taking risks they ought not to. People also use "dark play"—as in con-games, stings, or internet bullying—where only some of the players know that they are playing.

In terms of structure, Roger Caillois defined four types of games: *Agon*, or competition; *alea* or chance; mimicry or simulation; and *ilinx* or dizziness (1961). Many instances of playing combine some or all of these qualities. Poker combines the chance of the draw with the skill of betting and bluffing. A Greek tragedy draws on *alea* (fate) and *agon* (conflict). Carnival masking engages all four categories. Nor need all the players agree on what's happening. What's play for the cat is a slow terrifying death to the mouse.

For performance theorists, two aspects of play are of special interest: psychoanalyst D. W. Winnicott's notion of "transitional objects and phenomena" (1971) and sociologist Mihalyi Csikszentmihalyi's "flow" (1991). Transitional objects and phenomena are things and processes that do not belong to one person alone but are shared—such as the nursing mother's breasts. The infant and the mother merge during breast-feeding. In Winnicott's view, this kind of experience is never forgotten—as children develop, their earliest relations and attachments become unconscious but powerful players in ever-more complex operations that extend throughout adulthood (1971). These operations are at the basis of creativity—of inventing realities based on shared illusions, from God to cities to arts to science—all of culture. Csikszentmihalyi asserts that the merging of person and activity is extremely pleasurable. To be "in flow" is to be one with an activity. When people play deeply, they live in the flow; they create and merge with their creations; they become, if only temporarily, what they imagine (1991).

*Further reading*

Caillois (1961); Winnicott (1971).

*References*

Caillois, Roger. 1961. *Man, Play, and Games.* Translated by Meyer Barash. Bloomington, IN: University of Illinois Press.

Csikszentmihalyi, Mihalyi. 1991. *Flow: The Psychology of Optimal Experience.* New York: Harper Perennial.

Shakespeare, William. *King Lear*, edited by R.A. Foakes. In *The Arden Shakespeare*, London: Thomson Learning, 2005.

Winnicott, D.W. 1971. "Transitional Objects and Transitional Phenomena." In *Playing and Reality.* London: Tavistock Publications.

*Cross references*

"**Active analysis**" by Carnicke; "**Actor**" by Mee; "**Becoming *Kinocognophore***" by Bucher, Zeeb, with Cheng; "**Broad Spectrum Approach**" by Schechner; "**Circus**" by Tait; "**Communitas**" by Levine; "**Gaga Feminism**" by Halberstam; "**Intercultural performance**" by Alker; "**Masochism**" by O'Dell; "**Mimicry**" by Applebaum; ***"Reality Ends Here"*** by Watson.

***Reality Ends Here***

Jeff Watson

*Reality Ends Here* is a collaborative media making game played by students at the University of Southern California. Broadly conceived as a "peer discovery and serendipity accelerator" (Watson, n.d.), the game originated in 2011 as an informal learning initiative at the USC School of Cinematic Arts. The objective of this initiative was to speed up the rate at which incoming students could build interdisciplinary connections with one another, experiment with creative media, making using a range of practices and technologies, and establish relationships with upper-year students, alumni, and other mentors. Jeff Watson created *Reality Ends Here* as the core practical element of his doctoral research; and Simon Wiscombe and Tracy Fullerton collaborated with Watson to design the game.

Unlike many games deployed in educational settings, *Reality Ends Here* is an entirely optional experience. Students receive no official invitation to play, and faculty members are instructed to deny any knowledge of the game's existence. Once they discover the game, it is up to students themselves to divine how it works. In short, rather than being "pushed" into the experience in the manner of traditional education, students are "pulled" into the game through a variety of guerilla communications techniques. For example, during the 2012 run of the game, students received fortune cookies in lunches served at orientation sessions. Inside these fortune cookies were fragments of a code which, when assembled, led the students on a web- and real-world-based scavenger hunt. This scavenger hunt ultimately led to a nondescript office in a campus building, where students could meet members of the mysterious "Reality Committee" and sign up for the game proper. Myriad other approaches, such as a mysterious flag which intermittently flew in the central courtyard of the school, similarly enabled discovery and provided initiation pathways for students to join the game at any time over its semester-long run.

The core activity of *Reality Ends Here* is the public performance of prompt-driven collaborative media making. When students sign up for the game, they receive a packet containing 10 custom-made game cards. These cards, drawn from a master deck of over 700, can be combined—both with one another, and with cards belonging to other students—to generate creative prompts of varying complexity. Once a student or group of students has generated a prompt they find inspiring, they must create a media project based on that prompt, submit it to the game's website, and deliver an artist's statement (or "Justification") via webcam in order to score points. The more complex the creative prompt, the more points the project is worth, and all students who collaborate on a given project earn its full point value. Those who score the most points in a given week are treated to offbeat and personal encounters with alumni and other mentors active in the media arts industries, such as a home-cooked meal at a filmmaker's home, or a surprise meet-up with a game designer at a museum. All the projects created in the game are shared with the world via a publicly accessible website.

*Reality Ends Here* is a work of environmental game design—that is, it is a game designed to impact the way that a particular environment is perceived and used by its inhabitants. One of the principal ways that environmental games generate impact is by changing or broadening the ways that inhabitants perform in a given place. In so doing, such games can alter the behavioral spectacle of their target environment, surfacing new practices of living and possibilities for community engagement and participation.

Prior to the deployment of *Reality Ends Here* at USC, the environment at the School of Cinematic Arts had a muted relationship to interdisciplinary collaboration and discovery. The structure of the curriculum and the architectural constraints of the buildings housing the school kept students locked in their disciplinary silos, producing a spectacle of deep, yet narrow, specialization. Incoming students would encounter this spectacle and interpret it as a guideline for how they should perform, resulting in the replication and amplification of existing performative codes. *Reality Ends Here* intervenes on these codes first by providing students with a playful invitation to participate in self-directed, pro-social, and interdisciplinary media-making activities; and second, by creating a spectacle of these activities, both online, via social media and the game's web interface, and offline, via the various kinds of performance and social engagement involved in collaborative media-making and the sharing, trading, and combining of cards.

The design praxis of *Reality Ends Here* considers lived environments from a dramaturgical perspective. In this view, the ways that individuals and collectives behave in a given environment constitute a kind of performance. This performance serves to establish and maintain the environment's dramaturgical codes, which in turn shape the kinds of performances that are possible there. In many cases, such as that of a well-functioning library or hospital, this feedback loop can serve to optimize the efficiency and safety of the environment; however, the same loop can also entrench undesirable constraints on behavior and desire. To transform the dramaturgy of an environment requires intervention on the performances that take place within its boundaries, for it is through these performances that the environment acquires its identity.

In the words of Situationist writer Raoul Vaneigem, "[only] play can deconsecrate [and] open up the possibilities of total freedom" (1967/2001, 72) in lived environments. In part, this is because play—via designed or spontaneous games—is inherently an exercise of agency, and therefore uniquely capable of aligning with and channeling individual desire. It is also because play is imbued with a powerful kind of fiction-making power. "Let's pretend" is what we say both when we sit down to play a game, and when we set out to create a better world. At USC, we ushered in a new kind of community at the School of Cinematic Arts by creating a game that asked students to act *as if* the community they shared was something different than what it was. By performing this pretense, the students transformed an imaginary reality into a living and breathing creative community.

## References


Vaneigem, Raoul. 2001. *The Revolution of Everyday Life*. Translated by Donald Nicholson-Smith. Rebel Press. Originally published *Traité de savoir-vivre à l'usage des jeunes générations* (Gallimard, 1967).

Watson, Jeff. *Reality Ends Here*. http://www.remotedevice.net

## Postcolonial performance inquiry

Sudipto Chatterjee

The Random House dictionary dates the word "postcolonial" to have emerged between 1930 and 1935, identifying it as an adjective, "of or pertaining to the period following a state of colonialism." *The American Heritage Dictionary of the English Language* is more specific: "of, relating to, or being the time following the establishment of independence in a colony." The word continues, in a general sense, to work as a descriptive adjective in a geo-historical sense. Starting with the rise of the Négritude Movement, under the leadership of African and Black Caribbean intellectuals like Léopold Sédar Senghor, Aimé Césaire and Léon Damas in the 1930s, a critical discourse about colonialism developed among many non-European intellectuals that went hand in hand with independence movements in most colonial countries, stretching from Asia to the Americas. Most of these global movements revolved around the idea of an independent nation-state, marking a post-colonial era.

Following the Second World War and through the1950s and 1960s, most of the colonized countries attained their independence from the colonizing nations in Europe, mainly Britain, France, Portugal, Belgium and the Netherlands. Nevertheless, it was not until the 50s that post-colonialism emerged when Frantz Fanon (1925–1961), a psychiatrist, philosopher, revolutionary, and writer from the Caribbean island of Martinique, along with pioneering fellow citizen Aimé Césaire, started working out a more complex understanding of colonialism and its implications. In 1952, Fanon published *Black Skin, White Masks*, with Césaire adding *Discourse of Colonialism* in 1955. Albert Memmi, the Tunisian–Jewish theorist, contributed to the ongoing post-colonial conversation with his *The Colonizer and the Colonized* in 1957. In 1961, Fanon added *The Wretched of the Earth*. From the mid-1950s into the 1960s, revolutionary anti-colonial rhetoric and discourse on race and class, through the sharp interrogation of nationalist discourse and politics, gradually made way for an inclusive mode of inquiry now known as Postcolonial Studies.

The rise of Postcolonial Studies as a disciplinary field therefore coincides with the noticeable failure of nationalism as an effective answer to colonialism in the late 1960s and early 70s.

In 1978, the critique of imperialism inherent in the rise of Postcolonial Studies was further extended beyond the binary oppositions often suggested by the discourse of race and difference, into the field of culture and knowledge. An important marker was the arrival of Edward Said's *Orientalism* (1979), which tried "not so much to dissipate difference itself—for who can deny the constitutive role of national as well as cultural differences in the relations between human beings—but to challenge the notion that difference implies hostility." Instead, Said went on to suggest that Postcolonial Studies needed to go "beyond the stifling hold [ ... ] of some version of the master-slave binary dialectic" (Said 1994, 350–351). Homi K. Bhabha, in the early 1990s, added further wrinkles to the stretch of Postcolonial Studies. Invoking the political philosophy of Michel Foucault, along with Jacques Derrida and Jacques Lacan—Bhabha posited a critique of a tendency in Postcolonial Studies that flattened and homogenized the different colonial experiences and differing levels of ambiguities in the relations between the colonizer and colonized. In this regard, he drew attention to the notion of hybridity that created both collision and collusion between the parties involved in a colonial relationship. Bhabha also called into play—thereby making a more palpable and traceable link with performance—the idea of colonial mimicry, which he ascribed to be at the basis of colonial hybridity (1990). Other scholars like Robert Young and Michael Taussig pushed further Bhabha's deployment of the suggestive terms *mimicry* and *mimesis*, hybridity and the role of the narrative in the contact between colonizers and colonized. These incursions have, in turn, created a fertile ground for theatre and performance to contribute to the further development of Postcolonial Studies.

The heterogeneous findings of and political incursions affected by Postcolonial Studies have informed and inspired both theatrical performance as well as performance art. This is most clearly seen in traditional dramatic works by, to name just a few, Wole Soyinka, Athol Fugard, Utpal Dutt, Badal Sircar, Derek Walcott, Jack Davis, Mudrooroo, Ronnie Govinder, Dario Fo, Brian Friel, David Hare, Luis Valdez, and performance works by Guillermo Gómez-Peña, Reza Abdoh, Coco Fusco, James Luna, Renee Green, Lyle Ashton Harris and Renée Cox, Joyce Scott and Kay Lawal, Grace Jones, and Ong Keng Sen.

### *Further reading*

Appiah (1993); Benedict (1983); Bhabha (1990).

### *References*

Appiah, Kwame Anthony. 1993. *In My Father's House: Africa in the Philosophy of Culture.* Oxford: Oxford University Press.

Anderson, Benedict. 1983. *Imagined Communities: Reflections on the Origin and Spread of Nationalism.* London: Verso.

Bhabha, Homi. 1990. *Nation and Narration,* London: Routledge.

Césaire, Aimé. 1955. *Discourse on Colonialism.* Paris: Réclame.

Fanon, Frantz. 1952. *Black Skin, White Masks.* Translated by Richard Philcox. Reprint, 2008. New York: Grove Press.

Fanon, Frantz. 1961. *The Wretched of the Earth.* Translated by Richard Philcox. Reprint, 2004. New York: Grove Press.

Memmi, Albert. 1965. *The Colonizer and the Colonized.* Boston, MA: Beacon Press.

Said, Edward. 1979. *Orientalism.* New York: Vintage.

Said, Edward. 1994. *Culture and Imperialism.* New York: Random House.

### *Cross references*

"**Animal Studies**" by Chaudhuri; "**Identity politics**" by Adewunmi; "**The Internet**" and "**Performance in the digital age**" by Auslander; "**Guillermo Gómez-Peña attempts to explain performance art to people who may have never heard of it**" by Gómez-Peña; "**Multicentricity**" by Cheng; "**Performing body modifications**" by Henkes; "**Performing surveillance camera art**" by Nayar; "**Puppet and object performance**" by Bell.

## Postdramatic theater

Elinor Fuchs

"Postdramatic" is the term German theater theorist Hans-Thies Lehmann gives to a wide range of modernist theatre performances since the 1960s. With the publication of Lehmann's *Postdramatisches Theater* in Germany (1999), the term came into broad currency in central and western Europe. Since the publication of an abridged English translation (2006), the term has been increasingly adopted in the U.K. and the United States as a replacement for "postmodern" theatre as well as for the many loose designations under which such contemporary theatre has traveled, including "avant-garde," "experimental," "art performance," and "performance art," though the latter, despite stylistic and theoretical overlap, maintains a separate identity for smaller scale mixed-genre performance work. The term was first applied to the work of Robert Wilson and others in the 1980s by the Polish-German theater scholar Andrzej Wirth, founder in 1982 of the Institut für Angewandte Theaterwissenschaft [Institute for Applied Theater Studies] at the University of Giessen (Weiler 2005), and was earlier used by Richard Schechner (1988) in relation to Happenings. However, Lehmann was the first to use the term to denote not only a move away from dramatic dialogue, plot, or character (Fuchs 1996) but of the entire "fictive cosmos" traditionally associated with dramatic theatre (Lehmann 2006, 22–24).

Lehmann argues that the connecting link among performances as diverse as those created, for instance, by Tadeusz Kantor, Heiner Goebbels, Jan Lauwers, Jan Fabre, Societas Raffaello Sanzio, Richard Foreman, John Jesuran, and the Wooster

Group—as well as stagings by German directors such as Frank Castorf, Klaus Michael Gruber, and Einar Schleef—is their refusal of this key aspect of the dramatic: the creation of an internally coherent "world" in service to a dramatic text. Lehmann especially credits Robert Wilson with the creation and dissemination of postdramatic theater.

Lehmann builds on the core work of his mentor, the Hungarian theorist Peter Szondi, who in *Theory of the Modern Drama* argued that "drama" was a purely dialogic form arising in the seventeenth century and already beginning to shade into "epicization" (a term he derives from Brecht via Aristotle) by the late nineteenth century. Even Shakespeare, with his prologues, epilogues, and soliloquies, was to Szondi not yet entirely dramatic (Szondi 1987). Lehmann sees not Brecht, but Beckett, as marking the end of the dialogic, thus dramatic, form. It is important to note, however, that Lehmann's influential book does not follow the career of dramatic writing, or even of writing for the theatre, but is principally focused on the theatrical event.

Though shards of the fictive world may survive in postdramatic theatre, the theatre occasion becomes principally and self-consciously about the "situation" (Lehmann 2006, 128), the live interaction between audience and actors (2006, 127–128). Thus an outbreak of what Lehmann calls the "real" in the performance (2006, 99–104) becomes a central characteristic of this theatre. Lehmann associates a wide range of other traits with the postdramatic: the use of and inspiration by media, parataxis (the leveling of Aristotle's hierarchy of dramatic "elements") (2006, 86), polyglossia (2006, 147), the density of signs (2006, 89), the importance of "visual dramaturgy"(2006, 93), and the "cancellation" of an aesthetic synthesis (2006, 82).

While Lehmann's focus is largely on the postdramatic performance piece created by a group or an *auteur* director, and secondarily on postdramatic stagings of pre-existing texts, he mentions some playwrights as pointing the way to the postdramatic, for instance Gertrude Stein and the landscape play, Stanislaw Witkiewicz and the Theatre of Pure Form, and more recently and most of all, Heiner Müller. Subsequently, Rene Pollesch in Germany, Elfriede Jelinek in Austria, Martin Crimp in England, and Suzan-Lori Parks and Richard Maxwell in the U.S. have been described as creators of postdramatic texts.

Building not only on Szondi, but among others on Andrzej Wirth's theory of the transformation of dramatic dialogue into discourse, Lehmann points towards the extinction of the dramatic form without completely committing himself to this perspective. However it is possible to read another trajectory into his discussion, that the postdramatic is a belated eruption in the dramatic theater of impulses from cubism, Dada, and other modernist avant-gardes. On this view, such innovations are likely to follow the route of others in the history of changing theatrical styles and be reabsorbed into an enduring, if elastic, dramatic form. This latter route was followed by atonality in classical music, which came to coexist with the tonality it was thought to have banished, and by cubism and abstraction in painting, which at one time were thought to spell the end of figurative painting.

Despite the clarification that "postdramatic" brings to a confusing field for which the term "avant-garde" has surely been overused, Lehmann's book continues to stir controversy. Among its critics are Benjamin Bennett, who claims that Lehmann's definition of "drama" relies narrowly on late nineteenth-century literary style and staging (2005), and Bernd Stegemann, a professor of dramaturgy in Berlin, who, in an issue of *Theater Heute* observed the tenth anniversary of the German publication of *Postdramatic Theatre* with dueling essays defended dramatic theater's enduring talent for "believability" (2009).

## Further reading

Balme (2004); Bennett (2005), Fuchs (1996).

## References

Balme, Christopher. 2004. "Editiorial", *Theatre Research International*, 29.1: 1

Bennett, Benjamin. 2005. "Robert Wilson and the Work as an Empty Wavelength for its Own Public Discussion." In *All Theater is Revolutionary Theater*, 194–215. Ithaca and London: Cornell University Press.

Fuchs, Elinor. 1996. "The Death of Character: Perspectives on Theater After Modernism". In *Drama and Performance Studies*, edited by Timothy Wiles. Bloomington, IN: Indiana University Press.

Lehmann, Hans-Theis. 1999. *Postdramatic Theater*. Translated by Karen Jürs-Munby. Reprint, 2006. London and New York: Routledge.

Schechner, Richard. 1988. *Performance Theory*, London: Taylor & Francis.

Stegemann, Bernd. 2009. "After Postdramatic Theater." In *Theater*, translated by Michael Winter, 39.3: 11–23.

Szondi, Peter. 1987. *Theory of the Modern Drama*, edited and translated by Michael Hays. Minneapolis, MN: University of Minnesota Press.

Weiler. Christel 2005. "Postdramatisches Theater," in Erika Fischer-Lichte et. al. Eds. *Metzler Lexikon Theatertheorie*, Stuttgart: J.B. Metzler.

*Cross references*

"**Boychild**" by Halberstam; "**Feminist bloggins as activism and pedagogy**" by Dolan; "**Fluxus**" by Stiles; "**Happenings**" by Sandford; "**He Yunchang's limit acts**" by Cheng; "**Landscape theatre**" by Strahler Holzapfel; "**New genre public art**" by Irish; "**Performance, postmodernism, and beyond**" by Chin Davidson; "**The Wooster Group's *TO YOU, THE BIRDIE! (Phèdre)***" by Cody.

## The Wooster Group's *TO YOU, THE BIRDIE! (Phèdre)*

Gabrielle H. Cody

Long considered the masterpiece of French classical literature, *Phèdre*, along with Racine's other eleven plays, have not fared well outside of France. The neo-classical Alexandrine is a near-impossible poetic convention to translate. In the vernacular, it is muscular and smart. In translation, the baroque splendor of Racine's verse comes across as deadly logorrhea.

Unlike Shakespeare's populist theatricality, much of Racine's drama resides in the art of description. His plays were written for a court culture used to reading and eager to decipher through aphorisms the verbal behavior of his characters. Verisimilitude and the rules of decorum were state sponsored; stage actions were credible only if properly befitting rank. Similarly, in a genre in which language *is* action, actors were called upon to declaim rather than to enact their parts. First and foremost, the apparatus of tragedy served to put into relief the intimate pain of royal figures for whom the requirements of living in the private body of their passions cancelled out their ability to live in the public body of their caste. In Racine–unlike in Euripides and Seneca–Phèdre is bound by the moral rectitude of an idealized court ethos. It is no longer Phèdre who accuses Hippolytus, but her confidante Oenone. The French Hippolyte is not accused of rape, but merely of having thought of it.

The semiotic richness of Racine's work galvanized post-Second World War French intellectuals who recognized in his plays a profoundly modern pattern of obsessions, a fascination with (self-) alienation and the unconscious. Racine's cubistic optic was compared to the symbolists, even to Artaud. When he was not being championed as an existentialist, he was hailed as a postmodern. Roland Barthes's heady conclusion in *On Racine*, that "Racinian tragedy is merely a failure that speaks itself" echoes Beckett's self-acknowledged debt to the author of *Phèdre*.

The Wooster Group's *TO YOU, THE BIRDIE! (Phèdre)* (2002, New York City)–based on a compact translation by Paul Schmidt–baldly exposes all that in Racine is unseen and aphoristic. Elisabeth LeCompte and her company pry open the phantasmatic underbelly of Racine's poetic anatomy with a vengeance. To say

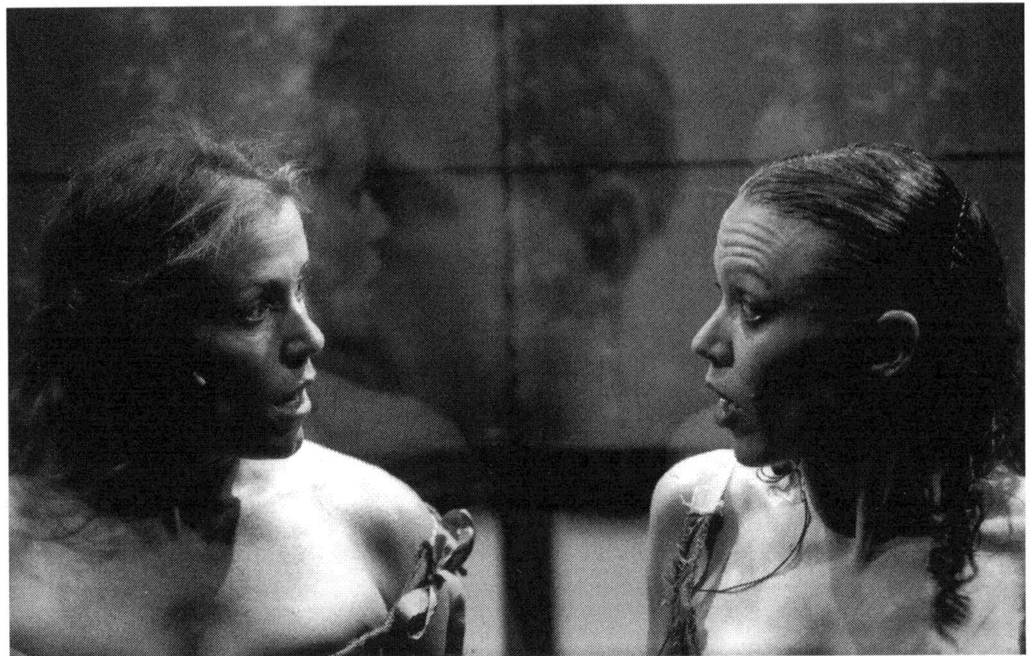

**Figure 34** The Wooster Group's *TO YOU, THE BIRDIE! (Phèdre)*. Directed by Elizabeth LeCompte. Pictured (l-r): Frances McDormand, Scott Shepherd, Kate Valk. Photo: © Mary Gearhart. Image courtesy of the photographer.

that *TO YOU, THE BIRDIE! (Phèdre)* eviscerates neo-classical decorum is to put it mildly. Two metaphors reign supreme in this posh, futuristic health spa for an ailing civilization that is LeCompte's reimagined Trozen: Phèdre's frequent and agonizing bowel movements and the macabre athletic regime of the badminton court. These literalizations of seventeenth-century court rituals–the performance of love's physical ravages (replete with enemas and bed pans) and "the game" of politics-as-sport–are incomparable ways of back-reading the signifiers of neo-classical myth-making.

Beneath the frenetic surface level of the Wooster Groups' anti-mimetic gymnastics is a dazzling distillation of the politics of tragic ethos. How the characters play the game of badminton says everything about where they stand on the scales of fate. Hippolytus (Ari Filakos) is a pro with a temper. Théramenes (Scott Shepard), his friend and tutor, hits the birdie with aggressive, military precision. Anemic Phèdre, played with exquisite timing and histrionic countenance by Kate Valk, cannot even hold the racket. All the while, Venus (Susie Roche), in a mechanical tone, keeps score ("let," "fault") for this pathetic humanity. The torments of erotic prohibition, the high stakes of noble falls, the stuff of great tragedy and national pedagogy, are ruthlessly lampooned.

As always, LeCompte and her crew distort and distend sound into a fantastical score, creating a fusion of techno-affects such as the massively amplified, steely trajectory of shuttlecocks inter-spliced with the prosaic chirping of birds. Far from gratuitous effects, the technical necromancy brutally comments on the cultivated artifice of her characters' mythic stature. An example of LeCompte's uncompromising look under the surface of decorum and court ideology is a hilarious prequel in which the homosocial pact at Trozen is neatly established. Hippolytus and his tutor Théramenes sit half-naked in a locker room sauna, towels veiling their virile manhood. Close-up images of their barely concealed genitals are projected on a small video screen, behind which the two men indiscriminately grope for each other's crotches as they, expressionless, face the audience. Similarly, when Valk and Filakos scandalously enact the moment of sexual transgression, Hippolytus displays the same groping indifference towards his Step Mother, who remains awkwardly compromised by a makeshift porta-potty throne.

Most of the time Phèdre does not have the agency of her own voice. When Scott Shepard is not playing Théramenes, his ironic voice interjects Phèdre's lines and melodramatic asides into an onstage microphone. At one point, Valk tries to drown her despair in the potentially curative powers of a pair of new red shoes (projected onto the screen) while Shepard whispers: "New clothes always make me feel good. But this isn't working." His exposed ventriloquism is as hilarious as it is devastating because Phèdre's petty interior monologues are physically offered by Valk as if she were pluming the depths of Phèdre's psyche. By estranging Phèdre's voice from the actor playing her, LeCompte is able to unapologetically satirize the cliché of Phèdre's tragic inner consciousness.

Valk's soon-to-be-suicided confidante (Frances McDormand) is given a brilliant social gestus by LeCompte. As part of the story's non-tragic personnel, she walks on her knees. McDormand also does some serious people-watching as she smokes her way through her hectic duties. One senses from her Oenone a wonderfully smug, snobbish servitude, the knowledge that she is on the Queen's payroll to dispense advice (however terrible) rather than Assisted Care.

The thunderous sound of gigantic footsteps and his repeated quip "look at this" punctuate Willem Dafoe's arrival, looking very much like an infomercial for Bowflex. But when Theseus, the great slayer of the Minautor lies down and a close-up of his torso is projected onto the plasma screen, Dafoe morphs into a marble statue. This moment is unexpectedly moving, and strangely erotic, as it uncovers for better or for worse a private moment of heroic solitude, the passage from flesh to marble, the cost of Apollonian perfection.

LeCompte and her company indict the ideological underpinnings of high tragedy by brilliantly inveighing against the histrionics of privileged and personal suffering. In this sense, *TO YOU, THE BIRDIE! (Phèdre)* is a remarkable piece of cultural history. Through their radically anti-psychological methods, the Wooster Group enables us to see past our own state-controlled media, and perhaps not coincidentally, the post-9/11/01 manufacturing of emotional affect and empathy: the right of some to suffer and grieve publicly, while others remain out of frame.

## Posthumanism

Pramod K. Nayar

Posthumanism in performance might be thought of as art forms that (i) explore the limits of the human, (ii) explore its possible trajectories of evolution, and (iii) foreground the human's irreducible species cosmopolitanism. Posthuman art almost always focuses on linkages of human form and function with something else.

Enhancement art, as we can think of Kevin Warwick and Stelarc's work, ponders over the ways and means through which the limitations of the human form might be overcome through technological, surgical, chemical intervention. Such work is the most obvious, or populist, manifestation of the posthuman—as a being whose identity and existence is lived through enhancing technologies.

Such enhancement art shares ideological and philosophical grounds with art that foregrounds the human-machine assemblage as not simply prosthetic condition but as speculating on the possible trajectories for evolution. Stelarc's work (*Third Ear*, 2007; *Exoskeleton*, 1999) and Isa Gordon's (*Psymbiote*, *Titanium Glove*, 2001–to date) examine the possibilities of the human form evolving in conjunction with prosthetic devices and processes, whether the internet or artificial skin. This is no mere technofetishism. Rather, they show how the old equation, human body+technological prosthesis, is no longer valid because humans have always evolved with technology in an assemblage. There is no originary body and techno-prosthetic. It becomes impossible to sort the origin and the prosthetic because the body itself has been evolved, shaped through extended engagements with nature (setting) and technology. In other words, the human form and function has always internalized the technological artifact or process for its purpose so that "human" and "machine" (where "machine" is a part of the external nonorganic world) are locked into a loop across which information flows. The technological object/process is no prosthesis: at the heart of the human is the prosthesis.

A third form of posthumanist art speculates about such human-machine or human-animal assemblages as evolving into chimerical forms. Eduardo Kac (*GFP Bunny*, 2000), Alexis Rockman (*The Farm*, 2000), Shen Shaomin (*Unknown Creature—Three Headed Monster*, 2002) and Bryan Crockett (*Ecce Homo*, 2000) examine the potential of mixed DNA to produce new forms of the human. The SymbioticA and Tissue Culture and Art projects (called BioArt) uses living tissue and genetic material in order to show the possibilities—and dangers—of genetic modification. Such art might be seen, as Pramod K. Nayar has elsewhere proposed as "monstrous" in the sense that they are revelatory ("monstrosity" comes from "monere", meaning warning, omen, portent, all indicating the future).

It is also possible to see this third kind of posthumanist art as grounded in a slightly different philosophical foundation. This foundation is the idea that since humans have always evolved *with* animal and other life forms, and where genes manifest as body shape, function or behavior based on their interactions with the environment (as demonstrated by biologist Lynn Margulis and more recently in evolutionary biology by Scott Gilbert), we need to consider the human form as co-evolving with other life forms. By emphasizing the possibilities of chimeras (life forms with multiple genetic origins), such art calls attention to the condition of species cosmopolitanism, Nayar's term for the boundary-crossing, multiorigin humanimal. Posthuman art of this variety denies the belief in the autonomous, bounded and coherent human (or any other form of life). The self/non-self model of the human is at stake in such art works because they emphasize the interconnectedness of life forms. Identity, argue Pradeu and Carosella, is based not on the *substance* of the human but on its *continuity* with the world outside and sharing space with other life forms (2010). Such art takes Alphonso Lingis' argument—that all life forms co-exist with other life forms where, in many cases, the basic functions of life are possible only because of this symbiotic relationship—seriously (2003). Such a posthumanist art posits a different model of the Self: as one that exists in continuity with the Other.

Posthumanist performance of the kinds inventoried above carries enormous ethical potential. First, it demolishes the Enlightenment ideal of the autonomous human, self-contained and coherent. Second, it interrogates the simplistic reduction of the human form to an "original" object to which secondary and prosthetic objects are added. Third, it emphasizes the "symbiogenetic" self that needs to respect other selves for survival (see Margulis and Sagan 2003). Fourth, such a question of respect for "companion species", as Donna Haraway terms them, is a rethinking of the ethical (2008): for it calls upon the human to recognize the Other not as a stranger but one with whom an ethical relation is forged due to our mutual dependency.

### Further reading

Braidotti (2013); Catts and Zurr (2002); Nayar (2007, 2013); Parker-Starbuck (2014).

### References

Braidotti, Rosi. 2013. *The Posthuman.* Cambridge: Polity.

Catts, Oran and Ionat Zurr. 2002. "Growing Semi-Living Sculptures: The Tissue Culture & Art Project." *Leonardo*, 35.4: 365–370.

Gordon, Isa. 2001–to date. "Psymbiote." *Psymbiote.* http://www.psymbiote.org

Haraway, Donna J. 2008. *When Species Meet.* Vol. 3 in *Posthumanities,* edited by Cary Wolfe. Minneapolis, MN: University of Minnesota Press.

Lingis, Alphonso. 2003. "Animal Body, Inhuman Face." In *Zoontologies: The Question of the Animal,* edited by Cary Wolfe, 165–182. Minneapolis, MN, and London: University of Minnesota Press.

Margulis, Lynn and Dorion Sagan 2003. *Acquiring Genomes: A Theory of the Origin of Species,* New York: Basic Books.

Nayar, Pramod K. 2007. "The New Monstrous: Digital Bodies, Genomic Arts and Aesthetics." *Nebula,* 4.2: 1–19.

Nayar, Pramod K. 2013. *Posthumanism.* Cambridge: Polity.

Parker-Starbuck, Jennifer. 2014. *Cyborg Theatre: Corporeal/Technological Intersections in Multimedia Performance.* New York: Palgrave Macmillan.

Pradeu, Thomas and Edgardo D. Carosella. 2010. *L'Identité: La Part de l'Autre.* Paris: Odile Jacob.

Stelarc. 1999. "Exoskeleton." http://stelarc.org/?catID=20227

Stelarc. 2007. "Third Ear." http://stelarc.org/?catID=20242

*Cross references*

"**Becoming *Kinocognophore***" by Bucher, Zeeb, with Cheng; "**Cybernetics**" and "**Performance in the digital age**" by Auslander; "**New Media Art**" by Cicchini; "**Performing surveillance camera art**" by Nayar; "**Prosthetic performance**" by Gass.

## Becoming *Kinocognophore*

Claudia Bucher and Yvonne Zeeb, with Meiling Cheng

*Prologue by a third observer, alias Meiling Cheng:*

Claudia Bucher's art thrives in the fluid intersection between body art, endurance art, sculpture, installation, technologic and ecological art. From enacting a make-believe cyborg to inventing an artificial transorganism, Bucher ventures into the realm of extended sentience with a conceptual sophistication complemented by her ability to fabricate formally elegant structures. Her performance-installation pieces often meld together narrative threads, embodied durational actions, with a sculptural environment. Bucher engages with the artist's role as, in her own coinage, a "scientartist," "an inventor, thinker, philosopher, activist, vision-quester."

The following excerpt documents a performative scientartist's installation, *Ecosystem #3* (2003), first exhibited in Track 16 Gallery in Santa Monica, California. Bucher transformed part of the gallery space into a habitat centrally occupied by a hanging structure. A network of tubes, transparent sacs, and suspended objects in an assortment of glass containers constituted the hanging structure, which was visually and systematically connected to three larger glass containers placed on a shelf hung close to the ground, suggesting a circulatory system in a crescent form, slanting from skyward to earthbound. Through her journal entries, Bucher reflects on the making of her *Ecosystem #3* and her ideas about the bio-ecological equivalence between her own body as a life form, other life forms contained within her synthetic life-sustaining architecture, and the artificial environment that she created as their joint ecosystem.

The excerpt itself is part of Bucher's massive intermedial project, *Kinocognophore* (2003-04), which included a sculptural installation first exhibited in the Art Center College of Design in Pasadena, California, and a fake scientific document entitled "Systems Poetics of a Physiological Imaginary as Applied to *Kinocognophore*" (2003), supposedly authored by Yvonne Zeeb, the Director of CTCI (the Center for Transcognitive Imaging). "*Kinocognophore*"–denoting

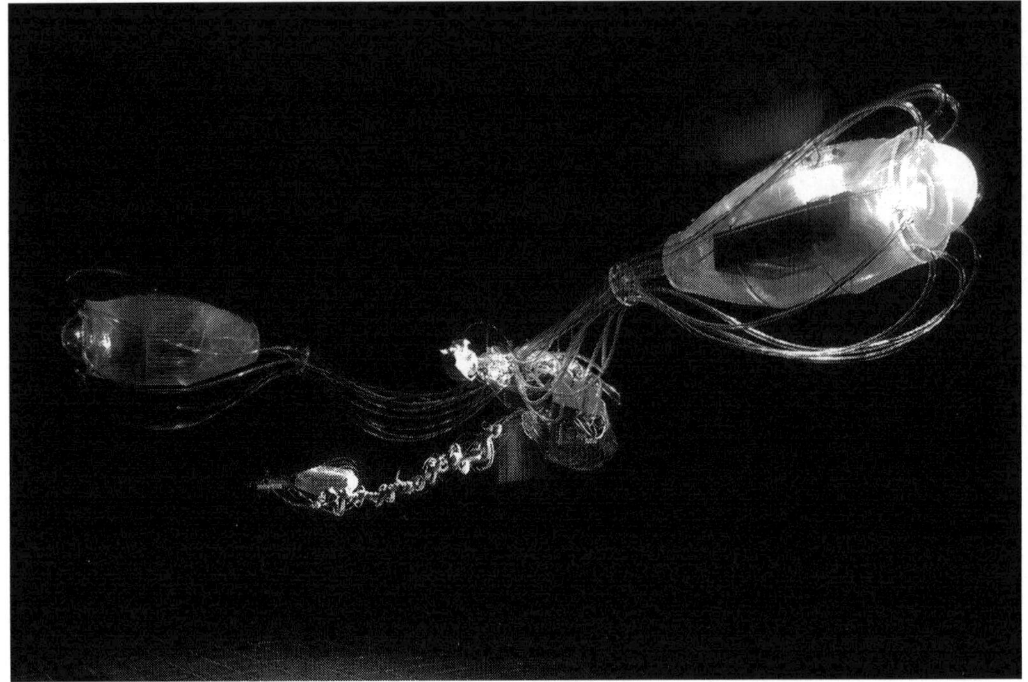

**Figure 35** *Kinocognophore* (2003). Photo by Joshua White. Image courtesy of the artist.

"a maker of cognitive images through cinematic means"—looks like a hybrid between a fiber-optic sea creature and a flying tripod, with a luminous ribbon of vertebrae supporting three heads, each a translucent sac that encloses a functioning cinematic projector. Just as *Kinocognophore* is a simulated artificial life form, so Yvonne Zeeb is Claudia Bucher's unacknowledged double, an alter ego constructed to critique Bucher's performative artwork from a neuro-cognitive perspective and to report on Bucher's eventual disappearance, as the scientartist allegedly became merged with her creation, *Kinocognophore*.

The selected journal entries and analytical treatise showcase the narrative parade of two personas: the scientartist Bucher, speculating on *Ecosystem #3*, her final performative experiment leading to *Kinocognophore*; and the transcognitive investigator Zeeb, commenting on her theory of the fusion between species, as envisioned in *Ecosystem #3*, to prepare for her startling "discovery" that Bucher has disappeared into—and become *Kinocognophore*.

A modified excerpt from "Systems Poetics," by Yvonne Zeeb, Director, CTCI.

The scientartist writes in her journal:

*March 2003*

I have to write about the desire to change form. I want to be an antiseptic corpse in an antiseptic body bag. I am thinking about all the corpses being produced in Iraq. Bright lights on clear vinyl, green, white and red fluid. My conversion system will be beautiful. My body/ my corpse will exist as bio-matter *in potentia*.

*April 2003*

Ecosystem #3 presents a suspended system of exchange. My body is contained within a clear vinyl biomorphic package that is suspended from the ceiling. Parallel to me is a succulent, a jade plant, also suspended in its own vinyl package. We are connected by tubing and are both leaking fluid. There are other components to the system that are also organic items

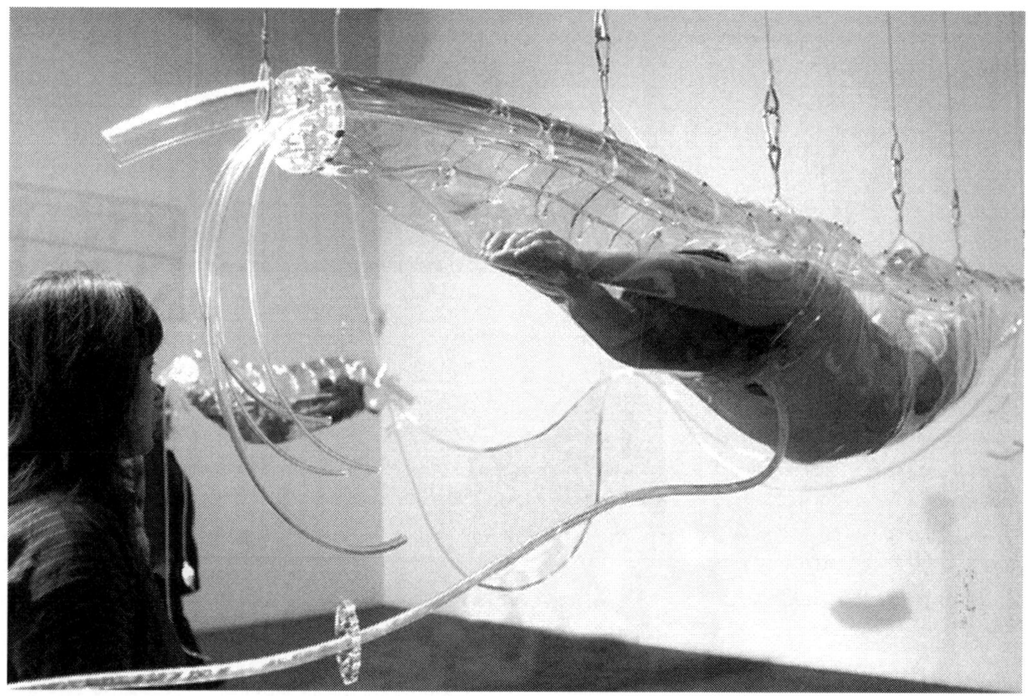

**Figure 36** *Ecosystem #3* (2003). Photo by Stephanie Allespach. Image courtesy of the artist.

contained within machine-cut plexiglass containers. The vinyl/plexiglass system is professionally made, carefully fabricated with machinic precision. The reference to medical/scientific packaging standards signifies the mastery of technology. The sculptural system materially represents the mastery of the human. However, what the system is presenting within its contents is saying something else about the human. In this antiseptic system, both plant and I are on a level playing field and we are both uprooted from our usual vertical orientation. We are both in suspended animation, oriented horizontally, disoriented by gravity. We have been taken out of our usual functioning context and placed in a system that could be devouring us by reducing our value to simple exchangeable metabolic material. This is representative of the collapse of species boundaries as implied by transgenic technologies.

Besides positioning two organisms on a parallel plane to create an equation of symbiosis of value, a positioning of secretions/fluids is also presented as a gauge for potential energy within the system. Suspended at a slightly lower level in front of me—as sac—is a shelf with three containers. The middle container collects my saliva as it drips down a tube coming from the sac. This container is flanked by two other containers of primary fluids, one that holds water, which is in the process of sustaining a plant, and one that holds automatic transmission fluid, which is in the process of floating a desiccated toad within a vitrinal flask.

The fluids function indexically and metaphorically; indexically in terms of the type of energy they represent, and metaphorically as a reiteration of the same leveling of types—here a leveling of the "organic" with the "machinic". In this case water is representing the organic and transmission fluid is representing the machinic, with saliva as somewhere in between.

However, transmission fluid is also fundamentally organic as a petroleum distillate, coming from the "blood of the earth", the residue of carbon-based physiological decay. Petroleum is a secretion produced by decay, which yet contains abundant potential energy. Saliva functions as a transmission fluid to the digestive process; it is an active agent of defense; and it facilitates speech. Its presence implies an energetic system as an origin.

*CTCI commentary*

*Ecosystem #3* was the last performative modeling experiment that the scientartist conducted before becoming *Kinocognophore*. With this investigation, we see an obvious trajectory beginning with *Ecosystem #1*, as *Ecosystem #3* takes the prior two investigations to their logical conclusion. *Ecosystem #3* presents the scientartist immobilized and suspended in a conversion sac parallel to a jade plant also suspended in a conversion sac. Both are secreting fluid, saliva and sap, into an interconnected system of tubes. As complimentary manifestations of a process of vital disruption or transformation, these two oozing sacs are bound by the same performative operation, functioning within a suspended system of display that subordinates everything to the equalizing language of exchange. In this equation of exchange, both organisms are yet cognitively separate individuals, but they are positioned within system parameters that will induce a becoming other within each of them. Each will hold within itself a metabolic image of the other, which will generate cognitive reverberations of empathic analysis. It is this cognitive condition that allowed the scientartist to become *Kinocognophore*.

*Ecosystem #3* also continued the investigation into the cybernetic concept of the self and the continuum between the natural and the synthetic, the machinic and the organic. Equalizing physiological exchange and horizontal transfer set the conditions for a redesign via symbiogenesis. "Metabolic dialogue and physical proximity led to incorporation, accommodation, and rearrangement" (Margulis and Sagan 2002, 97). Along this continuum that encompasses the relational mechanism of organisms, we must move from proximity to dialogue, to alliance, before reaching fusion. In an alliance, organisms are still separate, yet are on the verge of interdependence. The French philosophers Deleuze and Guattari cite the relationship between orchids with wasp-like markings and their pollen bearing wasps as an example of "the kind of unlikely alliance which can be struck in becomings" (Baker 2000, 126).

At this point in the continuum, the dynamic of exchange does not produce a merged hybrid but exists as a "creative alliance." *Ecosystem #3* enacts the dynamic of equalizing exchange and proximity between organisms that will lead to a "creative alliance." Colonial jellies, an organism that *Kinocognophore* is modeled on, are super-organisms. They are the emergent form generated by alliances that have moved towards fusion. As the artist Stelarc has said in regards to his own body extension experiments: "Only through a radical redesign of the body will we succeed in having significantly different thoughts and philosophies [...] Being human means being constantly redefined" (cited in Miglietti 2003, 194).

References

Baker, Steve. 2000. *The Postmodern Animal*. London: Reaktion.

Margulis, Lynn and Dorion Sagan. 2002. *Acquiring Genomes*. Reprint, New York: Basic, 2003.

Miglietti, Francesca Alfano. 2003. *Extreme Bodies: The Use and Abuse of the Body in Art*. Translated by Antony Shugaar. Milan: Skira.

## Puppet and object performance

John Bell

Puppets, defined by Paul McPharlin as "theatrical figure[s] moved under human control" (1949, 1), are global representatives of one of the most ancient human urges: to tell stories, entertain, and perform ritual actions by manipulating elements of the material world. They are part of a wide range of performing objects, defined by ethnologist Frank Proschan as "material images of humans, animals, or spirits that are created, displayed, or manipulated in narrative or dramatic performance" (1983, 4). The various forms of traditional puppetry differ according to the size of the figures and the techniques used to manipulate them, and include hand puppets, rod puppets, marionettes, shadow puppets, and giant puppets.

Most societies in global cultural history have nurtured one or more puppet or performing object traditions, usually with religious and ritual origins. Instead of the mutual focus of performers and audience on each other, object performance depends on the focus of both performers and audience on the dead matter of the material world being manipulated. Because puppet, mask, and object performances temporarily grant "life" to dead matter, they are often connected with religious beliefs and ritual, and puppeteers and other object performers have often been considered shamans.

Although puppet and object performance has been considered a central element of many Asian, African, and Native American cultures, modern culture in 16th- and 17th-century Europe began to consider performing objects as remnants of pagan and primitive societies, separate from high culture. In the latter part of the 19th century, this situation was augmented by the western concept that puppetry was particularly, if not solely, suited to children's entertainment and education. Moreover, the 19th-century invention of anthropology and folklore provided Europeans a scientific means of understanding the Asian, American, and African cultures (and some aspects of traditional European performance) that they considered primitive. As a result, these two disciplines provided the first in-depth western research into puppet, mask, and performing object forms.

But alternative performance trends existed in Europe as well. At the end of the 18th century, European artists connected with Romanticism (such as Kleist and Goethe) initiated a series of rediscoveries of puppets, masks, and performing objects that has continued to the present. The romantics saw puppets and masks as powerful embodiments of anti-rational forces, and thus inspiration for their embrace of nature and rejection of Enlightenment aims. At the end of the nineteenth century the symbolist movement, including playwrights Alfred Jarry and Maurice Maeterlinck, seized on puppets and masks as essential elements of symbolism, and proposed them as techniques for modern performance. The avant-garde performance movements of the twentieth century—including Futurism, Expressionism, Constructivism, the Bauhaus, Dada and Surrealism—all routinely used puppets, masks, and objects, taking inspiration from global traditions as well as a modernist sense of the importance of machines and manufactured objects.

Machines constitute a particular aspect of object performance. The earliest mechanical efforts of Hero of Alexandria (1st century CE) and Ibn al-Jazari (12th century) were directed towards the spectacular performance of religious rites as well as such important tasks as time-keeping, and incorporated mechanical representations of humans or animals, also known as automata. Such medieval mechanical inventions as clockworks routinely included automata as important aspects of their performance, a development that affected the growth of *karakuri-ningyo* performing machines in Japan by the 17th century. In the 19th century, the proliferation of new and increasingly sophisticated technologies for manufacture, construction, and performance led to cultural suspicions of technology and the invention of the term robot (which first appears in Karel Čapek's 1920 play *R.U.R.*) as a human-engineered figure capable of becoming autonomous. The late 20th-century appearance of information art continued the development of the performance possibilities of technology into the age of digital culture.

Beginning in the early 20th century, other disciplines joined folklore and anthropology in the study of objects as cultural performers. Psychologists Ernst Jentsch (1906) and Sigmund Freud (1919) considered the nature of performing objects to be "uncanny", a concept that re-invested objects with some of the mystery they hold in non-modern societies. Beginning in the 1920s, philosopher Martin Heidegger's studies of phenomenology focused particularly on the nature of "things" and the material world. At the same time, significant aspects of semiotic studies (especially from the Prague Linguistic School) advanced the functional analysis of puppet and object performance as sign systems. In 1971, D.W.

Winnicott's study of transitional objects provided another psychoanalytical perspective into the field in terms of childhood development. The development of material culture studies in the late 20th century has also offered critical perspectives on the importance of objects in culture; the same is true of object-oriented ontology, an early 21st-century continuation of Heidegger's phenomenology studies; and Actor-Network Theory, which considers the social significance of objects as well as humans. All of these recent analyses of the cultural meaning of objects—often in performance contexts—can offer useful insights into the nature of puppet and object performance.

Puppets and objects easily adapted to film, television, and digital media, and by the late twentieth century flourished in advertising, children's programming, and blockbuster films, merging into new technologies of special effects and computer-generated imagery. At the same time, performance innovators such as Peter Schumann, Jim Henson, and Julie Taymor combined the influences of global puppet and masks traditions to invent contemporary forms of live performance that reached back to puppetry's ritual, religious, and political roots.

### *Further reading*

Bell (2001, 2008); Blumenthal (2005).

### *References*


Bell, John, ed. 2001. *Puppets, Masks and Performing Objects*. Cambridge: MIT Press.

Bell, John. 2008. *American Puppet Modernism*. New York: Palgrave Macmillan.

Blumenthal, Eileen. 2005. *Puppetry: A World History*. New York: Abrams.

Freud, Sigmund. 1919. *The Uncanny.* Translated by David McLintock. Reprint, London: Penguin Books Ltd, 2003.

Jentsch, Ernst. 1906. *On the Psychology of the Uncanny*. Translated by Roy Sellars. doi: http://www.art3idea.psu.edu/locus/Jentsch_uncanny.pdf

McPharlin, Paul. 1949. *The Puppet Theatre in America, a History; With a List of Puppeteers, 1524–1948*. New York: Harper.

Proschan, Frank. 1983. *Puppets, Masks, and Performing Objets from Semiotic Perspectives.* Berlin: Mouton.

Winnicott, D.W. 1971. "Transitional Objects and Transitional Phenomena." In *Playing and Reality*. London: Tavistock Publications.


### *Cross references*

"**Animal Studies**" by Chaudhuri; "**Celebrity**" by Nayar; "**Circus**" by Tait; "**Destruction art**" by Stiles; "**Dramaturgy**" by Jannarone; "**Intermediality**" by Auslander; "**Readymade**" by Hoefer; "**Scenography**" by Smith.

## Racialization

Mike Sell

The dynamic, historically persistent, and regionally diverse relationship between performance and race is marked by paradox and irony. In the United States, the abolition of slavery in 1865 was followed by the emergence of a system of legal and cultural rules to govern the interaction of whites and blacks. Named after a song-and-dance hit on the blackface minstrelsy circuit, "Jim Crow" was especially attentive to public contact zones: theatres, restaurants, drinking fountains, grocery stores, bathrooms, swimming pools, public transportation, and the like. Rosa Parks and other anti-racist activists of the 1950s and 1960s broke these rules governing the performance of everyday life and catalyzed a broader movement against Jim Crow. However, recognition of the performative nature of race in the U.S., especially the performance of whiteness, has not resolved questions of ownership, authenticity, and propriety, as evidenced by the scandal caused by the Wooster Group's 1992 production of Eugene O'Neill's *Emperor Jones*, which featured performer Kate Valk in blackface, and by white actor Ted Danson's blackface performance at a Friar's Club roast in 1993, despite it being at the request of his friend, African-American comic Whoopi Goldberg. Recent studies of blackface show that such performance-based stereotypes provide a compelling, robust, yet perverse medium for the articulation of identity and nation (Lane 2005; Lott 1995).

Another example of race's ambivalent relationship with performance is the tradition of bohemianism. In the 1820s, a neighborhood in Paris developed a veritable counterculture. Marginalized by the French political, economic, and cultural systems, residents embraced the figurative identity of the "gypsy" ("bohemien"). A form of ethnic drag, bohemianism is an appropriation of certain, demonstrably stereotypical, aspects of Sinti (the term preferred to "gypsy") culture. Bohemian identity enabled culturally active urban subalterns to live with a sense of authenticity. It also promoted the identification, invention, and exploitation of cultural power through acts of public performance. "Bohemian" life is flamboyant life; "bohemians" rebel through dress, public acts of petty rebellion, and vociferous and highly visible presence at public art events (Sell 2007). Bohemians regularly transgress color lines, apparent among the negrophiles of the New Negro and Beat movements, and the multicultural hip-hop community.

In recent years, the concept of "strategic essentialism" has been devised to assess the performative ironies of race. Coined by theorist Gayatri Chakravorty Spivak (1995) and developed by queer and feminist artists, activists, and academics, strategic essentialism is a strategy of identity politics available to those disempowered and demeaned by stereotypes. Accepting the identity foisted upon one can provide useful forms of group identity, historical recovery, and cultural creativity, while also providing concrete opportunities for critique of that identity. However, it can also lead to new forms of essentialism such as "cultural racism," in which the specific experiences of a racialized group justify actions that demean and victimize others.

The desire to assess and engage the performative dimensions of racialized identity has prompted the rise of post-racial notions such as ethnicity, border performance, hybridity, and intercultural performance which, while emphasizing commonalities among group members, also account for differences in language, religious practice, cuisine, and so on. Still, racialized prejudices have not disappeared, as Guillermo Gómez-Peña and Coco Fusco discovered in 1992 when they performed the role of "undiscovered Amerindians" on display in a cage for museum visitors across Europe and the Americas. Reaction by audiences, museum personnel, and critics to their performances suggests, as Fusco puts it, "the desire to look upon predictable forms of Otherness from a safe distance persists" (Fusco 1995, 50).

### *Further reading*

Lott (1995); Sell (2007); Sieg (2002).

### *References*

Fusco, Coco. 1995. "The Other History of Intercultural Performance." In *English Is Broken Here: Notes on Cultural Fusion in the Americas.* New York: New Press.

Lane, Jill. 2005. *Blackface Cuba 1840–1895.* Philadelphia, NJ: University of Pennsylvania.

Lott, Eric. 1995. *Love and Theft: Blackface Minstrelsy and the American Working Class.* New York: Oxford University Press.

Sell, Mike. 2007. "Bohemianism, the 'Cultural Turn' of the Avant-Garde, and Forgetting the Roma." *TDR: The Drama Review*, 51.2: 41–59.

Sieg, Katrin. 2002. *Ethnic Drag: Performing Race, Nation, Sexuality in West Germany.* Ann Arbor, MA: University of Michigan Press.

Spivak, Gayatri. 1995. "Subaltern Studies: Deconstructing Historiography." In *The Spivak Reader: Selected Works of Gayatri Spivak*, edited by Donna Landry and Gerald MacLean. New York and London: Routledge.

### *Cross references*

"**The d/Deaf Performative**" by Pendgraft; "**Ethnic drag**" by Herrera; "**Hybridity**" by Mee;

"**Identity politics**" by Adewunmi; "**Postcolonial performance inquiry**" by Chatterjee; "**Sampling**" by Hodges Persley; "**Whiteness**" by Jones.

## Readymade

Rolf Hoefer

Marcel Duchamp (1887–1968) coined the term "readymade" in 1915 (see Stiles and Selz 1996, 819–820) as a concept celebrating a non-retinal, cerebral art at the service of the mind and ideas rather than for visual aesthetics. The necessary, sufficient, and tautological condition for a readymade artwork is that an artist *chooses* an object "already made" and *designates* it as art.

As Duchamp claimed, in his own practice, he typically chose on the basis of "visual indifference" to designate common, mass-produced industrial objects, such as shovels and urinals, as readymades. *Bicycle Wheel* (1913) was Duchamp's first "assisted" readymade—the wheel was overturned and mounted on a kitchen stool; hence, "altered," or "assisted" by the artist. *Bottle Rack* (1914) followed as his first "unassisted"—found and unaltered—readymade. Thereafter, Duchamp chose his readymade items and created their conceptual multivalence by "assisting" them with suggestive titles, slight physical or graphical alterations, and the relocation from mundane to artistic contexts (e.g. *Fountain*, 1917). The readymade allowed Duchamp to transgress the conventional criteria for art as a visually beautiful object, physically crafted by an artist who has masterful control over the artwork. His approach to art expanded art's established institutional boundaries and provided the conceptual wellspring for much of the twentieth-century avant-garde.

Duchamp's concept of readymade manages to relocate artists' practices and concerns from material to conceptual performance spaces. In this light, his series of readymades presents a methodology that foregrounds the artist's ideas. He reversed the conventional dominance of material appearance over conception in art by discarding—often humorously—preoccupations about retinal artworks. After Duchamp, as Joseph Kosuth argues, "art changed its focus from the form of the language to what was being said. Which means that it changed the nature of art from a question of morphology to a question of function" (1969, 164). The tension between these two questions is also evident in Duchamp's humorous rendition of a reciprocal readymade: "Use a Rembrandt as an ironing board!" (1961, 47). Taken to its extreme, the argument feeds into minimalism (e.g. see Sol LeWitt's work), conceptual art (e.g. see Joseph Kosuth's work), and contemporary performance art (e.g. see Meiling Cheng, *Beijing Xingwei*)—much of these later art genres attempt to minimize the gap between the idea that produces a "readymade" artwork and its material manifestation that becomes conceptually consumed during the exhibition process.

Aside from reformulating an ontological basis for art, the readymade as an enabling methodological device has inspired many influential artists and movements. By employing elements of everyday life, Duchamp's readymades transgressed the traditional separation between art and life à la anti-art, while encouraging subsequent artists to use all kinds of common materials for art. Thus, for example, Jasper Johns painted iconic objects (e.g. *Flag*, 1958), Andy Warhol iconic people (e.g. *Marilyn Diptych*, 1962), and Yves Klein the idea of painting (e.g. *IKB 191*, 1962). While these artists appropriated everyday concepts and images as artistically deployable "common materials," participants in art movements like Happenings and Fluxus appropriated readymade events and actions to compose their performance scores. Yet other artists appeared to both appropriate and subvert the concept of readymade by turning it into painterly techniques, such as the collages, assemblages, and photomontages developed by the Dadaists and Surrealists, or the well-known combines created by Robert Rauschenberg (e.g. *Monogram*, 1955).

As Duchamp elaborated later, readymades also implicate the audience member as a performer in the completion of a creative act, because an audience member cannot but "decipher and interpret" an artwork to co-create its meaning (see Stiles and Selz 1996, 818–819). John Cage, for example, reconceptualized music beyond mere notated sounds to include everyday sounds, even those randomly made by the audience (e.g. *4'33"*, 1952). Cage was less concerned with choosing any particular or beautiful sounds—his readymade sounds were chosen based on a certain "auditory indifference"—than with the audience's active participation in listening to music as "something to hear" (see Cage 1957). Applying the readymade to the work of Gertrude Stein, we can understand her "verbal indifference" in books like *Tender Buttons* (1914) as inviting the reader to complete the artwork by deciphering and interpreting its grammar-less text (see Perloff, 1996). The readymade thus enables not only the performance of artists, but also those of audiences in completing the creative act.

In sum, the readymade moves attention from technical execution to conceptual creation, from the material art object to its symbolic framing, from intentionality to chance, from originality to replication, and from the audience's passive aesthetic absorption to its active conceptual performance. At its core, the readymade has opened up new creative paths for artists; only the limit of an artist's imagination bounds its potential new uses and functions—still, please don't plagiarize this (readymade) entry for "artistic" purposes!

*Further reading*

Duchamp (1917); Goldsmith (1983); Nesbit (1986).

*References*

Cage, John. 1957. "Experimental Music." Lecture, Convention of the Music Teachers National Association. Chicago, IL.

Duchamp, Marcel. 1917. "The Richard Mutt Case." In *The Blind Man*, 2: 5. Reprinted in *Theories and Documents of Contemporary Art: A Sourcebook of Artists' Writings*, edited by Kristine Stiles and Peter Selz, 35: 817–818. Berkeley and Los Angeles: University of California Press, 1996.

Goldsmith, Steven. 1983. "The Readymades of Marcel Duchamp: The Ambiguities of an Aesthetic Revolution." *The Journal of Aesthetics and Art Criticism*, 42.2: 197–208.

Kosuth, Joseph. 1969. "Art after Philosophy [Part I]," *Studio International*, 178.915: 134–137. Reprinted in *Conceptual art: A critical anthology*, edited by Alexander Alberro and Blake Stimson, 158–170. Cambridge, MA: MIT Press, 1999.

Nesbit, Molly. 1986. "Ready-Made Originals: The Duchamp Model." *October*, 37: 53–64.

Perloff, Marjorie. 1996. "Of Objects and Readymades: Gertrude Stein and Marcel Duchamp." *Forum for Modern Language Studies*, Vol. XXXII.2: 137–154.

Stein, Gertrude. 1914. *Tender Buttons.* New York: Bartleby.

Stiles, Kristine and Peter Selz, eds. 1996. *Theories and Documents of Contemporary Art: A Sourcebook of Artists' Writings.* Berkeley, CA: University of California Press.

*Cross references*

"**Appropriation**" by Wong; "**Bodies in action**" by Stiles and O'Dell; "**Cindy Sherman's Real Fakery**" by Schneider; "**Experimental music**" by Henkes; "**Fluxus**" by Stiles; "**Installation art**" by Haidu; "**Minimalism**" by Lepecki; "**Multicentricity**" by Cheng; "**Photography and performance**" by Auslander; "**Proxemics**" by Cody.

## Rhetoric

Elise Morrison

In *Gorgias*, Plato framed rhetoric as a manipulative tool of oration and productive of "false belief," articulating a mistrust of the manipulative power of performers and performance that Jonas Barish has called an historical anti-theatrical prejudice (1981). Responding to his mentor's anti-theatricality in both *Poetics* and in *Rhetoric*, Aristotle re-framed rhetoric not as a tool of falsity but as a broadly applicable strategy of communication; he thus defined rhetoric as the art of using or the faculty of observing all available means of persuasion to communicate effectively with a given audience. Throughout its vast history in the fields of politics, orature, linguistics, and philosophy, classical rhetoric has typically referred to the making and giving of speeches through persuasive techniques in oration. Theatre and performance, as art forms that strategically employ techniques of representation and oration to communicate with audiences, have likewise employed rhetorical strategies to build effective performances, while simultaneously withstanding historical anti-theatrical accusations of falsity and manipulation.

Performance scholars have taken these classical understandings and uses of rhetoric and applied them as an analytical framework to investigate the role of performance within a wide range of cultural productions, while problematizing the status of truth and falsity in performance. Indeed, rhetoric has become an overarching concept linking diverse performance studies projects, elucidating relationships between linguistic acts and identity formation, architecture and everyday behavior, rituals and socio-political structures, and various forms of media in theatrical performances. J.L. Austin's speech act theory has been a central concept in what Shannon Jackson has called "the integration of theatrical and oral/rhetorical traditions" in performance studies (Jackson 2004, 10). In *How to Do Things With Words* (1962), Austin described speech as performative, analyzing the ways in which language operates reflexively, producing the world it simultaneously describes. Performance scholars have accordingly examined the reflexive interplay of language within social and political structures, connecting the practice of everyday life to linguistic rhetorical strategies (see Anzaldúa 1995; Butler 1997; Conquergood 2002b; Jackson 2004; Ong 1988).

In *The Practice of Everyday Life* (1984), Michel de Certeau recast the concept of rhetoric from linguistic strategy to a semiotics of space in order to theorize the relationships between spatial configurations, the behavior of subjects, and their political environments. Following Austin, de Certeau describes "pedestrian speech acts ... whose bodies follow the thicks and thins of an urban 'text' they write without being able to read it" (1984, 93). The ways in which these "urban texts" and "pedestrian speech acts" remain through traditions, ritual, and cultural uses of space have been studied by Performance studies scholars to write ongoing social and political histories of spaces and places, read through the embodied rhetoric of performance (see Roach 1996, Taylor 1997).

Studies of ritual performances as well as formal theatrical performance likewise analyze rhetorical systems of communication and meaning from both linguistic and socio-spatial perspectives. Kenneth Burke, in *A Grammar of Motives* (1945), parses performance into analytical ratios between scene, act, and agent, describing strategic uses of the various modes of communication available within the "container" of a given performance. In *The Anthropology of Performance* (1987), Victor Turner analyzes the rhetoric of rituals in everyday life, defining performance as "a complex sequence of symbolic acts" (1987, 75). His "social drama analysis," posits "daily living as a kind of theater, [...] a dramaturgical language about the language of ordinary role-playing and status-maintenance which constitutes communication in the quotidian social process" (1987, 76). Similarly, Clifford Geertz' and Erving Goffman's anthropological studies of the structures of behavior and performance in everyday life investigate the human faculty for observing and utilizing codified tools of persuasion and communication through a legible repertoire of verbal and non-verbal actions (see Geertz 1973; Goffman 1959, 1974). Goffman's *Frame Analysis* (1974) describes cognitive frames that encompass formal as well as everyday performative situations and within which participants "play" by a set of commonly understood rules and signals. Gregory Bateson, in his related theorization of play and metacommunication, argues that within such a frame a rhetorical substitution can be applied, in which an animal's playful nip connotes a more serious bite, while not actually being the bite itself (see Bateson 1972).

Drawing upon many of these anthropological studies, Richard Schechner's *Performance Theory* (1988) analyzes rhetorical strategies used to build connections between audiences, performers, texts, and the temporal and spatial aspects of restored, artistic-composed, and everyday behaviors. He describes the rich interplay of rhetorical schemas involved in the various aspects of performance: "drama, script, theater, and performance ... enclose one another, overlap, interpenetrate, simultaneously and redundantly arousing and using every channel of communication" (Schechner 1988, 94). In his schematizations of a wide variety of performance genres Schechner emphasizes the "rules of the game," be they linguistic, spatial, temporal, or gestural, which must be understood by all participants. Similarly, Eugenio Barba and the International School of Theater Anthropology have investigated the universal communicability of codified means of expression in various performance forms, examining gestures and facial expressions for rhetorical stability across cultural divides (Barba 1991).

Performance scholars have also applied the concept of rhetoric in analyses of poses and gestures in live performance, installation, and photographic works. Craig Owens coined the phrase "rhetoric of the pose" in his essay "Posing" (1992) in order to explore strategies of desire in photography across genres of pornography, surveillance, and self-portraiture. Other scholars, such as Amelia Jones, Andrea Cote, Rebecca Schneider, and Peggy Phelan, have used the concept of the "rhetoric of the pose" to identify strategic gestural choices in the self-portraiture of female artists (such as Hannah Wilke, Cindy Sherman, and Nikki S. Lee), that reveal and challenge relationships and power dynamics between the viewer, artist, posed body, and the concomitant histories of culture and media.

### Further reading

Bateson (1972); Schechner (1988).

### References


Anzaldúa, Gloria. 1995. *Borderlands/La Frontera*, New York: Touchstone.

Barba, Eugenio. 1991. *Dictionary of Theatre Anthropology: The Secret Art of the Performer*. London: Routledge.

Barish, Jonas A. 1981. *The Antitheatrical Prejudice*. Berkeley, CA: University of California Press.

Bateson, Gregory. 1972. *Steps to an Ecology of Mind*. New York: Ballantine.

Butler, Judith. 1997. *On Performativity from a Post-Structuralist Perspective*. London: Routledge.

Burke, Kenneth. 1945. *A Grammar of Motives*. Berkeley, CA: University of California Press.

Conquergood, Dwight. 2002b. "Performance studies: Interventions and Radical Research." *TDR: The Drama Review*, 46.2: 145–153.

De Certeau, Michel. 1984. *The Practice of Everyday Life*. Berkeley, CA: University of California Press.

Geertz, Clifford. 1973. *The Interpretation of Cultures*. Reprint, New York: Basic Books, 2000.

Goffman, Erving. 1959. *The Presentation of Self in Everyday Life*. New York: Anchor.

Goffman, Erving. 1974. *Frame Analysis*. Cambridge, MA: Harvard University Press.

Jackson, Shannon. 2004. *Professing Performance: Theatre in the Academy from Philology to Performativity*. Cambridge: Cambridge University Press.

Ong, Walter J. 1988. *Orality and Literacy: The Technologizing of the Word. New Accents*. Ed. Terence Hawkes. New York: Methuen.

Owens, Craig. 1992. *Beyond Recognition: Representation, Power, and Culture*. Berkeley, CA: University of California Press.

Roach, Joseph. 1996. *Cities of the Dead: Circum-Atlantic Performance*. New York: Columbia University Press.

Schechner, Richard. 1988. *Performance Theory*. Revised edition. London and New York: Routledge.

Taylor, Diana. 1997. *Disappearing Acts: Spectacles of Gender and Nationalism in Argentina's "Dirty War."* Durham: Duke University Press.

Turner, Victor W. 1987. *The Anthropology of Performance.* New York: PAJ.

*Cross references*

"**Cindy Sherman's Real Fakery**" by Schneider; "**Explicit body performance**" by McGinley; "**Gestus**" by Bial; "**Performativity**" by Pendgraft; "**Performing body modifications**" by Henkes; "**Play**" by Schechner; "**Proxemics**" by Cody; "**Quotation**" by Garrett.

## Sampling

Nicole Hodges Persley

Sampling, the practice of identifying and borrowing particular parts of a song and using them to create a new work, has the most visibility in Hip Hop music, one of the earliest and most enduring examples of the practice. DJs and producers research sounds across genres, cultures, and national spaces to identify parts of music that can be used to create sonic collages that may have no connection at all to the original. Joseph Schloss' *Making Beats: The Art of Sample Based Hip-Hop* (2004) is one of the first studies to chronicle the artistic process of Hip Hop DJs and producers searching for recorded sounds to create new music. Schloss examines the artistic and ethical ramifications of artists borrowing from previous works and making claims of authenticity and originality. Joanna Demers' work on sampling in Hip Hop music undergirds sampling's possibilities of theatricality in her theorization of sampling as an act of lineage between different times and spaces, genres and consciousness (2003). Such musical borrowings are performatively connected to the identities of the artists and have the capacity to incite literal and abstract connections between the music sampled and the remixed original.

Nicole Hodges Persley adapts sonic sampling in Hip Hop as a methodological and theoretical heuristic to read performance practices of artists in theatre, conceptual art and dance in her dissertation, *Sampling and Remixing Blackness in Hip Hop Theater and Performance* (2010). Hodges Persley focuses on Hip Hop as a site that both authorizes and sanctions the cross-racial and interracial performance of blackness. Identifying performative codes of racial and ethnic identity such as language, styles of self-adornment and embodied gestures, Hodges Persley explores the manipulation of embodied texts that indicate racial identity, here blackness, by artists across racial lines to construct performances. Hodges Persley observes that diverse artists inspired by the sampling aesthetic in Hip Hop borrow and reconfigure codes of identity connected to race, ethnicity, class, sexuality and nation through performance. Embodied exchanges of theatricality are facilitated by the artist's embodied improvisations of sampling to enable both liberatory and transgressive performances of identity that often transcend lived experiences. Used as a "mean and mode" of theatricality (Davis and Postlewait 2003, 2), sampling can be adopted as a subversive methodological and theoretical tool of identity construction, negotiation and representation by performers in theatre and everyday that allows them the opportunity to manipulate the boundaries and limitations of existing categories of difference and essentialist notions of being. Such individual and collective reconfigurations highlight the theatricality of identity as an ongoing "production" that is never complete (Hall 1993).

Tracy C. Davis and Thomas Postlewait's recognition of theatricality as a fluid, multivalent term that connects performance aesthetics with everyday life performances (Davis and Postlewait 2003, 2) is an important observation to consider when imagining bodies as archival sites of reproduction. The communicative power of bodies and voices to be used as sources of memory and recall, storage and suppression, is at the core of sampling as a mode of theatricality. Hodges Persley further theorizes sampling as an act of historical manipulation and revision. Offering the work of Suzan-Lori Parks as an example literary sampling across time, genres and shifting racial experiences, Hodges Persley contends that Parks' manipulation of history and existing texts "spins back to the breaks in history in order to show the practices of suture and overlap in existing discourses of blackness" (Hodges Persley 2011, 68). Exploring linguistic acts of sampling in the work of rap artist Jay-Z, Hodges Persley (2010) notes the artist's capacity to borrow from disparate oratorical traditions following the practices of many African American artists "from slavery to the present, who sample from a wide range of oratorical, literary and theatrical devices in order to articulate their experiences as Africans in the Americas" (2011, 67).

Improvised strategies of self-fashioning are available across racial lines through the theatrical act of sampling, permitting artists to manipulate their bodies, voices and existing texts to construct remixes of subjectivity. When used as a theatrical device to create and produce subjectivity through acts of selection and disavowal, sampling finds synergy with what Shannon Jackson argues as theatricality's claim on "flexible essentialism" (2003, 189) in that it allows us to explore theatricality's close relationship to performativity of race, ethnicity, gender, and sexuality that can occur in performance. Richard Shur identifies such theatrical practices of sampling of language, styles of self-adornment and gesture in the work of solo performer Anna Deavere Smith: "by sampling the words of her interviewees and then reconstructing them into a layered and flowing text, Smith interrogates who owned the performative spaces that the theater offers" (Schur 2010, 63).

Sampling, as a mode of theatricality, can be understood as a performer's capacity to use the body, voice and other senses to identify, borrow, produce and reproduce sonic, oral, visual, literary, and embodied codes of identity that highlight and potentially distort the performer's and the spectator's conscious and sub-conscious identification of such codes to construct identities. Such acts of sampling and remixing potentially reinscribe and/or subvert the saliency of categories of difference through performance.

## Further reading

Davis and Postlewait (2003); Schur and Lovalerie (2009).

## References


Davis, Tracy C. and Thomas Postlewait, eds. 2003. *Theatricality*. Cambridge: Cambridge University Press.

Demers, Joanna. 2003. "Sampling the 1970s in Hip-hop." *Popular Music*, 22.1: 41–56.

Hall, Stuart. 1993. "Cultural Identity and Diaspora." In *Colonial Discourse and Post-Colonial Theory. A Reader*, edited by Patrick Williams and Laura Chrisman, 392–403. New York: Harvester Wheatsheaf.

Hodges Persley, Nicole. 2010. "Sampling and Remixing: Hip-hop and Parks's History Plays." In *Suzan-Lori Parks: Essays on the Plays and Other Works*, edited by Philip C. Kolin. Jefferson, NC: McFarland.

Hodges Persley, Nicole. 2011. "A Urban Singer of Tales: The Freestyle Remixing of an Afro-Homeric Oral Tradition." *Jay-Z: Essays on Hip Hop's Philosopher King*, edited by Julius Bailey. Jefferson, NC: McFarland.

Jackson, Shannon. 2003. "Theatricality's Proper Objects: Genealogies of Performance and Gender." *Theatricality*, edited by Tracy Davis and Tom Postlewait. Cambridge: Cambridge University Press.

Schur, Richard. 2010. *Parodies of Ownership: Hip-hop Aesthetics and Intellectual Property Law*. Ann Arbor, MI: University of Michigan Press.

Schur, Richard and Lovalerie King, eds. 2009. *African American Culture and Legal Discourse*. New York: Palgrave Macmillan.

Schloss, Joseph G. 2004. *Making Beats: The Art of Sample-based Hip-Hop*. Middletown, CT: Wesleyan University Press.


## Cross references

"**Appropriation**" by Wong; "**Experimental music**" by Henkes; "**Feminist hip-hop fusion**" by Hodges Persley; "**Grace notes: Meredith Monk's *Songs of Ascension***" by Marranca; "**Intercultural performance**" by Alker; "**Post-linearity**" by Bay-Cheng; "**Readymade**" by Hoefer; "**Transnationalism**" by Yang.

## Feminist hip-hop fusion

Nicole Hodges Persley

Fusion, the process of joining two or more things together to form a single entity, is an effect of sampling in hip-hop. For over forty years, hip-hop music has been both a U.S.-based and global site of identity formation where diverse cultural identities find themselves in states of "becoming" and "being" (Hall 1993). The mid-2000s marks the rise of a generation of female artists playing at the sonic and cultural edges of hip-hop culture. Artists such as Nikki Minaj, Santigold, Iggy Azalea, and M.I.A. use their performances to challenge the saliency of categories such as race, gender, sexuality and nation. Forging intersections with hip-hop, electronica, soul, R&B, punk, classical, and so-called "world" music, their work "belongs to the future as much as to the past [...] transcending place, time, history and culture" (Hall 1993, 394) and forms a base for a transnational hip-hop feminist praxis that can account for productive coalition possibilities enabled by transgressive border crossings.

These places of fusion between cultural identities performed by women artists engaged with hip-hop indicate where it connects to the edges of other cultures. By sampling from diverse sonic, embodied, and visual cultures, they imagine new cultural identity formations that exist at what Stuart Hall calls "the unstable points of identification, or suture" (1993, 226), which challenge fixed ideas of race, gender, sexuality and hip-hop. Their music and aesthetic style play at the edge where similarities and dissonances between sonic and embodied manifestations of cultural identity are allowed to co-exist within and across national boundaries. As hip-hop artists, their radical black feminist practices challenge hyper-masculinist, heteronormative, and misogynist discourses that have dominated this art form's popular history and vexed present. The artists discussed here suggest that fused ideological positionings are always at play, confronting preconceived notions about hip-hop and blackness. Using their bodies and voices to assert alternative identities, their musical fusions acknowledge cross-racial solidarity within black "Hip-hop feminist" (Morgan 1999) frameworks, as they "rethink transnational feminist frameworks by creating new spaces for political and intellectual initiatives beyond disciplinary borders, artistic/activist divides, and North/South dichotomies" (Swarr and Nagar 2010, 15). Such a transnational hip-hop feminist praxis acknowledges the creative and subversive intellectual labor of women in the United States and abroad who theorize through artistic praxis about hip-hop's past and future relationships to blackness, gender, and freedom. Highlighting hip-hop as a transnational matrix that is equally informed by black feminist work and by the misogynistic representations of black women within it, these artists ask us to reconsider intellectual divides and value systems that presume hip-hop as antithetical to feminist praxis.

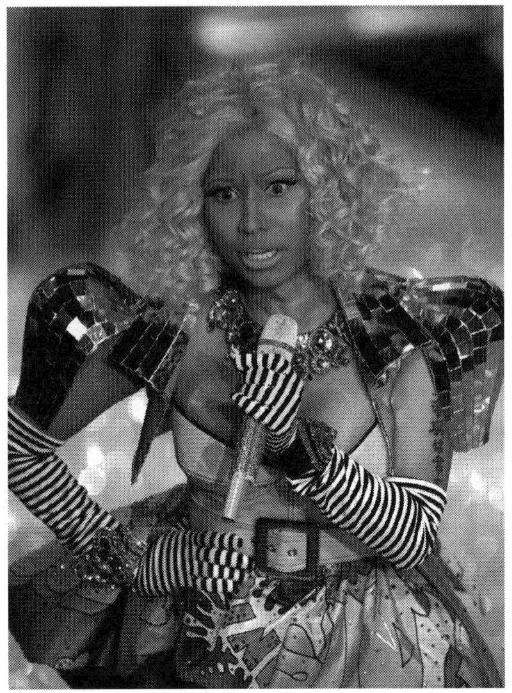

**Figure 37** Nicki Minaj performs on the runway during the 2011 Victoria's Secret Fashion Show at Lexington Avenue Armory on November 9, 2011 in New York City. Photo: Anton Oparin / Shutterstock.com © Anton Oparin.

Trinidadian-American Nikki Minaj challenges the conflation of blackness with African American culture as she deconstructs Eurocentric ideals of beauty by distorting them with African Diasporic perspectives. Using personal narratives of alterity, she addresses the advocates for LBGTQ youth and black women in hip-hop, using her body to show her audience where the edges of their perspectives connect. Minaj links music across time and genre to sample sounds from Stevie Wonder to Girl Talk. Alternating speaking in English, African American English, British Standard and Jamaican Patois, Minaj negotiates her blackness, sexuality, and femininity through a multiplicity of voices, embodying polyvocal notions of solidarity and paradox that transnational feminism promotes.

Likewise, Santigold, aka Santi White, is an African American artist who refuses any categorization except "pop music artist." Fusing ska, dub, hip-hop, electronica, rock and punk sounds, she sees herself as a "connector" between people (Ganz 2012). Santigold rejects most attempts to label her persona–racially, sexually, and/or musically. In a 2012 interview with *Spin* magazine, she contends, "I feel like I am pop, but I don't fit in this fucking formula, so nowadays, I don't know what I am" (Ganz 2012). Santigold destabilizes hip-hop by making the intersectional borders of its varied influences visible on her body. Her aesthetic styles and her music seek to unsettle assumptions of racial identity presupposing cultural identifications. Santigold's aesthetic has no center, just several circles intersecting. She refuses to pinpoint a style, wearing a broad range of fashions from deconstructed vintage clothing to skater chic. Her assertive approach to defining herself using terms that are outside of the discourse of race and nation is a subversive act. Her recent album cover for *Master of My Make-Believe (2012)* features the artist in a portrait painted by African American artist Kehinde Wiley. This cover marks the first time that the internationally recognized Wiley has ever painted a woman.

Iggy Azalea is a white rapper and former model from Australia. Raised in the New South Wales town of Mullumbimby, Azalea learned how to rap and to negotiate her feminist perspective through sonic engagements with African American MCs, namely Tupac Shakur. Though racially white, Azalea has immersed herself in African American culture. Her fluency in the cultural codes of U.S.-based expressions of blackness, (especially those of pro-woman female MCs), have earned her the title as the first woman to be named to *XXL's* freshman list. Azalea's overt sexuality and "hard core" verbal approach to hip-hop provide a disruptive contrast to her "supermodel" exterior. Her use of obscene language and braggadocio have earned her comparisons to provocative MCs such as Lil' Kim and MC Lyte. Azalea's feminist critique of U.S. class dynamics and popular stereotypes of "white" women in hip-hop with low-income trailer parks and female sexual promiscuity in her video *Work* (2013) attempts to unsettle fixed notions of white privilege and cultural practices as she makes visible the manual and sexual labor history shared by white and black women working to make it as lyricists in the hip-hop of industry. Azalea also raps in U.S.-based black vernacular in hip-hop to dislocate her racial and national identity into a liminal space of flux between the United States and Australia. Azalea asserts, "This is so weird that you're white, from another country, and you like black music. Why is it not weird for Keith Richards or Mick Jagger, but it's so weird and taboo for me?" (Harling 2013).

M.I.A., a U.K. rapper of Sri Lankan decent, began to rise to the top of the transnational hip-hop scene in 2005. Crossing time and geographic location, M.I.A.'s sonic and aesthetic mix fuses 1980s American and British pop culture references with African Diasporic shout-outs to 1990s Black Nationalist hip-hop. Remixing a swagger that owes as much to Indian culture as it does to 1970s African American television shows, M.I.A. creates transnational sonic collages that translate and connect the shared experiences of oppressed groups over time and across nations. Her 2013 song "The Message" critiques state policing of the Internet. This song constructs a performance that reveals the sonic and cultural dissonance that occurs when U.S.-based hip-hop inspired feminist agency is translated across borders to produce complimentary and contradictory sounds of chaos and order that resonate in transnational translation. *Time* magazine named M.I.A. one of the "World's Most Influential People" in 2009.

Hip-hop fusion artists such as Nikki Minaj, Santigold, Iggy Azalea, and M.I.A. choose transcultural approaches to art-making that disrupt static ideas of feminism, hip-hop, and blackness, refusing to limit their expression to stereotypical points of departure. These artists challenge the souvenir commodity culture of hip-hop by deconstructing stereotypical representations of feminist identity, blackness and nation to imagine new concentric identities. They use their art to question power and representation, forging new communities of solidarity.

### References

Ganz, Caryn. 2012. "Santigold's Killah Instinct," *Spin* (May-June) 58-62. Accessed June 16. 2015 http://www.spin.com/2012/05/santigolds-killah-instinct/

Hall, Stuart. 1993. "Cultural Identity and Diaspora." In *Colonial Discourse and Post-Colonial Theory. A Reader*, edited by Patrick Williams and Laura Chrisman, 392-403. New York: Harvester Wheatsheaf.

Harling, Danielle. 2013. "Iggy Azalea Defends her Status as a White Rapper." *Hip-Hop DX*, September 17. http://www.hiphopdx.com/index/news/id.25463/title.iggy- azalea- defends-her-status-as-a-white-rapper

Morgan, Joan. 1999. *When Chickenheads Come Home to Roost: My Life as a Hip-Hop Feminist*. New York: Simon & Schuster.

Swarr, Amanda and Richa Nagar. 2010. *Critical Transnational Feminist Praxis*. Albany, NY: SUNY Press.

## Semiotics/semiology

Timothy Scheie

Semiotics, sometimes called semiology, is the study of the organization, transmission, and reception of signs and signification. In semiotic analysis, a work of literary or artistic production understood as "the text" is approached as a network of signifying elements rather than as the direct reflection or expression of a truth or reality. More widely associated with the study of literature, semiotics has also found fertile ground for inquiry in, to use Roland Barthes's words, theatre's "density of signs" (1972, 25).

The origins of semiotics can be traced to the American philosopher Charles Sanders Peirce and the Swiss linguist Ferdinand de Saussure. However, it was the theorists of the Prague linguistic circle who, in the 1930s and 1940s, first analyzed how costumes, sets, lighting, props, stage directions, and acting styles signify richly in theatrical performance. Effectively unseating the dramatic text as the linchpin of meaning in theatre, the Prague theorists articulated the fundamental principle of *semiosis*: "all that is on stage is a sign" (Veltrusky 1964, 83–91). For example, a diamond ring off stage might signify wealth or marital engagement, but the validity of these meanings depends on the diamond's authenticity. On stage, a prop can signify "diamondness" and its connotations regardless of how obviously artificial or arbitrary the object-as-signifier may be, the signifying function within the production's system of meaning effectively eclipses the reality of the thing itself. The simplicity of this basic semiotic principle belies the Prague theorists' keen awareness of theatre's complex signifying functions. Their legacy is less a tidy method for explaining theatrical performance than the identification of conundrums that will vex later theorists: the non-arbitrary theatrical signifier, performance's ephemeral nature, the unsure distinction between intentional and non-intentional signification, and the performing body's singular resistance to semiosis.

During the 1960s and 1970s, semiotics rode the structuralist tide that swept through the humanities and social sciences. Identifying systems of meaning replaced the compounding of empirical data as the way towards a deeper understanding of a text, an epoch, psychology, or even the "human" itself. Borrowing heavily from linguistics and deploying dense scientific vocabulary, a new generation of semioticians charted the abstract codes that govern the profusion of meaning circulating on the stage. At their most ambitious, semiotic studies of this era ring with positivist optimism and suggest the possibility of an exhaustive semiotic account of the theatrical phenomenon.

Nevertheless, semiotics cuts a far narrower swath in theatre studies than in literary analysis. Semiotic inquiry frequently focuses on relatively conventional productions of dramatic texts, and has often been less attuned to avant-garde experimentation or broader conceptions of performance that radically depart from theatrical tradition. Some semioticians, including authors of magistral studies in the 1970s and 1980s, more recently concede the epistemological limits of semiotic analysis for theatre. Semioticians continue to pursue a post-structuralist semiotics in which the spectator navigates an open performance text, but they do so alongside other theorists who locate the powerful ontology of performance in what resists, exceeds, or undoes the codes and meanings that would contain it. When performance is understood as a crisis in signification that contests the theatrical medium itself, the charge of theatre semiotics invites reconsideration.

*Further reading*

Elam (1980); Matejka and Titunik (1976).

*References*

Barthes, Roland. 1972. "Baudelaire's Theater." In *Critical Essays*, trans. Richard Howard, 25–31. Evanston: Northwestern University Press.
Elam, Keir. 1980. *The Semiotics of Theater and Drama*. London: Routledge.
Matejka, Ladislav and Irwin R. Titunik, eds. 1976. *Semiotics of Art: Prague School Contributions*, Cambridge: MIT Press.
Veltruský, Ladislav. 1964. *Peněžní Oběh a úvěr v Kapitalistických Státech: Určeno Pro Posl. Fak. Polit. Ekonomie*. Prague: SPN.

*Cross references*

"**Bodies in action**" by Stiles and O'Dell; "**Double-coding**" and "**Gestus**" by Bial; "**Environmental Theatre**" by Alker; "**Minimalism**" by Lepecki; "**Mise-en-scène**" by Jannarone; "**Rhetoric**" by Morrison.

## Bodies in action

Kristine Stiles and Kathy O'Dell

Parsing the characteristic features of body art from other performance genres permits consideration of their syntactic roles within the history of performativity. While body art emerged in the 1960s as a unique genre, in 1918 Oskar Schlemmer had already identified "the new artistic medium [to be] the human body" (1972, 50), including "voice, gestures, and movements" (Gropius 1961, 22). In "Man in the Sphere of Ideas" (ca. 1928), Schlemmer described sensory perception as appropriate material for art: from "psychical impulses [to] the sensate, psycho-sexual mechanical," and the "dematerialized aspects of human reality" to the "laws" of the human organism that "reside in the invisible workings of his inner self [...] the heartbeat, circulation, respiration, the activities of the brain and nervous system" (Lehman and Richardson 1986, 15). Schlemmer's theories linked his goals to those of artists, who, for millennia, sought to animate inanimate objects and move art beyond mimesis to kinesis in order to better approximate the phenomenological conditions of the body and stimulate awareness of the noumenal–or the philosophically inexpressible, non-narrative, inchoate–emotions, moods, and thoughts of an artist. The five qualities of body art that follow suggest subtle distinctions between a performer executing a scored task or dialogue and a visual artist realizing a body action without a score or narrative.

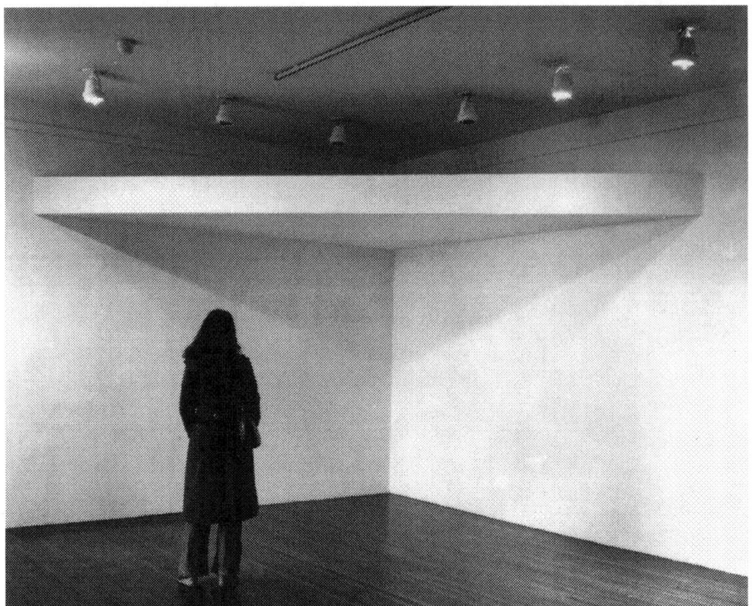

CHRIS BURDEN
White Light/White Heat, 1975

Ronald Feldman Fine Arts
New York
February 8-March 1, 1975

For my one-man show at Ronald Feldman, I requested that a large triangular platform be constructed in the southeast corner of the gallery. The platform was ten feet above the floor and two feet below the ceiling; the outer edge measured eighteen feet across. The size and height of the platform were determined by the requirement that I be able to lie flat without being visible from any point in the gallery. For twenty-two days, the duration of the show, I lay on the platform. During the entire piece, I did not eat, talk, or come down. I did not see anyone, and no one saw me.

CHRIS BURDEN STUDIO

**Figure 38** *White Light/White Heat* (1975) by Chris Burden. © Chris Burden. Courtesy Gagosian Gallery.

1: *Subject/object function*: Starting in the 1960s, artists created body art actions in an effort to remove material art objects from purely formal and commercial concerns, to immerse viewers in psychophysical, cognitive-intuitional dynamics, and transmute acts into corporeal events. Art-as-action amplified representation with presentation, making the body-as-subject an equally discrete object to be viewed. In this way, body art actions augmented the metaphorical capacity of visual art to include metonymical identification between acting and viewing subjects. While many artists could be cited for their body actions, in this short essay two actions by Chris Burden serve as examples. In *White Light/White Heat* (1975), Burden remained invisible on an elevated platform in the Ronald Feldman Gallery in New York for twenty-two days without coming down or interacting with the public. Although invisible, Burden's action identified the artist's body as the subject and the object of an interpersonal, proprioceptive encounter with viewers. This action transformed the public into subjects viewing the installation while imagining and sensing the artist's body. In this way, Burden's action invigorated the mediating interstice between subjects-as-subjects and subjects-as-objects in a manner comparable to the role of the "commissure." Derived from the Latin "commissural" (meaning to join together) and "committere" (connect, entrust, or give in trust), the term commissure defines the juncture of eyelids and of lips, and the band where the two hemispheres of the brain meet. While understood as a commissure, body action in art functions as a communicative modality joining artists with viewers. Distinguished from communion (exchange) and communitas (equality), the commissure (connection and commitment) enlivens awareness of intersubjective identification between subjects, and enhances comprehension of the significance, consequence, and potential of interaction in cultural and sociopolitical contexts.

2: *Noumenal and phenomenal aspects*: The presentation of body action in art emerged, in part, as an effort to convey the artist's noumenal, or inchoate states of mind–in conjunction with his or her phenomenal–or sensate and perceptual–corporeal experiences. By communicating through presence, body artists deployed their bodies as a medium of mediation between their own and a viewer's emotional and intellectual states. Emphasis on the communication of an artist's psychophysical experience in body art both impels viewers to consider the actual life experiences of an artist, specifically his/her biography, and galvanizes the interpersonal mechanisms of communication. This combination of forces cultivates commitment (intrinsic to "commissure") and the unspoken agreement (between a viewer and the artist) that is fundamental to body art actions.

3: *Contractual exchange*: To view a body action entails a tacit pact to watch, ponder, participate in, and respond to art as a durational event. The stakes rise when actions challenge physical and psychological limits, calling upon viewers to choose to stay, leave, or intervene. In *Doomed* (1975), at Chicago's Museum of Contemporary Art, Burden lay on his back under a 5' x 8' sheet of glass tilted against a wall, without having communicated his intentions to remain in this position until someone in the audience intervened. After almost four days, museum employee Dennis O'Shea, concerned for the artist's survival, placed a pitcher of water near the glass. Burden immediately rose, smashed the glass and the clock on the wall, ending the piece and marking his endurance of the work's duration: 45 hours and 10 minutes. In a manner that few other art forms do, body art evinces the contractual underpinnings of everyday life and how one negotiates when, or even whether, to take action in the interest of others.

4: *Documenation as proof*: Artists have documented the ephemeral practices of body art since its inception, understanding such records to be delimited by the temporal and material capacities of the medium (text, photography, video, audio). Body art actions, therefore, are known primarily through fragments–a photograph capturing a fraction of a second, hearsay, critics' analyses, or more extensive coverage that inevitably fails to represent a work's totality or complexity. Documentation may serve as a form of proof that underscores the legalistic contractual conditions of body actions, but can also dupe observers-and has often done so.

5: *Moral and ethical contingency of an artist's biography*: The conventions of mise-en-scène, according to Umberto Eco, establish the performative statement: "I am acting," and "[b]y this implicit statement the actor tells the truth since he announces that *from that moment on* he will lie" (1976, 115). "I am acting" allows viewers to suspend disbelief and participate in the narrative of the creative inventions of theatre and performance. Body art participates in this semiotic while turning it inside out. Using the verity of the artist's corporeal and psychical being as material, body art actions convey the truth of being in action.

## References

Eco, Umberto. 1976. "Semiotics of Theatrical Performance." *The Drama Review: TDR*, 21.1: 107–117.

Gropius, Walter. 1961. *The Theater of the Bauhaus*. Translated by Arthur S. Wensinger. Middletown, CT: Wesleyan University Press.

Lehmann, Hans-Theis and Brenda Richardson. 1986. *Oskar Schlemmer*. Baltimore, MA: Baltimore Museum of Art.

Schlemmer, Oskar. 1972. *The Letters and Diaries of Oskar Schlemmer*, edited by Tut Schlemmer and translated by Krishna Winston. Middletown, CT: Wesleyan University Press.

## Terrorism and performance

Jeanne Colleran

Barely a week after the September 11th attack on the World Trade Center, Karlheinz Stockhausen, the German composer, observed that "what happened there [...] is the biggest work of art there has ever been." Stockhausen's comments immediately ignited outrage even as he attempted to explain that he was referring to the creative destruction at work in epic confrontations. With distance, it is possible to understand that if a work of art is thought to be great because it has completely realized its ambition, producing an effect that spectators experience as unprecedented, singular, or life-changing, then Stockhausen's comments are less provocative. Understanding terrorism as a symbolic and performative act through which political power asserts itself provides a critical framework with which to approach a phenomenon that often has appeared to exceed civic discourse. Simply put: according to Brian Jenkins, author of *International Terrorism*, "Terrorism is theater" (1975, 4).

There is little agreement about an exact meaning of "terrorism," despite many efforts by the United Nations to produce an internationally acceptable definition. This lack of consensus reveals both the difficulty of determining who is a "legitimate combatant" and the reluctance of nations to posit an equivalence between state-sponsored and non-state-sponsored acts of violence. Ultimately, distinguishing a "freedom fighter" from a "terrorist" is a political rather than legal determination, but since 9/11, the term "terrorist" has become synonymous with Muslim enemies of the U.S. Thus emptied virtually of meaning, the word has been politically deployed both to assert Manichean distinctions and to denominate any political enemy or violent act. As Noam Chomsky points out, only crimes committed against the West are terrorist actions, "not our own comparable or worse ones" (2001, 119). Since the events of 9/11 have been portrayed as exceptional—without cause, without ground, without provocation—a myth of unprecedented injury has been perpetuated to justify all manners of self-defense against categorical evil, from curtailing constitutional rights to unlimited, unending warfare.

Terrorists leverage lesser political power against a greater one through a display of intended or already committed violence against victims of symbolic importance. Terrorism is, as Anthony Kubiak has described it, "an extreme, theatricalized violence that operates in what Roland Barthes would have termed 'the regime of the signifier'" (Kubiak 1991, 21). While this definition applies to any terrorist act, the advent of "media terrorism," has made it possible for anyone with cheap filming equipment and an envelope addressed to a news outlet to commit terrorism. In fact, terrorism may be differentiated from other criminal or war actions by its fundamental desire to attract publicity and amass a target audience; killing or torturing a victim is only a means to the primary goal of shocking those who are watching. The first time a terrorist act is broadcast, it immediately interrupts all other activity, assembling an audience that is *obliged* to watch by this tacit claim of importance and immediacy. When the actual violence of the terrorist act has been videotaped and replayed, act and artifact merge, producing a mixture of effects that may combine horror and skepticism, shock and de-sensitivity. The replication and dissemination may cause feelings of greater vulnerability or it may diminish the observer's sense of the real pain inflicted on an actual body, effectively upping the ante for the next provocative action.

Like minimalist theatre, terrorist acts are efficient, economical, and brief, employing strategies of appearance and disappearance, visibility and invisibility. As a spectacle, terrorism may be on a grand or small scale, but a terrorist act is essentially fragmentary, employing a strategic ambiguity to dissemble its power even as its produces fear about unpredictable replication. If, as Guy DeBord has observed, the spectacle is as an "instrument of unification" (1987: 3), terrorist spectacles serve to widen the gulf between antagonists, positing irreconcilable political and cultural differences. "What terrorism tends to be about," writes Anthony Kubiak, "is what theatre tends to be about: the means of circulating power and its currency as spectacle" (1991, 150).

A terrorist act inevitably provokes an equally theatrical political response, whether it is a full-dress pageant such as George Bush's "Mission Accomplished" speech on board the U.S.S. *Abraham Lincoln* in May, 2003 or a presidential address to Congress where "extras" such as ally Tony Blair or a Muslim first-time voter are called upon to support the male lead. While these speeches are commonly viewed as the usual partisan ploys, they are nonetheless consequential. As Diana Taylor has pointed out, Bush's speeches meet the conditions for "happy"—that is, successful—speech acts since they are uttered by someone in authority in an appropriate context. If theatricality is thought to be ephemeral, there should be no mistake about the actual lasting material and political consequences of these performances. Theatre artists respond by demystifying the political use of theatricality and by devising alternative performances meant to counter both terrorist spectacles and political performances.

### Further reading

Chomsky (2001); DeBord (2005); Jenkins (1975); Kubiak (1991).

### References


Chomsky, Noam. 2001. *9/11*. New York: Seven Stories Press.

DeBord, Guy and Alice Becker-Ho. 1987. *The Game of War*. Translated by Donald Nicholson-Smith. Reprint, London: Atlas Press, 2008.

DeBord, Guy. 2005 *The Society of Spectacle*. Translated by Ken Knabb. Oakland, CA: AK Press.

Jenkins, Brian M. 1975. *International Terrorism*. Los Angeles, CA: Crescent Publications.

Kubiak, Anthony. 1991. *Stages of Terror: Terrorism, Ideology, and Coercion as Theater History*. Bloomington, IN: Indiana University Press.


### Cross references

"**Ai Weiwei's transnational public spheres**" by Zheng; "**Audience**" by Cody; "**Global censorship**" by Shea; "**Happenings**" by Sandford; "**Media**" by Colleran; "**Sisters of Survival Signal S.O.S.**" by Gaulke; "**Surveillance**" by Morrison; "**War**" by Mike Sell.

## Theatre of images

Bonnie Marranca

The idea of a theatre of images grew out of a particular historical period of the 1970s in New York influenced by Happenings, Fluxus, mixed-media, painting and sculpture, Buddhism, the Judson Dance Theater, experimental film, and the compositional strategies of Merce Cunningham and John Cage. These numerous currents revolutionizing artistic process had been spreading throughout the experimental arts in the 1950s, 1960 and 1970ss, creating an "American" art in the post-war period. The contemporary arts in this era were also rooted in the heritage of the avant-garde between the wars, namely symbolism, dada, surrealism and the Bauhaus, as well as in Eastern thought, generating an approach to art making that intermingled high and popular culture, and American, European and Asian sources.

In 1977, in a volume entitled *The Theatre of Images*, Bonnie Marranca wrote about a new vision of theatre exemplified by specific works of Robert Wilson (*A Letter for Queen Victoria*), Richard Foreman (*Pandering to the Masses: A Misrepresentation*), and Lee Breuer (*The Red Horse Animation*). Her intention was both to explore the theatrical vocabulary for what was considered a radical change in American theatre and to develop new critical terms of analysis.

As outlined in Marranca's book, this theatre was characterized by a turn away from the play as the hierarchical element of theatre. On the contrary, theatre now moved toward the recognition that there were many more languages of the stage than the text, resulting in the integration of image-movement-design-poetry-music-technology. This theatre has sometimes been misread as anti-text, but that is not the case. Language plays an important role in these works, and it remains part of a larger field of theatrical elements. Likewise, in this historical period the development of imagery predates by several years the theatre's absorption in images through the use of digital media. In the theatre of images, the human figure still predominated, and the debates surrounding what constitutes "live" or "presence" did not yet exist. For the most part, the theatre of images was more concerned with the plane than the screen.

The new production values of the theatre of images embraced the integration of theatre and the visual arts, the development of imagery free of obvious psychological symbols, the use of sound as material and text as texture. Movement was tuned to the architecture of the theatre and the construction of space and time, in what was termed performance space rather than setting. In this highly formal approach to theatre, abstract performance styles replaced realistic acting, and experimental poetics and textual practices overrode dramatic literature. In its interdisciplinarity and intertextuality, art was understood as a language. This generation of artists began to work outside of conventional theatres, instead moving into galleries, museums and lofts. Visual artists, poets, filmmakers, musicians, dancers, and those interested in avant-garde values constituted the audiences in the "downtown" spaces where these performances took place.

The theatre of images vocabulary defined the stage picture and tableau as units of composition, framing the plastic qualities of performers through the articulation of space, a focus on process, and the dematerialization of the object. Other attributes manifested themselves as slowness, silence, flattening of the image and speech, and multiplicity of perspectives. One of the keys to this theatre was the audience interest in new modes of perception and consciousness.

Besides those featured in *The Theatre of Images* volume, several other artists created work in this period that could be considered under the concept, which freely crossed boundaries of theatre, dance, and performance art. They include Meredith Monk, Laurie Anderson, The Wooster Group, The Structuralist Workshop, and Stuart Sherman. Robert Wilson's *Einstein on the Beach*, Meredith Monk's *Quarry*, and Laurie Anderson's *United States*—all premiering in the 1970s—could be considered "classics" in this kind of theatre. Of artists working today, besides Robert Wilson, the Italian director Romeo Castellucci retains a link to the theatre of images in the fine art sensibility of his work.

### Further reading

Breuer (1979); Fairbrother (1991); Holmberg (1996).

### References

Breuer, Lee. 1979. *Animations: A Trilogy for Mabou Mines*. New York: Performing Arts Journal.

Fairbrother, Trevor. 1991. *Robert Wilson's Vision*. Boston, MA: Museum of Fine Arts.

Holmberg, Arthur. 1996. *The Theatre of Robert Wilson*, Cambridge: Cambridge University Press.

Marranca, Bonnie. 1977. *The Theatre of Images*. New York: Drama Book Specialists.

### Cross references

"**Cultural production**" by Colleran; "**Expanded cinema**" by Jarosi; "**Grace notes: Meredith Monk's Songs of Ascension**" by Marranca; "**Invisible theatre**" by Cody; "**Mediaturgy**" by Marranca; "**Romeo Castellucci's *Hey Girl!***" by Sack.

## Transcontextual

Charles R. Garoian and Yvonne M. Gaudelius

*Transcontextuality* is based on anthropologist Gregory Bateson's (1972) characterization of "ecology of mind," a way of thinking where disparate and disjunctive, impossible ideas and images interplay and enable epistemological shifts and links across contexts. Such thinking constitutes a critical form of consciousness capable of empathic stewardship among humans and biological others. Conversely, the loathing of such impossibility is made possible by inertia of mind, cognitive states yoked to reified and often fanatical assumptions that preclude differential possibilities for sustainability.

Insofar as assumptions are bound by familiarity, they represent an "explanatory world of *substance* [that] can invoke no differences and no ideas but only forces and impacts" (Bateson 1972, 271). As Bateson argues, contrary to the familiar, possible, and explainable, there exists a "world of *form* and communication [that] invokes no things, forces, impacts but only differences and ideas" (1972, 271). To characterize a differential ecology of mind, he turns to "double bind theory," which "asserts that there is an experiential component in the determination or etiology of schizophrenic symptoms and related behavioral patterns, such as humor, art, poetry, etc.," and that are indistinguishable (1972, 272). His metaphor of schizophrenia signifies a "genus of [non-pathological] syndromes," an ecology of mind that he refers to as "transcontextual."

> Both those whose life is enriched by transcontextual gifts and those who are impoverished by transcontextual confusions are alike in one respect: for them there is always or often a "double take." A falling leaf, the greeting of a friend, or a "primrose by the river's brim" is not "just that and nothing more." Exogenous experience may be framed in the contexts of dream, and internal thought may be projected into the contexts of the external world. And so on. For all this, we seek a partial explanation in learning and experience. (Bateson 1972, 272–273)

The disjunctions of impossible tasks and fragmented narratives of performance art create "double-take" responses, partial familiarities and explanations that lead us to our memories and cultural histories to interpret the performance. Such double-take responses occur, for example, when experiencing Tehching Hsieh's film *Time Piece* (1980–1981) of a yearlong performance. Both Hsieh's film and the live performance constitute transcontextualization inasmuch as the segmented montage of his body quaking while laboring, persistently, to punch a time clock, parodies the time-management and surveillance practices of corporate capitalism. In doing so, Hsieh's repetitive, incongruous labor, the by-product of which is the film, corresponds with critical theorist Linda Hutcheon's characterization of transcontextualization as "imitation with critical ironic distance" (1985, 37).

Hutcheon's "critical ironic distance" and Bateson's "partial explanation" suggest knowledge is impenetrable unless it is compared and contrasted with knowledge that is unfamiliar and impossible. "Thinking out of the box" and "breaking the boundaries" between what is known, familiar, and habitual, and what is not requires "feedback loops [...] a process of *trial and error* and a mechanism of comparison" (Bateson 1972, 274). As such, *trial-and-error* cannot be denied as a mechanism of transcontextual comparison insofar as it challenges and resists those outcomes and experiences that have become rarified, habitual, and rigid. In this light, the double-take of performance art constitutes a process of transcontextual inquiry and practice.

## Further reading

Barad (2007); Bateson (1972); Deleuze and Guattari (1987).

## References

Barad, Karen. 2007. *Meeting the Universe Halfway: Quantum Physics and the Entanglement of Matter and Meaning.* Durham: Duke University Press.

Bateson, Gregory. 1972. *Steps to an Ecology of Mind.* New York: Ballantine.

Deleuze, Gilles and Felix Guattari. 1987. "Becoming Intense, Becoming Animal and Becoming Imperceptible." In *A Thousand Plateaus: Capitalism and Schizophrenia*. Translated by Brian Massumi. Minneapolis, MN: University of Minnesota Press.

Hutcheon, Linda. 1985. *A Theory of Parody: The Teachings of Twentieth-century Art Forms*. New York: Methuen.

*Cross references*

"**Active Analysis**" by Carnicke; "**Broad Spectrum Approach**" by Schechner; "**Double-coding**" by Bial; "**Goat Island's *The Sea and Poison***" by Garoian and Gaudelius; "**Hybridity**" by Mee; "**Intermediality**" by Auslander; "**Multicentricity**" by Cheng; "**Paradox**" by Fabião.

## Goat Island's *The Sea & Poison*

Charles R. Garoian and Yvonne M. Gaudelius

*Pandemonium* ... a mass of bodies, dressed in brown, double-breasted suits, parading contiguously with a complex of other masses, their tangle of movements choreographed differently and yet the same, occurring live on the oval field of a stadium surrounded by eighty thousand viewers, a massive caldron of incongruity ... a fiery crucible tips and pours channeling a river of molten metal blazing along a serpentine trajectory filling an immense horizontal, circular mold in the midst of seven, towering industrial smokestacks and bodies with dirty faces, performing menial labor rhythmically, adjacent to large grimy belts and pulleys, their mechanical gyrations generating power, their bodies repeating the movements of these machines amongst scattered detritus underfoot ... muscle-bound bodies, wearing dark goggles, toiling round the ring's circumference, wielding hoes, removing scum, prodding the blazing flow into the mold ... another team of hooded brawn brandishes sledge hammers, the arc and blow of their synchronized exertions tempering the ring into steel ... a steam ship circumnavigates the caldron while a haughty male mob in frock coats, stirrup pants, boots, and tall stovepipe hats, struts the forceful movements of their machinery ... these barons smiling smugly, industrialists miming while impelling the human motor, exploiting the power of labor, forging bodies into mechanical efficiency forging the progress of industry, while marching women, bannered suffragists, advocate for labor and demand equal rights ... disparate/stratified masses, laborers/bosses, men/women, foreigners/natives ... their bodily movements, fine-tuned machine components driving the stratified new world order ... working class, middle class, upper class ... smoke, steam, fog, and in the background, a din of sentimental music fills the air stoking the pandemonium, forging its sublime object ... then, from the horizontal mold five fiery, golden rings emerge, ascend, and suspend above the stadium ... five colossal rings raining their radiance, reigning supreme ...

*Pandemonium*, the opening ceremony of the 2012 Summer Olympic Games in London, consisted of a celebration of nationalistic pride in England as the birthplace of the "Industrial Revolution." The naming of the ceremony was appropriated from the seventeenth-century English poet John Milton's naming of the capital city of Hell in his epic poem *Paradise Lost*. Historically reductive, and lacking any attempt at parody and critique, its Romantic metanarrative unabashedly commemorated the pandemonic forces of the Industrial Revolution and the promise of Capitalism while ignoring the devastations perpetrated on human life and the life of the planet over the course of the last two centuries. The spectacle that unfolded was one of unfettered pleasure, and the actions written on bodies were reducible and interchangeable, whether they were forging a ring of celebration or protesting inequality.

While the repetitive, disjunctive bodies performing the Industrial Revolution segment of *Pandemonium* brought to our minds transcontextual associations with Goat Island's performance *The Sea & Poison* (Garoian and Gaudelius 2008), further comparisons failed due to their creative and ideological differences. The impact

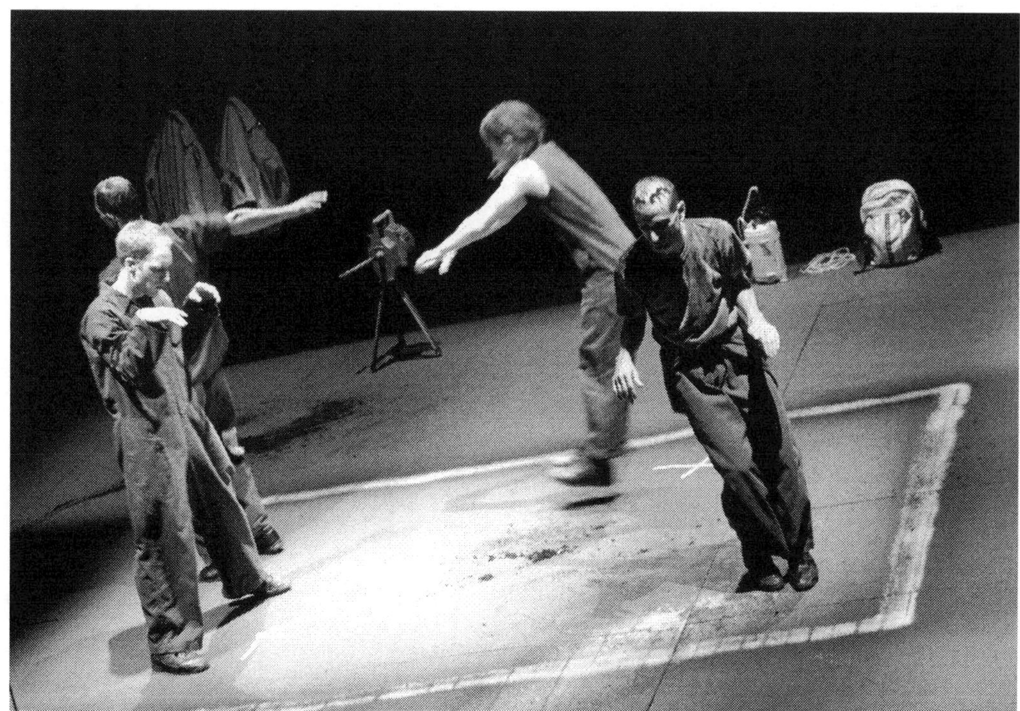

**Figure 39** Goat Island performing *The Sea & Poison* (1999). Photo by Claude Giger. Image courtesy of Goat Island.

on the performing bodies may have been equally strenuous, and the pain of repetitive motion may have been felt across all of them, but the similarities end here—in the hollow echo of pomp and circumstance—for it is not merely the form of the repeated laboring bodies, but the critique those bodies perform that mark the works of Goat Island.

Considering that the exploitation of resources initiated by the Industrial Revolution constituted a campaign against the all-encompassing "body," the body human, the body politic, and the body earth, Goat Island's "eco-performance" *The Sea & Poison* challenges our understanding of images and their power to affect our lives and the life of the planet. What this performance suggests is an attainment often deemed impossible: a compassionate, non-violent, interdependent and sustainable relationship with the earth. As such, what Goat Island called *"impossible tasks"*—the physical exertions of their bodies as well as the disjunctive encounters and alliances performed in *The Sea &* Poison—serve as transcontextual ecological imperatives focusing not on the "known but of the unknown; of things impossible; of limits and barriers which cannot be crossed" (Barrow 1998, 1). Paradoxically, the physical and conceptual challenges in Goat Island's performance work "make possible" liminal, contingent, and ephemeral spaces, within which social, cultural, and historical understandings can be exposed, examined and critiqued.

Goat Island performers Karen Christopher, Matthew Goulish, Bryan Saner, and Mark Jeffreys, dressed in dark factory-like uniforms, entered the compressed space of *The Sea & Poison*. They commenced their exhausting, turbulent, non-virtuoso erratic movements, forcefully twitching, gyrating, leaping, twisting, stretching, and thus exposing their bodies' vulnerability and limitations. Karen rose from a table, walked to Matthew, began leaping, jumping up and down. Matthew followed her, as did Bryan and Mark. They formed a quadrangle while jumping in unison. Matthew then danced a variation rotating his body while bending his knees, followed by Karen, Bryan and Mark performing the same actions.

After they completed their parts, they returned to their leaping, jumping up and down in unison, taking turns rotating on the floor, covering their eyes, flailing their arms. Their bodies were hysterical and desperate yet ironically choreographed in their structured movements.

Matthew, Brian and Karen STOPPED, stood still, Mark lay on the floor, his body writhing, his hands persistently slapping the floor. Mark stood up. All four spread their legs and spun their bodies onto the floor in unison. Karen and Mark leaped to their feet and returned to jumping. Bryan and Matthew joined in. As they continued this routine, their bodies tired, the crescendo of their heavy breathing resonated throughout the space. Matthew and Bryan stayed in place, jumped their bodies as Karen and Mark walked to a corner, somersaulted, laid on their bellies, and wriggled their torsos with their arms lifted. The sounds of their shoes were like those of marching troops. Their punctuated sounds of heavy breathing suggested "danger" to the body on the one hand, and "desperation" of the body on the other.

While performing these impossible tasks, a complex narrative, a "sea" of disjunctive images and ideas about eco-terrorism began to rage, implying trans-contextual associations between nature and culture, the earth and the human body, and their mutual poisoning, degradation, and death (Bateson 1972, 272-273). According to Stephen J. Bottoms, "The world of *The Sea & Poison* is not the shiny, exciting, virtual world of information superhighways, but the dirty, sweaty, poisoned, exhausted physical world of expanding global capitalism" (2000, 4). Unlike the portrayal of work given to us in the Olympian moment, the narrative of *The Sea & Poison* never leads to a completed whole, to shining rings, to the fulfillment of the spectacle. It is not about ceremony as a surface stand-in for impacts on the environment.

Goat Island's performances signify through simultaneous, transcontextual linguistic processes. One concept is used to represent another as impossible: exhausting tasks and disjunctive narratives that serve as metaphors of struggle and survival. Moreover, Goat Island's physical and conceptual exertions function as metonymy as the Goats are exhausted, thus creating a space of contiguity where multiple encounters, movements and alliances between and among disparate and disjunctive actions resist intellectual closure and challenge "the body's submission to socially prescribed behavioral patterns" (Bottoms 2000, 10). Compared with Goat Island's impossibly enacted "dance of resistance" to ideological closure, in *Pandemonium* we experience socially and historically constructed representations that lack metonymic contiguity. Instead, *Pandemonium* presents a flawless ontological narrative of never-ending progress played out on the passive bodies of the performers.

Thus, there exist ethical differences between the conceptual, emotional, and physical collisions performed by Goat Island and those of *Pandemonium*. Unlike the singular hypnotic assault of *Pandemonium*, Goat Island's images, ideas, and actions in performances like *The Sea & Poison* encourage critical reflection and social responsibility. They challenge us to resist reified ideologies for the purpose of sustaining an open-ended dialogue within our families, neighborhoods, and the global community. Such a dialogue resists ideological closure and provides a means by which to reclaim our socially and historically determined identities, and to address the wounds of its inscription upon and oppression of our bodies critically. In doing so, the potential exists that the hubris and fanaticism of rarified cultural representations such as *Pandemonium*, and the deployment of intoxicating entertainments that anesthetize introspection and reproach, are exposed to ethical examination and transformation.

The ambiguities and incompleteness in Goat Island's performances are open for immanent critique and interpretation. As we free-associate the transcontextual elements in performances like *The Sea & Poison*, we participate in a sustainable ecology wherein our differing yet interdependent cultural perspectives enable multiple yet interconnected interpretations. Thus, unlike the spectacle of *Pandemonium*, Goat Island's performance of humility implies struggle to achieve peaceful coexistences among biological others. Such a desire is predicated upon interdependency and contains the re-enchanting promise of Goat Island's impossible ecology.

References

Barrow, John D. 1998. *Impossibility: The Limits of Science and the Science of Limits*. London: Oxford University Press.

Bateson, Gregory. 1972. *Steps to an Ecology of Mind*. New York: Ballantine.

Bottoms, Stephen J. 2000. "Biochemically stressed: Goat Island, the body, technology and poison." Paper presented at "Performative Sites: Intersecting Art, Technology, and the Body" Symposium at Pennsylvania State University, University Park, Pennsylvania, October 26.

Garoian, Charles R., and Yvonne Gaudelius. 2008. "The Sea and Poison." *Spectacle Pedagogy: Art, Politics, and Visual Culture*. Albany, NY: State University of New York.

Garoian, Charles R. and Yvonne Gaudelius. 2008. *Spectacle Pedagogy: Art, Politics, and Visual Culture*. Albany, NY: State University of New York.

## Transnationalism

Haiping Yan

The general usage of transnationalism as a term is traceable to the early years of the twentieth century (Bourne 1916). As a critical analytic, it has been gaining academic currency across humanistic and social studies primarily since the 1990s. In contemporary performance, a transnational impulse is not only discernable but constitutive of otherwise discrete discourses including those of the postcolonial, diasporic, feminist and intercultural. Scholars specializing in drama of the sub-Saharan Africa and trans-oceanic regions, led by Biodun Jeyifo and Teju Olaniyan, open up Pan-African inflected horizons that cut across nationally predicated categories (Olaniyan 1995; Jeyifo 2004). Through gender-informed analyses of postcolonial plays, Helen Gilbert and Joanne Tompkins offer a style of critical inquiry, in the light of which lived experiences and cultural articulations of the colonized, colonial, and decolonizing subjects are shown to be inherently intertwined across a range of countries (Gilbert and Tompkins 1996). Alicia Arrizon's "Mestizaje" in the Latina/Chicana theatre, much as Yvonne Yarbro-Bejarano's female subject implicated in the Chicano theatre, leverages the notion of Third World feminism into a mobilizing sphere of artistic activity within the heartland of the US and beyond its marked national territory, grounding an activist analytic that is trans-ethnically embodied (Yarbro-Bejarano 1994; Arrizon 1999, 2006). Tracing the diasporic figurations of immigrants in North America arriving from colonial and postcolonial India, Aparna Dharwadker views their practices of theatre as fundamentally contingent upon their variable patterns of migration across the Pacific. Here, "the diasporic" functions as a register of the structured problematic of the Nation vs. its Other as it originated in colonial Europe in variable displacement and reinvention (Dharwadker 2003). Daphne Lei looks into the genealogies of Chinese theatre in the US as the loci of diasporic survival, under the ethnocentric regime of intelligibility that works to inscribe the diasporic as the limit (the eternal foreignness), against which an European identity is established as the regulating code for normal nationality and an American identity is invented as the commanding sign of human normality (Lei 2003). Artists and theorists such as Erika Fischer-Lichte, Marvin Carlson, Peter Brook, Eugenio Barba, Richard Schechner, gather under the intercultural call and work with resources chosen from not only different nations, countries, but also continents and civilizations, de-linking the dynamics of cultures from the signature of nation-states, and pointing toward a "Third Culture" (Brook's term), an un-fixated site of limitless human potential in connective creativity (Pavis 1996). Diverse in their critical orientations and cognitive politics, these analytics converge in a mobilization that destabilizes the vocabulary of modernity predicated on ethnocentric rubrics of the nation, the nation-state, and the national culture, giving rise to powerfully trans-ethnic, transnational processes of cultural hybridization.

Brian Singleton's attention to "the countless refugees" in the twenty-first century registers a distinct moment in the academic making of transnational discourses. Informed by Loren Kruge's research group working on the diasporic theatre of the US, Singleton turns to contemporary scenes across Europe and characterizes "the perpetual state of liminal rootlessness" of those refugees as indicative of a vast movement in which the world and its human geography are embattled and sent unraveling (Singleton 2003). This movement is called globalization, commonly understood as economic expansion and featuring the logic of the capital. In response to the motions of globalization, Katrin Sieg examines the issues of gender, sexuality and race in contemporary performance driven by unprecedented patterns of migration in Germany, evoking a transnational feminist genealogy and activating its analytic to "knit" scenes that expose and resist the power relations shaped by global capital, across the global, national and local sites (Sieg 2003). Rustom Bharucha's critique of interculturalism as a neocolonial enterprise includes the Singaporean arts city variant and advocates an intracultural-cum-transnational aesthetic working within and across "New Asia" and the world, in constant contestation with the ambitions of global capital and its power relations (Bharucha 2004).

Recognition of the fundamental instability of the category of the nation-state and its expressive vocabulary works as a cognitive center of gravity in the special issues of three leading journals in performance and theatre studies, published in 2005 and 2006. Edited by Jen Harvie and Dan Rebellato, the 2006 special issue of *Contemporary Theatre Review* presents a group of essays that revisit the site-specific nature of the performing arts and of human performance, posing it as a question of a new kind in an era where the national analytic as the sovereign code for culture, identity, community and knowledge production—just as the nation-state as the primary unit for modern economy and social existence—appears "increasingly irrelevant" amid an "intensely accelerated integration of the world into a single market" (Harvie and Rebellato 2006). Paul Rae's essay in the issue unpacks three performances mounted in "global arts cities" such as Singapore and London to re-contextualize the unraveling conditions for performing human identity in relations, producing personalized meanings within a history of the world, and re-utilizing the transnational "border-thinking" (a la Guillermo Gómez-Peña) with a globally mobile, at once "located and expansive" articulation at odds with "the churning instability of (globalizing) capitalism" (Rae 2006).

The 2005 special issue of *Theatre Journal* focuses on theorizing globalization through theatre and performance. In her editorial comment, Jean Graham-Jones foregrounds the category of "glocalization" to designate an interactive and interpenetrative relationship between the global and the local as the primary terrain for critical inquiry into the "excess, exclusion, and remains" of globalization, as well as for re-figurations of aesthetic politics in search of social efficacy (Graham-Jones 2005). Essays in the issue respectively re-organize the performative practices of distinct cultural traditions or ethnic forms into a glocalizing context in variation, located in a traumatized area (Gulu), a traveling route (Europe), a "most globalized nation" (Singapore), a glocal city (New York or Las Vegas), and an imperialist region ("the American Pacific"). Shifting the configurations of the body national and their relations involved therein, these essays also evoke the ethnic-leveraged trans-regional paradigm articulated in works by Joseph Roach (1996) and Diana Taylor (2003).

The 2005 special issue of *Modern Drama*, edited by Yan Haiping with an introductory essay, foregrounds the category of the nation-state and its form-giving function in the selected performances of human survival and creative energy discussed by the essays in the issue, as paradigmatic scenes of a global human geography enacted across multiple contexts of the Asian diaspora. Yan theorizes the ways in which each essay situates its subject of study in the shifting social matrixes of a historically shaped nationality that has been fundamentally transnationalized within and across different parts of the globe, as a subject in search of her intelligibility and her variable specific vocabulary in the confluences of "nations in transformation" or "trans-nations" worldwide (Yan 2005a). Essays by Ban Wang, Stephanie Ng, and Esther Kim Lee map out the contradictory demands of profit-driven logic of the capital and its cultural rubrics, as loci of a specified instance of humanity in modern displacement. The heightened performative dynamics of a displaced humanity show itself as the real engines or fuels of global change and productivity, rather than the capital and the supremacy of capital that seem to monopolize the processes and definitions of globalization. Yan calls for performance studies scholars to serve as "a living conduit" to unleash such human dynamics for transnational knowledge production.

Diverse in their composition and signification, essays in these special issues and other recent works suggest an organizational method that takes the sites of "trans-nation" in human performance as the primary terrain wherein scholars dialogue with the emerging and multiplying scenes of interactions that link people, communities, or institutions across the borders of nation-states, as co-existing with national and global formations (Aston and Case 2007; Reinelt 2006; Yan 2005). The connotation of such a transnational method is not merely different from but also incommensurate with definitions that pivot on linking the transnational to concepts of hybridity, for it is cognizant of the changing function or relative weight of nation-state as such, and rather than emphasizing the more elusive parameters of cultural belonging that have been associated with the nation as an ethnic form (Adelson 2001). Bilateral or multilateral institutional building for cross-border scholarly collaborations, as embodied in the establishment of the Hemispheric Institute (founded by Diana Taylor) and the Cornell University-East China Normal University Center for Cultural Studies (founded by Yan Haiping), while indicating certain scenarios of such a transnational method in practice, may give rise to new possibilities for producing transnational culture, identity, social relations, and humanistic knowledge in the era of Globalization.

### Further reading

Taylor (2003); Yan (2005).

### References

Adelson, Leslie. 2001. "Against Between: A Manifesto." In *Unpacking Europe*, edited by Salah Hassan and Iftikhar Dadi, 244–255. Rotterdam: NAi.

Arrizon, Alicia. 1999. "Transculturation and Gender in US Latina Performance." *Theater Research International*, 24.3: 288–292.

Arrizon, Alicia. 2006. *Queering Mestizaje.* Ann Arbor, MN: University of Michigan Press.

Aston, Elaine and Sue Ellen Case, eds. 2007. *Staging International Feminisms.* New York: Palgrave Publishers.

Bharucha, Rustom. 2004. "Foreign Asia/Foreign Shakespeare: Dissenting Notes on New Asian Interculturality, Postcoloniality, and Recolonization." *Theatre Journal*, 56.1: 1–28.

Bourne, Randolph S. 1916. "Trans-national America." *The Atlantic*, July 1.

Dharwadker, A. 2003. "Diaspora and the Theatre of the Nation," *Theatre Research International*, 28.3: 303–325.

Gilbert, Helen and Joanne Tompkins. 1996. *Post-Colonial Drama: Theory, Practice, Politics.* London: Routledge.

Graham-Jones, Jean. 2005. "Theorizing Globalization Through Theater and Performance." *Theater Journal*, 57.3: viii–xvi.

Harvie, Jen and Dan Rebellato, eds. 2006. *Contemporary Theater Review*, Vol. 16.1: 62–70.

Jeyifo, Biodun. 2004. *Wole Soyinka: Politics, Poetics, and Postcolonialism.* Cambridge: Cambridge University Press.

Lei, Daphne. 2003. "The Production and Consumption of Chinese Theater in

Nineteenth-Century California." *Theater Research International*, 28.3: 1–14.
Olaniyan, Tejumola. 1995. *Scars of Conquest/Masks of Resistence: The Invention of Cultural Identities in Africa, African American, and Caribbean Drama*. New York: Oxford University Press.
Pavis, Patrice, ed. 1996. *Intercultural Performance Reader*. New York: Routledge.
Rae, Paul. 2006. "Where is the Cosmopolitan Stage?" *Contemporary Theatre Review*, 16.1: 4–19.
Reinelt, Janelle. 2006. "To the Editor," *Theater Survey*, 47.2: 167–173.
Roach, Joseph. 1996. *Cities of the Dead: Circum-Atlantic Performance*. New York: Columbia University Press.
Sieg, Katrin. 2003. "Indians: the Globalized Woman on the Community Stage." *Theater Journal*, 55.2: 291–315.
Singleton, Brian. 2003. "Editorial." *Theater Research International*, 28.3: 227–228.
Taylor, Diana. 2003a. "Bush's Happy Performative." *TDR: The Drama* Review, 47.3: 5–8.
Taylor, Diana. 2003b. *The Archive and the Repertoire: Performing Cultural Memory in the Americas*. Durham: Duke University Press.
Yan, Haiping, ed. 2005a. "Other Transnationals: Asian Diaspora in Performance." *Modern Drama*, XLVIII.2, special issue.
Yan, Haiping. 2005b. *Staging Global Vagrancy: A Genealogy of Transnational Performance*. Ann Arbor, MN: University of Michigan Press.
Yarbro-Bejarano, Yvonne. 1994. "The Female Subject in Chicano Theater: Sexuality, Race, and Class." In *Performing Feminisms: Feminist Critical Theory and Theater*, edited by Sue-Ellen Case, 131–149. Minneapolis, MN: University of Minnesota.

*Cross references*

"**Ai Weiwei's transnational public spheres**" by Zheng; "**Global censorship**" by Shea; "**Guillermo Gómez-Peña attempts to explain performance art to people who may have never heard of it**" by Gómez-Peña; "**Hybridity**" by Mee; "**Intercultural performance**" by Alker; "**Postcolonial performance inquiry**" by Chatterjee.

## Whiteness

Amelia Jones

Whiteness is the relational concept that, in societies structured and dominated by European values (including those of North America, New Zealand, and Australia), works covertly to define any ethnic group not perceived as white to be "raced." As writers from Toni Morrison to Edward Said have pointed out, whiteness is deeply binary in its logic, relying for its power on its invisibility as well as on its opposition to various categories (such as Black, Oriental, "of color," Latino, Asian, etc.) which function as its debased, marginalized, negative other. Whiteness is part of a structure of belief predicated on the idea that race can be identified via the visual appearance of the body and is an essential, and ultimately genetically verifiable, aspect of identity.

Whiteness studies (or "critical white studies") grew in the 1990s out of critical race studies, an academic movement to historicize and provide critical models for examining the formations of race, which had developed out of the rights movements from the 1950s to the 1970s. Whiteness studies generally has as its goal the denaturalization of whiteness—the *making visible* of white as a racial category in order to question its unspoken privileging cultures dominated by European values. While the first wave of whiteness studies was largely based in the USA, the insights of whiteness studies began having an impact on scholarship in the humanities in the mid- to late 1990s, with British scholarship in cultural studies showing particular sensitivity to incorporating its insights (viz. Richard Dyer's groundbreaking 1997 book in film and visual culture studies, *White*). Meanwhile in the USA whiteness studies has largely been dominated by scholars in the social sciences, although some attention has been paid to whiteness in art and performance discourse, due to the strong impact of identity politics on the art world in the 1980s and

1990s and the primacy of *visuality* in sustaining the myth of whiteness (see Bowles 2001).

The legal scholar Ian F. Haney López argues in his 1996 book *White by Law* that whiteness "is contingent, changeable, partial, inconstant, and ultimately social" (1996, xiv). Whiteness, in other words, is understood as a construction, as a *performative* that takes place relationally to construct those defined or perceived as non-white as *other*. In spite of the centrality of the concept of construction or performance to the understanding of whiteness, however, performance studies (founded in the 1990s as well) has not always attended to race as a critical issue—although it has consistently foregrounded gender and sexuality in articulating a theory of identity as performative.

Judith Butler's foundational essay "Performative Acts and Gender Constitution" (1988)—reworked into her book *Gender Trouble*—which was hugely influential to the development of performance theory, typifies the tendency to apply concepts from phenomenology and linguistics to articulate a convincing model of the subject's gendered identity as "instituted through a *stylized repetition of acts*" (Butler 1988, 519), while largely ignoring other aspects of identification such as race, ethnicity, and class. Since the late 1990s, however, insights from whiteness studies have been usefully linked by performance scholars to the concept of performativity—which insists that all identifications, racial or otherwise, are *performed* in a process of intersubjective meaning-making rather than innate. This work suggests that whiteness, like "Blackness" or other racial identifications, takes place through similar "stylized repetitions of acts" to those identified by Butler as key to gender (and sex) identification.

Feminist performance scholar Peggy Phelan had raised the otherwise repressed specter of whiteness, and critiqued the clichéd notion of identity politics that visibility confers social power, by noting in her groundbreaking 1993 book *Unmarked* that "[i]f representational visibility equals power, then almost-naked young white women should be running Western culture" (1993, 10). Subsequently to Phelan's brief but crucial mention of whiteness in *Unmarked*, other scholars such as José Esteban Muñoz have explored the performativity of race, using insights from critical race and whiteness studies.

As Muñoz's work indicates, through the felicitous linking of the insights of whiteness studies to the theory of performativity (or more loosely the social construction of identity), a crucial political critique of often unacknowledged privileges attached to whiteness in European-based societies (and beyond) has thus been developed across disciplines. Crucially, as noted, the key to a critical practice is largely seen as the *making visible* of whiteness: the "outing" of whiteness, as it were, exposes the ideological force of its privileges, denaturalizing its "invisible" but ubiquitous claim to power.

### Further reading

Butler (1988); Bowles (2001); Phelan (1993).

### References

Bowles, John P. 2001. "Blinded by the White: Art and History at the Limits of Whiteness." *Art Journal*, 60.4: 38

Butler, Judith. 1988. "Performative Acts and Gender Constitution: An Essay in Phenomenology and Feminist Theory." *Theatre Journal*, 40.4: 519–531.

Dyer, Richard. 1997. *White: Essays on Race and Culture*. New York and London: Routledge.

López, Ian Haney. 1996. *White by Law: The Legal Construction of Race*. New York: New York University Press.

Phelan, Peggy. 1993. *Unmarked: The Politics of Performance*. New York: Routledge.

### Cross references

**"35 Years of Living Art (Excerpts from Linda Mary Montano's blog, Thursday, December 6, 2012)"** by Montano; "**Aging**" by Port; "**Hierarchy**" by Luber; "**Identification/dis-identification**" by Muñoz; "**Identity politics**" by Adewunmi; "**Postcolonial performance inquiry**" by Chatterjee; "**Racialization**" by Sell.

## The Muslim performative

Demir Barlas

Islam begins as an explicit command to perform for God: "Read, in the name of thy Sustainer!" was the first Qur'anic verse (Chapter 96: Verse 1) revealed to Muhammad, the prophet of Islam, by the angel Gabriel. By tradition, the illiterate Muhammad trembled with fear, as he could not read and was therefore unable to obey the divine; but, after God repeated the command thrice, Muhammad miraculously became literate.

Echoing the scriptural experience of Muhammad, Muslims become so not by birth but by reciting the phrase "There is no god but Allah and Muhammad is Allah's prophet" before witnesses. Just as Muhammad first bore witness to Allah's message in the presence of Gabriel, each Muslim acknowledges Allah's divinity and Muhammad's mission in the presence of other Muslims. This is done not only via the initial declaration of faith but also in the ongoing performance of congregational prayer, which reinforces the individual Muslim's membership in the global Islamic community (the *Ummah*) in servitude of Allah.

The Muslim performative is not limited to theological utterances, for the Qur'an also instructs Muslims as to how they are to perform sexually (2:222 forbids sex with menstruating women and reminds men that the God-ordained model of sex is penetrative-vaginal), socially (31:19 emphasizes the importance of speaking with a soft voice), appetitively (dietary codes

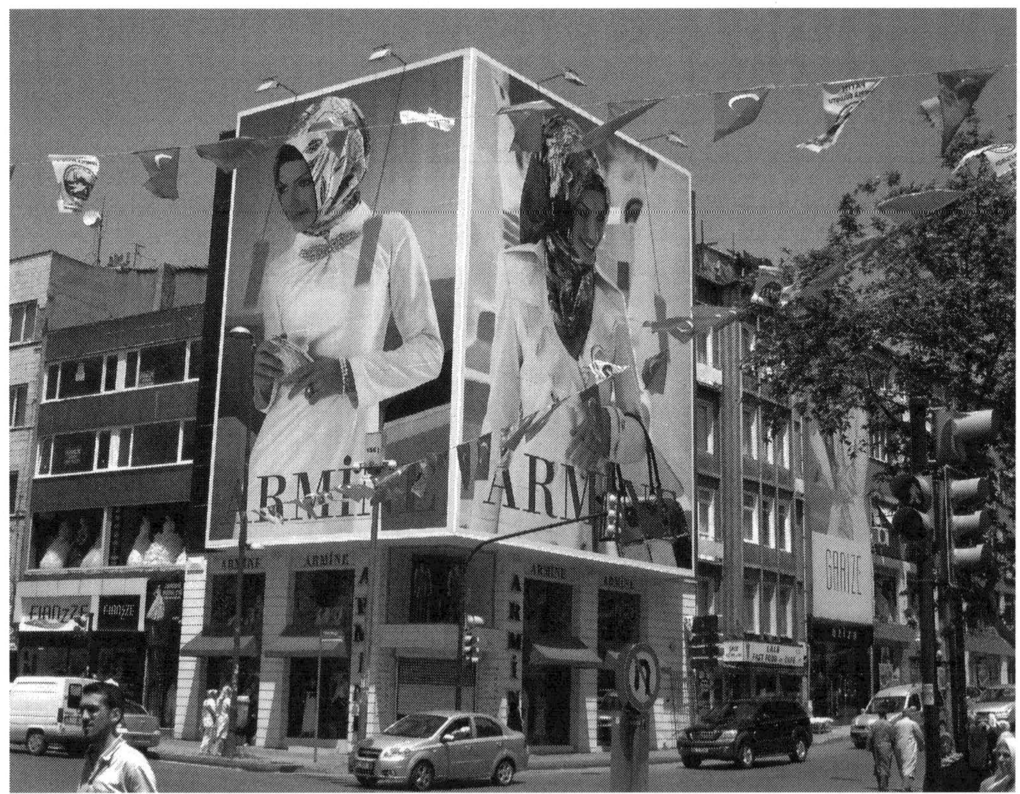


**Figure 40** Armine storefront on Fevzipaşa Caddesi, Fatih, Istanbul (2009). Photo by Anna Secor. Image courtesy of the photographer.

are enumerated in 5:3 and elsewhere), legally (in 2:282, Muslims are instructed to write down all elements of the marriage contract, and in Muslim tradition divorce is effected when a man says *I divorce you* three times to his wife), and aesthetically (24:31 instructs women in how to dress). In each of these cases, it is not sufficient that the Muslim approach a particular event–such as sex, marriage, the closet, or the dining table–with a particular intention; the intention must be marked with a performance, an outward sign that conveys obeisance to God. By the same token, mere performance without pious intent or prior introspection on God's signs (21:32 and elsewhere) is also insufficient.

The Qur'an itself acknowledges that some hypocritical Muslims "seek to deceive God" by, for example, praying "only to be seen and praised" (4:142). Islam's numerous rules and rituals thus generate a potential to confuse the signifier (the performative) with the signified (belief). Specifically, the issue of female veiling illustrates why the Muslim performative remains central to what Marshall Hodgson, in another context, terms the venture of Islam.

In 24:31, Allah instructs Muslim women in a number of practices that later became codified as veiling. Women are, particularly, to draw a covering over their breasts (fashionably displayed in pre-Muslim Arabia) and to refrain from swinging their hips as they walk; more generally, women are told not to convey their "charms" to men outside their immediate family. In practice, veiling can range from extreme, such as the wearing of a head-to-foot black covering, complete with black gloves, that utterly hides the wearer, to the salacious, such as the practice (increasingly common in Turkey) of assuming license to wear tight, revealing clothing as long as a light headscarf–more decorative than modest–is on the woman's head.

The original goal of the veil is to reflect God-consciousness (7:26) while sending a signal to potential observers that the veiled woman is a pious Muslim. The attainment of this goal is complicated by the fact that to please God while retaining consciousness of being watched is, in the Qur'anic view, impossible. As in 4:124, religious performance is irretrievably corrupted when the Muslim is aware that someone is watching; this awareness unfailingly tempts the Muslim to perform for the sake of the human observer, not the divine. The veil acquires an increasing number of what the Qur'an might call hypocritical significances and plays a prominent role in a kind of mummery. In Iran, for example, some veiled women defend oral sex–outside of marriage, a mortal sin in Islam–as religiously acceptable because it is, in an instantiation of Clintonian logic, not really sex. By the same standard, a Turkish woman who wears a skintight skirt but tops her outfit with a headscarf believes that, in hewing however marginally to the letter of God's performative command, she has escaped the need for the second component of Muslim belief, the internalization–not merely performance!–of God's rules.

The complexities of the Muslim performative, already countenanced by the Qur'an in the early seventh century CE, intensify in post-modernity, where issues of identity, technology, transnationalism, and cultural hybridity further vex Muslim performance. For example, there have been numerous cases of Muslim men divorcing their wives via text message, raising the question of what it means to "pronounce" divorce in an electronic age. However, all such problems are secondary to the original paradox of the Muslim performative. The real problematic of Muslim performance is not so much whether a particular performance is genuinely Islamic practice, the knot at the heart of the Muslim performative is how to perform for two incommensurate audiences, God and human, while remaining on the right side of what the Qur'an deems hypocrisy.

# Methodologies/turning points and paired case studies bibliography


Abram, David. 1996. *The Spell of the Sensuous: Perception and Language in a More- than-Human World*. New York: Pantheon Books.

Adelson, Leslie. 2001. "Against Between: A Manifesto." In *Unpacking Europe*, edited by Salah Hassan and Iftikhar Dadi, 244–255. Rotterdam: NAi.

Agamben, Giorgio. 2004. *The Open: Man and Animal*. Stanford, CA: Stanford University Press.

Albright, Daniel. 2000. *Untwisting the Serpent: Modernism in Music, Literature, and Other Arts*. Chicago, IL: University of Chicago Press.

Albright, Daniel. 2003. *Beckett and Aesthetics*. Cambridge: Cambridge University Press.

Albright, Daniel. 2004. *Modernism and Music: An Anthology of Sources*. Chicago, IL: University of Chicago Press.

Althusser, Louis. 1971. *Lenin and Philosophy and Other Essays*. Reprint, New York: Monthly Review Press, 2001.

Anderson, Benedict. 1983. *Imagined Communities: Reflections on the Origin and Spread of Nationalism*. London: Verso.

Appiah, Kwame Anthony. 1993. *In My Father's House: Africa in the Philosophy of Culture*. Oxford: Oxford University Press.

Arbeau, Thoinot. 1589. *Orchesography*. Translated by Mary Stewart Evans. Reprint 2012, The Noverre Press.

Aristotle. 1987. *The Poetics of Aristotle: Translation and Commentary*, edited by Stephen Halliwell. Chapel Hill, NC: University of North Carolina Press.

Arons, Wendy and Theresa J. May, eds. 2012. *Readings in Performance and Ecology*. New York: Palgrave Macmillan.

Arrizon, Alicia. 1999. "Transculturation and Gender in US Latina Performance." *Theater Research International*, 24.3: 288–292.

Arrizon, Alicia. 2006. *Queering Mestizaje*. Ann Arbor, MN: University of Michigan Press.

Artaud, Antonin. 1958 [1938]; *The Theater and Its Double*. New York: Grove Press Inc.

Aston, Elaine and Sue Ellen Case, eds. 2007. *Staging International Feminisms*. New York: Palgrave Publishers.

Austin, J.L. 1962. *How To Do Things With Words*. Oxford and New York: Oxford University Press.

Badiou, Alain. 2005. *The Century*. Reprint, Cambridge, England and Malden, Massachussets: Polity, 2011. Originally published as *Le Siècle*, Paris: Éditions du Seuil, 2005.

Baker, Steve. 2000. *The Postmodern Animal.* London: Reaktion.

Balme, Christopher. 2004. "Editorial"" *Theatre Research International,* 29.1: 1.

Barad, Karen. 2007. *Meeting the Universe Halfway: Quantum Physics and the Entanglement of Matter and Meaning.* Durham: Duke University Press.

Barba, Eugenio. 1991. *Dictionary of Theatre Anthropology: The Secret Art of the Performer.* London: Routledge.

Barish, Jonas A. 1981. *The Antitheatrical Prejudice.* Berkeley, CA: University of California Press.

Barrow, John D. 1998. *Impossibility: The Limits of Science and the Science of Limits.* London: Oxford University Press.

Barthes, Roland. 1972. "Baudelaire's Theater." In *Critical Essays,* translated by Richard Howard, 25–31. Evanston: Northwestern University Press.

Barthes, Roland. 1981. *Camera Lucida: Reflections on Photography.* Translated by Richard Howard. New York: Hill and Wang.

Basting, Anne Davis. 1991. *The Stages of Age: Performing Age in Contemporary American Culture.* Reprint, 1998. Ann Arbor, MN: University of Michigan Press.

Basting, Anne Davis. 2013. "The Penelope Project." *The Penelope Project.* http://www.thepenelopeproject.com

Bateson, Gregory. 1972. *Steps to an Ecology of Mind.* New York: Ballantine.

Bauman, H.-Dirksen L. 2007. "On The Disconstruction of (Sign) Language in Western Tradition: A Deaf Reading of Plato's *Cratylus.*" In *Open Your Eyes: Deaf Studies Talking,* edited by H.-Dirksen L. Bauman, 127–166. Minneapolis, MN: University of Minnesota Press.

Bell, John, ed. 2001. *Puppets, Masks and Performing Objects.* Cambridge: MIT Press.

Bell, John. 2008. *American Puppet Modernism.* New York: Palgrave Macmillan.

Benjamin, Walter. 1936. "The Work of Art in the Age of Mechanical Reproduction." In *Illuminations: Essays and Reflections,* edited by Hannah Arendt and translated by Harry Zohn. Reprint, New York: Schocken 1969.

Benjamin, Walter. 1986. *Reflections: Essays, Aphorisms, Autobiographical Writings,* edited by Peter Demetz. New York: Schocken Books.

Bennett, Benjamin. 2005. "Robert Wilson and the Work as an Empty Wavelength for its Own Public Discussion." In *All Theater is Revolutionary Theater,* 194–215. Ithaca and London: Cornell University Press.

Bentivoglio Leonetta, and Francesco Carbone. 2003. *Pina Bausch vous appelle.* Reprint, L'Arche, 2007.

Berger, John. 1980. "Why Look at Animals?" In *About Looking.* New York: Pantheon.

Berghaus, Günter. 2005. *Theatre, Performance, and the Historical Avant-garde.* New York: Palgrave Macmillan.

Berlant, Lauren. 2011. *Cruel Optimism.* Durham: Duke University Press.

Berson, Jessica. 2010. "Old Dogs, New Tricks: Intergenerational Dance." In *Staging Age: The Performance of Age in Theatre, Dance, and* Film, edited by Leni Marshall and Valerie Barnes Lipscomb, 164–189. New York: Palgrave Macmillan.

Besel, Richard D., and Jnan A. Blau, eds. 2013. *Performance on Behalf of the Environment.* New York: Rowen and Littlefield Publishing Group.

Bhabha, Homi K. 1984. "Of Mimicry and Man: The Ambivalence of Colonial Discourse." *October,* 28.1: 125–133.

Bhabha, Homi K. 1994. *The Location of Culture.* London: Routledge.

Bharucha, Rustom. 1992. *Theatre and the World: Essays on Performance and Politics of Culture.* New Delhi: Manohar Publishers.

Bharucha, Rustom. 2004. "Foreign Asia/Foreign Shakespeare: Dissenting Notes on New Asian Interculturality, Postcoloniality, and Recolonization." *Theatre Journal,* 56.1: 1–28.

Black, Joel. 1984. "Idolology: The Model in Artistic Practice and Critical Theory." In *The Literary and Philosophical Debate.* Vol. 1 in *Mimesis in Contemporary Theory,* edited by Mihal Spariosu. Philadelphia, NJ: John Benjamins.

Blessing, Jennifer and Nancy Spector. 1997. *Rrose is a Rrose is a Rrose: Gender Performance in Photography*. New York: The Solomon R. Guggenheim Foundation.

Bloom, Ina. 2002. "Shifting Affiliations & Conflicting Visions: A Short Note on Fluxus in Scandinavia." In *Q que é Fluxus? O que Não é! O porqué. What's Fluxus? What's Not? Why*, edited by Jon Hendricks, 111–112. Rio de Janeiro and Detroit: Centro Cultural Banco do Brasil and The Gilbert and Lila Silverman Fluxus Collection Foundation.

Blumenthal, Eileen. 2005. *Puppetry: A World History*. New York: Abrams.

Boenisch, Peter M. 2006. "Aesthetic Art to Aisthetic Act: Theatre, Media, Intermedial Performance." In *Intermediality in Theatre and Performance*, edited by Freda Chapple and Chiel Kattenbelt. Amsterdam and New York: Editions Rodopi B.V.

Bottoms, Stephen J. 2000. "Biochemically stressed: Goat Island, the body, technology and poison." Paper presented at "Performative Sites: Intersecting Art, Technology, and the Body" Symposium at Pennsylvania State University, University Park, Pennsylvania, October 26.

Bourne, Randolph S. 1916. "Trans-national America." *The Atlantic*, July 1.

Bowles, John P. 2001. "Blinded by the White: Art and History at the Limits of Whiteness." *Art Journal*, 60.4: 38.

Braidotti, Rosi. 2013. *The Posthuman*. Cambridge: Polity.

Brecht, Bertolt. 1964. *Brecht on Theatre*. Translated by John Willett. New York: Hill & Wang.

Breuer, Lee. 1979. *Animations: A Trilogy for Mabou Mines*. New York: Performing Arts Journal.

Briginshaw, Valerie A. and Ramsay Burt. 2009. *Writing Dancing Together*. Basingstoke: Palgrave Macmillan.

Burke, Kenneth. 1945. *A Grammar of Motives*. Berkeley, CA: University of California Press.

Butler, Judith. 1988. "Performative Acts and Gender Constitution: An Essay in Phenomenology and Feminist Theory." *Theatre Journal*, 40.4: 519–531.

Butler, Judith. 1990. *Gender Trouble: Feminism and the Subversion of Identity*. New York: Routledge.

Butler, Judith. 1993a. *Bodies that Matter*. Routledge: New York.

Butler, Judith. 1993b. "Imitation and Gender Insubordination." In *The Lesbian and Gay Studies Reader*, edited by Henry Abelove, Michele Aina Barale, and David M. Halperin, 307–320. New York: Routledge.

Butler, Judith. 1997. *On Performativity from a Post-Structuralist Perspective*. London: Routledge.

Cage, John. 1957. "Experimental Music." Lecture, Convention of the Music Teachers National Association. Chicago, IL.

Caillois, Roger. 1961. *Man, Play, and Games*. Translated by Meyer Barash. Bloomington, IN: University of Illinois Press.

Carlson, Marvin A. 1996. *Performance: A Critical Introduction*. New York: Routledge.

Carlson, Marvin A. 2001. *The Haunted Stage: The Theatre as Memory Machine*. Ann Arbor, MN: University of Michigan Press.

Catts, Oran and Ionat Zurr. 2002. "Growing Semi-Living Sculptures: The Tissue Culture & Art Project." *Leonardo*, 35.4: 365–370.

Césaire, Aimé. 1955. *Discourse on Colonialism*. Paris: Réclame.

Chaudhuri, Una. 1994. "'There Must Be a Lot of Fish in That Lake': Toward an Ecological Theater." *Theater*, 25.1: 23–31.

Chaudhuri, Una. 2003. "Animal Geographies: Zooësis and the Space of Modern Drama." *Modern Drama*, 46.4: 646–662.

Chaudhuri, Una and Holly Hughes, eds. 2014a. *Animal Acts: Performing Species Today*. Ann Arbor, MN: University of Michigan Press.

Chaudhuri, Una and Shonni Enelow, eds. 2014b. *Ecocide: Research Theatre and Climate Change*. New York: Palgrave Macmillan.

Cheng, Meiling. 1998. "*Les Demoiselles d/L.A.*: Sacred Naked Nature Girls' *Untitled Flesh*." *TDR: The Drama Review*, 42.2: 70–97.

Cheng, Meiling. 2002. *In Other Los Angeleses: Multicentric Performance Art*. Berkeley, CA: University of California Press.

Cheng, Meiling. 2013. *Beijing Xingwei: Contemporary Chinese Time-based Art*. Greenford: Seagull London.

Chomsky, Noam. 2001. *9/11*. New York: Seven Stories Press.

Climenhaga, Royd. 2008. "Pina Bausch." In *Routledge Performance Practitioners*, edited by Franc Chamberlain. New York: Routledge.

Climenhaga, Royd. 2010. "'Realigned Presence': A Reflection on Pina Bausch." HotReview: a peer-reviewed online journal of theater. http://www.hotreview.org/articles/realignedpresence.htm

Coates, Emily. 2010. "Beyond the Visible: The Legacies of Merce Cunningham and Pina Bausch." *PAJ: A Journal of Performance and Art*, 32.2: 1–7.

Cody, Gabrielle H.. 1998. "Woman, Man, Dog, Tree: Two Decades of Intimate and Monumental Bodies in Pina Bausch's Tanztheater." *TDR: The Drama Review*, 42.2: 115–131.

Coetzee, J.M. 1999. *The Lives of Animals*. Princeton, NJ: Princeton University Press.

Conquergood, Dwight. 2002a. "Lethal Theatre: Performance, Punishment, and the Death Penalty." *Theatre Journal*, 54.3: 339–367.

Conquergood, Dwight. 2002b. "Performance studies: Interventions and Radical Research." *TDR: The Drama Review*, 46.2: 145–153.

Cornell, Drucilla. 1995. *The Imaginary Domain: Abortion, Pornography and Sexual Harassment*. New York: Routledge.

Cristofovici, Anca. 1999. "Touching Surfaces: Photography, Aging, and an Aesthetics of Change." In *Figuring Age: Women Bodies*, Generations, edited by Kathleen Woodward, 268–293. Bloomington, IN: Indiana University Press.

Csikszentmihalyi, Mihalyi. 1991. *Flow: The Psychology of Optimal Experience*. New York: Harper Perennial.

Dalí, Salvador. 1958. *Anti-Material Manifesto*. New York: Carstairs Gallery.

Davidson, Michael. 2008. "Hearing Things: The Scandal of Speech in Deaf Performance." In *Concerto for the Left Hand: Disability and the Defamiliar Body*. Ann Arbor, MN: University of Michigan Press.

Davis, Tracy C. and Thomas Postlewait, eds. 2003. *Theatricality*. Cambridge: Cambridge University Press.

Dawkins, Richard. 1989. *The Selfish Gene*. Oxford: Oxford University Press.

De Certeau, Michel. 1984. *The Practice of Everyday Life*. Berkeley, CA: University of California Press.

De Lauretis, Teresa. 1984. *Alice Doesn't: Feminism, Semiotics, Cinema*. Bloomington, IN: Indiana University Press.

Debord, Guy. 2005 *The Society of Spectacle*. Translated by Ken Knabb. Oakland, CA: AK Press.

DeBord, Guy and Alice Becker-Ho. 1987. *The Game of War*. Translated by Donald Nicholson-Smith. Reprint, London: Atlas Press, 2008.

DeGrazia, David. 1996. *Taking Animals Seriously: Mental Life and Moral Status*. Cambridge: Cambridge University Press.

Deleuze, Gilles. 1988. *Fold: Leibniz and the Baroque*. Minneapolis, MN: University of Minnesota Press.

Deleuze, Gilles and Felix Guattari. 1983. *Anti-Oedipus: Capitalism and Schizophrenia*. Translated by Robert Hurley, Mark Seem, and Helen Lane. Minneapolis, MN: University of Minnesota Press. Originally published in France: Les Éditions de Minuit, 1972.

Deleuze, Gilles and Felix Guattari. 1987. "Becoming Intense, Becoming Animal and Becoming Imperceptible." In *A Thousand Plateaus: Capitalism and Schizophrenia*. Translated by Brian Massumi. Minneapolis, MN: University of Minnesota Press.

Demers, Joanna. 2003. "Sampling the 1970s in Hip-hop." *Popular Music*, 22.1: 41–56.

Derrida, Jacques. 1991. *Who Comes after the Subject?*, edited by Eduardo Cadava, Peter Connor, and Jean-Luc Nancy. New York: Routledge.

Dharwadker, Aparna Bhargava. 2005. *Theatres of Independence: Drama, Theory, and Urban Performance in India Since 1947*. Iowa City, IA: University of Iowa Press.

Diamond, Elin. 1997. *Unmaking Mimesis: Essays on Feminism and Theatre*, New York: Routledge.

Diderot, Denis. 1957. *The Paradox of Acting*. New York: Hill and Wang.

Doane, Mary Anne. 1982. "Film and the Masquerade: Theorizing the Female Spectator." In *Writing on the Body: Female Embodiment and Feminist Theory*, edited by Katie Conboy, Nadia Medina, and Sarah Stanbury. New York: Columbia University Press.

Dolan Jill. 1988. *Feminist Spectator as Critic*. Ann Arbor, MN: University of Michigan Press.

Dubuffet, Jean. 1951. "Anticultural Positions." Lecture at The Arts Club of Chicago, Chicago, IL, December 20.

Duchamp, Marcel. 1917. "The Richard Mutt Case." In *The Blind Man*, 2: 5. Reprinted in *Theories and Documents of Contemporary Art: A Sourcebook of Artists' Writings*, edited by Kristine Stiles and Peter Selz, 35: 817–818.
Berkeley and Los Angeles: University of California Press, 1996.

Dyer, Richard. 1997. *White: Essays on Race and Culture*. New York and London: Routledge.

Eco, Umberto. 1976. "Semiotics of Theatrical Performance." *The Drama Review: TDR*, 21.1: 107–117.

Elam, Keir. 1980. *The Semiotics of Theater and Drama*. London: Routledge.

*Embracing Earth: Dances with Nature*. 1995. Directed by Andy Abrahams Wilson. Performed by Anna Halprin. Sausalito, CA: Open Eye Pictures.

Eshelman, Raoul. 2001. "Performatism, or the End of Postmodernism." *Anthropoetics* 6.2. http://www.anthropoetics.ucla.edu/ap0602/perform.htm

Fairbrother, Trevor. 1991. *Robert Wilson's Vision*. Boston, MA: Museum of Fine Arts.

Fanon, Frantz. 1952. *Black Skin, White Masks*. Translated by Richard Philcox. Reprint, 2008. New York: Grove Press.

Fanon, Frantz. 1961. *The Wretched of the Earth*. Translated by Richard Philcox. Reprint, 2004. New York: Grove Press.

*Fantastic Mr. Fox*, film. 2009. Directed by Wes Anderson. Performed by George Clooney, Meryl Streep, Bill Murray. Screenplay by Wes Anderson and Noah Baumbach. Twentieth Century Fox, Indian Paintbrush, Regency Enterprises.

Fernandes, Ciane. 2005. *Pina Bausch and the Wuppertal Dance Theatre: The Aesthetics of Repetition and Transformation*. New York: Peter Lang.

Feuillet, Raoul-Auger. 1700. *Chorégraphie, ou l'art de décrire la danse par caracteres, figures et signes demonstratifs*, Paris: Self-published.

Flynt, Henry. 1975. *Blueprint for a Higher Civilization*. Milano: Multhipla Edizioni.

Foster, Susan Leigh. 2010. *Choreographing Empathy: Kinesthesia in Performance*. New York: Routledge.

Foucault, Michel. 1969. *The Archaeology of Knowledge*. Translated by A.M. Sheridan Smith. London: Routledge.

Foucault, Michel. 1977. *Discipline and Punish: The Birth of the Prison*. Translated by Alan Sheridan. New York: Vintage.

Frazer, James George. 1922. *The Golden Bough*. New York: Macmillan.

Freud, Sigmund. 1919. *The Uncanny*. Translated by David McLintock. Reprint, London: Penguin Books Ltd, 2003.

Fried, Michael. 1967. "Art and Objecthood." In *Art and Objecthood: Essays and Reviews*. Chicago, IL: University of Chicago Press, 1998.

Fried, Michael. 1998. *Art and Objecthood: Essays and Reviews*. Chicago, IL: University of Chicago Press.

Fuchs, Elinor. 1996. "The Death of Character: Perspectives on Theater After Modernism." In *Drama and Performance Studies*, edited by Timothy Wiles. Bloomington, IN: Indiana University Press.

Fudge, Erica. 2000. *Perceiving Animals: Humans and Beasts in Early Modern English Culture*. New York: Basingstoke.

Fusco, Coco. 1995. "The Other History of Intercultural Performance." In *English Is Broken Here: Notes on Cultural Fusion in the Americas*. New York: New Press.

Fusco, Coco. 2008. *A Field Guide for Female Interrogators*. New York: Seven Stories Press.

Ganz. Caryn. 2012. "Santigold's Killah Instinct." *Spin Magazine*, May 17. http://www.spin.com/articles/santigolds-killah-instinct/

Garoian, Charles R., and Yvonne Gaudelius. 2008a. "The Sea and Poison." *Spectacle Pedagogy: Art, Politics, and Visual Culture*. Albany, NY: State University of New York.

Garoian, Charles R. and Yvonne Gaudelius. 2008b. *Spectacle Pedagogy: Art, Politics, and Visual Culture*. Albany, NY: State University of New York.

Geertz, Clifford. 1973. *The Interpretation of Cultures*. Reprint, New York: Basic Books, 2000.

Gilbert, Helen and Joanne Tompkins. 1996. *Post-Colonial Drama: Theory, Practice, Politics*. London: Routledge.

Goffman, Erving. 1959. *The Presentation of Self in Everyday Life*. New York: Anchor.

Goffman, Erving. 1974. *Frame Analysis*. Cambridge, MA: Harvard University Press.

Goldberg, Marianne. 1989. "Artifice and Authenticity: Gender Scenarios in Pina Bausch's Dance Theatre." *Women & Performance: A Journal of Feminist Theory*, 4.2: 104–117.

Goldsmith, Steven. 1983. "The Readymades of Marcel Duchamp: The Ambiguities of an Aesthetic Revolution." *The Journal of Aesthetics and Art Criticism*, 42.2: 197–208.

Gómez-Peña, Guillermo. 1989. "The Multicultural Paradigm: An Open Letter to the National Arts Community." *High Performance*, 12.3: 18–27.

Gómez-Peña, Guillermo. 1993. *Warrior for Gringostroika: Essays, Performance Texts, and Poetry*. St. Paul, MN: Graywolf Press.

Gordon, Isa. 2001–to date. "Psymbiote." *Psymbiote*. http://www.psymbiote.org

Gordon, Avery F. and Christoper Newfield, eds. 1996. *Mapping Multiculturalism*. Minneapolis, MN: University of Minnesota Press.

Graham-Jones, Jean. 2005. "Theorizing Globalization Through Theater and Performance." *Theater Journal*, 57.3: viii–xvi.

Green, David and Joanna Lowry. 2006. *Stillness and Time: Photography and the Moving Image*. Brighton: Photoworks/Photoforum.

Gropius, Walter. 1961. *The Theater of the Bauhaus*. Translated by Arthur S. Wensinger. Middletown, Connecticut: Wesleyan University Press.

Groys, Boris. 2012. *Introduction to Antiphilosophy*. London and New York: Verson.

Gullette, Margaret Morganroth. 2004. *Aged by Culture*. Chicago, IL: University of Chicago Press.

Halberstam, J. Jack. 2012. *Gaga Feminism: Sex, Gender, and the End of Normal*. Boston, MA: Beacon Press.

Halberstam, Judith. 1998. *Female Masculinity*. Durham and London: Duke University Press.

Hall, Stuart. 1993. "Cultural Identity and Diaspora." In *Colonial Discourse and Post-Colonial Theory. A Reader*, edited by Patrick Williams and Laura Chrisman, 392–403. New York: Harvester Wheatsheaf.

Halliwell, Stephen. 1987. *The Poetics of Aristotle: Translation and Commentary*. Chapel Hill, NC: University of North Carolina Press.

Harling, Danielle. 2013. "Iggy Azalea Defends her Status as a White Rapper." *Hip-Hop DX*, September 17. http://www.hiphopdx.com/index/news/id.25463/title.iggy- azalea-defends-her-status-as-a-white-rapper

Haraway, Donna J. 2008. *When Species Meet*. Vol. 3 in *Posthumanities*, edited by Cary Wolfe. Minneapolis, MN: University of Minnesota Press.

Harvie, Jen and Dan Rebellato, eds. 2006. *Contemporary Theater Review*, Vol. 16.1: 62–70.

Hatfield, Jackie. 2003. "Expanded Cinema and Its Relationship to the Avant-Garde: Some Reasons for a Review of the Avant-Garde Debates Around Narrativity." *Millenium Film* Journal, 39/40: 50–65.

Hendricks, Jon, ed. 1988. *Fluxus Codex*. New York: Harry N. Abrams.

Hendricks, Jon, ed. 2002. *Q que é Fluxus? O que Não é! O porqué. What's Fluxus? What's Not? Why.* Rio de Janeiro and Detroit: Centro Cultural Banco do Brasil and The Gilbert and Lila Silverman Fluxus Collection Foundation.

Higgins, Dick. 1965a. "Intermedia." In *Foew & Ombwhnw: A Grammar of the Mind and a Phenomenology of Love and a Science of the Arts as Seen by a Stalker of the Wild Mushroom*, 11–29. New York, Barton, VT, and Cologne: Something Else Press, Inc.

Higgins, Dick. 1965b. "Synesthesia and Intersenses: Intermedia." In *Horizons: The Poetics and Theory of the Intermedia*. Carbondale, IL: Southern Illinois University Press.

Higgins, Dick. 1969. *Foew & Ombwhnw: A Grammar of the Mind and a Phenomenology of Love and a Science of the Arts as Seen by a Stalker of the Wild Mushroom*. New York: Something Else Press.

Higgins, Dick. 1984. *Horizons, the Poetics and Theory of the Intermedia*. Carbondale, IL: Southern Illinois University Press.

Hodges Persley, Nicole. 2010. "Sampling and Remixing: Hip-hop and Parks's History Plays." In *Suzan-Lori Parks: Essays on the Plays and Other Works*, edited by Philip C. Kolin. Jefferson, NC: McFarland.

Hodges Persley, Nicole. 2011. "A Urban Singer of Tales: The Freestyle Remixing of an Afro-Homeric Oral Tradition." *Jay-Z: Essays on Hip Hop's Philosopher King*, edited by Julius Bailey. Jefferson, NC: McFarland.

Holmberg, Arthur. 1996. *The Theatre of Robert Wilson*, Cambridge: Cambridge University Press.

Humphries, Tom. 2007. "Talking Culture and Culture Talking." In *Open Your Eyes: Deaf Studies Talking*, edited by H.-Dirksen L. Bauman, 35–41. Minneapolis, MN: University of Minnesota Press.

Hutcheon, Linda. 1985. *A Theory of Parody: The Teachings of Twentieth-century Art Forms*. New York: Methuen.

Huyssen, Andreas. 1984. "Mapping the Postmodern." *New German Critique*, 33: 5–52.

Irigaray, Luce. 1985. *Speculum of the Other Woman*. Translated by Gillian C. Gill. Ithaca: Cornell University Press.

Jackson, Shannon. 2003. "Theatricality's Proper Objects: Genealogies of Performance and Gender." *Theatricality*, edited by Tracy Davis and Tom Postlewait. Cambridge: Cambridge University Press.

Jackson, Shannon. 2004. *Professing Performance: Theatre in the Academy from Philology to Performativity*. Cambridge: Cambridge University Press.

Jameson, Frederic. 1991. *Postmodernism, Or, The Cultural Logic of Late Capitalism*. Durham: Duke University Press.

Jarosi, Susan. 2012. "Recycled Cinema as Material Ecology: Raphael Montanez Ortiz's Found-footage Films and Computer-Laser-Videos." *Screen*, 53.3: 228–245.

Jeff, Paul. 2006. "Performed Photography: The Map is not the Terrain." Paper presented at the Land/Water Symposium, Plymouth, University of Plymouth, June.

Jenkins, Brian M. 1975. *International Terrorism*. Los Angeles, CA: Crescent Publications.

Jentsch, Ernst. 1906. *On the Psychology of the Uncanny*. Translated by Roy Sellars. doi: http://www.art3idea.psu.edu/locus/Jentsch_uncanny.pdf

Jeyifo, Biodun. 2004. *Wole Soyinka: Politics, Poetics, and Postcolonialism*. Cambridge: Cambridge University Press.

Jones, Amelia. 1998. *Body Art/performing the Subject*. Minneapolis, MN: University of Minnesota Press.

Jones, Amelia and Andrew Stephenson, eds. 1999. *Performing the Body/Performing the Text*. London and New York: Routledge.

Kapchan, Deborah A. 1999. *Theorizing the Hybrid*. Arlington, VA: American Folklore Society.

Kaprow, Allan. 1961. *Essays on the Blurring of Art and Life*. Reprint, Berkeley, CA: University of California Press, 1993.

Karnad, Girish, 1971. *Hayavadana*. In *Collected Plays, Volume I*. Reprint, New Delhi: Oxford University Press, 2005.

Kirshenblatt-Gimblett, Barbara. 1999. "Performance Studies." Rockefeller Foundation: *Culture and Creativity*, September.

Kortenaar, Neil Ten. 1995. "Beyond Authenticity and Creolization: Reading Achebe Writing Culture." *PMLA*, 110.1: 30–42.

Kosuth, Joseph. 1969. "Art after Philosophy [Part I]," *Studio International*, 178.915: 134–137. Reprinted in *Conceptual art: A critical anthology*, edited by Alexander Alberro and Blake Stimson, 158–170. Cambridge, MA: MIT Press, 1999.

Kraidy, Marwan M. 2005. *Hybridity: Or the Cultural Logic of Globalization*. Philadelphia, NJ: Temple University Press.

Kubiak, Anthony. 1991. *Stages of Terror: Terrorism, Ideology, and Coercion as Theater History*. Bloomington, IN: Indiana University Press.

Kuppers, Petra. 2003. *Disability and Contemporary Performance: Bodies on Edge.* New York: Routledge.

Ladd, Patty. 2007. "Colonialism and Resistance: A Brief History of Deafhood." In *Open Your Eyes: Deaf Studies Talking*, edited by H.-Dirksen L. Bauman, 42–59. Minneapolis, MN: University of Minnesota Press.

Lane, Jill. 2005. *Blackface Cuba 1840–1895*. Philadelphia, NJ: University of Pennsylvania.

Lehmann, Hans-Theis. 1999. *Postdramatic Theater*. Translated by Karen Jürs-Munby. Reprint, 2006. London and New York: Routledge.

Lehmann, Hans-Theis and Brenda Richardson. 1986. *Oskar Schlemmer.* Baltimore, MA: Baltimore Museum of Art.

Lei, Daphne. 2003. "The Production and Consumption of Chinese Theater in Nineteenth-Century California." *Theater Research International*, 28.3: 1–14.

Lepecki, André. 2006. *Exhausting Dance: Performance and the Politics of Movement.* New York: Routledge.

Lingis, Alphonso. 2003. "Animal Body, Inhuman Face." In *Zoontologies: The Question of the Animal*, edited by Cary Wolfe, 165–182. Minneapolis, MN, and London: University of Minnesota Press.

Lippard, Lucy R. and John Chandler. 1968. "The Dematerialization of Art." *Art International*, 12:2: 31–36.

Lippit, Akira Mizuta. 2000. *Electric Animal: Toward a Rhetoric of Wildlife*. Minneapolis, MN: University of Minnesota Press.

Lipscomb, Valerie Barnes. 2004. *Act Your Age: The Performance of Age in Modern and Postmodern Drama*. PhD diss., University of South Florida, Tampa, FL.

Lipscomb, Valerie Barnes and Leni Marshall, eds. 2010. *Staging Age: The Performance of Age in Theatre, Dance, and Film*. New York: Palgrave.

Loomba, Ania. 2007. *Colonialism/Postcolonialism*. London and New York: Routledge.

López, Ian Haney. 1996. *White by Law: The Legal Construction of Race*. New York: New York University Press.

Lott, Eric. 1995. *Love and Theft: Blackface Minstrelsy and the American Working Class*. New York: Oxford University Press.

Lyotard, Jean-François. 1984. *The Postmodern Condition: A Report on Knowledge*. Minneapolis, MN: University of Minnesota Press.

Mac Low, Jackson and La Monte Young, eds. 1963. *An Anthology of Chance Operations*, USA: Jackson Mac Low.

Manning, Susan Allene. 1986. "An American Perspective on Tanztheater." *TDR: The Drama Review*, 30.2: 57–79.

Margulis, Lynn and Dorion Sagan. 2002. *Acquiring Genomes*. Reprint, New York: Basic, 2003.

Marranca, Bonnie. 1977. *The Theatre of Images*. New York: Drama Book Specialists.

Matejka, Ladislav and Irwin R. Titunik, eds. 1976. *Semiotics of Art: Prague School Contributions*, Cambridge: MIT Press.

May, Theresa J. 2007. "Beyond Bambi: Toward a Dangerous Ecocriticism in Theater Studies." *Theatre Topics*, 17.2: 95–110.

McEvilley, Thomas. 2005. *The Triumph of Anti-Art: Conceptual and Performance Art in the Formation of Post-Modernism.* New York: McPherson & Co.

McKenzie, Jon. 2001. *Perform or Else: From Discipline to Performance.* New York: Routledge.

McKenzie, Jon. 2009. "Counter-Perfomatives: Economic Meltdowns, Techno-Snafus, and Beyond." In *Performance Studies International,* 15: Misperformance: Misfiring, Misfitting, Misreading.

McPharlin, Paul. 1949. *The Puppet Theatre in America, a History; With a List of Puppeteers, 1524–1948.* New York: Harper.

Mekas, Jonas. 1972. *Movie Journal: The Rise of a New American Cinema, 1959– 1971.* New York: Macmillan.

Memmi, Albert. 1965. *The Colonizer and the Colonized.* Boston, MA: Beacon Press.

Metzger, Gustav. 1959. "Auto-Destructive Art." Radical Art. Accessed February 4, 2015. http://radicalart.info/destruction/metzger.html

Meyer, James. 2004. *Minimalism: Art and Polemics in the Sixties.* New Haven, CT: Yale University Press.

Miglietti, Francesca Alfano. 2003. *Extreme Bodies: The Use and Abuse of the Body in Art.* Translated by Antony Shugaar. Milan: Skira.

Minh-Ha, Trinh T. 1997. "Not You/Like You: Post-Colonial Women and the Interlocking Questions of Identity and Difference." In *Dangerous Liaisons: Gender, Nation, and Postcolonial Perspectives,* edited by Anne McClintock, Aamir Mufti and Ella Shohat, 415–419. Minneapolis, MN: University of Minnesota Press.

Moore, Bridie. 2014. "Depth, Significance, and Absence: Age-Effects in New British Theatre." *Age, Culture, Humanities: An Interdisciplinary* Journal, 1. http://ageculturehumanities.org/WP/depth-significance-and-absence-age-effects- in-new-british-theatre/

Morgan, Barbara. 1941. *Martha Graham; Sixteen Dances in Photographs.* New York: Duell, Sloan & Pearce.

Morgan, Joan. 1999. *When Chickenheads Come Home to Roost: My Life as a Hip-Hop Feminist.* New York: Simon & Schuster.

Morris, Robert. 1964. "Notes on Sculpture." *Artforum,* 4.6: 223.

Moten, Fred. 2003. *In the Break: The Aesthetics of the Black Radical Tradition.* Minneapolis, MN: University of Minnesota Press.

Mulvey, Laura. 1975. "Visual Pleasure and Narrative Cinema." *Screen,* 16.3: 6–18.

Muñoz, José Esteban. 1999. *Disidentifications: Queers of Color and the Performance of Politics.* Minneapolis, MN: University of Minnesota Press.

Muñoz, José Esteban. 2009. *Cruising Utopia: The Then and There of Queer Futurity.* New York: New York University Press.

Nayar, Pramod K. 2007. "The New Monstrous: Digital Bodies, Genomic Arts and Aesthetics." *Nebula,* 4.2: 1–19.

Nayar, Pramod K. 2009. *Seeing Stars: Spectacle, Society, Celebrity Culture.* New Delhi: Sage.

Nayar, Pramod K. 2013. *Posthumanism.* Cambridge: Polity.

Nayar, Pramod K. *Unique Identity: Surveillance and Citizenship in India.* Preprint, Cambridge: Cambridge University Press.

Nesbit, Molly. 1986. "Ready-Made Originals: The Duchamp Model." *October,* 37: 53–64.

Niwa, Harumi. 2009. "My Grandmothers: The Resonance of Memory." *Miwa Yanagi.* Tokyo: Tokyo Metropolitan Museum of Photography.

Olaniyan, Tejumola. 1995. *Scars of Conquest/ Masks of Resistence: The Invention of Cultural Identities in Africa, African American, and Caribbean Drama.* New York: Oxford University Press.

Ortiz, Rafael Montañez. 1962. "Destructivism: A Manifesto." In *Rafael Montañez Ortiz: Years of the Warrior, Years of the Psyche, 1960–1988* by Kristine Stiles, 52. New York: El Museo del Barrio, 1988.

Owens, Craig. 1983. "The Discourse of Others: Feminists and Postmodernism." *The Anti-Aesthetic: Essays on Postmodern Culture.* Seattle, WA: Bay Press.

Owens, Craig. 1992. *Beyond Recognition: Representation, Power, and Culture.* Berkeley, CA: University of California Press.

*Pangaean Dreams: A Shamanic Journey*, DVD. 2001. Directed by Rachel Rosenthal. Rachel Rosenthal Company.

Parker-Starbuck, Jennifer. 2014. *Cyborg Theatre: Corporeal/Technological Intersections in Multimedia Performance.* New York: Palgrave Macmillan.

Pavis, Patrice, ed. 1996. *Intercultural Performance Reader.* New York: Routledge.

Perloff, Marjorie. 1996. "Of Objects and Readymades: Gertrude Stein and Marcel Duchamp." *Forum for Modern Language Studies*, Vol. XXXII.2: 137–154.

Perreault, John. 1967. "Minimal Abstracts." *The Village Voice*, 260.

Phelan, Peggy. 1988. "Feminist Theory, Poststructuralism, and Performance." *TDR: The Drama* Review, 32.1: 107–127.

Phelan, Peggy. 1993. *Unmarked: The Politics of Performance.* New York: Routledge.

Phelan, Peggy and Jill Lane, eds. 1998. *The Ends of Performance.* New York: New York University Press.

*Pina*, documentary. 2011. Directed by Wim Wenders. Written by Wim Wenders. Performed by Pina Bausch, Regina Advento, Malou Airaudo. Neue Road Movie, Eurowide Film Production, Zweites Deutsches Fersehen.

Pina Bausch Foundation (website). "*Pina Bausch Foundation.*" Accessed February 2, 2015. http://www.pinabausch.org/en/home

Plato. 2003. *The Republic.* Translated by Desmond Lee. 2nd edn. London: Penguin.

Port, Cynthia. 2012. "No Future? Aging, Temporality, History, and Reverse Chronologies." *Occasion*, 4: 1–19.

Potolsky, Matthew. 2006. *Mimesis.* New York and London: Routledge.

Pradeu, Thomas and Edgardo D. Carosella. 2010. *L'Identité: La Part de l'Autre.* Paris: Odile Jacob.

Proschan, Frank. 1983. *Puppets, Masks, and Performing Objets from Semiotic Perspectives.* Berlin: Mouton.

Rae, Paul. 2006. "Where is the Cosmopolitan Stage?" *Contemporary Theatre Review*, 16.1: 4–19.

Rainer, Yvonne. 1999. *A Quasi Survey of Some "Minimalist" Tendencies in the Quantitatively Minimal Dance Activity Midst the Plethora, or an Analysis of Trio A.* Baltimore, MA: Johns Hopkins University Press.

Read, Alan, ed. 2000. "On Animals." *Performance Research*, Vol. 5.2, special issue.

Reinelt, Janelle. 2006. "To the Editor," *Theater Survey*, 47.2: 167–173.

Reinelt, Janelle. 2007. "The Limits of Censorship." *Theatre Research International*, 32.1: 3–15.

Richter, Hans. 1964. *Dada: Art and Anti-Art.* Reprint, New York: Thames and Hudson Inc., 1985.

Ritvo, Harriet. 1987. *The Animal Estate: The English and Other Creatures in the Victorian Age.* Cambridge, MA: Harvard University Press.

Roach, Joseph. 1996. *Cities of the Dead: Circum-Atlantic Performance.* New York: Columbia University Press.

Robertson, Roland. 1995. "Glocalization: Time-Space and Homogeneity-Heterogeneity." In *Global Modernities*, edited by Mike Featherstone, Scott M. Lash and Roland Robertson, 25–44. London: Sage Publication Ltd.

Rosenthal, Rachel. 2001. *Rachel's Brain and Other Storms. Rachel Rosenthal: Performance Texts*, edited by Una Chaudhuri. London: Continuum.

Said, Edward. 1979. *Orientalism.* New York: Vintage.

Said, Edward. 1994. *Culture and Imperialism.* New York: Random House.

Sandahl, Carrie and Philip Auslander, eds. 2005. *Bodies in Commotion: Disability and Performance.* Ann Arbor, MN: University of Michigan Press.

Schechner, Richard. 1982. "An Introduction" *TDR: The Drama Review*, 26.2: 3–4.

Schechner, Richard. 1985. *Between Theatre and Anthropology.* Philadelphia, NJ: University of Pennsylvania Press.

Schechner, Richard. 1988. *Performance Theory.* Revised edition. London and New York: Routledge.

Schechner, Richard. 2002. *Performance Studies: An Introduction.* London: Routledge.

Schechner, Richard. 2006. *Performance Studies: An Introduction.* New York: Routledge.

Schechner, Richard and Willa Appel, eds. 1990. *By Means of Performance: Intercultural Studies of Theatre and Ritual.* Cambridge: Cambridge University Press.

Schlemmer, Oskar. 1972. *The Letters and Diaries of Oskar Schlemmer*, edited by Tut Schlemmer and translated by Krishna Winston. Middletown, CT: Wesleyan University Press.

Schloss, Joseph G. 2004. *Making Beats: The Art of Sample-based Hip-Hop*. Middletown, CT: Wesleyan University Press.

Schmidt, Jochen. 2002. *Pina Bausch: Tanzen gegen die Angst.* Munich: Econ.

Schur, Richard. 2010. *Parodies of Ownership: Hip-hop Aesthetics and Intellectual Property Law*. Ann Arbor, MI: University of Michigan Press.

Schur, Richard and Lovalerie King, eds. 2009. *African American Culture and Legal Discourse.* New York: Palgrave Macmillan.

Schwarz, Arturo. 1969. *The Complete Works of Marcel Duchamp.* London: Thames and Hudson Inc.

Sell, Mike. 2007. "Bohemianism, the 'Cultural Turn' of the Avant-Garde, and Forgetting the Roma." *TDR: The Drama Review*, 51.2: 41–59.

Shakespeare, William. *King Lear*, edited by R.A. Foakes. In *The Arden Shakespeare*, London: Thomson Learning, 2005.

Shohat, Ella and Robert Stam. 1993. *Unthinking Eurocentrism: Multiculturalism and the Media.* London and New York: Routledge.

Sieg, Katrin. 2002. *Ethnic Drag: Performing Race, Nation, Sexuality in West Germany*. Ann Arbor, MA: University of Michigan Press.

Sieg, Katrin. 2003. "Indians: the Globalized Woman on the Community Stage." *Theater Journal*, 55.2: 291–315.

Silverman, Kaja. 1996. *The Threshold of the Visible World.* New York: Routledge.

Singleton, Brian. 2003. "Editorial." *Theater Research International*, 28.3: 227–228.

Spivak, Gayatri. 1995. "Subaltern Studies: Deconstructing Historiography." In *The Spivak Reader: Selected Works of Gayatri Spivak*, edited by Donna Landry and Gerald MacLean. New York and London: Routledge.

Stegemann, Bernd. 2009. "After Postdramatic Theater." In *Theater*, translated by Michael Winter, 39.3: 11–23.

Stein, Gertrude. 1914. *Tender Buttons.* New York: Bartleby.

Stein, Gertrude. 1935. *Lectures in America.* New York: Random House.

Stelarc. 1996. "Ping Body." http://v2.nl/events/ping-bod

Stelarc. 1999. "Exoskeleton." http://stelarc.org/?catID=20227

Stelarc. 2007. "Third Ear." http://stelarc.org/?catID=20242

Stiles, Kristine. 1987. "Synopsis of The Destruction in Art Symposium (DIAS) and Its Theoretical Significance." *The Act*, Vol. 1 (Spring 1987): 22–31.

Stiles, Kristine. 1990. "Notes on Rudolf Schwarzkogler's Images of Healing." *WhiteWalls: A Magazine of Writings by Artists.* Chicago, IL: White Walls.

Stiles, Kristine. 1992. "Survival Ethos and Destruction Art." *Discourse: Journal for Theoretical Studies in Media and Culture*, 14.2: 74–102.

Stiles, Kristine and Peter Selz, eds. 1996. *Theories and Documents of Contemporary Art: A Sourcebook of Artists' Writings.* Berkeley, CA: University of California Press.

Swarr, Amanda and Richa Nagar. 2010. *Critical Transnational Feminist Praxis.* Albany, NY: SUNY Press.

Swinnen, Aagje and John A. Stotesbury, eds. 2012. *Aging, Performance, and Stardom: Doing Age on the Stage of Consumerist Culture.* Berlin: Lit.

Szondi, Peter. 1987. *Theory of the Modern Drama*, edited and translated by Michael Hays. Minneapolis, MN: University of Minnesota Press.

Taylor, Diana. 1997. *Disappearing Acts: Spectacles of Gender and Nationalism in Argentina's "Dirty War."* Durham: Duke University Press.

Taylor, Diana. 2003a. "Bush's Happy Performative." *TDR: The Drama* Review, 47.3: 5–8.

Taylor, Diana. 2003b. *The Archive and the Repertoire: Performing Cultural Memory in the Americas*. Durham: Duke University Press.

Todorov, Tzvetan. 1983. *Theories of the Symbol*. Translated by C. Porter. Ithaca: Cornell University Press.

Turner, Victor W. 1987. *The Anthropology of Performance*. New York: PAJ.

Vaneigem, Raoul. 2001. *The Revolution of Everyday Life*. Translated by Donald Nicholson-Smith. Rebel Press. Originally published *Traité de savoir-vivre à l'usage des jeunes générations* (Gallimard, 1967).

Veltruský, Ladislav. 1964. *Peněžní Oběh a úvěr v Kapitalistických Státech: Určeno Pro Posl. Fak. Polit. Ekonomie*. Prague: SPN.

Watson, Jeff. *Reality Ends Here*. http://www.remotedevice.net

Wiener, Norbert. 1961. *Cybernetics, or Control and Communication in the Animal and the Machine*. Cambridge, MA: MIT Press.

*Wildness*, documentary. 2012. Directed by Wu Tsang. Screenplay by Wu Tsang and Roya Rastegar.

Winnicott, D.W. 1971. "Transitional Objects and Transitional Phenomena." In *Playing and Reality*. London: Tavistock Publications.

Wolfe, Cary. 2003. *Animal Rites: Animal Culture, the Discourse of Species, and Posthumanist Theory*. Chicago, IL: University of Chicago Press.

Woodward, Kathleen. 1991. *Aging and its Discontents: Freud and Other Fictions*. Bloomington, IN: Indiana University Press.

Woodward, Kathleen. 2006. "Performing Age, Performing Gender." In *NWSA Journal*, 18.1: 162–189.

Yan, Haiping, ed. 2005a. "Other Transnationals: Asian Diaspora in Performance." *Modern Drama*, XLVIII.2, special issue

Yan, Haiping. 2005b. *Staging Global Vagrancy: A Genealogy of Transnational Performance*. Ann Arbor, MN: University of Michigan Press.

Yanagi, Miwa. 2006. *Elevator Girls*. Art Space Niji, Kyoto.

Yarbro-Bejarano, Yvonne. 1994. "The Female Subject in Chicano Theater: Sexuality, Race, and Class." In *Performing Feminisms: Feminist Critical Theory and Theater*, edited by Sue-Ellen Case, 131–149. Minneapolis, MN: University of Minnesota.

Youngblood, Gene. 1970. *Expanded Cinema*. New York: Dutton.

# Index of essays

# Index

Page numbers in *italic* indicate figures.